W9-ADQ-688

# JUSTICE ADMINISTRATION

# JUSTICE ADMINISTRATION
## Police, Courts, and Corrections Management

*Fourth Edition*

**KENNETH J. PEAK**
*University of Nevada, Reno*

PEARSON

Prentice
Hall

Upper Saddle River, New Jersey 07458

**Library of Congress Cataloging-in-Publication Data**
Peak, Kenneth J.
   Justice administration : police, courts, and corrections management /
Kenneth J. Peak.—4th ed.
      p. cm.
Includes bibliographical references and index.
   ISBN 0-13-112300-9
   1.  Criminal justice, Administration of—United States.    2.  Law
enforcement—United States.    3.  Prison administration—United States.
I. Title.
   HV9950 .P43 2004
   364.973—dc21

                                        2003000334

**Editor-in-Chief:** Stephen Helba
**Executive Editor:** Frank Mortimer, Jr.
**Assistant Editor:** Sarah Holle
**Production Editor:** Karen Berry, Pine Tree
   Composition
**Production Liaison:** Barbara Marttine Cappuccio
**Director of Production and Manufacturing:**
   Bruce Johnson
**Managing Editor:** Mary Carnis
**Manufacturing Buyer:** Cathleen Petersen
**Creative Director:** Cheryl Asherman

**Cover Design Coordinator:** Miguel
   Ortiz
**Cover Designer:** Joseph Sengotta
**Cover Image:** G.K. and Vicky Hart,
   Stone
**Editorial Assistant:** Barbara Rosenberg
**Marketing Manager:** Tim Peyton
**Formatting and Interior Design:** Pine
   Tree Composition
**Printing and Binding:** Phoenix Book
   Tech Park

**Copyright © 2004, 2001, 1998, 1995 by Pearson Education, Inc., Upper Saddle River,
New Jersey 07458.** Pearson Prentice Hall. All rights reserved. Printed in the United States of
America. This publication is protected by Copyright and permission should be obtained from the
publisher prior to any prohibited reproduction, storage in a retrieval system, or transmission in
any form or by any means, electronic, mechanical, photocopying, recording, or likewise. For information regarding permission(s), write to: Rights and Permissions Department.

**Pearson Prentice Hall**™ is a trademark of Pearson Education, Inc.
**Pearson**® is a registered trademark of Pearson plc
**Prentice Hall**® is a registered trademark of Pearson Education, Inc.

Pearson Education LTD.
Pearson Education Singapore, Pte. Ltd
Pearson Education, Canada, Ltd
Pearson Education–Japan
Pearson Education Australia PTY, Limited
Pearson Education North Asia Ltd
Pearson Educaçion de Mexico, S.A. de C.V.
Pearson Education Malaysia, Pte. Ltd

10   9   8   7   6   5   4   3   2   1
ISBN 0-13-112300-9

*To the memory
of Bill Peak,
who has gone to a better place—
and most likely been discussing the finer points
of horses and hunting with heaven's top administrator*

# CONTENTS

## *Chapter 2*

## Organization and Administration: Principles and Practices                22

## *PART II*

## THE POLICE                59

## *Chapter 3*

## Police Organization and Operation                61

## Chapter 4

## Police Personnel Roles and Functions                                    87

## Chapter 7
## Court Personnel Roles and Functions                         167

## Chapter 8
## Court Issues and Practices                                   189

## PART IV

# CORRECTIONS                                                      205

### Chapter 9
### Corrections Organization and Operation                         207

## PART V

## ISSUES SPANNING THE JUSTICE SYSTEM: ADMINISTRATIVE CHALLENGES AND PRACTICES

### Chapter 13
### Ethical Considerations

## Chapter 14
## Rights of Criminal Justice Employees 324

## Chapter 15
## Special Challenges: Discipline, Labor Relations, and Liability 356

### Chapter 18
**Peeking over the Rim: What Lies Ahead?**                                                    **440**

# PREFACE

This fourth edition of *Justice Administration: Police, Courts, and Corrections Management* continues to be the sole book of its kind: a single author's examination of all facets of the criminal justice system as well as several related matters of interest to prospective and actual administrators. The author has held several administrative and academic positions in a criminal justice career spanning more than 30 years; thus, this book's chapters contain a palpable "real world" flavor not found in most textbooks.

More than 30 case studies are disseminated throughout the text; these case studies are intended to allow the reader to experience some of the kinds of problems confronted daily by justice administrators; with a fundamental knowledge of the system, and a reading of the chapters in the respective book part, readers should be in a position to arrive at several feasible solutions to each problem that is presented.

In addition to the chapters concerning police, courts, and corrections administration, also included are chapters on personnel and financial administration, rights of criminal justice employees, technology, discipline and liability, and futures. Articles from *Law Enforcement News* and other sources are interspersed throughout the book, and this edition also includes a new chapter concerning ethics in criminal justice. Other chapter sections that have been added or expanded deal with bioterrorism, racial profiling, school violence, vehicle pursuits, judicial selection, jury administration, gender bias, and women in corrections. Also new to this edition are key terms and concepts and chapter learning objectives, which appear at the beginning of each chapter.

Criminal justice is a people business. This book reflects that fact as it looks at human foibles and some of the problems of personnel and policy in justice administration. Thanks to many innovators in the field, however, a number of exciting and positive changes are occurring. The general goal of the book is to inform the reader of the primary *people, practices*, and *terms* that are utilized in justice administration.

There may well be activities, policies, actions, and my own views with which the reader will disagree. This is not at all bad, because in the management of people and agencies there are no absolutes, only ideas and endeavors to make the system better.

From its beginning (which includes an introduction by the president of the National Judicial College, Hon. William F. Dressel) through its final chapter, the reader is provided with a comprehensive and penetrating view of what is certainly one of the most difficult and challenging positions that one can occupy in America: the administration of a criminal justice agency.

I kindly solicit your input concerning any facet of this textbook; feel free to contact me if you have ideas for improving it.

# Acknowledgments

This edition, like its three predecessors, is the result of the professional assistance of several people. First, I continue to benefit by the guidance of the staff at Prentice Hall. This effort involved Frank Mortimer, acquisitions editor, and I was quite fortunate in being able to work with project coordinator, Karen Berry. Copyediting was masterfully accomplished by Linda Benson. The author also wishes to acknowledge the invaluable assistance of Clyde Cronkhite, Western Illinois University, Macomb, Ill.; Mary Stohr, Boise State University, Boise, Ida.; Vivian Lord, University of North Carolina–Charlotte, Charlotte, N.C.; and Patricia O'Donnell Brummett, California State University–Northridge, Northridge, Calif., whose reviews of this fourth edition resulted in many beneficial additions and modifications.

Ken Peak
peak_k@unr.edu

# ABOUT THE AUTHOR

Ken Peak is a full professor and former chairman of the Department of Criminal Justice, University of Nevada, Reno, where he has been named "Teacher of the Year" by the university's Honor Society. He served as chairman of the Police Section of the Academy of Criminal Justice Sciences from 1997 to 1999 and has served as president of the Western and Pacific Association of Criminal Justice Educators. He entered municipal policing in Kansas in 1970 and subsequently held positions as a nine-county criminal justice planner for southeast Kansas, director of a four-state Technical Assistance Institute for LEAA, director of university police at Pittsburg State University, and assistant professor of criminal justice at Wichita State University. His earlier books include *Policing America: Methods, Issues, Challenges* (4th ed.), *Policing Communities: Understanding Crime and*

*Solving Problems—An Anthology* (with R. Glensor and M. Correia), *Community Policing and Problem Solving: Strategies and Practices* (3d ed., with Ronald W. Glensor), *Police Supervision* (with Ronald W. Glensor and L. K. Gaines), *Kansas Temperance: Much Ado About Booze, 1870–1920* (Sunflower University Press), and *Kansas Bootleggers* (with P. G. O'Brien, Sunflower University Press). He also has published more than 50 journal articles and additional book chapters. His teaching interests include policing, administration, victimology, and comparative justice systems. He holds a doctorate from the University of Kansas.

# INTRODUCTION

*Judge William F. Dressel\**
*President, National Judicial College, Reno, Nevada*

It is generally assumed that the administration of justice embraced management concepts for many years. However, the truth is that justice management is in its infancy. Management experts who have studied the administration of justice

---

*Judge Dressel became President of the National Judicial College in November 2000. He obtained his juris doctorate degree from the University of Denver Law School. From 1966–1978 he was in private practice in both Denver and Fort Collins, Colorado, specializing in trial practice. He was a Judge to the 8th Judicial District, State of Colorado, from 1978 to 2000. Judge Dressel has been president of the Colorado District Judges' Association and chair of the Colorado Trial Judges' Council; from 1992 to 1993 he chaired

pointedly comment on the divisive nature of the justice system. This observation is often based on the political independence of the three entities examined in this book. However, this observed divisiveness arises more due to the impact of outside influences and involvement with other institutions/professions who have discordant views as to what the real mission of police, courts, and corrections should be. For example, courts often do not have agreed upon goals; and where goals do exist, special interest groups, defense counsel, prosecutors, rights groups, and so on, often work to see that the goals are never achieved.

Independence of these agencies aside, the administration of justice requires the three to work together, which is achieved through collaboration. The challenge is to bridge these entities in a manner that they are able to support each other. While there is without a doubt interface between each of these entities at the "street" level in the nature of a service relationship, the bridge that makes the justice system work is at the administrative level. It is there that the services to be provided and "terms of engagement" are negotiated whereby each entity meets the needs of the others. It may be argued that the courts dominate the relationship based on judicial authority to dictate the behavior of the other two. For instance, courts "instruct" police as to how they may arrest, what they must advise a person upon being arrested, how and under what conditions they may interview an individual, and what must occur in order to detain. Corrections are told what services they must provide and whether they can take any type of disciplinary action. It is with the acceptance of the authority of the courts that these three independent agencies do come together with their separate resources to reach an accommodation as to how justice will be provided to the citizenry. Whether the reader chooses a career with the police, courts, or corrections, you will need to understand the role and responsibility of each of these entities. This fourth edition goes beyond simply describing the entities in Parts 2, 3 and 4, but also explores the evolving role of each from community policing, problem solving/community courts, or innovative training/work programs for convicted offenders, to other forms of innovation.

In an introduction to another of Dr. Peak's textbooks, Reno, Nevada Chief of Police, Jerry Hoover, has described what faces law enforcement:

> What we are finding is that the challenges for the twenty first century are more likely to be an extension of our present issues: technology and crime, organization of police agencies, external social issues and ideology. There exist crimes based upon technology that did not exist a few years ago requiring police employees with different knowledge and skills. The philosophy of policing is steadily evolving. Some administrators subscribe to a community policing model, others to a problem-

---

the National Conference of State Trial Judges (and from 1987 to 1993 chaired its Court Delay Reduction Committee). He is principal author of the Trial Management Standards adopted by the American Bar Association House of Delegates in 1992. Judge Dressel has served as an adjunct professor at the University of Denver Law School; he served as a faculty of the National Judicial College from 1989 to 1993, and, prior to becoming its president, he was a member of its Board of Trustees. In 1998 he received the Justice Management Institute's Ernest C. Friesen Award of Excellence.

oriented policing approach; still others consider one a philosophy and the other a tactic and do both. An emerging debate exists regarding problem-oriented policing versus outcome-based policing. There is no correct answer as to which philosophy or tactic should be used by a department. The style of policing will depend upon various factors, such as the size and structure of the agency, the resources and technology available, the values of the community, and the social and criminal problems encountered.

Courts face the challenge of having to interpret laws adopted in different times to laws crafted to meet current issues, changing behavior, technology, and demands of society. Most courts are beginning to accept responsibility for an individual once he or she is arrested. Probable cause determinations are made within forty-eight hours of arrest and prosecuting attorneys given twenty-four to seventy-two hours to file charges as the courts have embraced the philosophy of the American Bar Association court delay standards which provides:

> From the commencement of litigation to its resolution, whether by trial or settlement, any elapsed time other than reasonably required for pleadings, discovery and court events, is unacceptable and should be eliminated. To enable just and efficient resolution of cases, the court, not the lawyers or litigants, should control the pace of litigation. A strong judicial commitment is essential to reducing delay and, once achieved, maintaining a current docket.

Utilizing innovative approaches, courts experiment with methods to manage their cases, their dockets, and trials with varying degrees of success. As discussed in this textbook, courts are led by presiding judges who have little training for the leadership role and who must learn to use persuasion to obtain action or conformity from their fellow judges who are essentially independent. The emerging role of the court manager is becoming critical as the court manager and presiding judge work together to administer justice. The National Association of Court Managers will be publishing core competencies of court managers in ten areas in early 2003: 1) caseflow management, 2) resources, budget and finance, 3) visioning and strategic planning, 4) leadership, 5) purposes and responsibilities of courts, 6) human resources management, 7) information technology management, 8) education, training and development, 9) court/community communication, and 10) essential components.

Corrections remain a great mystery of the justice system to many. Facilities are subject to the "not in my backyard" syndrome and the public does not want to know what occurs behind the walls or fences of a corrections facility. Fortunately, in some communities, those walls and fences are becoming transparent with local jails being viewed as a community asset or reflection of the values of the community. The public is being invited in to work with correctional facilities that are learning how to deal with a different population. The most striking example is the graying of persons in corrections due to mandatory sentences, sentence enhancements, and other measures. In response, corrections is looking to innovative programs whereby risk assessment can allow placement in alternative supervisory community settings. Privatization is seen by some as the balm to cure the growing prison population problem. Private prisons, private jails, and community corrections facilities are contracting with government agencies to hold those to be separated from society or supervised under conditions deemed appropriate to address risk and rehabilitation issues. The debate continues whether privatization is a cure.

There is no one perfect system for the administration of justice. When the reader of this book goes into a particular jurisdiction or state, you will have to step back to get the "lay of the land" and determine how what is described herein applies to that locale, as well as how the three entities interrelate with each other. Fortunately, many jurisdictions are installing an integrated criminal justice information system wherein records can be constructed from the first contact by police, through court determination of status, up to the ultimate decision of whether to incarcerate or place on community supervision. Information systems will be one of the true bridges that bring the three entities together if for no other reason than to lessen the burden of creating and maintaining valid data.

While there has been significant improvement, the administration of justice must address issues such as: unequal treatment in the justice system, effective judicial leadership in all segments of the judiciary, public understanding and the media, high cost of access to justice for all, and unfair and inconsistent judicial process.[1] It will be the challenge of those involved in the administration of justice to address these issues and more in the twenty-first century. This excellent work by Dr. Ken Peak frames those issues in the context of police, courts, and corrections.

---

[1]Conference of Chief Justices and National Association of Court Managers, "Public Trust and Confidence Issues for the 21st Century," Williamsburg, VA, June 2000.

# JUSTICE ADMINISTRATION

# PART I

# JUSTICE ADMINISTRATION
## An Introduction

*This part, consisting of two chapters, sets the stage for our later analysis of criminal justice agencies and their issues, problems, functions, and challenges in Parts II through V. Chapter 1 examines the scope of justice administration and why we study it. Chapter 2 discusses organization and administration in general, looking at both how organizations are managed and how people are motivated. The introductory section of each chapter provides specific chapter content.*

# Chapter 1

# The Study and Scope of Justice Administration

## Key Terms and Concepts

Administration

Conflict model

Consensus model

Criminal justice network

Criminal justice nonsystem

Criminal justice process

Due process

Manager

Social contract

Supervisor

System fragmentation

## Learning Objectives

As a result of reading this chapter, the student will:

- learn the concepts of *administration, manager,* and *supervisor*
- understand and be able to distinguish between criminal justice process, network, and nonsystem
- understand system fragmentation and how it affects the amount and type of crime
- be familiar with consensus and conflict theorists
- understand the two goals of the American criminal justice system
- be able to distinguish between extrinsic and intrinsic rewards and how they relate to the criminal justice system

> *[T]he ordinary administration of criminal and civil justice . . . contributes, more than any other circumstance, to impressing upon the minds of the people affection, esteem, and reverence towards the government.*
>
> —Alexander Hamilton, *The Federalist* No. 17

> *If men were angels, no government would be necessary.*
>
> —James Madison, *Federalist* No. 51

# Why Study Justice Administration?

The new millennium began by putting many administrators on the defensive or in a negative (even criminal) light. The lengthening list of disgraced and prosecuted chief executive officers brought a crisis of corporate leadership that affected all executives, as average citizens began paying attention to the litany of CEOs who failed in corporate governance—and indicated their disgust through actions that dramatically affected the stock markets. Administration has never been easy, and in the face of this public outrage against executives in the private sector, criminal justice administrators in the public sector must wonder whether they, too, will be pressured to put stricter controls in place and to bring greater accountability to their own organizations.

Many of us may find it difficult when we are young to imagine ourselves assuming a leadership role in later life. As one person quipped, we may even have difficulty envisioning ourselves serving as captain of our neighborhood block watch program. The fact is, however, that organizations increasingly seek people with a high level of education and experience as prospective administrators. The college experience, in addition to transmitting knowledge, is believed to make people more tolerant and secure and less susceptible to debilitating stress and anxiety than those who do not have this experience. We also assume that administration is a science that can be taught; it is not a talent that one must be born with. Unfortunately, however, administrative skills are often learned through on-the-job training; many of us who have worked for a boss with inadequate administrative skills can attest to the inadequacy of this training.

## *Purpose of the Book and Key Terms*

This book alone, as is true for any other single work on the subject of administration, cannot instantly transform the reader into a bona fide expert in organizational behavior and administrative techniques. It alone cannot prepare anyone to accept the reins of administration, supervision, or leadership; formal education, training, and experience are also necessary for such undertakings.

Many good, basic books about administration exist; they discuss general aspects of leadership, the use of power and authority, and a number of esoteric subjects that are beyond the reach of this book. Rather, here we simply consider some of the major theories, aspects, and issues of administration, laying the foundation for the reader's future study and experience.

Many textbooks have been written about *police* administration; a few have addressed administering courts and corrections agencies. Even fewer have analyzed justice administration from a *systems* perspective, considering all of the components of the justice system and their administration, issues, and practices. This book addresses that perspective. Further, most existing books on administration are immersed in "pure" administrative theory and concepts; in doing so, the *practical* criminal justice perspective is often lost on many college and university students. Conversely, many books dwell on minute concepts, thereby obscuring the administrative principles involved. This book, which necessarily delves into some theory and esoteric subject matter, is intended to focus on the practical aspects of justice administration.

*Justice Administration* is not written as a guidebook for a major, sweeping reform of the U.S. justice system. Rather, its primary intent is to familiarize the reader with the methods and challenges of criminal justice administrators. It also challenges the reader, however, to consider what reform is desirable or even necessary and to be open-minded and visualize where changes might be implemented.

Although the terms *administration, manager,* and *supervisor* are often used synonymously, each is a unique concept that is related to the others. **Administration** encompasses both management and supervision; it is the process by which a group of people is organized and directed toward achieving the group's objective. The exact nature of the organization will vary among the different types and sizes of agencies, but the general principles and the form of administration are similar. Administration focuses on the overall organization, its mission, and its relationship with other organizations and groups external to it.

*Managers,* who are a part of administration, are most closely associated with the day-to-day operations of the various elements within the organization. *Supervisors* are involved in the direction of staff members in their daily activities, often on a one-to-one basis. Confusion may arise because a chief administrator may act in all three capacities. Perhaps the most useful and easiest description is to define top-level personnel as administrators, mid-level personnel as managers, and those who oversee the work as it is being done as supervisors.[1] In policing, although we tend to think of the chief executive as the administrator, the bureau chiefs or commanders as managers, and the sergeants as supervisors, it is important to note that often all three of these roles are required of one administrator.

The terms *police* and *law enforcement* are generally used interchangeably. Many people in the police field believe, however, that the police do more than merely enforce laws; they prefer to use the term *police.*

## *Organization of the Book*

To understand the challenges that administrators of justice organizations face, we first need to place justice administration within the "big picture." Thus, in Part I, "Justice Administration: An Introduction," we discuss the organization, administration, and general nature of the U.S. justice system; the state of our country with respect to crime and government control; and the evolution of justice administration in all of its three components: police, courts, and corrections.

Parts II, III, and IV, which discuss contemporary police, courts, and corrections administration, respectively, follow the same organization: The first chapter of each part deals with the *organization and operation* of the component, followed in the second chapter by an examination of the component's *personnel roles and functions,* and in the third chapter, a discussion of *issues and practices.* Each of these chapters concludes with some case studies. As indicated in the Preface, these case studies present the kinds of problems confronted daily by justice administrators. Several discussion questions follow each case study. With a fundamental knowledge of the system and a reading of the chapters in each part, readers should be able to engage in some critical analysis—even, it is hoped, some spirited discussions—and arrive at several feasible solutions to the problems presented.

Part V examines administrative problems and factors that influence the entire justice system, including the rights of criminal justice employees, financial administration, technology, and the future.

This initial chapter sets the stage for later discussions of the criminal justice system and its administration. We first consider whether the justice system comprises a "process," a "network," a "nonsystem," or a true "system." A discussion about the legal and historical bases for justice and administration follows (an examination of what some great thinkers have said about governance in general is provided at the end of the book, in Appendix II). The differences between public-sector and private-sector administration are reviewed next, and the chapter concludes with a discussion of policymaking in justice administration. After completing this chapter, the reader will have a better grasp of the structure, purpose, and foundation of our criminal justice system.

# A True *System* of Justice?

What do justice administrators—police, courts, and corrections officials—actually *administer*? Do they provide leadership over a system that has succeeded in accomplishing its mission? Do individuals within the system work amiably and communicate well with one another? Do they all share the same goals? Do their efforts result in crime reduction? In short, do they compose a *system*? We now turn to these questions, taking a fundamental yet expansive view of justice administration.

The U.S. criminal justice system attempts to decrease criminal behavior through a wide variety of uncoordinated and sometimes uncomplementary efforts. Each system component—police, courts, and corrections—has varying degrees of responsibility and discretion for dealing with crime. Each system component fails, however, to engage in any coordinated planning effort; hence, relations among and between these components are often characterized by friction, conflict, and deficient communication. Role conflicts also serve to ensure that planning and communication are stifled.

For example, one role of the police is to arrest suspected offenders. Police typically are not judged by the public on the quality (for example, having probable cause) of arrests, but on their number. Prosecutors often complain that police provide case reports of poor quality. Prosecutors, for their part, are partially judged by their success in obtaining convictions; a public defender or defense attorney is judged by success in getting suspected offenders' charges dropped. The courts are very independent in their operation, largely sentencing offenders as they see fit. Corrections agencies are torn between the philosophies of punishment and rehabilitation, and in the view of many wind up performing neither function with any large degree of success. These agencies are further burdened with overcrowded conditions, high caseloads, and antiquated facilities.[2] Unfortunately, this situation has existed for several decades and continues today.

This criticism of the justice system, or process—that it is fragmented and rife with role conflicts and other problems—is a common refrain. Following are several views of the criminal justice system as it currently operates: the process, network, and nonsystem points of view. Following our discussion of those three viewpoints, we consider whether or not criminal justice truly represents a system.

## *A Criminal Justice* Process?

What is readily seen in the foregoing discussion is that our criminal justice system may not be a system at all. Given its current operation and fragmentation, it might be better described as a **criminal justice process.** As a process, it involves the decisions and actions taken by an institution, offender, victim, or society that influence the offender's movement into, through, or out of the justice system.[3] In its purest form, the criminal justice process occurs as shown in Figure 1.1. Note that the horizontal effects result from factors such as the amount of crime, the number of prosecutions, and the type of court disposition affecting the population in correctional facilities and rehabilitative programs. Vertical effects represent the primary system steps or procedures.[4]

At one end of this process are the police, who understandably may view their primary role as getting lawbreakers off the street. At the other end of the process are the corrections officials, who may see their role as being primary custodial in nature. Somewhere between are the courts, which try to ensure a fair application of the law to each case coming to the bar.

As a process, the justice system cannot reduce crime by itself, nor can any of the component parts afford to be insensitive to the needs and problems of the other parts. In criminal justice planning jargon, "You can't rock one end of the boat." In other words, every action has a reaction, especially in the justice process. If, say, a bond issue for funds to provide 10 percent more police officers on the streets is passed in a community, the additional arrests made by those added police personnel will have a decided impact on the courts and

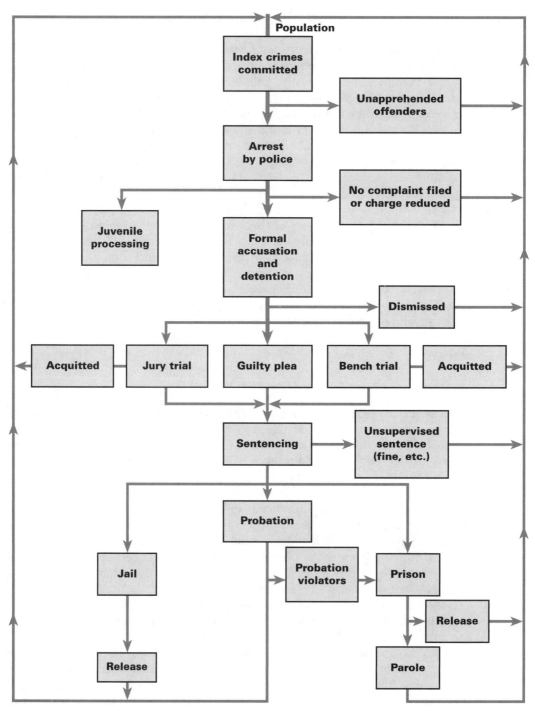

**Figure 1.1**

Criminal justice model. *Source:* Adapted from the President's Commission on Law Enforcement and Administration of Justice, *The Challenge of Crime in a Free Society.* Washington, D.C.: U.S. Government Printing Office, 1967, pp. 262–263.

corrections components. Obviously, although each component operates largely on its own, the actions and reactions of each with respect to crime will send ripples throughout the process.

Much of the failure to deal effectively with crime may be attributed to organizational and administrative fragmentation of the justice process. Fragmentation exists among the components of the process, within the individual components, among political jurisdictions, and among persons.

## *A Criminal Justice* Network?

Other observers contend that U.S. justice systems constitute a **criminal justice network.**[5] Steven Cox and John Wade believe that the justice system functions much like a television or radio network whose stations share many programs, but each station also presents programs that the network does not air on other stations. The network appears as a three-dimensional model in which the public, legislators, police, prosecutors, judges, and correctional officials interact with one another and with others who are outside the traditionally conceived criminal justice system.[6]

Furthermore, the criminal justice network is said to be based on several key yet erroneous assumptions, including the following:

1. The components of the network cooperate and share similar goals.
2. The network operates according to a set of formal procedural rules to ensure uniform treatment of all persons, the outcome of which constitutes "justice."
3. Each person accused of a crime receives due process and is presumed innocent until proven guilty.
4. Each person receives a speedy, public trial before an impartial jury of his or her peers and is represented by competent legal counsel.[7]

Cox and Wade assert that these key assumptions are erroneous because

1. The three components have incompatible goals and are continually competing with one another for budgetary dollars.
2. Evidence indicates that blacks and whites, males and females, and middle-class and lower-class citizens receive differential treatment in the criminal justice network.
3. Some persons are prosecuted, some are not; some are involved in plea bargaining, others are not; some are convicted and sent to prison, whereas others convicted of the same type of offense are not. A great deal of the plea negotiation process remains largely invisible, such as "unofficial probation" with juveniles. Also, Cox and Wade argue, considerable evidence points to the fact that criminal justice employees do not presume their clients or arrestees to be innocent.

4. Finally, these proponents for a "network" view of the justice process argue that the current backlog of cases does not ensure a speedy trial, even though a vast majority (at least 90 percent) of all arrestees plead guilty prior to trial.[8]

Adherents to this position, therefore, believe that our criminal justice system is probably not a just network in the eyes of the poor, minority groups, or individual victims. Citizens, they also assert, may not know what to expect from such a network. Some believe that the system does not work as a network at all and that this conception is not worth their support.[9]

## *A Criminal Justice* Nonsystem?

Many observers argue that the three components of the justice system actually comprise a **criminal justice nonsystem.** They maintain that the three segments of the U.S. system that deal with criminal behavior do not always function in harmony and that the system is neither efficient enough to create a credible fear of punishment nor fair enough to command respect for its values.

Indeed, these theorists are given considerable support by the President's Commission on Law Enforcement and the Administration of Justice (commonly known as the *Crime Commission*), which made the following comment:

> The system of criminal justice used in America to deal with those crimes it cannot prevent and those criminals it cannot deter is not a monolithic, or even a consistent, system. It was not designed or built in one piece at one time. Its philosophic core is that a person may be punished by the Government, if, and only if, it has been proven by an impartial and deliberate process that he has violated a specific law. Around that core, layer upon layer of institutions and procedures, some carefully constructed and some improvised, some inspired by principle and some by expediency, have accumulated. Parts of the system—magistrates, courts, trial by jury, bail—are of great antiquity. Other parts—juvenile courts, probation and parole, professional policemen—are relatively new. Every village, town, county, city and State has its own criminal justice system, and there is a Federal one as well. All of them operate somewhat alike, no two of them operate precisely alike.[10]

Alfred Cohn and Roy Udolf stated that criminal justice "is not a system, and it has little to do with justice as that term is ordinarily understood."[11] Also in this school of thought are Burton Wright and Vernon Fox, who asserted that "the criminal justice system . . . is frequently criticized because it is not a coordinated structure—not really a system. In many ways this is true."[12]

These writers would probably agree that little has changed since 1971, when *Newsweek* stated in a special report entitled "Justice on Trial" that

> America's system of criminal justice is too swamped to deliver more than the roughest justice—and too ragged really to be called a system. "What we have," says one former government hand, "is a non-system in which the police don't catch criminals, the courts don't try them, and the prisons don't reform them. The system, in a word, is in trouble. The trouble has been neglect. The paralysis of the civil courts, where it takes five years to get a judgment in a damage suit . . . the courts—badly managed,

woefully undermanned and so inundated with cases that they have to run fast just to stand still."[13]

Unfortunately, in many jurisdictions, those words still ring true. Too often, today's justice administrators cannot be innovators or reformers, but rather simply "make do." As one law professor stated, "Oliver Wendell Holmes could not survive in our criminal court. How can you be an eminent jurist when you have to deal with this mess?"[14]

Those who hold that the justice system is in reality no system at all can also point to the fact that many practitioners in the field (the police, judges, prosecutors, correctional workers, private attorneys) and academicians concede that the entire justice system is in crisis, even rapidly approaching a major breakdown. They can cite problems everywhere—high numbers of police calls for service, and overcrowded court dockets and prison populations. In short, they contend that the system is in a state of dysfunction, largely as a result of its fragmentation and lack of cohesion.[15]

**System fragmentation** is largely believed to directly affect the amount and type of crime that exists. Contributing to this fragmentation are the wide discretionary powers possessed by actors of the justice system. For example, police officers (primarily those having the least experience, education, and training) have great discretion over whom they arrest and are effectively able to dictate policy as they go about performing their duties. Here again, the Crime Commission was moved to comment, realizing that how the police officer moves around his or her territory depends largely on this discretion:

> Crime does not look the same on the street as it does in a legislative chamber. How much noise or profanity makes conduct "disorderly" within the meaning of the law? When must a quarrel be treated as a criminal assault: at the first threat, or at the first shove, or at the first blow, or after blood is drawn, or when a serious injury is inflicted? How suspicious must conduct be before there is "probable cause," the constitutional basis for an arrest? Every [officer], however sketchy or incomplete his education, is an interpreter of the law.[16]

Judicial officers also possess great discretionary latitude. State statutes require judges to provide deterrence, retribution, rehabilitation, and incapacitation—all in the same sentence. Well-publicized studies of the sentencing tendencies of judges—in which participants were given identical facts in cases and were to impose sentences based on the offender's violation of the law—have demonstrated considerable discretion and unevenness in the judges' sentences. The nonsystem advocates believe this to be further evidence that a basic inequality exists—an inequality in justice that is communicated to the offender.[17]

Finally, fragmentation also occurs in corrections—the part of the criminal justice process that the U.S. public sees the least of and knows the least about. Indeed, as the Crime Commission noted, the federal government, all 50 states, the District of Columbia, and most of the country's 3,047 counties now engage in correctional activities of some form or another. Each level of government acts independently of the others, and responsibility for the administration of corrections is divided within given jurisdictions as well.[18]

With this fragmentation comes polarity in identifying and establishing the primary goals of the system. The police, enforcing the laws, emphasize community protection; the courts weigh both sides of the issue—individual rights and community needs; and corrections facilities work with the individual. Each of these groups has its own perception of the offender, creating goal conflict; that is, the goal of the police and prosecutor is to get the transgressor off the street, which is antithetical to the "caretaker" role of the corrections worker, who often wants to rehabilitate and return the offender to the community. The criminal justice process does not allow many alternative means of dealing with offenders. Eventually, the nonsystem adherent believes that the offender will become a mere statistic, more important on paper than as a human being.[19]

Because the justice process lacks sufficient program and procedural flexibility, these adherents argue, its workers can either circumvent policies, rules, and regulations or they can adhere to organizational practices they know are, at times, dysfunctional. (As evidence of the former, they point to instances of *informal* treatment of criminal cases; for example, a police officer "bends" someone's constitutional rights in order to return stolen property to its rightful owner; or a juvenile probation officer, without a solid case but with strong suspicion, warns a youth that any further infractions will result in formal, court-involved proceedings.)

## *Or a True Criminal Justice* System?

That all of the foregoing perspectives on the justice system are grounded in truth is probably evident by now. In many ways, the police, courts, and corrections components work and interact to function like a process, a network, or even a nonsystem. However, the justice system may still constitute a true system. As Willa Dawson stated, "Administration of justice can be regarded as a system by most standards. It may be a poorly functioning system but it does meet the criteria nonetheless. The systems approach is still in its infancy."[20] J. W. La Patra added that "I do believe that a criminal justice system does exist, but that it functions very poorly. The CJS is a loosely connected, nonharmonious, group of social entities."[21]

To be fair, however, perhaps this method of dealing with offenders is best after all; it may be that having a well-oiled machine—in which all activities are coordinated, goals and objectives are unified, and communication between participants is maximized, all serving to grind out "justice" in a highly efficacious manner—may not be what we truly want or need in a democracy.

We hope that we have not belabored the subject; however, it is important to establish early in this book the type of system and components that you, as a potential criminal justice administrator, may encounter. You can reconcile for yourself the differences of opinion described earlier. In this book, we adhere to the notion that even with all of its disunity and lack of fluidity, what criminal justice officials administer in the United States is a system. Nonetheless, it is good to look at its operation and shortcomings and, as stated earlier, force ourselves to confront the criminal justice system's (CJS) problems and possible areas for improvement.

Now that we have a systemic view of what it is that criminal justice managers actually administer, it would be good to look briefly at how they go about doing it. We first consider the legal and historical bases that created the United States as a democracy regulated by a government and by a system of justice; we include the consensus-conflict continuum, with the social contract on one end and the maintenance of the status quo/repression on the other. Next, we distinguish between administration and work in the public and private sectors because the styles, incentives, and rewards of each are, by their very nature, quite different. This provides the foundation for the final point of discussion, a brief look at the policymaking process in criminal justice agencies.

# The Foundations of Justice and Administration: Legal and Historical Bases

Given that our system of justice is founded on a large, powerful system of government, these questions must be addressed: From where is that power derived? How can governments presume to maintain a system of laws that effectively governs its people and, furthermore, a legal system that exists to punish persons who willfully suborn those laws? We now consider the answers to those questions.

## *The Consensus Versus Conflict Debate*

U.S. society has innumerable lawbreakers. Most of them are easily handled by the police and do not challenge the legitimacy of the law while being arrested and incarcerated for violating it. Nor do they challenge the system of government that enacts the laws or the justice agencies that carry them out. The stability of our government for more than 200 years is a testimony to the existence of a fair degree of consensus as to its legitimacy.[22] Thomas Jefferson's statements in the Declaration of Independence are as true today as the day when he wrote them and are accepted as common sense:

> We hold these truths to be self-evident, that all men are created equal, that they are endowed by their Creator with certain inalienable Rights, that among these are Life, Liberty and the pursuit of Happiness—That to secure these rights, Governments are instituted among Men, deriving their just powers from the consent of the governed. That whenever any Form of Government becomes destructive of these ends, it is the Right of the People to alter or abolish it.

The principles of the Declaration were almost a paraphrase of John Locke's *Second Treatise on Civil Government,* which justified the acts of government on the basis of Locke's theory of **social contract.** In the state of nature, people, according to Locke, were created by God to be free, equal, independent, and with inherent inalienable rights to life, liberty, and property. Each person had the right of self-protection against those who would infringe on these liberties. In Locke's view, although most people were good, some would be likely to prey on their fellows, who in turn would constantly have to be on guard against such evildoers. To avoid this brutish existence, people joined together, forming governments to which they surrendered their rights of self-protection. In return, they received governmental protection of their lives, property, and liberty. As with any contract, each side has benefits and considerations; people give up their rights to protect themselves and receive protection in return. Governments give protection and receive loyalty and obedience in return.[23]

Locke believed that the chief purpose of government was the protection of property. Properties would be joined together to form the commonwealth. Once the people unite into a commonwealth, they cannot withdraw from it, nor can their lands be removed from it. Property holders become members of that commonwealth only with their express consent to submit to the government of the commonwealth. This is Locke's famous theory of *tacit consent:* "Every Man . . . doth hereby give his *tacit Consent,* and is as far forth obliged to Obedience to the Laws of the Government."[24] Locke's theory essentially describes an association of landowners.[25]

Another theorist connected with the social contract theory is Thomas Hobbes, who argued that all people were essentially irrational and selfish. He maintained that people had just enough rationality to recognize their situation and to come together to form governments for self-protection, agreeing "amongst themselves to submit to some Man, or Assembly of men, voluntarily, on confidence to be protected by him against all others."[26] Therefore, they existed in a state of consensus with their governments.

Jean-Jacques Rousseau, a conflict theorist, differed substantively from both Hobbes and Locke, arguing that "Man is born free, but everywhere he is in chains."[27] Like Plato, Rousseau associated the loss of freedom and the creation of conflict in modern societies with the development of private property and the unequal distribution of resources. Rousseau described conflict between the ruling group and the other groups in society, whereas Locke described consensus within the ruling group and the need to use force and other means to ensure the compliance of the other groups.[28]

Thus, the primary difference between the consensus and conflict theorists, with respect to their view of government vis-à-vis the governed, concerns their evaluation of the legitimacy of the actions of ruling groups in contemporary societies. Locke saw those actions as consistent with natural law, describing societies as consensual and arguing that any conflict was illegitimate and could be repressed by force and other means. Rousseau evaluated the actions of ruling groups as irrational and selfish, creating conflicts among the various groups in society.[29]

This debate is important because it plays out the competing views of humankind toward its ruling group; it also has relevance with respect to the kind of justice system (or process) we have. The systems model has been criticized for implying a greater level of organization and cooperation among the various agencies of justice than actually exists. The word *system* conjures an idea of machinelike precision in which wasted effort, redundancy, and conflicting actions are nearly nonexistent; our current justice system does not possess such a level of perfection. As mentioned earlier, conflicts among and within agencies are rife, goals are not shared by the system's three components, and the system may move in different directions. Therefore, the systems approach is part of the **consensus model** point of view, which assumes that all parts of the system work toward a common goal.[30] The **conflict model,** holding that agency interests tend to make actors within the system self-serving, provides the other approach. This view notes the pressures for success, promotion, and general accountability, which together result in fragmented efforts of the system as a whole, leading to a criminal justice nonsystem.[31]

This debate also has relevance for criminal justice administrators. Assume a consensus-conflict continuum, with social contract (the people totally allow government to use its means to protect them) on one end and class repression on the other. That our administrators *not* allow their agencies to "drift" too far to one end of the continuum or the other is of paramount importance. Americans cannot allow the compliance or conflict that would result at either end; the safer point is toward the middle of the continuum, where people are not totally dependent on their government for protection and maintain enough control to prevent totalitarianism.

## *Crime Control Through Due Process*

Both the systems and nonsystems models of criminal justice provide a view of agency relationships. Another way to view American criminal justice is in terms of its goals. Two primary goals are: (1) the need to enforce the law and maintain social order and (2) the need to protect people from injustice.[32] The first, often referred to as the crime control model, values the arrest and conviction of criminal offenders. The second, because of its emphasis on individual rights, is commonly known as the due process model. **Due process**—found in the Bill of Rights, particularly in the Fourteenth Amendment—is a central and necessary part of our system. It requires a careful and informed consideration of the facts of each individual case. Due process seeks to ensure that innocent people are not convicted of crimes.

The dual goals of crime control and due process are often suggested to be in constant and unavoidable opposition to each other. Many critics of criminal justice, as it exists in the United States, argue that our attempt to achieve "justice" for offenders too often occurs at the expense of due process. Other, more conservative observers believe that our system is too lenient with its clients, coddling offenders rather than protecting the innocent.

We are never going to be in a position to avoid ideological conflicts such as these. However, some observers, such as Frank Schmalleger, believe it is realistic to think of the U.S. system of justice as representative of *crime control through due process.*[33] This model of crime control is infused with the recognition of individual rights, which provides the conceptual framework for this book.

## Public-Sector versus Private-Sector Administration

That people derive positive personal experiences from their work has long been recognized.[34] Because work is a vital part of our lives and carries tremendous meaning in terms of our personal identity and happiness, the right match of person to job has long been recognized as a determinant of job satisfaction.[35] Factors such as job importance, accomplishment, challenge, teamwork, management fairness, and rewards become very important.

People in both the public (i.e., government) and private (e.g., retail business) sectors derive positive personal satisfactions from their work. The means by which they arrive at those positive feelings and are rewarded for their efforts, however, are often quite different. Basically, whereas private businesses and corporations can use a panoply of *extrinsic* (external) rewards to motivate and reward their employees, people working in the public sector must achieve job satisfaction primarily through *intrinsic* (internal) rewards.

Extrinsic rewards include perquisites such as financial compensation (salary and benefits package), private office, key to the executive washroom, bonuses, trips, company car, awards (including designations such as the employee of the month or the insurance industry's "million-dollar roundtable"), expense account, membership in country clubs and organizations, and job title. The title assigned to a job can affect one's general perceptions of the job regardless of actual job content. For example, the role once known disparagingly as "grease monkey" in a gasoline service station has commonly become known as "lubrication technician," garbage collectors have become "sanitation engineers," and so on. Enhancement of job titles is done to add job satisfaction and extrinsic rewards to what may often be lackluster positions.

Corporations often devote tremendous sums of time and money to bestowing extrinsic rewards, incentives, and job titles to employees to enhance their job satisfaction. These rewards, of course, cannot and do not exist in the public sector anywhere near the extent that they do in the private sector.

As indicated earlier, public-sector workers must seek and obtain job satisfaction primarily from within—through intrinsic means. These workers, unable to become wealthy through their salaries and to be in a position that is filled with perks, need jobs that are gratifying and that intrinsically make them feel good about themselves and what they accomplish. Practitioners often characterize criminal justice work as intrinsically rewarding, providing a sense of worth in making the world a little better place in which to live. These employees also seek appreciation from their supervisors and co-workers and generally enjoy challenges.

To be successful, administrators should attempt to understand the personalities, needs, and motivations of their employees and attempt to meet those needs and provide motivation to the extent possible. The late Sam Walton, the multibillionaire founder of Wal-Mart Stores, provided a unique example of the attempt to do this. One night, Walton could not sleep, so he went to a nearby all-night bakery (in Bentonville, Arkansas), bought four dozen doughnuts, and took them to a distribution center where he chatted with graveyard shift Wal-Mart employees. From that chat, he discovered that two more shower stalls were needed at that location.[36] Walton obviously solicited—and valued—employee input and was concerned about their morale and working conditions. Although Walton was known to be unique in his business sense, these are elements of administration that can be applied by all public administrators.

## Policymaking in Justice Administration

Imagine the following scenario. Someone in criminal justice operations (e.g., a city or county manager or a municipal or criminal justice planner) is charged with formulating an omnibus policy with respect to crime reduction. He or she might begin by trying to list all related variables that contribute to the crime problem: poverty; employment; demographics of people residing within the jurisdiction; environmental conditions (such as housing density and conditions and slum areas); mortality, morbidity, and suicide rates; educational levels of the populace; and so on.

The administrator would request more specific information from each justice administrator within the jurisdiction to determine where problems might exist in the practitioners' view of the police, courts, and corrections subsystems. For example, a police executive would contribute information concerning calls for service, arrests, and crime data (including offender information and crime information—time of day, day of week, methods, locations, targets, and so on). The status of existing programs, such as community policing and crime prevention, would also be provided. From the courts, information would be sought concerning the sizes of civil and criminal court dockets and backlogs ("justice delayed is justice denied"). Included in this report would be input from the prosecutor's office concerning the quality and quantity of police reports and arrests, as well as data on case dismissals and conviction rates at trial. From corrections administrators would come the average officer caseload and recidivism and revocation rates. Budgetary information would certainly be solicited from all subsystems, as well as miscellaneous data regarding personnel levels, training levels, and so on. Finally, the administrator would attempt to formulate a crime policy, setting forth goals and objectives for addressing the jurisdiction's needs.

As an alternative, the policymaker could approach this task in a far less complex manner, simply setting, either explicitly or without conscious thought, the relatively simple goal of "keeping crime down." This goal might be compromised or complicated by other factors, such as a bullish economy. This administrator could in fact disregard most of the other variables discussed earlier as being beyond his or her current needs and interest and would not even attempt to consider them as immediately relevant. The criminal justice practitioners would not be pressed to attempt to provide information and critical analyses. If pressed for time (as is often the case in these real-life scenarios), the planner would readily admit that these variables were being ignored.[37]

Because executives and planners of the alternative approach expect to achieve their goals only partially, they anticipate repeating endlessly the sequence just described as conditions and aspirations change and as accuracy of prediction improves. Realistically, however, the first of these two approaches assumes intellectual capacities and sources of information that people often do not possess; further, the time and money that can be allocated to a policy problem are limited. Public agencies are in effect usually too hamstrung to practice the first method; it is the second method that is followed. Curiously, however, the literature on decision making, planning, policy formulation, and public administration formalizes and "preaches" the first approach.[38] The second method is much neglected in this literature.

In the United States, probably no part of government has attempted a comprehensive analysis and overview of policy on crime (the first method just described). Thus, making crime policy is at best a rough process. Without a more comprehensive process, we cannot possibly understand how a variety of problems—education, housing, recreation, employment, race, and policing methods—might encourage or discourage juvenile delinquency. What we normally engage in is a comparative analysis of the results of similar past policy decisions. This explains why justice administrators often believe that outside experts or academics are not helpful to them—why it is safer to "fly by the seat of one's pants." Theorists often urge the administrator to go the long way to the solution of his or her problems, following the scientific method, when the administrator knows that the best available theory will not work. Theorists, for their part, do not realize that the administrator is often in fact practicing a systematic method.[39] So, what may appear to be mere muddling through is both highly praised as a sophisticated form of policymaking and decision making as well as soundly denounced as no method at all. What society needs to bear in mind is that justice administrators possess an intimate knowledge of past consequences of actions that "outsiders" do not. While seemingly less effective and rational, this method, according to policymaking experts, has merit. Indeed, this method is commonly used for problem solving in which the means and ends are often impossible to separate, aspirations or objectives undergo constant development, and drastic simplification of the complexity of the real world is urgent if problems are to be solved in reasonable periods of time.[40]

## Summary

This chapter presented the foundation for the study of justice administration. We also established the legal existence of governments, our laws, and the justice agencies that administer them. It was demonstrated that each of the three components of the justice system is independent and fragmented and often works at odds with one another toward the accomplishment of the system's overall mission.

## Questions for Review

1. Do the three justice components (police, courts, and corrections) constitute a true system or are they more appropriately described as a process or a true nonsystem? Defend your response.
2. What are the legal and historical bases for a justice system and its administration in the United States? Why is the conflict versus consensus debate important?
3. What are some of the substantive ways in which public-sector and private-sector administration are similar? How are they dissimilar?
4. Which method—a rational process or just muddling through—appears to be used in criminal justice policymaking today? Which method is probably best, given real-world realities? Explain your response.

## Notes

1. For a more thorough explication of these terms and roles, particularly as applied in policing, see Richard N. Holden, *Modern Police Management* (Englewood Cliffs, N.J.: Prentice Hall, 1986).
2. Michael E. O'Neill, Ronald F. Bykowski, and Robert S. Blair, *Criminal Justice Planning: A Practical Approach* (San Jose, Calif.: Justice Systems Development, Inc., 1976), p. 5.
3. Ibid., p. 12.
4. Ibid.
5. Steven M. Cox and John E. Wade, *The Criminal Justice Network: An Introduction,* 2d ed. (Dubuque, Iowa.: Wm. C. Brown, 1989), p. 1.
6. Ibid., p. 4.

7. Ibid., p. 12.

8. Ibid., pp. 13-14.

9. Philip H. Ennis, "Crime, Victims, and the Police," *Transaction* 4 (June 1967):36-44.

10. The President's Commission on Law Enforcement and the Administration of Justice, *The Challenge of Crime in a Free Society* (Washington, D.C.: U.S. Government Printing Office, 1967), p. 7.

11. Alfred Cohn and Roy Udolf, *The Criminal Justice System and Its Psychology* (New York: Van Nostrand Reinhold, 1979), p. 152.

12. Burton Wright and Vernon Fox, *Criminal Justice and the Social Sciences* (Philadelphia: W. B. Saunders, 1978).

13. "Justice on Trial: A Special Report," *Newsweek* (March 8, 1971):16.

14. Ibid., p. 18.

15. Alan R. Coffey and Edward Eldefonso, *Process and Impact of Justice* (Beverly Hills, Calif.: Glencoe Press, 1975), p. 32.

16. The President's Commission, *The Challenge of Crime in a Free Society,* p. 5.

17. Coffey and Eldefonso, *Process and Impact of Justice,* p. 35.

18. Ibid., p. 39.

19. Ibid., p. 41.

20. Willa Dawson, "The Need for a System Approach to Criminal Justice," in Donald T. Shanahan (ed.), *The Administration of Justice System—An Introduction* (Boston: Holbrook, 1977), p. 141.

21. J. W. La Patra, *Analyzing the Criminal Justice System* (Lexington, Mass.: Lexington Books, 1978), p. 75.

22. Alexander B. Smith and Harriet Pollack, *Criminal Justice: An Overview* (New York: Holt, Rinehart and Winston, 1980), p. 9.

23. Ibid., p. 10.

24. Ibid., p. 366.

25. Thomas J. Bernard, *The Consensus-Conflict Debate: Form and Content in Social Theories* (New York: Columbia University Press, 1983), p. 78.

26. Thomas Hobbes, *Leviathan* (New York: E. P. Dutton, 1950), pp. 290-291.

27. Jean-Jacques Rousseau, "A Discourse on the Origin of Inequality," in G. D. H. Cole (ed.), *The Social Contract and Discourses* (New York: E. P. Dutton, 1946), p. 240.

28. Bernard, *The Consensus-Conflict Debate,* pp. 83, 85.

29. Ibid., p. 86.

30. Frank Schmalleger, *Criminal Justice Today,* 7th ed. (Upper Saddle River, N.J.: Prentice Hall, 2003), p. 28.

31. One of the first publications to express the nonsystems approach was the American Bar Association's *New Perspective on Urban Crime* (Washington, D.C.: ABA Special Committee on Crime Prevention and Control, 1972).

32. Schmalleger, *Criminal Justice Today,* pp. 27-28.

33. Ibid.

34. Fernando Bartolome and Paul A. Lee Evans, "Professional Lives versus Private Lives: Shifting Patterns of Managerial Commitment," *Organizational Dynamics* 7 (1982):2-29; Ronald C. Kessler and James A. McRae Jr., "The Effect of Wives' Employment on the Mental Health of Married Men and Women," *American Sociological Review* 47 (1979): 216-227.

35. Robert V. Presthus, *The Organizational Society* (New York: Alfred A. Knopf, 1962).

36. Joseph A. Petrick and George E. Manning, "How to Manage Morale," *Personnel Journal* 69 (October 1990):87.

37. This scenario is modeled on one set out by Charles E. Lindblom, a Harvard economist, in "The Science of 'Muddling Through,'" *Public Administration Review* 19 (Spring 1959):79–89.

38. Ibid., p. 80.

39. Ibid., p. 87.

40. Ibid., p. 88.

# Chapter 2

# Organization and Administration
## Principles and Practices

## Key Terms and Concepts

Autocratic leaders

Consciously coordinated

Decoding

Democratic leader

Empathy

Encoding

Feedback

Grapevine

Laissez-faire leader

Maintenance or hygiene factors

Medium

Motivational factors

Organization

Reception

Relatively identifiable-boundary

Social entity

Transmission

Unity of command

## Learning Objectives

As a result of reading this chapter, the student will:

- be familiar with the elements of organization
- know the different principles of organizational structure
- understand the term *management*

- be familiar with the different aspects of communication and their role in the criminal justice system
- understand the barriers to effective communication
- be familiar with and be able to distinguish between the different historical approaches to management
- know the different primary leadership theories
- be familiar with the types of leadership skills
- have an understanding of the different managerial theories

> *We are born in organizations, educated by organizations, and most of us spend much of our lives working for organizations. We spend much of our leisure time paying, playing, and praying in organizations. Most of us will die in an organization, and when the time comes for burial, the largest organization of all—the state— must grant official permission.*
>
> —Amitai Etzioni

# Introduction

It is no surprise that *Dilbert*—one of today's most popular cartoon strips and television programs—portrays downtrodden workers, inconsiderate bosses, and dysfunctional organizations. Scott Adams's cartoon "hero," a mouthless engineer with a perpetually bent necktie, is believed by many Americans to be representative of today's workers. They believe that the Dilbert principle—the most ineffective workers are systematically moved to the place where they can do the least damage—is alive and well. Although a sizable majority of U.S. workers routinely indicate that their workplace is a pleasant environment, more than 70 percent also experience stress at work because of red tape, unnecessary rules, poor communication with management, and other causes. Indeed, what gives Adams grist for the Dilbert mill is the way managers mishandle their employees and carry out downsizing.[1]

This chapter examines organizations and the employees within them and how they should be managed and motivated. The chapter offers a general discussion of organizations, focusing on their definition, theory and function, and structure. Included are several approaches to managing and communicating within organizations.

We review historical schools of thought concerning management and examine organizational leadership theories. We then focus on one of the most important aspects of leadership, personnel administration. We conclude with a discussion of several motivational techniques for employees based on findings by major theorists in the field.

# Defining Organizations

Like *supervision* and *management*, the word *organization* has a number of meanings and interpretations that have evolved over the years. We think of organizations as entities of two or more people who cooperate to accomplish an objective(s). In that sense, certainly, the concept of organization is not new. Undoubtedly, the first organizations were primitive hunting parties. Organization and a high degree of coordination were required to bring down huge animals, as revealed in fossils from as early as 40,000 B.C.[2]

An **organization** may be formally defined as "a consciously coordinated social entity, with a relative identifiable boundary, that functions on a relatively continuous basis to achieve a common goal or set of goals."[3] The term **consciously coordinated** implies management. **Social entity** refers to the fact that organizations are composed of people who interact with one another and with people in other organizations. **Relatively identifiable boundary** alludes to the organization's goals and the public served.[4] Using this definition, we can consider many types of formal groups as full-blown organizations. Four different types of formal organizations have been identified by asking the question "Who benefits?" Answers include (1) mutual benefit associations, such as police labor unions; (2) business concerns, such as General Motors; (3) service organizations, such as community mental health centers, where the client group is the prime beneficiary; and (4) commonweal organizations, such as the Department of Defense and criminal justice agencies, where the beneficiaries are the public at large.[5] The following analogy is designed to help the reader to understand organizations.

An organization corresponds to the bones that structure or give form to the body. Imagine that the hand is a single mass of bone rather than four separate fingers and a thumb made up of bones joined by cartilage to be flexible. The single mass of bones could not, because of its structure, play musical instruments, hold a pencil, or grip a baseball bat. A criminal justice organization is analogous. It must be structured properly if it is to be effective in fulfilling its many diverse goals.[6]

It is important to note that no two organizations are exactly alike. Nor is there one best way to run an organization.

# Organizational Theory and Function

## Elements of an Organization

Max Weber (1864–1920), known as the *father of sociology*, explored in depth the organizational structure as well as the dynamics related to bureaucracy. He argued that if a bureaucratic structure is to function efficiently, it must have the following elements:

1. *Rulification and routinization.* Organizations stress continuity. Rules save effort by eliminating the need for deriving a new solution for every problem. They also facilitate standard and equal treatment of similar situations.
2. *Division of labor.* This involves the performance of functions by various parts of an organization along with providing the necessary authority to carry out these functions.
3. *Hierarchy of authority.* Each lower office is under the control and supervision of a higher one.
4. *Expertise.* Specialized training is necessary. Only a person who has demonstrated adequate technical training is qualified to be a member of the administrative staff.
5. *Written rules.* Administrative acts, decisions, and rules are formulated and recorded in writing.[7]

Bureaucracies are often criticized on two grounds. First, they are said to be inflexible, inefficient, and unresponsive to changing needs and times. Second, they are said to stifle the individual freedom, spontaneity, and self-realization of their employees.[8] James Q. Wilson referred to this widespread discontent with modern organizations as the "bureaucracy problem," where the key issue is "getting the frontline worker . . . to do 'the right thing.'"[9] In short, then, bureaucracies themselves can create problems.

### Organizational Inputs/Outputs

Another way to view organizations is as systems that take *inputs*, process them, and thus produce *outputs*. These outputs are then sold in the marketplace or given free to citizens in the form of a service. A police agency, for example, processes reports of criminal activity and, like other systems, attempts to satisfy the customer (crime victim). Figure 2.1 demonstrates the input/output model for the police and private business. There are other types of inputs by police agencies; for example, a robbery problem might result in an input of newly created robbery surveillance teams, the processing would be their stakeouts, and the output would be the number of subsequent arrests by the team. Feedback would occur in the form of conviction rates at trial.

## Organizational Structure

All organizations have an organizational structure or table of organization, be it written or unwritten, very basic or highly complex. An experienced manager uses this organizational chart or table as a blueprint for action. The size of the organization depends on the demand placed on it and the resources available to it. Growth precipitates the need for more personnel, greater division of labor, specialization, written rules, and other such elements.

**BUSINESS ORGANIZATION**

| Inputs | Processes | Outputs |
|---|---|---|
| Customer takes photos to shop to be developed. | Photos are developed and packaged for customer to pick up. | Customer picks up photos and pays for them. |

**Feedback**
Analysis is made of expenses/revenues and customer satisfaction.

**LAW ENFORCEMENT AGENCY**

| Inputs | Processes | Outputs |
|---|---|---|
| A crime prevention unit is initiated. | Citizens contact unit for advice. | Police provide spot checks and lectures. |

**Feedback**
Target hardening results; property crimes decrease.

**COURT**

| Inputs | Processes | Outputs |
|---|---|---|
| A house arrest program is initiated. | Certain people in pre- and post-trial status are screened and offered the option. | Decrease in number of people in jail, speeding up court process. |

**Feedback**
Violation rates are analyzed for success; some offenders are mainstreamed back into the community more smoothly.

**Figure 2.1**

The organization as an input-output model.

**PROBATION/PAROLE AGENCIES**

| Inputs | Processes | Outputs |
|---|---|---|
| Parole guidelines are changed to shorten length of incarceration and reduce overcrowding. | Qualified inmates are contacted by parole agency and given new parole dates. | A higher number of inmates are paroled into the community. |

| Feedback |
|---|
| Parole officer's caseload and revocation rates might increase; less time to devote per case. |

**Figure 2.1**

(*continued*)

In building the organizational structure, the following principles should be kept in mind:

1. *Principle of the objective.* Every part of every organization must be an expression of the purpose of the undertaking. You cannot organize in a vacuum; you must organize for something.
2. *Principle of specialization.* The activities of every member of any organized group should be confined, as far as possible, to the performance of a single function.
3. *Principle of authority.* In every organized group, the supreme authority must rest somewhere. There should be a clear line of authority to every person in the group.
4. *Principle of responsibility.* The responsibility of the superior for the acts of his or her subordinates is absolute.
5. *Principle of definition.* The content of each position, the duties involved, the authority and responsibility contemplated, and the relationships with other positions should be clearly defined in writing and published for all concerned.
6. *Principle of correspondence.* In every position, the responsibility and the authority to carry out the responsibility should correspond.
7. *Span of control.* No person should supervise more than six direct subordinates whose work interlocks.[10]

A related, major principle of hierarchy of authority is **unity of command,** which refers to placing one and only one superior officer in command or in control of every situation and employee. When a critical situation occurs, it is imperative that someone be responsible and in charge. The unity of command principle ensures that multiple and/or conflicting orders are not issued to the same police officers by several superior officers. For example, a patrol sergeant might arrive at a hostage situation, deploy personnel, and give all appropriate orders, only to have a shift lieutenant or captain come to the scene and countermand the sergeant's orders with his or her own orders. This type of situation would obviously be counterproductive for all concerned. All officers must know and follow the chain of command at such incidents. Every person in the organization should report to one and only one superior officer. When the unity of command principle is followed, everyone involved is aware of the actions initiated by superiors and subordinates. A simple structure indicating the direct line of authority in a chain of command is shown in Figure 2.2.

An organization should be developed through careful evaluation of its responsibilities, or the agency may become unable to respond efficiently to client needs. For example, the implementation of too many specialized units in a police department (e.g., community relations, crime analysis, media relations) may obligate too many personnel to these functions and result in too few patrol officers. As a rule of thumb, at least 55 percent of all sworn personnel should be assigned to patrol.[11]

The classical pyramidal design is shown in Figure 2.3. The pyramidal structure has the following characteristics:

1. Nearly all contacts take the form of orders going *down* and reports of results going *up* the pyramid.
2. Each subordinate must receive instructions and orders from only one boss.
3. Important decisions are made at the top of the pyramid.
4. Superiors have a specific "span of control," supervising only a limited number of people.
5. Personnel at all levels except at the top and bottom have contact only with their boss above them and their subordinates below them.[12]

**Figure 2.2**

Chain of command.

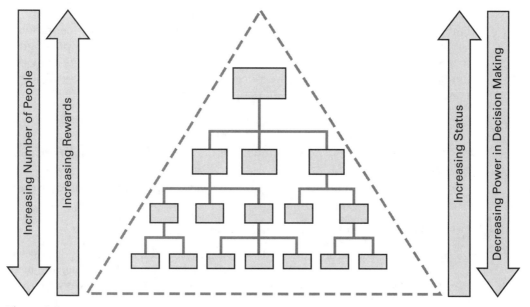

**Figure 2.3**

Organization pyramid. *Source:* Adapted from L. R. Sayles and G. Strauss, *Human Behavior Organizations*. Englewood Cliffs, N.J.: Prentice Hall, 1966, p. 349.

## Managing the Organization

The success of any organization normally depends on the quality of work life within the agency. Peter Drucker, often referred to as the *business guru*,[13] observed that "nothing quenches motivation as quickly as a slovenly boss. People expect and demand that managers enable them to do a good job. . . . People have . . . a right to expect a serious and competent superior."[14] Unfortunately, as Drucker was implying, some leaders do not succeed because their subordinates see them as untrained, uncaring, unfit, and/or unwilling to have the mantle of leadership thrust upon them.

We now look at leaders and what they can do to motivate their subordinates.

### *What Is Management?*

Probably since the dawn of time, when cave dwellers clustered into hunting groups and some particularly dominant person assumed a leadership role over the party, administrators have received advice on how to do their jobs from those around them. Even today, manuals for managers and upwardly mobile executives abound, offering quick studies in how to govern others. Although many have doubtless been profitable for their authors, most of these how-to primers on leading others enjoy only a brief, ephemeral existence.

To understand management, we must first define the term. This is an important and fairly complex undertaking, however. Perhaps the simplest definition is to say that management is "getting things done through people." Ralph Stogdill, in a review of 3,000 leadership studies, noted that "there are almost as many definitions of leadership as there are persons who have attempted to define the concept."[15] Among the most recent definitions are the following:

- "The process of influencing the activities of an individual or a group in efforts toward goal achievement in a given situation."[16]
- "Working with and through individuals and groups to accomplish organizational goals."[17]
- "The activity of influencing people to strive willingly for group objectives."[18]
- "The exercise of influence."[19]

Others have said the manager is viewed variously as a

team captain, parent, steward, battle commander, fountain of wisdom, poker player, group spokesperson, gatekeeper, minister, drill instructor, facilitator, initiator, mediator, navigator, candy-store keeper, linchpin, umbrella-holder and everything else between nurse and Attila-the-Hun.[20]

In criminal justice organizations, leadership might best be defined as "the process of influencing organizational members to use their energies willingly and appropriately to facilitate the achievement of the [agency's] goals."[21] We discuss management in greater length later in this chapter and in Chapter 4.

# Organizational Communication

## *Definition and Characteristics*

Communication is one of the most important dynamics of an organization. Indeed, a major role of today's administrators and other leaders is communication. Managers of all types of organizations spend an overwhelming amount of their time in the process of—and coping with problems in—communication.

Today we communicate via e-mail, facsimile machines, video camcorders, cellular telephones, satellite dishes, and on and on. We converse orally, in written letters and memos, through our body language, via television and radio programs, through newspapers and meetings. Even private thoughts—which take place four times faster than the spoken word—are communication. Every waking hour, our minds are full of ideas. Psychologists say that nearly 100,000 thoughts pass through our minds every day, conveyed by a multitude of media.[22] Communication becomes exceedingly important and sensitive in nature in a criminal justice organization because of the nature of information that is processed by practitioners—particularly police officers, who often see people at their worst and when they are in the most embarrassing and compromising situations. To "communicate" what is known about these kinds of behaviors could be devastating to the parties concerned. A former Detroit police chief lamented several decades ago that "many police officers, without realizing they carry such authority, do pass on rumors. The average police officer doesn't stop to weigh what he says."[23] Certainly the same holds true today and extends to courts and corrections personnel, especially in view of the very high-tech communications equipment now in use.

Studies have long shown that communication is the primary problem in administration, and lack of communication is employees' primary complaint about their immediate supervisors.[24] Mark Twain once said that "The difference between the right word and the almost right word is the difference between lightning and lightning bug."[25]

Managers are in the communications business. It has been said that

> Of all skills needed to be an effective manager/leader/ supervisor, skill in communicating is *the* most vital. In fact, more than 50 percent of a [criminal justice] manager's time is spent communicating. First-line supervisors usually spend about 15 percent of their time with superiors, 50 percent of their time with subordinates, and 35 percent with other managers and duties. These estimates emphasize the importance of communications in everyday . . . operations.[26]

Several elements compose the communication process: encoding, transmission, medium, reception, decoding, and feedback.[27]

*Encoding:* To convey an experience or idea, we translate, or encode, that experience into symbols. We use words or other verbal behaviors or nonverbal behaviors such as gestures to convey the experience or idea.

*Transmission:* This element involves the translation of the encoded symbols into some behavior that another person can observe. The actual articulation (moving our lips, tongue, etc.) of the symbol into verbal or nonverbal observable behavior is transmission.

*Medium:* Communication must be conveyed through some channel or medium. Media for communication include sight, hearing, taste, touch, or smell. Some other media are television, telephone, paper and pencil, and radio. The choice of the medium is important. For example, a message that is tranmitted via formal letter from the chief executive officer will carry more weight than if the same message is conveyed via a secretary's memo.

*Reception:* The stimuli, the verbal and nonverbal symbols, reach the senses of the receiver and are conveyed to the brain for interpretation.

*Decoding:* The individual who receives the stimuli develops some meaning for the verbal and nonverbal symbols and decodes the stimuli. These symbols are translated into some concept or experience for the receiver. Whether or not the receiver is familiar with the symbols or whether or not interference such as any noise or physiological problem occurs determines how closely the message that the receiver has decoded approximates the message that the sender has encoded.

*Feedback:* When the receiver decodes the transmitted symbols, he or she usually provides some response or feedback to the sender. If someone appears puzzled, we repeat the message or we encode the concept differently and transmit some different symbols to express the same concept. Feedback that we receive acts as a guide or steering device and lets us know whether the receiver has interpreted our symbols as we intended. Feedback is obviously a crucial element in guaranteeing that the proper meaning that the sender intended was in fact conveyed to the receiver.

## Communication Within Criminal Justice Organizations

An organization's systems of communication are usually created by establishing formal areas of responsibility and explicit delegations of duties, including statements of the nature, content, and direction of the communications that are necessary for the group's performance. Most criminal justice administrators prefer a formal system, regardless of how cumbersome it may be, because they can control it and because it tends to create a record for future reference. Several human factors, however, affect the flow of communication. Employees typically communicate with those persons who can help them to achieve their aims; they avoid communicating with those who do not assist, or may retard, their accomplishing those goals; they tend to avoid communicating with people who threaten them and make them feel anxious.[28] Other barriers to effective communication are discussed later.

Communication within a criminal justice organization may be downward, upward, or horizontal. There are five types of *downward* communication within a criminal justice organization:

1. *Job instruction*—communication relating to the performance of a certain task
2. *Job rationale*—communication relating a certain task to organizational tasks
3. *Procedures and practice*—communication about organizational policies, procedures, rules, and regulations (discussed in Chapter 3)
4. *Feedback*—communication appraising how an individual performs the assigned task
5. *Indoctrination*—communication designed to motivate the employee[29]

Other reasons for communicating downward—implicit in this list—are opportunities for administrators to spell out objectives, to change attitudes and mold opinions, to prevent misunderstandings from lack of information, and to prepare employees for change.[30]

*Upward* communication in a criminal justice organization may be likened to a trout trying to swim upstream: With its many currents of resistance, it is a much harder task than to float downstream. Several deterrents restrict upward communication. The physical distance between superior and subordinate impedes upward communication. Communication is often difficult and infrequent when superiors are isolated and seldom seen or spoken to. In large criminal justice organizations, administrators may be located in headquarters that are removed from the operations personnel. The complexity of the organization may also cause prolonged delays of communication. For example, if a corrections officer or a patrol officer observes a problem that needs to be taken to the highest level, normally this information must first be taken to the sergeant, then to the lieutenant, captain, deputy warden or chief, and so on. At each level, these higher individuals will reflect on the problem, put their own interpretation on it (possibly including how the problem might affect them professionally or even personally), and possibly even dilute or distort the problem. Thus, delays in communication are inherent in a bureaucracy. Delays could mean that problems are not brought to the attention of the chief executive for a long time. The more levels the communication passes through, the more it is filtered and diluted in its accuracy.

There is also the danger that administrators have a "no news is good news" or "slay the messenger" attitude, thereby discouraging the reception of information. Unless the superior does in fact maintain an open-door atmosphere, subordinates are often reluctant to bring, or will temper, bad news, unfavorable opinions, and mistakes or failures to the superior.[31] Administrators may also believe that they know and understand what their subordinates want and think, and that complaints from subordinates are an indication of disloyalty.

For all of these reasons, administrators may fail to take action on undesirable conditions brought to their attention; this will cause subordinates to lose faith in their leaders. Many time-consuming problems could be minimized or eliminated if superiors would take the time to listen to their employees.

*Horizontal* communication thrives in an organization when formal communication channels are not open.[32] The disadvantage in horizontal communication is that it is much easier and more natural to achieve than vertical communication and, therefore, it often replaces vertical channels. The horizontal channels are usually of an informal nature and include the grapevine, discussed next. The advantage is that horizontal communication is essential if the subsystems within a criminal justice organization are to function in an effective and coordinated manner. Horizontal communication among peers may also provide emotional and social bonds that build morale and feelings of teamwork among employees.

## The Grapevine

In addition to the several barriers to effective communication just discussed, the so-called **grapevine**—termed as such because it zigzags back and forth across organizations—can also serve to hinder communication. Communication includes rumors, and probably *no* type of organization in our society has more grapevine "scuttlebutt" than police agencies. Departments even establish "rumor control" centers during major crisis situations. Compounding the usual barriers to communication is the fact that policing, prisons, and jails are 24-hour, 7-day operations, so that rumors are easily carried from one shift to the next.

The grapevine's most effective characteristics are that it is fast; it operates mostly at the place of work; and it supplements regular, formal communication.

On the positive side, it can be a tool for management to get a feel for employees' attitudes, to spread useful information, and to help employees vent their frustrations. However, the grapevine can also carry untruths and be malicious. Without a doubt, the grapevine is a force for adminstrators to reckon with on a daily basis.

## Oral and Written Communication

Our society tends to place considerable confidence in the written word within complex organizations. It establishes a permanent record, but transmitting information in this way does not necessarily ensure that the message will be clear to the receiver. Often, in spite of the writer's best efforts, information is not conveyed clearly to the receiver. This may be due in large measure to shortcomings with the writer's skills. Nonetheless, criminal justice organizations seem to increasingly rely on written communication, as evidenced by the proliferation of written directives found in most agencies.

This tendency for organizations to promulgate written rules, policies, and procedures has been caused by three contemporary developments. First is the *requirement for administrative due process* in employee disciplinary matters, encouraged by federal court rulings, police officer bill of rights legislation, and labor contracts. Another development is *civil liability*. Lawsuits against local governments and their criminal justice agencies and administrators have become commonplace; written agency guidelines prohibiting certain acts provide a hedge against successful civil litigation.[33] Written communication is preferred as a medium for dealing with citizens or groups outside the criminal justice agency. This means of cmmunication provides the greatest protection against the growing number of legal actions taken against agencies by activists, citizens, and interest groups.

Finally, a third stimulus is the *accreditation movement*. Agencies that are either pursuing accreditation or have become accredited must possess a wealth of written policies and procedures.[34]

In recent years, electronic mail (e-mail) has proliferated as a communication medium in criminal justice organizations. E-mail provides an easy-to-use and almost instantaneous communication with anyone possessing a personal computer—in upward, downward, or horizontal directions. For all its advantages, however, e-mail messages can lack security and can be ambiguous—not only with respect to content meaning, but also with regard to what they represent. Are such messages, in fact, mail, to be given the full weight of an office letter or memo, or should they be treated more as offhand comments?[35]

## Other Barriers to Effective Communication

In addition to the barriers just discussed, several other potential barriers to effective communication exist. Some people, for example, are not good listeners. Unfortunately, listening is one of the most neglected and the least understood of the communication arts.[36] We allow other things to obstruct our communication, including time, inadequate or too great a volume of information, the tendency to say what we think others want to hear, failure to select the best word, prejudices, and strained sender-receiver relationships.[37] Also, subordinates do not always have the same "big picture" viewpoint that superiors possess and also do not always communicate well with someone in a higher position who is perhaps more fluent and persuasive than they are.

### *Cultural Empathy*

It is important to note that at least 90 percent of communication is *nonverbal* in nature, involving posture, facial expressions, gestures, tone of voice ("it's not what you say, but how you say it"), and so on.[38] People learn to interpret these nonverbal messages by growing up in a particular culture, but not every culture interprets nonverbal cues in the same way.

For example, in some cultures the avoidance of eye contact by looking to the ground is meant to convey respect and humility. Making what to some people are exaggerated hand gestures may be a normal means of communication in some cultures, and social distance for conversation for some societies may be much closer than it is in the United States. Someone from Nigeria, for example, may stand less than 15 inches from someone while conversing, whereas about two feet is a comfortable conversation zone for Americans. These few examples demonstrate why criminal justice practitioners must possess cultural empathy and understand the cultural cues of citizens from other nations.

## Historical Approaches to Management

According to Ronald Lynch,[39] the history of management can be divided into three approaches and time periods: (1) scientific management (1900–1940), (2) human relations management (1930–1970), and (3) systems management (1965–present).

### *Scientific Management*

Frederick W. Taylor, who first emphasized time and motion studies, is known today as the *father of scientific management*. Spending his early years in the steel mills of Pennsylvania, Taylor became chief engineer and later discovered a new method of making steel; this allowed him to retire at age 45 to write and lecture. He became interested in methods to get greater productivity from workers and was hired in 1898 by Bethlehem Steel, where he measured the time it took workers to shovel and carry pig iron. Taylor recommended giving workers hourly breaks and going to a piecework system, among other adjustments. Worker productivity soared; the total number of shovelers needed dropped from about 600 to 140, and worker earnings increasing from $1.15 to $1.88 per day. The average cost of handling a long ton (2,240 pounds) dropped from $0.072 to $0.033.[40]

Taylor, who was highly criticized by unions for his management-oriented views, proved that administrators must know their employees. He published a book, *The Principles of Scientific Management*, in 1911. His views caught on, and soon emphasis was placed entirely on the formal administrative structure; terms such as *authority, chain of command, span of control*, and *division of labor* were coined.

In 1935, Luther Gulick formulated the theory of POSDCORB, an acronym for planning, organizing, staffing, directing, coordinating, reporting and budgeting (Figure 2.4); this philosophy was emphasized in police management for many years. Gulick stressed the technical and engineering side of management, virtually ignoring the human side.

The application of scientific management to criminal justice agencies was heavily criticized. It viewed employees as passive instruments whose feelings were completely disregarded. In addition, employees were considered to be motivated by money alone.

PLANNING: working out in broad outline what needs to be done and the methods for doing it to accomplish the purpose set for the enterprise;

ORGANIZING: the establishment of a formal structure of authority through which work subdivisions are arranged, defined, and coordinated for the defined objective;

STAFFING: the whole personnel function of bringing in and training the staff and maintaining favorable conditions of work;

DIRECTING: the continuous task of making decisions, embodying them in specific and general orders and instructions, and serving as the leader of the enterprise;

COORDINATING: the all-important duty of interrelating the various parts of the organization;

REPORTING: informing the executive and his assistants as to what is going on, through records, research, and inspection;

BUDGETING: all that is related to budgeting in the form of fiscal planning, accounting, and control.

**Figure 2.4**

Gulick's POSDCORB. *Source:* Luther Gulick and Lyndall Urwick, *Papers on the Science of Administration*. New York: Institute of Public Administration, 1937.

## Human Relations Management

Beginning in 1930, people began to realize the negative effects of scientific management on the worker. A view arose in policing that management should instill pride and dignity in officers. The movement toward human relations management began with the famous studies conducted during the late 1920s through the mid-1930s by the Harvard Business School at the Hawthorne plant of the Western Electric Company.[41] These studies, which are discussed in more detail later in this chapter, found that worker productivity is more closely related to *social* capacity than to physical capacity, that noneconomic rewards play a prominent part in motivating and satisfying employees, and that employees do not react to management and its rewards as individuals but as members of groups.[42]

In the 1940s and 1950s, police departments began to recognize the strong effect of the informal structure on the organization; agencies began using techniques such as job enlargement and job enrichment to generate interest in policing as a career. Studies indicated that the supervisor who was "employee centered" was more effective than one who was "production centered." Democratic or participatory management began to appear in police agencies. The human relations approach had its limitations, however. With the emphasis placed on the employee, the role of the organizational structure became secondary; the primary goal seemed to many to be social rewards, with little attention given to task accomplishment. Many police managers saw this trend as unrealistic. Employees began to give less and expect more in return.[43]

## Systems Management

In the mid-1960s, features of the human relations and scientific management approaches were combined in the *systems management* approach. Designed to bring the individual and the organization together, it attempted to help managers use employees to reach desired production goals. The systems approach recognized that it was still necessary to have some hierarchical arrangement to bring about coordination, that authority and responsibility were essential, and that overall organization was required.

The systems management approach combined the work of Abraham Maslow,[44] who developed a hierarchy of needs; Douglas McGregor,[45] who stressed the general theory of human motivation; and Robert Blake and Jane Mouton,[46] who developed the "managerial grid," which emphasized two concerns—for task and for people—that managers must have. (These theories are discussed in greater detail later.) In effect, the systems management approach holds that to be effective, the manager must be interdependent with other individuals and groups and have the ability to recognize and deal with conflict and change. More than mere technical skills are required; managers require knowledge of several major resources: people, money, time, and equipment.[47] Team cooperation is required to achieve organizational goals.

Several theories of leadership also have evolved over the past several decades, the most common being trait theory, leadership styles, and situational approaches. Each is discussed briefly next.

# Primary Leadership Theories

## *Trait Theory*

*Trait theory* was popular until the 1950s. This theory was based on the contention that good leaders possessed certain character traits that poor leaders did not. Those who developed this theory, Stogdill and Goode, believed that a leader could be identified through a two-step process. The first step involved studying leaders and comparing them to nonleaders to determine which traits only the leaders possessed. The second step sought people who possessed these traits to be promoted into managerial positions.[48]

A study of 468 administrators in 13 companies found certain traits in successful administrators. They were more intelligent and better educated; had a stronger need for power; preferred independent activity, intense thought, and some risk; enjoyed relationships with people; and disliked detail work more than their subordinates.[49] Figure 2.5 shows traits and skills commonly associated with leader effectiveness, according to Gary Yuki. Following this study, a review of the literature on trait theory revealed the traits most identified with leadership ability: intelligence, initiative, extroversion, sense of humor, enthusiasm, fairness, sympathy, and self-confidence.[50]

| Traits | Skills |
|---|---|
| Adaptable to situations | Clever (intelligent) |
| Alert to social environment | Conceptually skilled |
| Ambitious and achievement oriented | Creative |
| Assertive | Diplomatic and tactful |
| Cooperative | Fluent in speaking |
| Decisive | Knowledgeable about group task |
| Dependable | Organized (administrative ability) |
| Dominant (desire to influence others) | Persuasive |
| Energetic (high activity level) | Socially skilled |
| Persistent | |
| Self-confident | |
| Tolerant of stress | |
| Willing to assume responsibility | |

**Figure 2.5**

Traits and skills commonly associated with leadership effectiveness.
*Source:* Gary Yuki, *Leadership in Organizations.* Englewood Cliffs, N.J.: Prentice Hall, 1981, pp. 70, 121–125.

Trait theory has lost much of its support since the 1950s, partly because of the basic assumption of the theory that leadership cannot be taught. A more important reason, however, is simply the growth of new, more sophisticated approaches to the study of leadership. Quantifiable means to test trait theory were limited. What does it mean to say that a leader must be intelligent? By whose standards? As compared with persons within the organization or within society? How can traits such as sense of humor, enthusiasm, fairness, and the others listed earlier be measured or tested? The inability to measure these factors was the real flaw in and reason for the decline of this theory.

## Style Theory

A study at Michigan State University investigated how leaders motivated individuals or groups to achieve organizational goals. The study determined that leaders must have a sense of the task to be accomplished as well as the environment in which their subordinates work. Three principles of leadership behavior emerged from the Michigan study:

1. Leaders must assume the leadership role and give task direction to their followers.
2. Closeness of supervision directly affects employee production. High-producing units had less direct supervision; highly supervised units had lower production. Conclusion: Employees need some area of freedom to make choices. Given this, they produce at a higher rate.
3. Leaders must be employee oriented. It is the leader's responsibility to facilitate employees' accomplishment of goals.[51]

In the 1950s, Edwin Fleishman began studies of leadership at Ohio State University. After focusing on leader behavior rather than personality traits, he identified two dimensions of basic principles of leadership that could be taught: *initiating structure* and *consideration* (Figure 2.6).[52] Initiating structure

Initiating structure

Autocratic

Democratic

Consideration

? ◄── Laissez-faire

**Figure 2.6**

Style theory. *Source:* Richard N. Holden, *Modern Police Management*. Englewood Cliffs, N.J.: Prentice Hall, 1986, p. 40.

referred to supervisory behavior that focused on the achievement of organizational goals, and consideration was directed toward a supervisor's openness toward subordinates' ideas and respect for their feelings as persons. High consideration and moderate initiating structure were assumed to yield higher job satisfaction and productivity than high initiating structure and low consideration.[53]

The major focus of style theory is the adoption of a single managerial style by a manager based on his or her position in regard to initiating structure and consideration. Three pure leadership styles were thought to be the basis for all managers: autocratic, democratic, and laissez-faire.

**Autocratic leaders** are leader centered and have a high initiating structure. They are primarily authoritarian in nature and prefer to give orders rather than invite group participation. They have a tendency to be personal in their criticism. This style works best in emergency situations in which strict control and rapid decision making are needed. The problem with autocratic leadership is the organization's inability to function when the leader is absent. It also stifles individual development and initiative, because subordinates are rarely allowed to make an independent decision.[54]

The **democratic leader** tends to focus on working within the group and strives to attain cooperation from group members by eliciting their ideas and support. Democratic managers tend to be viewed as consideration oriented and strive to attain mutual respect with subordinates. Democratic leaders operate within an atmosphere of trust and delegate much authority. This style is useful in organizations in which the course of action is uncertain and problems are relatively unstructured. It often taps the decision-making ability of subordinates. In emergency situations requiring a highly structured response, however, democratic leadership may prove too time consuming and awkward to be effective. Thus, although the worker may appreciate the strengths of this style, its weaknesses must be recognized as well.[55]

The third leadership style, **laissez-faire,** is a hands-off approach in which the leader is actually a nonleader. The organization in effect runs itself, with no input or control from the manager. This style has no positive aspects, as the entire organization is soon placed in jeopardy. In truth, this may not be a leadership style at all; instead, it may be an abdication of administrative duties.

### Situational Leadership

Situational leadership theory recognizes that the workplace is a complex setting subject to rapid changes. Therefore, it is unlikely that one way of managing these varying situations would be adequate. In this view, the best way to lead depends on the situation.

In 1977, Paul Hersey and Kenneth Blanchard[56] presented a model of situational leadership that has been used for training by many major corporations and the military. Their model emphasizes the leader's behavior in relationship to followers' behavior (see Figure 2.7). The situational leadership requires the leader

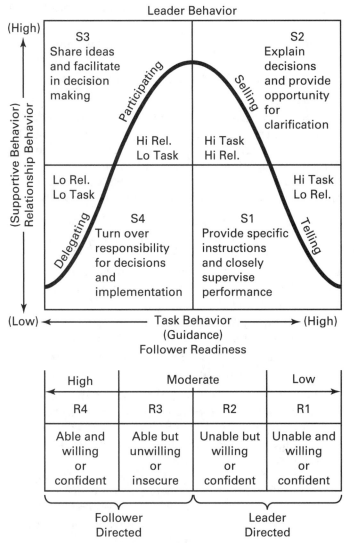

Leader Behavior

(High)

(Supportive Behavior)
Relationship Behavior

| S3 Share ideas and facilitate in decision making | S2 Explain decisions and provide opportunity for clarification |
|---|---|
| *Participating* | *Selling* |
| Hi Rel. Lo Task | Hi Task Hi Rel. |
| Lo Rel. Lo Task | Hi Task Lo Rel. |
| *Delegating* S4 Turn over responsibility for decisions and implementation | S1 Provide specific instructions and closely supervise performance *Telling* |

(Low) ◄──────── Task Behavior ────────► (High)
(Guidance)
Follower Readiness

| High | Moderate | | Low |
|---|---|---|---|
| R4 | R3 | R2 | R1 |
| Able and willing or confident | Able but unwilling or insecure | Unable but willing or confident | Unable and willing or confident |

Follower Directed ⏜ | Leader Directed ⏜

**Figure 2.7**

Situational leadership. *Source:* Copyrighted material. Reprinted with permission of Center for Leadership Studies, Escondido, CA 92025. All rights reserved.

to evaluate follower readiness in two ways; willingness (motivation) and ability (competence).

Situational leadership takes into account worker readiness; readiness is defined as the capacity to set high but attainable goals, the willingness to take responsibility, and the education and/or experience of the individual or the group. Figure 2.7 depicts the various levels of follower maturity, which are defined as:

R1: The followers are neither willing nor able to take responsibility for task accomplishment.

R2: The followers are willing but are not able to take responsibility for task accomplishment.

R3: The followers are not willing but are able to take responsibility for task accomplishment.

R4: The followers are willing and able to take responsibility for task accomplishment.

Task behavior, shown in Figure 2.7, is essentially the extent to which a leader engages in one-way communication with subordinates; relationship behavior is the extent to which the leader engages in two-way communication (by providing positive reinforcement, emotional support, and so on).

There are four basic styles of leadership that are associated with task accomplishment; the definition of these four styles of leadership are as follows:

S1: *Telling*. High task/low relationship style characterized by one-way communication in which the leader defines the roles of followers and tells them what, how, when, and where to do various tasks.

S2: *Selling*. High task/high relationship behavior is provided by two-way communication and socioemotional support to get followers to voluntarily buy into decisions that have been made.

S3: *Participating*. High relationship/low task behavior indicates both leader and follower have the ability and knowledge to complete the task.

S4: *Delegating*. Low relationship/low task behavior gives followers the opportunity to "run their own show" with little supervision.

The bell-shaped curve in the style-of-leader portion of Figure 2.7 means that, as the readiness level of followers develops, the appropriate style of leadership moves correspondingly. For example, a police supervisor who has a subordinate whose maturity is in the R3 range (able but unwilling) would be most effective employing an S3 (participating) style of leadership.

Hersey and Blanchard asserted that leaders could reduce their close supervision and direction of individuals and increase delegation as followers' readiness to complete tasks increased. The difficulty of this style of leadership is its dependence on leaders to diagnose the ability of followers and then adjust their leadership style to the given situation. This is often easier said than done.

# The Managerial Grid

In 1964, Blake and Mouton developed their managerial grid from the studies done by Edwin Fleishman and others at Ohio State University. The Ohio team used two variables, focus on task (initiating structure) and focus on relationships (consideration), to develop a management quadrant describing leadership behavior. The managerial grid (Figure 2.8) includes five leadership styles based on concern for output (production) and concern for people. Using a specially developed testing instrument, researchers can assign a numerical

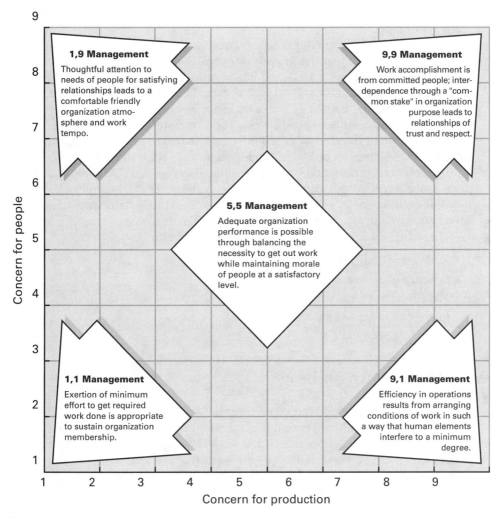

**Figure 2.8**

Management grid. *Source:* Reprinted by permission of *Harvard Business Review*
[Nov.-Dec. 1964]. An exhibit from "Breakthrough in Organizational
Development" by Robert R. Blake, Jane S. Mouton, Louis B. Barnes, and Larry
E. Greiner. Copyright 1964 by the President and Fellows of Harvard
College; all rights reserved.

score based on subjects' concern for each variable. Numerical indications such
as 9,1; 9,9; 1,1; and 5,5 are then plotted on the grid using the scales on the
horizontal and vertical axes. The grid is read like a map, right and up. Each
axis is numbered 1 to 9, with 1 indicating the minimum effort or concern and
9 the maximum. The horizontal axis represents the concern for production

and performance goals, and the vertical axis represents the concern for human relations or empathy.

The points of orientation are related to styles of management. The lower-left-hand corner of the grid shows the 1,1 style (representing a minimal concern for task or service and a minimal concern for people). The lower-right-hand corner of the grid identifies the 9,1 style. This type of leader would have a primary concern for the task or output and a minimal concern for people. Here, people are seen as tools of production. The upper-left-hand corner represents the 1,9 style, often referred to as "country club management," with minimum effort given to output or task. The upper right, 9,9, indicates high concern for both people and production—a "we're all in this together," common-stake approach of mutual respect and trust. In the center—a 5,5, "middle-of-the-road" style—the leader has a "give a little, be fair but firm" philosophy, providing a balance between output and people concerns.[57]

These five leadership styles can be summarized as follows:[58]

- Authority-compliance management (9,1)
- Country club management (1,9)
- Middle-of-the-road management (5,5)
- Impoverished management (1,1)
- Team management (9,9)

## Types of Leadership Skills

In 1974, Robert Katz identified three essential skills that leaders should possess: technical, human, and conceptual. Katz defined a *skill* as the capacity to translate knowledge into action in such a way that a task is accomplished successfully.[59] Each of these skills (when performed effectively) results in the achievement of objectives and goals, which is the primary task of management.

*Technical skills* are those a manager needs to ensure that specific tasks are performed correctly. They are based on proven knowledge, procedures, or techniques. A police detective, a court administrator, and a probation officer have all developed technical skills directly related to the work they perform. Katz wrote that a technical skill "involves specialized knowledge, analytical ability within that specialty, and facility in the use of the tools and techniques of the specific discipline."[60] This is the skill most easily trained for. A court administrator, for example, has to be knowledgeable in areas such as computer applications, budgeting, caseload management, space utilization, public relations, and personnel administration; a police detective must possess technical skills in interviewing, fingerprinting, and surveillance techniques.[61]

*Human skills* involve working with people, including being thoroughly familiar with what motivates employees and how to utilize group processes. Katz visualized human skills as including "the executive's ability to work effectively as a group member and to build cooperative effort within the team he leads."[62]

Katz added that the human relations skill involves tolerance of ambiguity and empathy. *Tolerance of ambiguity* means that the manager is able to handle problems when insufficient information precludes making a totally informed decision. **Empathy** is the ability to put oneself in another's place. An awareness of human skills allows a manager to provide the necessary leadership and direction, ensuring that tasks are accomplished in a timely fashion and with the least expenditure of resources.[63]

*Conceptual skills*, Katz said, involve "coordinating and integrating all the activities and interests of the organization toward a common objective."[64] Katz considered such skills to include "an ability to translate knowledge into action." For example, in a criminal justice setting, a court decision concerning the admissibility of evidence would need to be examined in terms of how it affects detectives, other court cases, the forensic laboratory, the property room, and the work of the street officer.

Katz emphasized that these skills can be taught to actual and prospective administrators; thus, good administrators are not simply born but can be trained in the classroom. Furthermore, all three of these skills are present in varying degrees for each management level. As one moves up the hierarchy, conceptual skills become more important and technical skills less important. The common denominator for all levels of management is *human* skills. In today's litigious environment, it is inconceivable that a manager could neglect the human skills.

# Motivating Employees

One of the most fascinating subjects throughout history is how to motivate people. Some have sought to do so through justice (Plato), others through psychoanalysis (Freud), some through conditioning (Pavlov), some through incentives (Taylor), and still others through fear (any number of dictators, czars, pharaohs, and despots). From the industrial revolution until today, managers have been trying to get a full day's work from their subordinates. The controversy in the early 1990s caused by Japanese businessmen who stated that American workers were lazy certainly raised our collective ire; many U.S. businesspeople and managers would probably agree that better worker motivation is needed. As Donald Favreau and Joseph Gillespie stated: "Getting people to work, the way you want them to work, when you want them to work, is indeed a challenge."[65]

Many theories have attempted to explain motivation. Some of the best known are those resulting from the Hawthorne studies and those developed by Abraham Maslow, Douglas McGregor, and Frederick Herzberg, all of which are discussed here along with the expectancy and contingency theories.

## *The Hawthorne Studies*

As mentioned earlier, one of the most important studies of worker motivation and behavior, launching intense interest and research in those areas, was the Western Electric Company's study in the 1920s. In 1927, engineers at the

# EXHIBIT 2.1
# Leadership's Bond of Trust

*By Lawrence B. Kokkelenberg*

The old military dogma, one also quite familiar to many areas of the private sector, was "I am the boss you are the subordinate, just do what I tell you to do. You don't have to trust me, in fact you don't even have to like me. Just follow orders." Many old adages support this paradigm: "Leadership is a lonely position." "A manager's job is to manage, not run a popularity contest." "If you are going to lead, then lead." "When I tell you to jump, just go up, I'll tell you when to come down."

This autocratic approach worked well for America for 200 years, but that was back in the days when life was simple. Back then if you did not work, you did not eat. Today if you don't work, you can make a pretty good living. We are not economically or financially bound by a job today as we were then. Back then, having a job was only a means to an end (providing for your family). Today, having a meaningful career is an important end in itself. Back then, we worked for someone; today we want to work with someone. (Today there are no "employees"; everyone is an "associate.") Back then, work came first, then family. For many workers today, family is first and work second. Back then there was [*sic*] little, if any, civil rights laws, today, everyone has rights.

Times have changed, people's values have changed. People today are more sophisticated and more mature than the workers of 50 years ago. In fact, the entire culture has changed, and if leadership does not change its style then it is the leadership that is out of sync with the culture and the desires of the American work force. The new Generation X'ers will only serve to prove the above even further and more rapidly than the current generation.

More than ever before in the history of American management, values are critical. . . . A leader's values color the entire organization or country. . . . Values drive the behavior and therefore the culture of an organization. All organizations have values, whether they know it or not. Simply watch how people are treated in any organization and you'll see their informal values. Trust is one of those critical values.

Why is trust important? Because all good sustained relationships require trust. Think about this: Would you voluntarily follow anyone you did not trust? We learned this lesson in Vietnam about not trusting our military leaders. Look what happened to those individuals.

To be a leader, you must have followers. So the question to ask yourself is why in the world would anyone choose to voluntarily follow you. What traits or characteristics do you possess that would encourage people to say, "I'll go with you anywhere"? Here is the acid test. If you left your current department or agency and went to another, would you have people who would want to transfer with you, or would the remaining staff now have a party because you're gone?

---

Certainly one of the key characteristics of an effective leader is that followers trust him or her. Have you ever worked for someone you did not trust? What was the atmosphere like? How would you characterize your relationship with him or her? What were some of the qualities or traits of this boss? Contrast this with someone you did trust. What was this atmosphere like? How would you characterize this trusting relationship? What were some of the qualities or traits of this boss?

Leadership is not about position, title or rank; it is about developing, possessing or acquiring the necessary traits to encourage people to voluntarily follow us. We tend to trust those individuals who have integrity, solid values and a strong character ethic. We tend not to trust those individuals who are duplicitous, upholding the law for others while violating it themselves. How many officers speed on their way to and from work every day, and then write tickets for citizens who do the same? . . .

If you want to be a trusted leader, work on your character and be trustworthy. Over time, establish yourself as an individual of great character and moral strength, walk the talk, have integrity, be honest and fair, do the right things and you will be a trusted leader.

*Source:* Reprinted with permission from *Law Enforcement News*, May 15, 2001, pp. 9, 10. John Jay College of Criminal Justice (CCNY), 555 West 57th St., New York, NY 10019.

Hawthorne Plant of Western Electric near Chicago conducted an experiment with several groups of workers to determine the effect of illumination on production. The engineers found that when illumination was increased in stages, production increased. To verify their findings, they reduced illumination to its previous level; again, production increased. Confused by their findings, they contacted Elton Mayo and his colleague Fritz Roethlisberger from Harvard to investigate.[66] First, the researchers selected several experienced women assemblers for an experiment. Management removed the women from their formal group and isolated them in a room. The women were compensated on the basis of the output of their group. Next, researchers began a series of environmental changes, each discussed with the women in advance of its implementation. For example, breaks were introduced and light refreshments were served. The normal six-day week was reduced to five days and the workday was cut by one hour. *Each* of these changes resulted in increased output.[67] To verify these findings, researchers returned the women to their original working conditions; breaks were eliminated, the six-day workweek was reinstituted, and all other work conditions were reinstated. The results were that production again increased!

Mayo and his team then performed a second study at the Hawthorne plant. A new group of 14 workers—all males who worked in simple, repetitive telephone coil-winding duties—were given variations in rest periods and workweeks.[68] The men were also put on a reasonable piece rate—that is, the more they produced, the more money they would earn. The assumption was that the workers would strive to produce more since it was in their own economic interest to do so.

The workers soon split into two informal groups on their own, each group setting its own standards of output and conduct. The workers' output did not increase. Neither too little nor too much production was permitted, and peers exerted pressure to keep members in line. The values of the informal group appeared to be more powerful than the allure of bigger incomes:

1. Don't be a "rate buster" and produce too much work.
2. If you turn out too little work, you are a "chiseler."
3. Don't be a "squealer" to supervisors.
4. Don't be officious; if you aren't a supervisor, don't act like one.[69]

Taken together, the Hawthorne studies revealed that people work for a variety of reasons, not just for money and subsistence. They seek satisfaction for more than their physical needs at work and from their co-workers. For the first time, clear evidence was gathered to support workers' social and esteem needs. As a result, this collision between the human relations school, begun in the Hawthorne studies, and traditional organizational theory sent researchers and theorists off in new and different directions. At least three major, new areas of enquiry evolved: (1) what motivates workers (leading to the work of Maslow and Herzberg), (2) leadership (discussed earlier), and (3) organizations as behavioral systems.

## *Maslow's Hierarchy of Needs*

Abraham H. Maslow (1908–1970), founder of the humanistic school of psychology, conducted research on human behavior at the Air University, Maxwell Air Force Base, Alabama, during the 1940s. His approach to motivation was unique in that the behavior patterns analyzed were those of motivated, happy, and production-oriented people—achievers, not underachievers. He studied biographies of historical and public figures, including Abraham Lincoln, Albert Einstein, and Eleanor Roosevelt; he also observed and interviewed some of his contemporaries—all of whom showed no psychological problems or signs of neurotic behavior.

Maslow hypothesized that if he could understand what made these people function, it would be possible to apply the same techniques to others, thus achieving a high state of motivation. His observations were coalesced into a *hierarchy of needs.*[70]

Maslow concluded that because human beings are part of the animal kingdom, their basic and primary needs or drives would be physiological: air, food, water, sex, and shelter. These needs are related to survival. Next in order of importance are needs related to safety or security: protection against danger, murder, criminal assault, threat, deprivation, and tyranny. At the middle of the hierarchy is belonging, or social needs: being accepted by one's peers, and association with members of groups. The next level on the hierarchy are the needs or drives related to ego: self-esteem, self-respect, power, prestige, recognition, and status. Located at the top of the hierarchy is self-realization or actualization: self-fulfillment, creativity, becoming all that one is capable of becoming.[71] Figure 2.9 depicts this hierarchy.

Unlike the lower needs, the higher needs are rarely satisfied. Maslow suggested that to prevent frustration, needs should be filled in sequential order. A satisfied need is no longer a motivator. Maslow's research also indicated that once a person reaches a high state of motivation (i.e., esteem or self-realization levels), he or she will remain highly motivated, will have a positive attitude toward the organization, and will follow a "pitch in and help" philosophy.

## McGregor's Theory X/Theory Y

Douglas McGregor (1906–1967), who served as president of Antioch College and then on the faculty of the Massachusetts Institute of Technology, was one of the great advocates of humane and democratic management. At Antioch, McGregor tested his theories of democratic management. He noted that behind every managerial decision or action are assumptions about human behavior. He chose the simplest terms possible with which to express them, designating one set of assumptions as Theory X and the other Theory Y.[72]

*Theory X* managers hold traditional views of direction and control, such as the following:

- The average human being has an inherent dislike of work and will avoid it if possible. This assumption has deep roots, beginning with the punishment of Adam and Eve and their banishment into a world where they had to work for a living. Management's use of negative reinforcement and the emphasis on "a fair day's work" reflect an underlying belief that management must counter an inherent dislike for work.[73]

- Because of this human characteristic of dislike of work, most people must be coerced, controlled, directed, or threatened with punishment to get them to put forth adequate effort toward the achievement of organizational objectives. The dislike of work is so strong that even the promise of rewards is not generally enough to overcome it. People will accept the rewards and demand greater ones. Only the threat of punishment will work.[74]

- The average human being prefers to be directed, wishes to avoid responsibility, has relatively little ambition, and wants security above all. This assumption of the "mediocrity of the masses" is rarely expressed so bluntly. Although much lip service is paid to the "sanctity" of the worker and human beings in general, many managers reflect this assumption in practice and policy.

(*Note:* Theory X managers would be autocratic and classified as a 9,1 on the managerial grid.)

| Self-Realization Needs | Job-Related Satisfiers |
|---|---|
| Reaching Your Potential<br>Independence<br>Creativity<br>Self-Expression | Involvement in Planning<br>Your Work<br>Freedom to Make Decisions<br>Affecting Work<br>Creative Work to Perform<br>Opportunities for Growth<br>and Development |

| Esteem Needs | Job-Related Satisfiers |
|---|---|
| Responsibility<br>Self-Respect<br>Recognition<br>Sense of Accomplishment<br>Sense of Competence | Status Symbols<br>Merit Awards<br>Challenging Work<br>Sharing in Decisions<br>Opportunity for Advancement |

| Social Needs | Job-Related Satisfiers |
|---|---|
| Companionship<br>Acceptance<br>Love and Affection<br>Group Membership | Opportunities for Interaction<br>with Others<br>Team Spirit<br>Friendly Co-workers |

| Safety Needs | Job-Related Satisfiers |
|---|---|
| Security for Self and Possessions<br>Avoidance of Risks<br>Avoidance of Harm<br>Avoidance of Pain | Safe Working Conditions<br>Seniority<br>Fringe Benefits<br>Proper Supervision<br>Sound Company Policies, Programs,<br>and Practices |

| Physical Needs | Job-Related Satisfiers |
|---|---|
| Food<br>Clothing<br>Shelter<br>Comfort<br>Self-Preservation | Pleasant Working Conditions<br>Adequate Wage or Salary<br>Rest Periods<br>Labor-Saving Devices<br>Efficient Work Methods |

**Figure 2.9**

Maslow's hierarchy of human needs. *Source:* A. H. Maslow, *Motivation and Personality*, 2d ed. New York: Harper & Collins, 1970.

*Theory Y managers* naturally take the opposite view of the worker:

- The expenditure of physical and mental effort in work is as natural as play or rest. The average human being does not inherently dislike work; it may even be a source of satisfaction, to be performed voluntarily.
- External control and the threat of punishment are not the only means for bringing about effort toward organizational objectives.
- Commitment to objectives is a function of the rewards associated with their achievement. The most significant of such rewards—satisfaction of ego and self-actualization needs—can be direct products of effort directed toward organizational objectives.
- Under proper conditions, the average human being learns not only to accept but to seek responsibility. Under this view, the avoidance of responsibility, lack of ambition, and the emphasis on security are general consequences of experience, not inherent human characteristics.
- The capacity to exercise a high degree of imagination, ingenuity, and creativity in the solution of organizational problems is widely, not narrowly, distributed in the population.
- Under the conditions of modern industrial life, the intellectual potentialities of the average human being are only partially utilized.

## Herzberg's Motivation-Hygiene Theory

During the 1950s, Frederick Herzberg conducted a series of studies in which he asked workers, primarily engineers, to describe the times when they felt particularly good and particularly bad about their jobs. The respondents identified several sources of satisfaction and dissatisfaction in their work. Then, from these findings, Herzberg isolated two vital factors found in all jobs: maintenance or hygiene factors and motivational factors.

**Maintenance or hygiene factors** are those elements in the work environment that meet an employee's hedonistic need to avoid pain. Hygiene factors include the necessities of any job (e.g., adequate pay, benefits, job security, decent working conditions, supervision, interpersonal relations). Hygiene factors do not satisfy or motivate; they set the stage for motivation. They are, however, a major source of dissatisfaction when they are inadequate.[75]

**Motivational factors** are those psychosocial factors that provide intrinsic satisfaction and serve as an incentive for people to invest more of their time, talent, energy, and expertise in productive behavior. Examples include achievement, recognition, responsibility, the work itself, advancement, and potential for growth. The absence of motivators does not necessarily produce job dissatisfaction.[76]

Although these needs are obviously related, they represent totally different dimensions of satisfaction.

## EXHIBIT 2.2
## Real Leadership Is More than Just a Walk in the Park

*By Lawrence D. Kokkelenberg*

"If you think you're a leader, but nobody is following you, then you are just out for a walk."

Bosses have subordinates, but true leaders have followers regardless of their rank or title. Historically, when individuals thought of leadership, they thought of rank. For rookies, it was the field training officer and for everyone else it was the level(s) above their rank. That perception, along with a top-down chain of command, caused a lot of people to believe that they cannot or should not do anything about reoccurring or organizational problems. Organizational problems were beyond their authority, even if they saw departmental problems and solutions; they simply waited for those above them to resolve it.

In many police academies we teach the recruits to have good independent judgment and decision-making out on the street. But when it comes to department or agency issues, we enforce a chain-of-command approach. Today, departments and agencies are telling their employees that you are a leader regardless of your position, title or rank; if you see a problem, solve it or bring it to your boss's attention. . . .

Leadership begins with self-discipline or leadership of self. You must have self-confidence, self-worth, a sense of purpose and direction in your life, and established values that you choose to live by, before you can effectively have interdependence and work well with others.

Today many departments and agencies are adopting a cradle-to-grave approach to leadership. It begins with recruits at the academy and ends with senior law enforcement executives. There are essentially four levels of leadership and at each level different knowledge and skill sets are necessary. There is a different focus at each level, yet there is a common thread running through the entire program, and each level builds on the one before it.

1. At the core is personal leadership, which is leadership of self. Included here are ethics, developing values, self-confidence, and character development. Every recruit class and every academy should spend considerable time teaching and demonstrating ethics, value development, character development and the consequences that attend to the lack of these traits. Background checks are not sufficient. They only cull out the obvious and recent problem applicants. Avoiding the recruitment of felons is not the same as character development.

2. At the next level—FTO's, sergeants, lieutenants—the focus is on leadership of others, or interpersonal leadership. This level includes a wide variety of supervisory and management skills—most importantly, what it takes to lead others, what are the traits of effective leaders, and how to develop those traits. The recognition

that leadership is a choice, not a position, is critical here.

3. Next comes the management level of leadership (shift commanders, bureau chiefs, etc.). At this level there is broader responsibility, yet not at the senior command level. Leadership entails an understanding of organizational psychology and organizational effectiveness, systems, structure and their impact on behavior. Managerial style, mission vision and values development and their impact on the department's performance are a part of this level's skills to be learned.

4. The fourth level is the organizational level, and is for senior law enforcement executives who deal more with a large-scale or big-picture perspective. Strategy development, systems design, process mapping, re-engineering, leading organizational change and the development of agency culture are a part of this level's skill set.

For decades, leadership development has been looked at as a single training program, not a progression; as an event, not a process. For years we have promoted individuals to leadership positions simply because they were in the right spot at the right time, or because they were friends with someone above them. For years some departments have promoted the wrong people simply because they needed the position filled (crisis hiring on the belief that anyone is better than no one).

Many police agencies are now paying the price for past and current management and leadership malpractice. Police reputations and citizen trust are low, we are having trouble attracting high quality candidates to the profession, citizen suspicions and complaints, police turnover and police prosecutions are all up—the list goes on. Lack of leadership certainly contributed to the current problems and it will be the new leadership that helps reestablish policing as the noble profession it is, and regains citizen and world respect.

*Source:* Reprinted with permission from *Law Enforcement News*, February 14, 2001, p. 9. John Jay College of Criminal Justice (CCNY), 555 West 57th St., New York, NY 10019.

## *Expectancy and Contingency Theories*

In the 1960s, *expectancy theory* was developed, holding that employees will do what their managers or organizations want them to do if the following are true:

1. The task appears to be possible (employees believe they possess the necessary competence).

2. The reward (outcome) offered is seen as desirable by the employees (intrinsic rewards come from the job itself; extrinsic rewards are supplied from others).

3. There is a perception in the mind of employees that performing the required behavior or task will bring the desired outcome.

4. There is a good chance that better performance will bring greater rewards.[77]

Expectancy theory will work for an organization that specifies what behaviors it expects from people and what the rewards or outcomes will be for those who exhibit such behaviors. Rewards may be pay increases, time off, chances for advancement, a sense of achievement, or other benefits. Managers and organizations can find out what their employees want and see to it that they are provided with the rewards they seek. Walter Newsom[78] said that the reality of the expectancy theory can be summarized by the "nine C's": (1) capability (does a person have the capability to perform well?), (2) confidence (does a person believe that he or she can perform the job well?), (3) challenge (does a person have to work hard to perform the job well?), (4) criteria (does a person know the difference between good and poor performance?), (5) credibility (does a person believe the manager will deliver on promises?), (6) consistency (do subordinates believe that all employees receive similar preferred outcomes for good performance, and vice versa?), (7) compensation (do the outcomes associated with good performance reward the employee, with money and other types of rewards?), (8) cost (what does it cost a person, in effort and outcomes forgone, to perform well?), and (9) communication (does the manager comunicate with the subordinate?).

Later, in the 1970s, Morse and Lorsch built on McGregor's and Herzberg's theories with their theory of motivation called *contingency theory*. This theory sought to determine the fit between the organization's characteristics and its tasks and the motivations of individuals. The basic components of the contingency theory are that (1) among people's needs is a central need to achieve a sense of competence, (2) the ways in which people fulfill this need will vary from person to person, (3) competence motivation is most likely to be fulfilled when there is a fit between task and organization, and (4) a sense of competence continues to motivate people even after competence is achieved. In essence, we all want to be competent in our work. Contingency theory contends that people performing highly structured and organized tasks perform better in Theory X organizations and that those who perform unstructured and uncertain tasks perform better under a Theory Y approach. This theory tells managers to tailor jobs to fit people or to give people the skills, knowledge, and attitudes they will need to become competent.[79]

# Summary

Most young people entering the labor force would probably like to retain their individuality, feel free to express themselves, have a sense of being an important part of the team, and realize both extrinsic and intrinsic rewards from their work. The reality is, however, that a majority of people entering the job market will work within the structure of an organization that will not meet all of their personal needs.

We have seen that many organizations have a highly refined bureaucracy. Whether an organization will meet one's individual needs depends largely on its administrative philosophy. Therefore, our discussions in this chapter covered the structure and function of organizations and, just as important, how adminis-trators and subordinates function within them. Also shown to be of major impor-tance is the need for effective communication.

The point to be made above all else is that administrators must know their people. In addition to covering several prominent theories that have withstood the test of time, we pointed out some approaches that have not succeeded. One can learn much from a failed approach or even from a poor boss who failed to appreciate and understand subordinates and practiced improper or no motiva-tional techniques.

## Questions for Review

1. Define *organization*. What is its function and structure?
2. What are the three historical approaches to management? Distinguish be-tween the historical approaches to management and the more "enlight-ened," contemporary view.
3. What are some of the skills that strong leaders will commonly possess (use the Katz model) and some of the common weaknesses in leadership?
4. What are three major theories concerning the motivation of employees?
5. What does *communication* mean? What is its importance in organizations? Explain some of the major barriers to effective communication and why it can be particularly problematic in criminal justice agencies.
6. Objectively assess what kind of leader you would be likely to be (if helpful, use the management grid). Is it an effective style? What are some of the pos-sible advantages and disadvantages of that style?

## Notes

1. Steven Levy, "Working in Dilbert's World," *Newsweek* (August 12, 1996):52–57.
2. David A. Tansik and James F. Elliott, *Managing Police Organizations* (Monterey, Calif.: Duxbury Press, 1981), p. 1.
3. Stephen P. Robbins, *Organizational Theory: Structure, Design and Applications* (Engle-wood Cliffs, N.J.: Prentice Hall, 1987).
4. Larry K. Gaines, Mittie D. Southerland, and John E. Angell, *Police Administration* (New York: McGraw-Hill, 1991), p. 5.
5. Peter W. Blau and W. Richard Scott, *Formal Organizations* (Scranton, Pa.: Chandler, 1962), p. 43.
6. Gaines, Southerland, and Angell, *Police Administration*, p. 9.
7. Max Weber, *The Theory of Social and Economic Organization*, trans. A. M. Henderson and Talcott Parsons (New York: Oxford University Press, 1947), pp. 329–330.

8. James Q. Wilson, *Varieties of Police Behavior* (Cambridge, Mass.: Harvard University Press), pp. 2–3.

9. Ibid., p. 3.

10. Adapted from Lyndall F. Urwick, *Notes on the Theory of Organization* (New York: American Management Association, 1952).

11. Gaines, Southerland, and Angell, *Police Administration*, p. 9.

12. Leonard R. Sayles and George Strauss, *Human Behavior in Organizations* (Englewood Cliffs, N.J.: Prentice Hall, 1966), p. 349.

13. See, for example, Samuel C. Certo, *Principles of Modern Management: Functions and Systems*, 4th ed. (Boston: Allyn and Bacon, 1989), p. 103.

14. Quoted in Charles R. Swanson, Leonard Territo, and Robert W. Taylor, *Police Administration*, 2d ed. (New York: Macmillan, 1988), p. 127.

15. Quoted in Wayne W. Bennett and Karen Hess, *Management and Supervision in Law Enforcement* (St. Paul, Minn.: West, 1992), p. 61.

16. Paul Hersey and Kenneth H. Blanchard, *Management of Organizational Behavior*, 3d ed. (Englewood Cliffs, N.J.: Prentice Hall, 1977), p. 12.

17. Ibid.

18. Quoted in Bennett and Hess, *Management and Supervision in Law Enforcement*, p. 61.

19. Ibid.

20. Roger D. Evered and James C. Selman, "Coaching and the Art of Management," *Organizational Dynamics* (Autumn 1989):16.

21. Swanson, Territo, and Taylor, *Police Administration*, 2d ed., p. 61.

22. Ibid., p. 86.

23. Louis A. Radelet, *The Police and the Community: Studies* (Beverly Hills, Calif.: Glencoe, 1973), p. 92.

24. *Interpersonal Communication: A Guide for Staff Development* (Athens, Ga.: Institute of Government, University of Georgia, August 1974), p. 15.

25. Quoted in Swanson, Territo, and Taylor, *Police Administration*, 2d ed., p. 161.

26. Bennett and Hess, *Management and Supervision in Law Enforcement*, p. 85.

27. See R. C. Huseman, ibid., pp. 21–27. Material for this section was also drawn from Charles R. Swanson, Leonard Territo, and Robert W. Taylor, *Police Administration: Structures, Processes, and Behavior*, 4th ed. (Upper Saddle River, N.J.: Prentice Hall, 1998).

28. Charles R. Swanson, Leonard Territo, and Robert W. Taylor, *Police Administration: Structures, Processes, and Behavior*, 3d ed. (New York: Macmillan, 1993), p. 203.

29. D. Katz and R. L. Kahn, *The Social Psychology of Organizations* (New York: John Wiley & Sons, 1966), p. 239. As cited in P. V. Lewis, *Organizational Communication: The Essence of Effective Management* (Columbus, Ohio: Grid, 1975), p. 36.

30. Lewis, *Organizational Communication*, p. 38.

31. Swanson, Territo, and Taylor, *Police Administration*, 3d ed., p. 206.

32. See R. K. Allen, *Organizational Management Through Communication* (New York: Harper & Row, 1977), pp. 77–79.

33. Swanson, Territo, and Taylor, *Police Administration* (3d ed.), p. 248.

34. Stephen W. Mastrofski, "Police Agency Accreditation: The Prospects of Reform," *American Journal of Police*, 5:3 (1986):45–81.

35. Alex Markels, "Managers Aren't Always Able to Get the Right Message Across with E-Mail." *The Wall Street Journal*, August 6, 1996, p. 2.

36. Robert L. Montgomery, "Are You a Good Listener?" *Nation's Business* (October 1981): 65–68.

37. Bennett and Hess, *Management and Supervision in Law Enforcement*, p. 101.

38. G. Weaver, "Law Enforcement in a Culturally Diverse Society," *FBI Law Enforcement Bulletin*, September 1992.

39. Ronald G. Lynch, *The Police Manager: Professional Leadership Skills*, 3d ed. (New York: Random House, 1986), p. 4.

40. Certo, *Principles of Modern Management*, p. 35.

41. See Elton Mayo, *The Human Problems of an Industrial Civilization* (New York: Macmillan, 1933).

42. Paul M. Whisenand and Fred Ferguson, *The Managing of Police Organizations*, 3d ed. (Englewood Cliffs, N.J.: Prentice Hall, 1989), pp. 218-219.

43. Lynch, *The Police Manager*, pp. 5-6.

44. Abraham H. Maslow, *Motivation and Personality* (New York: Harper & Row, 1954).

45. Douglas McGregor, *The Human Side of Enterprise* (New York: McGraw-Hill, 1960).

46. Robert R. Blake and Jane S. Mouton, *The Managerial Grid* (Houston: Gulf Publishing Company, 1964).

47. Lynch, *The Police Manager*, pp. 7-8.

48. Richard Holden, *Modern Police Management,* 2d ed. (Upper Saddle River, N.J.: Prentice Hall, 1994), p. 47.

49. Thomas A. Mahoney, Thomas H. Jerdee, and Alan N. Nash, "Predicting Managerial Effectiveness," *Personnel Psychology* (Summer 1960):147-163.

50. Joe Kelly, *Organizational Behavior: An Existential Systems Approach*, rev. ed. (Homewood, Ill.: Richard D. Irwin, 1974), p. 363.

51. Bennett and Hess, *Management and Supervision in Law Enforcement*, pp. 65-66.

52. Edwin Fleishman, "Leadership Climate, Human Relations Training and Supervisory Behavior," *Personnel Psychology* 6 (1953):208-222.

53. Stephen M. Sales, "Supervisory Style and Productivity: Review and Theory," in Larry Cummings and William E. Scott (eds.), *Readings in Organizational Behavior and Human Performance* (Homewood, Ill.: Richard D. Irwin, 1969), p. 122.

54. Holden, *Modern Police Management*, pp. 39-40.

55. Ibid., pp. 41-42.

56. Paul Hersey and Kenneth H. Blanchard, *Management of Organizational Behavior* (Englewood Cliffs, N.J.: Prentice Hall, 1977).

57. Donald F. Favreau and Joseph E. Gillespie, *Modern Police Administration* (Englewood Cliffs, N.J.: Prentice Hall, 1978), p. 80.

58. Bennett and Hess, *Management and Supervision in Law Enforcement*, p. 66.

59. Robert L. Katz, "Skills of an Effective Administrator," *Harvard Business Review* 52 (1975):23.

60. Ibid., p. 23.

61. Dan L. Costley and Ralph Todd, *Human Relations in Organizations* (St. Paul, Minn.: West, 1978).

62. Ibid., p. 24.

63. James M. Higgins, *Human Relations: Concepts and Skills* (New York: Random House, 1982).

64. Ibid., p. 27.

65. Favreau and Gillespie, *Modern Police Administration*, p. 85.

66. Warren Richard Plunkett, *Supervision: The Direction of People at Work* (Dubuque, Iowa: Wm. C. Brown, 1983), p. 121.

67. Elton Mayo, *The Social Problems of an Industrial Civilization* (Boston: Division of Research, Graduate School of Business Administration, Harvard University, 1945), pp. 68–86.

68. Favreau and Gillespie, *Modern Police Administration*, pp. 100–101.

69. Frederick J. Roethlisberger and William J. Dickson, *Management and the Worker* (Cambridge, Mass.: Harvard University Press, 1939), p. 522.

70. Favreau and Gillespie, *Modern Police Administration*, p. 87.

71. Ibid.

72. Ibid., p. 88.

73. Ibid., p. 89.

74. Ibid.

75. Harry W. More and W. Fred Wegener, *Behavioral Police Management* (New York: Macmillan, 1992), pp. 163–164.

76. Frederick Herzberg, "One More Time: How Do You Motivate Employees," in Walter E. Netemeyer (ed.), *Classics of Organizational Behavior* (Oak Park, Ill.: Moore, 1978).

77. Randall S. Schuler, *Personnel and Human Resources Management* (St. Paul, Minn.: West, 1981), pp. 41–43.

78. Walter B. Newsom, "Motivate, Now!" *Personnel Journal* (February 1990):51–55.

79. Plunkett, *Supervision*, pp. 131–132.

# PART II

# THE POLICE

*This part consists of three chapters. Chapter 3 examines the organization and operation of police departments. Chapter 4 covers personnel roles and functions, and Chapter 5 discusses police issues and practices. The introductory section of each chapter provides specific chapter content, while case studies in police administration appear at the end of each chapter.*

# Chapter 3

# Police Organization and Operation

## Key Terms and Concepts

Bureaucracy

COPPS

Organization

S.A.R.A.

Specialization

## Learning Objectives

As a result of reading this chapter, the student will:

- understand the five ways in which police agencies organize their personnel and activities
- understand specialization and the advantages it has in relation to the police department
- be familiar with the disadvantages of Frederick Taylor's scientific management theory
- understand COPPS and be able to distinguish the different ways it has been implemented in police agencies
- be familiar with the S.A.R.A. process
- know the components of problem analysis
- know the importance of a supervisor, chief executive, and mid-level manager

*Blessed are the peacemakers.*

—Matthew 5:8

# Introduction

To perform smoothly (at least as smoothly as society, resources, politics, and other influences will permit), police agencies are organized to enhance the accomplishment of their basic mission and goals. This chapter examines contemporary police organization and operations.

First, we consider how police agencies are defined and how they operate as bona fide organizations. We then review the traditional bureaucratic as well as the contemporary organizations of police departments. Included are several examples of basic as well as more specialized organizational structures for police agencies.

We then discuss the need to develop appropriate policies, procedures, rules, and regulations. Following that, we examine the influence of research findings on contemporary policing operations, including how some "sacred cows" of policing have been shown to be ineffectual.

Next, we examine the now prevalent concept in police operations: community oriented policing and problem solving, or COPPS; this approach has caused many changes in the traditional organization and administration of police agencies. We define the term and discuss the problem-solving process, with emphasis on evaluating outcomes. Several case studies are included in this chapter section. Then we review what must occur in order for police organizations to change, including the roles of chief executives, mid-level managers, and first-line supervisors.

The chapter concludes with two case studies, for which the reader needs to consider how implementing community policing and problem solving would help solve neighborhood problems.

# Police Agencies as Organizations

## *Organizing: The Grouping of Activities*

An **organization** is an artificial structure created to coordinate either people or groups and resources to achieve a mission or goal.[1] Certainly police agencies fit this definition. First, the organization of these agencies includes a number of specialized units (e.g., patrol, traffic, investigation, records). The role of chief executives, mid-managers, and first-line supervisors is to ensure that these units work together to reach a common goal; allowing each unit to work independently would lead to fragmentation, conflict, and competition and would subvert the entire organization's goals and purposes. Second, police agencies consist of people who interact within the organization and with external organizations.

Through mission statements, policies and procedures, and management style, among other factors, police administrators attempt to ensure that the organization meets its overall goals of investigating and suppressing crime and that the organization works amiably with similar organizations. As the organization becomes larger, the need for people to cooperate to achieve the organizational goals increases. The formal organizational charts discussed later in this chapter assist in this endeavor by spelling out areas of responsibility and lines of communication and by defining the chain of command.

Police administrators modify or design the structure of their organization to fulfill their mission. An organizational structure reflects the formal organization of task and authority relationships determined to be most suited to accomplishing the police mission (organizational structures are discussed and shown later in this chapter). Organizing allows police agencies to group personnel and activities in five ways:

1. *By clientele:* In a police organization, personnel are assigned by the type of clientele to be served or monitored, such as juveniles, senior citizens, or gang members. Officers become familiar with the specific enforcement problems and patterns associated with different client populations.

2. *By style of service:* A police organization usually has a uniformed patrol bureau and a plainclothes detective bureau. The former is grouped by the nature of its services (conspicuous, preventive patrol, and preliminary investigations), and the latter by the same principle (follow-up investigations). This form of grouping takes advantage of specialized knowledge and skill and pinpoints responsibility.

3. *By geography:* When activities occur over a wide area, it is often beneficial to group people and functions together; examples include smaller city precincts or state police posts located throughout a state. Even in headquarters buildings, such functions as records, communications, and crime analysis usually share the same floor. This allows administrators to become familiar with the problems of related units.

4. *By time:* Some functions or services need to be performed beyond the normal workday, so that the next shift can continue the effort. Patrolling is an obvious example: It is divided into three shifts. This form of grouping tends to create problems of communication and coordination, however, because top administrators normally work the day shift, and many of their subordinates work evenings or nights. The need to delegate authority is critical under these circumstances.

5. *By process:* All personnel who use a particular type of equipment are placed in one function, such as crime laboratory personnel, automotive maintenance units, and special weapons units.[2]

## *Specialization in Police Agencies*

The larger an agency, the greater the need for specialization and the more vertical (taller) its organizational chart becomes. Some 2,300 years ago, Plato observed that "each thing becomes . . . easier when one man, exempt from other tasks, does one thing."[3]

**Specialization,** or the division of labor, is one of the basic features of traditional organizational theory.[4] Specialization produces different groups of functional responsibilities, and the jobs allocated to meet these different responsibilities are held by people who are considered to be especially well qualified to perform those jobs. Thus, specialization is crucial to effectiveness and efficiency in large organizations.[5]

Specialization makes the organization more complex, however, by complicating communication, increasing the units from which cooperation must be obtained, and creating conflict among different units. Specialization creates an increased need for coordination because it adds to the hierarchy, which can lead to narrowly defined jobs that stifle the creativity and energy of their incumbents. Police administrators are aware of these potential shortcomings of specialization and attempt through various means to inspire their employees to the extent possible. For example, personnel can be rotated to various jobs and given additional responsibilities that challenge them. In addition, in a medium-sized department serving a community of 100,000 or more, a police officer with 10 years of police experience could have had the responsibilities of dog handler, motorcycle officer, detective, and/or traffic officer while being a member of special weapons or hostage negotiation teams.

In sum, the advantages to specialization in large police departments include the following:

- *Placement of responsibility:* The responsibility for the performance of given tasks can be placed on specific units or individuals. For example, the traffic division investigates all accidents and the patrol division handles all calls for service.
- *Development of expertise:* Those who have specialized responsibilities receive specialized training. Homicide investigators can be sent to forensic pathology classes; special weapons and tactics teams train regularly to deal with terrorists or hostage situations.
- *Group esprit de corps:* Groups of specially trained persons share a camaraderie and depend on one another for success; this leads to cohesion and high morale.
- *Increased efficiency and effectiveness:* Specialized units have a high degree of proficiency in job task responsibility. For example, a specially trained financial crimes unit normally is more successful with complex fraud cases than is a general detective division.[6]

# Traditional and Contemporary Police Organization

## *The Traditional Bureaucratic Model*

By the 1950s, some police chiefs began to demonstrate that good administration could make a difference in a police organization's efficiency.[7] These administrators stressed military organization; for them, efficiency meant close supervision and strong internal discipline. This movement improved police service and probably appealed to most police officers, many of whom were military veterans.[8]

Frederick Taylor's scientific management theory was in vogue in the 1950s, but its task-oriented approach to worker productivity was not universally popular. Ronald Lynch[9] stated the major criticisms of the scientific management theory as it relates to policing:

1. Officers were considered passive instruments; their personal feelings were completely disregarded. Any differences, especially regarding motivation, were ignored; all officers were treated basically alike.
2. The employee was considered to be an "economic man" who could be motivated through wage incentives or fear of job loss.
3. The focus was on technical efficiency, not the effectiveness of the organization.
4. Efficiency of operation was to be obtained only through division of labor (breaking the job down into small parts), specialization of police activities, rigid structure of line and staff departments, and the use of a span of control whereby supervisors had only a few subordinates.

The scientific management theory, as many police officers know, is alive and well today in some police agencies where employees are still motivated by fear and administrators practice a "do as I say and not as I do" philosophy.

A **bureaucracy** is an organization with specialized functions, adherence to fixed rules, and a hierarchy of authority. Police organizations in the United States are bureaucracies, as are virtually all large organizations in modern society, such as the military, universities, and private corporations. To a large extent, the structure and management process of most police agencies are similar. The major agency differences occur between large and small departments; the former are more complex, reflect more specialization, have a taller hierarchical structure, and use an authoritarian style of command to a greater degree.

The administration of most police organizations is based on the traditional, pyramidal, quasi-military organizational structure containing to one extent or another the elements of a bureaucracy noted earlier. The appropriateness of the tall, hierarchical, quasi-military organizational structure of bureaucracies is often being challenged, especially with the relatively recent advent and rapid spread of **COPPS** (community oriented policing and problem solving). The California Department of Justice provided the following definition for COPPS:

Community-oriented policing and problem solving is a philosophy, management style, and organizational strategy that promotes proactive problem solving and police-community partnerships to address the causes of crime and fear as well as other community issues.[10]

The reasons for this disillusionment include the quasi-military discipline of police organizations; the inability of management to match talent and positions; the organizational restrictions on personal freedom of expression, association, and dress; communication blockage in the tall structure; the outmoded methods of operation that organizations cling to; the lack of management flexibility and real challenge of the job; and the narrow job descriptions in the lower ranks of police organizations.

The traditional hierarchical organizational structure found in policing represents strong barriers to COPPS. Therefore, before a meaningful transition can occur, the very core of an organization's culture must change. To ensure that COPPS becomes a part of the organizational culture, police agencies must link COPPS to how they recruit, hire, train, evaluate, promote, reward, and discipline their employees.[11] (See the example of Hayward, California, later; COPPS is examined more thoroughly later in this chapter.)

## *Attempts to Reform the Traditional Model*

Attempts to reform the traditional, tall hierarchical structure of police organizations and their inherent rank structure have been described as "attempts to bend granite."[12] Because the rank structure controls the incentives of pay, status, and power, it seriously hinders attempts to provide incentives for the officer on the street. Some attempts have been made, however, such as using expanded pay scales or salary incentives for the patrol officer (with step or ladder increases), and adopting skill attainment plans, which provide incentive pay for the patrol officer rank on the basis of longevity, certification in a skill, an academic degree, or a job assignment requiring a particular skill.

As noted in Chapter 2, in the 1940s and 1950s, some police departments began to recognize the needs of the employees within the organization; agencies began using techniques such as job enlargement and job enrichment to generate interest in policing as a career. Democratic or participatory management began to be used in police agencies as private industry also began to move away from the pyramid-shaped, tall organizational structure to a flatter structure.

This human relations approach had its limitations, however. By emphasizing the employee, the organizational structure became secondary. The primary goal of this approach seemed to many to be social rewards rather than accomplishing tasks. Employees began to give less and expect more in return.[13]

In the late 1960s, the military model was replaced by one that stressed bureaucratic accountability. In the 1970s, experts on police organization, such as Egon Bittner, contended that the military-bureaucratic organization of the police, which emphasized chain of command, adherence to rules, and unquestioned authority, created obstacles to communication and the development of a truly professional police system.[14]

Disenchantment with the traditional bureaucratic structure of police organizations may exist, but that structure continues to prevail. Many administrators still consider it the best one, especially when rapid leadership and division of labor are required in times of crises.

### A Fresh Approach: Hayward, California

A number of agencies—especially, again, with the spread of COPPS—have experimented with other organizational philosophies and approaches, with good results, flattening their organizational structure and functioning in nontraditional ways. Hayward, California, provides a good example of how the organization can change its structure, culture, and operation. After altering the organizational structure, replacing the traditional structure, and making the decision to shift its policing philosophy, the administration's initial focus was on personnel systems: recruiting, hiring, training, performance appraisal evaluations, and promotability. The following questions were explored:

1. Overall, what type of candidate, possessing what types of skills, is being recruited?

2. What specific knowledge, skills, and abilities reflect the COPPS philosophy—particularly problem-solving abilities and sensitivity to the needs of the community?

3. How can these attributes best be identified through the initial screening process?[15]

Administrators also analyzed the city's demographics, finding that the city had a diverse ethnic composition. To promote cultural diversity and sensitivity to the needs of the community, a psychologist was employed to develop a profile of an effective COPPS officer. These considerations became an integral part of the department's hiring process.[16]

Next, the training and performance evaluation systems were reappraised. All personnel—both sworn and civilian—had to receive COPPS training that provided a clear and thorough understanding of the history, philosophy, and transition to COPPS. The department's initial training was directed to management and supervisory personnel and designed to assist these employees in accomplishing the department's goals of reinforcing COPPS values, modifying the existing police culture, strategically transitioning the organization from traditional policing to the new philosophy, and focusing on customer relations.[17] Rank-and-file officers were given 40-hour blocks of instruction.

Performance and reward practices for personnel were modified to reflect the new criteria. Emphasizing quality over quantity (e.g., arrest statistics, number of calls for service, response times), new criteria included an assessment of how well a call for service was handled and what type of problem-solving approach was used to reach a solution for the problem.[18] Promotional processes were also retooled; a new phase was added to the department's promotional test to evaluate the candidate's decision-making abilities, analytical skills, communication skills, interpersonal skills, and professional contributions.[19]

Such examples demonstrate how a break from the traditional policing organizational structure and philosophy can assist—and is often indispensable toward accomplishing—a shift in agency mission and goals.

# Examples of Organizational Structures

An organizational structure helps departments carry out the many complex responsibilities of policing. It should be noted, however, that organizational structures will vary from one jurisdiction to another and are fluid in nature. The highly decentralized nature and the different sizes of police departments in the United States, as well as turnover in the chief executive officer (chief of police or sheriff) position, cause these structures to change. It is possible, however, to make certain general statements about all agencies to characterize a "typical" police organization.

As mentioned earlier, the police traditionally organize along military lines with a rank structure that normally includes the patrol officer, sergeant, lieutenant, captain, and chief. Many departments, particularly larger ones, employ additional ranks, such as corporal, major, and deputy chief, but there is a legitimate concern that these departments will become top heavy. The military rank hierarchy allows the organization to designate authority and responsibility at each level and to maintain a chain of command. The military model also allows the organization to emphasize supervisor-subordinate relationships and to maintain discipline and control.

Every police agency, regardless of size, has a basic plan of organization. In addition, every such agency, no matter how large or small, has an organizational chart. A visitor to the police station or sheriff's office may even see this organizational chart displayed prominently on a wall. Even if it is not on paper, such a chart exists. A basic organizational chart for a small agency is shown in Figure 3.1.

Operational or line elements involve policing functions in the field and may be subdivided into primary and secondary line elements. The patrol function—often called the "backbone" of policing—is the primary line element because it is the major law enforcement responsibility within the police organization. Most small police agencies, in fact, can be described as patrol agencies with the patrol forces responsible for all line activities.[20] Such agencies provide routine patrol, conduct criminal and traffic investigations, and make arrests. These agencies are basically generalists. In a community that has only one employee—for example, a marshal, he or she obviously must perform all the functions just listed. This agency's organizational chart is a simple horizontal one with little or no specialization.

Investigative and youth activities are the secondary operational elements. These functions would not be needed if the police were totally successful in their patrol and crime prevention efforts—an obviously impossible goal. Time

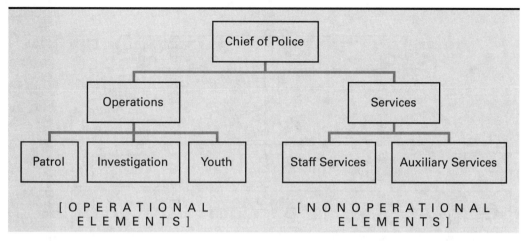

**Figure 3.1**

Basic police organizational structure.

and area restrictions on the patrol officers, as well as the need for specialized training and experience, require some augmenting of the patrol activity.

The nonoperational functions and activities can become quite numerous, especially in a large community. These functions fall within two broad categories: *staff services* (also known as administrative) and *auxiliary* (or technical) *services.* The staff services are usually people oriented and include recruitment, training, promotion, planning and research, community relations, and public information services. Auxiliary services involve the types of functions that a non-police person rarely sees, including jail management, property and evidence handling, crime laboratory services, communications (dispatch), and records and identification. Many career opportunities exist for persons interested in police-related work who cannot or do not want to be a field officer.

The basic organizational structure of the Portland, Oregon, Police Bureau (PPB) is shown in Figure 3.2. Portland has a population of about 530,000, and the PPB has about 1,300 total personnel, 999 of whom are sworn. The police budget is more than $120 million.[21] Some of the PPB functions are parochial—unique to that city—and are explained in an endnote.[22]

Portland's and other cities' organizational structures are designed to fulfill five functions: apportioning the workload among members and units according to a logical plan; ensuring that lines of authority and responsibility are as definite and direct as possible; specifying a unity of command throughout, so there is no question as to which orders should be followed; placing responsibility and authority, and if responsibility is delegated, the delegator is held responsible; and coordinating the efforts of members so that all will work harmoniously to accomplish the mission.[23] In sum, this structure establishes the chain of command and determines lines of communication and responsibility.

# Portland Police Bureau
## Organizational Chart

**Figure 3.2**

Portland Police Bureau organizational chart. Reprinted with permission.

# Policies, Procedures, Rules, and Regulations in Policing

Policies, procedures, rules, and regulations are important for defining role expectations for all police officers. The officers are granted an unusually strong power in a democratic society; because they possess such extraordinary powers, police officers pose a potential threat to individual freedom. Thus, because police agencies are service oriented in nature, they must work within well-defined, specific guidelines designed to ensure that all officers conform to behavior that will enhance public protection.[24]

Related to this need for policies, procedures, rules, and regulations is the fact that police officers possess a broad spectrum of discretionary authority in performing their duties. This fact, coupled with the danger posed by their work and the opportunities to settle problems informally, work against having narrow, inflexible job requirements.

Thus, the task for the organization's chief executive is to find the middle ground between unlimited discretion and total standardization. The police role is much too ambiguous to become totally standardized, but it is also much too serious and important to be left completely to the total discretion of the patrol officer. As Gary Sheehan and Gary Cordner put it, the idea is for chief executives to "harness, but not choke, their employees."[25]

Organizational *policies* are more general than procedures, rules, or regulations. Policies are basically guides to the organization's philosophy and mission and help to interpret those elements to the officers.[26] Policies should be committed to writing, then modified according to the changing times and circumstances of the department and community.

*Procedures* are more specific than policies; they serve as guides to action. A procedure is "more specific than a policy but less restrictive than a rule or regulation. It describes a method of operation while still allowing some flexibility within limits."[27]

Many organizations are awash in procedures. Police organizations have procedures that cover investigation, patrol, booking, radio communications, filing, roll-call, arrest, sick leave, evidence handling, promotion, and others. Such procedures are not totally inflexible, but they do describe in rather detailed terms the preferred methods for carrying out policy.

Some procedures are mandated by the U.S. Supreme Court. A good example is the Court's 1985 decision in *Tennessee v. Garner*. This decision resulted in a new policy concerning the use of deadly force. Officers are allowed to use deadly force only when a "suspect threatens the officer with a weapon or there is probable cause to believe that [the suspect] has committed a crime involving the infliction or threatened infliction of serious physical harm."[28]

Some police executives have attempted to run their departments via flurries of memos containing new procedures. This path is often fraught with difficulty. An abundance of standardized procedures can stifle initiative and imagination, as well as complicate jobs.[29] On the positive side, procedures can decrease the time wasted in figuring out how to accomplish tasks and thereby increase productivity. As they do with policies, chief executives must seek the middle ground in drafting procedures and remember that it is next to impossible to have procedures that cover all possible exigencies.

*Rules and regulations* are specific managerial guidelines that leave little or no latitude for individual discretion; they require action (or in some cases, inaction). Some require officers to wear their hats when outside their patrol vehicle, check the patrol vehicle's oil and emergency lights before going on patrol, not consume alcoholic beverages within 4 hours of going on duty, and arrive in court 30 minutes before sessions open or at roll call 15 minutes before scheduled duty time. Rules and regulations are not always popular, especially if perceived as unfair or unrelated to the job. Nonetheless, they contribute to the total police mission of community service.

Rules and regulations should obviously be kept to a minimum because of their coercive nature. If they become too numerous, they can hinder action and give the message that management believes that it cannot trust the rank and file to act responsibly on their own. Once again, the middle range is the best. As Thomas Reddin, former Los Angeles police chief, stated:

> Certainly we must have rules, regulations and procedures, and they should be followed. But they are no substitutes for initiative and intelligence. The more a [person] is given an opportunity to make decisions and, in the process, to learn, the more rules and regulations will be followed.[30]

# The Influence of Research on Police Functions

## *The Mid-1970s: Crises Stimulate Progress*

Little research concerning police functions and methods was conducted until 1964.[31] In fact, little substantive research examining police methods actually occurred until the mid-1970s. Two reasons account for this lack of inquiry into policing. First, the police agencies tended to resist outside scrutiny. Functioning in a bureaucratic environment, they—like other bureaucracies—were sensitive to outside research. Many police administrators perceived research studies as a threat to personal careers and the organization's image, and they were concerned as to the legitimacy of the research. Administrators were naturally reluctant to invite trouble. Given these obstacles, sociologists were often reluctant to attempt to penetrate the walls of what appeared to be a closed fortress.

Second, few police administrators saw any benefit to the research for them. They had no need to challenge traditional methods of operation. The "if it ain't broke, don't fix it" attitude prevailed, particularly among old-school administrators. Some ideas—additional police personnel and vehicles equaled more patrolling and therefore less crime, a quicker response rate, and a happier private citizenry—were etched in stone. The methods and effectiveness of detectives and their investigative techniques and the old myths of good policing were not even open to debate.

Then, as the police faced crises, things began to change. As Herman Goldstein stated,

> Crises stimulate progress. The police came under enormous pressure in the late 1960s and early 1970s, confronted with concern about crime, civil rights demonstrations, racial conflicts, riots and political protests.[32]

A 1985 national survey probed the effect of budget limits or cuts on police forces in the 1970s and 1980s. It found that 44 percent of police and sheriff's departments had the same number or fewer personnel than they had five years earlier.[33] As a result, police administrators came under increasing pressure to use personnel and equipment in the most efficient fashion—to do more with less. This pressure may explain why police administrators became more willing to challenge traditional assumptions and beliefs and to open the door to researchers. That willingness to allow researchers to examine traditional methods led to the growth and development of two important policing research organizations, the Police Foundation and the Police Executive Research Forum (PERF).[34]

George Kelling and a research team at the Police Foundation conducted the best-known study of the assumptions concerning patrolling in Kansas City, Missouri, in 1973. The researchers divided the city into 15 beats, which were then categorized into five groups of three matched beats each. Each group was composed of neighborhoods that were similar in terms of population, crime characteristics, and calls for police services. Patrolling techniques used in the three beats varied; there was no preventive patrolling in one (police responded only to calls for service); preventive patrol activity in another was two or three times the typical amount; and the third beat maintained the usual level of service. Citizens were interviewed and crime rates measured during the one-year period of the Kansas City Preventive Patrol Experiment. The results showed no significant differences in the crime rates or citizens' perceptions of safety as a result of the type of preventive patrol an area received. Similar results were obtained in studies in St. Louis and Minneapolis. These studies also found that the police can stop routinely patrolling their beats for up to a year without necessarily being missed by the residents and without a rise in crime rates in the patrol area.[35]

Police response time has also been analyzed. According to the long-standing assumption concerning police response time, the ability to arrest perpetrators decreased proportionately as response time increased. Thus, conventional wisdom held, the more police on patrol in rapid vehicles, the more quickly they can reach the crime scene and make arrests. In 1977, the National Institute of Justice (NIJ) funded a project to analyze the effect of response time on the outcome of police services (arrests, citizen injury, witness availability, and citizen satisfaction). Again, the site of the research was Kansas City, Missouri. Over a two-year period, the police department collected information on crimes in 56 of its 207 beats; observers rode with police officers and collected travel-time data. The results indicated that police response time was unrelated to the probability of making an arrest or locating a witness, and neither dispatch nor travel time was strongly associated with citizen satisfaction. The time it takes to *report* a crime, the study found, is the major determining factor of whether an on-scene arrest takes place and whether witnesses are located.[36]

## *Rethinking "Sacred Cow" Traditions*

On the basis of these two major studies of patrol methods and effectiveness, many police executives began rethinking their "sacred cow" traditions that have kept the old myths in a protective shroud. Researchers examined another sacred cow—the methods of criminal investigations used by police and their effectiveness. Police departments have always ranked criminal investigation—attempting to link a crime with a suspect—as one of their most critical duties. The belief—largely perpetuated by the movies—that most crimes can be solved, that most cases involving unknown criminals are solved through good detective work, and that detectives should be assigned to follow-up investigation of all but the most minor criminal cases has historically surrounded the area of investigation.[37]

Until 1975, the criminal investigation function itself had never been investigated. The NIJ hired the RAND Corporation to study the investigative function. The study surveyed 150 large police agencies by interviewing and observing investigators in more than 25 police departments. At about the same time, the Stanford Research Institute (SRI) conducted another study of investigations; it found that in Alameda County, California, in more than 50 percent of the burglaries in which the burglar was arrested, the arrest was made within 48 hours of the report of the burglary. Both the RAND and SRI study results suggested that detectives actually played a relatively minor role in solving burglaries and that the information provided by patrol officers from their preliminary investigations was an important determining factor in whether a follow-up investigation would result in an arrest.[38]

As a result of these findings, NIJ funded more studies of the investigation process in the late 1970s in Santa Monica, California; Cincinnati, Ohio; and Rochester and Syracuse, New York. Several consistent findings emerged: Many serious crimes are not solved; patrol officers are responsible, directly or indirectly, for most arrests (either arresting the suspect at the scene or obtaining helpful descriptions from victims or witnesses); and only a small percentage of arrests are made by detectives with specialized training and skill.[39]

In 1983, PERF published the results of its own look at the investigative function, including the following:

> Changes have occurred in investigative management as a result of the earlier studies; all of them had a profound influence on investigative management today. For instance, there has been a greater emphasis on case screening and on improving the role of patrol officers in investigations—policy changes that were recommended by many of the earlier studies.[40]

These studies proved that if not all cases can be solved, not all cases should be pursued as vigorously as others. The SRI research produced "predictors of case closure," an index to be used by the police for estimating the solvability of burglaries. Included are elements such as the estimated range of time when the crime occurred, whether a witness reported the offense and an eyewitness was present, if usable fingerprints were retrieved, and if a suspect was described or named. Using this yardstick, police can better manage the burglary caseload and determine which burglaries have little or no chance of being solved. Obviously, using the solvability factors of this predictor can prevent the expenditure of tremendous amounts of time and resources on dead-end investigations.

## *Other Major Findings*

Other major research findings have shaken old assumptions about policing. The following points are now accepted in most quarters as part of the common wisdom of policing:

1.  The police do much more than deal with crime; they deal with many forms of behavior that are not defined as criminal.
2.  In the past, too much dependence has been placed on the criminal law (using arrests only) in order to get the police job done; arrest and prosecution are simply not effective ways to handle much of what constitutes police business.
3.  Police use a wide range of methods—formal and informal—to do their jobs. Law enforcement is only one method among many.
4.  The police (contrary to the desires of earlier advocates of the "professional" model) are not autonomous. The sensitive function they perform requires that they be accountable, through the political process, to the community.
5.  Individual police officers exercise a great deal of discretion in deciding how to handle the tremendous variety of circumstances they confront.[41]

We now know that two-person patrol cars are no more effective than one-person cars in reducing crime or apprehending criminals. Furthermore, injuries to police officers are not more likely to occur in one-person cars. And, most officers on patrol do not stumble across felony crimes in progress—only "Dirty Harry" does so.[42]

Although the results of research studies reported here should not be viewed as being conclusive—different results could be obtained in different communities—they do demonstrate that traditional police methods should be viewed cautiously. The "we've always done it this way" mentality, still pervading policing to a large extent, may not only be an ineffective means of organizing and administering a police agency, but may also be a costly squandering of valuable human and financial resources.

A police agency can perform different types of research provided that it has the desire to do it and the personnel to implement it. For example, research could be conducted into the best way to create beats. Traditionally, many city beats have been determined by using a conveniently located major street or river in town. It would be far better if the geographical boundaries for beats were drawn after analyzing where most crimes have been committed and with a view to making the workload more equal among available officers.

In the same vein, it would be a better use of resources to assign personnel according to the time of day and day of week when most crimes and calls for service occur rather than to set the goals as reducing response time, which has not been found to increase arrests. Other types of in-house research that can be performed involve the number of crimes that are cleared by arrest, the number of officers per 1,000 population, conviction rates, types of crimes committed and value of items taken, and crime projections.

Next we discuss COPPS, including some evaluation and research efforts.

# Community Oriented Policing and Problem Solving

## *Today's Dominant Philosophy*

Community oriented policing and problem solving—COPPS, defined earlier in this chapter—has emerged as the dominant strategy of policing. It is an approach to crime detection and prevention that provides police officers and supervisors with new tools for addressing recurrent problems that plague communities and consume a majority of police agency time and resources.

Two principal and interrelated components emerge from this definition: community engagement (partnerships) and problem solving. With its focus on collaborative problem solving, COPPS seeks to improve the quality of policing. The S.A.R.A. process discussed next provides the police with the tools necessary to accomplish these tasks.

## *The S.A.R.A. Process*

**S.A.R.A.** (*S*canning, *A*nalysis, *R*esponse, *A*ssessment) (Figure 3.3) provides officers with a logical step-by-step framework to identify, analyze, respond to, and evaluate crime, fear of crime, and neighborhood disorder. This approach, with its emphasis on in-depth analysis and collaboration, replaces officers' short-term, reactive responses with a process vested in longer-term outcomes.

**Figure 3.3**

A problem-solving process. *Source:* John E. Eck and William Spelman, *Problem-Solving: Problem-Oriented Policing in Newport News* (Washington, D.C.: U.S. Department of Justice, National Institute of Justice, 1987), p. 43.

### *Scanning: Problem Identification*

Scanning involves problem identification. It initiates the problem-solving process by conducting a preliminary inquiry to determine if a problem really exists and whether further analysis is needed. A problem may be defined as a cluster of two or more similar or related incidents that are of substantive concern to the community and to the police. If the incidents to which the police respond do not fall within the definition of a problem, then the problem-solving process is not applicable.

Numerous resources are available to the police for identifying problems, including calls for service data—especially repeat calls, crime analysis information, police reports, and officers' own experiences. Scanning helps the officer determine whether a problem really exists before moving on to more in-depth analysis.

### *Analysis: Determining the Extent of the Problem*

Analysis is the heart of the problem-solving process. It is the most difficult and important step in the S.A.R.A. process. Without analysis, long-term solutions are unlikely and the problem will persist.

Here, officers gather as much information as possible from a variety of sources. A complete and thorough analysis consists of officers identifying the seriousness of the problem, all persons affected, and the underlying causes. Officers should also assess the effectiveness of current responses.

Many tools are available to assist with analysis. Crime analysis may be useful in collecting, collating, analyzing, and disseminating data relating to crime, incidents not requiring a report, criminal offenders, victims, and locations. Mapping and geographic information systems (GIS) can identify patterns of crime and "hot-spots." Police offense reports can also be analyzed for suspect characteristics, victim characteristics, and information about high-crime areas and addresses. Computer-aided dispatch (CAD) is also a reliable source of information, as it collects data on all incidents and specific locations from which an unusual number of incidents require a police response.

Generally, three elements are needed for a problem to occur: an *offender*, a *victim*, and a *location*. The problem analysis triangle, shown in Figure 3.4, helps officers visualize the problem and understand the relationship between the three elements. The three elements must be present for a crime or harmful

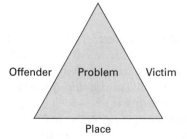

**Figure 3.4**

Problem analysis triangle.
*Source*: Bureau of Justice Assistance, U.S. Department of Justice, *Comprehensive Gang Initiative: Operations Manual for Implementing Local Gang Prevention and Control Programs* (Draft, October 1993), pp. 3–10.

event to occur; removing one or more of these elements will remove the problem. Strategies for removing one of these elements are only limited to an officer's ability to develop responses, and available resources.

### Response: Formulating Tailor-Made Strategies

Once a problem has been clearly defined, officers may seek the most effective responses. Developing long-term solutions to problems is of paramount importance with COPPS; however, officers cannot ignore the fact that more serious situations may require immediate action. In the case of an open-air drug market involving rival gang violence, police may initially increase the number of patrols in the area to arrest offenders, gain control of public space, and secure the safety of residents and officers. Once this is accomplished, long-term responses, which include the collaborative efforts of officers, residents, and other agencies, may be considered.

Administrators must bear in mind that responses to substantive problems rarely involve a single agency or tactic or a quick fix. Arrest is often viewed as the only response to a problem even though it is rarely sufficient to provide more permanent resolutions. More appropriate responses often involve the police and public and other appropriate actors, including businesses, private and social service organizations, and other government agencies.

Patrol officers have many options to use to respond to problems, but they should not expect to eliminate every problem they take on. With some social problems, such as gangs and homelessness, elimination is impractical and improbable.

Another important prevention tool for COPPS is crime prevention through environmental design (CPTED). CPTED teaches officers how building space, architectural design, lighting, and other such features of the environment contribute to criminal opportunities. Both situational crime prevention and CPTED provide officers with tools necessary to employ comprehensive prevention strategies.

### Assessment: Evaluating Overall Effectiveness

The final stage of the S.A.R.A. process is assessment. Here, officers evaluate the effectiveness of their actions and may use the results to revise their responses, collect more data, or even redefine the problem.

## Evaluation and Research

Although many assessments of COPPS initiatives have been performed, the lack of a formal evaluation of outcomes remains one of the most prevalent and enduring criticisms of those initiatives; furthermore, few police agencies employ personnel who are adequately trained and educated for conducting program evaluations. Thus, this is one area that sorely needs "shoring up."

A COPPS initiative that is not reinforced by an evaluation process may have difficulty establishing whether or not it succeeded and thus should continue to receive resources. Therefore, rigorous evaluation is an essential component of the COPPS initiative. Evaluations provide knowledge; key decision makers in the jurisdiction need a gauge of the strategy's impact and cost effectiveness.[43]

Broken down into simplified steps, evaluation asks some or all of the following questions:

- What is the problem? (defined by measures such as community indicators, police data, and public surveys)
- How does the project intend to address the problem? (look at the project's goal statements and objectives)
- How does the project carry out its objectives? (look at collaborative efforts among the police, other governmental agencies, and private businesses)
- What impact (over time) does the prevention project have on the problem? (reported crimes increased or decreased by what percentage)[44]

## *Two Illustrations: Chicago, Illinois, and Lawrence, Massachusetts*

The following two case studies provide views of COPPS evaluations for Chicago, Illinois, and Lawrence, Massachusetts.

### *Chicago, Illinois*

The Chicago Alternative Policing Strategy (CAPS) initiative was field tested in 1993 in five selected districts (and later implemented on a citywide basis) to cultivate problem solving and to reorganize policing around the city's 279 police beats. In 1995, researchers found that perceived crime problems had decreased significantly in all five districts; furthermore, physical decay had declined in three districts, and citizen assessments of police had improved significantly.[45]

A more recent evaluation of CAPS was conducted in 1999 with funding from the U.S. Department of Justice and the Illinois Criminal Justice Information Authority. Some of the findings were as follows:

- Since 1996, recognition of CAPS had grown from 53 percent to 79 percent; the greatest source of information was television.
- Involvement continued to be strong among some of the city's poorest and most crime-ridden communities. Attendance at beat meetings was highest in predominately African American areas. Overall, 14 percent of Chicagoans said they had attended a beat meeting in the past year.
- Police officers who attended beat community meetings reported satisfaction with the effectiveness of the meetings. More than three-quarters were happy with levels of attendance.
- Community policing had become a routine aspect of the city's life. Within the police department, the strategy was no longer described as "just smoke and mirrors."[46]

### Lawrence, Massachusetts

Lawrence, Massachusetts, is a dense, urban center of 70,000 people, 28 miles north of Boston, whose residents live in an area of about seven square miles. The police department recently began to explore new philosophies for delivering police service and to generally reform its operations.

The police chief and a nine-member management team began rethinking their basic strategies. A bilingual community questionnaire was designed to identify crime and disorder issues important to citizens. Next, a citizen advisory committee was established to get more direct input about the needs of the consumers.[47] The management team then began to develop a "vision" for the department; from this process, new mission and values statements were written. The department then began to explore how to strategically address problems, choosing a 45-square-block neighborhood consisting mostly of multiple-family residential units and small single-family housing. A team of six community police officers (CPOs) was assigned to seek citizen input, analyze problems, and develop intervention strategies. Questionnaires were again used to identify problems and concerns in the area. Returns of these questionnaires produced a lot of valuable information on drug dealers' operations while also raising the fear level of dealers. A public education campaign was launched in the area, as was enhanced police activity.

A 60-item citizen survey was distributed to 3,676 households (with a 30.3 percent response rate). Using this procedure, a summary measure of disorder for each neighborhood was obtained. The findings indicated that residents experienced substantial reductions in their fear and perceptions of crime and disorder.[48]

## Effecting Change in Policing

As indicated earlier, bringing about change in policing is not always easy. It can and does occur, however. But as we will see, several key individuals—starting with the first-line supervisor—must carve out the path.

### Change Begins with the Supervisor

Organizational change begins or ends with an agency's supervisors. The link between street officers and the organization is their sergeant. Indeed, the quality of an officer's daily life is often dependent on the supervisor. There is, however, some cause for supervisors' reluctance to change.

A difficult hurdle that supervisors must overcome is the idea that giving line officers the opportunity to be creative and take risks does not diminish the role or authority of the supervisor. Risk taking and innovation require mutual trust between supervisors and line officers. The supervisor's role changes from being a "controller," primarily concerned with rules, to being a "facilitator" and "coach" for officers engaged in COPPS work. Supervisors must also be well skilled in problem solving, especially in the analysis of problems and evaluation of efforts. Conducting workload analysis and finding the time for officers to solve problems and engage the community are important aspects of supervision. A supervisor must also be prepared to intercede and remove any roadblocks to officers' problem-solving efforts. A supervisor should assist officers with managing their beats and time utilized for COPPS activities. Also, supervisors should not contribute to the COPPS initiative becoming a mere public relations campaign; the emphasis is always on results.[49]

To gain time for officers to engage in COPPS functions, departments should review their patrol plan to determine whether units are fielded in proportion to workload. Delaying response time to calls for service can also provide more time for officers. Response time research has determined that rapid responses are not needed for most calls. Furthermore, dispatchers can set citizens' expectations of when an officer will arrive. Slower police responses to nonemergency calls has been found to be satisfactory to citizens if dispatchers tell them an officer might not arrive at their home right away. Managers have also garnered more time for officers by having nonsworn employees handle noncrime incidents.[50]

## The Chief Executive and Mid-Level Manager

Major change in philosophy and practices is required within a police organization before a major shift such as COPPS can be made. We briefly examine how the chief or sheriff and the captain and lieutenant are all key figures in effecting such a major transformation.

First, the police organization needs a viable change agent; the person at the top is responsible for setting both the policy and tone of the organization. The chief executive must be both visible and credible and create a climate conducive to change. Employees must be involved in the change process. Gauging the pace and degree of change is also necessary. It is essential, however, that chief executives communicate the idea that COPPS is department-wide in scope and encourage and guide all officers to engage in problem solving.

Mid-level managers also play a crucial role in the implementation of a COPPS philosophy. They must not view COPPS as a threat to their power. Middle managers are essential to the process of innovation, much of which can originate only at their level.[51] As George Kelling and William Bratton observed,

> Ample evidence exists that when a clear vision of the business of the organization is put forward, when mid-managers are included in planning, when their legitimate self-interests are acknowledged, and when they are properly trained, mid-managers can be the leading edge of innovation and creativity.[52]

Mid-level managers and first-line supervisors are discussed in greater detail in Chapter 4.

# CASE STUDIES

The following two case studies will help the reader understand and apply some of this chapter's materials in a real-world context.

## Dismal City P.D.'s Command to "Do More With Less"*

Dismal City, USA, is a rapidly growing community of 50,000 residents located in the southern part of the state along the ocean. The city gains a population of 10,000 to 20,000 visitors a day during the summer months, when ocean recreation is a popular activity. The city's demographics are changing rapidly. Its Hispanic and Asian populations are growing at a tremendous rate. However, most of these new residents work outside the city. The downtown area has slowly degenerated over the past few years resulting in increased crime and disorder. A property tax cap has resulted in reduced revenues to local jurisdictions, and the recent recession has also taken a substantial toll on the city's budget. The result has been significant reductions in staffing. The city's two attempts to have voters approve bond issues for increased taxes and police officers have failed. The police department has experienced its share of budget cuts and reduced staffing levels. The chief recently retired because of continued problems with the city council, the budget, and low morale in the agency. As a result of these problems, relations between the community and the department have been tense at best. The police department has experienced a continued reduction in staffing over the past five years. The reduction is not expected to continue, but increases also are not expected. The morale of the department is at its worst and is fueled by the increase in workload and what is perceived as an uncaring chief. The increase in violent crime only aggravates the problems, as officers believe that their safety is in jeopardy as a result of the lower staffing levels. Furthermore, the increase in Hispanic and Asian residents creates an additional burden as the department consists largely of white male officers. The department has no bilingual officers.

You have been hired as the new chief and will begin work in two weeks. The city manager and council have asked for a meeting with you to discuss the future of the department. At this meeting, they explain the situation to you and request a staff report within one month of your reporting to work. The manager and several council members recently attended a conference that presented several workshops on the implementation of community policing. They are convinced that this trend, now apparently sweeping the nation, would result in a

---

*Contributed by Deputy Chief Ronald W. Glensor, Ph.D., Reno, Nevada, Police Department.

more efficient police department. The manager and governing board enthusiastically seek your views on community policing, its potential for Dismal City, and how you might approach its implementation. They inform you that the police officers' union has heard rumors of this idea and has made it clear that it probably would not want anything to do with changing the organization at a time when resources are strained.

## Questions for Discussion

1. In your report, how will you respond concerning whether or not community policing is the panacea for the city's financial and demographic woes? Will it help the department?
2. Do you envision any problems with "traditional thinking" supervisors and community policing. If so, how do you handle their concerns?
3. What would you do to mend the poor relations between labor and management?
4. Would the community need to be involved in the design and implementation of community policing? If so, how?
5. How might community policing provide more effective delivery of services?
6. Would you anticipate that the officers' workload would be reduced or increased under this strategy?
7. What types of information would you use to evaluate the progress of your community policing initiative for city hall?

## Sins and the City

Officers assigned to your district have been responding to a number of noise complaints, reckless driving, and fight calls in the area of 7500 Commercial Row. This area contains a number of restaurants, bars, and several strip malls that attract juveniles and young adults. Within the past week, there have also been three gang-related drive-by shootings and seven gas drive-offs. A majority of the underaged adults are attracted to the area by a dance club located in one of the strip mall centers and two all-night fast-food restaurants. All three locations attract large crowds that loiter and drink alcohol in their parking lots. The owners of the shopping centers and restaurants have also complained about thousands of dollars in vandalism by the loitering youths.

## Questions for Discussion

1. How would you use the S.A.R.A. process to address the problem?
2. Would the problem analysis triangle be of assistance in addressing this problem? If so, how?

## Summary

This chapter explored traditional and contemporary models of police organization; the policies, procedures, rules, and regulations that guide them; and the results of research into policing methods.

The burgeoning nature of community oriented policing and problem solving as an operational strategy was emphasized. This approach has caused many changes in the traditional organization and administration of police agencies. It was clearly demonstrated that this shift in philosophy and strategies has brought with it a fresh, new look at how police organizations must be structured and function, and how these initiatives must be evaluated in order to see "what works."

## Questions for Review

1. What are the distinctions among policy, procedure, and rules and regulations? Why are they necessary in law enforcement agencies? What are their relationship and role vis-à-vis police discretion?

2. What aspects of law enforcement agencies make them bureaucracies? Can such a form of organization ever be eliminated?

3. What is the basic police organizational structure? How have contemporary police organizations changed from the more traditional, bureaucratic form?

4. What are some of the major, recent research findings concerning policing? How have they affected the field?

5. What role do innovation and values play in police organizations?

6. What is meant by *community-oriented policing and problem solving*? How does this concept differ from past policing methods? How can its outcomes be evaluated? Under this strategy, what important roles are played by chief executives, mid-level managers, and first-line supervisors?

## Notes

1. Wayne W. Bennett and Karen M. Hess, *Management and Supervision in Law Enforcement*, 3d ed. (Belmont, Calif.: Wadsworth, 2001), p. 2.
2. Adapted from Charles R. Swanson, Leonard Territo, and Robert W. Taylor, *Police Administration: Structures, Processes, and Behavior*, 5th ed. (Upper Saddle River, N.J.: Prentice Hall, 2001), pp. 183–184.
3. *The Republic of Plato*, trans. Allen Bloom (New York: Basic Books, 1968), p. 7.
4. See Luther Gulick and L. Urwick, eds., *Papers on the Science of Administration* (New York: Augustus M. Kelley, 1969).
5. Swanson, Territo, and Taylor, *Police Administration*, p. 177.
6. Ibid., p. 178.

7. Egon Bittner, *The Functions of the Police in a Modern Society*, Public Health Service Publication 2059 (Washington, D.C.: U.S. Government Printing Office, 1970), p. 53.

8. John J. Broderick, *Police in a Time of Change* (Prospect Heights, Ill.: Waveland Press, 1987), p. 231.

9. Ronald G. Lynch, *The Police Manager: Professional Leadership Skills*, 3d ed. (New York: Random House, 1986), p. 4.

10. California Department of Justice, *COPPS: Community-Oriented Policing and Problem Solving*. Office of the Attorney General, Crime Violence Prevention Center (Sacramento, Calif.: Author, 1995).

11. For related discussion, see Kenneth J. Peak and Ronald W. Glensor, *Community Policing and Problem Solving: Strategies and Practices*, 3d ed. (Upper Saddle River, N.J.: Prentice Hall, 2002), primarily Chapters 6 and 7.

12. Dorothy Guyot, "Bending Granite: Attempts to Change the Rank Structure of American Police Departments," *Journal of Police Science and Administration* 7 (1979):253-284.

13. Lynch, *The Police Manager*, pp. 5-6.

14. Bittner, *The Functions of the Police in a Modern Society*, p. 51.

15. Ibid., p. 72.

16. Ibid., p. 73.

17. Ibid.

18. Ibid., pp. 74-75.

19. Ibid.

20. Ibid., p. 18.

21. Personal communication, Marsha R. Palmer, Planning and Support Division, City of Portland, Oregon, Bureau of Police, July 20, 2001.

22. In the Portland Police Bureau organizational structure shown in Figure 3-2, DPSST is the Department of Public Safety Standards and Training, to which the PPB loans officers; PPA is the Portland Police Association, or the bureau's collective bargaining agent; the Management Services Division manages the bureau's facilities, liability, and loss control; the Sunshine Division includes personnel who work to provide food, clothing, and toys to needy families; the HAP liaisons and Safety Action Team include officers assigned to the Housing Authority of Portland; Douglas and Parkrose liaisons are officers working in school districts; APP liaison is a private association of businesses that fund one officer position for downtown; the Public Utility Commission includes grant-funded positions for conducting traffic enforcement along interstate corridors; ROCN is the Regional Organized Crime and Narcotics task force; and WomenStrength is a program to teach women self-defense tactics.

23. President's Commission on Law Enforcement and Administration of Justice, *Task Force Report: The Police* (Washington, D.C.: U.S. Government Printing Office, 1967), p. 46.

24. Robert Sheehan and Gary W. Cordner, *Introduction to Police Administration*, 2d ed. (Cincinnati, Ohio: Anderson, 1989), pp. 446-447.

25. Ibid., p. 449.

26. Ibid.

27. O. W. Wilson and Roy C. McLaren, *Police Administration*, 3d ed. (New York: McGraw-Hill, 1972), p. 79.

28. 471 U.S. 1 (1985).

29. Raymond O. Loen, *Manage More by Doing Less* (New York: McGraw-Hill, 1971), pp. 86-89.

30. Thomas Reddin, "Are You Oriented to Hold Them? A Searching Look at Police Management," *The Police Chief* (March 1966):17.

31. Peter K. Manning, "The Researcher: An Alien in the Police World," in Arthur Niederhoffer and Abraham S. Blumberg (eds.), *The Ambivalent Force: Perspectives on the Police*, 2d ed. (Hinsdale, Ill.: Dryden Press, 1976), pp. 103–121.

32. Herman Goldstein, *Problem-Oriented Policing* (New York: McGraw-Hill, 1990), p. 9.

33. Joan Petersilia, "The Influence of Research on Policing," in Roger C. Dunham and Geoffrey P. Alpert (eds.), *Critical Issues in Policing: Contemporary Readings* (Prospect Heights, Ill.: Waveland Press, 1989), p. 230.

34. Ibid.

35. Ibid., pp. 231–232.

36. Ibid., p. 235.

37. Ibid., p. 237.

38. Ibid.

39. Ibid., p. 238.

40. John E. Eck, *Solving Crimes: The Investigation of Burglary and Robbery* (Washington, D.C.: Police Executive Research Forum, National Institute of Justice, 1983), p. xxiii.

41. Goldstein, *Problem-Oriented Policing*, pp. 8–11.

42. Jerome H. Skolnick and David H. Bayley, *The New Blue Line, Police Innovation in Six American Cities* (New York: Free Press, 1986), p. 4.

43. U.S. Department of Justice, Bureau of Justice Assistance, The Community Policing Consortium, *Understanding Community Policing: A Framework for Action* (Washington, D.C.: Author, 1993), p. 82.

44. Adapted from ibid., p. 4.

45. U.S. Department of Justice, National Institute of Justice Research Preview, "Community Policing in Chicago: Year Two" (Washington, D.C.: Author, October 1995), pp. 1–2.

46. Institute for Policy Research, *Northwestern Study Shows Great Strides in Community Policing Program* (Evanston, Ill.: IPR News, May 1999, pp. 1–2. A 120-page report on Years Five–Six of CAPS is available at: http://www.new.edu/IPR/news/CAPS99release.html

47. Allen W. Cole and Gordon Bazemore, "Police and the 'Laboratory' of the Neighborhood: Evaluating Problem-Oriented Strategies in a Medium Sized City," *American Journal of Police*, forthcoming.

48. Ibid., p. 31.

49. Police Executive Research Forum. *Supervising Problem-solving* (Washington, D.C.: Author, training outline), 1990.

50. John Eck and William Spelman. "A Problem-oriented Approach to Police Service Delivery," in Dennis Jay Kenney (ed.), *Police and Policing: Contemporary Issues* (New York: Praeger, 1989), pp. 95–111.

51. John Eck and William Spelman, *Solving Problems: Problem Oriented Policing in Newport News*. Research in Brief. (Washington D.C.: U.S. Department of Justice, National Institute of Justice, January 1987).

52. George L. Kelling and William J. Bratton, *Implementing Community Policing: The Administrative Problem* (Washington, D.C.: Police Executive Research Forum, June 1992), p. 11.

# Chapter 4

# Police Personnel Roles and Functions

## Key Terms and Concepts

Captain

Chief executive officer (CEO)

Chief of police

Conceptual skill

Dissemination

Disturbance-handler

Entrepreneur

Figurehead role

First-line supervisor

Human skill

Leadership role

Liaison role

Lieutenant

Middle managers

Monitoring/inspecting

Negotiator

Resource-allocator

Spokesperson

Technical skill

## Learning Objectives

After reading this chapter, the student will:

- be able to describe each of Mintzberg's three main roles of the chief executive officer (CEO)
- know the steps taken by an assessment center to obtain the most capable chief executive and the skills the executive must possess

- have an idea of the duties and qualifications for the office of chief of police
- know the duties performed by the sheriff's office
- be familiar with the criteria used to evaluate CEOs
- know the tasks performed by middle managers (captains and lieutenants)
- be familiar with the criteria for a first-line supervisor (patrol sergeant) position as well as its roles and tasks
- understand the tasks of patrol officers and be able to name the 12 qualities imperative for entry-level officers
- know the roles and functions performed by all personnel in COPPS

> *The police are the public and the public are the police.*
>
> —Robert Peel

# Introduction

Some of the most important and challenging positions in our society are those of a police administrator, manager, or supervisor. Given the weight of contemporary social problems, personnel issues, and the constant specter of liability, persons occupying these positions assume greater levels of responsibility than ever before.

This chapter examines the roles and functions of law enforcement chief executives (chiefs of police and county sheriffs), middle managers (typically captains and lieutenants), first-line supervisors (sergeants), and patrol officers. First, we examine in general terms the roles of law enforcement chief executives, adapting Mintzberg's model of chief executive officers (CEOs), which are applicable to practically any position of leadership. Next, we review the assessment center process, a comparatively sophisticated means used for hiring and promoting people into police positions, and then we explore in detail the positions of chief of police and sheriff. Several appropriate methods of assessing chief executive performance are described as well. Then, we consider the roles and functions of middle managers (captains and lieutenants), supervisors (sergeants), and patrol officers.

Figure 4.1 shows the hierarchy of managers within the typical police organization and the inverse relationship between rank and number of personnel; in other words, as rank increases, the number of persons at that rank decreases.

The chapter concludes with two case studies.

# Roles of the Police Executive: The Mintzberg Model of CEOs

A police chief executive fills many roles. Henry Mintzberg[1] described a set of behaviors and tasks of chief executive officers in any organization. Following is an adaptation of Mintzberg's model used to examine the three main roles of the

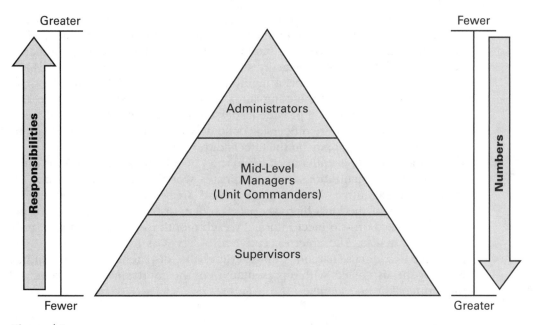

Greater

Fewer

Responsibilities

Numbers

Administrators

Mid-Level
Managers
(Unit Commanders)

Supervisors

Fewer

Greater

**Figure 4.1**

Hierarchy of managers within the typical police organization. *Source:*
Larry K. Gaines, Mittie D. Southerland, and John E. Angell, *Police
Administration*. New York: McGraw-Hill, 1991, p. 11. Reproduced
with permission of The McGraw-Hill Companies.

**chief executive officer (CEO)** (the chief of police or sheriff): the interpersonal, the informational, and the decision-maker roles.

## *The Interpersonal Role*

The *interpersonal* role has three components: (1) the figurehead, (2) leadership, and (3) liaison duties.

In the **figurehead role,** the CEO performs various ceremonial functions. He or she rides in parades and attends civic events, speaks to school and university classes and civic organizations, meets visiting officials and dignitaries, attends academy graduations and swearing-in ceremonies and certain weddings and funerals, and visits injured officers. Like a city's mayor, whose public responsibilities include cutting ribbons and kissing babies, the police CEO performs these duties simply because of his or her title and position within the organization. Although chiefs or sheriffs are not expected to attend the grand opening of every retail or commercial business and other such events to which they are invited, they are certainly obligated from a professional standpoint to attend many civic functions and ceremonies.

The **leadership role** requires the CEO to motivate and coordinate workers while resolving various goals and needs within the department and the community. A chief or sheriff may have to urge the governing board to enact a code or ordinance that, whether or not popular, is in the best interest of the jurisdiction. For example, a chief in a western state recently led a drive to pass an ordinance that prohibited parking by university students in residential neighborhoods surrounding the campus. This was a highly unpopular undertaking, but the chief was prompted because of the complaints about hardships suffered by the area residents. The CEO also may provide leadership by taking stands on bond issues (seeking funds to hire more officers or build new buildings, for example) and by advising the governing body on the effects of proposed ordinances.

The **liaison role** is undertaken when the CEO of a police organization interacts with other organizations and coordinates work assignments. It is not uncommon for executives from a geographical area—the police chief, sheriff, ranking officer of the local highway patrol office, district attorney, campus police chief, and so on—to meet informally each month to discuss common problems and strategies. The chief executive also serves as liaison to regional law enforcement councils, narcotics units, crime labs, dispatching centers, and so on. He or she also meets with representatives of the courts, juvenile system, and other criminal justice agencies.

## *The Informational Role*

Another role identified by Mintzberg's model is the *informational* one. In this capacity, the CEO engages in tasks relating to (1) monitoring/inspecting, (2) dissemination, and (3) spokesperson duties.

In the **monitoring/inspecting** function, the CEO constantly reviews the department's operations to ensure that it is operating smoothly (or as smoothly as police operations can be expected to be). This function is often referred to as "roaming the ship"; many CEOs who isolated themselves from their personnel and the daily operations of the agency can speak from sad experience of the need to be involved and present. For example, a Midwestern sheriff of a small county was voted out of office in part because it was revealed that two deputies on the graveyard shift were engaged in a "Batman and Robin" style of police work that included using an M-16 automatic rifle and a police dog; the deputies had received no formal training in the use of either tool. The sheriff, unaware of these covert activities and preferring to administer by looking the other way, was eventually caught in a tidal wave of opposition. Many police executives use daily staff meetings to acquire information about their jurisdictions, especially criminal and other activities during the previous 24 hours.

**Dissemination** tasks involve distributing information to members of the department via memoranda, special orders, general orders, and policies and procedures as described in Chapter 3. The **spokesperson** function is related to the dissemination task but is focused more on providing information to the news media. This is a difficult task for the chief executive; news organizations, especially the television and print media, are competitive businesses that seek to obtain the most complete news in the shortest amount of time, which often translates to wider viewership and therefore greater advertising revenues for them. From one perspective, the media must appreciate that a criminal investigation can be seriously compromised by premature or excessive coverage. From the other perspective, the public has a legitimate right to know what is occurring in the community, especially matters relating to crime. Therefore, the prudent police executive attempts to have an open and professional relationship with the media in which each side knows and understands its responsibilities. The prudent chief executive also remembers the power of the media and does not alienate them; as an old saying goes, "Never argue with someone who buys his ink by the barrel." Unfortunately, many police executives (a good number who involuntarily left office) can speak of the results of failing to develop an appropriate relationship with the media.

An example of the good-bad relationship that often exists between the police and the media is the Washington, D.C.-area sniper investigation of late 2002. Although Montgomery County, Maryland, Police Chief Charles Moose was at times very frustrated by leaks of confidential information to the media, he also used the media to communicate with the snipers—who eventually were captured after the suspects' photographs and a vehicle description were broadcast.

## *The Decision-Maker Role*

In the decision-maker role, the CEO of a police organization serves as (1) an entrepreneur, (2) a disturbance-handler, (3) a resource-allocator, and (4) a negotiator.

In the capacity of **entrepreneur,** the CEO must sell ideas to the members of the governing board or the department—perhaps helping them to understand a new computer or communications system, the implementation of a policing strategy, or different work methods, all of which are intended to improve the organization. Sometimes roles blend, as when several police executives band together (in their entrepreneurial and liaison functions) to lobby the state attorney general and the legislature for new crime-fighting laws.

As a **disturbance-handler,** the executive's tasks range from resolving minor disputes between staff members to dealing with major events such as riots, continued muggings in a local park, or the clean up of the downtown area. Sometimes the executive must solve intradepartmental disputes, which can reach major proportions. For example, the chief executive must intervene when friction develops between different units, as when the patrol commanders' instruction to street officers to increase arrests for public drunkenness causes a strain on the resources of the jail division's commander.

As a **resource-allocator,** the CEO must clearly understand the agency's budget and its budgetary priorities. The resource-allocator must consider requests for funds from various groups. Personnel, for example, will ask for higher salaries, additional officers, and better equipment. Citizens may complain about speeding motorists in a specific area, which would require the allocation of additional resources to that neighborhood. In the resource-allocator role, the CEO must be able to prioritize requests and to defend his or her choices.

As a **negotiator,** the police manager resolves employee grievances and, through an appointed representative at the bargaining table, tries to represent the best interests of both the city and labor during collective bargaining. In this role, the CEO must consider rank and file's request for raises and increased benefits as part of budget administration. If funds available to the jurisdiction are limited, the CEO must negotiate with the collective bargaining unit to reach an agreement. At times, contract negotiations reach an impasse or deadlock.

We will elaborate on some of these chief executive functions later in the chapter; furthermore, labor relations—including unionism and collective bargaining—are discussed more fully in Chapter 14.

# Police Executives

Prior to examining the role and functions of contemporary police executives, we first consider how such persons are selected for these positions. Given the responsibilities placed on those who occupy such positions, the means employed to test applicants for or to promote individuals into them becomes important.

## *Obtaining the Best: The Assessment Center*

To obtain the most capable people for chief executive positions (and also for middle-management and even supervisory positions) in policing, the assessment center method has surfaced as an efficacious means of hiring and promoting personnel. (*Note*: Sheriffs are normally elected, not hired or promoted into their position; thus, the assessment center is of little use for that position.) The assessment center method is now increasingly utilized for selecting people for all management or supervisory ranks. The assessment center process may include interviews; psychological tests; in-basket exercises; management tasks; group discussions; role-playing exercises, such as simulations of interviews with subordinates, the public, and news media; fact-finding exercises; oral presentation exercises; and written communications exercises (each is discussed in this section).

The first step is to identify behaviors important to the successful performance of the position. Job descriptions listing responsibilities and skills should exist for all executive, midmanagement, and supervisory positions (such as chief, captain, lieutenant, sergeant, and so on). Then each candidate's abilities and skill levels should be evaluated using several of the techniques mentioned.

Individual and group role-playing provides a hands-on exercise during the selection process. Candidates may be required to perform in simulated police-community problems (they conduct a "meeting" to hear concerns of local minority groups), to react to a major incident (explaining what they would do and in what order in a simulated shooting or riot situation), to hold a news briefing, or to participate in other such exercises. They may be given an in-basket situation in which they receive an abundance of paperwork, policies, and problems to be prioritized and dealt with in a prescribed amount of time. Writing abilities may also be evaluated: Candidates may be given 30 minutes to develop a use-of-force policy for a hypothetical or real police agency. This type of exercise not only illustrates candidates' written communications skills and understanding of the technical side of police work but also shows how they think cognitively and build a case.

During each exercise, several assessors or raters analyze each candidate's performance and record some type of evaluation; when the assessment center process ends, each rater submits his or her individual rating information to the person making the hiring or promotional decision. Typically selected because they have held the position for which candidates are now vying, assessors must not only know the types of problems and duties incumbent in the position but also should be keen observers of human behavior.

Assessment centers are logistically more difficult to conduct as well as more labor-intensive and costly than traditional interviewing procedures; but they are well worth the extra investment. Monies invested at the early stages of a hiring or promotional process can help avoid selecting the wrong person and can prevent untold problems for years to come. Good executives, mid-managers, and supervisors make fewer mistakes and are probably sued less often.

### Skills of Good Managers

To expand on the discussion of leadership skills in Chapter 2, the police executive must develop certain basic management skills. First is **technical skill,** which involves specialized knowledge, analytical ability, and facility in the use of tools and techniques of the specific discipline. This is the skill most easily trained for. Examples in policing include budgeting, computer usage, and fundamental knowledge of some specialized equipment, such as radar or breathalyzer machines.

Second is the **human skill,** which is the executive's ability to work effectively as a group member and build cooperation; this includes being sensitive to the needs and feelings of others, tolerating ambiguity, and being able to empathize with different views and cultures. Finally, **conceptual skills** involve coordinating and integrating all the activities and interests of the organization into a common objective: in other words, being able to translate knowledge into action.[2]

These skills can be taught, just as other skills can, which proves that good administrators are not simply born but can be trained in the classroom and by practicing the skills on the job.

# Chiefs of Police

What do law enforcement executives do? In contrast to Mintzberg's rather sophisticated model described earlier, Ronald Lynch stated the primary tasks of these executives in simple terms:

They listen, talk, write, confer, think, decide—about [personnel], money, materials, methods, facilities—in order to plan, organize, direct, coordinate, and control their research service, production, public relations, employee relations, and all other activities so that they may more effectively serve the citizens to whom they are responsible.[3]

Next, we look at what the city officials and community expect of police chiefs, as well as how they ascend to this position.

## Expectations of Government and Community

The **chief of police** (also known as the *commissioner* or *superintendent*) is generally considered to be one of the most influential and prestigious persons in local government. Indeed, people in this position often amass considerable power and influence in their jurisdiction. Mayors, city managers and administrators, members of the agency, labor organizations, citizens, special-interest groups, and the media all have differing role expectations of the chief of police that often conflict.

The mayor or city manager likely wants the chief of police to promote departmental efficiency, reduce crime, improve service, and so on. Others appreciate the chief who simply keeps morale high and citizens' complaints low.

The mayor or city manager also expects the chief to communicate with city management about police-related issues and to be part of the city management team; to communicate city management's policies to police personnel; to establish agency policies, goals, and objectives and put them in writing; to develop an administrative system of managing people, equipment, and the budget in a professional and businesslike manner; to set a good example, both personally and professionally; to administer disciplinary action consistently and fairly when required; and to select personnel whose performance will ably and professionally adhere to the organization's objectives.

Members of the agency also have expectations of the chief executive: to be their advocate, supporting them when necessary and representing the agency's interests when dealing with judges and prosecutors who may be indifferent or hostile. Citizens tend to expect the chief of police to provide efficient and cost-effective police services while keeping crime and tax rates down (often an area of built-in conflict) and preventing corruption and illegal use of force. Special-interest groups expect the chief to advocate policy positions that they favor. For example, Mothers Against Drunk Driving (MADD) would desire strong anti-DUI measures by the police. Finally, the media expect the chief to cooperate fully with their efforts to obtain fast and complete crime information.

## Qualifications

Qualifications for the position of police chief vary widely, depending on the size of the agency and the region of the country. Small agencies, especially those in rural areas, may not have any minimum educational requirement for the job. In the early 1970s, the National Advisory Commission on Criminal Justice Standards and Goals surveyed police chiefs and their superiors to determine the essential qualities for the job. Education was found to be an important consideration; today, many agencies require a college education plus several years of progressively responsible police management experience. A survey by the Police Executive Research Forum of 358 police chiefs in jurisdictions of 50,000 or more residents found that chiefs were generally highly educated—87 percent held a bachelor's degree and 47 percent had a master's—and were more likely to be chosen from outside the agencies they headed, but they spent less than five years in the position.[4]

Police chief executives also need several types of important management skills. The National Advisory Commission asked police chiefs and their superiors to rate, on a scale of 1 to 10, the importance of 14 desirable management skills. The ability to motivate and control personnel and to relate to the community was considered most important. A survey today would probably yield similar results.[5]

Many cities finding themselves in need of a police chief have had to consider whether it would be better to promote someone from within the ranks or hire from outside (perhaps using the assessment center process, described earlier). Although it is perhaps more economical and certainly less trouble to select a police chief from within the organization as opposed to arranging an assessment center, both methods have advantages and disadvantages. One study of police chiefs promoted from within or hired from outside indicated only one significant difference in qualification: educational attainment. The outsiders were more highly educated. No differences were found with respect to other aspects of their background, attitudes, salary, tenure in current position or in policing, the size of agency or community, and current budget.[6] Some states, however, have made it nearly impossible for an outsider to come in. California has mandated that the chief be a graduate of its own Peace Officers Standards and Training (POST) academy; New Jersey and New York also encourage "homegrown" chiefs.[7]

## *Job Protection, Termination, and the Political Arena*

Traditionally, the job tenure of police chiefs has been short. A federal study in the mid-1970s found that the average length in office by chiefs of police was 5.4 years.[8] Another PERF study in the mid-1980s found the average to be practically unchanged, 5.5 years. That figure has not varied much in contemporary times.[9] This short tenure of police chiefs has several negative consequences; it prevents long-range planning, results in frequent new policies and administrative styles, and prohibits the development of the chief's political power base and local influence.

Police chiefs would of course prefer to possess some type of job protection against their arbitrary and unjustified removal from office by an elected or political officeholder.[10] In fact, some police chiefs have resigned and reverted back to their former position as assistant or deputy chief, simply to have some job protection until retirement.

In some states, statutory protections against such actions exist, or special boards or commissions have been created for the sole purpose of establishing recruitment, selection, and retention policies for chiefs of police. Other states require written notice of the basis for the proposed termination, a hearing on the charges, and a finding of cause before the dismissal can be effected. Still, police chiefs across the country are looking for job protections in local civil service codes, municipal ordinances, and such individual employment contracts as they can negotiate.[11]

Losing a job as police chief is not difficult to do. Although some, of course, lose their positions because of their own shortcomings, others leave their post as a result of situations and conflicts outside their control. These conflicts have been termed *political arenas* and can be divided into three types based on their duration, intensity, and pervasiveness: (1) confrontation, (2) shaky alliance, and (3) a politicized organization.[12]

The first type of political arena, *confrontation*, occurs when the situational conflict is intense but brief and confined. An obvious example is the 1991 incident involving Rodney King, which put an end to Los Angeles Chief of Police Daryl Gates. The second arena is the *shaky alliance*, in which conflict is less intense but still pervasive. Again, an example involves a former Los Angeles police chief, Willie Williams—Gates's successor and the first outsider appointed as chief in that city in more than 40 years. Williams had to deal with both external (the impact of the King incident on the public) and internal (the resentful feelings from his own officers) pressures. This was a shaky alliance, and soon Williams's contract was not renewed.

The third type of political arena, a *politicized organization*, features pervasive but muted conflict that is tolerable for a time. This kind of conflict is commonplace in American policing, and in this situation, the chief's survival will depend on external support. Examples would be a riot resulting from allegations of police brutality or a lengthy, unsuccessful, and possibly botched homicide investigation. For example, in the JonBenet Ramsey investigation, the Boulder, Colorado, chief of police had little support from the media, divided political support within the city council, and little support from his officers (he received a 2-1 vote of no confidence by the troops) and was forced to step down by an acting city manager.

The advent of community policing has also presented some risks for police chiefs; that element is discussed more later in the section concerning the chief executive.

# The Sheriff

The position of sheriff has a long tradition, rooted in the time of the Norman conquest of England (in 1066), and it played an important part in the early law enforcement activities of colonial America. Unfortunately, because of television and movie depictions, many people today view the county sheriff as a bumbling, cruel, overweight, or corrupt individual, wearing a cowboy hat and sunglasses while talking with a Southern drawl (see, for example, movies such as *Smoky and the Bandit*, *Mississippi Burning*, *The Dukes of Hazzard*, *Walking Tall*, and many others).

This image is both unfair and highly inaccurate. Next, we examine the real role of today's county sheriffs.

## *Role and Functions*

Because of the diversity of sheriff's offices throughout the country, it is difficult to describe a "typical" sheriff's department; those offices run the gamut from the traditional, highly political, limited-service office to the modern, fairly nonpolitical, full-service police organization. It is possible, however, to list functions commonly associated with the sheriff's office:

1. Serving and/or implementing civil processes (divorce papers, liens, evictions, garnishments and attachments, and other civil duties, such as extradition and transportation of prisoners)
2. Collecting certain taxes and conducting real estate sales (usually for nonpayment of taxes) for the county
3. Performing routine order-maintenance duties by enforcing state statutes and county ordinances, arresting offenders, and performing traffic and criminal investigations
4. Serving as bailiff of the courts
5. Maintaining and operating the county correctional institutions[13]

Sheriffs, therefore, have a unique role in that they typically serve all three components of the justice system: (1) law enforcement (with patrol, traffic, and investigative functions), (2) the courts (as civil process servers and bailiffs), and (3) corrections (in the county jails). In many urban areas, civil process duties consume more time and resources than those involving law enforcement.[14]

Sheriffs are elected in all but two states; thus, they tend to be aligned with a political party. As elected officials, sheriffs are important political figures and, in many rural areas, represent the most powerful political force in the county. As a result, sheriffs are far more independent than appointed municipal police chiefs, who can be removed from office by the mayors or city managers who appoint them. However, because they are elected, sheriffs receive considerable media scrutiny and are subject to state accountability processes.

Because of this electoral system, it is possible that the only qualification for getting into the office is the ability to get votes. In some areas of the country, the sheriff's term of office is limited to one 2-year term at a time (a sheriff cannot succeed himself or herself); thus, the office has been known to be rotated between the sheriff and undersheriff. In most counties, however, the sheriff has a four-year term of office and can be reelected.

The sheriff enjoys no tenure guarantee, although one study found that sheriffs (averaging 6.7 years in office) had longer tenure in office than chiefs of police (5.4 years). This politicization of the office of sheriff can result in high turnover rates of personnel who do not have civil service protection. The uncertainty as to tenure is not conducive to long-range (strategic) planning. Largely as a result of the political nature of the office, sheriffs tend to be older, less likely to have been promoted through the ranks of the agency, and less likely to be college graduates and to have specialized training than police chiefs have. Research has also found that sheriffs in small agencies have more difficulty with organizational problems (field activities, budget management) and that sheriffs in large agencies find dealing with local officials and planning and evaluation to be more troublesome.[15]

# Rating Chief Executive Performance

How good is your police chief or sheriff? The answer probably depends on whom you ask. To some, the police chief executive or CEO is the best thing that ever happened to the community or county; to others, he or she is the worst thing. Rating the CEO's performance in this complex job involves several potential "traps." CEOs are human; they do make mistakes, but citizen perceptions of them and their performance are often wrong. Therefore, it is difficult to assess accurately how the CEO is performing; no litmus test or simple fill-in-the-boxes exercise exists. Several broad, general guidelines can be applied, however, when evaluating these CEOs.

## *Inappropriate Evaluation Criteria*

As pointed out by Jerald Vaughn, former police chief and author of a report for PERF,[16] inappropriate criteria can be used to evaluation CEOs, such as the following:

1. *Personal popularity.* The longer the CEO's tenure, the greater the chance that people within and without the department will have complaints about something the CEO did or did not do.
2. *Department morale.* Morale is a fragile thing; Peter Drucker wrote that morale does not mean that "people get along together"; the test is performance, not conformance.[17] Like soldiers and other workers in bureaucratic organizations, police officers can become chronic and notorious complainers; the "grapevine" normally keeps people stirred up, and a certain amount of griping will occur even when things are running smoothly. Thus, the morale of a department is not necessarily the result of the CEO's leadership.
3. *Controversy surrounding the CEO.* Some CEOs may become involved in controversial local issues. Controversy and conflict can be productive, causing people to challenge old ideas and methods. CEOs are highly visible and

influential; they should be allowed to speak out and provide leadership on matters that concern the public safety.

4. *A rising crime rate.* The former chief of Madison, Wisconsin, David Couper, observed that social and economic factors have a large influence on community crime levels.[18] To blame the chief executive for the crime rate is to miss the point. When a serious crime rate or public concern about crime exists, however, the chief executive should develop programs and strategies to combat it rather than merely watching crime statistics soar and engaging in mere bean counting.

5. *Single issues: "Run the bum out of town."* Occasionally, a single, critical event or issue, such as a police beating or shooting of a citizen or promotional policy, will arise that can mushroom into a call to oust the CEO. Sometimes the chief executive survives the incident if his or her overall performance is reviewed. On other occasions, the passion of the moment may prevail. Indeed, in some incidents the chief may deserve to be relieved of command; however, more often a multidimensional review of the chief's total performance should be made. The ouster of the chief does not ensure that the basic problem causing the upheaval will be eliminated.

## *Appropriate Evaluation Criteria*

A police executive's evaluation should focus only on the qualities, characteristics, and behavior required to do the job. Honesty and integrity are probably the chief's most important qualities, followed by leadership effectiveness. The direction of the department, its commitment to professional and ethical standards, and its basic values emanate from the chief's leadership role. The chief's ability to motivate and inspire people both inside and outside the department should also be considered.

Any assessment of the chief executive must consider leadership effectiveness. The chief's ability to be a good follower and take a subordinate position to the mayor and city manager/council is also important. It is important that the chief know where the lines are drawn, when it is time to quit leading and start following.

CEOs manage a significant number of resources—human and financial, equipment, and physical facilities. CEOs must make timely and responsible decisions, as well as realize the impact and legal ramifications of those decisions. The chief executive must also delegate authority and decision making to others rather than taking on too much, which often results in a sluggish operation. Finally, a chief executive must be innovative and think creatively. Today's CEO must be willing to keep up with the challenges facing law enforcement and the need to move the agency into a new era of research, experimentation, and risk taking.[19]

Several other areas of the chief executive's performance must be evaluated. The first relates to departmental values: Do the department's values reflect a commitment to the rights of individuals, including its employees? Does the CEO manage force carefully and aggressively to ensure that the public is not subjected to unlawful or unwarranted physical force by police? Does the CEO require the agency to have clear policies, rules, and procedures to guide employees? Are those directives constantly updated and enforced fairly and consistently? Has the CEO introduced or implemented crime strategies to make the community safer?

The labor climate of the organization is an especially difficult area for today's police executive; civil service, unions, appeal boards, the courts, and the changing profile of today's police officer have made managing labor relations a constant challenge.[20]

Finally, the CEO's understanding of where the department stands with the community should be evaluated. No other sector of government in our society has more frequent and direct contact with the public than the police. As Darlene Walker and Richard Richardson observed:

> Whatever the citizen thinks of the police, they can hardly be ignored. Whereas other police bureaucrats are often lost from the public's view, locked in rooms filled with typewriters and anonymity, police officers are out in the world—on the sidewalks and in the streets and shopping malls, cruising, strolling, watching, as both state protectors and state repressors.[21]

## Middle Managers: Captains and Lieutenants

Few police administration books contain information about the **middle-managers** of a police department, the captains and **lieutenants.** This is unfortunate because they are too numerous and too powerful within police organizations to ignore. Opinions vary toward these mid-management personnel, however, as we discuss later.

Leonhard Fuld, one of the early progressive police administration researchers, said in 1909 that the **captain** is one of the most important officers in the organization. Fuld believed that the position had two broad duties—policing and administration. The captain was held responsible for preserving the public peace and protecting life and property within the precinct. Fuld defined the captain's administrative duties as being of three kinds: clerical, janitorial, and supervisory.[22]

Although every ranking officer in the police department exercises some managerial skills and duties, here we are concerned with the managers to whom first-line supervisors report, for they generally are unit commanders. In a mid-sized or large police agency, a patrol shift or watch may be commanded by a captain, who will have several lieutenants reporting to him or her. The lieutenants may assist the captain in running the shift, but when there is a shortage of sergeants as a result of vacations or retirements, the lieutenant may assume the duties of a first-line supervisor. In some respects, the lieutenant's position in some departments is a training ground for future unit commanders (captain rank or higher).

Perhaps the best way to understand what these shift commanders do is to examine the tasks they perform in a medium-sized police department. First, we examine the tasks generally performed by the captain, using the Lexington, Kentucky, Police Department as an example. The 15 most critical or important tasks performed by captains are as follows:

1. Issuing assignments to individuals and units within the section
2. Receiving assignments for section/unit
3. Reviewing incoming written complaints and reports
4. Preparing routine reports
5. Reviewing final disposition of assignments
6. Ensuring that subordinates comply with general and special orders
7. Monitoring crime and other activity statistics
8. Evaluating the work of individuals and units within the section
9. Maintaining sector facilities
10. Discussing concerns and problems with people
11. Attending various staff meetings
12. Maintaining working contacts and responding to inquiries from other sections of the division
13. Reviewing and approving overtime in section/unit
14. Monitoring section/unit operations to evaluate performance
15. Fielding and responding to complaints against subordinates

A review of these tasks shows that captains have more administrative responsibilities than lieutenants or sergeants, with 9 of the 15 tasks being administrative in nature. Captains spend a substantial amount of time coordinating their units' activities with those of other units and overseeing the operation of their units. As an officer progresses up the chain of command, his or her responsibilities become more administrative. At the same time, captains also have supervisory responsibilities (tasks 1, 3, 5, 6, 8, and 15). Whereas a sergeant or lieutenant may be supervising individual officers, a captain is more concerned with individual tasks, unit activities, and the overall performance of the officers under his or her command.

Every commander and administrator in the department, including the police chief, possesses administrative and supervisory responsibilities to some extent. As can be seen from the previous list, the unit commander functions to some extent like a police chief. The unit commander has many of the same responsibilities as the chief, but on a smaller scale. The chief performs these functions for the total department, while the unit commander is concerned only with one unit.

Next, we examine the tasks generally performed by the **lieutenant,** again using the Lexington Police Department as an example. The 15 most important responsibilities for lieutenants include the following (this list is based on the frequency they are performed and their urgency):

1. Assisting in supervising or directing the activities of the unit
2. Performing the duties of a police officer
3. Ensuring that departmental and governmental policies are followed
4. Preparing duty roster
5. Reviewing the work of individuals or groups in the section
6. Responding to field calls requiring an on-scene commander
7. Holding roll call
8. Preparing various reports
9. Reviewing various reports
10. Coordinating the activities of subordinates on major investigations
11. Meeting with superiors concerning unit operations
12. Maintaining time sheets
13. Notifying captain/bureau commander of significant calls
14. Answering inquiries from other sections/units, divisions, and outside agencies
15. Serving as captain/bureau commander in absence of same

Notice that some of the tasks performed by the lieutenants are purely administrative in nature (tasks 4, 7, 8, and 12). These are administrative activities that occur in every operational unit in the police department. The lieutenants in Lexington also perform supervisory functions (tasks 1, 3, 5, 6, and 9). These functions include overseeing officers and sergeants to ensure that different tasks are completed. Here, direct supervision generally focuses on the most critical tasks or those tasks that when performed incorrectly can result in dire consequences. Tasks 11, 13, 14, and 15 are managerial in nature. These responsibilities are generally vested with a unit commander, but many lieutenants perform them, especially in the absence of the captain. Finally, lieutenants perform the duties of a police officer (task 2). With their supervisory and managerial responsibilities, they engage in a limited amount of police work. The list shows that lieutenants are involved in a wide range of supervisory, managerial, and police duties.[23]

One potential problem of police organizations is that they may become top-heavy, with too many administrative, management, and supervisory personnel in general, or too many who are working in offices and not on the streets. Such structures can hinder the accomplishment of goals and objectives. Too often, middle managers become glorified paper pushers, especially in the present climate that requires a myriad of reports, budgets, grants, and so on.

The agency should determine what administrative, management, and supervisory functions are essential, and how many captains, lieutenants, and sergeants are needed to perform them. Some communities, such as Kansas City, Missouri, have eliminated the rank of lieutenant; they found that this move had no negative consequences.[24]

# First-Line Supervisors: Becoming a Patrol Sergeant

## *Seeking the Gold Badge*

Sometime during the career of a patrol officer (provided that he or she acquires the minimal years of experience), the opportunity for career advancement is presented—the chance to wear the sergeant's "gold badge." This is a difficult position to occupy because at this middle level, **first-line supervisors** are caught between upper management and the rank-and-file officers.

This initial promotional opportunity to attain the rank of sergeant is normally quite attractive. It is not uncommon for 60 to 65 percent or more of those who are eligible to take the test for promotion; thus, competition for the sergeant openings in most departments is quite keen.

Becoming a sergeant often involves an assessment center process, discussed earlier, and departmental and civil service procedures that are intended to guarantee legitimacy and impartiality in the process. Officers are often told it is best to rotate into different assignments before testing for sergeant, to gain exposure to a variety of police functions and supervisors. The promotional system, then, favors well-rounded officers; furthermore, being skilled at test taking is often of tremendous assistance, so even if one fails the first or several times, going through the testing process can be invaluable. As with the chief executives' hiring process, an assessment center, which includes critical-incident, problem solving, in-basket, disciplinary problems, role-playing exercises and/or other components, will provide candidates with valuable training and testing experience. Other factors that might come into play as part of the promotional process include education and training, years of experience, supervisory ratings, psychological evaluations, and departmental commendations.

## *Assuming the Position: General Roles and Functions*

Administrative personnel know that a good patrol officer is not automatically a good supervisor. Since supervisors are promoted from within the ranks, they are often placed in charge of their friends and peers. Longstanding relationships are put under stress when a new sergeant suddenly has official authority over former equals. Leniency or preferential treatment oftentimes is expected of new sergeants by their former peers.

When new supervisors attempt to correct deficient behavior, their own previous performance may be recalled as a means of challenging the reasonableness or legitimacy of their supervisory action. Supervisors with any skeletons in their closets can expect to hear those skeletons rattling as they begin to use their new-found authority. This places a great deal of pressure on the supervisor. A new supervisor must, therefore, go through a transitional phase to learn how to exercise command and get cooperation from subordinates.

The new supervisor is no longer responsible solely for her or his own personal behavior but instead is responsible for the behavior of several other employees. The step from officer to supervisor is a big one and calls for a new set of skills and knowledge largely separate from those learned at lower levels in the organization.

Supervision is not only challenging in policing but also in corrections, where supervisors must follow federal and state laws and court decisions that concern the custody, care, and treatment of inmates. Their subordinates, however, expect them to be understanding, to protect them from prison management's potentially unreasonable expectations and arbitrary decisions, and to represent their interests.

The supervisor's role, put simply, is to get his or her subordinates to do their very best. This task involves a host of actions, including communicating, motivating, leading, team building, training, appraising, counseling, and disciplining. Getting them to do their very best includes figuring out each subordinate's strengths and weaknesses, defining good and bad performance, measuring performance, providing feedback, and making sure that subordinates' efforts coincide with the organization's mission, values, goals, and objectives.

Supervising a group of subordinates is made more difficult because of the so-called "human element." People are complex and sometimes unpredictable. Rules and principles for communicating and leading and other supervisory tasks are rarely hard-and-fast because different people react differently. What works for a supervisor in one situation may not work for that supervisor in another situation, much less for some other supervisor. Thus, supervisors have to learn to "read" subordinates and diagnose situations before choosing how to respond. Supervisors have to become students of human behavior and of such behavioral science disciplines as psychology and sociology.

Effective supervision is also difficult because the job is dynamic, not static. Even without any turnover of personnel, one's subordinates change over time as they age, grow, mature, and experience satisfaction and dissatisfaction in their personal and work lives. In addition, turnover is common as a result of retirements, promotions, and transfers to other units within the department. When new subordinates come under the supervisor's wing, the supervisor must learn the best way to handle these new subordinates and also be attuned to the new officers' effects on other subordinates and on the work group as a whole.

It is not only one's subordinates who change; the organization and its environment change over time. The organization's rules and expectations may change. The public may make new demands. Societal values evolve and change. Effective supervision over the long haul requires continuous monitoring and adaptation. The department expects the supervisor to keep up with such changes in order to better supervise subordinates. Subordinates, on the other hand, expect the supervisor to help them interpret and adapt successfully to this changing environment. The nature of the supervisor's job is reflected in Table 4.1.

**TABLE 4.1**   Management's and Officers' Expectations of Supervisors

*MANAGEMENT'S EXPECTATIONS*

- Interpret departmental policies, procedures, and rules, and ensure that officers follow them
- Initiate disciplinary action when officers fail to follow policies
- Ensure that officers' paperwork and reports are accurate and filed on a timely basis
- Train officers when they are deficient or unskilled
- Complete performance evaluations
- Ensure that officers treat citizens respectfully, professionally, and impartially
- Ensure that officers' equipment and appearance is in order
- Backup officers and review their performance when officers answer calls for service
- Take charge of high risk or potential critical incident situations
- Make assignments to ensure that the objectives of the unit are met

*OFFICERS' EXPECTATIONS*

- Interpret departmental policies, procedures, and rules to meet the needs of the officers
- Handle disciplinary actions informally rather than taking direct action, especially regarding minor infractions
- Advocate for officers when they request vacation or time off
- Support them when there is a conflict with citizens
- Provide them support and backup at high risk calls
- Assist them in getting better assignments and shifts
- Emphasize law enforcement activities over other activities such as providing services, community policing activities, or mundane assignments such as traffic control
- Understand that officers need to take breaks and sometimes attend to personal needs while on duty

## *Basic Tasks*

The following 9 tasks are most important for police supervisors; they are listed with the most important first:

1. Supervises subordinate officers in the performance of their duties
2. Disseminates information to subordinates
3. Ensures that general and special orders are followed
4. Reviews and approves various reports
5. Listens to problems voiced by officers
6. Answers calls
7. Keeps superiors apprised of ongoing situations
8. Provides direct supervision for potential high-risk calls or situations
9. Interprets policies and informs subordinates

Tasks 1 and 8 on this list are global supervisory tasks that incorporate both direction and control. Tasks 2 and 9 are aspects of the directing function, while tasks 3, 4, and 5 are elements of control. Thus, six of these top 9 sergeant's tasks involve directing and controlling. The remaining three tasks provide interesting glimpses into some of the other duties and responsibilities performed by police supervisors: listening to subordinates' problems, notifying superiors of problems, and directly assisting subordinates in performing their work. Police supervisors provide an important communications link in the hierarchy between workers and management, as well as a sounding board for problems and grievances. They also get involved in performing street police work from time to time.

Supervisory tasks can range from the mundane (such as typing and filing reports, operating dictation equipment) to the challenging (assigning priorities to investigations, training personnel in forced entry procedures and barricaded person situations). Tasks may be administrative (preparing monthly activity reports, scheduling vacation leave), operational (securing major crime scenes, assisting stranded motorists), general (maintaining inventory of equipment, training subordinates), or specialized (conducting stakeouts, training animals for use in specialized units).

## *Types of Supervisors*

Robin S. Engel[25] studied police supervisors and found four distinct types: traditional, innovative, supportive, and active. Each of these types can be found in any police department. A particular supervisor's style is largely dependent on his or her experiences on the job, training, and the department's organizational climate.

The first type, *traditional*, is law enforcement oriented. Traditional supervisors expect their subordinates to produce high levels of measurable activities, such as traffic citations and arrests. They expect officers to respond to calls for service efficiently, place a great deal of emphasis on reports and other paperwork, and provide officers with a substantial amount of instruction and oversight. To a great extent, traditional supervisors are task oriented. They tend to place greater emphasis on punishment than rewards and often believe that they do not have a great deal of power in the department. These supervisors see their primary role as controlling subordinates. Traditional supervisors often have morale and motivation problems with their subordinates.

The second type is the *innovative* supervisor, who is most closely associated with community policing. To some extent, innovative supervisors are the opposite of traditional supervisors. Innovative supervisors generally do not place a great deal of emphasis on citations or arrests. They also depend more on developing relationships with subordinates as opposed to using power to control or motivate. Innovative supervisors usually are good mentors, and they tend to coach rather than order. They are open to new ideas and innovations. Their ultimate goal is to develop officers who can solve problems and have good relations with citizens. Innovative supervisors sometimes have problems with officers who are task oriented or who emphasize enforcement and neglect community relations.

The third type of supervisor is the *supportive* supervisor, who, like the innovate supervisor, is concerned with developing good relations with subordinates. The primary difference is that the supportive supervisor is concerned with protecting officers from what are viewed as unfair management practices. They see themselves as a buffer between management and officers. They attempt to develop strong work teams and motivate officers by inspiring them. Their shortcoming is that they tend to see themselves as "one of the boys," and they sometimes neglect emphasizing departmental goals and responsibilities.

The final category of supervisors according to Engel is the *active* supervisor, who tends to work in the field. Active supervisors sometimes are police officers with stripes or rank. They often take charge of field situations rather than supervise them, although they are active supervisors in most situations. They are able to develop good relations with subordinates, because they are perceived as being hard working and competent. Their shortcoming is that by being overly involved in some field situations, they do not give their subordinates the opportunity to develop.

Engel[26] found that the four types of supervision were fairly evenly distributed in the departments. The most effective supervisor was the active supervisor. Subordinates working for active supervisors performed better in a number of areas, including problem solving and community policing. This led Engel to conclude that active supervisors were able to develop a more productive work unit because of their leading by example. It seems that working supervisors inspire subordinates to work and be productive.

Engel did identify one issue with active police supervisors: a higher incidence of use of force relative to the other types. Since active supervisors are very involved in the provision of police services, efforts should be made to ensure that they follow policies as well as that subordinates adhere to policies and procedures. Supervisors must not only be well trained and selected carefully, but they too must receive a measure of supervision from their superior. If the supervisor fails to make sure that employees perform correctly, the unit will not be successful, causing difficulties for the manager, the lieutenant, or the captain.

A police department is really nothing more than the sum total of all its units, and one problem unit can adversely affect other units and detract from the department's total effectiveness. This is particularly true for police organizations, since there is substantial interdependence among the various units in a police department. For example, if patrol officers do a poor job of writing reports when they respond to crimes, the workload of detectives who later complete the case's follow-up investigation will increase.

# The Patrol Officer

Countless books and articles have been written about and other chapters in this book deal in part with the beat officer. Here, we briefly discuss the nature of this position.

## *Basic Tasks*

Many people believe that the police officer has the most difficult job in America. When broken down to fundamental terms, the police perform four basic functions: (1) enforcing the laws, (2) performing services (such as maintaining or assisting animal control units, reporting burned out street lights or stolen traffic lights and signs, delivering death messages, checking the welfare of people in their homes, delivering blood), (3) preventing crime (patrolling, providing the public with information on locks and lighting to reduce the opportunity for crime), and (4) protecting the innocent (by investigating crimes, police are systematically removing innocent people from consideration as crime suspects).[27]

Because police officers are solitary workers, spending much of their time on the job unsupervised, and because those officers who are hired today will become the supervisors of the future, police administrators must attempt to attract the best individuals possible. A major problem of police administration today involves personnel recruitment.

## *Problems with Getting the Best*

Whether one blames a generally weak national economy, higher educational requirements, or noncompetitive wages and benefits, police and sheriff's departments in virtually every region of the country agree that the generous pool of applicants from which they once sought qualified candidates is becoming increasingly shallow.[28]

Recruiting and retaining females in police service remains particularly problematic. Gender bias (reflected in the absence of women being hired and then promoted into policymaking roles) and sexual harassment concerns prevent many women from applying and cause many female officers to leave—and quickly: About 60 percent of female officers who leave their agency do so between their second and fifth year on the job.[29]

Some agencies have successfully addressed recruitment dilemmas. For example, the New York State Police (NYSP) learned that people sought job enrichment in an occupation and were motivated to enter police work by the chance to help others and to serve the community. These two factors are now emphasized in the NYSP mission and values statements, as well as in recruitment drives. Other recruiting methods employed by police agencies include seeking applicants far from home, having application forms on the Web where they can be easily downloaded, and allowing some applicants to substitute work experience for college credits.[30]

# What Traits Make a "Good Cop"?

Although it may be difficult for the average police administrator to articulate what qualities are needed in a "good" officer, some psychological characteristics can be identified. According to psychologist Lawrence Wrightsman,[31] it is important that good officers be *incorruptible*, of high moral character. They should be *well adjusted*, able to carry out the hazardous and stressful tasks of policing without "cracking up," and thick-skinned enough to operate without defensiveness. They also should be *people oriented* and able to respond to situations without becoming emotional, impulsive, or overly aggressive; they need to exercise restraint. They also need *cognitive skills*, to assist in their investigative work.

Chief Dennis Nowicki[32] compiled 12 qualities that he believes are imperative for entry-level police officers:

1. *Enthusiasm:* believes in what he or she is doing and goes about even "routine" duties with a certain vigor that is almost contagious
2. *Good communications skills:* highly developed speaking and listening skills; ability to interact equally well with people from all socioeconomic levels
3. *Good judgment:* wisdom and analytical ability to make good decisions based on an understanding of the problem
4. *Sense of humor:* ability to laugh and smile, to help officers cope with the regular exposure to human pain and suffering
5. *Creativity:* ability to use creative techniques by placing themselves in the mind of the criminal and legally accomplishing arrests
6. *Self-motivation:* making things happen, proactively solving difficult cases, creating their own luck
7. *Knowing the job and the system:* understanding the role of a police officer, the intricacies of the justice system, what the administration requires, and using both formal and informal channels to be effective
8. *Ego:* believing they are good officers, having self-confidence that enables solving difficult crimes
9. *Courage:* ability to meet physical and psychological challenges, thinking clearly during times of high stress, admitting when they are wrong, standing up for what is difficult and right
10. *Understanding discretion:* enforcing the spirit of the law, not the letter of the law; not being hard nosed, hard headed, or hard hearted; giving people a break and showing empathy
11. *Tenacity:* staying focused; seeing challenges, not obstacles; not viewing failure as a setback, but as an experience
12. *A thirst for knowledge:* staying current of new laws and court decisions, always learning (from the classroom but also via informal discussions with other officers)

# Roles and Functions of All Personnel in COPPS

Next, we briefly examine the roles of chief executive, middle manager, supervisor, and patrol officer under community oriented policing and problem solving (COPPS, discussed in Chapter 3)—all of which are extremely important if this strategy is to succeed.

## *The Chief Executive*

Much has been written about how the chief executive of a police agency must lead the organization in terms of changing its entire mission, values, culture to effect the COPPS strategy. The advent of community policing has brought new challenges for police chiefs, calling for new skills and attitudes and even an ability to be an entrepreneur.[33]

First, the police chief executive is ultimately responsible for all the facets of COPPS, from implementation to training to evaluation. Therefore, what is needed are chief executives who are willing to do things that have not been done before, in other words, "risk takers and boat rockers within a culture where daily exposure to life-or-death situations makes officers natural conservators of the status quo."[34] These are chief executives who become committed to getting the police and neighborhoods to work together to attack the roots of crime. For them, "Standing still is not only insufficient . . . it is going backwards."[35]

Therefore, police executives must be *viable change agents*. In any hierarchy, the person at the top is responsible for setting both the policy and the tone of the organization. Within a police agency, the chief or sheriff has the ultimate power to make change, particularly as substantive a one as COPPS. The chief executive must be both visible and credible and must create a climate conducive to change. Under COPPS, chief executives must focus on the values, mission, and long-term goals of policing in order to create an organizational environment that enables officers, government officials, and community members to work together. By building consensus, they can establish programs, develop timelines, and set priorities. They should honor the good work done in the past but exhibit a sense of urgency about implementing change while involving people from the community and the department in all stages of the transition.

In sum, the chief executive's roles and responsibilities during the change to COPPS include the following:

- Articulating a clear vision to the organization
- Understanding and accepting the depth of change and time required to implement COPPS
- Assembling a management team that is committed to translating the new vision into action
- Being committed to removing bureaucratic obstacles whenever possible

An interesting point of view regarding chiefs of police, change, and COPPS has been offered by Charles Gain, former chief of the Oakland, California, Police

Department, who observed that most top police executives reach their position as chief in the twilight of their policing careers. They tend to resist organizational change, Gain said, because they fear the loss of the position to which they have so long aspired; and, as they are in the final stages of their career, they engage in a "holding action."[36] Gain further asserted that when chiefs make it to the top, they might be reluctant to jeopardize their position—especially without some form of contract protection—by setting new goals and moving ahead.[37]

## Middle Managers

Middle managers—lieutenants and captains—also play a crucial role in the operation of a COPPS philosophy. COPPS's emphasis on problem solving necessitates that middle managers draw on their familiarity with the bureaucracy to secure, maintain, and use authority to empower subordinates, helping officers to actively and creatively confront and resolve issues, and sometimes using unconventional approaches on a trial-and-error basis.

Middle managers must *build on the strengths* of their subordinates, capitalizing on their training and competence.[38] They must "cheerlead," encouraging supervisors and patrol officers to actually solve the problems they are confronting.[39] The lieutenants are the "gatekeepers" and must develop the system, resources, and support mechanisms to ensure that the officers/detectives and supervisors can achieve the best results. The officers and supervisors cannot perform without the necessary equipment, resources, and reinforcement.[40]

In sum, the roles and responsibilities of middle managers during the change to COPPS include

- Assuming responsibility for strategic planning
- Eliminating red tape and bottlenecks that impede the work of officers and supervisors
- Conducting regular meetings with subordinates to discuss plans, activities, and results
- Assessing COPPS efforts in a continuous manner

## First-Line Supervisors

Perhaps the most challenging aspect of changing the culture of a police agency lies in changing first-line supervisors. Supervisors must be convinced that COPPS makes good sense in today's environment.

The roles and responsibilities of first-line supervisors during a change to COPPS include

- Understanding and practicing problem solving
- Managing time, staff, and resources
- Encouraging teamwork
- Helping officers mobilize stakeholders

- Tracking and managing officers' problem solving
- Providing officers with ongoing feedback and support

## *Rank-and-File Officers*

All experts on the subject of police innovation and change emphasize the importance of empowering and using the input from the street officers. The patrol officer becomes a *problem solver.* There is an emphasis on practical intelligence—the ability to quickly analyze key elements of a situation and identify possible courses of action to reach logical conclusions. In order to formulate a response, the officer must define the problem and address the motivations of the offenders.[41]

Under COPPS, the patrol officer is expected to recognize when old methods are inadequate and new and different solutions are needed. The officer is expected to display many of the skills demanded in higher-level personnel, such as detectives, including being creative, flexible, and innovative; working independently; and maintaining self-discipline. Communication skills are also vital. The officer must possess the ability to work cooperatively with others to solve problems and to listen.[42]

# CASE STUDIES

The following two case studies deal with CEO functions and disciplinary problems and assist the reader in understanding and applying administrative challenges in a real-world context.

## The Chief Executive's Busy Days

You have been the Park City police chief for six months, overseeing an agency of 60 sworn officers in a community of 80,000 people; your city abuts another larger city, with a population of 160,000. These populations are deceptive, however, soaring during the summertime, as your area is a tourist-based gaming destination. Today is July 3rd, and at 8:00 A.M. you briefly attend a staff meeting of detectives, led by a deputy chief of operations, to learn the latest information concerning a highly publicized kidnapping. In the afternoon, you plan to deliver a news release concerning the case status. Then you will give the graduation speech at the area police academy, which is followed by your attending a meeting of the Tri-County Regional Major Case Squad, where you will discuss the latest intelligence information concerning a ring of circulating slot machine cheaters in your jurisdiction. You then learn from Communications that one of your motorcycle officers has gone down, and you speed to the hospital emergency room to wish him well. You then meet with your events staff and other city officials to finalize security and traffic plans for tomorrow's huge fireworks display, as last year's event resulted in huge numbers of alcohol-related traffic and fighting arrests. You are also scheduled to ride in a car in the holiday parade. At day's end, you make final preparations for your July 5th presentation to the City Council concerning the need for a modern 800-megahertz communications system, which you hope to convince the council to purchase. You also will be attending a special ceremony at a city park that honors area law enforcement officers who have been killed in the line of duty.

### Questions for Discussion

1. Using Mintzberg's model for CEOs, classify each of the functions mentioned in the case study into the interpersonal, informational, and decision-maker roles.
2. More specifically, which of this chief executive's tasks or activities would fall within the figurehead, leadership, liaison, monitoring/inspecting, dissemination, spokesperson, entrepreneur, disturbance-handler, resource-allocator, and negotiator functions? Explain.

# Intruding Ima and the Falsified Report

An eight-year employee of your police agency, Officer Ima Goodenough, is a patrol officer who often serves as field training officer. Goodenough is generally capable and experienced in both the patrol and detective divisions. She takes pride in being of the "old school" and has evolved a clique of approximately 10 people with whom she gets along, while mostly shunning other officers. As an officer of the old school, she typically handles calls for service without requesting cover units or backup. She has had six complaints of brutality lodged against her during the past three years. For Ima and her peers, officers who call for backup are "wimps." She has recently been involved in two high-speed pursuits during which her vehicle was damaged when she attempted to run the offender off the road. Ima will notify a supervisor only when dealing with a major situation. She is borderline insubordinate when dealing with new supervisors. She believes that, generally speaking, the administration exists only to "screw around with us." You, her shift commander, have been fed up with her deteriorating attitude and reckless performance for some time and have been wondering if you will soon have occasion to take some form of disciplinary action against her. You have also learned that Ima has a reputation among her supervisors as being a "hot dog." Some of her past and present supervisors have even commented that she is a "walking time bomb" who is unpredictable and could "blow" at any time.

One day while bored on patrol, Ima decides to go outside her jurisdiction, responding to a shooting call that is just across the city limit and in the county. She radios the dispatcher that she is out "assisting," then walks into the home where paramedics are frantically working on a man with a head wound lying on the floor. Nearby on the floor is a large, foreign-made revolver; Ima holds and waves the revolver in the air, examining it. A paramedic yells at her, "Hey! Put that down, this may be an attempted homicide case!" Ima puts the revolver back on the floor. Meanwhile, you have been attempting to contact Ima via radio to get her back into her jurisdiction. Later, when the sheriff's office complains to you about her actions at their crime scene, you require that she write a report of her actions. She completes a report describing her observations at the scene but denies touching or picking up anything. Looking at Ima's personnel file, you determine that her performance evaluations for the past eight years are "standard"—average to above average. She has never received a suspension from duty for her actions. While verbally expressing their unhappiness with her for many years, Ima's supervisors have not expressed that disdain in writing.

## Questions for Discussion

1. What are the primary issues involved in this situation?
2. Do you believe that there are sufficient grounds for bringing disciplinary action against Goodenough? If so, what would be the specific charges? What is the appropriate punishment?

3. Do you believe that this is a good opportunity, and do grounds exist, for termination?

4. Does the fact that her supervisors have rated her as standard have any bearing on this matter or create difficulties in bringing a case for termination? If so, how?

## Summary

Clearly, those who hold positions of authority in law enforcement also hold the reins of tremendous responsibility. This chapter has noted the awesome roles and challenges that are inherent in these positions. Police executives, managers, and supervisors must decide what the best leadership method is, and how to execute each role in the best way. They must be concerned with their agency's performance and standing with the community, governing board, and rank and file. It is no wonder that countless police supervision and management seminars are conducted by federal, state, and local training academies, as well as universities and colleges across the nation.

## Questions for Review

1. What are some of a police executive's primary roles? (Use the three major categories of the Mintzberg model of chief executive officers in developing your response.)

3. What are some elements of the police chief's position that make it attractive and unattractive? Do you think that contemporary qualifications for the position are adequate?

4. How do chiefs and sheriffs differ in role and background?

5. How is the performance of chiefs and sheriffs evaluated? Are there other, better criteria that could be used? What personal traits are most important for persons occupying or seeking these offices?

6. How do the role and function of sergeants differ from those of upper or middle management?

7. What are the three types of political arena conflicts that can cause police chief executives to lose their job?

## Notes

1. Henry Mintzberg, "The Manager's Job: Folklore and Fact," *Harvard Business Review* 53 (July/August 1975):49–61.

2.  Robert Katz, "Skills of an Effective Administrator," *Harvard Business Review* (January/February 1955):33–41.

3.  Ronald G. Lynch, *The Police Manager*, 3d ed. (New York: Random House, 1986), p. 1.

4.  "Survey Says Big-City Chiefs Are Better-Educated Outsiders," *Law Enforcement News*, April 30, 1998, p. 7.

5.  Ibid.

6.  Janice K. Penegor and Ken Peak, "Police Chief Acquisitions: A Comparison of Internal and External Selections," *American Journal of Police* 11 (1992):17–32.

7.  Richard B. Weinblatt, "The Shifting Landscape of Chiefs' Jobs," *Law and Order* (October 1999):50.

8.  National Advisory Commission on Criminal Justice Standards and Goals, *Police Chief Executive* (Washington, D.C.: U.S. Government Printing Office, 1976), p. 7.

9.  Weinblatt, "The Shifting Landscape of Chiefs' Jobs," p. 51.

10. For an excellent compilation of articles concerning the chief's role, see *Police Leadership in America: Crisis and Opportunity*, William Geller (ed.) (New York: Praeger, 1985).

11. Janet Ferris, "Present and Potential Legal Job Protections Available to Heads of Agencies," *Florida Police Chief* 14 (1994):43–45.

12. Henry Mintzberg, *Power In and Around Organizations* (Englewood Cliffs, N.J.: Prentice Hall, 1983).

13. Ibid., pp. 50–53.

14. Charles R. Swanson, Leonard Territo, and Robert W. Taylor, *Police Administration*, 5th ed. (Upper Saddle River, N.J.: Prentice Hall, 2001), p. 94.

15. Colin Hayes, "The Office of Sheriff in the United States," *The Prison Journal* 74 (2001):50–54.

16. Jerald R. Vaughn, *How to Rate Your Police Chief* (Washington, D.C.: Police Executive Research Forum, 1987), pp. 7–14.

17. Peter Drucker, *Management, Tasks, Responsibilities, and Practices* (New York: Harper & Row, 1974), p. 85.

18. David C. Couper, *How to Rate Your Local Police* (Washington, D.C.: Police Executive Research Forum, 1973).

19. Vaughn, *How to Rate Your Police Chief*, pp. 15–20.

20. Ibid., pp. 23–29.

21. N. Darlene Walker and Richard J. Richardson, *Public Attitudes Toward the Police* (Chapel Hill, N.C.: Institute for Research in Social Science, 1974), p. 1.

22. Leonhard F. Fuld, *Police Administration* (New York: G.P. Putnam's Sons, 1909), pp. 59–60.

23. See Kenneth J. Peak, Larry K. Gaines, and Ronald W. Glensor, *Police Supervision and Management: In an Era of Community Policing* (Upper Saddle River, N.J.: Prentice Hall, forthcoming), Chapter 2, generally.

24. Richard N. Holden, *Modern Police Management*, 2d ed. (Englewood Cliffs, N.J.: Prentice Hall, 1994), pp. 294–295.

25. Robin S. Engel, "Patrol Officer Supervision in the Community Policing Era," *Journal of Criminal Justice*, 30 (2002):51–64.

26. Robin S. Engel, "Supervisory Styles of Patrol Sergeants and Lieutenants," *Journal of Criminal Justice*, 29 (2001):341–355.

27. Kenneth J. Peak, *Policing America: Methods, Issues, Functions*, 4th ed. (Upper Saddle River, N.J.: Prentice Hall, 2003), pp. 57–58.

28. Jennifer Nislow, "Is Anyone Out There?" *Law Enforcement News*, October 31, 1999, p. 1.

29. "Plenty of Talk, Not Much Action," *Law Enforcement News* (January 15/31, 1999):1.

30. "Police Chiefs Try Many Recruiting Strategies to Boost Applicant Pool," *Crime Control Digest* (February 2, 2001):1-2.

31. Lawrence S. Wrightsman, *Psychology and the Legal System* (Monterey, Calif.: Brooks/Cole Publishing Company, 1987), pp. 85-86.

32. Adapted from Dennis Nowicki, "Twelve Traits of Highly Effective Police Officers," *Law and Order* (October 1999):45-46.

33. See, for example, Kenneth J. Peak and Ronald W. Glensor, *Community Policing and Problem Solving: Strategies and Practices*, 3d ed. (Upper Saddle River, N.J.: Prentice Hall, 2002).

34. Mike Tharp and Dorian Friedman, "New Cops on the Block," *U.S. News and World Report* (August 2, 1993):23.

35. John Eck, quoted in ibid., p. 24.

36. As discussed in J. Ruiz, *The Return of the Ultimate Outsider: A Civilian Administrator at the Top* (Unpublished paper, 1997).

37. Ibid.

38. William A. Geller and Guy Swanger, *Managing Innovation in Policing: The Untapped Potential of the Middle Manager* (Washington, D.C.: Police Executive Research Forum, 1995), p. 105.

39. Ibid., p. 109.

40. Ibid., p. 112.

41. Ibid., p. 116.

42. Ibid., pp. 119-120.

# Chapter 5

# Police Issues
# and Practices

## Key Terms and Concepts

Bioterrorism                          Exception principle
Counterterrorism                      Terrorism
Ecoterrorism

## Learning Objectives

After reading this chapter, the student will:

- be familiar with the definition and types of terrorism
- know the three categories of the current international terrorist threat
- have an understanding of bioterrorism
- be familiar with administrative responses to terrorism
- have an understanding of the ramifications of racial profiling
- know the three types of abuse committed by police officers
- be familiar with violence in the schools and how the police and community can help prevent it

*In utrumque paratus / Seu versare dolos seu certae occumbere morti.*

*[Prepared for either event, to set his traps or to meet with certain death.]*

—Virgil, 70–19 B.C.

# Introduction

It was often stated tongue-in-cheek that in the earlier days of policing, "a size 3 hat and a size 43 jacket" were the only qualifications for entering and doing the work of policing. Given the challenging and dangerous issues and problems that accompany this occupation—several of which are discussed in this chapter—that description could never have been further from the truth than it is today.

The chapter begins with an examination of terrorism, including tactical and administrative responses. Next is another "hot button" issue: racial profiling, and what is being done by administrators to track, identify, and it is hoped eliminate it. The chapter then examines police management of the use of force, including deadly force and domestic violence by police. Then, we discuss police roles and functions in the school violence problem. We next examine vehicular pursuits by police. Following that, we review what needs to occur when patrol officers find a situation too overwhelming to handle: the *exception principle* of management. The chapter concludes with three challenging case studies.

Also note that other issues concerning the development and use of technology are discussed in Chapter 17.

## *A Cautionary Note*

Much of what is described in this chapter tends to portray the police in a negative light. It would be well to remember, however, that only a small proportion of the nation's more than 700,000 sworn police officers violate their oath of office. Furthermore, what is often overlooked is violence that is directed *toward* the police. Each year about 70 police officers are killed[1] and more than 55,000 are assaulted (about 7,500 with a dangerous weapon)[2] in the line of duty. Indeed, police officers are the victims of aggravated assaults at a rate of 29 per 1,000 workers—more than three times the rate for any other occupational field.[3] Given the high number of drug-addicted people on the streets (of particular danger are those who use methamphetamine) and the tremendous amount of firepower now in the possession of criminals, this occupation is more dangerous than ever before.

For their part, many police officers see the United States as a mean and dangerous place. As William A. Westley wrote in *Violence and the Police*,

> The policeman's world is spawned of degradation, corruption and insecurity. He sees man as ill-willed, exploitative, mean and dirty; himself a victim of injustice . . . he walks alone, a pedestrian in Hell.[4]

Many police officers' day is like a foray into a combat zone. Indeed, the inner-city streets have been likened to a domestic war zone. Instead of facing some foreign enemy, however, the foes of these officers include gang members, homicidal killers, and drug addicts. Police adversaries are more heavily armed and more arrogant than ever.

# Terrorism

## *Definition and Types*

Title 22, Section 265f(d) of the United States Code states the following: **Terrorism** "means premeditated, politically motivated violence perpetrated against noncombatant targets by subnational groups or clandestine agents, usually intended to influence an audience."[5] The FBI defines terrorism as "the unlawful use of force against persons or property to intimidate or coerce a government, the civilian population, or any segment thereof, in furtherance of political or social objectives."[6]

The threat of terrorism has changed and become more deadly. Over the past several years, a new trend has developed in terrorism within the United States: a transition from more numerous low-level incidents to less frequent but more destructive attacks, with a goal to produce mass casualties and attract intense media coverage. While the number of terrorist attacks in the United States declined during the 1990s, the number of persons killed and injured increased.[7]

Such attacks in the United States are caused by both foreign and domestic terrorists. Examples of the former are the attacks in September 2001 that crashed hijacked jetliners into the World Trade Center buildings in New York and the Pentagon in Virginia, with around 3,000 people killed or missing. Other examples include the bombing of the World Trade Center in New York City in February 1993, killing six and injuring 1,000 people. An example of the latter is the April 1995 bombing of the Murrah Building in Oklahoma City by Timothy McVeigh, killing 168 people and injuring more than 500.[8] (McVeigh was executed in June 2001.)

Combating terrorism is expensive: The U.S. Congress appropriated more than $60 billion from September 2001 to January 2002 to combat terrorism at home and abroad, including $1.5 billion for the new Homeland Security Office.[9] Law enforcement resources available to fight terrorism have also greatly increased. From 1993 to 2001, the FBI (which created a new Counterterrorism Division in April 2000) saw its **counterterrorism** budget increase from $77 million to $376 million[10]—or 388 percent (the most significant increase followed the Oklahoma City bombing). The costs of trying to secure the nation's people and places are projected to skyrocket even more in the aftermath of 9/11—$150 billion more by 2010.[11]

Terrorism can take many forms and does not always involve bombs and guns. For example, the Earth Liberation Front (ELF) and a sister organization, the

Animal Liberation Front, have been responsible for the majority of terrorist acts committed in the United States for several years. These proponents of **ecoterrorism** have burned greenhouses, tree farms, logging sites, ski resorts, and new housing developments. The groups' members have eluded capture, have no centralized organization or leadership, and are so secretive as to be described as "ghosts" whose organizations are more difficult to infiltrate than organized crime.[12]

U.S. embassies abroad have also been singled out for terrorist attacks; in 1998, bombings of embassies in Kenya and Tanzania left 224 dead and resulted in the placement of Saudi Arabian millionaire Osama bin Laden at the top of the FBI's most wanted list, as well as the conviction in June 2001 of four of bin Laden's foot soldiers.[13]

The FBI divides the current international terrorist threat into three categories:

1. *Foreign sponsors of international terrorism.* Seven countries—Iran, Iraq, Syria, Sudan, Libya, Cuba, and North Korea—are designated as sponsors and view terrorism as a tool of foreign policy. They fund, organize, network, and provide other support to formal terrorist groups and extremists.

2. *Formalized terrorist groups.* Autonomous organizations (such as bin Laden's al Qaeda, Afghanistan's Taliban, Iranian-backed Hezbollah, Egyptian Al-Gama'a Al-Islamiyya, and Palestinian HAMAS) have their own infrastructures, personnel, finances, and training facilities.

3. *Loosely affiliated international radical extremists.* These terrorists do not represent a particular nation, but they may pose the most urgent threat to the United States because they remain relatively unknown to law enforcement agencies.[14] Members of these groups attacked the World Trade Center towers and the Pentagon in 2001 and bombed the World Trade Center in 1993.

These international groups now pose another source of concern to law enforcement agencies: They are cooperating with one another. For example, a terrorist manual is circulating among them, and al Qaeda is known to maintain close ties with Hezbollah.[15] Another concern is their choice of weapons; although terrorists continue to rely on conventional weapons such as bombs and small arms, there are indications that terrorists and other criminals may consider using unconventional chemical (including nerve gas, sarin, or other chemical cocktails whose ingredients are readily available) or biological weapons in an attack on the United States at some point in the future.[16]

With regard to domestic terrorism, many people living in the United States are determined to use violence to advance their agendas. Domestic terrorism seems to have hit a high-water mark from 1982 to 1992, when a majority of the 165 terrorist incidents were conducted by domestic terrorist groups. One current troubling branch of right-wing extremism is the militia or patriot movement. Members of this group generally are law-abiding citizens who have become intolerant of what they perceive as violations of their constitutional rights.[17]

## *A Looming Threat: Bioterrorism*

The use of anthrax in the United States in late 2001 left no doubt about people's vulnerability to **bioterrorism**—and the intention of some people to develop and use it. Smallpox, botulism, and plague also constitute major threats, and many experts believe that it is only a matter of time before biological weapons get into the wrong hands and are used like explosives in the past.[18]

All of this brings to mind a real-life *Andromeda Strain* movie scenario: a toxic agent is genetically engineered in large quantities in the laboratory and sprayed into the population; that agent then reproduces itself and kills many people. This is the most worrisome aspect of bioterrorism: the possibility of terrorists releasing an infectious, self-replicating microorganism into the population that spreads to many millions of other individuals. The person who controls this toxin could then sell it to terrorists. One has to wonder why international terrorists have not already done so. This form of terrorism is easy for a biochemist to accomplish and can wipe out an entire civilization. All that is required is a toxin that can be cultured and put into a spray form that can be disseminated into the population. Fortunately, they *are* extremely difficult for all but specially trained individuals to make in large quantities and in the correct dosage; they are tricky to transport, in that live organisms are delicate; and they must be dispersed in a proper molecule size to infect the lungs of the target. Like chemical weapons, they are also dependent on the wind and the weather and are difficult to control.[19]

Police supervisors, middle managers, and administrators must be prepared for such eventualities; training for these leaders, and for the rank-and-file officers, is of the utmost importance. With respect to biological agents, the role of the police will vary depending on whether or not they are the first responder. Police must become knowledgeable about bio-weapons and how to ascertain if the agent is transmittable, as well as the appropriate agencies to get involved. Then, if an agent is deployed overtly and therefore discovered quickly, the police will respond immediately; if covert (and, say, hospitals do not begin to see cases until many days after the agent is released), the police will be responsible for conducting a later investigation. If hundreds of people are showing up at hospitals, then the police will also have to maintain order.[20]

## *Tactical and Administrative Responses*

There are several possible means by which the police can address domestic terrorism, particularly following the 2001 attacks in New York City and Washington, D.C. First, and perhaps the most fruitful, is military support of domestic law enforcement. The Posse Comitatus Act of 1878 generally prohibits using the military to execute the laws; the military may be called upon, however, to provide personnel and equipment for certain special support activities, such as domestic terrorist events involving weapons of mass destruction.[21]

Additional changes in security measures or activities—several of which are already in place—include loosening restrictions on FBI surveillance; giving more

## Exhibit 5.1
## Under the Glare of Scrutiny, FBI Gets Ready for a Makeover

FBI officials, under harsh criticism for failing to "connect the dots" when internal and external intelligence reports warned prior to Sept. 11 that an attack on American soil might be coming, are now seeking to redefine the bureau's mission with a massive overhaul of both its philosophy and organizational structure.

FBI Director Robert S. Mueller III outlined a proposal in June that will shift the bureau's traditional focus from crime fighting to terrorism prevention. "First, and foremost, the FBI must protect and defend the United States against terrorism and foreign intelligence threats," he said in a statement before a Senate committee. Its second duty is to enforce the nation's criminal laws, said Mueller, and third, to provide assistance to state, local and international law enforcement, as well as to other federal agencies.

### Red Flags and Unconnected Dots

"I cannot say for sure that there wasn't a possibility we could have come across some lead that would have led us to the hijackers," he conceded. While insisting that there was no specific warning, Mueller said, "that doesn't mean that there weren't red flags out there, that there weren't dots that should have been connected to the extent possible."

The FBI makeover, which has yet to be approved by Congress, calls for the hiring of 900 new agents by September; the permanent reassignment of 500 agents from such activities as bank robbery, white-collar crime and narcotics investigations to intelligence, and the increase from 153 counterterrorism agents to 682 over the next two years.

Involvement in drug investigations—which the FBI long resisted and only reluctantly undertook beginning in 1981—will be reduced, as will the bureau's participation in white-collar and violent crime investigations. The decision to limit the involvement in narcotics cases, said Mueller, came after consultation with the FBI's special agents in charge, federal prosecutors, state and local law enforcement officials and others. Where in the past, 10 to 12 agents might have participated in joint task forces, now that number may be half that. . . .

Among the other key features of the reorganization will be:

A restructuring and expansion of the bureau's Counterterrorism Division to include a National Joint Terrorism Task Force that will improve collaboration and information sharing with other agencies and local field offices.

The establishment of a new Office of Intelligence, which will initially be staffed by CIA analysts until the bureau can recruit, train, hire and build its own "analytic cadre."

A Cyber Division, which will operate out of FBI headquarters to coordinate, oversee and facilitate investigations in which the Internet, on-line services and computer systems and networks "are the principal instruments or targets of foreign intelligence or terrorists and for criminal violations where the use of such systems is essential to the illegal activity."

Also planned is splitting the bureau's Laboratory Division into two parts: Investigative Technologies and Laboratory Division. While the Laboratory Division will continue to focus on evidence analysis, training and forensic research, Investigative Technologies will provide a variety of technical and tactical support services.

*Source:* Reprinted with permission from *Law Enforcement News,* June 15, 2002, pp. 1, 6. John Jay College of Criminal Justice (CCNY), 555 West 57th St., New York, NY 10019.

power to law enforcement agencies to conduct wiretaps, detain foreigners, and track money-laundering cases; recruiting and paying overseas agents linked to terrorist groups, for the purpose of infiltration; lifting a 1976 executive order banning U.S. involvement in foreign assassinations; establishing a counterterrorism czar within the White House; expanding the intelligence community's ability to intercept and translate messages in Arabic, Farsi, and other languages;[22] fortifying cockpits to prevent access by hijackers; placing federal air marshals on commercial flights; eliminating curbside check-in; and instituting more intensive screening of luggage.[23]

Police supervisors, managers, and administrators must provide new types of training in a much more security-oriented environment. For example, the first responding patrol officer at a scene that might involve a terrorist incident should know the following:

- If it is a terrorist event, the terrain was last controlled by the terrorist; it is to be treated as a minefield, with a clear view of the scene and emphasis put on the safety of the first responders.
- Before entering the scene, make an assessment of what happened: damage, injuries, any existing threats. Map a safe lane through the scene.
- Keep witnesses and victims in a safe area.[24]
- Remain aware of the possibility of chemical agents while at the scene.[25]

Police personnel are the key to successful critical incident management following terrorist acts. A federal report stated the following: "Emergencies can only be managed by people at the site. They can't be managed back in Washington. Expect the unexpected and be prepared to adjust accordingly."[26]

## Technology Needs

A particular concern for law enforcement administrators is the gap between technologies available to the police and those used by persons and groups planning terrorist acts. The National Institute of Justice conducted a survey of law enforcement technology needs for combating terrorism, interviewing 198 individuals representing 138 agencies from the 50 states. The interviewees were queried about their needs in areas such as intelligence gathering; surveillance; command, control, and communication (C3); site hardening; detecting, disabling, and containing explosive devices; and defending against weapons of mass destruction [i.e., nuclear, biological, chemical (NBC) devices] and cyber-terrorism.[27]

By far, the most pressing technology need concerned ready access to current intelligence—a national terrorism intelligence database accessible to all state and local law enforcement agencies. Improved means to detect and analyze explosive devices were also a major need, as was better NBC protective gear (such as masks, suits, and gloves); C3 was another area of greatest need.

# A "Hot Button Issue": Racial Profiling

A contemporary, volatile issue in which police find themselves open to criticism and even disciplinary action involves racial profiling. This issue has driven a deep wedge between the police and minorities, many of whom claim to be victims of this practice. Indeed, a New Jersey state police superintendent was fired by that state's governor in March 1999 for statements concerning racial profiling that were perceived as racially insensitive.

Many people remain convinced that the justice system unfairly draws minorities into its web, and that police methods are at the forefront of this practice. Racial profiling—also known as "Driving While Black or Brown" (DWBB)—occurs when a police officer, acting on a personal bias, stops a vehicle simply because the driver is of a certain race.[28]

Anecdotal evidence of racial profiling has been accumulating for years, and now many people and groups (such as the American Civil Liberties Union) believe that all "pretext" traffic stops are wrong, because the chance that racism and racial profiling will creep into such stops is very high.

For their part, many police executives defend such tactics as an effective way to focus their limited resources on likely lawbreakers; they argue that profiling is based not on *prejudice* but on *probabilities*—the statistical reality that young minority men are disproportionately likely to commit crimes. As explained by Bernard Parks, an African American and former police chief of Los Angeles,

> We have an issue of violent crime against jewelry salespeople. The predominant suspects are Colombians. We don't find Mexican-Americans, or blacks, or other immigrants. It's a collection of several hundred Colombians who commit this crime. If you see six in a car in front of the Jewelry Mart, and they're waiting and watching people with briefcases, should we play the percentages and follow them? It's common sense.[29]

Still, it is difficult for the police to combat the public's perception that traffic stops of minorities simply on the basis of race is widespread and prejudicial in nature.

The best defense and advice for police administrators may be summarized in two words: *collect data.*[30] Collecting traffic stop data helps chiefs and commanders determine whether officers are stopping or searching a disproportionate number of minorities and enables them to act on this information in a timely fashion.[31] In 1999, Connecticut was the first state to require all of its municipal police agencies and the state police to collect race data for every police-initiated traffic stop;[32] by mid-2001, at least 34 states had either enacted laws that included data collection or were considering data-collection legislation, and Congress has enacted federal racial profiling legislation. It is anticipated that eventually all states will require the tracking of race data for all contacts. Technology such as mobile data computers and wireless handheld devices is being adapted for this purpose.[33]

Figure 5.1 shows a race data traffic stops form for the state of Connecticut.

## State of Connecticut
### Traffic Stops Statistics

Department — ORI: _____    Town: _____

Date: _____/_____/_____        Time:_____:_____        Age:_____

Gender:  Male   Female   Unknown

Race:          W - White                                    Ethnicity:    H - Hispanic
(Circle One)   B  - Black                                   (Circle One)  N - Not Hispanic
               I   - Indian Amer./Alaskan Native                          U - Unknown
               A  - Asian/Pacific Islander
               U  - Unknown

Stop Nature: I-Investigation, Criminal        Statute: _____

Vehicle Search:
(Circle One)   Y - Yes
               N - No
               V - Violation, Motor Vehicle
               E  - Equipment, Motor Vehicle

Disposition:  U - Uniform Arrest Report          Event Number: _____
(Circle One)  M- Misdemeanor Summons             (as defined by your department)
              I  - Infraction Ticket
              V - Verbal Warning
              W- Written Warning
              N - No Disposition

**Figure 5.1**

State of Connecticut traffic stops statistics.

The International Association of Chiefs of Police recently issued a comprehensive policy statement on biased policing and data collection. The association "believes that any form of police action that is based solely on the race, gender, ethnicity, age, or socioeconomic level of an individual is both unethical and illegal," but that data-collection programs "must ensure that data is being collected and analyzed in an impartial and methodologically sound fashion."[34]

# Managing the Use of Force

## *Power That Is to Be Used Judiciously*

A young black man is videotaped from across the street as he is being beaten by a white police officer, who claims the youth was resisting arrest. After the videotape is made public, the case immediately receives national attention. The minority community is outraged, convinced the incident is the result of racism by the police, and the U.S. Department of Justice launches an investigation into the case. This is *not* a synopsis of the March 1991 beating of Rodney King in Los Angeles. Rather, these are the apparent facts in an incident involving 16-year-old Donovan Jackson in Inglewood, California, in July 2002. This case and others similar to it raise the question in the public mind as to how often such incidents occur that are *not* videotaped. They also show how wide the rift between the police and public can be and demonstrate how critical effective police administration is in this country.

Unfortunately, these two incidents are not the only ones. Amadou Diallo, a 22-year-old, unarmed West African street vendor was shot 19 times by four New York police officers who mistook him for a serial rapist. Abner Louima, a Haitian emigre, was beaten and sodomized by four Brooklyn, New York, police officers. Such celebrated cases are comparatively rare; most instances of police brutality involve relatively minor abuse: discourtesy, name calling, racial or ethnic slurs, or a shove that leaves no injury.[35] Still, these incidents raise the collective ire of all Americans, result in public demonstrations and protests, foster calls for the firing of police executives, and even provoke widespread rioting. If any good can come from such unfortunate incidents, perhaps it is educational in nature: that the public and police leadership realize that they must be aware of the potential for the use of excessive force by officers.

Americans and their judicial system bestow a tremendous amount of authority on their police officers. The police are the only element of our society (except for the military, under certain circumstances) who are allowed to use force against its citizens, up to and including that which is lethal in nature. The quid pro quo, however, is that the police are given this power and authority with the expectation that they will use it judiciously, only when necessary and as a last resort. A serious problem arises, however, when officers deploy this force improperly.

Regardless of the type of force used, police officers must use it in a legally accepted manner. Police officers are allowed to use only that force necessary to effect an arrest. Thus, the amount of force that a police officer uses is dependent on the amount of resistance demonstrated by the person being arrested. This concept is taught to police officers in training academies through a use-of-force continuum, which includes actions ranging from verbal commands to deadly force. Figure 5.2 contains the use-of-force continuum.

The use-of-force continuum attempts to illustrate how officers respond to suspects' actions. For example, if a suspect attempts to physically assault an officer using his or her fists, an officer possibly is justified in using a police baton,

| LEVELS OF RESISTANCE | LEVELS OF CONTROL OR FORCE |
|---|---|
| **Suspect's Actions** | **Officer's Response** |
| Psychological Intimidation<br>Non-verbal clues which indicate<br>a subject's attitude, appearance,<br>physical readiness | Officer presence<br>Verbal direction |
| Verbal Noncompliance<br>Verbal responses indicating<br>unwillingness attitude | Officer presence<br>Verbal direction<br>Telling suspect what you want him to do |
| Passive Resistance<br>Physical actions that do not prevent<br>officer's attempt to control, dead<br>weight, active passiveness | Officer presence<br>Verbal direction<br>Soft empty hand techniques<br>Wrist locks, pressure point control |
| Defensive Resistance<br>Physical actions that prevent<br>officer's control without<br>attempting to harm the officer. | Officer presence<br>Verbal direction<br>Soft empty hand techniques<br>Strikes with hands, feet, knee, elbow<br>in response to defensive resistance,<br>this level of control should only be<br>used after lesser force has proved<br>ineffective in controlling the suspect<br>and applied only to non-vital areas. |
| Active Aggression<br>Physical assault on the officer | Officer presence<br>Verbal direction<br>Soft empty hand techniques<br>Hard empty hand techniques<br>Soft and hard intermediate<br>weapons. Soft shall include<br>radial arm locks, arm bars,<br>etc. Hard shall include strikes<br>with baton to non-vital areas. |
| Aggravated Active Aggression | Any of the above and Lethal Force |
| Deadly force encounters | Firearms, strikes to the head and<br>other vital areas with impact weapons. |

**Figure 5.2**

Use of force continuum for law enforcement.

pepper spray, or some other less-than-lethal means to ward off the attack and subdue the suspect. On the other hand, if the suspect is brandishing a knife, the officer may be justified in using a firearm. In addition to using force that is necessary to effect the arrest, the officer must also respect the suspect's life. In 1985, the U.S. Supreme Court ruled that the shooting of any unarmed, nonviolent fleeing felony suspect violated the Fourth Amendment to the Constitution.[36] As a result, almost all major urban police departments enacted restrictive policies regarding deadly force.

## A Typology of Abuse of Authority

The use-of-force continuum shows the range of force that officers can employ. David Carter[37] looked at officers' abuse of authority and provided a typology, which includes (1) physical abuse/excessive force, (2) verbal/psychological abuse, and (3) legal abuse/violations of civil rights.

### Physical Abuse and Excessive Force

As noted earlier, police use of physical force often results in substantial public scrutiny. Local incidents may not receive national media coverage, but they oftentimes have the same dramatic, chilling effect in a community. All police officers are judged by the actions of one or a few officers, and—history has shown—such incidents can also result in rioting by citizens.

The application of deadly force can be a form of excessive force. When a police officer deliberately kills someone, a determination is made as to whether or not the homicide was justified to prevent imminent death or serious bodily injury to the officer or another person. According to a federal report on justifiable homicides by police,[38] from 1976 to 1998, 8,578 felons were justifiably killed by police in the United States; the largest number of such killings in one year was 459 (1994), and the smallest was 296 (1987). On average, 373 felons are lawfully killed by police each year. What is *not* reported, however, are the number of so-called "bad" shootings, for which the subsequent investigation ruled that the police officer did not kill a citizen with justification.

### Verbal and Psychological Abuse

Police officers sometimes abuse citizens by berating or belittling them. They antagonize citizens knowing that as police officers they are wrapped in the shroud of authority, and that citizens must take the abuse. One of the most common methods used by police officers to verbally abuse citizens is profanity. Research indicates that profanity is used for a variety of reasons: as a source of power to control others,[39] as a weapon to degrade or insult others,[40] as a method of alienating others,[41] as a method of labeling others,[42] and as a way of defying authority.[43] Unfortunately, profanity has become a part of the police culture and many officers' everyday speech. When profanity is used liberally in the work setting, it increases the likelihood that it will be used inappropriately.

Profane language tends to polarize a situation. A citizen will either passively submit or respond aggressively—in either case, causing the citizen to distrust and dislike the police. When police officers use profanity, especially in an aggressive manner, the focus shifts from the problem to the officer's language; and when it is used aggressively, profanity can easily create greater physical risks to the officer. Furthermore, even if the officer intended to resolve the situation, it may no longer be possible because of the harm caused by the language. And, because it can incite situations, profanity also increases the potential for liability and citizens' complaints; therefore, it also heightens the possibility of the officer's facing administrative action.[44]

For all of these reasons, profanity by the police toward citizens is not justified, wise, or advised. Supervisors should discourage its use and review every instance when an officer used it with a citizen.

### Legal Abuse and Violations of Civil Rights

Legal abuse and civil rights violations consist of police actions that violate citizens' constitutional or statutory rights. This abuse usually involves false arrest, false imprisonment, and harassment. For example, a police officer may knowingly make an unlawful search, charge the suspect with a crime, and then lie about the nature of the search. Another example occurs when police officers hassle a criminal to gain information or hassle a businessowner to obtain some monetary gain.

Supervisors and managers play a key role in preventing legal abuse and violations of citizens' civil rights. Supervisors frequently back up officers when responding to calls and observe situations that lead to an arrest. They should ensure that officers' decisions to arrest are based on probable cause, not some lesser standard. They should also review arrest reports and question officers when arrests are not observed to ensure that the arrests meet the probable cause standard.

Officers should provide the same level of services to all citizens, and they should use consistent decision-making criteria when deciding to make an arrest regardless of race, gender, or social standing.

## Domestic Violence by Police

A relatively new issue for administrators involves domestic violence by police officers. The 1996 Domestic Violence Offender Gun Ban bars anyone—including police and military personnel—from carrying firearms if they have a misdemeanor conviction for domestic violence. Hundreds of police officers across the nation have lost their jobs as a result of the law.[45]

No one denies that a police officer who physically assaults a spouse or child should be terminated from his or her position. Critics of the law, however, including many politicians, police administrators and associations, and unions, argue that the law is too broad. Assume, as in one actual case, that a female police officer tells her 15-year-old son he cannot leave the house to go "hang out" with some kids she knows to be using drugs. Her son calls her names and attempts to leave, at which time she grabs him by the arm and sits him down. The youth is not injured except for a bruise on his arm, but he calls the police. A report is filed, and the female officer is convicted of misdemeanor assault in a trial by judge with no right to trial by jury. Because of the domestic violence law, she loses her right to carry a gun; thus, her career is ended.[46]

The issue is not whether abusive police officers should be terminated, but whether the law, as it is written, is effective and legal. Congress has considered several proposals that would amend the law to soften its impact on the police, and in August 1998 the District of Columbia Circuit Court of Appeals declared the law unconstitutional (this decision being applicable only in the District of Columbia). Because police agencies typically have no unarmed positions, unless the law is amended it in effect ends the careers of officers who are affected by it.

# School Violence

## *What's Happened to Our Children?*

Recent shootings and other forms of violence on school campuses have all of America wondering what has happened to its children. In one 6-year period, 1992 to 1998, there were 225 school-associated violent deaths.[47] (This figure excludes the April 1999 massacre of 13 people at Columbine High School in Littleton, Colorado.)

Today the possibility that a disagreement among students will be settled with some type of weapon has increased significantly. About 5 percent of today's students are chronic rule breakers and are generally out of control most of the time. Students in schools where violence occurs may not focus on studies, perform at high academic levels, or even stay in school.[48]

Common traits among the perpetrators of school violence include an orientation toward violent shows, videos, and music; a feeling of inferiority or being picked on, with a grudge against some student or teacher; easy access to weapons; suicidal tendencies and above-average intelligence; and the presence of ample warning signs, either in writing or talking about killing others.[49] Exhibit 5.2 discusses some measures that can be taken to address school violence.

## *Leadership Rejoinder*

Police leaders can partner with school administrators toward being prepared for acts of school violence and creating safer schools. First, they can ensure that basic crime prevention techniques are being employed by having all school visitors check in at the office, monitoring campus perimeters and hallways, making certain that area police agencies have maps or site plans of schools as well as

# EXHIBIT 5.2
# Doing What Works to Fight School Violence

*By Lawrence W. Sherman*

School violence cannot be separated from youth violence. Both problems are heavily concentrated in a small number of schools in urban poverty areas. . . . These incidents are terrible tragedies that should and do produce valuable national dialogue, but in setting long-term public policy, we need to focus on where the core of the problem lies.

Not all children are equal in their risk of being murdered, either in school or out. Seventeen percent of schools in cities report at least one violent incident in a year, compared to 11 percent on the urban fringe, 8 percent of rural schools and 5 percent of schools in small towns.

The best predictor of the safety of a school is the safety of its neighborhood. Research on school safety shows that the causes of violence and drug abuse in schools have only a modest connection to what goes on within their walls. . . .

Serious violence in this country is heavily concentrated in a small number of neighborhoods in a small number of cities. Yet the lowest level of crime prevention spending per homicide is found in those areas, while most Federal funding is actually spent in *low-risk* areas. . . . Our national rates of serious crime—in and out of schools—are heavily determined by what happens in our most violent census tracts. With very few exceptions, however, Federal policy does not focus funding on those areas where the most violence occurs.

The mismatching of Federal funds and the problem of violence is not the policy of any Federal agency, but of the legislative formulas used to allocate the funding. . . . Put bluntly, the formulas put violence-prevention funding where the votes are, not where the violence is.

We should invest Safe and Drug-Free Funds in more police around violent schools. . . .

Police can make a difference. More police can mean less crime. More specifically, research shows that putting police at the hot spots at the hot times reduces crime. Three percent of the addresses in this country produce half the crime. Using computerized crime-mapping software, police departments can accurately measure and analyze the nature of crime and provide valuable guidance to police and community leaders. Several scientific studies have shown the strength of programs that take illegally carried guns off of our streets, particularly from youth near parks, playgrounds and schools. Several cities and counties have done these programs in ways that reduce crime in a manner that is constitutional and has the support of the residents of high-crime areas. Doing this in collaboration with school-based officers could make them even more effective. Until Federal, state and local leaders concentrate their time and resources in areas where most of the crime occurs, we will not make substantial progress in ensuring safe schools.

*Source:* Reprinted with permission from *Law Enforcement News*, May 15/31, 1999, p. 13, John Jay College of Criminal Justice (CCNY), 555 West 57th St., New York, NY 10019.

master keys to all school classrooms and offices, having a warning signal when a school encounters a threat or emergency, and ensuring that the police and school personnel remain in constant contact during a crisis.[50]

It is also recommended that representatives from the police, the schools, and the community come together to sign memorandums of understanding (MOU) that clearly define what each organization or agency will do from the beginning if a school-violence crisis occurs.[51]

An interesting approach to school violence was recently attempted in Charlotte, North Carolina, where the National Institute of Justice sponsored a research project on school safety in a high school. The program had three major components: regular meetings among faculty, administrators, and the police; problem-solving classes for the students; and regular reviews by the police and teachers to identify problem students. The curriculum was based on the S.A.R.A. problem-solving process (discussed in Chapter 3) to be student-driven with teachers acting as mentors and facilitators. Students identified fighting and disorder in the lunchroom as a major issue. The root of the problem was that the entire school population—as many as 1,500 students—was released for lunch at the same time. Students proposed several solutions (an open campus policy was rejected by the administration); students met with lunchroom workers, who agreed to open additional lines and improve the food-serving system. Police calls for service at the school, fear levels of students, and actual incidents of violence dropped, as did incidents of vandalism, theft, and obscene threats and gestures.[52]

Furthermore, police can (and often must) take gang-suppression measures into the elementary and secondary schools. Studies have found that the percentage of 12- to 17-year-old students reporting the presence of gangs at school nearly doubled during the mid-1990s; indeed, about 8 percent of students surveyed reported that gangs were involved in three types of crimes at their schools: assault, drug sales, or gun carrying.[53]

Other strategies have been suggested for preventing school violence:

- Publicizing the philosophy that a gang presence will not be tolerated, and institutionalizing a code of conduct
- Alerting students and parents about school rules and punishments for infractions
- Creating alternative schools for those students who cannot function in a regular classroom
- Training teachers, parents, and school staff to identify children who are most at risk for violent behavior
- Developing community initiatives focused on breaking family cycles of violence, and providing programs on parenting, conflict resolution, anger management, and recovery from substance abuse
- Establishing peer counseling in schools to give troubled youths the opportunity to talk to someone their own age

• Teaching children that it is not "tattling" to go to a school teacher or staff member if they know someone who is discussing "killing."[54]

# Vehicular Pursuits

## A High-Stakes Operation

Few patrol operational issues are of greater concern to police leadership than police pursuits. Civil litigation arising out of collisions involving police pursuits reveals it to be a high-stakes undertaking with serious and sometimes tragic results. Several hundred people are killed each year during police pursuits;[55] many of the resulting deaths and injuries involved innocent third parties or stemmed from minor traffic violations. The U.S. Supreme Court, as discussed in the next section, has strengthened most progressive chase policies, but the Court has also conferred a responsibility that must be borne by the police.

Pursuits place the police in a delicate balancing act. On one hand is the need to show that flight from the law is no way to freedom. If a police agency completely bans high-speed pursuits, its credibility with both law-abiding citizens and law violators may suffer; public knowledge that the agency has a no-pursuit policy may encourage people to flee, decreasing the probability of apprehension.[56] Still, according to one author, because of safety and liability concerns, "A growing number of agencies have the position that if the bad guy puts the pedal to the metal, it's a 'freebie.' They will not pursue him."[57]

On the other hand, the high-speed chase threatens everyone within range of the pursuit, including suspects, their passengers, or other drivers or bystanders. One police trainer asks a simple question of officers to determine whether or not to continue a pursuit: "Is this person a threat to the public safety other than the fact the police are chasing him?" If the officer cannot objectively answer "yes," the pursuit should be terminated.[58] Exhibit 5.3 elaborates on the concept of training for vehicular pursuits.

## The Supreme Court's View

In May 1990, two Sacramento County, California, deputies responded to a fight call. At the scene, they observed a motorcyle with two riders approaching their vehicle at high speed; turning on their red lights, the deputies ordered the driver to stop. The motorcycle operator began to elude the officers, who initiated a pursuit reaching speeds of more than 100 miles per hour over about 1.3 miles. The pursuit ended when the motorcycle crashed; the deputies' vehicle could not stop in time and struck the bike's passenger, killing him; his family brought suit, claiming the pursuit violated the crash victim's due process rights under the Fourteenth Amendment.

In May 1998, the U.S. Supreme Court, in *County of Sacramento v. Lewis*,[59] ruled that the proper standard to be employed in these cases is whether or not the officer's conduct during the pursuit was conscience shocking; it further determined that high-speed chases with no intent to harm suspects do not give rise

## EXHIBIT 5.3
## Pursuit Simulation Training Is No Ordinary Crash Course

While it is no substitute for actual driving experience, a driving simulator used by the Medina County, Ohio, Sheriff's Department has proven to be an effective means of determining how and when a pursuit should be called off. . . .

More than 70 officers were trained in October when the department leased the simulator for a week. During his session, Deputy Dave Swinehart swerved around a computerized image of a transit bus, past a produce truck and a minivan as a BMW pulled ahead of him, roaring through two red lights.

Swinehart, a 10-year veteran who has been involved in actual high-speed pursuits, pulled left, dodging a pickup truck that had pulled over, then right, to avoid a child on a skateboard. When the BMW whipped left into a school zone, however, Swinehart tapped his brakes, ending the simulated pursuit.

It was the right decision, said driving instructor Daryll Rocklin. "Good recognition. You're not going to chase through a school zone."

Miller recalled that when he started in law enforcement 25 years ago, a pursuit policy was about a paragraph long. The Medina County department's now runs approximately two pages, due mainly to the addition of examples and instances of when a chase should be cut off. By using the simulator, Miller said, police saw how frequently unexpected obstacles could appear on the road.

Driver training, said Strongsville Police Chief Charles Goss, should make police better thinkers, not NASCAR drivers. His department has used the simulator, he told The Cleveland Plain Dealer, as have other law enforcement agencies in the area. . . .

*Source:* Reprinted with permission from *Law Enforcement News*, November 15, 2000, p. 6. John Jay College of Criminal Justice (CCNY), 555 West 57th St., New York, NY 10019.

to liability under the Fourteenth Amendment.[60] The Court left unanswered many important questions, such as whether an innocent third party can file a claim against the police for damages, or whether a municipality can be held liable for its failure to train officers in pursuit issues.

### *Leadership Rejoinder*

The following incidents demonstrate the dangerous nature of police pursuits:

- In Omaha, Nebraska, a 70 mile-per-hour pursuit through a residential neighborhood of a motorcyclist for expired license plates ended when the motorcyclist ran a stop sign, crashing into another vehicle and killing the female passenger on the motorcycle.

- A sheriff's deputy in Florida intentionally rammed a vehicle during a pursuit for an outstanding misdemeanor warrant, causing a collision and killing a backseat passenger.
- A police officer pursuing a shoplifter in Mobile, Alabama, crashed into a mall security vehicle, seriously injuring the guard.

These and other tragic stories are all too common, and certainly the onus is on police chief executives to develop pursuit policies that consider input from line personnel, supervisors and managers, and attorneys versed in civil liability and remain vigilant in seeing that they are enforced. Pursuit policies provide general guidelines for the officer and supervisor. The courts will evaluate these policy issues when considering whether or not an agency or its officers or supervisors should be held culpable for damages or injuries resulting from pursuits.

The membership at the International Association of Chiefs of Police (IACP) Annual Conference in 1996 adopted a resolution and model pursuit policy to serve as a guideline for police executives. The resolution and policy, based on recommendations from the National Commission on Law Enforcement Driving Safety, were provided to the IACP's Highway Safety Committee. The resolution and policy as shown in Figure 5.3 are purposely generic in nature so that agencies can individualize them to their specific needs.

The responsibility falls to the field supervisor to see that proper methods are employed by patrol officers during pursuits, whether the pursuit involves simply a primary pursuing officer and a backup or a more elaborate scenario.

Two rather elaborate methods of pursuit termination may be used. The first is *boxing*: Three police vehicles are positioned during the chase at the front, rear, and side of the suspect vehicle; the three police vehicles slow in unison, causing the offender to slow and eventually stop. This technique can result in damage to any or all of the vehicles involved. The second termination tactic, *precision immobilization technique*, involves a police vehicle making contact with a suspect vehicle. The officer gently pushes one of the rear quarter panels of the suspect vehicle in order to displace its forward motion, causing it to spin. This technique also involves considerable risk to the officer and suspect.[61] Both of these methods, as well as other tactics employed during pursuits, are potentially perilous and require extensive officer training to obtain proficiency.

Oversight of pursuits enables a third, neutral party, the supervisor, to guard against what has been termed a *pursuit fixation*, wherein pursuing officers act recklessly.[62] Supervisors need to set the rules on what will be tolerated and what level of performance is expected during a pursuit. They must clearly establish that once the pursuit team is in place, other officers not directly involved should drive parallel to the pursuit, obeying all traffic laws.[63]

Supervisors depend on other officers to give them the information needed to make the decisions demanded by the courts. The supervisor needs to know the speed and direction of the fleeing suspect vehicle; the offense, suspected offense, or status (i.e., warrants) of the suspect; the number of police units

Following are selected portions of the Sample Vehicular Pursuit Policy that was approved at the 103rd Annual Conference of the International Association of Chiefs of Police in Phoenix, Arizona, on September 30, 1996. Note the responsibilities of the supervisor as they pertain to communications, coordination, participation, and possible termination as they relate to the pursuit:

I. *Purpose*
   The purpose of this policy is to establish guidelines for making decisions with regard to pursuits.
II. *Policy*
   Vehicular pursuit of fleeing suspects can present a danger to the lives of the public, officers, and suspects involved in the pursuit. It is the responsibility of the agency to assist officers in the safe performance of their duties. To fulfill these obligations, it shall be the policy of this law enforcement agency to regulate the manner in which vehicular pursuits are undertaken and performed.
III. *Procedures*
   A. Initiation of Pursuit
      1. The decision to initiate pursuit must be based on the pursuing officer's conclusion that the immediate danger to the officer and the public created by the pursuit is less than the immediate or potential danger to the public should the suspect remain at large.
      2. Any law enforcement officer in an authorized emergency vehicle may initiate a vehicular pursuit when the suspect exhibits the intention to avoid apprehension by refusing to stop when properly directed to do so. Pursuit may also be justified if the officer reasonably believes that the suspect, if allowed to flee, would present a danger to human life or cause serious injury.
      3. In deciding whether to initiate pursuit, the officer shall take into consideration:
         a. Road, weather, and environmental conditions.
         b. Population density and vehicular and pedestrian traffic.
         c. The relative performance capabilities of the pursuit vehicle and the vehicle being pursued.
         d. The seriousness of the offense.
         e. The presence of other persons in the police vehicle.
         Upon engaging in a pursuit, the officer shall notify communications of the location, direction, and speed of the pursuit, the description of the pursued vehicle, and the initial purpose of the stop. When engaged in pursuit, officers shall not drive with reckless disregard for the safety of other road users.
   C. Supervisory Responsibilities
      1. When made aware of a vehicular pursuit, the appropriate supervisor shall monitor incoming information, coordinate and direct activities as needed to ensure that proper procedures are used, and have the discretion to terminate the pursuit.
      2. Where possible a supervisory officer shall respond to the location where a vehicle has been stopped following a pursuit.

**Figure 5.3**

IACP model vehicular pursuit policy. *Source:* International Association of Chiefs of Police, Sample Vehicle Pursuit Policy, *Police Chief* (January 1997), p. 20.

involved in the pursuit; and the suspect's actions (is he or she close to putting others in danger with his or her driving?).[64] Supervisors serve as the "safety officer" of the pursuit—a role they may not wish to take because they do not want to be unpopular with their officers, but one that is far better than attending an officer's funeral or visiting one in the hospital.

It is obvious the liabilities associated with police pursuits should be a primary concern of every police chief executive officer. The courts have awarded numerous six- and seven-figure settlements to plaintiffs seeking redress for injuries, damages, or deaths resulting from police pursuits. The development of pursuit policies and officer and supervisor training can help to protect agencies against liability suits.

It is the responsibility of command personnel and supervisors to ensure that officers thoroughly understand and comply with pursuit policies. In addition to the policy issues and supervisory information identified earlier, other factors considered by the courts to evaluate pursuit liability involve the following:

> *The Reason for the Pursuit.* Does it justify the actions taken by the officer?
>
> *Driving Conditions.* Any factor that could hinder an officer's ability to safely conduct a pursuit should be considered sufficient reason to terminate.
>
> *The Use of Police Warning Devices.* Typically, lights and siren are required by state statutes.
>
> *Excessive Speed.* This often depends on conditions of the environment. For example, a 30 mile-per-hour pursuit in a school zone may be considered excessive and dangerous.
>
> *Demonstrations of Due Regard in Officers' Actions.* Officers who choose the course of safety will create the least danger to all parties affected and maintain the highest degree of protection from liability.
>
> *The Use of Deadly Force.* There are few instances in which officers can justify driving tactics that result in the death of a fleeing driver; such situations include roadblocks, boxing in, and ramming.
>
> *Departmental Policies and State Law.* These must be obeyed; to do otherwise greatly increases the potential liability of both the officer and department.
>
> *Appropriate Supervision and Training.* In the absence of such measures, the department will be subject to a finding of negligence, and liability will attach.[65]

Police pursuits represent an ongoing, hazardous problem. Therefore, efforts must continue to develop electromagnetic-field devices that officers can place on the roadway and use to interrupt the electronic ignition systems in suspect vehicles and terminate pursuits. In the meantime, tire deflation devices, which can end chases by slowly deflating one or more tires of a suspect's vehicle, have been welcomed by the police.

# When all Hell Breaks Loose: Notifying Supervisors, Managers, and Administrators

Police supervisors, managers, and administrators cannot work 24 hours a day, seven days per week. Nonetheless, the types of critical incidents discussed in this chapter may well be occasions when ranking personnel should be notified, as the task at hand is too overwhelming for subordinates. This is known as the **exception principle** of management: Each rank should handle only the situations that its subordinate officers lack the authority and capacity to handle. If the officer has handled a similar situation but it is one that may have further complications, a superior officer must be notified for guidance.[66]

Although subject to change depending on local custom and guidelines (which should be put in writing), police supervisors and/or managers should be appropriately notified when incidents involve

- Serious injuries to officers or employees
- Use of force (when death or serious injury occurs as a result of officer actions)
- Multijurisdictional officers (from other jurisdictions beyond the geographic boundaries assigned to a particular police manager or commander; such notification can prevent jurisdictional or "turf" problems from flaring up later)
- Off-duty officer conduct that is unusual or unlawful in nature
- Serious crimes (the term *serious* will vary in meaning from one jurisdiction to the next)
- Prominent public figures (from politicians to rock stars, the interest generated by such incidents often becomes highly publicized)[67]

# CASE STUDIES

The following three case studies involve the role of police sergeant, racial profiling, and personnel problems, respectively. They enable the reader to examine some of the issues and problems that are presented in today's police arena.

## Adapting to the Responsibilities of the Role

Sgt. Tom Gresham is newly promoted and assigned to patrol on the graveyard shift; he knows each officer on his shift, and several are close friends. Sgt. Gresham was an excellent patrol officer and prided himself on his reputation and ability to get along with his peers. He also believed this trait would benefit him as a supervisor. From the beginning, Sgt. Gresham believed that he could get more productivity from his officers by relating to them at their level. He made an effort to socialize after work and took pride in giving his team the liberty of referring to him by his first name. Sgt. Gresham also believed that it was a supervisor's job to not get in the way of "good" police work. In his view, his team responded tremendously, generating the highest number of arrest and citation statistics in the entire department. Unfortunately, his shift was also generating the highest number of citizen complaints for abusive language and improper use of force, but few complaints were sustained by internal affairs. It was Gresham's opinion that complaints are the product of good, aggressive police work. He had quickly developed the reputation among subordinates as being "a cop's cop."

One Monday morning, Sgt. Gresham is surprised when called in to see you, his patrol captain. The internal affairs lieutenant is also present. You show Gresham a number of use-of-force complaints against his team over the past week while Sgt. Gresham was on vacation. Despite your efforts to describe the gravity of the situation, Gresham fails to grasp the seriousness of the complaints, and how his supervisory style may have contributed to them.

### Questions for Discussion

1. What do you believe are some of Sgt. Gresham's problems as a new supervisor?
2. As his captain, what advice would you give to Gresham?
3. What corrective action must Sgt. Gresham take immediately with his team of officers?

# Racial Profiling or Good Police Work?

Officer James and Sergeant Drummond are on surveillance in a strip mall. A detective received an anonymous tip that a credit union might be robbed at 3:00 P.M. The detective also related to the patrol division that the person providing the tip is a known drug addict and not at all reliable, but given that there have been a string of credit union robberies during the past two months, Drummond decides to surveil the area with Officer James. The predominant suspects in the credit union robberies are Asians, and the officers have stopped and talked with several Asian people in the area, taking their names and other identifying information. At approximately 2:45 P.M., Drummond and James are notified by Communications that a security officer reported hearing a gunshot in the parking lot of a nearby grocery store where he is working. Since they are nearby, and there might be a connection to the credit union robberies, Drummond and James decide to take the call. Upon arriving at the scene, the security officer meets the two officers and informs them that he "might have" heard a small-caliber pistol shot in the parking lot; he also believes that a young black man who walked into the grocery store a few minutes ago might be carrying a gun under his coat. About 10 minutes later, a 30-year-old black man comes walking out of the store. The officers draw their guns and order him down to the asphalt and then order him to crawl to their vehicle. At that time, an Asian woman carrying a child approaches the officers, yelling at them that the man is her husband and demanding to know what they are doing to him. The officers order her to her car, whereupon she faints on the asphalt while suffering an epileptic seizure. The black man, seeing his wife and child on the ground, now becomes very agitated; the officers use considerable force to subdue and handcuff him. He is arrested for resisting arrest and a host of other offenses; later he sues for violation of his civil rights.

## Questions for Discussion

1. Did the officers have just cause to be engaged in the initial (credit union) surveillance? To question Asian people in the area? Defend your answer.
2. Did the officers violate the black man's civil rights? Why or why not? If yes, would you support (as the chief of police) some form of disciplinary action against them?
3. Should the woman be entitled to collect damages? Why or why not?
4. In which (if any) aspects of this scenario do you believe the officers are guilty of engaging in racial profiling? Explain your answer.
5. Assume that this case led to a public outcry for a citizen review board to examine questionable police activities and recommend disciplinary and policy actions. Would you support the creation of such a board? Why or why not?

# "Racin' Ray, Graveyard Shift Gadabout"*

Members of the Pineville County Sheriff's Department have been involved in several vehicle pursuits within the past year. One such incident resulted in the death of a 14-year-old juvenile who crashed during a pursuit while he was joyriding in his parents' car. This tragedy sparked a massive public outcry and criticism of the police department for using excessive force. A lawsuit against the department and individual officers involved in the pursuit is pending. The sheriff immediately changed the department's policy regarding pursuits. The policy now requires that a supervisor cancel any pursuit that does not involve a violent felony crime or other circumstances that would justify the danger and potential liability. All officers have been trained in the new policy. A separate policy prohibits the firing of warning shots unless "circumstances warrant." Last night at 1:00 A.M., Deputy Raymond "Racin' Ray" Roadhog was patrolling an industrial park in his sector. Deputy Roadhog, freshly graduated from the police academy and field training, engages in pursuits at every opportunity; also, unbeknown to the sheriff and other supervisors, he occasionally takes along his pet German Shepherd dog for use in building checks; he also has a TASER stun device that delivers 50,000 volts on contact in his trunk (he has not been trained in or authorized to carry this weapon). He was providing extra patrol as a result of reports of vandalism and theft of building materials in that area of the county. Generally, after 6:00 P.M., he believes that no one should have any reason to be in any construction area. A parked vehicle attracts his attention because private vehicles are not normally parked in the area at this time. As Roadhog approaches the vehicle with his cruiser's lights off and spotlight on, he notices the brake lights on the vehicle flash on and off. Roadhog immediately gets out of his vehicle for a better view and calls dispatch for backup assistance in the event that there is a burglary or theft in progress. At this point, the vehicle takes off at a high rate of speed, in Roadhog's direction. Roadhog, out of his vehicle and seeing the vehicle coming at him from about 30 yards, fires a warning shot into the ground. When it is about 15 yards away, the vehicle veers away from him and then leaves at a high rate of speed. As the escaping vehicle crosses the path of his spotlight, Roadhog sees that there are two young people inside, a man driving and a woman in the passenger's seat. Roadhog yells for the driver to halt, then lets loose another warning shot, this time into a nearby fire hydrant. He then takes off in pursuit of the vehicle. The officer radios dispatch to inform him of his observations and of his present pursuit. You, the shift commander—a patrol lieutenant—hear this radio transmission.

## Questions for Discussion

1. What are the central issues involved?
2. Is the deputy in compliance with the use-of-force policy? Defend your answer.

---

*Contributed by Deputy Chief Ronald W. Glensor, Ph.D., Reno, Nevada, Police Department.

3. Are you going to "shut down" Roadhog's pursuit? Explain.

4. Should the deputy have fired warning shots? Why or why not?

5. Assuming that all of the information comes to light, will the sheriff be likely to begin disciplinary action against Roadhog? Why or why not?

6. Do the policies appear to be sound as written? Are additional policies needed? Explain your answers.


## Summary

This chapter opened with a discussion of terrorism and also explored the issues of racial profiling, the use of force, school violence, and vehicular pursuits. Clearly these contemporary matters will continue to challenge police administrators for years to come. Indeed, some of the issues have long been simmering in the public mind, while others have only recently come to the forefront of the public's attention.

Perhaps just as important as having administrators today who understand and deal with these problems are the subordinates of tomorrow; those who will wear the mantle of leadership in the future must likewise attempt to grasp the means of addressing these issues.


## Questions for Review

1. What is terrorism, and how does it pose exceedingly powerful challenges (especially in terms of biological weaponry) as well as demand new technologies to cope with it?

2. What is racial profiling, and what can police leadership do to address it?

3. What types of issues are involved in Carter's typology of abuse of police authority?

4. What are the various steps and methods employed in the use-of-force continuum?

5. In what ways can police leaders become engaged with school administrators before and during acts of school violence?

6. What is the problem with police vehicle pursuits, and what has the U.S. Supreme Court stated about them? What responsibilities do patrol supervisors possess in regard to pursuits?

7. How does the 1996 Domestic Violence Offender Gun Ban affect policing in general, and administrators in particular?

8. What is meant by the term *exception principle of management,* and in what kinds of incidents should patrol officers notify supervisors and/or managers?

# Notes

1. U.S. Department of Justice, Federal Bureau of Investigation Press Room, Press Release, http://www2.fbi.gov/pressrel/pressrel02/keoka2000/1prelim.htm (accessed July 13, 2002).

2. U.S. Department of Justice, Federal Bureau of Investigation, *Law Enforcement Officers Killed and Assaulted, 2000, FBI Uniform Crime Reports* (Washington, D.C.: Author, 2001).

3. *Law Enforcement News*, "A Dangerous Place to Work" (January 15/31, 2002):1.

4. William A. Westley, *Violence and the Police: A Sociological Study of Law, Custom, and Morality* (Cambridge, Mass.: MIT Press, 1970), p. 5.

5. C. Jylland-Halverson, R. Stoner, and S. Till, "Terrorism: The Hostage Negotiator's Ultimate Challenge," *Law Enforcement Trainer* (January/February 2000):14–43.

6. M. K. Rehm and W. R. Rehm, "Terrorism Preparedness Calls for Proactive Approach," *The Police Chief* (December 2000):38–43.

7. J. F. Lewis Jr., "Fighting Terrorism in the 21st Century," *FBI Law Enforcement Bulletin* (March 1999):3.

8. Ibid.

9. A. Fram, "Terror's $60 Billion Price Tag," Associated Press, January 7, 2002.

10. C. Ragavan, "FBI, Inc.: How the World's Premier Police Corporation Totally Hit the Skids," *U.S. News and World Report* (June 18, 2001):14.

11. Fram, "Terror's $60 Billion Price Tag."

12. D. Westneat, "Terrorists Go Green," *U.S. News and World Report* (June 4, 2001):28.

13. K. R. Doane, "It's Hardly Terror Inc.," *U.S. News and World Report* (June 11, 2001):31.

14. Lewis, "Fighting Terrorism in the 21st Century," p. 3.

15. Doane, "It's Hardly Terror Inc.," p. 31.

16. Lewis, "Fighting Terrorism in the 21st Century," p. 3.

17. Ibid.

18. K. Strandberg, "Bioterrorism: A Real or Imagined Threat?" *Law Enforcement Technology* (June 2001):88–97.

19. D. Rogers, "A Nation Tested: What Is the Terrorist Threat We Face and How Can We Train for It?" *Law Enforcement Technology* (November 2001):16–21.

20. Strandberg, "Bioterrorism," p. 97.

21. D. G. Bolgiano, "Military Support of Domestic Law Enforcement Operations: Working Within Posse Comitatus," *FBI Law Enforcement Bulletin* (December 2001):16–24.

22. W. Pincus and D. Eggen, "Ashcroft Seeks New Surveillance Powers." *The Washington Post* (September 16, 2001):1A.

23. J. Morris, "Task Forces Formed to Recommend Means to Improve Aviation Security," *The Dallas Morning News* (September 16, 2001):1A.

24. J. Carlson, "Critical Incident Management in the Ultimate Crisis," *FBI Law Enforcement Bulletin* (March 1999):19.

25. M. Begert, "The Threat of Domestic Terrorism." *The Police Chief* (November 1998):36–38.

26. Quoted in Carlson, "Critical Incident Management in the Ultimate Crisis," p. 19.

27. U.S. Department of Justice, National Institute of Justice Research in Brief, "Inventory of State and Local Law Enforcement Technology Needs to Combat Terrorism." (Washington, D.C.: Author, January 1999).

28. R. Neubauer, quoted in Keith W. Strandberg, "Racial Profiling," *Law Enforcement Technology* (June 1999):62.

29. Quoted in Randall Kennedy, "Suspect Policy," *The New Republic* (September 13, 1999): 30-35.

30. See, for example, Aether Systems, Mobile Government Division, "Special Report II: Overcoming the Perception of Racial Profiling," *Law and Order* (April 2001):94-101; J. A. Oliver, "Lessons Learned: Collecting Data on Officer Traffic Stops," *The Police Chief* (July 2001):23-29.

31. R. L. Garrett, "Changing Behavior Begins with Data," *Law Enforcement Technology* (April 2001):103.

32. S. M. Cox, "Racial Profiling: Refuting concerns About Collecting Race Data on Traffic Stops," *Law and Order* (October 2001):61-65.

33. Aether Systems, "Special Report II," pp. 94-101.

34. G. Voegtlin, "Biased-Based Policing and Data Collection," *The Police Chief* (October 2001):8.

35. Samuel Walker, *Police Accountability: The Role of Citizen Oversight* (Belmont, Calif.: Wadsworth, 2001), p. 141.

36. *Tennessee v. Garner*, 471 U.S. 1, 105 S.Ct. 1694, 85 L. Ed.2d 1 (1985).

37. David Carter, "Theoretical Dimensions in the Abuse of Authority," in T. Barker and D. Carter (eds.), *Police Deviance* (Cincinnati: Anderson, 1994), pp. 269-290.

38. J. M. Brown and P. A. Langan, *Policing and Homicide, 1976-1998: Justifiable Homicide by Police, Police Officers Murdered by Felons* (Washington, D.C.: U.S. Department of Justice, Bureau of Justice Statistics, March 2001).

39. G. W. Selnow, "Sex Differences in Uses and Perceptions of Profanity," *Sex Roles* 12 (1985):303-312.

40. D. L. Paletz and W. F. Harris, "Four-letter Threats to Authority," *Journal of Politics* 37 (1975):955-979.

41. Selnow, "Sex Differences in Uses and Perceptions of Profanity," p. 306.

42. D. W. Warshay and L. H. Warshay, "Obscenity and Male Hegemony." Paper presented at the annual meeting of International Sociological Association (no month, 1978), Detroit, Michigan.

43. Paletz and Harris, "Four-letter Threats to Authority," p. 955.

44. Ibid.

45. "Beat Your Spouse, Lose Your Job," *Law Enforcement News* (December 31, 1997):9.

46. Adapted from Jerry Hoover, "Brady Bill Unfair in Broad Approach to Police Officers," *Reno Gazette Journal* (September 25, 1998):11A.

47. G. Marlin and B. Vogt, "Violence in the Schools." *The Police Chief* (April 1999):169-172.

48. "An Overview of Violence in the Schools." http://eric-web.tc.columbia.edu/monographs/uds107/preventing_introduction.html (accessed June 14, 2001).

49. T. Egan, "Killing Sprees at Nation's Schools Share Number of Common Traits," *The Springfield State-Journal Register* (June 1998):9.

50. D. Bridges, "Safeguarding Our Schools," *FBI Law Enforcement Bulletin* (September 1999):21-23.

51. S. R. Band and J. A. Harpold, "School Violence: Lessons Learned," *FBI Law Enforcement Bulletin* (September 1999):10.

52. Dennis Kenney, *Crime in the Schools: A Problem-Solving Approach* (Washington, D.C.: National Institute of Justice Research Preview, August 1998).

53. J. C. Howell and J. P. Lynch, *Youth Gangs in Schools* (Washington, D.C.: U.S. Department of Justice, Office of Juvenile Justice and Delinquency Prevention Programs, August 2000).

54. Marlin and Vogt, "Violence in the Schools," p. 169.

55. National Highway Traffic Safety Administration, *National Highway Traffic Safety Administration Statistics* (Washington, D.C.: Author, 1995).

56. C. B. Eisenberg, "Pursuit Management," *Law and Order* (March 1999):73–77.

57. A. Belotto, "Supervisors Govern Pursuits," *Law and Order* (January 1999):86.

58. G. T. Williams, "When Do We Keep Pursuing? Justifying High-Speed Pursuits," *The Police Chief* (March 1997):24–27.

59. 118 S.Ct. 1708

60. Ibid. at p. 1720.

61. Eisenberg, "Pursuit Management," p. 77.

62. E. M. Sweeney, "Vehicular Pursuit: A Serious—and Ongoing—Problem," *The Police Chief* (January 1997):16–21.

63. Belotto, "Supervisors Govern Pursuits," p. 86.

64. Williams, "When Do We Keep Pursuing?" p. 27.

65. D. N. Falcone, M. T. Charles, and E. Wells, "A Study of Pursuits in Illinois," *The Police Chief* (March 1994):59–64.

66. Roger Fulton, "Supervisory Notifications," *Law Enforcement Technology* (November 1998):66.

67. Ibid.

# PART III

# THE COURTS

*This part consists of three chapters. Chapter 6 examines court organization and operation; Chapter 7 covers personnel roles and functions; and Chapter 8 discusses court issues and practices. The introductory section of each chapter provides specific chapter content. Case studies in court administration appear at the end of each chapter.*

# Chapter 6

# Court Organization and Operation

## Key Terms and Concepts

Adversarial system

Alternative dispute resolution

Arbitration

Functional organization

Litigation

Mediation

Policy

## Learning Objectives

As a result of reading this chapter, the student will:

- have an understanding of how courts are different from bureaucracies
- be familiar with court organization
- know the four components of court unification
- understand the importance of court decor and decorum
- be familiar with the ramifications of the adversarial system
- have an understanding of policymaking and the influence of courts upon it
- understand why the legal system has become overwhelmed
- know the importance of Alternative Dispute Resolution (ADR) and why it is the "wave of the future"
- be familiar with the components of arbitration and mediation
- know the importance of citizen groups in the courtroom

> *The place of justice is a hallowed place.*
>
> —Francis Bacon
>
> *Courts and camps are the only places to learn the world in.*
> —Earl of Chesterfield

# Introduction

Courts have existed in some form for thousands of years. Indeed, the ancient trial court of Israel, and the most common tribunal throughout its biblical history, was the "court at the gate," where elders of each clan resolved controversies within the kin group. Then, in the fourth century B.C., courts in Athens, Greece, dealt with all premeditated homicides and heard constitutional cases. Since then, the court system has survived the dark eras of the Inquisition and the Star Chamber (which, in England during the 1500s and 1600s, without a jury enforced unpopular political policies and meted out severe punishment, including whipping, branding, and mutilation). The U.S. court system developed rapidly after the American Revolution and led to the establishment of law and justice on the western frontier.

This chapter opens with some quantitative information concerning the number of federal courts and cases disposed of per annum. Next, we go "inside" the courts, considering their special nature in our country, as well as typical courtroom decor and decorum. Then, we discuss how the courts attempt to get at truth within the controversial adversary system of justice. Courts as organizations is the topic examined next, including some court organizational structures and whether or not the courts represent bureaucracies in the usual sense. Then, we discuss the role of courts as policymaking bodies, followed with a review of a relatively new and promising concept, alternative dispute resolution, which addresses the overcrowded court dockets. Then, we examine both historical and current arguments and recommendations for reforming court organizations. The chapter concludes with a case study concerning court administration.

# By the Numbers: Court Organizational Statistics

There are currently 208 statewide general (meaning they can hear all types of cases) and limited (restricted types of cases) jurisdiction court systems in the United States. About 9,065 full-time judges serve in the 71 statewide trial court systems of general jurisdiction alone. There are also about 327 drug courts in 43 states; all but 17 states have family courts with jurisdiction over domestic and marital matters.[1]

It is impossible to gauge with any certainty the number of criminal cases begun, terminated, and pending in all of these courts, particularly at the local level. It is reported, however, that the U.S. Supreme Court disposes of about

7,500 cases annually,[2] with the U.S. district courts' 655 judges disposing of about 63,000—18,000 (or 29 percent) of which are drug related.[3] Furthermore, each year there are nearly 1 million felony convictions in state courts, more than a third of which are drug related.[4]

# Inside the Courts: A Look at Decor, Decorum, Citizens

## *Hallowed Places*

Practically everything one sees and hears in an American courtroom is intended to convey the sense that the courtroom is a hallowed place in our society. Alexis de Tocqueville, in his study of the United States more than a century ago, observed the extent to which our legal system permeates our very lives:

> Scarcely any political question arises in the United States that is not resolved, sooner or later, into a judicial question. Hence all parties are obliged to borrow, in their daily controversies, the ideas, and even the language, peculiar to judicial proceedings. [T]he spirit of the law, which is produced in the schools and courts of justice, gradually penetrates beyond their walls into the bosom of society, where it descends to the lowest classes, so that at last the whole people contract the habits and the tastes of the judicial magistrate.[5]

The physical trappings and demeanor one finds in the courts convey this sense of importance. On their first visit, citizens often are struck by the court's high ceilings, ornate marble walls, and comparatively expensive furnishings.

A formalized level of decorum is accorded this institution. All people must rise when the judge enters the courtroom; permission must be granted before a person can approach the elevated bench; and a general air of deference is granted the judge. A vitriolic utterance that could lawfully be directed to the president of the United States could result in the utterer's being jailed for contempt of court when directed to a judge.

The design of the courtroom, although generally dignified in nature, also provides a safe, functional space that is conducive to efficient and effective court proceedings. The formal arrangement of the participants and furnishings reflects society's view of the appropriate relationships between the defendant and judicial authority. The courtroom must accommodate judges, court reporters, clerks, bailiffs, witnesses, plaintiffs, defendants, attorneys, juries, and spectators, as well as police officers, social workers, probation officers, guardians ad litem, interpreters, and the press. Space must also be allotted for evidence, exhibits, recording equipment, and computers.

Judges and court staff now may require high-technology audiovisual equipment and computer terminals to access automated information systems. Chapter 17 discusses the kinds of technologies that are now commonly used in the nation's courtrooms.

## *Justice in the Eye of the Beholder*

Whether or not justice is done in the courtrooms depends on the interests or viewpoints of the affected or interested parties. A victim may not agree with a jury's verdict; a "winner" in a civil case may not believe that he or she received an adequate sum of money for the suffering or damages involved. Thus, since "justice" is not always agreed on, the courts must *appear* to do justice. The court's responsibility is to provide a fair hearing, with rights accorded to all parties to speak or not to speak, to have the assistance of counsel, to cross-examine the other side, to produce witnesses and relevant documents, and to argue their viewpoint. This process, embodied in the due process clause, must appear to result in justice.[6]

Certainly, many people today are put off with accounts of what they perceive as coddling of offenders and the ravages of the "law's delay," discussed thoroughly in Chapter 8. People tell their neighbors of long waits at the courthouse to take care of business or of having been summoned for jury service. They hear victims and witnesses talk of having been treated badly at the hands of the justice system. Being summoned for, and serving jury duty is for many people, however, an enjoyable and educational experience—one they feel is their civic duty (which it is, from a legal standpoint).

Several citizen's groups interested in reforming the system have engaged in court-watching efforts; such groups include Mothers Against Drunk Drivers, the League of Women Voters, and the National Council of Jewish Women.

## *Seeking Truth in an Adversarial Atmosphere*

Ralph Waldo Emerson stated that "every violation of truth . . . is a stab at the health of human society."[7] Certainly, most people would agree that the traditional, primary purpose of our courts is to provide a forum for seeking and—through the adversarial process—obtaining the truth. Indeed, the U.S. Supreme Court declared in 1966 in *Teban v. United States ex rel. Shott*[8] that "the basic purpose of a trial is the determination of truth."

Today, however, increasing numbers of Americans have the impression that truth is being compromised and even violated with regularity in the trial, plea bargaining, and appellate apparatus of our justice system, thereby "stabbing at the health of human society."

High on their list of impediments is the **adversary system** itself—perhaps reaching its apex following the O. J. Simpson trial, which included jury nullification (acquitting a defendant because it disagrees with a law or the evidence), lawyer grandstanding, improper and racist police procedures, and a general circus atmosphere allowed by the judge and engaged in by the media. Although many people would argue that such a system is vital to a free democratic society, under this system the courtroom becomes a battleground where participants often have little regard for guilt or innocence; rather, concern centers on whether or not the state is able to prove guilt beyond a reasonable doubt. To many people, this philosophy flies in the face of what courts were intended to accomplish. In the adversary system, the desire to win can become overpowering. As one state supreme court justice put it, prosecutors "are proud of the notches on their gun."[9] Defense counsel enjoy winning equally. The attention can shift from the goal of finding truth to being effective game players.

Should this system be modified or replaced? That is an important and difficult question. As one law professor observed: "Lawyers are simply not appropriate to correct the defects of our adversary system. Their hearts will never be in it; it is unfair to both their clients and themselves to require them to serve two masters."[10]

It would appear, however, that the adversarial system is here to stay. Indeed, several safeguards have been put in place to enable this system to reach the truth. First, evidence is tested under this approach, through cross-examination of witnesses. Second, power is lodged with several different people; each courtroom actor is granted limited powers to counteract those of the others. If, for example, the judge is biased or unfair, the jury can disregard the judge and reach a fair verdict. If the judge believes the jury has acted improperly, he or she can set aside the jury's verdict and order a new trial. Furthermore, both the prosecuting and defense attorneys have certain rights and authority under each state's constitution. This series of checks and balances is aimed at curbing misuse of the criminal courts.

# Courts as Organizations

## *A Nonbureaucratic Work Group*

In the view of many academics, the courts have erroneously been characterized as bureaucracies.[11] Bureaucracies have separate divisions tied together by a distinctive authoritarian structure, or hierarchy. They also have well-defined organizational rules governing the disposition of particular tasks, including individually defined, specialized ones.[12] These characteristics do not apply to courts.

Here, we examine how courts differ from the typical organization and how court administration is made more complex because of this uniquely informal structure and organization. Indeed, courts are relatively autonomous single work units that do not function in a bureaucratic manner. A trial court is an entity that does not report to a single authority figure in a chain of command. It often ignores formal rules in favor of shared decision making among judges, prosecutors, and defense attorneys.[13]

Rather than being bureaucracies, trial courts are informal work groups in which interaction among members occurs on a continuing basis. Court participants have discretion in carrying out their tasks; they are interdependent but also have the ability to modify formal rules and procedures so that participants can complete their assignments successfully. A professional bond exists because most of the participants are lawyers. A bureaucratic management style generally would be inappropriate for the courts. In fact, the more a judge insists on being treated with great deference, the more that work group's cohesion diminishes. More important, participants' roles are interchangeable: Defense attorneys may become prosecutors or judges, and vice versa.[14]

Formal authority is modified in trial courts in many ways. For example, whereas the judge has the authority to make the major decisions—setting bail, determining guilt, and imposing sentence—he or she often relies on input from others. Also, because they know more about cases coming to court, the judges' subordinates (prosecutors and defense attorneys) can influence his or her decisions by selective information flow.[15]

For these informal work groups to be effective, group norms must be enforced. Group members who comply with the norms of behavior are rewarded; those who do not are subject to sanctions. Defense attorneys who do not file unnecessary motions or avoid pushing for "unreasonable" plea bargains may be rewarded, such as being allowed more time to read the police reports of their cases. Similarly, prosecutors may receive more time to talk with witnesses or defense counsel. Conversely, sanctions for defense attorneys who violate group norms may include less access to case information, not being appointed to represent indigents in future cases, or harsher sentences imposed on their clients. Furthermore, prosecutors may not receive requested continuances (most requests for continuances come from the district attorney's office).[16] In sum, it is important to remember that the courtroom work group is a social organization, with people interacting, with cooperation between the actors, and with a commonly understood set of practices.[17]

## *Organizational Structure*

Chapter 3 discussed organizational structures, both in general and as concerns police agencies. Courts are organized in similar fashion, providing a more **functional organization** by spelling out areas of responsibility and lines of communication and defining the chain of command.

Figure 6.1 shows an organizational structure for a county district court serving a population of 300,000. Note the variety of functions and programs that exist in addition to the basic court role of hearing trials and rendering dispositions.

Court organization can be quite complicated and technical. Even lawyers who regularly use the courts sometimes find the details of court organization confusing. Terms that refer to the court system include many shorthand phrases that are confusing to the outsider.[18]

Three concepts—jurisdiction, trial versus appellate courts, and the dual court system—underlie court organization.

1. *Jurisdiction:* Court structure is largely determined by the types of cases a court may hear and decide. Jurisdiction is the power of a court to decide a dispute. It has three subcomponents:
   - *Geographical*—Courts are authorized to hear and decide disputes within a specified geographical area; thus, a New York court normally has no jurisdiction to try a person accused of committing a crime in New Jersey.

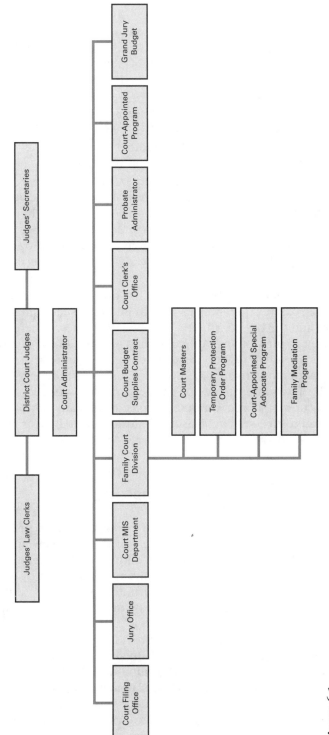

**Figure 6.1**

Organizational structure for a district court serving a population of 300,000.

- *Subject matter*—Trial courts of *limited* jurisdiction hear a restricted category of cases, typically misdemeanors and civil suits involving small sums of money. Trial courts of *general* jurisdiction are empowered to hear all other types of cases within their jurisdiction.
- *Hierarchical*—This term refers to different court functions and responsibilities. *Original* jurisdiction means that a court has the authority to try a case and decide it; *appellate* jurisdiction means a court can review cases that have already been decided by another court.

2. *Trial and Appellate Courts:* Virtually all cases, whether civil or criminal, begin in the trial court. The losing party in the trial court generally has the right to request an appellate court review of the case. The appellate court's primary function is to ensure that the trial court correctly interpreted and applied the law. It reexamines old rules, devises new ones, and interprets unclear language of past court decisions or statutes. Appellate and trial courts are organized and operate quite differently, because their roles are different.

3. *Dual Court System:* The United States has both a single, national court system and a separate court systems in each of the 50 states, plus the District of Columbia and the U.S. territories. This effectively means there are more than 50 different court systems. Although they may be similar in structure, their operations are anything but identical; each court system has its own structure and law enforcement and correctional systems; there will be variations in how the law is interpreted and applied, and how offenders are sentenced. This dual court system contributes a considerable amount of complexity to the criminal justice system, causing confusion in such areas as the constitutional prohibition against double jeopardy.[19]

# The Influence of Courts in Policymaking

The judicial branch has the responsibility to determine the legislative intent of the law and to provide public forums—the courts—for resolving disputes. This is accomplished by determining the facts and their legal significance in each case. If the court determines the legal significance of the facts by applying an existing rule of law, it is engaging in pure dispute resolution.[20] "But if to resolve the dispute the court must create a new rule or modify an old one, that is law creation."[21]

Determining what the law says and providing a public forum involve the courts in policymaking. **Policy** can be defined as choosing among alternative choices of action, particularly in the allocation of limited resources "where the chosen action affects the behavior and well-being of others who are subject to the policymaker's authority."[22] The policy decisions of the courts affect virtually all of us in our daily living. And in recent decades, the courts have been asked to deal with issues that previously were within the purview of the legislative and judicial branches. Because many of the Constitution's limitations on government are couched in vague language, the judicial branch must eventually deal with potentially volatile social issues, such as those involving prisons, abortion, and schools.[23]

U.S. Supreme Court decisions have dramatically changed race relations, resulted in the overhaul of juvenile courts, increased the rights of the accused, prohibited prayer and segregation in public schools, legalized abortion, and allowed for destruction of the U.S. flag. State and federal courts have together overturned minimum residency requirements for welfare recipients, equalized school expenditures, and prevented road and highway construction from damaging the environment. They have eliminated the requirement of a high school diploma for a firefighter's job and ordered increased property taxes to desegregate public schools. The only governmental area that has not witnessed judicial policymaking since the Civil War is foreign affairs. Cases in which courts make policy determinations usually involve government, the Fourteenth Amendment, and the need for equity—the remedy most often used against governmental violations of law. Recent policymaking decisions by the judicial branch have not been based on the Constitution, but rather, on federal statutes concerning the rights of the disadvantaged and consumers and the environment.[24]

Perhaps nowhere have the nation's courts had more of an impact than in the prisons—from which nearly 60,000 prisoner petitions are filed each year in the U.S. district courts.[25] Among these accomplishments of judicial intervention have been extending recognized constitutional rights of free speech, religion, and due process to prisoners; abolishing the South's plantation model of prisons; accelerating the professionalization of U.S. correctional managers; encouraging a new generation of correctional administrators more amenable to reform; reinforcing the adoption of national standards for prisons; and promoting increased accountability and efficiency of prisons. The only failure of judicial intervention has been its inability to prevent the explosion in prison populations and costs.[26]

The courts have become particularly involved in administrative policy, because of public–interest group litigation. For example, legislation was enacted allowing citizen lawsuits when certain federal regulatory agencies, such as the Environmental Protection Agency (EPA), failed to perform certain duties as required by statute. Thus a citizens' environmental group was allowed to sue the EPA.

It may appear that the courts are over broad in their review of issues. However, it should be remembered that judges "cannot impose their views . . . until someone brings a case to court, often as a last resort after complaints to unresponsive legislators and executives."[27] And plaintiffs must be truly aggrieved, or have *standing.* The independence of the judicial branch, particularly at the federal court level at which judges enjoy lifetime appointments, allows the courts to champion the causes of the underclasses: those with fewer financial resources, votes (by virtue of, say, being a minority group), or a positive public profile.[28] It is also important to note that the judiciary is the "least dangerous branch," having no enforcement powers. And the decisions of the courts can be overturned by legislative action. Even decisions based on the Constitution can be overruled by subsequent constitutional amendment. Thus, the judicial branch depends on a perception of legitimacy surrounding its decisions.[29]

# Decreasing Litigation: Alternative Dispute Resolution

This chapter began with a statistical overview of the nation's courts and their annual caseloads. Although these lawsuits—both criminal and civil—have arguably resulted in better safety and quality of life in the United States, the fact remains that the weight of this litigation has imposed a tremendous workload on the nation's courts.

Several methods are now being proposed to reduce the number of lawsuits in this country. One is to limit punitive damages, with only the judge being allowed to levy them. Another is to force losers to pay the winners' legal fees. The process of discovery also warrants examination. This process involves exchange of information between prosecutors and defense attorneys, to ensure that the adversary system does not give one side an unfair advantage over the other. Many knowledgeable people believe that the process of discovery wastes much time and could be revamped.[30]

Another proposal that is already in relatively widespread use is **alternative dispute resolution** (ADR). Realizing that the exploding backlog of both criminal and civil cases pushes business cases to the back of the queue, many private corporations are attempting to avoid courts and lawyers by using alternative means of resolving their legal conflicts. Some corporations have even opted out of litigation altogether; about 600 top corporations have signed pledges with other companies to consider negotiation and other forms of ADR prior to suing other corporate signers.[31]

ADR is appropriate when new law is not being created. ADR can provide the parties with a forum to reach a resolution that may benefit both sides. **Litigation** is adversarial; ADR can resolve disputes in a collaborative manner that allows parties' relationship to be maintained. Furthermore, ADR proceedings are normally confidential, with only the final agreement being made public. ADR is also much more expedient and less costly than a trial.[32]

## *ADR Options: Arbitration and Mediation*

The two most common forms of ADR used today are arbitration and mediation. **Arbitration** is similar to a trial, though less formal. An arbitrator is selected or appointed to a case; civil court rules generally apply. Parties are usually represented by counsel. The arbitrator listens to testimony by witnesses for both sides; then, after hearing closing remarks by counsel, the arbitrator renders a verdict. Arbitration may be mandatory and binding, meaning that the parties abandon their right to go to court once they agree to arbitrate. The arbitration award is usually appealable. Types of disputes commonly resolved through arbitration include collective bargaining agreements, construction and trademark disputes, sales contracts, warranties, and leases.[33]

**Mediation** is considerably less formal and more "friendly" than arbitration. Parties agree to negotiate with the aid of an impartial person who facilitates the settlement negotiations. A mediation session includes the mediator and both parties; each side presents his or her position and identifies the issues and areas of dispute. The mediator works with the parties until a settlement is reached or the negotiations become deadlocked; in the latter case, the matter may be continued in court. Mediation is not binding or adversarial; instead, mediation encourages the parties to resolve the dispute among themselves. Mediation is commonly used when the parties in dispute have a continuing relationship, such as landlord-tenant disputes, long-term employment/labor disputes, and disputes between businesses.[34]

The leading ADR firm is Judicial Arbitration & Mediation Services, Inc. (JAMS), based in Orange, California, and started in 1979. It employs a panel of about 200 former judges. Washington-based Endispute, Inc., and the Philadelphia-based Judicate, Inc., are rapidly growing in the field as well. These private arbitration and mediation firms charge $300 to $350 per hour, a huge savings from the $300 an hour that a battery of lawyers might each charge litigants.[35]

Given the increasing number of lawsuits in this country, it appears that ADR is the wave of the future; as one law professor noted, "In the future, instead of walking into a building called a courthouse, you might walk into the Dispute Resolution Center."[36]

# Attempts at Reforming Court Organization

The current status of state court systems—both courts of last resort and intermediate courts of appeals—is shown in Figures 6.2 and 6.3. It will be seen that there is widespread variation in terms of these courts' names and the number of judges for each.

Historically, court reform has centered on implementing a unified court system. Indeed, since the beginning of the 1900s, the organization of U.S. courts has been a primary concern of court reformers who believe the multiplicity of courts is inefficient.

A unified court system would, first and foremost, shift judicial control to centralized management. The loose network of independent judges and courts would be replaced by a hierarchy with authority concentrated in the state capital.

Other perceived benefits of court unification would include the following four general principles:[37]

1. *Simplified Court Structure:* Court reformers stress the need for a simple, uniform court structure for the entire state. In particular, the multiplicity of

| Supreme Court | Alabama (9), Alaska (5), Arizona (5), Arkansas (7), California (7), Connecticut (7), Delaware (5), Florida (7), Georgia (7), Hawaii (5), Idaho (5), Illinois (7), Indiana (5), Iowa (9), Kansas (7), Kentucky (7), Louisiana (8), Michigan (7), Minnesota (9), Mississippi (9), Missouri (7), Montana (7), Nebraska (7), Nevada (5), New Hampshire (5), New Jersey (7), New Mexico (5), North Carolina (7), North Dakota (5), Ohio (7), Oklahoma[a] (9), Oregon (7), Pennsylvania (7), Rhode Island (5), South Carolina (5), South Dakota (5), Tennessee (5), Texas[a] (9), Utah (5), Vermont (5), Virginia (7), Washington (9), Wisconsin (7), Wyoming (5) |
|---|---|
| *Court of Appeals* | District of Columbia (9), Maryland (7), New York (7) |
| *Supreme Judicial Court* | Maine (7), Massachusetts (7) |
| *Court of Criminal Appeals* | Oklahoma (3),[a] Texas (9)[a] |
| *Supreme Court of Appeals* | West Virginia (5) |

[a]Two courts of last resort in these states.

**Figure 6.2**

Courts of last resort in U.S. states.

minor and specialized courts, which often have overlapping jurisdiction, would be consolidated; therefore, variations between counties would be eliminated. There would be a three-tier system: a state supreme court at the top, an intermediate court of appeal, and a single trial court.

Looking at a system that has become unified on a statewide basis is instructive. Kansas, which unified its court system in 1977, has a supreme court (with seven justices and appellate and original jurisdiction); an intermediate court of appeals (seven justices who hear appeals from district courts); a district court (70 district, 64 associate district, and 76 district magistrate judges; general original jurisdiction in all civil and criminal matters, hearing appeals from lower courts); and municipal courts (384 judges who handle city ordinance violation, with no jury trials).[38] This is actually about as simple as court unification can be.

Witness the Kansas court system *prior to* unification: a supreme court; 29 district courts (no intermediate court of appeals); 93 county courts, handling civil cases, felony preliminaries, misdemeanors, and jury trials; 8 city courts hearing civil matters, felony preliminaries, misdemeanors, and jury trials; 5 magistrate courts hearing civil cases, felony preliminaries, and misdemeanors; 109 probate courts; 109 juvenile courts; 4 common pleas courts handling civil cases, felony preliminaries, and misdemeanors; and 384 municipal courts, hearing city ordinance violations, including traffic, resulting in less than one-year imprisonment.[39] Note the several different titles and types of courts, with similar yet different roles and jurisdiction. Imagine the confusion, redundancy, and fragmentation that existed.

| | |
|---|---|
| *Appeals Court* | Massachusetts (14) |
| *Appellate Court* | Connecticut (9), Illinois (42) |
| *Appellate Division of Superior Court* | New Jersey (28) |
| *Appellate Divisions of Superior Court* | New York (48) |
| *Appellate Terms of Supreme Court* | New York (15) |
| *Commonwealth Court* | Pennsylvania (9) |
| *Court of Appeals* | Alaska (3), Arizona (21), Arkansas (6), Colorado (16), Georgia (9), Idaho (30), Indiana (5), Iowa (6), Kansas (10), Kentucky (14), Michigan (24), Minnesota (16), Missouri (32), Nebraska (6), New Mexico (10), North Carolina (12), North Dakota (3)[b], Ohio (65), Oklahoma (12)[a], Oregon (10), South Carolina (6), Tennessee (12)[a], Utah (7), Virginia (10), Washington (23), Wisconsin (15) |
| *Court of Appeal* | California (88), Louisiana (55), Texas (80) |
| *Court of Civil Appeals* | Alabama (3) |
| *Court of Criminal Appeals* | Alabama (5), Tennessee (9) |
| *Court of Special Appeals* | Maryland (13) |
| *District Court of Appeals* | Florida (57) |
| *Intermediate Court of Appeals* | Hawaii (3) |
| *Superior Court* | Pennsylvania (15) |

[a]Civil only
[b]Temporary

**Figure 6.3**

Intermediate courts of appeal.

2. *Centralized Administration:* Reformers envision the state supreme court working with state and county court administrators and providing leadership for the state court system.

3. *Centralized Rule Making:* Reformers argue that the state supreme court should have the power to adopt uniform rules that would be followed by all courts in the state, including procedures for meting out discipline against attorneys and setting time standards for disposing of cases. This change would shift control from the legislatures to judges and lawyers.

4. *Centralized Budgeting:* With unification would come centralized budgeting by the state judicial administrator, who would report to the state supreme court. A single budget would be prepared for the entire state judiciary and sent to the state legislature. The governor's power to recommend a judicial budget would be eliminated. Lower courts would be dependent on the supreme court for their monies.

While judicial reformers have achieved considerable success in these regards, with many states substantially unifying their court systems, they believe there is still much that needs to be accomplished. For example, statewide financing has not fared well. In many states, the county still finances the major trial courts to a significant degree.

Why have reform proposals been rejected? One must look to the political arena for the answer to this question. First, support for court reform is concentrated among the "legal elites" of the legal system—including the American Bar Association and the American Judicature Society, and even middle-class reform organizations such as the League of Women Voters. Their efforts are often greeted with disinterest or skepticism; judges and other court personnel often resist the idea of forced change, especially when it involves many new procedures. Rural politicians and lawyers typically see no problems in their courts, nor do they believe there would be any benefit to reorganizing them. The general public has little interest in seeing the courts' organizational structures changed, and political parties that are in power see court reform as bringing the loss of patronage positions.[40]

# CASE STUDY

The following case study will help the reader consider real-world court problems—an embattled court system and personnel issues.

## Chief Judge Cortez's Embattled Court*

You have just been hired as the new court administrator for a medium-sized court with approximately 90 employees. Once on the job, you discover that you have been preceded by two heavy-handed court administrators who together lasted less than a year on the job, because of their inability to handle employee conflicts and to achieve a minimal level of productivity. They were more or less forced to resign because of a lack of employee cooperation and increasing talk of unionization. There is general turmoil and distrust throughout the organization. Employees do not trust each other, and as a group, they do not trust management. The courthouse runs on gossip and inertia. There is very little official communication throughout the organization. Prior court administrators made no attempt to solicit employee opinions or ideas. The judges are all aware of the problem, but they have formed no clear consensus as to how to respond to it. In fact, there is turmoil and conflict among the judges themselves. They engage in "turf protection" with operating funds and the court's cases and often take sides in office squabbles. As a result, they are unable to come to any clear consensus or to provide the court administrator with any guidance. The chief judge, Dolores Cortez, has served in that capacity for 10 years and is known to be exceedingly fair, compassionate, and competent; however, she is approaching retirement (in six months) and appears unwilling to take a firm stand on, or a strong interest in, addressing intraoffice disputes and difficulties. In fact, she is not altogether convinced that there is a problem. Furthermore, in past years she has been quite reluctant to intervene in arguments between individual judges.

### Questions for Discussion

1. As the "new kid on the block," how would you respond to this organizational problem? What is the first issue you would address, and how would you address it? What additional problems require your attention?
2. As court administrator, how would you respond to the inability of the judges to develop a consensus? How could the decision-making process be improved?

---

*Contributed by Dennis Metrick, Management Analyst, Court Services Department, Administrative Office of the Courts, Phoenix, Arizona.

3. What techniques could be employed to improve communication through the organization, lessen tension and strife, and generally create a more harmonious work environment?

4. What would be your general approach to Judge Cortez? To her successor?

## Summary

This chapter reviewed the distinctive nature of the courts and their organization. U.S. courts, which have thus far resisted attempts to be bureaucratized, have comparatively little formalized, hierarchical structure or chain of command but are composed of informal work groups and are largely autonomous.

Several areas of concern were highlighted as well. One increasing concern has to do with the burgeoning caseloads of the courts; alternative dispute resolution was proposed as a means of helping in this area of courts' operation. Another problem presented in this chapter is the need for court reform; many notable authorities believe changes are necessary to improve court efficiency. It is clear that until a number of political impediments are overcome, widespread court reform is unlikely.

## Questions for Review

1. How do the courts differ from the police or other traditional bureaucracies in their organization? How and why do courts eschew the usual characteristics found in a bureaucracy?

2. In what ways are courts unique in terms of their decor and decorum?

3. In what ways does alternative dispute resolution hold promise for reducing the current avalanche of lawsuits?

4. What are some perceived benefits of unifying the state court systems? How would a unified state court system be organized?

5. What are some hindrances to court reform?

6. Why is the adversarial system of justice believed to impede the determination of truth in the courtroom? What are some safeguards that argue for continuation of this system?

## Notes

1. U.S. Department of Justice, Bureau of Justice Statistics, "Court Organization Statistics." Web page: http://www.ojp.usdoj.gov/bjs/courts.htm (accessed May 17, 2002).

2. U.S. Department of Justice, Bureau of Justice Statistics, *Sourcebook of Criminal Justice Statistics 2000* (Washington, D.C.: U.S. Government Printing Office, 2001), p. 472.

3. Ibid., p. 413.

4. Ibid., p. 456.

5. Alexis de Tocqueville, *Democracy in America,* Vol. 1, trans. H. Reeve, (New York: D. Appleton, 1904), pp. 283–284.

6. H. Ted Rubin, *The Courts: Fulcrum of the Justice System* (Santa Monica, Calif.: Goodyear, 1976), p. 3.

7. Stephen Whicher and R. Spiller, eds., *The Early Lectures of Ralph Waldo Emerson* (Philadelphia: University of Pennsylvania Press, 1953), p. 112.

8. 382 U.S. 406 (1966), 416.

9. Thomas L. Steffen, "Truth as Second Fiddle: Reevaluating the Place of Truth in the Adversarial Trial Ensemble," *Utah Law Review* 4 (1988):821.

10. W. Alschuler, "The Preservation of a Client's Confidences: One Value Among Many or a Categorical Imperative?" 52 *U. Colo. L. Rev.* (1981):349.

11. Edward J. Clynch and David W. Neubauer, "Trial Courts as Organizations: A Critique and Synthesis," in Stan Stojkovic, John Klofas, and David Kalinich (eds.), *The Administration and Management of Criminal Justice Organizations: A Book of Readings,* 3d ed. (Prospect Heights, Ill.: Waveland Press, 1999), pp. 69–88.

12. Peter M. Blau and Marshall W. Meyer, *Bureaucracy in Modern Society* (New York: Random House, 1971), Chapter 2.

13. Clynch and Neubauer, "Trial Courts as Organizations," p. 43.

14. Ibid., pp. 46–48.

15. Ibid., pp. 49–50.

16. Ibid., pp. 51–52.

17. David W. Neubauer, *America's Courts and the Criminal Justice System,* 7th ed. (Upper Saddle River, N.J.: Prentice Hall, 2002), p. 16.

18. Ibid., p. 59.

19. Adapted from ibid., pp. 59–61.

20. Howard Abadinsky, *Law and Justice: An Introduction to the American Legal System,* 4th ed. (Chicago: Nelson-Hall, 1999), p. 33.

21. Richard A. Posner, *The Federal Courts: Crisis and Reform* (Cambridge, Mass.: Harvard University Press, 1985), p. 3.

22. Harold J. Spaeth, *Supreme Court Policy Making: Explanation and Prediction* (San Francisco: W. H. Freeman, 1979), p. 19.

23. Abadinsky, *Law and Justice,* p. 174.

24. Ibid., p. 170.

25. U.S. Department of Justice, *Sourcebook of Criminal Justice Statistics 2000,* p. 467.

26. Malcolm M. Feeley and Edward L. Rubin, *Judicial Policy Making and the Modern State: How the Courts Reformed America's Prisons* (New York: Cambridge University Press, 1998).

27. Stephen L. Wasby, *The Supreme Court in the Federal System,* 3d ed. (Chicago: Nelson-Hall, 1989), p. 5.

28. Abadinsky, *Law and Justice,* p. 171.

29. Ibid., p. 166.

30. Bob Cohn, "The Lawsuit Cha-Cha," *Newsweek* (August 26, 1991): 59.

31. Michele Galen, Alice Cuneo, and David Greising, "Guilty!" *Business Week* (April 13, 1992): 63.

32. American Bar Association, "Dispute Resolution: A 60-Minute Primer" (Washington, D.C.: Author, 1994), pp. 1–2.
33. Ibid., p. 3.
34. Ibid., p. 4.
35. Quoted in ibid.
36. Ibid., p. 64.
37. Neubauer, *America's Courts and the Criminal Justice System,* pp. 100, 102.
38. William E. Hewitt, Geoff Gallas, and Barry Mahoney, *Courts That Succeed* (Williamsburg, Va.: National Center for State Courts, 1990), p. vii.
39. Ibid., p. vii.
40. Neubauer, *America's Courts and the Criminal Justice System,* pp. 104–105.

# Chapter 7

# Court Personnel Roles and Functions

## Key Terms and Concepts

Appointment

Court administration

Court clerk

Court Executive Development
  Program (CEDP)

Court management

Judicial administration

Merit selection

Nonpartisan election

Partisan election

## Learning Objectives

As a result of reading this chapter, the student will:

- be able to define and understand judicial administration and court administration
- be familiar with the selection process needed to become a judge
- have an understanding of partisan elections, nonpartisan elections, merit selection, and appointment
- know the benefits and problems encountered by judges, including the three problems faced by newly appointed judges
- be familiar with the three phases of the court development program
- understand the duties of judges as court managers
- know the importance of court clerks

- understand the six major duties of court administrators
- be familiar with the conflict between judges and court administrators and the sources of these disagreements
- know the five strategies that judges follow in determining the quality of work by administrators
- understand the components of jury administration

*The justice or injustice of the cause is to be decided by the judge.*
—Samuel Johnson

## Introduction

Chapter 6 looked at the "hallowed" nature of the courts, and how the courts and judges—with gavels, flowing robes, ornate surroundings, and other aspects of decor and decorum that are accorded their office—are enveloped by a mystique of importance and authority. This chapter expands that discussion, focusing more on judges and other key personnel who are involved in court administration.

The administration of the judicial process is probably the least understood area of justice administration—and possibly all of criminal justice. This lack of understanding is compounded by the fact that, very often, even judges and court administrators themselves are not formally trained in their roles. Furthermore, few judges would probably "like to spend all day or most of the day handling union grievances or making sure that employees know what their benefits are."[1] Opportunities to receive training and education are expanding, however, and this chapter addresses some of the means by which that can be accomplished.

We begin by defining and distinguishing the terms *judicial administration* and *court administration* and then consider judges themselves: how they ascend to the bench, benefits and problems of the position, and their role as the ultimate judicial administrator. The historically important role of court clerks is then reviewed, including the unique role played by those clerks in rural communities. Next, we examine the relatively new position of the specially trained court administrator, including training and duties, judges' evaluation criteria, and conflict among judicial administrators. Then, an overview follows of the problems court administrators might confront with composing and maintaining juries, especially during sequestration and notorious trials. The chapter concludes with a case study.

## Defining Judicial Administration

The purpose of judicial independence is to mitigate arbitrariness in judging. But what is the purpose of **judicial administration**? That is more difficult to define. Consequently, as Russell Wheeler noted, "many court administrators today find themselves under the inevitable strain of not knowing for certain what their purpose is."[2]

Most works on judicial administration point to Roscoe Pound as the chief thinker in the field of judicial administration, as a result of his 1906 essay, "The Causes of Popular Dissatisfaction with Administration of Justice." However, the field should properly regard as just as much a founding document a major essay by Woodrow Wilson written 19 years earlier (in 1887), entitled "The Study of Administration." Wilson stressed that the vocation of administration was a noble calling, not a task for which every person was competent.[3] He emphasized that policy and administration are two different matters and, with great foresight, wrote that judges were responsible for judging and "establishing fundamental court policy," and that a third task was for a "trained executive officer, working under the chief judge or presiding judge, [to] relieve judges generally [of] the function of handling the numerous business and administrative affairs of the courts."[4] Courts have *not* always regarded administration as a noble calling, but they have always been a bastion in defense of the distinction Wilson drew between policy and administration.[5]

Wilson's essay certainly gives intellectual respectability to the field of administration. However, it also poses two troubling problems. First, although it may be accurate in the abstract to state that a wall exists between administration and policy, almost every administrator and policymaker knows, as Wheeler phrased it, that "the wall is full of many gaps and is easily scaled."[6] Policy decisions inevitably intertwine with administrative decisions. Second, trying to honor this policy-administration dichotomy would leave the administrator adrift when confronted with inevitable policy decisions. For example, today's court administrator must often set policy for dealing with such issues as celebrity cases, evidence, case scheduling, and the use of cameras in the courtroom—the kinds of issues that are discussed in Chapter 8.

The difficulty of defining judicial administration became obvious during the 1970s, when it nevertheless became an attractive vocation. Various people and commissions tried to define it but seemed capable only of listing the duties of the office. For example, the National Advisory Commission on Criminal Justice Standards and Goals stated in 1973 that "the basic purpose of court administration is to relieve judges of some administrative chores and to help them perform those they retain."[7] Furthermore, in 1974, the American Bar Association specified a variety of functions for the court administrator to perform "under the authority of the judicial council and the supervision of the chief justice."[8]

The problem of definition continued into the 1980s; one law professor who had conducted a large amount of research in the field believed in 1986 that the safest approach was "not . . . to attempt a definition" but simply "to accept that it is a sub-branch of administration—more precisely of public administration."[9]

To assist in this dilemma and provide more clarity, a good working definition of judicial administration was advanced by Russell Wheeler and Howard Whitcomb; this definition allows an analysis from a variety of perspectives: "The direction of and influences on the activities of those who are expected to contribute to just and efficient case processing—except legal doctrinal considerations, insofar as they dispose of the particular factual and legal claims presented in a case."[10] This definition also separates the judicial and nonjudicial functions of the court and implies that a *set* of people share a role norm and that judicial administration constitutes *all* of the factors that direct and influence those people.[11]

Notably, however, the term **court administration** might be conceived of loosely as the specific activities of those persons who are organizationally responsible for manipulating these various judicial administration directions and influences.[12] This term is more commonly used in this chapter, as we focus on the development of the role and functions of the *individual trial court administrator.* This will become clearer as the chapter unfolds and the judge's and court administrator's relationship is discussed.

# The Jurists

## *Those Who Would Be Judge: Methods of Selection*

To a large extent, the quality of justice Americans receive depends on the quality of the judges who dispense it. Whereas we would like to believe that judges are objective, incorruptible, and unbiased in their application of the laws and the constitutions, indeed, the personality of the judge is also of the utmost importance. There is no agreed-upon set of criteria about what personality traits good judges should have, however. Many factors have a bearing on the quality of judicial personnel: salary, length of term, prestige, independence, and personal satisfaction with the job. But the single most important factor considered by court reformers is judicial selection.[13]

A variety of methods are used to select judges: partisan elections, nonpartisan elections, merit selection, or appointment. Figure 7.1 depicts regional patterns in the methods of judicial selection. It shows that partisan elections are concentrated in the South, nonpartisan elections in the West and upper Midwest, legislative elections and executive appointments in the East, and merit selection west of the Mississippi River. How selection is conducted determines who becomes a judge.[14]

In some states, judges are selected using **partisan elections** (the nominee's party is listed on the ballot). Historically, this method enabled party bosses to use judicial posts as patronage to reward the party faithful. In other states, judges are selected using **nonpartisan elections** (no party affiliations are listed on the ballot). Nevertheless, even in these elections, partisan influences are often present: Judicial candidates are endorsed or nominated by parties, receive party support during campaigns, and are identified with party labels. Campaigns for judgeships are normally low key and low visibility, with an absence of controversy and low voter turnout. In recent years, however, some contests—particularly for state supreme court seats—have been contentious and costly election battles, involving millions of dollars. The general lack of information

| Partisan Election | Nonpartisan Election | Merit | Appointment |
|---|---|---|---|
| Alabama | California | Alaska | Maine (G) |
| Arkansas | Florida | Arizona | New Hampshire (G) |
| Illinois | Georgia | Colorado | New Jersey (G) |
| Indiana | Idaho | Connecticut | Rhode Island (G) |
| Louisiana | Kentucky | Delaware | South Carolina (L) |
| Mississippi | Michigan | District of Columbia | Virginia (L) |
| Missouri* | Minnesota | Hawaii | |
| New York | Montana | Iowa | |
| North Carolina | Nevada | Kansas | |
| Pennsylvania | North Dakota | Maryland | |
| Tennessee | Ohio | Massachusetts | |
| Texas | Oklahoma | Nebraska | |
| West Virginia | Oregon | New Mexico | |
| | South Dakota | Utah | |
| | Washington | Vermont | |
| | Wisconsin | Wyoming | |

L = Legislative appointment; G = Gubernatorial appointment
*Partisan election in nonmetropolitan circuits.

**Figure 7.1**

Initial selection of state judges (trial courts of general jurisdiction).
*Source:* American Judicature Society, *Judicial Selection in the United States: A Compendium of Provisions,* 2d ed. (Chicago: American Judicature Society, 1993).

about judges and the low levels of voter interest, however, give incumbent judges important advantages in running for reelection. The prestigious title of "judge" is often listed on the ballot in front of the judge's name or on political signs and billboards. Few sitting judges are even opposed for reelection.[15]

**Merit selection** has been favored by court reformers wanting to "remove the courts from politics!" They point to three problems with popular elections of judges: (1) Elections fail to encourage the ablest lawyers to seek judicial posts, while discouraging qualified persons who want to avoid the rigors (if not the ordeal) of a campaign; (2) elections may provide an incentive for judges to decide cases in a popular manner; and (3) the elective system is a contest in which the electorate is likely to be uninformed about the merits of the candidates. To solve these problems, reformers advocate merit selection, also known as the Missouri Bar Plan. At present, 34 states and the District of Columbia use the merit system, and a number of other states have considered it. Merit selection involves the creation of a nominating commission whenever a vacancy occurs for any reason; the commission is composed of lawyers and laypersons; this group suggests a list of qualified nominees (usually three) to the governor, who chooses one person as judge. After serving a period on the bench, the new judge stands uncontested before the voters. The sole question on the ballot is, "Should Judge X be retained in office?" If the incumbent wins a majority of the votes, then he or she earns a full term of office, and each subsequent term is secured through another uncontested "retention ballot." Most judges are returned to office by a healthy margin.[16]

With the **appointment** method at the state level, governors tend to nominate those persons who have been active in their campaigns. In recent years, some governors have allowed bar associations to examine the qualifications of potential nominees, but they still have the ability to ignore the bar association's advice.

The question is often raised as to which method is best for choosing judges. A key criterion is whether one system produces better judges than the others. In short, methods of judicial selection are not related to judges' personal characteristics. No evidence exists that one selection system produces better judges than another system.[17]

## *Benefits and Problems*

Judges enjoy several distinct benefits of office, including life terms for federal positions and in some states. Ascending to the bench can be the capstone of a successful legal career for a lawyer, even though a judge's salary can be less than that of a lawyer in private practice. Judges certainly warrant a high degree of respect and prestige as well; from arrest to final disposition, the accused face judges at every juncture involving important decisions about their future: bail, pretrial motions, evidence presentation, trial, punishment.

Although it would seem that judges are the primary decision makers in the court, such is not always the case. Judges often accept recommendations from others who are more familiar with the case—for example, bail recommendations from prosecutors, plea agreements struck by prosecuting and defense counsels, and sentence recommendations from the probation officer. These kinds of input are frequently accepted by judges in the kind of informal courtroom network that exists. Although judges run the court, if they deviate from the consensus of the courtroom work group, they may be sanctioned: Attorneys can make court dockets go awry by requesting continuances or by not having witnesses appear on time.

Other problems can await a new jurist-elect or appointee. Judges who are new to the bench commonly face three general problems:

1. *Mastering the breadth of law they must know and apply.* New judges would be wise, at least early in their career, to depend on other court staff, lawyers who appear before them, and experienced judges for invaluable information on procedural and substantive aspects of the law and local court procedures. Through informal discussions and formal meetings, judges learn

how to deal with common problems. Judicial training schools and seminars have also been developed to ease the transition into the judiciary. For example, the National Judicial College, located on the campus of the University of Reno, Nevada, is a full-time institution offering more than 90 educational sessions per year for more than 3,300 state judges, including judges from around the world (the box on p. 175; also see the website for the NJC, provided in Appendix I. The NJC is discussed more fully later).

2. *Administering the court and the docket while supervising court staff.* One of the most frustrating aspects of being a judge is the heavy caseload and corresponding administrative problems. Instead of having time to reflect on challenging legal questions or to consider the proper sentence for a convicted felon, trial judges must move cases. They can seldom act like a judge in the "grand tradition". As Abraham Blumberg noted several years ago, the working judge must be politician, administrator, bureaucrat, and lawyer in order to cope with the crushing calendar of cases.[18] Judges are required to be competent administrators, a fact of judicial life that comes as a surprise to many new judges. One survey of 30 federal judges found that 23 (77 percent) acknowledged having major administrative difficulties upon first assuming the bench. Half complained of heavy caseloads, stating that their judgeship had accumulated backlogs and that other adverse conditions compounded the problem. A federal judge maintained that it takes about four years to "get a full feel of a docket."[19] Likewise, the NJC offers several courses that can assist judges in better administering their courts. The following one-week courses are currently available:

- Court Management for Judges and Court Administrators (covering topics such as managing human resources, conflict resolution, team building, budgeting, data collection, public relations)
- Management Skills for Presiding Judges
- Judges as Change Agents: Problem Solving Courts

The National Center for State Courts in Williamsburg, Virginia, also has a program designed specifically for management and leadership in the courts: the Institute for Court Management's **Court Executive Development Program (CEDP).** Those who successfully complete the four phases of the CEDP earn the distinction of being a fellow in the institute; currently there are about 900 fellows in the United States and abroad. The CEDP's four phases are

a. Management of Court Operations (comprised of six courses)

b. Leadership and Management in the Courts and Justice Environment (focusing on roles and purposes of courts and modern leadership and management theory and practice)

c. Court Improvement Project (an independent study segment in which a master's level research paper is written)

d. Concluding Seminar[20]

3. *Coping with the psychological discomfort that accompanies the new position.* Most trial judges experience psychological discomfort on assuming the bench. Seventy-seven percent of new federal judges acknowledged having psychological problems in at least one of five areas: maintaining a judicial bearing both on and off the bench, the loneliness of the judicial office, sentencing criminals, forgetting the adversary role, and local pressure. One aspect of the judicial role is that of assuming a proper mien, or "learning to act like a judge." One judge remembers his first day in court: "I'll never forget going into my courtroom for the first time with the robes and all, and the crier tells everyone to rise. You sit down and realize that it's all different, that everyone is looking at you and you're supposed to do something."[21] Like police officers and probation and parole workers, judges complain that they "can't go to the places you used to. You always have to be careful about what you talk about. When you go to a party, you have to be careful not to drink too much so you won't make a fool of yourself."[22] And the position can be a lonely one: "After you become a . . . judge some people tend to avoid you. For instance, you lose all your lawyer friends and generally have to begin to make new friends. I guess the lawyers are afraid that they will some day have a case before you and it would be awkward for them if they were on too close terms with you."[23] Judges frequently describe sentencing criminals as the most difficult aspect of their job: "This is the hardest part of being a judge. You see so many pathetic people and you're never sure of what is a right or a fair sentence."[24]

## Judges as Court Managers

The Administrative Office of the United States Courts coordinates and administers the operations of the federal courts. In the states, judges assume three types of administrative roles: (1) statewide jurisdiction for state supreme court chief justices; (2) local jurisdiction—a trial judge is responsible for administering the operations of his or her individual court; and (3) "presiding" or "chief" judge—supervising several courts within a judicial district.

Having a judge preside over several courts within a district developed as early as 1940 when Dean Roscoe Pound recommended that a chief or presiding judge of a district or a region be responsible for case and judge assignment.[25] Today, these judges assume "general administrative duties over the court and its divisions" and are typically granted authority over all judicial personnel and court officials.[26] The duties of the presiding judge are numerous and include personnel and docket management and case and judge assignments; coordination and development of all judicial budgets; the convening of *en banc* (judges meeting as a whole) court meetings; coordination of judicial schedules; creation and use of appropriate court committees to investigate problems and handle court business; interaction with outside agencies and the media; the drafting of local

# Judges Must Train to Take the Bench

At the National Judicial College (NJC) in Reno, Nevada, classroom bells—not gavels and bailiffs—rule the day. And the underlying message rings loud: Wearing a black robe alone does not a judge make. In times when the legal profession and the courts are coming under increased scrutiny and public criticism, the weight of judicial robes can be heavy.

At the judicial college, the goal is not only to coach lawyers on how to be judges, but to teach veteran judges how to be better arbiters of justice. For many lawyers, the move to the other side of the bench is an awesome transition. "Judges aren't born judges," said U.S. Supreme Court Justice Sandra Day O'Connor, who attended the NJC on her election as an Arizona Superior Court judge in 1974. She recalled her anxieties the first time she assumed the bench: "It was frightening, really. There was so much to think about and to learn."

Justice Anthony M. Kennedy, who is on the judicial college's faculty, described the college as

> an institutional reminder of the very basic proposition that an independent judiciary is essential in any society that is going to be based on the rule of law. Judicial independence cannot exist unless you have skilled, dedicated, and principled judges. This leads to so many different areas—judicial demeanor, how to control a courtroom, basic rules of civility, how to control attorneys. These are difficult skills for judges to learn. They're not something judges innately have. Judges have to acquire these skills.

Founded in 1963, the college put on its first course the following year in Boulder, Colorado. It is the only full-time institution in the country that provides judicial training primarily for state judges. It is affiliated with the American Bar Association, which pays about 10 percent of the college's annual budget. Other money comes from an endowment fund, donations, and program tuition and fees. Regular curriculum includes courses on courtroom technology; dealing with jurors; courtroom disruptions; domestic violence; managing complex cases; death penalty issues; mediation; family law; forensic, medical, and scientific evidence; and opinion writing.

As legal issues become increasingly complex and courts become overloaded with cases, judicial training becomes more critical. As stated by Joseph R. Weisberger, chief justice of the Rhode Island Supreme Court and an NJC instructor for 30 years, "It is the judiciary that transforms constitutional rights and liberties from a piece of parchment and printed words into living, breathing reality."

---

Adapted from Sandra Chereb, Associated Press, "Judges Must Train to Take the Bench," *Reno Gazette-Journal,* May 28, 1996, pp. 1B, 5B. Used with permission of the Associated Press.

court rules and policies; the maintenance of the courts' facilities; and the issuing of orders for keeping, destroying, and transferring records.[27]

A basic flaw in this system is that the chief or presiding judge is actually a "first among equals" with his or her peers. The title of chief judge is often assigned by seniority; therefore, there is no guarantee that the chief judge will have the interest, temperament, or skills needed to manage a large court system.[28]

From a court administrator's standpoint, the office of and person serving as presiding judge are of utmost importance. As one judge put it, "the single most determinative factor of the extent of the administrator's role, aside from his personal attributes, is probably the rate of turnover in the office of the presiding judge."[29]

# Court Clerks

## *Key Individuals*

Not to be overlooked in the administration of the courts is the **court clerk,** also referred to as a prothonotary, registrar of deeds, circuit clerk, registrar of probate, and even auditor. Most courts have de facto court administrators in these clerks, even if they have appointed administrators. These are key individuals in the administration of local court systems. They docket cases, collect fees and costs, oversee jury selection, and maintain court records. These local officials, elected in all but six states, can amass tremendous power.[30]

From the beginning of English settlement in North America, court clerks were vital members of society. "Clerks of writs" or "clerks of the assize" existed in early Massachusetts, where people were litigious primarily because of land boundaries. Hostility toward lawyers carried over from England, and the clerk was the intermediary between the litigants and the justice of the peace. During the late seventeenth century, American courts became more structured and formalized. Books were available that imposed English court practices in the colonies, and clerks, judges, and attorneys were provided proper forms that had to be used. In fact, some of the forms used by clerks 200 years ago are similar to those in use today.[31]

Clerks have traditionally competed with judges for control over local judicial administration. In fact, one study found that the majority (58.9 percent) of elected clerks perceived themselves as colleagues and equal with the judges.[32] Court clerks have not as a rule been identified with effective management, however:

> Generally they are conservative in nature and reflect the attitudes and culture of the community. Their parochial backgrounds coupled with their conservative orientation, in part accounts for this resistance to change. This resistance often compels judicial systems to retain archaic procedures and managerial techniques.[33]

### *The Forgotten Majority: Clerks in Rural Courts*

Much of the United States is rural in nature. Nearly four-fifths of its courts exist in rural counties. A *rural court* is any trial court of general jurisdiction having fewer than two full-time judges authorized.[34] An enormous difference in court administration exists between urban courts and rural courts.

The small scale of rural courts affects the type of person who serves as clerk. Urban courts pay high salaries to obtain specially trained and educated court administrators, but rural clerks often have less training and education and receive lower salaries.[35]

Although ultimately accountable for caseflow management, the clerk actually has little power to control the calendar. In most rural courts, lawyers actually review the proposed calendar before it is final. Clerks in rural courts are challenged by conditions such as a single court reporter who is responsible for courtroom work in a large area, the lack of a local crime laboratory, the need to bring expert witnesses from outside, and the limited availability of the trial judge, often only a few days each month.

Other duties of rural court clerks include keeping tradition by maintaining records concerning the land grants of the town ancestors and the naturalization of the people who broke the sod and of births, deaths, marriages, and divorces in the community.

## Trained Court Administrators

### *Development and Training*

One of the most recent and innovative approaches to solving the courts' management problems has been the creation of the position of court administrator. This relatively new criminal justice position began to develop in earnest during the 1960s; since that time, the number of practicing trial court administrators has increased tenfold and continues to expand. Actually, this concept has its roots in early England where, historically, judges have abstained from any involvement in court administration. This fact has not been lost on contemporary court administrators and proponents of this occupation: "It seems to be a very valuable characteristic of the English system that the judges expect to *judge* when they are in the courthouse . . . it does not allow time for administrative distractions."[36]

The development of the position of court administrator has been sporadic. In the early 1960s, probably only 30 people in the United States worked as court administrators. By 1970, there were fewer than 50 such specially trained employees.[37] Estimates differ concerning the expansion of the administrator's role during the 1980s. One expert maintained that by 1982 between 2,000 and 3,000 people were in the ranks of court managers;[38] another argued that there were only about 500.[39] At any rate, most estimators agree that more than twice as many of these positions were created between 1970 and 1980 than in the pre-ceding six decades.[40]

We also know that by the 1980s every state had established a statewide court administrator, normally reporting to the state supreme court or the chief justice of the state supreme court. The three primary functions of state court ad-ministrators are preparing annual reports summarizing caseload data, preparing budgets, and troubleshooting.[41]

Today, few, if any, metropolitan areas are without full-time court administra-tors[42] (the court organization chart shown in Chapter 6 demonstrates the breadth of responsibilities held by court administrators). An underlying premise and justification for this role is that by having a trained person performing the tasks of court management, judges are left free to do what they do best: decide cases. Indeed, since the first trial court administrative positions began to appear, "there was little doubt or confusion about their exact purpose."[43] (As will be seen later, however, there has been doubt and confusion concerning their proper role and functions.)

As court reformers have called for better trained specialists (as opposed to political appointees) for administering court processes, the qualifications for this position have come under debate. The creation of the Institute for Court Man-agement in 1970 was a landmark in the training for this role, legitimizing its standing in the legal profession. Many judges, however, still believe that a law degree is essential, whereas others prefer a background in business administra-tion. There will probably never be total agreement concerning the skills and background necessary for this position, but the kind of specialized training that is offered by the institute and a few graduate programs in judicial administration across the country would seem ideal.

Court administrators are trained specifically to provide the courts with the expertise and talent they have historically lacked. This point was powerfully made by Bernadine Meyer:

> Management—like law—is a profession today. Few judges or lawyers with severe chest pains would attempt to treat themselves. Congested dockets and long delays are symptoms that court systems need the help of professionals. Those professionals are managers. If court administration is to be effective, judicial recognition that man-agerial skill and knowledge are necessary to efficient performance is vital.[44]

### General Duties

Trial court administrators generally perform six major duties:

1. *Reports:* Administrators have primary responsibility for the preparation and submission to the judges of periodic reports on the activities and state of business of the court.
2. *Personnel administration:* Court administrators serve as personnel officers for the court's nonjudicial personnel.
3. *Research and evaluation:* This function is to improve court business methods.

4. *Equipment management:* Administrators are engaged in procurement, allocation, inventory control, and replacement of furniture and equipment.

5. *Preparation of court budget*

6. *Training coordination:* Court administrators provide training for nonjudicial personnel.[45]

Other duties that are assumed by the trained court administrator include jury management, case flow or calendar management, public information, and management of automated data processing.[46]

# Conflict Among Judicial Administrators

## *A Difficult Dichotomy*

The nature of the administrative relationship between the court administrator and the clerk can be an area of concern. Administrators often view clerks as a threat and as an intrusion into their business. Clerks, therefore, have assumed a central role in resisting the creation of a court administrator position, but the court administrator often depends on receiving information that only the clerk can provide, such as the names of prospective jurors.[47]

Some conflicts occur between the judge and the court administrator. Sometimes, the judge usurps the administrator's role and makes most management decisions unilaterally, defeating the purpose of having an administrator. Judges should delegate sufficient responsibility to the administrator so that the former is getting the help he or she needs, and the latter is doing what he or she was trained to do. On the other hand, judges sometimes totally abdicate their responsibilities, delegating too much of the court's work to the administrator and exercising virtually no oversight of the latter's performance. Abdication is particularly prevalent when judges and administrators are in separate buildings or cities. In this instance, the court administrator will in effect be unsupervised.[48]

Tension and conflict may arise between the judge and the court administrator because some judges are reluctant to delegate responsibility over major aspects of court operations—budgeting and case scheduling, for example. In many courts, however, the court administrator has been given full responsibility, including the latitude to be extremely innovative. Unfortunately, substantial confusion still exists over the proper role of the court administrator.[49]

The rift that can exist between judges and court managers also relates to the resistance that judges and courts have to bureaucracy:

> The integration of professionals into a professional bureaucracy has always been problematic. Because professionals identify more with their occupations than with their organizations, because they often control their own certification and performance standards, and because they have separate sources of legitimacy within their organizations, they often have functioned somewhat autonomously from and at odds with administrators.[50]

Judges resist measures of performance; their productivity is an intensely personal and private matter to them. The ultimate, and perhaps only, test of judicial performance occurs when voters are asked to retain or reject them or during the appointment process. There are no merit salary programs or incentive or performance appraisal systems. Judges need autonomy and discretion. Conversely, for the court administrator, accountability is the bottom line.[51]

Figure 7.2 depicts on a continuum how all court administration activities could be distributed and performed, and where collaboration between judge and administrator would be required.

Unfortunately, the relationship between court administrators and judges can involve a "clash between two cultures." Judges and their court administrators not only differ in background, education, and training, but also approach their job roles from very different perspectives.[52]

## Sources of Disagreement

Larry Mays and William Taggart examined court administrators' perceptions of the sources of conflict in managing the courts. The major source of conflict was case-flow management, one of the crucial elements in any court's administrative process. Respondents commented on postponement of cases, judges' rescheduling the calendar, docketing, judicial assignments, and backlogs.[53] This finding

**Administrator-centered**                                                                **Judge-centered**

| Administration | | Adjudication |
|---|---|---|
| Administrator makes the decisions without consulting the judge | Joint decision making or information sharing; "a shared role" | Judge makes the decisions without consulting the administrator |

**Examples of Activities**

| | | |
|---|---|---|
| Budgeting | Agency relationships | Case decisions |
| Training for nonjudicial personnel | Legislative relationships | Directing meetings of judges |
| Purchasing | Public information | Assigning judges |
| Accounting | Planning committees | Training for judges |
| Statistics | Research on rules and procedures | Selecting law-trained support personnel |
| Report preparation | Probation | Supervising screening and instructing of jurors |
| Systems analysis and research | Case processing | Record creation |
| Record keeping | Financial policy | |
| | Personnel rules | |

**Figure 7.2**

Continuum of administrative-judicial activities. *Source:* E. Keith Stott Jr.,
"The Judicial Executive: Toward Greater Congruence in an Emerging
Profession." *The Justice System Journal* 7[2] (1982): 152–179.

generally concurred with that of other researchers: Case-flow management was one of the 10 least-delegated duties of presiding judges. One explanation for this finding is that case-flow management is one function that "judges would be reluctant to delegate," as it is a duty that "might be considered judicial in nature."[54] Thus, although case-flow management is described by many authors[55] as one of the primary functions of court managers, it is also one that is grudgingly delegated by judges and is a leading source of conflict within the courtroom work group.

Mays and Taggart found that conflict in court management revolved around financial issues and personnel matters. Financial issues included accounting problems and methods, unbudgeted expenditures, procurement policies, and budget cutbacks. Among the personnel issues most often cited by respondents were employee evaluations, salary disputes, lack of adequate staffing, and the competency of staff.[56]

It is perhaps ironic that the more court managers attempt to control the administrative processes, the wider the gap may become between themselves and judges and lawyers. These two groups can have widely divergent perspectives on *what* is to be done and *how* it is to be accomplished.[57]

## How Judges Evaluate Administrators

Like other administrative mortals, judges and court administrators often see the world through "rose-colored glasses." As one Arizona judge observed:

> Judges and court administrators are not likely to view themselves in a negative light. As part of an organization that creates a certain amount of respect and awe for itself, it is not surprising that the [judge] and the court administrator may believe that they are better than they actually are. As a result, their top members frequently believe that the awe displayed toward them is intrinsic to their person, and not to the office.[58]

This view of the world can be an impediment to objective assessment and clear decision making. Still, the judge needs to be able to determine whether his or her court administrator is performing competently and effectively.

According to John Greacen,[59] judges follow several basic strategies in determining the quality of work performed by their administrators:

1. *The judge looks for indications of good management.* A well-managed organization will have a number of plans and procedures in place, including personnel policies, recruitment and selection procedures, an orientation program for new employees, performance evaluation procedures, a discipline and grievance process, case management policies, financial controls, and other administrative policies (such as for facilities and records management).

2. *The judge should be getting regular information.* Critically important reports and data on the court's performance, plans, activities, and accomplishments should be provided to the judge on a routine basis. The judge should be notified of the number of case filings, terminations, and pending cases;

financial information; staff performance; long- and short-range plans; and other statistical data.

3. *Judges should be watching carefully.* Judges observe a lot of the staff's activities. They alone can make an assessment of their administrator's strengths and weaknesses. How does the administrator respond to problems and crises? Does he or she show initiative?

4. *Judges must often ask others about the performance of the administrator.* This includes soliciting input from lawyers, other judges, and other court staff members.

# Jury Administration

Certainly, the jury system has been in the forefront of the public's mind in recent years, primarily as a result of the jury nullification concept (the right of juries to nullify or refuse to apply law in criminal cases despite facts that leave no reasonable doubt that the law was violated).[60] Here, however, we focus on the responsibilities of the court administrator in ensuring that a jury is properly composed and sustained during trials. Elements of the jury system that involve court administration include jury selection, sequestration, comfort, and notorious cases.

Regarding jury selection, the court administrator is responsible for compilation of a master jury list; this is a large pool of potential jurors compiled from voter registration, driver's license, or utility customer or telephone customer lists to produce a representative cross section of the community. From that master list, a randomly selected smaller venire (or jury pool) is drawn; a summons is mailed out to citizens, asking them to appear at the courthouse for jury duty. There, they will be asked questions and either retained or removed as jury members.

Here is where juror comfort enters in. Unfortunately, many jurors experience great frustration in the process, being made to wait long hours, possibly in uncomfortable physical surroundings, while receiving minimal compensation and generally being inconvenienced. Courts in all states now have a juror call-in system, enabling jurors to dial a phone number to learn whether their attendance is needed on a particular day; in addition, many jurisdictions have reduced the number of days a juror remains in the pool.

Some trials involving extensive media coverage require jury sequestration—jurors remain in virtual quarantine for sometimes many weeks and are compelled to live in a hotel together. This can be a trying experience for jurors and certainly poses greater logistical problems for court administrators. The court administrator must also consider security issues (protecting the jury from outside interference and providing for conjugal visits, room searches, transportation, and so on) as well as jurors' personal needs (such as entertainment and medical supplies).[61]

The existence of notorious cases—those involving celebrities or particularly egregious crimes—has always been a part of, and caused problems in, courtrooms: the trials of O. J. Simpson, Susan Smith, Mike Tyson, William Kennedy Smith, Oliver North, Marion Barry, Bernhard Goetz, John Gotti, Manuel Noriega, and the police officers who were tried for assaulting Rodney King were clearly "notorious."[62] Court administrators and other court staff members must deal with media requests; courtroom and courthouse logistics for handling crowds, the media, and security; and the management of the court's docket of other cases. A notorious trial may also require that a larger courtroom be used and many attorneys accommodated.[63] A number of other issues must be considered: Are identification and press passes and entry screening devices needed? Do purses, briefcases, and other such items need to be searched? Perhaps the most important task in managing notorious cases is communication with the media, often by setting aside a certain time when reporters may discuss the case.[64]

# CASE STUDY

The following case study will help the reader consider some of this chapter's materials, specifically concerns about court budgeting and operations.

## The Court Administrator and the Prudent Police Chief*

You are the court administrator in a system that has the following procedure for handling traffic matters:

1. All persons who are given a traffic citation are to appear in court at 9:00 A.M. on either Monday or Wednesday within two weeks of their citation date. They are given a specific date to appear.

2. Persons cited are not required to appear, either at the return date or at trial; they have the option of staying home and simply forfeiting their bond, which has been posted in advance of their initial appearance.

3. At the initial appearance, the arresting agency is represented by a court officer who has previously filed copies of all the citations with the clerk of the court.

4. The clerk, prior to the return date on the citation, prepared a file for each citation.

5. The clerk calls each case, and those persons appearing are requested by the court to enter a plea; if the plea is "not guilty," the matter is set for trial at a future date.

6. One case is scheduled per each hour. On the trial date, the prosecutor and arresting officer are required to appear, ready for trial.

7. Statistics show that 75 percent of those persons pleading not guilty in this jurisdiction fail to appear for trial.

The chief of police in the court's jurisdiction is concerned about overtime for officers. He communicates with you, the court administrator, about this concern and explains that all police officers who appear in court for trial are entitled to the minimum two hours of overtime when they are not appearing during their regular shift. He views this as a tremendous and unnecessary expense to the city, in view of the fact that most of the officers are not needed because the defendants do not appear. He recognizes that defendants have a right to post bond under the law and simply forfeit it at the initial appearance or on the trial date.

---

*Contributed by Hon. Burton A. Scott, former associate dean of the National Judicial College, Reno, Nevada.

He is interested, however, in devising some system to save the city the tremendous cost for all the officers' overtime. He explains that other municipalities are faced with similar problems.

## Questions for Discussion

1. What kind of a system would you propose to address the problem, and how would you go about accomplishing this end? In creating a modified system, you are to work within the existing law, with no changes in statutes or ordinances.
2. After you have completed designing a system and explaining how you would go about obtaining the cooperation of the judges, prosecutors, clerk's office, and other law enforcement agencies as well as that of the defense bar, discuss any proposed changes in the law you think might improve the system further.
3. How would you go about accomplishing other *significant* changes for improvement in the procedures and operation of this system? Consider the creation of an ongoing mechanism or committee that would propose, discuss, adopt, and carry out changes for the benefit of the system as a whole.

## Summary

Today, the court administrator's functions are quite different from the "house-keeping chores" seen in its earlier times and involve policymaking as well. Judicial administration possesses a basic body of practical knowledge, a rudimentary theoretical perspective, and a concern for professional ethics.

It was also shown that several obstacles still exist in the total acceptance of court administration as an integral part of the judiciary. The extent of actual and potential areas of conflict between judges and administrators was seen as a major source of problems.

Court administration is a rapidly developing field. While it still has its detractors, it is apparent that it has come far from its roots and is evolving into a bona fide element of the American justice system.

## Questions for Review

1. Why is the term *judicial administration* multifaceted? What would be a good working definition for this term? For *court administration?*
2. How might judges and court administrators receive training for their roles?

3. How have court clerks traditionally assumed and performed the role of court administrator? What are some of the unique problems of being a court clerk in a rural area?

4. What are some common areas of conflict among judges, court administrators, and court clerks?

5. What criteria may be employed by judges to evaluate the effectiveness of their administrators?

6. What are the court administrator's duties in general? What issues must the court administrator address in composing or sequestering a jury? For notorious cases?

# Notes

1. Robert C. Harrall, "In Defense of Court Managers: The Critics Misconceive Our Role," *Court Management Journal* 14 (1982):52.

2. Russell Wheeler, *Judicial Administration: Its Relation to Judicial Independence* (Williamsburg, Va.: National Center for State Courts, 1988), p. 19.

3. Woodrow Wilson, "The Study of Administration," *Political Science Quarterly* 2 (1887):197; reprinted in *Political Science Quarterly* 56 (1941):481.

4. Quoted in Paul Nejelski and Russell Wheeler, *Wingspread Conference on Contemporary and Future Issues in the Field of Court Management* 4 (1980).

5. Wheeler, *Judicial Administration,* p. 21.

6. Ibid., p. 22.

7. National Advisory Commission on Criminal Justice Standards and Goals, *Courts* (Washington, D.C.: U.S. Government Printing Office, 1973), p. 171.

8. American Bar Association, *Standards on Court Organization,* Standard 1.41 (1974).

9. Ian R. Scott, "Procedural Law and Judicial Administration," *Justice System Journal* 12 (1987):67–68.

10. Russell R. Wheeler and Howard R. Whitcomb, *Judicial Administration: Text and Readings* (Englewood Cliffs, N.J.: Prentice Hall, 1977), p. 8.

11. Ibid.

12. Ibid., p. 9.

13. David W. Neubauer, *America's Courts and the Criminal Justice System,* 7th ed. (Belmont, Calif.: Wadsworth, 2002), p. 198.

14. Barbara Luck Graham, "Do Judicial Selection Systems Matter? A Study of Black Representation on State Courts," *American Politics Quarterly* 18 (1990):316–336.

15. Neubauer, *America's Courts and the Criminal Justice System,* pp. 200–201.

16. Ibid.

17. Craig Emmert and Henry Glick, "The Selection of State Supreme Court Justices," *American Politics Quarterly* 16 (1988):445–465.

18. Abraham Blumberg, *Criminal Justice* (Chicago: Quadrangle Books, 1967).

19. Wheeler and Whitcomb, *Judicial Administration,* p. 370

20. National Center for State Courts Web page, http://www.ncsc.dni.us/ICM/cedp/program.html

21. Wheeler and Whitcomb, *Judicial Administration*, p. 372.

22. Ibid.

23. Ibid.

24. Ibid., p. 373.

25. Roscoe Pound, "Principles and Outlines of a Modern Unified Court Organization," *Journal of the American Judicature Society* 23 (April 1940):229.

26. See, for example, the Missouri Constitution, Article V. Sec. 15, paragraph 3.

27. Forest Hanna, "Delineating the Role of the Presiding Judge," *State Court Journal* 10 (Spring 1986):17–22.

28. Neubauer, *America's Courts and the Criminal Justice System*, p. 117.

29. Robert A. Wenke, "The Administrator in the Court," *Court Management Journal* 14 (1982):17–18, 29.

30. Marc Gertz, "Influence in the Court Systems: The Clerk as Interface," *Justice System Journal* 2 (1977):30–37.

31. Robert B. Revere, "The Court Clerk in Early American History," *Court Management Journal* 10 (1978):12–13.

32. G. Larry Mays and William Taggart, "Court Clerks, Court Administrators, and Judges: Conflict in Managing the Courts," *Journal of Criminal Justice* 14 (1986):1–7.

33. Larry Berkson, "Delay and Congestion in State Systems: An Overview," in Larry Berkson, Steven Hays, and Susan Carbon (eds.), *Managing the State Courts: Text and Readings* (St. Paul, Minn.: West, 1977), p. 164.

34. Kathryn L. Fahnestock and Maurice D. Geiger, "Rural Courts: The Neglected Majority," *Court Management Journal* 14 (1982):4–10.

35. Ibid., pp. 6, 8.

36. Ernest C. Friesen and I. R. Scott, *English Criminal Justice* (Birmingham, Eng.: University of Birmingham Institute of Judicial Administration, 1977), p. 12.

37. Harvey E. Solomon, "The Training of Court Managers," in Charles R. Swanson and Susette M. Talarico (eds.), *Court Administration: Issues and Responses* (Athens, Ga.: University of Georgia, 1987), pp. 15–20.

38. Ernest C. Friesen, "Court Managers: Magnificently Successful or Merely Surviving?" *Court Management Journal* 14 (1982):21.

39. Solomon, "The Training of Court Managers," p. 16.

40. Harrall, "In Defense of Court Managers," p. 51.

41. Neubauer, *America's Courts and the Criminal Justice System*, p. 117.

42. Ibid.

43. Geoffrey A. Mort and Michael D. Hall, "The Trial Court Administrator: Court Executive or Administrative Aide?" *Court Management Journal* 12 (1980):12–16, 30.

44. Bernadine Meyer, "Court Administration: The Newest Profession," *Duquesne Law Review* 10 (Winter 1971):220–235.

45. Mort and Hall, "The Trial Court Administrator," p. 15.

46. Ibid.

47. Neubauer, *America's Courts and the Criminal Justice System*, p. 117.

48. John M. Greacen, "Has Your Court Administrator Retired? Without Telling You?" National Association for Court Management, conference papers from the Second National Conference on Court Management, *Managing Courts in Changing Times*. Phoenix, Ariz., September 9–14, 1990, pp. 1–20.

49. E. Keith Stott, "The Judicial Executive: Toward Greater Congruence in an Emerging Profession," *Justice System Journal* 7 (1982):152–179.

50. Quoted in R. Dale Lefever, "Judge-Court Manager Relationships: The Integration of Two Cultures," *The Court Manager* 5 (Summer 1990):8–11.

51. Ibid., p. 10.

52. Ibid., p. 9.

53. Mays and Taggart,"Court Clerks, Court Administrators, and Judges," p. 3.

54. Mort and Hall, "The Trial Court Administrator," p. 14.

55. See W. LeBar, "The Modernization of Court Functions: A Review of Court Management and Computer Technology," *Journal of Computers and Law* 5 (1975):97–119; Burton W. Butler, "Presiding Judges' Perceptions of Trial Court Administrators," *Justice System Journal* 3 (1977):181; J. M. Scheb, "Florida Conference Examines Education of Court Administrators," *Judicature* (1981):465–468; David Saari, *American Court Management: Theories and Practice* (Westport, Conn.: Quorum Books, 1982).

56. Mays and Taggart,"Court Clerks, Court Administrators, and Judges," p. 4.

57. Ibid., p. 7.

58. James Duke Cameron, Isaiah M. Zimmerman, and Mary Susan Downing, "The Chief Justice and the Court Administrator: The Evolving Relationship," 113 *Federal Rules Decisions* 443 (1987).

59. Greacen, "Has Your Court Administrator Retired?," p. 18.

60. Darryl Brown, "Jury Nullification Within the Rule of Law," *Minnesota Law Review* 81 (1997):1149–1200.

61. Ibid., pp. 53, 73.

62. Timothy R. Murphy, Genevra Kay Loveland, and G. Thomas Munsterman, *A Manual for Managing Notorious Cases* (Washington, D.C.: National Center for State Courts, 1992), pp. 4–6. See also Timothy R. Murphy, Paul L. Hannaford, and Kay Genevra, *Managing Notorious Trials* (Williamsburg, Va.: National Center for State Courts, 1998).

63. Murphy, Loveland, and Munsterman, *A Manual for Managing Notorious Cases,* p. 23.

64. Ibid., pp. 27–30.

# Chapter 8

# Court Issues
and Practices

## Key Terms and Concepts

Crime control model

Due process model

Exclusionary rule

Individual calendar system

Juveniles tried as adults

Master calendar system

Plea bargaining

Trial delay

## Learning Objectives

As a result of reading this chapter, the student will:

- understand the differences between the due process and crime control models
- be familiar with the problems and consequences of unnecessary trial delays
- understand some solutions to the problem of delayed trials
- be familiar with the two systems used in scheduling cases
- understand why gender bias is a concern in the court system
- be familiar with the concerns of juveniles being tried as adults

*Justice is such a fine thing that we cannot pay too dearly for it.*
*—Alain Rene LeSage*

# Introduction

In reality, many of the topics discussed previously, primarily in Chapter 6—such as reforming court organization and unification, use of the adversary system, and alternative dispute resolution—could have been included in this chapter. They are problem areas. This chapter, however, examines additional contemporary issues and practices.

It is helpful for court administrators to view court issues and practices through the lenses of the crime control and due process models of criminal justice; these models represent what might be termed the "hard-line" and the "soft-line" approaches toward offenders and how the justice system should deal with them. Therefore, the chapter begins with an overview of those case-processing models. Then the following six issues are discussed: the dilemma of delay (including its consequences, suggested solutions, and two systems of scheduling cases), gender bias, juveniles being tried as adults, and whether the exclusionary rule, use of cameras in courtrooms, and plea bargaining should be banned or modified.

After presenting an example of how good court administration can reform the practices of a virtually unworkable court system, the chapter concludes with a case study.

# Justice from the Due Process and Crime Control Perspectives

As noted earlier, several of the issues and practices discussed later in this chapter will be viewed in terms of the crime control and due process models of criminal justice. The main points of these two philosophies are presented here.

In 1968, Herbert Packer[1] presented these two now-classic, competing models, which describe how criminal cases are processed. The **due process model** holds that defendants should be presumed innocent, that the courts' first priority is protecting suspects' rights, and that granting too much freedom to law enforcement officials will only result in the loss of freedom and civil liberties for all Americans. Therefore, each court case must involve formal fact finding in order to uncover mistakes by the police and prosecutors. This view also stresses that crime is not a result of individual moral failure but is the result of social influences (such as unemployment, racial discrimination, and other factors that disadvantage the poor); thus, courts that do not follow this philosophy are fundamentally unfair to these defendants. Furthermore, rehabilitation will prevent further crime.

Standing in contrast is the **crime control model,** which views crime as a breakdown of individual responsibility and places the highest importance on repressing criminal conduct, thus protecting society. Those persons who are charged are presumed guilty, and the courts should not hinder effective enforcement of the laws; rather, legal loopholes should be eliminated and offenders swiftly punished. The police and prosecutors should have a high degree of discretion. Punishment will deter crime, so there must be speed and finality in the courts in order to ensure crime suppression.

# The Dilemma of Delay

There is no consensus as to how long is too long with respect to bringing a criminal case to trial, and the test is a balancing one with regard to the prosecutor's and defense attorney's conduct.[2] Still, a point at which Packer's models begin to diverge involves **trial delay.** The crime control model inherently calls for swift justice in order to protect society by incarcerating offenders, whereas due process advocates would call for a more thoughtful and careful approach.

The principle that "justice delayed is justice denied" says much about the long-standing goal of processing court cases with due dispatch. Charles Dickens condemned the practice of slow litigation in nineteenth-century England, and Shakespeare mentioned "the law's delay" in *Hamlet.* More recently, delay in processing cases has remained one of the most long-standing problems of U.S. courts. The public often hears of cases that have languished on court dockets for years. This can only erode public confidence in the judicial process.[3] The overload in our bloated court system has been building for years, with the most immediate source of pressure for the courts being the intensifying drug war; with increasing drug arrests, backlogs are growing.

Case backlog and trial delay affect many of our country's courts. The magnitude of the backlog and the length of the delay vary greatly, however, depending on the court involved. It is best to view delay not as a problem but as a symptom of a problem.[4] Generally, the term *delay* suggests abnormal or unacceptable time lapses in the processing of cases. Yet some time is needed to prepare a case. What is a concern is *unnecessary* delay. However, there seems to be no agreed upon definition concerning what unnecessary delay is.

## *The Consequences*

The consequences of delay can be severe. It can jeopardize the values and guarantees inherent in our justice system. Delay deprives defendants of their Sixth Amendment right to a speedy trial. Lengthy pretrial incarceration pressures can cause a defendant to plead guilty.[5] In contrast, delay can strengthen a defendant's bargaining position; prosecutors are more apt to accept pleas to a lesser charge when dockets are crowded. Delays cause pretrial detainees to clog the jails, police officers to appear in court on numerous occasions, and attorneys to expend unproductive time appearing on the same case.

One contributing factor to court delay is the lack of incentive to process cases speedily. Although at least 10 states require cases to be dismissed and defendants to be released if they are denied a speedy trial,[6] the U.S. Supreme Court has refused to give the rather vague concept of a "speedy trial" any precise time frame.[7] The problem with time frames, however, is twofold: First, more complex cases legitimately take a long time to prepare; second, these time limits may be waived due to congested court dockets. In sum, there is no legally binding mechanism that works.

## Suggested Solutions

The best-known legislation addressing the problem is the Speedy Trial Act of 1974, amended in 1979. It provides firm time limits: 30 days from the point of arrest to indictment and 70 days from indictment to trial. Thus, federal prosecutors have a total of 100 days from the time of arrest until trial. This speedy trial law has proven effective over the years.

Unfortunately, however, laws that attempt to speed up trials at the state level have had less success than this federal law, because most state laws fail to provide the courts with adequate and effective enforcement mechanisms. As a result, the time limits specified by speedy trial laws are seldom followed in actual practice.[8]

A number of proposals have emerged to alleviate state and local courts' logjams, ranging from judicial jury selection and limits on criminal appeals to six-person juries. The latter was actually suggested more than two decades ago as a means of relieving congestion of court calendars and reducing court costs for jurors.[9] Thirty-three states have specifically authorized juries of fewer than 12, but most allow smaller juries only in misdemeanor cases. In federal courts, defendants are entitled to a 12-person jury unless the parties agree in writing to a smaller one.[10]

Some reformers suggest that the courts' greatest need is for better management and efficiency. In considering how the courts could function better, however, we need to bear in mind that justice must be served. Where justice ends and expediency begins can be a difficult distinction to comprehend. Courthouse officials are to both "do justice" and move cases.

One experiment that seems to have great promise toward unclogging courts and reducing delay was launched in Detroit, Michigan's largest district court. Known as "pre-exam waiver hearings," the program allows defendants facing drug, gun, or auto theft charges (which compose more than half of all criminal cases) to waive their preliminary examinations one week earlier than normal. This program has thus far unclogged the courts, kept police and witnesses from showing up in court for proceedings that never occurred, and saved the court more than a half million dollars annually. The program causes police and prosecutorial personnel to present their reports much more quickly; the jails save money by reducing the time defendants spend behind bars, and police save tens of thousands of dollars in overtime pay because officers do not have to attend waived hearings.[11]

## Case Scheduling: Two Systems

A key part of addressing case delay concerns the ability of the court administrator to set a date for trial. Scheduling trials is problematic because of forces outside the administrator's control: slow or inaccurate mail delivery, which can result in notices of court appearances arriving after the scheduled hearing; an illegible address that prevents a key witness or defendant from ever being contacted about a hearing or trial; or a jailer's inadvertent failure to include a defendant on a list for transportation. If just one key person fails to appear, the matter must be rescheduled. Furthermore, judges have limited ability to control the actions of personnel from law enforcement, probation, or the court reporter's offices, all of which have scheduling problems of their own.[12]

The two primary methods by which cases are scheduled by the courts are the individual calendar and the master calendar.

### Individual Calendar System

The simplest procedure for scheduling cases is the **individual calendar system.** A case is assigned to a single judge, who oversees all aspects of it from arraignment to pretrial motions and trial. The primary advantage is continuity; all parties to the case know that a single judge is responsible for its conclusion. There are other important advantages as well. Judge shopping (where attorneys try to get their client's case on a particular judge's docket) is minimal, and administrative responsibility for each case is fixed. Also, it is easier to pinpoint delays, because one can easily compare judges' dockets to determine where cases are moving along and where they are not.

This system, however, is often affected by major differences in "case stacking," because judges work at different speeds. Also, if a judge draws a difficult case, others must wait. Because most cases will be pleaded, however, case stacking is not normally a major problem unless a judge schedules too many cases for adjudication on a given day. Conversely, if a judge stacks too few cases for hearing or adjudication each day, delay will also result. If all cases settle, the judge has dead time, with a large backlog and nothing to do for the rest of the day.

### Master Calendar System

The **master calendar system** is a more recent development. Here, judges oversee (usually on a rotating basis) given stages of a case: preliminary hearings, arraignments, motions, bargaining, or trials. A judge is assigned a case from a central or master pool; once he or she has completed that phase of it, the case is returned to the pool. The primary advantage with this system is that judges who are good in one particular aspect of litigation (such as preliminary hearings) can be assigned to the job they do best. The disadvantage is that it is more difficult to pinpoint the location of or responsibility for delays. Judges also have less incentive to keep their docket current because when they dispose of one case, another appears. Also, the distribution of work can be quite uneven. If, for example, three judges are responsible for preliminary hearings and one is much slower than the others, an unequal shifting of the workload will ensue; in other words, the two harder-working judges will be penalized by having to work more cases.

### Which System Is Best?

Each of the calendar systems has advantages and disadvantages, but a running debate has developed over which is best. The answer probably depends on the nature of the court. Small courts, such as the U.S. district courts, use the individual calendar system more successfully. But largely because of their complex dockets, metropolitan and state courts almost uniformly use the master calendar system. Research indicates that courts using the master calendar experience the greatest difficulty. Typical problems include the following: (1) Some judges refuse to take their fair share of cases; (2) the administrative burden on the chief judge is often great; and (3) as a result of these two factors, a significant backlog of cases may develop. In those courts where the master calendar system was discontinued in favor of the individual system, major reductions in delay were realized.[13]

## Gender Bias

Another concern for judges who administer the courts concerns accusations of gender bias. As we have become a more diverse society, so have problems increased in this regard. Indeed, at least 36 states have created task forces to investigate gender bias in the legal system.[14] These task forces consistently found problems in gender bias in four areas of the legal system: domestic violence, sexual assault, divorce, and behavior toward female workers.

Domestic violence is one area in which the state task forces found gender bias to be the most common. Some members of the courtroom work group believe that domestic violence is a private matter and should not be dealt with in the court system. As an example, a New York woman was assaulted by her husband who used a telephone to hit her; from the bench the judge said, "What's wrong with that? You've got to keep them in line once in a while."[15]

Sexual assault is another area that is still problematical. Sexual assault is underreported because women think they will not be believed and will themselves be blamed or will have their sexual history thrown open to scrutiny. Divorce cases were found by the task forces to make women suffer in terms of awarding alimony, division of property, and child support (the outcomes were biased against men, however, in child custody awards).[16]

With respect to court workers, female lawyers (who now constitute anywhere from one-third to one-half of all law students and more than 10 percent of the nation's judges) and court employees report offensive and intolerable actions toward women participants in the legal system. Judges and attorneys address female lawyers in a demeaning manner, using terms such as "sweetie," "little lady lawyer," "pretty eyes," and "dear." Sexist remarks or jokes are also heard.[17] Gender bias can also affect hiring and promotions. Many female lawyers perceive that it is harder to get hired, and once hired they are paid less and have fewer opportunities for promotion.

Sometimes "black robe disease"—overstepping the bounds of propriety due to ignorance or arrogance—is more of a problem of machismo. For example, a 22-year-old Michigan coed was awaiting sentencing by a 54-year-old judge for a DUI charge; the judge asked her to meet him at a bar on a Saturday night to discuss her case.[18] Other cases concerning judicial ethics are discussed in Chapter 13.

Although it is difficult to estimate the true extent of gender bias, it is important to recognize and deal with it whenever it occurs. Perceptions of gender bias are a serious matter because they affect litigants' view of the fairness of the justice system.

# Should Juveniles Be Tried as Adults?

During the mid-1990s, the nation's focus on crime began to shift from drugs to juvenile crime, particularly violent crime. Beginning in the mid-1980s, a juvenile crime wave that would be like none other was predicted to be on the horizon; a "superpredator" form of juvenile offender was anticipated to prey on society in large numbers, bolstered by the realization that the juvenile population would increase from 27 million to 39 million in 2000. That prediction, however, never came to pass.[19]

Numerous states are responding to public perceptions that violent juvenile crime is a growing menace, however, by making it easier to transfer juveniles from the relatively "protective shroud" of juvenile court to the jurisdiction of adult courts. The philosophy and treatment of juveniles is quite different in the latter, where the process is adversarial instead of amicable, and punitive rather than treatment oriented.

States are also lowering the age and increasing the list of crimes for which juveniles can be transferred. The state of Georgia, for example, enacted a mandatory transfer for juveniles 13 years and older who have been charged with specified serious offenses (if convicted, a 13-year-old may face a minimum 10-year prison sentence). Today, at least 24 states have laws sending violent juveniles to adult courts.[20]

Concerns regarding due process include that this approach carries the possibility of juveniles being incarcerated with adult offenders, and possibly being raped or assaulted by the older inmates. Advocates of restorative justice emphasize that juvenile matters are the prime example of efforts at reconciliation being likely to yield more positive results than punitive measures.[21]

Should juveniles be prosecuted as adults? If so, under what conditions should they be sentenced and incarcerated? Should potential and traditional rehabilitative philosophies and functions of the juvenile court be taken into account? These questions must be addressed, not only in light of the hardened nature of today's violent juvenile offenders, but also in terms of what the future holds for juvenile violence.

## Should the Exclusionary Rule Be Banned?

The **exclusionary rule** quickly became controversial for both crime control and due process advocates when it was adopted in 1961 by the U.S. Supreme Court in *Mapp v. Ohio.*[22] The view of the crime control model—as expressed by former President Ronald Reagan in 1981—was, and is, that the rule "rests on the absurd proposition that a law enforcement error, no matter how technical, can be used to justify throwing an entire case out of court. The plain consequence is a grievous miscarriage of justice: the criminal goes free."[23]

But to many legal experts who are inclined toward the due process model, illegal conduct by the police cannot be ignored. They believe that a court that admits tainted evidence tolerates the unconstitutional conduct that produced it and demonstrates an "insufficient commitment to the guarantee against unreasonable search and seizure."[24]

While the exclusionary rule remains controversial, the nature of the debate has changed. Initially, critics called for complete abolition of the rule; now, they suggest modifications. Former Chief Justice Warren Burger has urged an "egregious violation standard," whereby the police could be attacked in civil suits when believed to be in error. Others support an exception for reasonable mistakes by the police. In fact, the U.S. Supreme Court has recognized an "honest mistake" or "good faith" exception to the rule only in extremely narrow and limited circumstances.[25] Furthermore, the Rehnquist Court includes six justices who have publicly criticized *Mapp*. This majority, however, has not been able to fashion a means of replacing *Mapp* while prohibiting truly bad-faith searches by the police. As a result, predicting the future of the exclusionary rule is difficult at best.

Should the exclusionary rule be abolished outright? Modified? Kept in its present form? These are compelling questions that our society and its courts may continue to ponder for many years to come.

## Should Cameras Be Banned?

As the trial of actor Robert Blake (charged with murdering his wife, Bonny Lee Bakley) was being prepared in 2002, the controversy over whether or not cameras should be allowed in court—with a well-known actor playing himself in a real-life courtroom drama—was rekindled. The widely televised trial of O. J. Simpson clearly caused rethinking about whether or not cameras should be allowed in courtrooms.

Perceptions that Simpson's lawyers played to the cameras apparently had an impact in several highly publicized cases that followed: A judge refused to allow broadcasts in the trial of Susan Smith, a South Carolina woman accused of drowning her two young sons in 1995,[26] and a California judge barred cameras in the trial of Richard Allen Davis, who kidnaped and killed Polly Klaas in 1993.

By the late 1990s, however, despite the Simpson trial backlash, opposition cooled; a study found that four of every five television requests were approved by judges in California in 1998 and 1999.[27] Indeed, a judge allowed coverage of the trial of four police officers accused (and acquitted) of murdering Amadou Diallo in New York City in 2000.

The Blake trial once again brought to center stage all of the concerns that have been lodged against the practice of televising high-publicity trials. Opponents of cameras in court—including due process advocates—complain that televising trials distorts the process by encouraging participants to play to the cameras, and that by covering only sensational trials and presenting only dramatic moments of testimony, the trial is not portrayed accurately.[28] They argue that in celebrity cases even the witnesses "exaggerate things to give themselves a bigger role."[29] Supporters of the concept, conversely, maintain that televising trials has an educational value, providing the public with a firsthand view of how court proceedings operate. Indeed, studies have found that viewers of a television trial of moderate interest became more knowledgeable about the judicial process.[30]

The question of publicizing high-profile cases is not a new one. Cameras or recording devices were forbidden in the courthouse following the excessive press coverage of German immigrant Bruno Hauptman, who was accused of kidnaping and murdering the son of famous aviator Charles Lindbergh in the 1930s. This case is the reason that television stations began to hire artists to provide sketches of courtroom participants.

Restrictions on cameras in the courtroom are changing, however. The Supreme Court unanimously held that electronic media and still photographic coverage of public judicial proceedings does not violate a defendant's right to a fair trial; states are therefore free to set their own guidelines. Today, only two states prohibit all forms of electronic coverage of criminal trial proceedings, while 35 states allow electronic coverage of criminal trials.[31] The remaining states are as yet undecided on the issue.

In order to prevent disruption of the proceedings and to prohibit camera operators from moving about the courtroom while the trial is in session, states include limitations on this electronic coverage. Furthermore, some states require the consent of the parties, meaning either side can veto coverage of the proceedings. In others, the news media need only receive permission from the trial judge to broadcast the proceedings.[32]

The lingering question is whether cameras are an asset or a liability in the courtroom. To answer, one must determine whether or not their value as a tool of education and publicity overcomes the potential liabilities.

# Does Plea Bargaining Belong?

Some people within the court system believe the institution of **plea bargaining** reduces the courthouse to something akin to a Turkish bazaar, where people barter over the price of copper jugs.[33] They see it as justice on the cheap. Others believe that plea bargaining works to make the job of the judge, prosecutor, and defense attorney much easier. Primary opposition to plea bargaining involves ideological preferences. No matter on which side of the issue one stands, however, it is ironic that both the police and the civil libertarians oppose plea bargaining, but for different reasons.

The police and others in the crime control camp view plea bargaining as undesirable because defendants can avoid conviction for crimes they actually committed, while pleading to and receiving a sentence for lesser offenses. The police see victims at their worst and are highly chagrined when, for example, an accused rapist is allowed to plead guilty to a lesser charge because a prosecutor believes that evidence is lacking for a rape conviction. These advocates of crime control would much prefer to see the defendant convicted for the crime charged.

Similarly, civil libertarians and supporters of the due process model oppose plea bargaining because when agreeing to plead to a crime(s), the accused forfeits a long list of due process protections afforded under the Bill of Rights: the presumption of innocence; the government's burden of proof; and the rights to face one's accuser, to testify and present witnesses in one's defense, to have an attorney, to appeal, and so on. Another concern is that an innocent defendant might be forced to enter a plea of guilty.

A bargained agreement on reduced charges may be the product of initial overcharging and/or of evidence problems that surface later. Furthermore, defendants who gain the most from plea bargaining are the less serious, marginal offenders, in cases lacking in evidence. By contrast, defendants in serious cases who have prior criminal histories do not benefit. In short, plea bargaining appears to reflect a rational rather than a coercive process.

Overall, does plea bargaining sacrifice the rights of the defendant? Or does justice suffer by giving too much benefit to guilty persons? These are the fundamental questions that have swirled around this concept since its inception.

# Court Administration Practice and Reform: A Model

Imagine that you are in a crowded main lobby of a courthouse; it is packed, with sweltering heat. Tempers are short, lines are long, and people appear frustrated; some are even angry. Many have been waiting several hours simply to pay a traffic-violation fine.

Inside the courtrooms, matters are little better. Cases are dismissed for want of a speedy trial because records are lost; continuances abound for the same reason. The calendar is in a shambles. In the office areas, the same condition prevails. Large sums of money frequently disappear; boxes of money orders, checks, and even cash are piled up because no one knows what they are intended to pay or where they go. There are also huge stacks of case files in 20 or more locations around the courthouse; dozens of cubic feet of warrants are piled in boxes in bathrooms and closets because they cannot be matched to case files. The data-entry section is at least 5,000 cases behind and the delay is growing. There is a large backlog of criminal cases. There are no written procedures, no forms management program, no employee performance reviews. Turnover is 50 percent and absenteeism is rampant. There is no training program. Public relations is a disaster, and complaints to the mayor and city council abound. This court does not work.[34]

Imagine that you return to the same court on a sweltering summer day three years later. Now, inside the lobby is a cool, white tile floor and ceiling fans; citizens cool off during an average 15-minute wait until being served by well-trained, motivated court staff members (citizens give them a 90 percent favorable rating). An express box now allows many to pay fines without waiting. In the courtrooms, action is fast paced but smooth flowing. The calendar is followed promptly and accurately; missing files now average less than 1 in 1,000. Dismissals due to speedy trial violations are now rare, and continuances are under control. No funds have disappeared from court offices in years, and cash security is tight. All payments are deposited within 24 hours; computer case records are updated within 48 hours. Loose paperwork is no problem, and each section has written procedures, lines of authority, flowcharts, and job standards. Comprehensive training is now provided to employees, who leave at an annual rate of only 4.5 percent and have comparatively little absenteeism. The public, attorneys, and media recently gave the court high marks for efficiency, and complaints to the politicians are minimal. The court now works very well.[35]

How has this program of court administration turned itself around? Some courts and their administrators, such as those in Tucson, Arizona, have done so; they have provided useful information for others to follow as a model. First, the presiding judge must delegate enough authority to the court administrator to get the job of reform started. In turn, the court administrator must respect the ultimate authority of the presiding judge. Second, the leadership must recognize that the currency of case filing is *the* priority for a high-volume court. All case files acted upon today must be processed (computer update, manual logging, mailing distribution, calendaring) and filed tomorrow.[36]

Third, all judicial administrators and staff must understand the fundamentals of court productivity. The clerk/judge ratio is of compelling importance. Ron Zimmerman observed that "it makes no difference how many competent, hardworking judges a court may have if it does not have enough clerks to process the cases arriving daily from the bench."[37] Zimmerman further noted that nine support staff for each full-time judge seems appropriate. The daily productivity of judges must be quantified according to the types of cases handled; then the average time to complete the case must be measured to determine how many hours of clerical time are involved in the actual actions received daily. With this information, the number of clerk positions needed can be calculated. Another factor contributing to court productivity is the number of total filings (complaints) per operations clerk. Zimmerman determined that a clerk can be expected to handle no more than 3,000 case filings per year. Thus, if each judge is found to handle all work derived from 15,000 complaints, each judge needs 5 clerical staff members to handle that aspect of his or her work output alone.[38]

Following the inception of this approach, Tucson courts reduced their case-processing backlogs from 25,000 to 40,000 cases to zero; the number of dismissals for lack of a speedy trial became statistically insignificant; and judicial backlogs were reduced from several thousand to zero. Furthermore, the average time to service persons at the counter dropped from more than 10 minutes to 2.5 minutes each. A new case-tracking and management system was installed, including automatic reporting to the state motor vehicle division, automatic surcharge calculation, revenue distribution, and court scheduling.[39]

These changes required more than four years to accomplish, and the job is still not complete. However, many years of failure to plan can require such a long effort; the benefits of changing from chaos to excellence are obvious. The message provided by a program of reform is that planning and, perhaps just as important, simplification are needed.[40]

# CASE STUDY

The following case study helps the reader consider some of this chapter's subject matter, specifically concerns about case delay and scheduling.

## An Unmanageable Case-Management Quandary*

You are court administrator for a court with 50 employees. This court, which used to dispose of about 700 cases per month, now hears an average of 100 criminal and 400 civil cases per month. Case filings have doubled in the past seven years. The present "hybrid" combination of the individual and master case-management systems has evolved over a long period of time through tradition and expediency. A growing caseload and increasing difficulties in avoiding a backlog, however, have prompted the judges to rethink their present system. Criminal cases that used to reach final disposition in a month now require two to three months. The situation shows no signs of improving in the foreseeable future. Again, the court has a mixed calendar system. Two judges are assigned to hear criminal cases and motions for a one-month period, while the remaining four judges hear all manner of civil matters on a random basis upon the filing of the civil complaint. The judges are responsible for the management of these cases until final disposition. At the end of the one-month period, the two judges hearing criminal cases return to the civil division and two other judges rotate onto the criminal bench; any pending criminal cases or motions are then heard by these two incoming criminal judges. One of the judges hears all juvenile-related matters in addition to any assignment in the criminal and civil divisions. The court collects statistics on the number of court filings and motions filed in each division on a month-to-month basis.

## Questions for Discussion

1. In a general way, discuss both the merits and difficulties posed by this case-management approach. Relate your response to the general advantages and disadvantages of both the individual and the master calendar systems.
2. What specific problems could arise in the criminal division? Why?

---

*Contributed by Dennis Metrick, Management Analyst, Court Services Department, Administrative Office of the Courts, Phoenix, Arizona.

3. What specific problems could be created by the permanent assignment of a judge to the juvenile division? What advantages?

4. What comments would you make with regard to the court's statistical report? Are other data needed for management purposes? If so, what kind?

## Summary

This chapter discussed several challenges involving the courts, generated from both internal and external sources.

It is obvious that today's court issues and operations carry tremendous responsibilities for administrators. Those who serve as court leaders must be innovative, open to new ideas, accountable, well trained, and educated for the challenges that lie ahead. Certainly, legislators and policymakers must also become more aware of the difficulties confronting the courts and be prepared to provide additional resources for meeting the increasing caseloads, issues, and problems of the future.

## Questions for Review

1. What are the possible consequences of and solutions for combating delay in the courts?

2. What are the two primary methods of case scheduling employed by the courts? What are advantages and disadvantages of each?

3. Should juveniles be tried as adults? Why or why not?

4. Should the exclusionary rule be banned? Why or why not?

5. What are some examples of gender bias in the courts? What might judges and administrators do to address the problem?

6. Should plea bargaining and courtroom cameras be kept or barred from our legal system? Why or why not?

## Notes

1. Herbert L. Packer, *The Limits of the Criminal Sanction* (Stanford, Calif.: Stanford University Press, 1968).

2. *Barker v. Wingo,* 407 U.S.514 (1972)

3. David W. Neubauer, *America's Courts and the Criminal Justice System,* 7th ed. (Belmont, Calif.: Wadsworth, 2002), pp. 127–128.

4. Ibid., p. 126.

5.  Ibid., p. 128.
6.  See *Barker v. Wingo,* 407 U.S. 514 (1972).
7.  Ibid., at p. 522.
8.  Neubauer, *America's Courts and the Criminal Justice System,* p. 130.
9.  National Advisory Commission on Criminal Justice Standards and Goals, *Courts* (Washington, D.C.: U.S. Government Printing Office, 1973), p. 12.
10. Neubauer, *America's Courts and the Criminal Justice System,* p. 352.
11. Jim Dyer, "Court Reform Unclogs Docket," *The Detroit News* (June 11, 1998):C1.
12. Steven Flanders, *Case Management and Court Management in the United States District Courts* (Washington, D.C.: Federal Judicial Center, 1977).
13. David W. Neubauer, Maria Lipetz, Mary Luskin, and John Paul Ryan, *Managing the Pace of Justice: An Evaluation of LEAA's Court Delay Reduction Programs* (Washington, D.C.: U.S. Government Printing Office, 1981).
14. Craig Hemmens, Kristin Strom, and Elicia Schlegel, "Gender Bias in the Courts: A Review of the Literature." Paper presented at the Academy of Criminal Justice Sciences, Louisville, Kentucky, March 1997.
15. Gail Diane Cox, "Judges Behaving Badly (Again)," *The National Law Journal* 21 (May 3, 1999):1-5.
16. Neubauer, *America's Courts and the Criminal Justice System,* p. 204.
17. Hemmens, Strom, and Schlegel, "Gender Bias in the Courts."
18. Cox, "Judges Behaving Badly (Again)," pp. 1-5.
19. Kevin Johnson and Gary Fields, "Juvenile Crime 'Wave' May Be Just a Ripple," *USA Today* (13 December 1996):3.
20. Neubauer, *America's Courts and the Criminal Justice System,* p. 510.
21. Ibid.
22. 367 U.S. 643
23. Quoted in Neubauer, *America's Courts and the Criminal Justice System,* p. 310.
24. Yale Kamisar, "Is the Exclusionary Rule an 'Illogical' or 'Unnatural' Interpretation of the Fourth Amendment?" *Judicature* 78 (1994):83-84.
25. See, for example, *U.S. v. Leon,* 486 U.S. 897 (1984) and *Illinois v. Krull,* 480 U.S. 340 (1987).
26. Jesse Holland, "Susan Smith Judge Bars TV Cameras from Murder Trial," *Times-Picayune* (25 June 1995):1A.
27. Zanto Peabody, "Blake Case Revives Issue of Cameras in Court," *Los Angeles Times,* (May 27, 2002):1A.
28. Paul Thaler, *The Watchful Eye: American Justice in the Age of the Television Trial* (Westport, Conn.: Praeger, 1994).
29. Peabody, "Blake Case Revives Issue of Cameras in Court," p. 1A.
30. S. L. Alexander, "Cameras in the Courtroom A Case Study," *Judicature* 74 (1991): 307-313; Paul Raymond, "The Impact of a Televised Trial on Individuals' Information and Attitudes," *Judicature* 57 (1992):204-209.
31. Alexander, "Cameras in the Courtroom."
32. Neubauer, *America's Courts and the Criminal Justice System,* p. 376.
33. Alvin Rubin, "How We Can Improve Judicial Treatment of Individual Cases Without Sacrificing Individual Rights: The Problems of the Criminal Law," *Federal Rules of Decisions* 70 (1976):176.

34. Adapted from Ron Zimmerman, "From Chaos to Excellence: Four Tough Years," *State Court Journal* 12 (Summer 1988):13–18.

35. Ibid.

36. Ibid., pp. 14–15.

37. Ibid.

38. Ibid., p. 15.

39. Ibid., p. 16.

40. Ibid., p. 18.

# PART IV

# CORRECTIONS

*This part includes four chapters about corrections administration. Chapter 9 examines corrections organization and operation, including in prisons and jails. Chapter 10 covers personnel roles and functions, and Chapter 11 discusses the administration of community corrections through probation and parole. Chapter 12 reviews corrections issues and practices. Specific chapter content is provided in the introductory section of each chapter. Case studies in corrections administration appear at the end of each chapter.*

# Chapter 9

# Corrections Organization and Operation

## Key Terms and Concepts

Central office

Custodial organization

Customer model

Due deference doctrine

Employer model

Hands-off doctrine

Manpower model

New generation jail

Punitive segregation

Rehabilitation

Social density

Spatial density

Treatment organization

Warden

## Learning Objectives

After reading this chapter, the student will:

- be familiar with the general features of the correctional organization
- have an idea of the personnel and divisions found in the central office and their functions
- be familiar with prison organization and the different responsibilities of the prison warden
- have an understanding of the different factors affecting prison and jail populations

- have an initial understanding of the rights of inmates
- understand the due deference doctrine
- know how the "new generation" jail differs from the traditional model
- be familiar with the research findings concerning correctional institutions

*Prisons are built with stones of Law.*

—William Blake

*The founders of a new colony . . . recognized it among their earliest practical necessities to allot a portion of the virgin soil as a cemetery, and another portion as the site of a prison.*

—Nathaniel Hawthorne

# Introduction

The subculture of prisons and jails has been the subject of television and movie fare in the United States for several decades. Most dramas about prison and jail life have portrayed prison administrators and their staff as cruel, bigoted, corrupt, and morally base. Prison literature, such as Jack Henry Abbott's *In the Belly of the Beast,* Eldridge Cleaver's *Soul on Ice,* George Jackson's *Soledad Brother,* and Malcolm Braly's *On the Yard,* among others, have presented similar views. Television programs, movies, and books reflect the public's interest in, and often contribute to its lack of accurate knowledge about, our correctional institutions. Even though past decades and even centuries may have witnessed cruel, autocratic corrections administration, this chapter presents its contempory, professional nature.

The "key facts" section below shows that corrections is now a boom industry in terms of both expenditures and employment; then, the chapter focuses on correctional agencies as organizations, generally, including a view of the statewide central offices overseeing prison systems and their related functions, as well as a typical individual prison's organization and administration. Next, we examine the causes and effects of prison crowding, which is followed by a discussion of inmate rights and civil litigation. We also look at the organization of local jails and conclude the chapter by examining research findings concerning the effects of several aspects of incarceration, including crowding, solitary confinement, and life on death row. The chapter ends with two case studies.

# Correctional Organizations, Generally

## Key Facts: Inmates, Employment, Expenditures

Even with the recent, widely reported decline in crime in the United States, corrections can still be regarded as a boom industry. The number of people under some form of correctional supervision has been increasing, and today about

Adult correctional populations, 1980–2000

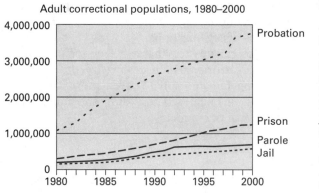

**Figure 9.1**

Adult correctional populations, 1980–2000. *Source:* Bureau of Justice Statistics Correctional Surveys (The Annual Probation Survey, National Prisoner Statistics, Survey of Jails, and The Annual Parole Survey) as presented in *Correctional Populations in the United States, 1997* and *Prisoners in 2000* (Washington, D.C.: Author, 2002), p. 1.

6.5 million people are in prison or jail or on probation or parole[1]—3.1 percent of all adult U.S. residents, or about 1 in every 32 adults.[2] Figure 9.1 depicts this increase.

In order of frequency, about 3,800,000 individuals are on probation; 1,312,000 are in prison (1,252,000 in state systems, the remainder in federal prisons); 725,000 are on parole; and 702,000 are in local jails awaiting trial or serving a sentence.[3] Correctional administrators are also responsible for holding about 3,600 persons on death rows; 38 states and the federal government have capital punishment statutes.[4]

There are about 717,000 correctional employees in the United States; most (about 450,000) are state employees and 228,000 are local.[5] The custody and treatment of criminals make corrections an expensive undertaking. It now costs nearly $50 billion per year for corrections activities in the United States, compared with $65 billion for the police functions and $32 billion for courts.[6]

## General Mission and Features

Correctional organizations are complex, hybrid organizations that utilize two distinct yet related management subsystems to achieve their goals: One is concerned primarily with managing correctional employees, and the other is concerned primarily with delivering correctional services to a designated offender population. The correctional organization, therefore, employs one group of people—correctional personnel—to work with and control another group—offenders.

The mission of corrections agencies has changed little over time. It is as follows: to protect the citizens from crime by safely and securely handling criminal offenders, while providing offenders some opportunities for self-improvement and increasing the chance that they will become productive and law-abiding citizens.[7]

An interesting feature of the correctional organization is that *every* correctional employee who exercises legal authority over offenders is a supervisor, even if the person is the lowest-ranking member in the agency or institution. Another feature of the correctional organization is that—as with the police—everything a correctional supervisor does may have civil or criminal ramifications, both for himself or herself and for the agency or institution. Therefore, the legal and ethical responsibility for the correctional (and police) supervisor is greater than it is for supervisors in other types of organizations.

Finally, two different philosophies exist as to what a correctional organization should be: (1) **custodial organizations,** which emphasize the caretaker functions of controlling and observing inmates and (2) **treatment organizations,** which emphasize rehabilitation of inmates. These different philosophies contain potential conflict for correctional personnel.

# Prisons as Organizations

As noted earlier in this chapter, the mission of most prisons is to provide a safe and secure environment for staff and inmates, and programs for offenders that can assist them after release.[8] This section describes how prisons are organized to accomplish this mission. First, we look at the larger picture—the typical organization of the central office within the state government that oversees *all* prisons within its jurisdiction, and then we look at the characteristic organization of an individual prison.

## *Statewide Central Offices*

The state's central organization that oversees its prison system is often called the **central office.** Some of the personnel and functions that are typically found in a central office are discussed in the following sections.

### *Office of the Director*
In addition to the director, the staff within the office of the director includes public or media affairs coordinations, legislative liaisons, legal advisers, and internal affairs representatives. As one of the largest state agencies, a tremendous demand for public information is made on correctional agencies. If a policy issue or a major incident is involved, the media will contact the director for a response. The office of public affairs also oversees the preparation of standards reports, such as an annual review of the department and its status, or information regarding a high-profile program or project. Also, because state correctional agencies use a large percentage of the state budget, the legislature is always interested in its operations. Therefore, there is usually an office of legislative affairs, which responds to legislative requests and tries to build support for resources and programs.[9]

Legal divisions, typically composed of four to six attorneys, often report to the director as well. The work of the legal division includes responding to inmate lawsuits, reviewing policy for its legal impact, and offering general advice regarding the implementation of programs in terms of past legal decisions. These attorneys will predict how the courts are likely to respond to a new program in light of legal precedents.

Finally, the director's office usually has an inspector or internal affairs division. Ethics in government is a major priority; corrections staff may be enticed to bring contraband into a prison or may be physically abusive to inmates. Whenever there is a complaint of staff misconduct by anyone, the allegation needs to be investigated.

### Administration Division

Two major areas of the administrative division of a corrections central office are budget development/auditing and new prison construction. The administration division collects information from all of the state's prisons, other divisions, and the governor's office to create a budget that represents ongoing operations and desired programs and growth. Once approved by the governor's office, this division begins to explain the budget to the legislative budget committee, which reviews the request and makes a recommendation for funding to the full legislative body. After a budget is approved, this division maintains accountability of funds and oversees design and construction of new and renovated facilities.[10]

### Correctional Programs Division

A central office will usually have a division that oversees the operation of correctional programs, such as security, education, religious services, mental health, and unit management. It is clear that

> Offenders enter prison with a variety of deficits. Some are socially or morally inept; others are intellectually or vocationally handicapped; some have emotional hangups that stem from . . . psychological problems; still others have a mixture of varying proportions of some or even all of these.[11]

Having to deal with inmates suffering from such serious and varied problems is a daunting task for correctional organizations. Prison culture makes the environment inhospitable to programs designed to rehabilitate or reform.

A major contemporary problem among persons entering prison is drug addiction. Drug-addicted offenders are currently subjected to one of three types of treatment programming which attempts to address the problem: punitive (largely involving withdrawal and punishment), medical (consisting of detoxification, rebuilding physical health, counseling, and social services), or the communal approach (using group encounters and seminars conducted by former addicts who serve as positive role models).[12] Chapter 12 discusses what prison administrators are doing to interdict drugs coming into prisons, and the kinds of treatment programs that are maintained in them.

### Medical or Health Care Division

One of the most complicated and expensive functions within a prison is health care. As a result, this division develops policy, performs quality assurance, and looks for ways to make health care more efficient for inmates and less expensive for the prison. It should be noted that one of the best outcomes for a corrections health care program involved HIV/AIDS. A widespread epidemic of HIV/AIDS cases was initially feared in prisons (through homosexual acts and prior drug use), but such an outbreak never happened: Today, the overall rate of confirmed AIDS among the nation's prison population is 0.6 percent, and has been growing at a much slower rate than that of the overall prison population.[13]

### Human Resource Management Division

The usual personnel functions of recruitment, hiring, training, evaluations, and retirement are accomplished in the human resource management division. Affirmative action and labor relations (discussed in Chapter 15) may also be included. Workplace diversity is important for corrections agencies, particularly with the growing number of African American and Hispanic inmates (4,848 black male inmates per 100,000 black males in the United States and 1,668 Hispanic male inmates per 100,000 Hispanic males, as compared with 705 white inmates per 100,000 white males).[14] Most states have a unionized workforce, and negotiating and managing labor issues are time consuming. Therefore, this division has staff with expertise in labor relations.

Figure 9.2 shows the organizational structure of a central office in a state of 3 million people.

## Prison Organization and Administration

Over time, prison organizational structures (Figure 9.3) have changed considerably in order to respond to external needs. Until the beginning of the twentieth century, prisons were administered by state boards of charities, boards composed of citizens, boards of inspectors, state prison commissions, or individual prison keepers. Most prisons were individual provinces; **wardens,** who were given absolute control over their domain, were appointed by governors through a system of political patronage. Individuals were attracted to the position of warden because it carried many fringe benefits, such as a lavish residence, unlimited inmate servants, food and supplies from institutional farms and warehouses, furnishings, and a personal automobile. Now most wardens or superintendents are civil service employees who have earned their position through seniority and merit.[15]

Attached to the warden's office are (possibly by some other title) an institutional services inspector and the institutional investigator who deal with inmate complaints against staff. As mentioned in the earlier section about the central office, prisons also need personnel who deal with labor contracts and the media and who will collect and provide this information to the central office. A computer services manager maintains the management information systems.

Also reporting to the warden are deputy or associate wardens, each of whom supervises a department within the prison. The deputy warden for operations will normally oversee correctional security, unit management, the inmate disciplinary committee, and recreation. The deputy warden for special services will typically be responsible for the library, mental health services, drug and

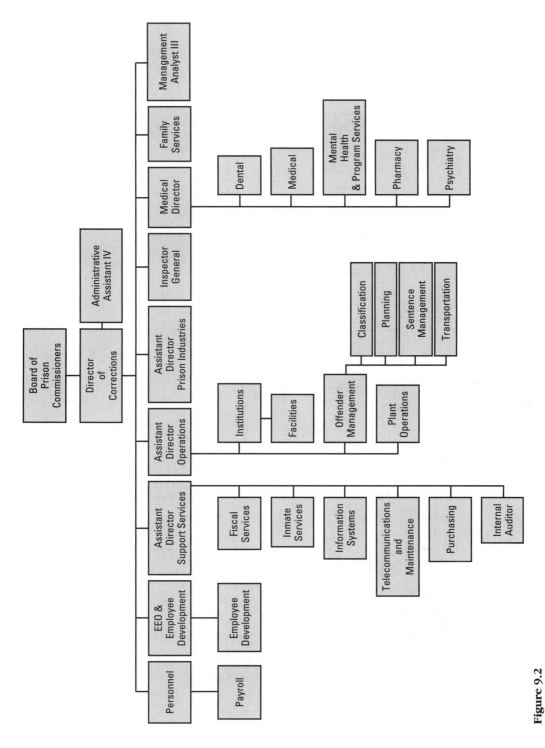

**Figure 9.2**

Organizational structure for a correctional central office.

**Figure 9.3**

Organizational structure for a maximum security prison.

*Correctional Emergency Response Team

alcohol recovery services, education, prison job assignments, religious services, and prison industries. The deputy warden for administration will manage the business office, prison maintenance, laundry, food service, medical services, prison farms, and the issuance of clothing.[16]

Correctional security, unit management, education, and penal industries are now discussed in greater detail:

- The *correctional security department* is normally the largest department in a prison, with 50 to 70 percent of all staff. It supervises all of the security activities within a prison, including any special housing units, inmate transportation, and the inmate disciplinary process. Security staff wear military-style uniforms; a captain normally runs each eight-hour shift, while lieutenants often are responsible for an area of the prison and sergeants oversee the rank-and-file correctional staff.

- The *unit management* concept was originated by the federal prison system in the 1970s and now is used in nearly every state to control prisons by providing a "small, self-contained, inmate living and staff office area that operates semi-autonomously within the larger institution."[17] The purpose of unit management is twofold: to decentralize the administration of the prison and to enhance communication among staff and between staff and inmates. Unit management breaks the prison into more manageable sections based on housing assignments; assignment of staff to a particular unit; and staff authority to make decisions, manage the unit, and deal directly with inmates. Units are usually composed of 200 to 300 inmates; staff are not only assigned to units, but their offices are also located in the housing area, making them more accessible to inmates and better able to monitor inmate activities and behavior. Directly reporting to the unit manager are "case managers," or social workers, who develop the program of work and rehabilitation for each inmate and write progress reports for parole authorities, classification, or transfer to another prison. Correctional counselors also work with inmates in the units on daily issues, such as finding a prison job, working with their prison finances, and creating a visiting and telephone list.[18]

- *Education departments* operate the academic teaching, vocational training, library services, and sometimes recreation programs for inmates. An education department is managed in similar fashion to a conventional elementary or high school, with certified teachers for all subjects that are required by the state department of education or are part of the General Education Degree (GED) test. Vocational training can include carpentry, landscaping or horticulture, food service, and office skills.

- *Penal industries* are legislatively chartered as separate government corporations and report directly to the warden, because there is often a requirement that the industry be self-supporting or operate from funds generated from the sale of products. Generally, no tax dollars are used to run the programs, so there is strict accountability of funds. A typical prison industry organizational structure is presented in Figure 9.4. Correctional administrators

**Figure 9.4**

Organizational structure for a prison industry. *Source: Correctional Administration: Integrating Theory and Practice* © 2002. Reprinted by permission of Pearson Education, Inc., Upper Saddle River, NJ.

report that joint ventures provide meaningful, productive employment that helps reduce inmate idleness and supplies companies with a readily available and dependable source of labor, as well as the partial return to society of inmate earnings to pay state and federal taxes, offset incarceration costs, contribute to the support of inmates' families, and compensate victims. Different types of business relationships have been developed. In the **personnel model,** prisoners are employed by the state division of correctional industries, which in turn charges the companies a fixed rate for their labor. In the **employer model,** the company employs the inmates, and private companies own and operate their prison-based businesses, with prison officials providing the space in which the companies operate as well as a qualified labor pool from which the companies hire employees. In the **customer model,** the company contracts with the prison to provide a finished product at an agreed-upon price. The correctional institution owns and operates the business that employs the inmates. To be sure, these joint ventures provide challenges and problems: absenteeism and rapid turnover of employees, limited opportunities for training, and logistical concerns. Still, many inmates participate in these programs, show up for their jobs on time, work hard during their shifts, and have been hired by companies after their release.[19]

## The Increase in Prison Populations

### *Rehabilitative Versus Lock-'Em-Up Philosophies and Truth in Sentencing Laws*

Several factors affect prison and jail populations, which now total about 2 million men and women.[20] First is the nation's drug problem. Data show that the number of persons admitted to state prisons for drug offenses has for several years exceeded the number entering for violent or property crimes. Other commonly cited factors include truth in sentencing laws, violence on television and in the movies, and a general deterioration of morals and of the family. In sum, the nation has become more punitive in nature.

Truth in sentencing for prison inmates began in 1984 in Washington State. The concept, which involves restriction or elimination of parole eligibility and good-time credits, quickly spread to other states after a determination in 1996 that prisoners were serving on average about 44 percent of their court sentence. To assure that offenders serve larger portions of their sentence, Congress authorized funding for additional state prisons and jails if states met eligibility criteria for truth in sentencing programs.[21] To qualify, states must require violent offenders to serve at least 85 percent of their prison sentence. By 1998, 27 states and the District of Columbia qualified; 14 states have abolished early parole board release for all offenders.[22]

A philosophical shift about the purpose of incarceration also contributed to prison crowding. In response to the apparent failure of **rehabilitation** policies, the now-prevailing philosophy sees prisons as places to incarcerate and punish inmates in an effort to deter crime. This philosophy has resulted in get-tough sentencing practices (including mandatory sentencing laws), which contribute to rising prison populations. Legislators have essentially removed the word *rehabilitation* from the penal code while focusing on fixed sentences. This shift from rehabilitating inmates to "just deserts" is based on the fact that offenders make "free will" decisions to commit crimes and, therefore, no longer deserve compassion and "correction." U.S. citizens, however, may be leaning more toward rehabilitative efforts. One survey found that about 48 percent of all Americans believed that it is more important to try to rehabilitate people who are in prison than merely to punish them (14.6 percent).[23]

Robert Martinson's well-publicized finding that "almost nothing works" in correctional treatment programs served to "ignite a firestorm of debate that has lasted" nearly two decades.[24] Although Martinson's methodology was brought into serious question and he later attempted to recant his findings, his assessment clearly had a major impact. Legislators and corrections administrators became unwilling to fund treatment programs from dwindling budgets, while academics and policymakers claimed that the medical model of correctional treatment programs failed to accomplish its goals. Paul Louis and Jerry Sparger noted that "perhaps the most lasting effect of the 'nothing works' philosophy is the spread of cynicism and hopelessness" among prison administrators and staff members.[25]

An even greater widening between rehabilitation and just deserts occurred in the 1980s. Ted Palmer[26] identified these modified positions as the "skeptical" and "sanguine" camps. The skeptics believed that relatively few prison programs work and that successful ones account for only negligible reductions in recidivism. Furthermore, they believed that rehabilitation programs had not been given an adequate chance in correctional settings because they were either poorly designed or badly implemented. The sanguine perspective is that although the existing rehabilitation programs have not been very effective to date, evidence indicates that many programs provide positive treatment for selected portions of the offender population. An assessment of Martinson's "nothing works" statement by Palmer and others has given new hope for rehabilitation. Palmer rejected Martinson's indictment of correctional treatment modalities and demonstrated that many of the programs initially reviewed by Martinson were actually quite successful.[27] Other research has supported Palmer's position.[28] Still, the rehabilitative philosophy is not expected to see a resurgence in the foreseeable future.

Some observers, however, also believe that the just deserts logic is defeated by a combination of demography and justice system inefficiency. Each year, a new crop of youths in their upper teens constitutes the majority of those arrested for serious crimes. As these offenders are arrested and removed from the crime scene, a new crop replaces them: "The justice system is eating its young. It imprisons them, paroles them, and re-arrests them with no rehabilitation in between," according to Dale Secrest.[29]

Still, large-scale, long-term imprisonment unquestionably keeps truly serious offenders behind bars, preventing them from committing more crimes.

# Inmate Litigation

## *Rights of Inmates*

Incarceration in prisons and jails entails stringent restrictions on freedom of movement and the loss of numerous privileges; however, inmates enjoy several important constitutional rights. The legal standing of prison inmates has changed tremendously since 1871 when the Virginia Supreme Court told Woody Ruffin, a convicted murderer, that he was a "slave of the state" with no rights that need be recognized.[30]

The demise of the **hands-off doctrine,** by which courts deferred to the expertise of correctional administrators in the operation of their institutions, began in the mid-1960s; in *Cooper v. Pate,*[31] the U.S. Supreme Court held that state inmates could bring lawsuits against prison authorities under Title 42, Section 1983 of the Civil Rights Act. This decision began a new era for inmates and represented the beginning of what has been an explosion in inmate litigation. During the 1971-1972 Supreme Court term, following the deadly prison riot at Attica, New York, additional court decisions expanded prisoners' rights and remedies. One of the major decisions was *Wolff v. McDonnell* (1974),[32] in which the U.S. Supreme Court stated that "there is no Iron Curtain drawn between the Constitution and the prisons of this country." Previous to *Wolff,* inmates had no universally recognized due process rights during disciplinary hearings; the widespread discretion given to correctional administrators was open to potential abuse. In *Wolff,* the Court gave inmates facing severe disciplinary action certain due process protections, including advance written notice of the charges, the right to a fair and impartial hearing, the right to present evidence and call witnesses in their behalf, the use of counsel, and a written statement of the decision reached, and reasons for it.

## *A Resurgence of the Hands-Off Doctrine?*

The turning point in this expansion of inmates' rights was the case of *Bell v. Wolfish*[33] in 1979, which considered, among other issues, double-bunking in the Metropolitan Correctional Center in New York City. The Court seemed to revert to the original hands-off doctrine, declaring in a 6–3 decision that jail management should be left to corrections personnel. In other words, the Court said that deference should be extended to persons with expertise in correctional matters, and administrative decisions should not be invalidated by the Court unless extreme circumstances required it.

## *Trends in Litigation*

In recent years, the attention and focus of the media and legislators have been on conditions *within* prisons. The current rhetoric advocates restoring fear to prisons, caning, making prisoners "smell like a prisoner," and returning executions to the county seat.[34] While some people might see federal and state court intervention as an erosion of the power of prison wardens, others believe that any progress inmates have made in the past quarter century in improved living conditions has been due, at least in part, to litigation.[35] Courts continue to be involved in reforming correctional institutions.

The volume of inmate litigation increased significantly following the *Cooper v. Pate* decision in 1964. In 1966, 218 petitions were filed, and the number increased to 16,741 in 1981.[36] In 1980, inmates in state and federal correctional institutions filed 23,287 petitions alleging both civil and criminal violations and seeking compensatory damages, injunctions, and property claims.[37] By 1990, the number of such petitions had swollen to nearly 43,000, and more than 64,000 petitions were filed in 1996.[38]

Prisoners sue primarily because they are either unwilling to accept their conviction or they wish to harrass their keepers.[39] Prisoner litigants fall into two categories. First are those who file a single suit during their entire period of incarceration (usually requiring the assistance of others to do it); one study found that 71 percent of all litigants filed only one action but accounted for about half of all litigation.[40] The other group is composed of inmates who make law a prison career—the so-called "jailhouse lawyers."[41]

There is an irony connected to this litigation explosion. Until the 1970s, conditions in many prisons were almost insufferable for both staff members and inmates; the former often had to battle the same vermin and insects and eat the same food (some of which was poisoned with lead peeling from the kitchen walls), and for at least eight hours per day, generally had to endure the same conditions as the inmates. The irony here, of course, was that many administrators and staff had to hope to be sued by inmates for violating their Eighth Amendment rights and to lose before working conditions could improve.

## *The Due Deference Doctrine*

As noted earlier, the Supreme Court's decision in *Bell v. Wolfish* (1976), the "cornerstone of the future edifice of correctional law,"[42] represented to many a reinstatement of the hands-off doctrine. From that point to the present, *federal* courts have generally deferred to the expertise of prison administrators in cases involving day-to-day operations (court activism concerning overcrowding notwithstanding). From 1979 to 1986, federal courts initiated a pattern of deciding cases with greater deference to correctional officials; cases decided from 1987 to 1994 made it even more difficult for prisoners to prevail in Section 1983 litigation.[43]

This was the emergence of the **due deference doctrine,** which refers to the courts' policy not to interfere in matters pertaining to prison administration. This doctrine has not been developed sufficiently, however, to determine for the courts when they should or should not intervene. Frequently, the result has been, as in *Bell,* that courts accept jurisdiction over prisoners' claims but fail to provide remedies to them.[44]

The media brought to light many past abuses inside prisons, but media attention may now be turning in another direction; media reports of trivial lawsuits filed by inmates (such as an inmate's suit for being sold a jar of creamy peanut butter when he had ordered chunky style, and a cruel and unusual punishment claim by an inmate when a guard refused to refrigerate his ice cream) have become commonplace. The expenses to defend against such lawsuits, coupled with the fact that the United States has the world's largest and costliest prison system[45] combine to foster public resentment against prisons and prisoners.

The judiciary, too, may be growing weary of inmate complaints and court intervention in corrections. As indicated earlier, more control over prisons has gradually been given back to the states, and the courts are displaying more tolerance for minor violations of prisoners' constitutional rights. Such a shift was exemplified in *Turner v. Safley,*[46] In which the U.S. Supreme Court stated that "when a prison regulation impinges on inmates' constitutional rights, the regulation is valid if it is reasonably related to legitimate penological interests." Some authors have characterized *Turner* as another reformulation of the hands-off doctrine. This decision was strengthened with a later one, *Wilson v. Seiter,*[47] which said that when an inmate claims that the conditions of his or her confinement violate the Eighth Amendment, he or she must show a culpable state of mind on the part of prison officials. Finally, a more recent case emphasized the Supreme Court's desire to give "deference and flexibility to state officials trying to maintain a volatile environment."[48] This decision made it "more difficult to bring constitutional suits challenging prison management."[49]

Taken together, then, recent U.S. Supreme Court decisions have stated clearly that the *federal* doors to prison litigation have all but closed. Under due deference, the federal courts appear to distinguish substantive prisoner rights claims from frivolous complaints against prison administrators.[50] This "judicial retreat" or gradual return to the *Bell* decision troubles some observers, however, as it may reverse what has been termed "the most important development in the prisoner's environment,"[51] which substitutes the rule of law and rational/legal decision making for arbitrary prison administration decision making.[52]

# Jails as Organizations

Across the United States, approximately 3,316 jails are locally administered.[53] Their organization and hierarchical levels are determined by several factors: size, budget, level of crowding, local views toward punishment and treatment, and even the levels of training and education of the jail administrator. An organizational structure for a jail serving a population of about 250,000 is suggested in Figure 9.5.

The administration of jails is frequently one of the major tasks of county sheriffs. Several writers have concluded that sheriff and police personnel primarily see themselves as law enforcers first and view the responsibility of organizing and operating the jail as an unwelcome task.[54] Therefore, their approach is often said to be at odds with advanced corrections philosophy and trends.

## *The "New Generation" Jail*

As noted previously, in the past the federal courts have at times abandoned their traditional hands-off philosophy toward prison and jail administration, largely in response to the deplorable conditions and inappropriate treatment of inmates. The courts became more willing to hear inmate allegations of constitutional violations ranging from inadequate heating, lighting, and ventilation to the censorship of mail. One of every five cases filed in federal courts was on behalf of prisoners[55] and 20 percent of all jails were a party in a pending lawsuit.[56]

In response to this deluge of lawsuits and in order to improve conditions, many local jurisdictions constructed new jail facilities. The court-ordered pressures to improve jail conditions afforded an opportunity for administrators to explore new ideas and designs. The term **new generation jail** was coined to characterize a style of architecture and inmate management totally new and unique to local detention facilities, and it represented a new era in correctional thought.[57] The concept was endorsed by the American Correctional Association and the Advisory Board of the National Institute of Corrections. W. Walter Menninger, director of law and psychiatry at the Menninger Foundation in Topeka, Kansas, observed that

> Careful studies of these new generation facilities have found significant benefits for inmates, staff and society at large. There are fewer untoward incidents and assaults, [a] greater level of personal safety for both staff and inmates, greater staff

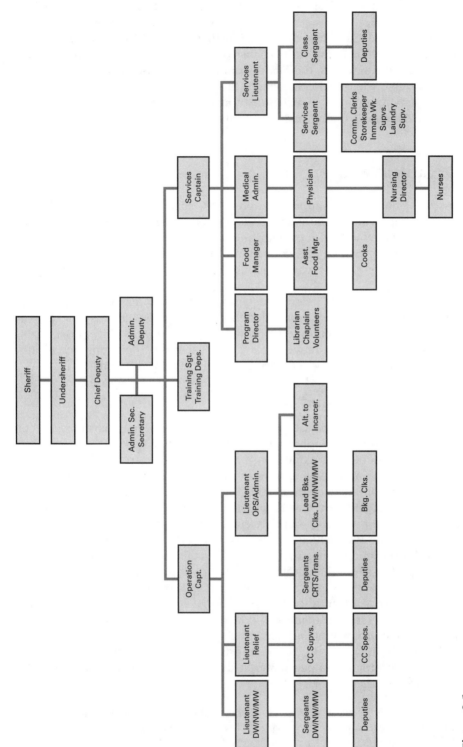

**Figure 9.5**

Organizational structure for a jail serving a county of 250,000 population.
(DW = day watch; NW = night watch; MW = mid-watch;
CC = conservation camps)

satisfaction, more orderly and relaxed inmate housing areas, [and] a better maintained physical plant. Finally, these facilities are cost effective to construct and to operate.[58]

According to corrections specialist Matt Leone, there are several reasons for the fact that new generation jails are not expanding in number, however. First, new jails are not typically built until old jails either wear out or become too small. Second, there is often a public perception that such facilities are "soft on crime." Finally, these facilities simply do not have the *appearance* of being a jail.[59] To the extent possible, symbols of incarceration were to be removed in these new jails, which were to have no bars in the living units; windows were to be provided in every prisoner's room; and padded carpets, movable furniture, and colorful wall coverings were to be used to reduce the facility's institutional atmosphere. Inmates were to be divided into small groups of approximately 40 to 50 for housing purposes. Officers were to interact with inmates rather than remain inside an office or behind a desk. The interior features of the facility were designed to reduce the "trauma" of incarceration.[60]

The most important features of many of these facilities were one cell per inmate; direct staff supervision; and "functional inmate living units," which were to locate all "sleeping, food, and hygiene facilities . . . in one self-contained, multi-level space."[61] A corrections officer was to be assigned to each unit to ensure direct and continuous supervision.

The first facility of the new generation style opened in the 1970s in Contra Costa County, California. This facility quickly became a success and was deemed cost effective to build and safer for inmates and staff.

## *Making Jails Productive*

The 1984 Justice Assistance Act removed some of the long-standing restrictions on interstate commerce of prisoner-made goods. By 1987, private sector work programs were under way in 14 state correctional institutions and two county jails.[62] Today, many inmates in U.S. jails are involved in productive work. Some simply work to earn privileges, and others earn wages applied to their custodial costs and compensation to crime victims. Some hone new job skills, improving their chances for success following release. At one end of the continuum is the trusty (an inmate requiring a low security level) who mows the grass in front of the jail and thereby earns privileges; at the other end would be those jail inmates working for private industry for real dollars.[63]

Some jails have undertaken training programs for their inmates, following the recommendations of the American Jail Association. For example, one state-of-the-art facility in the West trains inmates to operate a plastic-sign engraving machine and has plans to teach dog grooming at the local animal control center. The engraving equipment, as well as the facility's 24 computers for inmate use, cost taxpayers nothing; they were purchased through commissary funds (monies acquired from sales of canned goods, cigarettes, coffee, and other such items). This jail's inmates can also earn a GED, and the facility is considering programs in auto detailing, food service, book mending, mailing service, painting, printing, carpet installation, and upholstering.

# Research in Correctional Institutions

Many writers have painted a horrible picture of prisons, describing them as devoid of even the most basic elements of humanity,[64] and as detrimental to the humanity of the offender;[65] they generally issue a scathing indictment of prisons.[66]

The following research findings should help to determine the correctness of this assessment. Note that many of the research studies were conducted one or two decades ago. They are presented briefly, however, because they are important to the field of corrections administration and are not often discussed in the literature.

## *Prison and Jail Crowding*

Many correctional administrators see crowding as *the* major barrier to humane housing of offenders. Researchers see crowding as a complex phenomenon, with most agreeing that it can foster a psychological response to high population density, which is stress.[67] The inmates' age can play an important role: The relationship between misconduct and population density was more pronounced in institutions housing young offenders.[68] There are also indications that prison variables other than overcrowding may influence aggressive behavior; for example, crowded prisons may be poorly managed.[69] In summary, crowded prisons and jails may cause physiological and psychological stress among many inmates, although disruptive behavior depends on other factors such as age, institutional parameters (sudden shifts in the inmate membership), and the chronicity of the situation.[70] (We discuss possible administrative approaches to crowding in Chapter 10.)

## *Spatial and Social Densities*

The average number of square feet per inmate in a jail is referred to as **spatial density;** the average number of inmates per living unit is the **social density.** Organizing and managing jails becomes more difficult when a larger number of inmates are living in high-density situations. Maintaining high population densities can affect routine activities such as food service, visitation, recreation, medical care and sick call, inmate property management, and inmate movements to and from court or consultations with attorneys. A high spatial density facility is identified as one in which more than 40 percent of the inmates have less than 60 square feet per person in housing in which they are confined for 10 hours or more.[71] The standard for the highest social density residence category is an average of five persons per housing unit. Higher population densities are more common in jails holding 500 to 999 inmates;[72] inmate suicide rates are higher in small jails and highest in small jails with lower population densities (owing to the lower supervision levels of inmate by staff).[73]

## *Health Risks from Incarceration*

A number of studies have attempted to determine whether incarceration threatens the health of the confined; most have failed to find negative effects on inmate health as a result of incarceration.[74] In fact, two studies have found a significantly *lower* incidence of hypertension among inmates than in the general population.[75] Indeed, the evidence indicates that many prisons may actually be conducive to *good* health, because most prisons offer regular and nutritious diets, access to recreational exercise, opportunity to sleep, and available medical care.[76] In the United States, deaths due to homicide are actually less likely inside than outside prisons.[77]

## *Effects of Long-Term Incarceration*

What happens to people serving life terms in prison? Cognitive tests have been administered to long- and short-term inmates; the results indicated no differences in intellectual performance, but long-term inmates showed increased hostility and social introversion.[78] Other studies have found no evidence of psychological deterioration; in fact, these studies reported an improvement in intelligence over time and a decrease in hostility.[79] Timothy Flanagan found that the misconduct rate among long-term inmates was approximately half that of the short-term offenders.[80] Additional studies assessing lifers found no deterioration in health or intellect or any psychiatric symptoms.[81] Long-termers have reported that the earlier portion of their sentences was more stressful and that with time they had learned to cope effectively.[82] In summary, the evidence indicates little support for the notion that long-term imprisonment has detrimental effects on inmates' health.

## *Effects of Solitary Confinement*

Solitary confinement, also referred to as **punitive segregation,** has been described as "the most individually destructive, psychologically crippling, and socially alienating experience that could conceivably exist within the borders of [Canada]."[83] Is this scathing denouncement an accurate depiction? Studies using volunteers have found few detrimental effects for subjects placed in solitary confinement for periods of up to 10 days. Perceptual and motor abilities were not impaired, physiological levels of stress were lower than for control groups, and various attitudes toward the experience and the self did not worsen.[84] Studies using prison inmates have also found no detrimental effects. In general, inmates found the first 72 hours to be the most difficult but after that they adjusted quite well. Researchers found "no support for the claim that solitary confinement . . . is overwhelmingly aversive, stressful, or damaging to the inmates."[85]

## *Effects of Death Row*

Very little research concerning inmates' adjustment to death row is available. One study of 34 death row inmates, however, showed increased feelings of depression and hopelessness; severe disturbances (psychosis) were not observed.[86] Robert Johnson interviewed 35 men on death row and found them concerned about their powerlessness, fearful of surroundings, and feeling emotionally drained.[87] Other interviews found that most inmates exhibited well-intact defenses regarding their alleged guilt[88] and that *all* slept well and felt relatively good about themselves.[89]

# CASE STUDIES

The following two case studies will help the reader apply some of this chapter's materials to real-world issues of corrections organization and operations.

## As Bad as It Can Get

You are the deputy warden for operations in a comparatively small (500 inmates) maximum-security prison for adults. As is typical, you oversee correctional security, unit management, the inmate disciplinary committee, and recreation. One Wednesday at about 2:00 A.M., an inmate who is a minority group member with a history of mental health problems and violent behavior begins destroying his cell and injures himself by ramming into the walls. The supervisor in charge collects a group of four correctional officers, with the intention of removing the inmate from his cell and isolating, medicating, and checking him for injuries. The group of four—all fairly new on the job, untrained in cell extraction or self-defense, and without any specialized extraction equipment—prepares to enter the cell. When the officers open the cell door, the inmate charges at them, knocking down two of the officers. They finally wrestle the inmate to the floor, although he is still struggling. One officer attempts to subdue him by wrapping his arm around the inmate's neck, pressing on his carotid artery. Finally the inmate quiets down and is restrained and removed to another, larger cell. After 15 minutes, however, the inmate has failed to regain consciousness. A medical staff person rushes to the cell, sees the inmate in an unconscious state, and then has him taken to a local hospital. After the inmate has remained in a comatose condition for two months and has been classified as brain dead, the family opts to remove the life-support system that has sustained him.

### Questions for Discussion

1. What, if any, inmate rights are involved in this case?
2. Which, if any, of the inmate's rights were violated?
3. To what extent does the prison system's Central Office become involved? What kinds of policies need to be developed to cover any similar occurrences in the future?
4. As deputy warden, what disciplinary action would you consider against the officers? Was there intent present?
5. What policy needs and problems exist with regard to new policies? Facilities for mentally ill inmates? Officer training? Equipment?
6. Assume that about one month prior to this incident, a minority woman was fired from a high-profile position by the warden for incompetence, and thus

this incident adds more fuel to the flames. What would be your or the warden's responses to claims by minority groups that your institution has obviously been shown to be racist?

# When Politics Trumps Policy

For two years, you have been director of a prison system for adults in a medium-sized state. As a result of revenue shortfalls for several years, it has been a constant struggle to keep a full labor force in your state's 10 prisons and to lure professional staff members to work and live in the more rural areas where they are located. During the past six months, however, you have managed to assemble a fine staff of wardens and other subordinates in the prisons and have implemented a number of policies that provide for educational, vocational, and treatment opportunities—which have been gaining national attention for their effectiveness. Recidivism has been reduced to 30 percent, and your policies are beginning to be accepted by staff and citizens alike. Running a "Take Back the Streets" anticrime campaign, a politically inexperienced person (formerly a popular college quarterback at a state university) was recently elected governor. The new governor has just sent you a letter stating in effect that your institution is not the "Ritz" and demanding that all "frivolous, mamby-pamby programs like the ABCs and where cons learn how to hammer nails" be ceased immediately. He asks for your written response, a plan for tightening security, and the implementation of tougher inmate programs within one month.

## Questions for Discussion

1. How would you respond? Would you just capitulate and rescind some or all of these programs? Explain your answer.
2. Is there any room to negotiate with the governor? As a tradeoff, would you offer to put in place some programs that are known to be tough on inmates? If so, what kind?
3. Before dismantling your policies and programs, would you attempt to see how much internal and external support you have for them? If yes, whom would you contact, and how?
4. How might you go about demonstrating how successful your policies have been?

# Summary

This chapter presented an overview of corrections as a "boom" industry; correctional, prison, and jail organization and administration; inmate rights and litigation; and research findings concerning the effects of incarceration. The chapter also demonstrated how the times have changed with respect to the manner in which corrections is organized and administered and provided a glimpse into some of the kinds of issues and problems that challenge administrators, all of which are furthered examined in later chapters.

## Questions for Review

1. What is the typical organization of a "central office" that oversees the state's prison system? An individual prison?
2. What are some of the major administrative positions within a prison?
3. What factors contribute to an increase in the prison population in the United States?
4. What is a new generation jail, and how might it help reduce the effects of overcrowding and increase the quality of life in institutions?
5. What constitutional rights do inmates possess? What is the current doctrine concerning court oversight of prison administration?
6. What are some advantages for correctional administrators—and inmates— for having prison industry? What are the three models of such industries that now exist?
7. In what major ways do jails differ from prisons in their organization and administration?
8. What are some major findings in corrections research regarding prison life for inmates, and some implications for correctional administrators?

## Notes

1. U.S. Department of Justice, Bureau of Justice Statistics Web page, "Corrections Statistics," http://www.ojp.usdoj.gov/bjs/glance/corr2.htm (accessed June 24, 2002).
2. U.S. Department of Justice, Bureau of Justice Statistics Web page, "The number of adults in the correctional population has been increasing," http://www.ojp.usdoj.gov/bjs/correct.htm (accessed June 24, 2002).
3. U.S. Department of Justice, Bureau of Justice Statistics Web page, "Key Facts at a Glance: Correctional Populations," http://www.ojp.usdoj.gov/bjs/corr2tab.htm (accessed June 24, 2002).
4. U.S. Department of Justice, Bureau of Justice Statistics Web page, "Capital Punishment Statistics," http://www.ojp.usdoj.gov/bjs/cp.htm (accessed June 24, 2002).
5. U.S. Department of Justice, Bureau of Justice Statistics, *Justice Expenditure and Employment in the United States, 1999* (Washington, D.C.: February 2002), p. 6.
6. U.S. Department of Justice, Bureau of Justice Statistics Web page: http://www.ojp.usdoj.gov/bjs/glance/tables/exptyptab.htm (accessed June 24, 2002).
7. Richard P. Seiter, *Correctional Administration: Integrating Theory and Practice* (Upper Saddle River, N.J.: Prentice Hall, 2002), p. 11.

8. Ibid., p. 192.

9. Ibid., p. 189.

10. Ibid., pp. 190–191.

11. Robert Levinson, "Try Softer," in Robert Johnson and Hans Toch (eds.), *The Pains of Imprisonment* (Beverly Hills, Calif.: Sage Publications, 1982), p. 246.

12. T. Paul Louis and Jerry R. Sparger, "Treatment Modalities within Prison," in John W. Murphy and Jack E. Dison (eds.), *Are Prisons Any Better? Twenty Years of Correctional Reform* (Newbury Park, Calif.: Sage, 1990), pp. 147–162.

13. U.S. Department of Justice, Bureau of Justice Statistics Web page, "HIV in Prisons and Jails," http://www.ojp.usdoj.gov/bjs/abstract/hivpj99.htm (accessed June 24, 2002).

14. U.S. Department of Justice, Bureau of Justice Statistics Web page, "Prison Statistics," http://www.ojp.usdoj.gov/bjs/prisons.htm (accessed June 24, 2002).

15. James A. Inciardi, *Criminal Justice,* 7th ed. (Fort Worth, Tex.: Harcourt Brace, 2001), p. 454.

16. Ibid., p. 194

17. United States Bureau of Prisons, *Unit Management Manual* (Washington, D.C.: Author, 1977), p. 6.

18. Seiter, *Correctional Administration,* p. 196.

19. U.S. Department of Justice, National Institute of Justice, *Work in American Prisons: Joint Ventures with the Private Sector* (Washington, D.C.: USGPO, November 1995), pp. 2–3.

20. U.S. Department of Justice, Bureau of Justice Statistics Web page, http://www.ojp.usdoj.gov/bjs/correct.htm (accessed June 24, 2002).

21. See the Violent Offender Incarceration and Truth-in-Sentencing Incentive Grants program, Public Law 103–322, 108 Stat. 1796 (1994).

22. U.S. Department of Justice, Bureau of Justice Statistics Special Report, *Truth in Sentencing in State Prisons* (Washington, D.C.: Author, January 1999), pp. 1–3.

23. Kathleen Maguire and Ann L. Pastore, eds., *Sourcebook of Criminal Justice Statistics 1997* (U.S. Department of Justice, Bureau of Justice Statistics) (Washington, D.C.: U.S. Government Printing Office, 1998), p. 137.

24. Louis and Sparger, "Treatment Modalities Within Prison," p. 148.

25. Ibid., p. 149.

26. Ted Palmer, "The 'Effectiveness' Issue Today: An Overview," *Federal Probation* 42 (1983):3–10.

27. Ibid.

28. See D. A. Andrews, "Program Structure and Effective Correctional Practices: A Summary of the CAVIC Research," in Robert R. Ross and Paul Gendreau (eds.), *Effective Correctional Treatment* (Toronto, Ontario, Canada: Butterworth, 1980); R. Peters, *Deviant Behavioral Contracting with Conduct Problem Youth* (Kingston, Ontario, Canada: Queen's University, 1981).

29. Andrews, "Program Structure and Effective Correctional Practices," p. 42.

30. *Ruffin v. Commonwealth,* 62 Va. 790, 796 (1871).

31. 378 U.S. 546 (1964).

32. 418 U.S. 539 (1974).

33. 441 U.S. 520 (1979).

34. Adam Nossiter, "Making Hard Time Harder: States Cut Jail TV and Sports," *New York Times* (September 17, 1994): A1, A10.

35. Susan P. Sturn, "The Legacy and Future of Corrections Litigation," *University of Pennsylvania Law Review* 142 (2000):639–738. Also, for an excellent resource concerning

major cases in corrections, see Rolando V. del Carmen, Susan E. Ritter, and Betsy A. Witt, *Briefs of Leading Cases in Corrections,* 2d ed. (Cincinnati, Ohio: Anderson, 1998).

36. A. E. D. Howard, "The States and the Supreme Court," 31 *Catholic University Law Review* 375 (1982), 379.

37. Timothy J. Flanagan and Kathleen Maguire (eds.), *Sourcebook of Criminal Justice Statistics 1991* (U.S. Department of Justice, Bureau of Justice Statistics) (Washington, D.C.: U.S. Government Printing Office, 1992), p. 555.

38. Ibid. Also see Kathleen Maguire and Ann L. Pastore (eds.), *Sourcebook of Criminal Justice Statistics 1995.* (U.S. Department of Justice, Bureau of Justice Statistics) (Washington, D.C.: U.S. Government Printing Office, 1996), p. 177.

39. Jim Thomas, Kathy Harris, and Devin Keeler, "Issues and Misconceptions in Prisoner Litigation," *Criminology* 24 (1987):901–919.

40. Jim Thomas, "Repackaging the Data: The 'Reality' of Prisoner Litigation," *New England Journal of Criminal and Civil Confinement* 15 (1989):195–230.

41. Ibid., p. 50.

42. Charles H. Jones, "Recent Trends in Corrections and Prisoners' Rights Law," in Clayton A. Hartjen and Edward E. Rhine (eds.), *Correctional Theory and Practice* (Chicago: Nelson-Hall, 1992), pp. 119–138.

43. Darrell L. Ross, "Emerging Trends in Correctional Civil Liability Cases: A Content Analysis of Federal Court Decisions of Title 42 United States Code Section 1983," *Journal of Criminal Justice* 25 (1997):501–514.

44. Ibid., p. 120.

45. Francis X. Cline, "Prisons Run Out of Cells, Money and Choices," *New York Times* (May 28, 1993):B7.

46. 107 S. Ct. 2254 (1987), at 2254.

47. 111 S. Ct. 2321 (1991).

48. *Sandin v. Conner,* 115 S. Ct. 2321 (1995), at 2293.

49. Linda Greenhouse, "High Court Makes It Harder for Prisoners to Sue," *New York Times* (June 20, 1995):A11.

50. Jones, "Recent Trends in Corrections and Prisoners' Rights Law," pp. 121–122.

51. James Jacobs, *Stateville: The Penitentiary in Mass Society* (Chicago: University of Chicago Press, 1977).

52. Jones, "Recent Trends in Corrections and Prisoners' Rights Law," p. 122.

53. U.S. Department of Justice, Bureau of Justice Statistics Bulletin, *Prison and Jail Inmates at Midyear 1998* (Washington, D.C.: USGPO, 1999) pp. 1, 7.

54. For example, see James M. Moynahan and Earle K. Stewart, *The American Jail: Its Development and Growth* (Chicago: Nelson-Hall, 1980), p. 100; Clemens Bartollas, Stuart J. Miller, and Paul B. Wice, *Participants in American Criminal Justice: The Promise and the Performance* (Englewood Cliffs, N.J.: Prentice Hall, 1983), p. 59.

55. J. Moore, "Prison Litigation and the States: A Case Law Review," *State Legislative Report* 8 (1981):1.

56. National Sheriffs' Association, *The State of Our Nation's Jails, 1982* (Washington, D.C.: Author, 1982), p. 55.

57. Linda L. Zupan, *Jails: Reform and the New Generation Philosophy,* (Cincinnati, Ohio: Anderson, 1991), p. 71.

58. Quoted in William R. Nelson and M. O'Toole, *New Generation Jails* (Boulder, Colo.: Library Information Specialists, Inc., 1983), pp. 35–36.

59. Matt Leone, personal communication, March 16, 1997.

60. Zupan, *Jails Philosophy,* p. 67.

61. R. Wener and R. Olson, *User Based Assessments of the Federal Metropolitan Correctional Centers: Final Report* (Washington, D.C.: U.S. Bureau of Prisons, 1978), p. 4.

62. U.S. Department of Justice, National Institute of Justice Research in Brief, *Making Jails Productive* (Washington, D.C.: Author, 1987), p. 1.

63. *Ibid.,* p. 16.

64. Gresham Sykes, *The Society of Captives: A Study of a Maximum Security Prison* (Princeton, N.J.: Princeton University Press, 1958).

65. Milton G. Rector, "Prisons and Crime," *Crime and Delinquency* 28 (1982):505-507.

66. Jessica Mitford, *Kind and Unusual Punishment* (New York: Alfred A. Knopf, 1973).

67. Irwin Altman, "Crowding: Historical and Contemporary Trends in Crowding Research," in A. Baum and M. Y. M. Epstein (eds.), *Human Response to Crowding* (Hillsdale, N.J.: Lawrence Erlbaum, 1978), pp. 3-29.

68. James Bonta and Paul Gendreau, "Reexamining the Cruel and Unusual Punishment of Prison Life," *Law and Human Behavior* 14 (1990): 347-372.

69. See Gerald G. Gaes, "The Effects of Overcrowding in Prison," in Michael Tonry and Norval Morris (eds.), *Crime and Justice,* Vol. 6 (Chicago: University of Chicago Press, 1985), pp. 95-146.

70. Bonta and Gendreau, "Reexamining the Cruel and Unusual Punishment of Prison Life," p. 355.

71. U.S. Department of Justice, Bureau of Justice Statistics Special Report, *Population Density in Local Jails, 1988* (Washington, D.C.: USGPO, 1989), p. 4.

72. See *Manual of Standards for Adult Correctional Institutions* (College Park, Md.: American Correctional Association, August 1977), and *Federal Standards for Correction* (Washington, D.C.: U.S. Department of Justice, 1980).

73. U.S. Department of Justice, *Population Density in Local Jails: 1988,* pp. 2, 7.

74. See Seth B. Goldsmith, "Jailhouse Medicine: Travesty or Justice?" *Health Services Report* 87 (1972):767-774; R. A. Derro, "Administrative Health Evaluation of Inmates of a City-County Workhouse," *Minnesota Medicine* 61 (1978):333-337.

75. See L. Culpepper and J. Floom, "Incarceration and Blood Pressure," *Social Services and Medicine* 14 (1980):571-574; Lloyd F. Novick, Richard Della-Penna, Melvin S. Schwartz, Elaine Remlinger, and Regina Lowenstein, "Health Status of the New York City Prison Population," *Medical Care* 15 (1977):205-216.

76. Bonta and Gendreau, "Reexamining the Cruel and Unusual Punishment of Prison Life," p. 357.

77. R. Barry Ruback and Christopher A. Innes, "The Relevance and Irrelevance of Psychological Research: The Example of Prison Crowding," *American Psychologist* 43 (1988):683-693.

78. K. J. Heskin, F. V. Smith, P. A. Banister, and N. Bolton, "Psychological Correlates of Long-Term Imprisonment:II. Personality Variables," *British Journal of Criminology* 13 (1973): 323-330.

79. N. Bolton, F. V. Smith, K. J. Heskin, and P. A. Banister, "Psychological Correlates of Long-Term Imprisonment:IV. A Longitudinal Analysis," *British Journal of Criminology* 16 (1976): 36-47.

80. Timothy J. Flanagan, "Time Served and Institutional Misconduct: Patterns of Involvement in Disciplinary Infractions Among Long-Term and Short-Term Inmates," *Journal of Criminal Justice* 8 (1980):357-367.

81. W. Rasch, "The Effects of Indeterminate Sentencing: A Study of Men Sentenced to Life Imprisonment," *International Journal of Law and Psychiatry* 4 (1981):417-431.

82. Doris L. MacKenzie and Lynn Goodstein, "Long-Term Incarceration Impacts and Characteristics of Long-Term Offenders: An Empirical Analysis," *Criminal Justice and Behavior* 13 (1985):395–414.

83. M. Jackson, *Prisons of Isolation: Solitary Confinement in Canada* (Toronto, Ontario, Canada: University of Toronto Press, 1983), p. 243.

84. James Bonta and Paul Gendreau, "Reexamining the Cruel and Unusual Punishment of Prison Life," p. 360.

85. P. Suedfield, C. Ramirez, J. Deaton, and G. Baker-Brown, "Reactions and Attributes of Prisoners in Solitary Confinement," *Criminal Justice and Behavior* 9 (1982):303–340.

86. James H. Panton, "Personality Characteristics of Death Row Prison Inmates," *Journal of Clinical Psychology* 32 (1976):306–309.

87. Robert Johnson, "Life Under Sentence of Death," in Robert Johnson and Hans Toch (eds.), *The Pains of Imprisonment,* pp. 129–145.

88. Charles E. Smith and Richard Reid Felix, "Beyond Deterrence: A Study of Defenses on Death Row," *Federal Probation* 50 (1986):55–59.

89. Julius Debro, Komanduri Murty, Julian Roebuck, and Claude McCann, "Death Row Inmates: A Comparison of Georgia and Florida Profiles," *Criminal Justice Review* 12 (1987):41–46.

# Chapter 10

# Corrections Personnel Roles and Functions

## Key Terms and Concepts

Correctional officers (CO)

Hard liner

Loner

New old penology

People worker

Rule enforcer

Synthetic officer

## Learning Objectives

As a result of reading this chapter, the student will:

- know the duties of prison wardens
- be familiar with John J. DiIulio Jr.'s research and his six principles of good prison leadership
- have an understanding of the responsibilities of middle managers and supervisors
- know the duties of correctional officers
- be able to describe the five different types of correctional officers and the three residual types
- understand how jails are different from prisons
- be familiar with job satisfaction and dissatisfaction in correctional facilities
- be familiar with the benefits of having women employed in correctional facilities

*The mood and temper of the public in regard to the treatment of crime and criminals is one of the most unfailing tests of the civilization of any country.*

—Winston Churchill

# Introduction

This chapter focuses on personnel within correctional institutions. Presented first is a profile of prison wardens, recommendations for administering prisons, and an assessment of the diversification of correctional staff. After an overview of middle managers and supervisors, we examine in greater detail the front-line personnel in prisons: **correctional officers (COs).** This section includes a typology of the eight types of COs in terms of their overall orientation toward, and how they perform and view, their occupation. Then, we consider the "cousins" of prisons, the local jails: how jail personnel view their work by type of facility, employee job satisfaction and attrition, female detention personnel, and problems selecting people wanting detention as a career path. The chapter concludes with two case studies.

Two basic principles constitute the philosophy of prison and jail officers: First, whatever the reasons a person is incarcerated, he or she is not to suffer pains beyond the deprivation of liberty—confinement itself is the punishment. Second, regardless of the crime, the prisoner must be treated humanely and in accordance with his or her behavior; even the most heinous offender is to be treated with respect and dignity and given privileges if institutional behavior warrants it.[1] Our analysis of institutional management is predicated on these two principles.

# The Warden

## *Needed: A Balance of Power*

A state director of prisons once stated in the author's justice administration class that the job of prison warden is the most difficult in all of corrections;[2] this assessment is probably true, because the warden must take the director's general policies and put them into effect throughout the prison, while being responsible for the smooth day-to-day operation of the institution. These correctional executives also oversee the fastest growing agencies in state government; administer increasingly visible operations; and are held accountable by politicians, auditors, the press, organized labor, and numerous other stakeholders.[3] Wardens work within a field that has become more demanding, consumes an increasing share of public funds, and involves responsibility for the lives and safety of others.

Of course, both staff and inmates are sensitive to the warden's granting of what each side perceives to be a strengthened position for the other side. For example, if a policy is enacted that gives the staff more power over inmates, the inmates will be unhappy, perhaps even rebellious; conversely, if a policy is put into practice that the staff thinks affords too much additional freedom to inmates, the staff will feel sold out. Furthermore, the prison director, typically appointed by and serving at the pleasure of the state's governor, can impose on the warden all manner of political influences at any point in time.

## A Profile

A national survey by Timothy Flanagan, W. Wesley Johnson, and Katherine Bennett[4] of 641 prison wardens at adult state institutions provided the following demographic information: 86 percent were male, the mean age of respondents was 47 years, the majority (80 percent) were white, about half possessed a graduate degree or had some graduate work, and 54 percent had been correctional officers and had been in their current positions for an average of 5.7 years. Sixty-one percent of the respondents reported being "very satisfied" with their position and two-thirds stated that if free to go to any kind of job they wanted, they would keep their current one. More than three-fourths (76.2 percent) believed that if they had to decide all over again whether to take their present job, they would do so, and two-thirds (67.9 percent) said they would strongly recommend a warden's job to a friend. Taken together, the responses suggest that prison wardens are a highly satisfied occupational group.

Wardens who responded that the central office, inmates, and the media exerted more influence on prisons than they did themselves had lower job satisfaction scores. This finding was not surprising to Flanagan and colleagues, who observed that

> Correctional professionals are, in the final analysis, in the business of *control*. Because control (of inmates, of staff, and of the entire prison) is the *sine qua non* of the warden's job, it is perhaps not surprising that perceived loss of control and lower job satisfaction would be closely associated.[5]

## Administering Prisons

Throughout the nineteenth and the early part of the twentieth centuries, studies of prisons generally focused on the administrators rather than on the inmates. Beginning in the 1940s, however, an ideological shift from prison administration to the inmates occurred. The central reason for the shift seems to have been that these institutions were poorly managed or were what prison researcher John J. DiIulio Jr. referred to as "ineffective prisons."[6] Many writers expressed grave doubts about the efficacy of correctional administrators and expressed the idea that prison managers could do nothing to improve conditions behind bars.

It is not surprising that when contemporary researchers attempt to relate prison management practices to the quality of life behind bars, the results are normally quite negative: Prisons that are managed in a tight, authoritarian fashion are plagued with disorder and inadequate programs; those that are managed in a loose, participative fashion are equally troubled; and those with a mixture of these two styles are not any better.[7]

In a three-year study of prison management in Texas, Michigan, and California, however, DiIulio found that levels of disorder (rates of individual and collective violence, and other forms of misconduct), amenities (availability of clean cells, decent food, etc.), and service (availability of work opportunities and educational programs) did not vary with any of the following factors: a higher socioeconomic class of inmates, higher per capita spending, lower levels of crowding, lower inmate-to-staff ratios, greater officer training, more modern plant and equipment, and more routine use of repressive measures. DiIulio concluded that "all roads, it seemed, led to the conclusion that the quality of prison life depended mainly on the quality of prison management."[8]

DiIulio also found that prisons managed by a stable team of like-minded executives, structured in a paramilitary, security-driven, bureaucratic fashion had better order, amenities, and service than those managed in other ways, *even when* the former institutions were more crowded, spent less per capita, and had higher inmate/staff ratios: "*The only findings of this study that, to me at least, seem indispensable, is that . . . prison management matters*" (emphasis in original).[9]

Studies analyzing the causes of major prison riots found that they were the result of a breakdown in security procedures—the daily routine of numbering, counting, frisking, locking, contraband control, and cell searches—that are the heart of administration in most prisons.[10] Problems in areas such as crowding, underfunding, festering inmate-staff relations, and racial animosities may make a riot more *likely,* but poor security management will make riots *inevitable.*[11]

DiIulio offered six general principles of good prison leadership:

1. Successful leaders focus, and inspire their subordinates to focus, on results rather than process, on performance rather than procedures, on ends rather than means. In short, managers are judged on results, not on excuses.

2. Professional staff members—doctors, psychiatrists, accountants, nurses, and other nonuniformed staff—receive some basic prison training and come to think of themselves as correctional officers first.

3. Leaders of successful institutions follow the "management by walking around" (MBWA) principle. These managers are not strangers to the cellblocks and are always on the scene when trouble erupts.

4. Successful leaders make close alliances with key politicians, judges, journalists, reformers, and other outsiders.

5. Successful leaders rarely innovate, but the innovations they implement are far-reaching and the reasons for them are explained to staff and inmates well in advance. Line staff are notoriously sensitive to what administrators do "for

inmates" versus "what they do for us." Thus, leaders must be careful not to upset the balance and erode staff loyalty.

6. Successful leaders are in office long enough to understand and, as necessary, modify the organization's internal operations and external relations. DiIulio used the terms *flies, fatalists, foot soldiers,* and *founders.* The flies come and go unnoticed and are inconsequential. Fatalists also serve brief terms, always complaining about the futility of incarceration and the hopelessness of correctional reform. The foot soldiers serve long terms, often inheriting their job from a fly or fatalist and make consequential improvements whenever they can. Founders either create an agency or reorganize it in a major and positive way.[12]

To summarize, to "old" penologists, prison administrators were admirable public servants, inmates were to be restricted, and any form of self-government was eschewed. To "new" penologists, prison administrators are loathsome and evil, inmates are responsible victims, and complete self-government is the ideal. DiIulio calls for a **new old penology,** or a shift of attention from the society of captives to the government of keepers. He asserts that tight administrative control is more conducive than loose administrative control to decent prison conditions. This approach, he added, will "push administrators back to the bar of attention," treating them at least as well as their charges.[13]

## Does Diversifying Prison Staff Help?

To better manage the prison and be more consistent with the ratio of black to white inmates, many prison administrators have attempted to change the racial composition of correctional staff by increasing the number of minority correctional officers. It has been assumed that minority officers would share the same socioeconomic and cultural backgrounds of prisoners and be more sympathetic to inmates' rights and rehabilitation considerations. It has also been assumed that black correctional officers would have more positive attitudes toward black inmates.

One study[14] attempted to determine if these assumptions were accurate by examining interracial and intraracial disciplinary reports: whether or not black or white correctional officers wrote more disciplinary reports against black or white inmates. The study found *no* significant difference between black and white officers in the writing of disciplinary reports against *either* black or white inmates; one racial group of COs was not more likely than another to issue official sanctions through writing disciplinary reports. The findings suggest that perhaps the racial integration of the CO staff may be successful toward improving white COs' behavior toward prisoners. This finding supports the classic study in 1977 by Rosabeth Kanter, who found that when a minority group achieves some critical mass in an organization, it is able to influence the creation of the informal rules of the larger institution.[15]

# Middle Managers and Supervisors

Chapter 4 examined in detail the roles of *police* supervisors and managers. It would be repetitious to dwell at length here on those roles and functions, because most of them apply to *corrections* supervisors and managers as well. The reader is encouraged to review those roles and functions in Chapter 4.

Clearly, supervisors have one of the most demanding positions in correctional institutions. They must direct work activities, assign tasks, provide employee feedback, and serve as technical experts for the staff reporting to them. They serve as boss, adviser, counselor, mentor, coach, trainer, and motivator.

Middle managers, although not on the front lines, are also in challenging and important positions. They are responsible for organizing their departments, planning and developing goals and objectives, overseeing the efficient use of resources, and developing effective communication networks throughout the organization.

# "Thy Brother's Keeper": Correctional Officers

Subordinate to the institutional administrator, middle managers, and supervisors is the correctional staff itself—those who, in the words of Gordon Hawkins, are "the other prisoners."[16] Their role is particularly important, given that they provide the front-line supervision and control of inmates and constitute the level from which correctional administrators may be chosen.

## *An Ironic Comparison: Correctional Officers and Inmates*

One guard stated: "We're all doing time, some of us are just doin' it in eight-hour shifts."[17] Richard Hawkins and Geoffrey Alpert compared officers and inmates and found that both groups are likely to be drawn from lower- and working-class backgrounds; both are likely to be in their present roles because of lack of employment opportunities; both groups are largely invisible; both are closely watched and experience some depersonalization (e.g., they wear uniforms and are subject to psychological testing and probing into their past); both develop feelings of powerlessness; and both are fighting for their individual rights (conditions of employment and incarceration, respectively).[18]

Most applicants for positions as correctional officers may have had little knowledge of the job when they applied. A job description for the position might read something like this:

> [They] must prevent rape among two hundred convicts enraged by their powerlessness and sexual deprivation . . . prevent violence among the convicts . . . shake down all cells for contraband . . . know what is going on in the convicts' head and report it to their supervisors . . . account for all material entering or leaving each cellblock . . . maintain sanitation in each cell . . . give individual attention to all . . .

convicts . . . [and] prevent the suicide or running amok of the raped, the depressed, and the terrified . . . and look out for their own physical and psychological survival.[19]

In most assignments, correctional officers experience stimulus overload, are assailed with the sounds of "doors clanging, inmates talking or shouting, radios and televisions playing, and food trays banging . . . [and odors] representing an institutional blend of food, urine, paint, disinfectant, and sweat."[20]

Correctional officers are not allowed to provide informal counseling or to aid in the rehabilitative effort. Due process rights for prisoners have made corrections jobs even more difficult.[21] Therein lies what Hawkins and Alpert referred to as "the big bitch" of correctional officers: They are losing power and influence while inmates are gaining them as they are accorded more due process rights.[22] This frustration can be vented in physical ways. Although certainly not frequent today, beatings and even sexual attacks by some officers have been documented.[23]

## *A Typology: Eight Types of COs*

Correctional officers play an influential role in the lives of many inmates because of their direct and prolonged interaction. They are also responsible for creating and maintaining a humane environment in prisons and jails.

Mary Ann Farkas[24] categorized correctional officers into five types—rule enforcer, hard liner, people worker, synthetic officer, and loner—based on their orientation toward rule enforcement, extent of mutual obligations with colleagues, orientation toward negotiation or exchange with inmates, and their desire to incorporate human service activities into their approach. Farkas added three residual types that were identified by respondents in her study: officer friendly, lax officer, and wishy-washy. These eight types are discussed next.

**Rule enforcers,** about 43 percent of correctional officers, are the most common type in Farkas's sample. Rule enforcers are characterized as rule bound and inflexible in discipline and have an esprit de corps with others sharing their enforcement philosophy. They are more likely than other correctional officers to be younger than 25 and to have a baccalaureate degree; they tend to have less work experience and to work the evening or night shifts. They typically work on posts involving direct inmate contact, such as the regular housing units and in maximum-security or segregation units. They are more likely to have entered corrections for extrinsic reasons, including job security, benefits, and job availability. They possess a militaristic approach toward inmates, expecting deference to their authority and obedience to their orders. Rule enforcers are not willing to negotiate or use exchange as a strategy to gain inmate compliance.[25]

The **hard liners** are actually a subtype and an extreme version of the rule enforcers. They are hard, aggressive, power hungry, and inflexible with rules and possess little interpersonal skill. These officers are also more likely to be male, with a high school education or GED, and between ages 26 to 36. They also tend to work later shifts and in maximum-security or segregation units, and they endorse militaristic values and distinction and deference to rank and chain of command. At times, they may become abusive and aggressive toward inmates and perceive acting tough as the way a CO is supposed to act in order to maintain control and order.[26]

**People workers** (22 percent of COs) are characterized as "professionals trying to be social, responsible, and trying their very best." They have a more comfortable style with inmates, are more flexible in rule enforcement and disciplinary measures, use their own informal reward and punishment system and believe that the way to gain inmate compliance is through interpersonal communication and personalized relations. They regard an overreliance on conduct reports as an indication of one's inability to resolve difficult situations. They often discuss issues privately with inmates instead of embarrassing them in front of peers. They are concerned with conflict resolution, relying on verbal skills in defusing situations, enjoy the challenge of working with inmates, and actually prefer the posts with more inmate contact.[27]

The **synthetic officers** (14 percent) are essentially a synthesis of the rule enforcer and the people worker types. They are typically older (37 and over), more experienced officers who work in regular inmate housing units on the day shift. Synthetic officers try to modify the formalized policies and procedures to emphasize organizational directives and interpersonal skills. They follow rules and regulations closely, yet they try to consider the circumstances. They are careful not to deviate too far from procedure, however, which might cause sanctions for themselves. Strict enforcement of rules and flexibility in enforcement are juggled in their interactions with inmates.[28]

**Loners** (8 percent) are also similar to rule enforcers but differ in the motivation behind their policy of strict enforcement. Loners closely follow rules and regulations because they fear criticism of their performance. Female and black officers are more likely to be represented in this type. Loners are likely to be between the ages of 26 and 36 and less experienced COs and to work on solitary posts. Loners believe their job performance is more closely watched because of their female and/or minority status, as well as the need to constantly prove themselves. They do not feel accepted by other officers, nor do they identify with them. They are wary of inmates. There is a basic mistrust, even fear of working with inmates.[29]

The three residual types—the lax officer, officer friendly, and wishy-washy—are officers who reject the official values and goals of the formal organization. Their rule enforcement is erratic, inconsistent, or nonexistent.

The *lax* officers are described as passive, apathetic, or timid. They are generally veteran male COs who are weary of arguments with inmates and writing conduct reports. They are just "doing their time," wanting to get through the day with a minimum of effort. *Officer friendly* types are subtypes of people workers, wanting to be liked by all inmates and easily manipulated by inmates to give lots of "second chances." They negotiate with inmates to maintain order and gain compliance by overlooking minor violations or doing favors. They typically have little loyalty or affinity to other officers. *Wishy-washy* types are unpredictable, moody, and inconsistent. They communicate and help inmates at one time, then are distant and rule oriented at another. They are likely to be accused of favoritism and mistrusted by inmates because they do not follow through on promises.

To summarize, age and seniority are associated with officer types. Rule enforcers and hard liners tend to be younger, less experienced COs, whereas older, more experienced officers belong to the people worker or synthetic officer categories. Generally, as officers mature, they become more interested in service delivery.

Although one might assume that more educated officers are inclined toward rehabilitation and are less punitive or aggressive toward inmates, Farkas found that rule enforcers were more likely to hold baccalaureate or master's degrees; she suggests that education may not be a strong indicator of human service attitudes.[30] Considerable evidence suggests that higher education may lead to lower job satisfaction. One observer noted that "except for the somewhat disappointing finding that [correctional officers] with more education are less satisfied with their jobs, the overall picture shows that education is not related to any attitudinal variable examined thus far."[31] Other studies have determined that as officers' educational levels increased, so did their desire to become administrators, the less likely they were to feel a sense of accomplishment working as correctional officers or to want to make a career of corrections, the more likely they were to express dissatisfaction with the pace of career advancement, the more interest they had in counseling;[32] but the less willing they were to engage in rehabilitation activities.[33]

Shift and work assignment also affect one's orientation—the more custodial types of officers work later shifts because they are newer officers and are more likely to work on units with more difficult inmates (such as maximum-security, segregation, or units for inmates with behavioral problems). Finally, the reason for becoming a CO is related to officer type: People workers are attracted to intrinsic factors of correctional work, because of its interesting and challenging aspects. Rule enforcers and hard liners become officers for extrinsic reasons: job security and benefits of state employment and job availability.

These CO typologies are actually modes of accommodation or adaptation to the organizational factors of the correctional institutions, including overcrowded conditions, more troublesome inmates, and a more litigious environment.[34]

# Jail Personnel

## *Jail Purpose and Environment*

As noted in Chapter 9, about 700,000 persons are incarcerated in 3,316 local jails in the United States, either awaiting trial or serving a sentence.[35] Furthermore, about 229,000 people are employed in local jails.[36] The jail is the point of entry into the criminal justice system. While prisons hold persons who have committed felonies and have been sentenced to at least one year in prison, jails hold persons who are arrested and booked for criminal activity or are waiting for a court appearance if they cannot arrange bail, as well as those who are serving sentences of up to one year for misdemeanors. Jails also temporarily hold felons whose convictions are on appeal or who are awaiting transfer to a state prison.

Perhaps one of the most neglected areas in criminal justice research concerns individuals who are employed in local jails; what limited studies have been performed generally focus on the conditions of confinement. Jail employees, however, often must work in an environment that is unstable, uncertain, and unsafe. Therefore, it would be beneficial for jail administrators to become knowledgeable about why people choose to work in local jails, as well as jail employee job satisfaction and turnover.

## Choosing Jail Work and Type of Facility

Studies have fairly consistently shown that both male and female workers utilize a standard set of priorities in choosing the work they prefer: salary, autonomy, prestige, and location.[37] Although individual motivation will vary, certainly these factors, along with job security, will come into play when someone considers a jail career. Furthermore, research indicates that, given a choice, men and women apparently prefer predominantly male occupations, as they are generally better paying, more prestigious, carry more authority, and offer more opportunities for advancement than their female-dominated counterparts.[38]

One study of correctional officers in a southwestern state found that 83 percent of the COs expressed a preference for working in men's prisons because men are perceived as being easier to manage and more respectful (particularly of female officers).[39] Officers' overall view was that women are more prone than men to irrational outbursts.[40]

Correctional officers also see the women's facility as something less than a "real prison." Women's prisons typically have a much smaller inmate population than men's, with only one officer assigned to a dormitory, so officers are isolated from one another for the majority of their shifts. This situation differs markedly from men's prisons, where officers are almost never assigned alone; the strong team structure and the sense of being a member of a team that are thus present in men's prisons are primary reasons for both male and female correctional officers preferring to work with male inmates.[41]

## Employee Job Satisfaction and Attrition

Symptoms of dissatisfaction in corrections—not unlike other occupations—include increased absenteeism and decreased employee productivity. Feelings of accomplishment (such as competency and success on the job) reduce burnout.[42] One study found that a large majority of jail employees liked their superiors and co-workers and their work. However, they reported that dealing with aggressive groups or using force, being in hazardous situations while alone, insufficient personnel, and lack of support from the agency were major sources of job stress.[43]

Organizational factors, such as lack of agency support, have been found to be even more important for correctional officers than individual attributes or dealing with inmates for determining job satisfaction. Correctional officers who experience greater intrinsic and extrinsic rewards have greater job satisfaction. If available, intrinsic rewards of the job—such as freedom to plan work activities, freedom to exercise one's skills and talent, and personal growth—can lead to greater job satisfaction than extrinsic rewards of the job (such as pay, job security, fringe benefits, and promotional opportunities).[44] Finally, job satisfaction has been found to result in decreased turnover.[45]

Nevertheless, a recent study in one of Florida's five largest jails, holding nearly 2,000 inmates, found that 60 percent of the jail officer respondents were either "presently looking and planning to leave" or "seriously considering leaving in the near future"; 13 percent reported that they "probably" or "definitely" will leave. Half indicated that they would quit as soon they could find a better job, 60 percent reported that they often thought about quitting, and 60 percent also reported that they desired better promotion and opportunities.[46]

It is common for many local jails/sheriff's offices to initially hire people to perform detention-related functions often for three to five years before they can expect to transfer into what they believe is "real police work." Not surprisingly, the Florida study found that although many of the jail employees did not wish to continue their careers within the detention facility, they did want to continue working with the sheriff's office, hoping to transfer laterally to patrol functions as soon as possible.[47] Career paths and working in detention as opposed to being on road patrol are discussed more later.

This Florida study and others like it present a number of areas of concern for jail administrators: Employees believed that there are too few rewards for their work. More specifically, the lack of a fair chance at promotion, as well as an inability to get ahead, insufficient salary increases, and insufficient benefits were the primary sources of their dissatisfaction. They also identified serious morale problems—particularly bickering and fighting and lack of communication—as additional sources of dissatisfaction. Thus, situational factors within the work organization (an unsafe work environment, with insufficient resources to compensate for the work) conspired to be the primary sources of job stress and dissatisfaction among the jail workers examined.[48]

Detention officers could be allowed to have more direct involvement in jail decision-making processes that affect their work environment. Similarly, jail administrators should give careful consideration to opportunities for professional growth and development, which might compensate for the limited opportunities for extrinsic rewards associated with jail work.[49]

Regarding employee attrition, one survey[50] of 122 jails in 32 states reported an annual average jail employee turnover rate of 16 percent. And, similar to the Florida findings mentioned earlier, jail employees quit their jobs for a variety of reasons: low pay, inadequate benefits, dangerous/stressful working conditions, lack of autonomy, limited opportunities for advancement, and better job opportunities elsewhere.

## *Female Jail Deputies*

The primary stimulus for the employment of female officers in local jails has been the need to comply with federal guidelines on hiring, as well as with various court orders to implement hiring quotas to increase female representation or to rewrite entrance exams and requirements to encourage the employment of females.[51]

Several administrative factors have also driven the need for more female employees. First, jails must house both male and female inmates, and women are needed to supervise the female residents. Second, female officers are needed to conduct searches of female visitors. Third, a rapid expansion of the jail workforce has increased demand and opened job opportunities for qualified female applicants.[52]

Despite this increased female presence in jail work, the role of a female jail deputy is different from that in other work places, in that violence is prevalent in the work environment and it is perceived to be a highly sex-typed male job requiring dominance, authoritativeness, and aggressiveness. Studies have shown that, quite often, female deputies believe that they are judged as members of a gender class rather than as individuals—that male workers don't see them as equals.[53]

One of the most pervasive themes expressed by nearly every female officer in each of the jails studied was the perception that female staff members possess more effective communication skills than do male staff and that female officers rely more on their verbal skills. Male officers are more confrontational than are female officers. Men working in jails are more willing than female officers to employ threats, intimidation, and physical coercion in order-maintenance tasks.[54] It has also been determined that female jail deputies are more likely than males to develop friendly relationships with inmates to get inmates to follow the rules—often through the strategic use of humor.[55]

According to Nancy Jurik, perhaps the most demoralizing realization for women employed in jails is that their opportunities for advancement are limited. Women in corrections routinely experience exclusion, discrimination, and hostility from male supervisors and co-workers. Supervisors who are biased against women working as corrections officers use performance evaluations to discourage them and keep them in subordinate positions.[56]

## *Detention as a Career Path*

Because no single jail administrator is responsible for statewide jail management, detention officers may manage their jails according to vastly different perceptions and philosophies concerning their staffing and operation. Most jails are supervised by a sheriff's office, where career advancement may be quite limited. When jails are separate units of local government with their own director, they tend to attract more qualified administrators with greater career commitments. A separate, jail-related career path for correctional workers in jail administration is currently needed.

As mentioned earlier, many local jail facilities hire people first as detention officers who, after attending their basic academy training, may work for three to five years in detention; eventually, wanting to do "real police work," they transfer to the patrol division as soon as a vacancy becomes available and after attaining a sufficient amount of seniority within their law enforcement agency. This situation often results in tremendously high turnover rates in the jail, as well as large numbers of less experienced detention personnel and low job satisfaction on the part of jail employees. Or, many good officers also resign, being unwilling to serve a period of several years working in detention.

Jail administrators finding themselves in this situation—having difficulty in recruiting people into detention, and then experiencing high employee attrition and low job satisfaction in detention—would do well to take one of two approaches: (1) attempt to create two separate career paths—one in patrol and one in detention. Those who begin on one path can choose to remain in it, be promoted within it, and, it is hoped, even retire from it. Of course, the detention program of the agency must be made attractive enough for one to pursue this occupation as a career; (2) The administrative, middle management, and supervisory personnel can attempt to convince newly hired personnel to look at the "big picture": that only about 20 percent of their 20-year career will be spent working in detention, with the remaining 80 percent spent as a road deputy.

## *Employee Training*

Jail administrators and employees need to be thoroughly trained in all aspects of their job. Jail workers have been criticized for being untrained and apathetic, although most are highly effective and dedicated. One observer wrote that

> Personnel is still the number one problem of jails. Start paying decent salaries and developing decent training and you can start to attract bright young people to jobs in jails. If you don't do this, you'll continue to see the issue of personnel as the number one problem for the next 100 years.[57]

Training should be provided on the booking process, inmate management and security, general liability issues, policies related to AIDS, problems of inmates addicted to alcohol and other drugs, communication and security technology, and issues concerning suicide, mental health problems, and medication.

# CASE STUDIES

The following two case studies deal with personnel roles and functions and will help the reader consider some of the chapter information concerning employee behaviors. The first case study also shows the kinds of problems a middle manager faces and the ways in which he or she spends time during a tour of duty in a correctional institution.

## The Wright Way

Lieutenant Bea Wright has been in her current position in the state prison for one year and is shift supervisor on swing (evening) shift, with 20 officers on her shift. There is also a recreation and development lieutenant, who oversees the yard, commissary, and other high-participation activities during the shift. Wright begins at 4:00 P.M. by holding a roll call for officers, briefing them on the activities of the day, any unusual inmate problems or tensions in progress, and special functions (such as Bible study groups) that will be happening during the evening. Soon after roll call, Wright has the staff conduct the very important evening count—important because inmates have not been counted since morning. At about 5:00 P.M., Wright determines that there are only four correctional officers in the dining room with 1,000 inmates, so she contacts other units (such as education, library, recreation) to have them send available staff to the dining hall for support. After dinner, Wright finds a memo from the warden, asking her to recommend ways of improving procedures for having violent inmates in the Special Housing Unit (SHU) taken to the recreation area in the evening. Wright asks two of her top COs who work in the SHU to provide her with some preliminary information concerning the system in place, and any recommendations they might have. While walking the yard, Wright observes what appears to be an unusual amount of clustering and whispering by inmates, by race; she asks a sergeant to quietly survey the COs to determine whether there have also been unusual periods of loud music or large amounts of long-term foodstuffs purchased in the commissary (together, these activities by inmates might indicate that a race war is brewing, or an escape plan being developed). Furthermore, on the way to her office an inmate stops her, saying that a group of inmates is pressuring him to arrange to have drugs brought into the prison, and he fears for his safety. Wright arranges for him to be called out of the general population the next day under the guise of being transported to a prison law library, at which time he can privately meet with an investigator and thus not draw suspicion to himself for talking to the staff. At about 9:00, Anderson, a CO, comes to her office to report that he overheard another CO, Jones, making disparaging remarks to other staff members concerning Anderson's desire to go to graduate school and try to become a warden some day. Anderson acknowledges that he does not get along with Jones, is tired of his "sniping," and asks Wright to intercede. She also knows that Jones has been argumentative with other staff members and inmates of late and makes a mental note to visit with him later in the shift to see if he is having personal problems.

## Questions for Discussion

1. Does it appear that Lt. Wright, although fairly new in her position, has a firm grasp of her role and performs well in it?
2. In what ways is it shown that Wright seeks input from her subordinates?
3. How does she delegate and empower her subordinates?
4. Is there any indication that Wright is interested in her correctional officers' training and professional development?
5. In which instances does Wright engage in mediation? MBWA (management by walking around)?

# The Wraung Way*

Randall Wraung has been a shift supervisor at the Granite County Detention Facility for the past three years. He was promoted to sergeant, performed patrol duties, and had about 10 years' experience with the sheriff's office. Wraung enjoys taking new hires under what he terms his "unofficial tutelage," priding himself in the fact that he knows every aspect of the jail's operation.

Wraung is supervising a newly hired deputy, Tom Sharpe, who is a graduate of the local university's criminal justice program and, like all new hires, is initially assigned to detention. Sharpe finds Wraung to be an interesting and outspoken person. In their conversations about work in the jail, Wraung decides to give Tom some insights.

"I have some good advice for you, kid, and for anyone else going into this job." Wraung continues, "First, try to get out of the jail and into a patrol car as soon as you possibly can. Office politics are extremely bad in here, where you're surrounded and watched by brass all the time. Plus, you can't use any of your university education or academy training 'inside,' so you'll want to get out on a beat as soon as possible.

"Second, I find that you have to be realistic about your chances for having any positive influence with the scum who come through here. Oh, I've worked with lots of people who thought they could change the world in here. Me? Well, I'm a realist. Let's face it. We get the people everyone else has given up on, so what can we be expected to do? I tell visitors that 'We get the cream of the crap here,' and I mean it. Don't set your expectations very high, and you won't be

---

*Contributed by Ted Heim, Professor Emeritus, Washburn University, Topeka, Kansas.

disappointed. I have always been able to keep a good perspective. Hell, the top brass around here and the politicians over at the courthouse give us plenty to laugh at. All you need to do when you're down is look at some of the orders these clowns put out and some of the things our glorious leaders tell the public about treatment, efficiency, blah, blah, blah. I personally don't believe stuff like boot camp and the jail's educational and industry programs even belong here.

"The job tends to get you down if you let it. I have found that you have to find a relief from all the frustrations you experience and the problems created by some of the SOBs who come through here. About once a week, the gang and I hold 'choir practice' at a bar down the street. After about five or six beers, this place and the world look a helluva lot better. People who don't work in corrections can't understand the need to let off a little steam once in a while. Gladly, I am half way to being able to just retire and walk away from this place."

## Questions for Discussion

1. Assume that you are Wraung's lieutenant and, while standing in the hallway, you overhear this conversation. What would be your *immediate* reaction to Wraung's expression of his views of the job and the inmates? To Sharpe? What *long-term* actions would you take with Wraung and/or Sharpe?

2. If you were Wraung's supervisor, would you feel compelled to look into, leave alone, or halt the "choir practices"?

3. Assume that you are Sharpe; of all the points made by Wraung, are there any with which you agree? Disagree? Why or why not? Is there any value whatever to listening to such candor from someone like Wraung?

4. Is Wraung the sort of employee who should be supervising others? Dealing at all with the public?

5. Do you believe such cynicism is common in corrections? In criminal justice, generally? In most other occupations? Explain your answer.

## Summary

This chapter has examined those criminal justice employees who work in correctional institutions, with particular emphasis placed on administrators. Certainly, as noted in Chapter 9, substantial pressures are now placed on prison and jail administrators by the external and internal environments. They must maintain a secure environment while attempting to offer some degree of treatment to inmates, who should not leave the prison or jail experience in a much worse condition than when they entered. At the same time, another increasingly difficult challenge is that these administrators must constantly strive to maintain a competent, dedicated workforce that will also uphold the primary tenets of incarceration: providing a secure environment while also ensuring that inmates are treated with respect and dignity.

# Questions for Review

1. What is meant by the term *new old penology?*
2. What are some major principles of prison administration?
3. What are some of the major problems encountered by prison or jail employees? What factors contribute most to their low job satisfaction and high attrition, and what can their administrators do toward alleviating those problems?
4. What do correctional officers and inmates have in common?
5. What are the eight types of correctional officers? How do age, length of service, type of assignment, and education affect where one fits in this typology?
6. In the case study involving Lt. Wright, what are some of the major elements and problems of the role that are made evident?
7. What major aspects of the correctional officer's role should be made known to the administrator?
8. What are the functions of middle managers and supervisors in jails and prisons (see Chapter 3 if necessary)?
9. How would you describe the prison warden and his or her role?
10. Why is there often a detention/patrol dichotomy for new jail hires, and what can jail administrators do to try to convince employees that they should consider a career in the detention field?

# Notes

1. John J. DiIulio Jr., *Governing Prisons: A Comparative Study of Correctional Management* (New York: Free Press, 1987), p. 167.
2. Personal communication, Ron Angelone, director, Nevada Department of Prisons, April 27, 1992.
3. F. T. Cullen, E. J. Latessa, R. Kopache, L. X. Lombardo, and V. S. Burton Jr., "Prison Wardens' Job Satisfaction," *The Prison Journal* 73 (1993):141-161.
4. Timothy J. Flanagan, W. Wesley Johnson, and Katherine Bennett, "Job Satisfaction Among Correctional Executives: A Contemporary Portrait of Wardens of State Prisons for Adults," *The Prison Journal* 76 (December 1996):386-399.
5. Ibid., p. 395.
6. John J. DiIulio Jr., "Well Governed Prisons are Possible," in George F. Cole, Marc C. Gertz, and Amy Bunger, eds., *The Criminal Justice System: Politics and Policies,* 8th ed. (Belmont, Calif.: Wadsworth, 2002,) pp. 411-420.
7. Ibid., p. 449.
8. DiIulio, *Governing Prisons,* p. 256.
9. Ibid.
10. Bert Useem, *States of Siege: U.S. Prison Riots, 1971-1986* (New York: Oxford University Press, 1988).
11. DiIulio Jr., "Well Governed Prisons Are Possible," p. 413.

12. John J. DiIulio Jr., *No Escape: The Future of American Corrections* (New York: Basic Books, 1991), Chapter 1.

13. DiIulio, "Well Governed Prisons Are Possible," p. 456.

14. Marianne Fisher-Giorlando and Shanhe Jiang, "Race and Disciplinary Reports: An Empirical Study of Correctional Officers," *Sociological Spectrum* 20 (2000):169–194.

15. Rosabeth Kanter, "Some Effects of Proportions on Group Life: Skewed Sex Ratios and Responses to Token Women," *American Journal of Sociology* 82 (1977):965–990.

16. Gordon Hawkins, *The Prison* (Chicago: University of Chicago Press, 1976).

17. Cited in Eric D. Poole and Robert M. Regoli, "Alienation in Prison: An Examination of the Work Relations of Prison Guards," *Criminology* 19 (1981):251–270.

18. Richard Hawkins and Geoffrey P. Alpert, *American Prison Systems: Punishment and Justice* (Englewood Cliffs, N.J.: Prentice Hall, 1989), p. 338.

19. Adapted from Carl Weiss and David James Friar, *Terror in the Prisons* (Indianapolis, Ind.: Bobbs-Merrill, 1974), p. 209.

20. Ben M. Crouch, *The Keepers: Prison Guards and Contemporary Corrections* (Springfield, Ill.: Charles C Thomas, 1980), p. 73.

21. Hawkins and Alpert, *American Prison Systems,* p. 340.

22. Ibid., p. 345.

23. See Lee H. Bowker, *Prison Victimization* (New York: Elsevier, 1980), Chapter 7.

24. Mary Ann Farkas, "A Typology of Correctional Officers," *International Journal of Offender Therapy and Comparative Criminology* 44 (2000):431–449.

25. Ibid., pp. 438–439.

26. Ibid., pp. 439–440.

27. Ibid., pp. 440–441.

28. Ibid., p. 442.

29. Ibid., pp. 442–443.

30. Ibid.

31. Susan Philliber, "Thy Brother's Keeper: A Review of the Literature on Correctional Officers," *Justice Quarterly* 4 (1987):9–37.

32. Robert Rogers, "The Effects of Educational Level on Correctional Officer Job Satisfaction," *Journal of Criminal Justice* 19 (1991):123–137.

33. David Robinson, Frank J. Porporino, and Linda Simourd, "The Influence of Educational Attainment on the Attitudes and Job Performance of Correctional Officers," *Crime and Delinquency* 43 (1997):60–77.

34. Ibid., pp. 445–446.

35. U.S. Department of Justice, Bureau of Justice Statistics Web page: http://www.ojp.usdoj.gov/bjs/glance/tables/corr2tab.htm (accessed June 24, 2002).

36. U.S. Department of Justice, Bureau of Justice Statistics, *Justice Expenditure and Employment in the United States, 1999* (Washington, D.C.: Author, February 2002), p. 6.

37. See, for example, Christine Bose and Peter Rossi, "Gender and Jobs: Prestige Standings of Occupations as Affected by Gender," *American Sociological Review* 48 (1983): 316–330; Christopher Jencks, L. Perman, and Lee Rainwater, "What Is a Good Job? A New Measure of Labor Market Success," *American Journal of Sociology* 93 (1988): 1322–1357; D. Kaufman and M. Fetters, "Work Motivation and Job Values Among Professional Men and Women: A New Accounting," *Journal of Vocational Behavior* 16 (1980):251–262.

38. Christine L. Williams, *Still a Man's World: Men Who Do "Women's" Work* (Berkeley, Calif.: University of California Press, 1995).

39. Dana M. Britton, "Cat Fights and Gang Fights: Preference for Work in a Male-Dominated Organization," *The Sociological Quarterly* 40 (1999):455–474.

40. Ibid., p. 462.

41. Ibid., pp. 465–466.

42. C. Simmons, J. K. Cochran, and W. R. Blount, "The Effects of Job-Related Stress and Job Satisfaction on Probation Officers' Inclinations to Quit," *American Journal of Criminal Justice* 21 (1996):213–229.

43. Terry G. Byrd, John K. Cochran, Ira J. Silverman, and William R. Blount, "Behind Bars: An Assessment of the Effects of Job Satisfaction, Job-Related Stress, and Anxiety on Jail Employees' Inclinations to Quit," *Journal of Crime and Justice* 23 (2000):69–93.

44. J. R. Hepburn and P. E. Knepper, "Correctional Officers as Human Services Workers: The Effect on Job Satisfaction," *Justice Quarterly* 10 (1993):315–337.

45. C. W. Muller, J. E. Wallace, and J. L. Price, "Employee Commitment Resolving Some Issues," *Work and Occupation* 19 (1992):211–236; P. F. Spector, "Measurement of Human Service Staff Satisfaction: Development of the Job Satisfaction Survey," *American Journal of Community Psychology* 13 (1985):693–711.

46. Byrd, Cochran, Silverman, and Blount, "Behind Bars," p. 79.

47. Ibid.

48. Ibid., p. 85.

49. Ibid.

50. G. M. Camp and C. G. Camp, *The Corrections Yearbook, 1996: Jail Systems* (South Salem, N.Y.: Criminal Justice Institute, 1996).

51. Mark R. Pogrebin and Eric D. Poole, "Women Deputies and Jail Work," *Journal of Contemporary Criminal Justice* 14 (May 1998):117–134.

52. Ibid., pp. 117–118.

53. Ibid., p. 120.

54. Ibid.

55. Ibid., p. 125.

56. Nancy C. Jurik, "An Officer and a Lady: Organizational Barriers to Women Working as Correctional Officers in Men's Prisons," *Social Problems* 32 (1985):375–388.

57. Quoted in Advisory Commission on Intergovernmental Relations, *Jails: Intergovernmental Dimensions of a Local Problem* (Washington, D.C.: Author, 1984), p. 1.

# Chapter 11

# Community Corrections: Probation and Parole

## Key Terms and Concepts

Authoritarian

Consolidated model

Democratic

Diversion program

Independent model

Laissez-faire

Parole

Probation

Shock incarceration

Systems theory

## Learning Objectives

As a result of reading this chapter, the student will:

- be able to distinguish between the duties of probation and parole officers
- know the six different categories of probation systems
- have an understanding of systems theory and its resources, activities, and outcomes
- be familiar with probation administrators' management styles
- know the three services of parole agencies and the two models used for administering parole services
- know the advantages of the independent and consolidated models
- be familiar with the alternatives to incarceration

> *Even I/Regained my freedom with a sigh.*
>
> —Lord Byron

## Introduction

Community corrections originated in the years following World War II, when returning veterans encountered adjustment problems as they attempted to reenter civilian life.[1] It has also been stated that community corrections is "the last bastion of discretion in the criminal justice system."[2] Community corrections is typically viewed as a humane, logical, and effective approach for working with and changing criminal offenders. The President's Commission on Law Enforcement and Administration of Justice endorsed this model in 1967, saying that it

> includes building or rebuilding solid ties between the offender and the community, obtaining employment and education, securing in the large sense a place for the offender in the routine functioning of society. This requires . . . efforts directed towards changing the individual offender [and] mobilization and change of the community and its institutions.[3]

Changes in national ideological thought and other matters have combined to present difficulties in achieving these lofty ideals. As shown in the earlier chapters of Part IV, these factors also have compelled us at times in this nation to use incarceration instead of community-based corrections.

This chapter examines probation and parole and begins with what is perhaps the core issue: appropriate alternatives to imprisonment. Then, we examine the problem of large caseloads. The types of administrative systems and issues that are related to the administration of probation and parole are considered. Next, we analyze the relatively new alternatives to incarceration and conventional probation and parole, known as *intermediate sanctions:* intensive probation/parole supervision, electronic monitoring, shock probation or parole, boot camps/shock incarceration, and day reporting.

The chapter concludes with two case studies.

## Why Alternatives to Imprisonment?

Sanctions or mechanisms of social control for enforcing society's standards are most likely to deter violations of those standards if they meet two conditions: They injure "the social standing [of the perpetrator] by the punishment," and they make "the individual feel a danger of being excluded from the group."[4] The United States bases its assumptions about what constitutes punishment on the norms and living standards of society at large. This view overlooks several important facts: First, most serious offenders neither accept nor abide by those norms; and second, most incarcerated people today come from communities where conditions fall far below the living standards that most Americans would accept.[5] The grim fact and national shame are that for many people who go to prison, the conditions inside are not all that different from, and might even be better than, the conditions outside.

Social isolation is the second presumably punitive aspect of imprisonment. When a person goes to prison, however, he or she seldom feels isolated but is likely to find friends, if not family, already there.[6]

Furthermore, it seems plausible that prison life is not perceived as being as difficult as it once was. Inmates' actions speak loudly in this respect: More than 50 percent of today's inmates have served a prior prison term. Knowing what prison is like, these inmates evidently still believe the "benefits" of committing a new crime outweigh the costs of being in prison.[7] We must wonder how punitive the prison experience is for such offenders.

Finally, the stigma of having a prison record is not the same as in the past, because so many of the offenders' peers and family members also have done time. Many youths in state training schools had parents who had also been incarcerated. Imprisonment confers status in some neighborhoods. Gang members have repeatedly stated that incarceration was not a threat because they knew their sentence would be minimal. To many people, serving a prison term is a badge of courage. It also is their source of food, clothing, and shelter.[8]

We have thus begun our discussion of community sanctions with indications of the often ineffectiveness of prisons to punish criminal behavior. Society needs to determine if it is time to seriously consider alternatives to incarceration. Probation and parole administrators might question whether conventional **probation** and **parole** are effective alternatives to prison sentences in all cases or whether others—such as intensive supervision programs—should be implemented.

## The Burden of Large Probation and Parole Caseloads

The quality of service that a probation or parole officer can provide to his or her clients is related to that officer's caseload. *Caseload* refers to the average number of cases supervised in a given period. Each case represents an offender on probation or parole who is supervised by an individual officer. As John Conrad observed:

> There is much that a good probation/parole officer can do for the people on his or her caseload. A parole officer who makes it clear that "fellow, if you don't watch your step I'm gonna run your ass right back to the joint" is not in a position to be helpful as a counselor or facilitator. With the best intentions, a[n] officer struggling with the standard unwieldy caseload of 100 or more will deal with emergencies only, and sometime will not be able to do that very well.[9]

About 4 million adults are now on probation in the United States.[10] Although ideal caseloads for probation officers range from 25 to 50, many actually have caseloads of 200 or more. Because the quality of officers' contact with probationers is negatively affected by their inability to have regular face-to-face contact, probation is often judged unfairly as being ineffective as a deterrent to crime. Probation departments are often the last to be given additional funding to create new positions to handle increasing numbers of offenders. Few agencies or courts consider the negative implications of giving understaffed and underfunded probation departments increasing numbers of persons to supervise.[11]

Parole officers supervise about 731,000 parolees in the United States.[12] As with probation, the optimal caseload is about 25 to 50 parolees; but in some jurisdictions, the parolee/parole officer ratio is as high as 300 to 1.

Probation and parole administrators can probably do little about excessively high caseloads. Because they are at the end of the justice system process, they have little control over the number of people whom the police arrest, prosecutors formally charge, juries convict, or judges sentence to prison.

# Probation Systems

## *Types of Systems*

Figure 11.1 depicts an organizational structure for a regional probation and parole organization. Probation is the most frequently used sanction of all; it costs offenders their privacy and self-determination and usually includes some element of the other sanctions: jail time, fines, restitution, or community service.[13] Probation in the United States is administered by more than 2,000 different agencies. Its organization is a patchwork that defies simple explanation. In about three-fourths of the states, adult probation is part of the executive branch of state government.[14] By contrast, more than half of the agencies providing juvenile probation services are administered in juvenile courts on the local level.[15]

Furthermore, according to Howard Abadinsky, the administration of probation systems can be separated into six categories:

1. *Juvenile.* Separate probation services for juveniles are administered on a county, municipal, or state level.
2. *Municipal.* Independent probation units are administered by the lower courts under state laws and guidelines.
3. *County.* Under laws and guidelines established by the state, a county operates its own probation agency.
4. *State.* One agency administers a central probation system, which provides services throughout the state.
5. *State combined.* Probation and parole services are administered on a statewide basis by one agency.
6. *Federal.* Probation is administered as an arm of the federal courts.[16]

This patchwork nature of probation systems has raised two central organizational issues concerning the administration of probation services: Should probation be part of the judicial or the executive branch of government? Does the

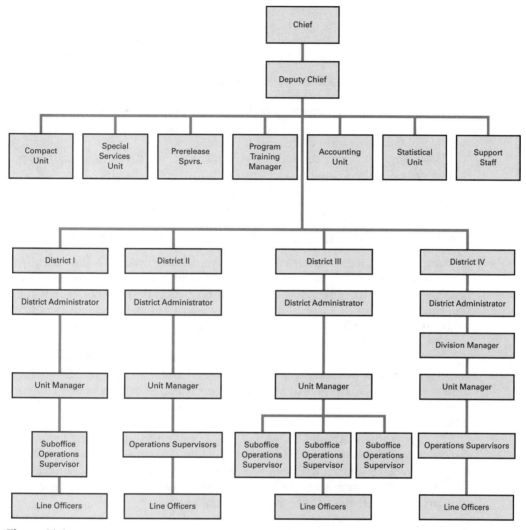

**Figure 11.1**

Organizational structure for a regional adult probation and parole agency.

lack of uniformity in administering probation make justice less equitable statewide?[17] These important and lingering issues were first considered nearly 40 years ago by the President's Commission.[18]

Abadinsky argues that probation administered by the judiciary on a *county* level promotes *diversity:*

> Innovative programming can be implemented more easily in a county agency since it has a shorter line of bureaucratic control than would a statewide agency. A county agency can more easily adapt to change, and the successful programs of one agency

can more easily be adopted by other probation departments . . . and unsuccessful programs avoided. Although the judiciary is nominally responsible for administering probation, the day-to-day operations are in the hands of a professional administrator—the chief probation officer.[19]

One problem with the county-level administration of probation services, however, is that of reduced oversight of operations. The officer/client ratios may differ from one county to another, which would probably not occur if services were monitored by a statewide agency whose personnel could easily be shifted from one county to another to equalize caseloads.

This brings us to the second issue concerning whether this lack of uniformity in providing probation services makes justice less equitable statewide. This issue has led states with county-based probation systems to create statewide bodies for better coordination and uniformity of services.

## *Probation Departments' Need for an Organizational Plan*

As early as 1924, a probation executive wrote that "without a consistent, orderly, and practical plan of organization, and without adequate, competent and sensible methods of supervising the staff, a probation department cannot function properly."[20] Studies discussed later indicate that these problems persist for probation departments in the new millennium: "What are my resources? How can I use them to maximize our supervision and services?" These questions constantly challenge the probation administrator but are seldom addressed directly, according to Patricia Hardyman, who performed a major study of probation administration. The answers would enable the probation administrator to better control limited resources, select supervision strategies, and pursue attainable outcomes.[21]

Each year administrators invest much time and effort in building and acquiring the capital to build office space for probation departments. This investment does not include the human resources invested by community volunteers and the families of probationers, yet little is known about how these resources are translated into activities or their outcomes and impacts.[22]

### *Systems Theory*

As with the administration of police, court, or prison organizations, the probation department administrator's goals may affect the services provided to the client, which in turn may have an impact on the client's request for services. This systematic interaction between an organization's resources and structure and the community has been referred to as its *sociotechnical environment,*"[23] meaning that the principles of the system are organized to execute the basic production technologies of the organization. Each probation administrator needs to recognize that the organization is a system of inputs, processes, and outputs. For probation, inputs would be clients coming into the office for counseling and supervision (the processes); outputs would be the probationer's obtaining employment, acquiring a skill, observing a curfew, and so on. This understanding of probation, using **systems theory,** provides a means to learn how probation departments function and interact with their environment, and to examine the resources, activities, and outcomes in a way that will identify the goals, describe the day-to-day activities, and link the department's activities to resources and outcomes.

According to systems theory, probation may be conceptualized as a network of interwoven resources, activities, and outcomes.[24] According to Hardyman, *resources* include the probation department's funding level, goals, policies and procedures, organizational structure, and caseload; the probation staff's characteristics; the services available to probationers; and the rates of unemployment, poverty, and crime in the county. *Activities* are supervision techniques, rewards, leadership style, contacts, and direct and indirect services provided by the probation department. *Outcomes* according to systems theory are the number of probationers who were arrested, incarcerated, and/or cited for a technical violation during the follow-up period, as well as the needs of probationers that were considered.[25]

## *Management Styles*

Hardyman's study of probation administrators also focused on their management style—the fundamental determinant of the nature of the probation organization—and was instructive in its description of the impact of this style on the department's operation. Few departments, even those with hierarchical organizational structure, had a pure management style; administrators vacillated among a variety of styles, including laissez-faire, democratic, and authoritarian. The degree to which administrators included the probation officers in the decision-making process and communicated with officers varied. The **authoritarian** administrator created emotional and physical distance between the officers and themselves. Officers in such systems reported feeling that they had little control over their cases and that policies and procedures were developed and enforced by people who were unconcerned with their problems and needs on the job.[26]

Surprisingly, the most common management style used by probation administrators was **laissez-faire.** Hardyman found that many probation administrators simply did not participate in the day-to-day activities and supervision strategies of the staff. They remained remote but made final decisions on critical policies and procedures.[27]

Hardyman also found that few probation administrators across the country operated with the **democratic** style. Those who did, of course, listened more to the concerns and suggestions of the line supervisors and officers. The administrator still made final decisions, but information was generally sought from the line staff and their opinions were considered. Officers working under this style had a greater sense that their opinions mattered and that the administrator valued their input. An additional benefit of the democratic style was that the administrators had power by virtue of both their position and their charisma, which inspired teamwork and task accomplishment.[28]

Hardyman also found several negative aspects of probation administration. Chaos was extremely high in urban, laissez-faire probation departments. She observed shouting matches between staff members, and officers reported conflicting departmental policies and standards of supervision. She noted a lack of communication between the administrator and the staff and an inability to create and finish projects. Changes were viewed as imposed from above and were therefore resisted; officers were convinced that their administrators would not listen. Even in democratic probation departments with an open and friendly environment, projects to address current crises were abandoned, and line staff and administrators frequently disagreed. None of the probation departments studied was proactive.[29]

# Parole Systems

## *Models for Providing Services*

The administration of parole is much less complex than probation because parole services are administered centrally on a statewide basis.[30] (It should also be noted that in about 20 states, probation officers also serve as parole officers; thus, much of the information presented in the previous section applies to parole as well.) One state agency administers the parole function on a statewide basis, except that in a number of states, parolees from a local jail come under the supervision of a *county* probation and parole department.[31]

A parole agency can provide three basic services: parole release, parole supervision, and executive clemency. In a number of states that have abolished parole release (such as California), parole officers continue to supervise offenders released by the prison itself on *good time* (reduction of sentence through good behavior).

The National Advisory Commission on Criminal Justice Standards and Goals delineated two basic models for administering parole services:

1. *The **independent model.*** A parole board is responsible for making release (parole) determinations as well as supervising persons released on parole (or good time). It is independent of any other state agency and reports directly to the governor.
2. *The **consolidated model.*** The parole board is a semiautonomous agency within a large department that also administers correctional institutions. Supervision of persons released on parole (or good time) is under the direction of the commissioner of corrections, not the parole board.[32]

Both models sometimes combine probation services with parole services in a single statewide agency.

The President's Commission summarized the advantages of the independent model:

1. The parole board is in the best position to promote the idea of parole and to generate public support and acceptance of it. Because the board is accountable for parole failures, it should be responsible for supervising parolees.
2. The parole board that is in direct control of administering parole services can evaluate and adjust the system more effectively.
3. Supervision by the parole board and its officers properly divorces parole release and parolees from the correctional institution.
4. An independent parole board in charge of its own services is in the best position to present its own budget request to the legislature.[33]

The advantages of including both parole services and institutions in a consolidated department of corrections were summarized by the President's Commission as follows:

1. The correctional process is a continuum; all staff, both institutional and parole, should be under a single administration rather than be divided, which avoids competition for public funds and friction in policies.
2. A consolidated correctional department has consistent administration, including staff selection and supervision.
3. Parole boards are ineffective in performing administrative functions; their major focus should be on case decision, not on day-to-day field operations.
4. Community-based programs that fall between institutions and parole, such as work release, can best be handled by a single centralized administration.[34]

Critics of the independent model contend that it tends to be indifferent or insensitive to institutional programs and that the parole board places undue emphasis on variables outside the institution. Critics of the consolidated model contend that the parole board is pressured to emphasize institutional factors in making parole decisions.[35] Clearly, the trend in this country, beginning in the late 1960s, has been in the direction of consolidation.

In the past, whether institution staff or independent agency should make the parole decision has been controversial. The arguments for staff deciding when to release inmates are based on the following: The staff knows the inmates better, independent agencies and parole boards are too far removed from institutions to know what goes on within them, and giving this responsibility to independent boards downgrades the professional competence of staff and is unnecessarily complicated. These arguments are countered by those contending that independent agencies granting paroles will eliminate irrational decision making by staff, that staff often lengthen stays for the violation of trivial and meaningless rules, and that staff may be secretive about the criteria for release and hold release over the heads of inmates.[36]

## *The Demise of Federal Parole*

The U.S. Sentencing Commission established a new set of sentencing guidelines that were instituted on November 1, 1987. The guidelines abolished parole for federal prisoners. Supervised release from prison was *not* discontinued entirely, however; in effect, something equivalent to parole is still in place, but the sentencing court is now the controlling authority over the inmate rather than a federal parole commission. The court has the authority to impose sanctions on released prisoners if they violate conditions of their release.

Many, if not most, prisoners sentenced under the new guidelines are still in prison (and have attempted a substantial amount of litigation attacking the new sentencing guidelines, most of which has been rejected by the courts). Prison wardens have undoubtedly experienced a higher inmate population that is serving longer terms because of this legislation; as a result, they must expend greater effort toward seeking alternatives to incarceration.

# Intermediate Sanctions

As this and preceding chapters have indicated, the overall health of corrections is not good. The criminal justice community, including probation agencies, is said to be involved in guerrilla warfare, meaning that the highest-risk probationers are out of control and generally reside in "out-of-control communities."[37] As one author observed, offenders may be smiling because "revolving door justice" has become an all-too-frequent fact of prison and jail life.[38] Institutional and community systems are being utilized beyond capacity. The United States is not soft on crime, but because prisons are not in a position to effect great change,[39] the search for solutions must include correctional programs in the community.

The demand for prison space has created a reaction throughout corrections. Many state systems have attempted to solve the problem by building more prisons or expanding existing ones; however, these reactive efforts have resulted in financial, legal, and administrative problems.[40] With the cost of prison construction now exceeding $200,000 per cell in maximum-security institutions, cost-saving alternatives are becoming more attractive if not necessary. Opening the gates of jails and prisons and liberating inmates is, of course, one solution to the overcrowding problem. But it is not a serious alternative. A real alternative to incarceration needs to have three elements to be effective: It must incapacitate offenders enough so that it is possible to interfere with their lives and activities to make committing a new offense extremely difficult; it must be unpleasant enough to deter offenders from wanting to commit new crimes; and it has to provide real and credible protection for the community.[41]

In addition to overcrowding, two interrelated developments characterize the state of corrections today and reflect major correctional problems: ideological restatement and, as a result, intermediate initiatives. In response to the criticisms and failures of rehabilitative philosophy and policies, the prevailing ideology of incapacitation, punishment, and deterrence has resulted in get-tough sentencing practices that contribute to rising prison populations. This shift from rehabilitating inmates to giving them their just deserts is based on the belief that offenders make free will decisions to commit crime and therefore no longer deserve compassion and correction. This ideology has brought an era of repressive social control, which attempts to banish, expel, and stigmatize the criminal deviant.[42] This is a vicious cycle, however; we have seen that these actions do little to deter crime.

## *Alternatives to Incarceration*

Probation and parole do not operate in a vacuum; their operations are affected by what occurs in the rest of the justice system and the actions of other justice administrators. As the number of crimes continues to increase, the availability of incarceration facilities decreases. The implication of this problem is not lost on offenders: If they commit more crimes, they cause more overcrowding, spend less time in an institution, and are quickly released to commit a new round of offenses.[43]

Much of the experimentation with community-based alternatives to imprisonment reflects the current crisis in our prisons. The tension between the get-tough philosophy and the realities of prison overcrowding has led to a "search for intermediate punishments . . . an attempt to find mid-range solutions."[44] This in turn has brought about the emergence of a new generation of programs, making community-based corrections, according to Barry Nidorf, a "strong, full partner in the fight against crime and a leader in confronting the crowding crisis. It is no longer considered a weak stepchild of the justice system."[45] Economic reality dictates that cost-effective measures be developed, and this is motivating the development of intermediate sanctions.[46]

A survey by the Association of State Correctional Administrators[47] found that 86 percent of all states used intensive supervision, 83 percent used electronic monitoring, and 34 percent used house arrest. Table 11.1 shows the numbers of persons under supervision by program type.

The growing interest in alternatives to incarceration is not based solely on the need to develop less expensive alternatives to prisons, although the economic realities cannot be overlooked.[48] Today's probation and parole administrators must have an arsenal of risk-control tools at their disposal. Community corrections agencies are using the programs described next.

### *Intensive Probation or Parole*

Intensive supervision has become the most popular program in probation and parole. Early versions were based on the premise that increased client contact would enhance rehabilitation while affording greater client control. Current programs are simply a means of easing the burden of prison overcrowding.[49]

Intensive supervision can be classified into two types: those stressing diversion, and those stressing enhancement. A **diversion** program is commonly

**TABLE 11.1**   Persons Under Jail Supervision, by Confinement Status and Type of Program, Midyear 1995, 1999–2001

| CONFINEMENT STATUS AND TYPE OF PROGRAM | NUMBER OF PERSONS UNDER JAIL SUPERVISION | | | |
|---|---|---|---|---|
| | *1995* | *1999* | *2000* | *2001* |
| **Total** | 541,913 | 687,973 | 687,033 | 702,044 |
| **Held in jail** | 507,044 | 605,943 | 621,149 | 631,240 |
| **Supervised outside a jail facility**[a] | 34,869 | 82,030 | 65,884 | 70,804 |
| Electronic monitoring | 6,788 | 10,230 | 10,782 | 10,017 |
| Home detention[b] | 1,376 | 518 | 332 | 539 |
| Day reporting | 1,283 | 5,080 | 3,969 | 3,522 |
| Community service | 10,253 | 20,139 | 13,592 | 17,561 |
| Weekender programs | 1,909 | 16,089 | 14,523 | 14,381 |
| Other pretrial supervision | 3,229 | 10,092 | 6,279 | 6,632 |
| Other work programs[c] | 9,144 | 7,780 | 8,011 | 5,204 |
| Treatment programs[d] | — | 8,500 | 5,714 | 5,219 |
| Other/unspecified | 887 | 3,602 | 2,682 | 7,729 |

—Not available.
[a]Excludes persons supervised by a probation or parole agency.
[b]Includes only those without electronic monitoring.
[c]Includes persons in work release programs, work gangs, and other work alternative programs.
[d]Includes persons under drug, alcohol, mental health, and other medical treatment.

*Source:* U.S. Department of Justice, Bureau of Justice Statistics, *Prison and Jail Inmates at Midyear 2001* (Washington, D.C.: Author, April 2002), p. 8.

known as a "front door" program because its goal is to limit the number of generally low-risk offenders who enter prison. *Enhancement programs* generally select already sentenced probationers and parolees and subject them to closer supervision in the community than they receive under regular probation or parole. These people have shown evidence of failure under routine supervision or have committed offenses deemed to be too serious for supervision on routine caseloads.[50]

As of 1990, jurisdictions in all 50 states had instituted *intensive supervision probation* (ISP). Persons placed on ISP are supposed to be those offenders who, in the absence of intensive supervision, would have been sentenced to imprisonment. In parole, intensive supervision is viewed as risk management—allowing for a high-risk inmate to be paroled but under the most restrictive of circumstances. In either case, intensive supervision is a response to overcrowding; although ISP is invariably more costly than regular supervision, the costs "are compared not with the costs of normal supervision but rather with the costs of incarceration."[51]

ISP is demanding for probationers and parolees and does not represent freedom; in fact, it may stress and isolate repeat offenders more than imprisonment does. Given the option of serving prison terms or participating in ISPs, many offenders have chosen prison.[52] Many offenders may prefer to serve a short prison term rather than spend five times as long in an ISP. Consider the alternatives now facing offenders in one western state:

> *ISP.* The offender serve two years under this alternative. During that time, a probation officer visits the offender two or three times per week and phones on the other days. The offender is subject to unannounced searches of his or her home for drugs and has his or her urine tested regularly for alcohol and drugs. The offender must strictly abide by other conditions as set by the court: not carrying a weapon, not socializing with certain persons, performing community service, and being employed or participating in training or education. In addition, he or she will be strongly encouraged to attend counseling and/or other treatment, particularly if he or she is a drug offender.
>
> [or]
>
> *Prison.* The alternative is a sentence of two to four years of which the offender will serve only about three to six months. During this term, the offender is not required to work or to participate in any training or treatment but may do so voluntarily. Once released, the offender is placed on a two-year routine parole supervision and must visit his or her parole officer about once a month.[53]

When choosing punishment for offenders, policymakers must consider the attitudes of this country's serious offenders. Imprisonment no longer represents a horrible punishment and therefore has lost much of its deterrent power. If fear of prison does not prevent criminal behavior, other methods should be tried.

Corrections administrators should note that the establishment of ISP was not based on careful research and evaluation but is simply a response to jail and prison overcrowding. Nonetheless, although evidence of the effectiveness of this program is lacking, it has been deemed a public relations success.[54] Intensive supervision is usually accomplished by severely reducing caseload size per probation/parole officer, leading to increased contact between officers and clients or their significant others (such as spouse or parents), and that this increased contact will improve service delivery and control and thus reduce recidivism.[55]

ISP for drug offenders in seven cities (Seattle, Washington; Des Moines, Iowa; Santa Fe, New Mexico; Atlanta, Georgia; Macon, Georgia; Waycross, Georgia; and Winchester, Virginia) did not, however, appear to impact recidivism. Research revealed no significant differences between the arrest rates for intensively supervised clients and a control group receiving regular supervision. Similar findings have been reported in studies in other cities.[56] Drawing conclusions from recidivism statistics can be misleading, however, because recidivism could

be a feature of the intensity of the supervision, which could increase the probability of new criminality being *discovered.*

Another problem to be considered by correctional administrators, policymakers, and sentencing judges concerns the potential for—and the reality of—
ISP being used inappropriately, and for the wrong reasons. Although such
supervision is intended for high-risk offenders, studies have determined that
many ISP programs appear to be accepting those offenders who are not at high
risk and who probably should have been on regular probation in the first instance. It is known that probation departments in some jurisdictions routinely
recommend inappropriate cases for ISP for two reasons: to deliver "good stats"
and to keep down regular caseloads by shifting some cases to probation officers
funded by special ISP allocations. Intensive supervision for such cases may actually be harmful to the client: an offender inappropriately identified as high risk
may indeed assume that role and conduct his or her behavior accordingly.
Judges should stringently refrain from sending probation-eligible offenders to
prison while using ISP for those who would be sentenced to probation in any
event.[57]

### Electronic Monitoring

Like ISP, the use of electronic monitoring began in the mid-1980s. In the early
1980s, Jack Love, a judge in New Mexico, saw a *Spiderman* comic in which evildoers placed an electronic monitor on Spiderman to track his whereabouts. Love
persuaded a friend to develop the idea and the technology; the rest is history.[58]

Electronic monitoring has become another form of intermediate sanction; it
applies to offenders whose crimes are less serious than those requiring long-
term incarceration but are more serious than those committed by persons serving standard probation. Electronic monitoring has been associated primarily
with probation, although its use in a parole setting has occurred in some states
(such as Utah) on a limited scale to supplement curfew restrictions.

Two basic types of electronic monitoring devices are available: active and
passive. The former are continuous signaling devices attached to the offender
that constantly monitor his or her presence at a particular location. A receiver-
dialer apparatus is attached to the offender's telephone and detects signals from
the transmitter. A central computer accepts reports from the receiver-dialer over
telephone lines, compares them with the offender's curfew schedule, and alerts
corrections officials to unauthorized absences.[59] Simpler, continuous signaling
systems that do not use a telephone consist of only two basic components: a
transmitter and a portable receiver. The transmitter, which is strapped to the offender's ankle or wrist or worn around the neck, emits a radio signal that travels
about one city block. By driving past the offender's residence, place of employment, or wherever he or she is supposed to be, the officer can verify his or her
presence with the handheld portable receiver.[60]

The passive type of electronic monitoring involves the use of programmed
contact devices that contact the offender periodically to verify his or her presence. Various manufacturing companies use a different method to assure that

the offender is the person responding to the call and is in fact at the monitored location as required. One system uses voice verification technology. Another system uses satellite technology. The subject wears an ankle bracelet and carries or wears a portable tracking device about the size of a small lunchbox, weighing 3.5 pounds. The Defense Department's Global Positioning System satellite constellation is able to establish an offender's whereabouts within 150 feet of his or her location 24 hours a day. The device can also warn an offender to "back off" if he or she has strayed too far from the assigned location. The cost of this system is many times that of the active systems already discussed.[61]

Such devices greatly aid in the use of home detention programs, which have been implemented for repeat drunk-driving and other types of offenders. Persons who would normally be incarcerated are allowed to remain in the community under probation supervision but are restricted to their homes during evening hours. A computer dials the client's home telephone number on random days; the client answers and by placing an electronic bracelet attached to his or her wrist to the telephone sends a code to the computer. The computer then asks several verifying questions of the client, and a report is sent to the office.

### Shock Probation/Parole

Shock probation is another less costly intermediate alternative to incarceration that is supported by many correctional administrators. This form of corrections combines a brief exposure to incarceration with subsequent release. It allows sentencing judges to reconsider the original sentence to prison and, upon motion, to recall the inmate after a few months in prison and place him or her on probation, under conditions deemed appropriate. The idea is that the "shock" of a short stay in prison will give the offender a taste of institutional life and will make such an indelible impression that he or she will be deterred from future crime and will avoid the negative effects of lengthy confinement.[62]

In many states, each candidate for shock probation/parole must obtain a community sponsor who will be responsible for the applicant's actions while in the community. The sponsor serves as an adjunct to and a resource for the probation officer. Specific activities for the sponsor can include providing transportation to work, checking on compliance with curfew and other restrictions, assisting with housing and employment problems, and maintaining contact with the probation officer. The offender may also be required to perform community service, usually physical labor.[63]

### Boot Camps/Shock Incarceration

Correctional boot camps, also called shock incarceration, were first implemented as an intermediate sanction in 1983. Since then, the political appeal of boot camp programs has led to their rapid proliferation across the United States for both adult and juvenile offenders.[64] These programs place offenders in a quasi-military program of three to six months' duration that is similar to a military basic training program. The intent is to avoid long-term incarceration and to instill discipline, routine, and unquestioning obedience to orders. Offenders serve a short institutional sentence and then are put through a rigorous regimen of drills, strenuous workouts, marching, and hard physical labor. To be eligible, inmates must generally be young, nonviolent offenders.

Proponents of the boot camp concept argue that many young offenders become involved in crime because they lack self-respect and are unable to structure their lives; consequently the boot camp model targets young first offenders who seem to be embarking on a path to sustained criminality.[65] It is also believed that these youths can benefit from a militarylike atmosphere that strips them of their street identity and allows them to experience improvements in self-esteem, educational achievement, and physical fitness.

Early evaluations of boot camps generally found, however, that this regimen and harsh atmosphere did little to overcome the problems that cause inner-city youths to get in trouble with the law in the first place. In fact, follow-up of boot camp graduates shows that they did no better than other offenders without this experience.[66] Only boot camps that were carefully designed, targeted the right offenders, and provided rehabilitative services and aftercare were deemed likely to save the state money and reduce recidivism.[67]

Skeptics of the jail or prison boot camp experience believe that such an approach is absurd in light of the fact that the military itself has dramatically changed in the way it trains recruits, moving away from abusive or degrading methods. Furthermore, they believe the boot camp approach runs the risk of turning out young men who are stronger and more aggressive than they would have been under routine imprisonment—and without receiving education or developing any additional employment skills. They add that this approach is simply a scam by political officials who want to show that they are "doing something" about crime and criminals. Others note that after boot camp, military personnel enter a stable environment that provides for their basic needs—a very different environment from the one to which most shock incarceration subjects will return.[68]

Notwithstanding all the criticisms and controversy swirling around the boot camp experience, the major question remaining is do they work to reduce recidivism? Generally, research has shown that offenders released from boot camps do not fare better after they return to the community.[69] As Doris MacKenzie[70] concluded:

> If the core components of boot camps reduced recidivism, we would have expected that the boot camp releasees in all states would do better than the offenders in the comparison groups. This did not happen. The military atmosphere does not appear to reduce recidivism.

### Day Reporting Centers

Another intermediate sanction that has gained recent popularity among correctional administrators and policymakers is the day reporting center. Such centers originated in Great Britain as a response to less serious but chronic offenders who lacked basic skills and were often dependent on drugs or alcohol. The British experience led several U.S. states to begin setting up day reporting centers in the mid-1980s. The purposes of day reporting centers are to heighten control and surveillance of offenders placed on community supervision, to increase offender access to treatment programs, to give officials more proportional and certain sanctions, and to reduce prison or jail crowding. Offenders report to the centers frequently (usually once or twice a day), and treatment services (job training and placement, counseling, and education) are usually provided on-site either by the agency running the program or by other human services agencies.[71]

One study of the effect of day reporting centers on recidivism found no significant reduction in the rate of rearrest. The author pointed out, however, that regardless of effect on recidivism, the center "empowers the individual offender by offering him or her literacy courses, GED preparation, substance abuse counseling, and anger management courses."[72]

# CASE STUDIES

The following two case studies will help the reader apply some of this chapter's materials concerning probation and parole. The first addresses a disgruntled employee and the second involves policy and publicity.

## "Cheerless Chuck" and the Parole Officer's Orientation Day*

"So, you're the new parole officer with a criminal justice degree from the university? Well, I hope you last longer than the last recruit I had. She meant well, but I guess her idealistic ideas about the job of parole officer couldn't handle the realities of the work. In a way, I understand what she went through. Same thing happened to me 12 years ago when I started this job. There I was, fresh out of college with a brand new diploma with "Social Work" written on it. I figured that piece of paper made me a social worker, and I better get right to work fixing society. It didn't take me long to realize that the real world was different from what I had learned in college. It was like I had been trained as a sailor, and I was about to set out on a voyage, but I couldn't take the time to steer the ship because I was so busy bailing water. The crises we deal with here make it darned difficult to do the work we all see needs to be done. Years ago, when I first started with the parole department, things were a lot better than they are now. Caseloads were lower, fewer people were getting parole who didn't deserve it, and the rest of the criminal justice system was in a lot better shape, which made our jobs a lot easier to do. Think about it. We vote in politicians who promise the public that they are going to 'get tough' on crime and the first thing they do is allot more money for law enforcement stuff: beat cops, car computers, helicopters, and so on. These things are great, but all they do is add more people into a system that is already overloaded. No one gets elected by promising to build more courts or add jail and prison space, or probation and parole officers. Eventually these added police officers arrest more people than the system can handle. The courts back up, which in turn messes up the prisons and the jails. The inmates stuck in these crowded places get tired of living like sardines, so they sue the prisons and jails. Remember, the Constitution prohibits cruel and unusual punishment. A lot of times inmates' complaints are legitimate, and they win. The judge orders the prison to lower its population to a reasonable level, which forces the parole board to consider more inmates for early release. They come knocking on our doors, hoping we can get them out of the mess that politics and budgets have created. Nobody mentions giving the

*Contributed by Matthew Leone, assistant professor of criminal justice, University of Nevada, Reno.

parole department more officers, or a bigger budget for added administrative help. No, the bucks go to the flashy, visible things like cops and cars. Meanwhile, in the past 10 years, our average caseload for a parole officer has increased 75 percent. We have more people who need supervision, and we are doing it on a budget that has not kept pace with the remainder of the criminal justice system. This wouldn't be so bad if the system was at least adding things to other areas, like the jail or the courts. The problem here is that we depend on the jail to hold our parolees who have violated their conditions. We catch some of them using booze or drugs, and we are *supposed* to bring them in to the county jail to wait for a hearing to decide if they are going back to prison, or back on the street. But the jail has its own set of problems. A couple of years ago the U.S. district court slapped a population cap on our jail. If it goes over that population, the jail will not accept our violators. So we send them home. If they get into more serious trouble, we call it a new crime, the police arrest them, and the jail has to take them. Then they have to sit and wait for the court to catch up, since the courts are not in much better shape than the jail. I guess the job would be easier if the prisons were doing their jobs, too. I can't really blame them, since the prisons are funded in much the same way that parole is. We are not 'glamorous' places to send your tax dollars, but if the prisons were getting more money, they might be able to improve the quality of inmate they send to us. Maybe a little more vocational training and substance abuse counseling, so they could stay off the booze and drugs. Possibly then fewer of these parolees would wind up back behind bars a few years later. The worst part about the job is the caseload. We presently have so many on parole that I am lucky if I can get a phone call to each of them once a week, and maybe a home visit once a month. You can't tell me that a phone call and a home visit are really keeping these guys from committing crimes. The sad part about it is that with the proper budget and staff, we could really make a difference. We spend so much time bailing water out of the boat, we don't realize that there is no one steering, and we are just drifting in circles. By the way, my name is Charlie Matthews, but everyone calls me Chuck. I'm a supervisor here as well as the designated new-employee orientation specialist and all-round public relations person. I hope I've not depressed you too much on your first day, but now is a good time to drop your idealism and get to work 'bailing.' What're *your* views and ideas?"

## Questions for Discussion

1. Should Chuck be retained as orientation coordinator? Why or why not?
2. How would changes in politics affect the parole system directly and indirectly?
3. How does an old criminal justice planning adage that "you can't rock one end of the boat" seem to be applicable to what Chuck says about law enforcement getting so much new political funding?

4. What kinds of administrative problems and practices might be responsible for this agency's situation?

5. Why do crowded jails and prisons make the job of parole officers more difficult?

6. How could practices of the jails and prisons change the success of the parole system?

7. Based on Chuck's assessment of the local situation, where do you believe the greatest misconceptions about courts and corrections exist?

## "Out of Town Brown" and the Besieged Probation Supervisor*

Joan Casey is a career probation officer. She majored in criminal justice as an undergraduate and plans to get her master's in criminology within the next few years. She holds memberships in several national correctional organizations, attends training conferences, and does a lot of reading on her own time to stay current in the field. Casey began working for the Collier County Probation Department soon after she graduated from college and was promoted to a supervisory position within five years, a remarkable accomplishment considering her relative lack of seniority in the organization. She supervises an adult probation unit consisting of eight seasoned probation officers, all of whom have been in the workforce longer than she has. The unit is responsible for investigating approximately 80 offenders a month and preparing presentence investigation reports on them. Collier County Probation Department has made the front page of the local newspapers twice in the past year. Both times it was a nightmare for the chief probation officer, Jack Brown, and the entire agency. "Collier County Soft on Crime!" screamed the first headline and then, just a month later, "Northside Stalker Gets Probation!" Brown called a management team meeting. It was short and to the point: "No more lousy publicity," he said, "or heads are gonna roll! Has everybody got it?" Everybody got it. No written policy concerning media relations exists, however, nor is any particular person authorized to release agency information. This week Brown is on annual leave, the assistant chief is out of state at an American Correctional Association meeting, and Joan Casey is the designated officer in charge. One of Casey's probation officers has recommended community-based treatment for a 16-year-old mentally retarded boy who was prosecuted as an adult. The youth murdered his stepfather with an axe after submitting to many years of physical and mental abuse. He had been an incest victim since he was five years old. Casey is aware of the probation officer's recommendation and agrees with it. After all, she reasons, the boy is a low risk for recidivism, and he is as much a victim of this offense as was his step-

*Contributed by Catherine Lowe, former director, California Center for Judicial Education and Research, Emeryville, California.

father. It is 4:45 P.M. on Thursday. Casey's phone rings; her secretary has put through a call from a reporter at a local newspaper. The reporter is a strong crusader in the local war against crime. He has his own byline weekly column at the paper. He knows that the "kiddie-killer" will be sentenced tomorrow.

### Questions for Discussion

1. What should Casey's response to the reporter be other than hanging up or telling him to call back?
2. If she elects to discuss her officer's recommendation, what should she say to justify it?
3. What should the chief probation officer do upon his return to work?
4. Was the probation officer's recommendation correct based on these facts?
5. Should a policy be immediately drafted for this situation? Should any personnel actions be taken?

## Summary

This chapter focused on probation, parole, and several new forms of diversion termed *intermediate sanctions.* It is clear that probation and parole agencies continue to bear the brunt of the combined effects of increased crime, tough mandatory sentencing laws leading to a increased incarceration of offenders, a get-tough public and justice system attitude toward crime that permeates the country, and tremendously overcrowded prisons. Given this situation, it is probably a credit to probation and parole administrators that they have managed to cope under such circumstances and have implemented several other, intermediate sanctions to address these problems.

## Questions for Review

1. What are the various types of probation systems being administered in the United States? Describe each.
2. Should probation services be placed within the judicial or executive branch of government? Defend your answer.
3. What are some of the major needs, problems, and concerns of probation administrators?
4. What are the two basic models of parole administration.
5. Why are intermediate sanctions being used so widely in probation and parole?
6. What do *intensive supervision* and *electronic monitoring* mean?

7. How can shock probation further the goals of corrections? Boot camps/ shock incarceration? What successes and problems have been found with these practices?

# Notes

1. Belinda McCarthy and Bernard McCarthy, quoted in Howard Abadinsky, *Probation and Parole: Theory and Practice,* 7th ed. (Upper Saddle River, N.J.: Prentice Hall, 2000), p. 196.

2. Todd R. Clear, "Punishment and Control in Community Supervision," in Clayton A. Hartjen and Edward E. Rhine (eds.), *Correctional Theory and Practice* (Chicago: Nelson-Hall, 1992), pp. 31–42.

3. See the President's Commission on Law Enforcement and Administration of Justice, *Task Force Report: Corrections* (Washington, D.C.: U.S. Government Printing Office, 1967), p. 7.

4. Franklin E. Zimring and Gordon J. Hawkins, *Deterrence: The Legal Threat in Crime Control* (Chicago: University of Chicago Press, 1973).

5. Joan Petersilia, "When Probation Becomes More Dreaded Than Prison," *Federal Probation* 54 (March 1990):23.

6. Ibid.

7. Ibid., p. 25.

8. Ibid., p. 24.

9. John Conrad, "The Pessimistic Reflections of a Chronic Optimist," *Federal Probation* 55 (June 1991):4–9.

10. U.S. Department of Justice, Bureau of Justice Statistics Web page, "Correctional Populations," http://www.ojp.usdoj.gov/bis/glance/tables/corr2tab.htm (accessed June 24, 2002).

11. Dean J. Champion, *Corrections in the United States: A Contemporary Perspective,* 2d ed. (Upper Saddle River, N.J.: Prentice Hall, 1998), p. 37.

12. U.S. Department of Justice, Bureau of Justice Statistics Web page, "Correctional Populations," http://www.ojp.usdoj.gov/bis/corr2tab.htm (accessed June 24, 2002).

13. Barry J. Nidorf, "Community Corrections: Turning the Crowding Crisis into Opportunities," *Corrections Today* (October 1989):82–88.

14. Abadinsky, *Probation and Parole,* p. 104.

15. Ibid., p. 57.

16. Ibid., pp. 104–105.

17. Ibid., pp. 106–107.

18. See President's Commission, *Task Force Report,* pp. 35–37.

19. Abadinsky, *Probation and Parole,* p. 107.

20. E. P. Volz, "Staff Supervision and Organization," in *Proceedings of the National Probation Association—1924* (New York: National Probation Association, 1924), pp. 103–105.

21. Patricia L. Hardyman, "Management Styles in Probation: Policy Implications Derived from Systems Theory," in Hartjen and Rhine, *Correctional Theory and Practice,* pp. 61–81.

22. David Duffee, "The Community Context of Probation," in Patrick McAnany, Doug Thompson, and David Fogel (eds.), *Probation and Justice: Reconsideration of Mission* (Cambridge, Mass.: Oelgeschlager, Gunn, and Hain, 1984).

23. Eric Trist, "On Socio-Technical Systems," in Kenneth Benne and Robert Chin (eds.), *The Planning of Change,* 2d ed. (New York: Holt, Rinehart and Winston, 1969), pp. 269–281.

24. Daniel Katz and Robert I. Kahn, *The Social Psychology of Organizations* (New York: John Wiley, 1966).
25. Hardyman, "Management Styles in Probation," p. 68.
26. Ibid., p. 70.
27. Ibid.
28. Ibid., p. 71.
29. Ibid., pp. 74–75.
30. Abadinsky, *Probation and Parole,* p. 223.
31. Ibid.
32. National Advisory Commission on Criminal Justice Standards and Goals, *Corrections* (Washington, D.C.: U.S. Government Printing Office, 1973), pp. 396–397.
33. President's Commission, *Task Force Report,* p. 71.
34. Ibid.
35. National Advisory Commission, *Corrections,* pp. 396–397.
36. President's Commission, *Task Force Report,* p. 65.
37. Donald Cochran, "Corrections' Catch 22," *Corrections Today* (October 1989):16–18.
38. Nidorf, "Community Corrections," p. 82.
39. John P. Conrad, "The Redefinition of Probation: Drastic Proposals to Solve an Urgent Problem," in McAnany, Thomson, and Fogel (eds.), *Probation and Justice,* p. 258.
40. Peter J. Benekos, "Beyond Reintegration: Community Corrections in a Retributive Era," *Federal Probation* 54 (March 1990):53.
41. Ibid.
42. Ibid.
43. Nidorf, "Community Corrections," p. 84.
44. Belinda R. McCarthy, *Intermediate Punishments: Intensive Supervision, Home Confinement, and Electronic Surveillance* (Monsey, N.Y.: Criminal Justice Press, 1987), p. 3.
45. Nidorf, "Community Corrections," p. 85.
46. Benekos, "Beyond Reintegration," p. 54.
47. Association of State Correctional Administrators, *Newsletter,* 16:3 (April 1999):4–5.
48. McCarthy, *Intermediate Punishments,* p. 3.
49. Abadinsky, *Probation and Parole,* p. 410.
50. Joan Petersilia and Susan Turner, *Evaluating Intensive Supervision Probation/Parole: Results of a Nationwide Experiment* (Washington, D.C.: National Institute of Justice, 1993).
51. Lawrence A. Bennett, "Practice in Search of a Theory: The Case of Intensive Supervision—An Extension of an Old Practice," *American Journal of Criminal Justice* 12 (1988):293–310.
52. Ibid., p. 293.
53. This information was compiled from ISP brochures and information from the Oregon Department of Correction by Joan Petersilia.
54. Todd R. Clear and Patricia R. Hardyman, "The New Intensive Supervision Movement," *Crime and Delinquency* 36 (January 1990):42–60.
55. Ibid., p. 44.
56. Petersilia and Turner, *Evaluating Intensive Supervision Probation/Parole.*
57. Abadinsky, *Probation and Parole,* pp. 422–423.
58. Keenen Peck, "High-Tech House Arrest," *The Progressive* (July 1988):26–28.
59. Annesley K. Schmidt, "Electronic Monitors: Realistically, What Can Be Expected?" *Federal Probation* 59 (June 1991):47–53.

60. Abadinsky, *Probation and Parole*, p. 428.

61. David Brauer, "Satellite 'Big Brother' Tracks Ex-Inmates," *Chicago Tribune* (December 18, 1998):31.

62. Jeanne B. Stinchcomb and Vernon B. Fox, *Introduction to Corrections*, 5th ed. (Upper Saddle River, N.J.: Prentice Hall, 1999), p. 165.

63. Abadinsky, *Probation and Parole*, p. 434.

64. Gaylene Styve Armstrong, Angela R. Gover, and Doris Layton MacKenzie, "The Development and Diversity of Correctional Boot Camps," in Rosemary L. Gido and Ted Alleman (eds.), *Turnstile Justice: Issues in American Corrections* (Upper Saddle River, N.J.: Prentice Hall, 2002), pp. 115–130.

65. Todd R. Clear and John E. Adamson, *American Corrections*, 6th ed. (Belmont, Calif.: Wadsworth, 2003).

66. Doris Layton MacKenzie, "Boot Camp Prisons and Recidivism in Eight States," *Criminology* 33:3 (1995):327–358.

67. Doris Layton MacKenzie and Alex Piquero, "The Impact of Shock Incarceration Programs on Prison Crowding," *Crime and Delinquency* 40:2 (April 1994):222–249.

68. Rudolf E. S. Mathias and James W. Mathews, "The Boot Camp Program for Offenders: Does the Shoe Fit?" *International Journal of Offender Therapy and Comparative Criminology* 35 (1991):322–327.

69. Armstrong, Gover, and MacKenzie, "The Development and Diversity of Correctional Boot Camps," p. 126.

70. Doris Layton MacKenzie, "Results of a Multistate Study of Boot Camp Prisons," *Federal Probation* 58 (June 1994):61.

71. Dale G. Parent, "Day Reporting Centers: An Evolving Intermediate Sanction," *Federal Probation* 60 (December 1996):51–54.

72. Liz Marie Marciniak, "The Addition of Day Reporting to Intensive Supervision Probation: A Comparison of Recidivism Rates," *Federal Probation* 64 (June 2000):34–39.

# Chapter 12

# Corrections Issues and Practices

## Key Terms and Concepts

Boot camps

Drug interdiction

Eighth Amendment

Privatization

Sexual victimization

## Learning Objectives

After reading this chapter, the student will:

- be familiar with victimization in correctional institutions
- have an understanding of prison chain gangs
- be familiar with shock incarceration programs
- be aware of issues concerning various inmate groups, including the mentally ill, female, and minority populations
- have an understanding of the Pennsylvania Plan
- be familiar with the treatment of drug problems in prisons
- understand the pros and cons of privatization in correctional operations and programs

> *Boredom is beautiful.*
>
> —Former Nevada prison warden

*I never saw a man who looked / With such a wistful eye / Upon
that little tent of blue / Which prisoners call the sky.*

—Oscar Wilde

## Introduction

The preceding three chapters addressed issues related to prisons and jails.
This chapter discusses additional challenges for contemporary correctional
administrators.

First, we examine both substantive (e.g., overcrowding and problems involving the inmate population) and administrative (budgeting, human resource management, planning, and projecting for the future) issues. Then, we
discuss the extent of, and methods for coping with, sexual coercion within
the institutional setting. Next, we consider whether, as some have suggested,
the use of chain gangs and boot camps constitutes cruel and unusual punishment. We then examine issues concerning several types of offender populations: the aging, juvenile, female, mentally ill, and minority inmates. Next is a
review of drug use, interdiction, and treatment in prisons, followed by an
overview of the privatization of prisons. The chapter concludes with two case
studies.

## Issues Facing Correctional Administrators

These are not times for weak-spirited corrections leaders and managers. Today's
correctional environment differs from that of the past in several ways. First, political involvement in correctional policy and practice are strong influences. Second, correctional agencies now use a large percentage of the public budget of
the federal, state, and local governments. Finally, because of the extensive media
coverage of high-profile crimes and sentencing practices, citizens develop a
strong interest in and opinion of criminals' treatment.[1]

To be successful, correctional administrators must be some of the best in
government service, as many practical issues confront them. Those issues may
be divided into two broad categories: substantive and administrative. We discuss
both next.

### Substantive Correctional Issues

Substantive issues involve matters and knowledge that are specific to the practice and profession of corrections, including factors such as dealing with increasingly overcrowded prisons and managing prisoners who are serving extremely
long terms.

Managers of community-based correctional operations must consider what
is often referred to as a new narrative for community supervision, one that deals

more with supervision and public safety than with assistance and counseling for offenders.[2] Both prison and community correctional staff must deal with offenders who are now younger, more violent, and more likely to be associated with gangs.

Increases in the number of prisoners in state and federal institutions (see Chapter 9) present several issues for administrators: the prediction of which offender categories will grow and by how much, the development of management policy for the expected increase (for example, added bed space or diversion of offenders?), public and political support for the approach, and the implementation of plans for managing the increase in offenders. Each year, the average length of prison confinement increases, as Congress and state legislatures adopt three strikes laws for repeat offenders and extend the number of crimes for which offenders must serve a "natural life" (their life span) sentence. Long sentences present administrators with several formidable problems because of the diversity of the prison population and the severity of offenses that result in these lengthy sentences. Not only must correctional administrators determine the appropriate design and construction of prisons to house these inmates, but they must also look at how these longer sentences affect traditional approaches for inmate discipline and rewards to promote safe environments for staff and other inmates.[3]

Proponents of longer sentences argue that such sentences maximize the correctional goals of incapacitation and deterrence; they suggest that these longer sentences effectively reduce crime and therefore justify the significant increase in the number of inmates.[4] Opponents, however, argue that this increase in prison terms creates collateral issues and unintended social consequences, such as the recruitment by seasoned offenders of younger individuals to replace those criminals arrested and incarcerated, and the deterioration of the family that results from removing the parent-age male from the home.[5]

For most of the 1990s, community supervision (probation and parole) underwent a transition from helping and counseling offenders to risk management and surveillance.[6] This new focus has been accompanied by additional allocations of resources for incarceration, rather than for probation and parole. In this view, crime is seen as a social phenomenon. Offenders are addressed not as individuals, but as aggregate populations.[7] Therefore, community corrections and prison administrators must confront a basic and critical issue: managing an offender population that has changed dramatically during the past 25 years. In sum, as Richard Seiter[8] observed:

> As a group, today's offenders are more prone to gang involvement and violence, are younger and more impulsive, are serving longer sentences, and have little hope or belief that they will successfully return to the community as law abiding citizens. Many more offenders are dealing with medical and mental health issues. Last, juvenile offenders increasingly act like adults in their sophistication and types of crimes.

## *Administrative Correctional Issues*

The kinds of administrative issues that must be confronted by today's corrections leaders include areas such as *budgeting, human resource management, planning,* and *projecting for the future.* As budgets have grown, demanding a larger share of governmental resources, political scrutiny has increased. In 1982, corrections expenditures in this nation totaled about $9 billion; today, the budgets for correctional agencies are more than $49 billion[9]—an increase of 449 percent (85 percent of those expenditures are for state and local governments combined, and the federal government spends the rest).[10]

The challenge for correctional administrators is twofold. First, they must convince elected officials that maintaining the same level of funding is essential and probably will need to increase as the number of offenders increases each year (as shown in Chapter 9). Second, as the private sector becomes involved in operating correctional programs, competition develops, and public correctional administrators must ensure that their budgets are not out of line with the operating expenses of the private sector companies.[11]

Another complex administrative issue involves human resource management problems and challenges that result from rapid expansion, such as recruitment, training and staff development, professionalizing staff, and labor relations. In periods of rapid growth, correctional agencies must add line staff, train them, and prepare them to take over challenging duties. Furthermore, each new prison or community-based agency needs supervisors, managers, and administrators. Rapid growth requires rapid development of staff, who must be prepared to advance in the organization and take over added responsibilities (corrections personnel were discussed thoroughly in Chapter 10). The human resources issues also include dealing with labor organizations, discussed in Chapter 15.

A third administrative issue involves planning for the future. Corrections agencies have had nearly two centuries of slow change; now they must prepare for more rapid change rather than dwell on the routine. Correctional administrators must constantly respond to changing circumstances in the internal and external environments. The external environment includes interest groups outside the correctional organization, such as the media, political supervisors, the legislature, other criminal justice and social service agencies, and a variety of interest groups that include victims and offender families. The philosophy of correctional issues will evolve into public policy from the input of this external arena.[12]

Today's correctional administrator must be more sophisticated than in the past and have a broad base of leadership skills, as well as

> the following qualities: well-grounded experientially and academically in correctional operations and theory; in management skills and techniques; and in major public policy development and political skills. Many have the first two; few have all three.[13]

Many correctional administrators bemoan the fact that they spend more time on issues external to the organization than on dealing with their agency's central mission. They regularly deal with interest groups, who either support or disagree with the agencies' policies. They often give media interviews to explain a policy or describe a situation or incident. They respond almost daily to their executive branch leaders or to members of the legislature.[14]

Corrections administrators must be both proactive as well as reactive. Proactive responses usually result from a challenge to an established policy or the administrator's interest in changing a policy. The administrator must be involved with education and coalition building. Reactive responses often result from a serious incident, such as a prison escape, a serious crime committed by a parolee, a disturbance or riot, or a union picket or walkout (collective bargaining in corrections is discussed in Chapter 15). Both types of issues require considerable time, and both require considerable patience, excellent communication skills, and a foundation of trust and confidence in the administrator by others.[15]

# Sexual Coercion in Correctional Institutions

Inmate sexual assault is not a subject that correctional administrators care to discuss; nevertheless, it remains an issue—one that has been termed "the plague that persists"[16]—and must be addressed.

## *The Extent of Victimization*

People serving terms in correctional institutions do not leave their sexuality at the front gate, and long ago researchers began studying and publishing their results about this issue. One scholar, Paul Tappan, even maintained that from a biological point of view, homosexuality is normal behavior in correctional institutions.[17] Homosexuality is a universal concomitant of sex-segregated living and a perennial issue in camps, boarding schools, single-sex colleges, training schools, and, of course, correctional facilities.[18]

Persons entering prisons and jails express their sexuality in many forms, some of which are innocuous and others violent. If placed on a continuum, solitary or mutual masturbation or the manufacturing of a sexual object (such as the so-called "Fifi bag" made from a rolled-up magazine and other objects) would be at one end, consensual homosexual behavior in the middle, and gang rapes at the other end.

The true extent of prison sexual assault is unknown; it is likely to be underreported for fear of reprisals and not wanting to be labeled a "snitch" or one who is weak.[19] One study, however, estimated that in one year, approximately 359,000 males and 5,000 females were sexually assaulted while in U.S. prisons.[20] Another study of sexual coercion rates in seven prisons for men found that 21 percent of the inmates had experienced pressured or forced sexual contact, and 7 percent had been raped.[21] Factors that appear to increase sexual coercion rates include large population size (more than 1,000 inmates), understaffed workforces, racial conflict, barracks-type housing, inadequate security (often with low-paid, undermotivated staff who fail to complete assigned rounds), and a high percentage of inmates incarcerated for crimes against persons.[22] Furthermore, inmates who are young, physically small or weak, suffering from mental illness, known to be "snitches," not gang affiliated, or convicted of sexual crimes are at increased risk of **sexual victimization.**[23]

### Administrators' Roles

Prison administrators are often incredulous as to how rapes can be occurring in their institutions, especially if their facility has a reputation for good management and few problems with violent inmates. These officials obviously play a major role in the prevention, intervention, and prosecution of sexual assaults. Identifying and segregating targets from perpetrators is a prevention tactic (but incidents still occur even in protective custody). Facilities may need to increase surveillance in vulnerable areas: transportation vans, holding tanks, shower rooms, stairways, and storage areas. Administrators may also need to install more security cameras. Finally, it is suggested that new inmates be informed of the potential for being sexually assaulted while incarcerated and be told about prevention and what medical, legal, and psychological help is available if they are targeted.[24]

## Chain Gangs and Boot Camps: Cruel and Unusual Punishment?

Two programs that have been challenged by some writers as being either mentally or physically abusive to inmates are chain gangs and boot camps. Each is discussed next in terms of its constitutionality.

### Chain Gangs Reintroduced

Chain gangs began to flourish in the United States in the late 1800s as a means of providing inexpensive inmate labor. Inmates, often laboring under barbaric and abusive conditions, worked on road projects and prison construction in some states for many years. Prison industry peaked in the early 1920s, but the emergence of organized labor in the late 1920s brought many complaints about competition with free inmate labor. In response to these concerns, Congress passed the Hawes-Cooper Act of 1929, which subjected prison products to the laws of the state to which they were shipped.[25] Following that, chain gangs were used sporadically in the nation until the late 1960s. In 1995, however, they began to reemerge in Alabama, Arizona, and Florida (where the official term is *restricted labor gangs*).[26] Florida instituted labor gangs in six prisons and one county jail, with about 210 inmates who violated prison rules but were not convicted of first degree murder or escape attempts.

Amnesty International and other writers[27] believe, however, that such use and treatment of inmates constitute cruel and degrading treatment. For opponents, the concept also evokes images of slavery and is in violation of international standards on the treatment of prisoners. They also argue that from a security standpoint, it is unsafe to have inmates armed with axes, shovels, blades, and rocks on the side of roads where they can distract drivers.[28]

For the present, the use of chain gangs is legal. Opponents will be buoyed, however, by a decision of the U.S. Supreme Court in mid-2002. The Court disallowed an Alabama practice of chaining disruptive inmates to outdoor "hitching posts" (the inmate plaintiff claimed that he was chained and also deprived of food and water). The Court also allowed nearly 400 inmates in Alabama to sue their guards and get a jury trial if they believe they were mistreated.[29]

### *Shock Incarceration*

Some observers believe that **shock incarceration** programs also violate the **Eighth Amendment.** These programs, known also as **boot camps,** have been used in jails and prisons since the 1980s and have even been instituted for women.[30] Although the U.S. Supreme Court has not passed judgment on this form of treatment, some authors believe that it is only a matter of time before an inmate brings an Eighth Amendment claim against such programs. Such a claim may or may not succeed in court, but it would be a case that could be costly for a government to defend.[31]

Skeptics maintain that the aggressive, confrontational military style of boot camps may lead to the physical and emotional abuse of inmates. In determining whether a punishment is in fact cruel and unusual, the Supreme Court has emphasized two general themes: The punishment must accord with "the dignity of man" and comport with "evolving standards of decency." Furthermore, the Court has held that an inmate need not suffer "serious" injuries in order for an Eighth Amendment violation to have occurred.

If an inmate can successfully claim that the prison "inflicted unnecessary and wanton pain and suffering," and if corrections officials can be shown to have been aware of this needless suffering yet demonstrated deliberate indifference, these officials may be found in violation of the Constitution.[32] At the very least, it is recommended that corrections administrators monitor these programs and carefully select and train staff, in order to ensure that these programs are more supportive of a rehabilitative philosophy.[33]

## Issues Concerning Inmate Populations

Not only must correctional administrators deal with issues such as institutional population and design, budgets and politics, the Eighth Amendment, and sexual predators, they must also cope with problems relating to the types of inmates who are under their supervision. Next, we discuss some of the problems surrounding the aging, juvenile, female, mentally ill, and minority inmate populations.

## *The Aging Offender*

Today about 8.4 percent of the inmates in state and federal prisons are age 55 or older.[34] Like the United States in general, the prison population is "graying" at a rapid rate.

Imagine an 86-year-old man using a walker as he shuffles down a prison hallway. Sentenced to life without parole for killing his wife's lover 30 years ago, he is still in a Pennsylvania prison—frail, depressed, and a threat to no one.[35] Such an inmate creates many questions in corrections administration: How can institutions provide for the greater health care needs of older offenders? Can older offenders be classified at a lower security level because they are less aggressive and more frail? Does it take a different type of staff or staff with different training to supervise older offenders?[36] There is also the issue of housing accommodations and assignments. Older inmates cannot climb into upper bunks and often do not wish to share a cell with younger inmates, who have different habits and preferences in music, television, or radio stations.

These questions have no easy or clear answers for corrections administrators, as the senior population in the nation's prisons increases.

## *Juvenile Offenders Sentenced as Adults*

With an increasing percentage of violent crimes being committed by youths, one of the outcomes of the just deserts perspective toward crime has been the movement to treat serious juvenile offenders as adults. Subsequently, the waiver of juveniles to adult courts has increased. Today, about 106,000 juveniles are in detention in the United States, 7,400 in state prisons; furthermore, 4,500 (61 percent) of them are incarcerated for committing a violent offense.[37]

The criminal processing of juveniles as adults creates many issues for correctional administrators. The crux of the problem concerns housing and programming: Should violent juvenile offenders be kept separate from older offenders? And should the institutions provide programs and activities designed to meet their needs as youths? If so, then in effect a new system is created, one that must be operated with almost separate resources and programs. Few adult correctional agencies have educational, vocational, and life-skills programs that meet the needs of young offenders. Similarly, most states do not have a large enough number of juveniles in their adult system to make the development of such programs cost effective. Meanwhile, problems involved in inmate movement, meal service, and medical care and other service and delivery program make total separation of juveniles an almost impossible task.[38]

Adult correctional administrators must now face philosophical, political, and operational issues as they try to deal with the onslaught of these youthful offenders.

## Female Offenders

Like the aged and juveniles in prison, females have also seen their numbers increasing. In 1990, 44,085 females were in state prisons; in 2000, there were 91,612, a 108 percent increase.[39] Furthermore, about 53,600 (59 percent) had minor children.[40]

In addition to the sexual abuse problems facing female inmates, a foremost issue for correctional administrators is how to provide the same quantity and quality of programs and service for female prisoners as are provided for male prisoners, including maintaining similar staff-inmate ratios; providing work, education, parent-child, and recreational program opportunities; providing comparable health care; and ensuring a satisfactory number of minimum-security spaces for females eligible for such placement.[41]

Most states have only one or two female prisons. This causes problems for families and children in terms of visiting (the majority of female inmates are mothers, many of whom harbor feelings of guilt and isolation)[42] and less separation of inmates by security classification. Many prisons have established parenting programs, which include training in improving parenting skills and finding ways to be parental figures, even while in prison.

Because female prisons have a different culture than that of male prisons (females expect and need a different style of communication with each other and with staff), correctional administrators must understand and be sensitive to this culture and the different needs and problems of female offenders.[43]

## Mentally Ill Offenders

Since the deinstitutionalization movement of the 1970s, the number of criminal offenders and inmates suffering from mental illness has been increasing. Today, it is estimated that 137,000 inmates held in 1,500 state correctional facilities are receiving therapy and/or counseling; about 10 percent of them are also taking psychotropic medications.[44]

In prison, these individuals pose a dual dilemma for administrators. They are often violent and may be serving a long period of incarceration. Therefore, they require a high security level placement and are housed with other offenders who have committed equally serious offenses who are serving equally long sentences. The presence of potentially violent, mentally ill prisoners in high-security and probably overcrowded institutions is a dangerous situation.[45]

Mental illness must be treated while inmates are incarcerated. The key to dealing with treatment involves partnerships between the state and local correctional agencies and state and local mental health services agencies. Local mental health agencies can be used to provide counseling and support to probationers. Many states have also developed excellent programs for inmates with mental health problems. The challenge for correctional administrators is to maintain a viable program to treat and control a difficult group of offenders. The treatment of this group requires resources, trained staff, and appropriate facilities.[46]

## Minority Inmates

Race and corrections remains perhaps one of the most controversial topics today, owing largely to the disproportionately high number of minorities in the criminal justice and correctional systems. Today there are 3,535 sentenced black males per 100,000 black males in the United States, compared to 1,177 sentenced Hispanic males per 100,000 Hispanic males and 462 white males per 100,000 white males.[47]

Many people believe that systemic racism confronts the minority offender who enters the judicial process;[48] studies show, however, that while racism may exist at some points in the justice system, systemwide discrimination does not exist.[49]

Minorities are disproportionately involved in crime, especially violent crime, both as the perpetrators and as the victims. Crime is linked with poverty, drug use, and blocked opportunity for legitimate approaches to economic success. Therefore, it appears that the disproportionate number of minorities under correctional supervision has more to do with social factors influencing crime and social class than with racism. Even so, the high numbers of minorities in correctional systems still create a phenomenon that causes problems for administrators, who must strive for effective affirmative action programs to have a workforce that mirrors, to the extent possible, the inmate population. This not only enhances the potential for positive communications between staff and offenders, but also reduces the perception by offenders that the system is racist and that they have a "right" to misbehave.

# Drug Use in Prisons: Interdiction and Treatment

More than half of all adult arrestees test positive for drug use at the time of their apprehension; their drug use prior to incarceration is typically chronic. More than three-fourths (78 percent) of state and federal prisoners have used drugs at some time in the past.[50]

Furthermore, offenders still manage to obtain illicit drugs during their incarceration, threatening the safety of inmates and staff while undermining the authority of correctional administrators, contradicting rehabilitative goals, and reducing public confidence.[51]

Next, we discuss Pennsylvania's **drug interdiction** plan to prevent illicit drugs from coming into the state's prisons. Then, we look at what can be done toward treating offenders' substance abuse problems inside the institution.

## The Pennsylvania Plan

The state of Pennsylvania was compelled to acknowledge that drug use was pervasive in several of its prisons. Six inmates died from overdoses in a two-year period, and assaults on corrections officer and inmates had increased. To combat the problem, the state first adopted a zero-tolerance drug policy: Inmates caught with drugs were to be criminally prosecuted, and those testing positive (using hair testing) were to serve disciplinary custody time. Highly sensitive drug detection equipment was employed to detect drugs that visitors might try to smuggle into the prison, to inspect packages arriving in the mail, and to detect drugs that correctional staff might try to bring in. New policies were issued for inmate movement and visitation, and a new phone system was installed to randomly monitor inmates' calls.[52]

The results were impressive. The state's 24 prisons became 99 percent drug free. The number of drug finds during cell searches dropped 41 percent; assaults on staff decreased 57 percent; inmate-on-inmate assaults declined 70 percent; and weapons seized during searches dropped from 220 to 76. Marijuana use dropped from 6.5 percent before interdiction to 0.3 percent, and there were significant declines in the use of other types of drugs. Pennsylvania now believes that the foundation has been laid for inmates to abstain from drug use during service of their sentences—a necessary first step toward long-term abstinence and becoming a better citizen for their families and communities.[53]

## *Treating the Problem in Prisons*

During the past several years, a number of aggressive federal and state initiatives have been undertaken to expand substance treatment within correctional settings. These initiatives have been fueled by the high rates of substance abuse among offenders, and the view that intensive, prison-based treatment efforts can significantly reduce post-prison substance use and recidivism.[54]

Several barriers remain for correctional administrators in implementing substance treatment programs, however. First, institutions tend to use limited criteria (such as any lifetime drug use, possession, drug sales, trafficking) to determine the need for treatment, leading to a large portion of the treatment population who have not severely abused substances; conversely, many inmates who legitimately need treatment may be excluded for reasons unrelated to their substance abuse problems (gang affiliation or the commission of a sexual or violent offense). Treatment staff should be involved in the selection of candidates to ensure the appropriateness of the program population.[55]

Second, it is difficult to locate and recruit qualified and experienced staff in the remote areas where prisons are often located. Also, counselors who are well suited for community-based treatment programs will not necessarily be effective in the prison setting. They often resist the rigid custody regulations that are common in institutional settings. For these reasons, limited human resources and high turnover rates for drug abuse treatment counselors make staffing an ongoing problem for prison administrators.[56]

Possible solutions to this staffing problem include offering sufficient wages and other amenities to induce counselors to move to and stay with the prison; recruiting and training "lifers" as inmate counselors and mentors; and professionalizing treatment positions for correctional officers. With the use of counselors, certification and financial incentives would help toward retaining staff, as well as enhancing their professional development for the treatment setting.[57]

# The Move Toward Privatization

## *Emergence of the Concept*

Perhaps the most controversial approach to reducing the cost of corrections has been the **privatization** of correctional operations and programs. Private vendors not only supply health care services, educational and vocational training, and an array of other services to public institutions,[58] but they also construct and/or manage prisons and detention facilities. The largest and most prominent of the private corporations attempting to operate correctional institutions is Corrections Corporation of America (CCA), formed in 1983.[59]

## *Arguments For and Against*

Proponents for privatization of prisons and jails believe that it will be able to offer a greater diversity of programs and facilities and increase the ability to handle special inmate populations or offer special rehabilitative or training programs.[60] The strongest argument for the concept, however, is the belief that private industry can respond more quickly than governmental bureaucracies and in a more cost-effective manner to the current pressure for more prison space because they are not bound by state civil service rules or by employee unions. Proponents maintain that a private prison will charge the state less per day to hold each inmate than the publicly operated facility will by reducing building and labor costs and using economies of scale. They also argue that the profit motive creates an inherent efficiency.[61] Finally, one study in Florida found that inmates released from private prisons had lower recidivism rates (10 percent) than those released from public institutions (19 percent), and that those released from private prisons who reoffended committed less serious subsequent offenses than did their public prison counterparts.[62]

Those who have studied the operation of private prisons since they were initiated have identified 10 key issues that should be part of any deliberations regarding the use of private prisons:

1. *Propriety:* Can the punishment of offenders be delegated to nonpublic agencies?
2. *Cost and efficiency:* Are private prisons operated less expensively than public prisons?
3. *Quality:* Does the profit motive diminish the drive for delivery of quality services and programs to inmates?
4. *Quantity:* Does the involvement of the private sector to make a profit encourage the expansion of imprisonment beyond what is in the public interest?

5. *Flexibility:* Does the private sector's not having to follow bureaucratic governmental policies for purchasing and personnel management increase efficiency?

6. *Security:* Does an emphasis on profits and cost cutting undermine security for inmates, staff, and community?

7. *Liability:* What impact does contracting with a private firm have on governmental liability for violation of inmates' constitutional rights?

8. *Accountability and monitoring:* How will private contractors be monitored to fulfill requirments and be held responsible if they do not?

9. *Corruption:* Without restraints found in government to reduce the likelihood of corruption, will there be an increase in corrupt activities by personnel in private prisons?

10. *Dependence:* Will the public sector become dependent on the private sector contract, and if so, how will it affect decision making?[63]

At this time, there are no firm conclusions about the cost efficiency and overall superiority of private prisons versus public prisons. The most important element for correctional administrators considering contracting with the private sector is to be extremely specific in the Request For Proposal (RFP) regarding minimal levels of programs and to build in procedures to monitor and hold the private sector accountable for meeting these levels.

# CASE STUDIES

The following two case studies will help the reader apply some of this chapter's materials toward addressing real-world issues concerning external relations and a problem inmate.

## Prisons, Politics, Poverty, and the Rebellious Rurals*

It is time to prepare the annual budget for the Department of Prisons for the legislature. The entire country is suffering a recession, and your state is no different. Tax revenues are down. All state agencies, including the Department of Corrections, have suffered a blanket 10 percent cut in their budget during the current fiscal year. For the prison system, this meant the closing of a prison and the firing of more than 100 staff members. Your state is overwhelmingly urban in distribution of population and political power. The director of the prison system has just returned from the governor's cabinet meeting, where he has been told that the governor will recommend to the legislature an even lower budget amount for prisons next year. This is very troubling, given that the legislature will be considering a budget that will not even begin for another 18 months, and that the inmate population is sure to grow during that time. Meetings within the prison system over the next several days result in a three-part proposal to live within the smaller budget:

1. Closing all minimum-custody work camps in the rural areas of the state
2. Operating the remaining institutions and facilities at the absolute limit of their capacity
3. Proposing the enactment of an emergency release bill that would parole inmates who are closest to discharge 60 days earlier to keep from exceeding prison capacity

The early-release proposal is approved by the governor and is now being presented to the legislature. At present, the state's prison system houses 12,000 inmates. According to population projections, it is estimated that 800 inmates would be eligible for release under this program: two-thirds from the minimum-custody institutions, one-fourth from camps, and the remainder from medium- or maximum-security facilities. Upon learning of this plan, a tremendous outcry is heard from the rural areas of the state over the closing of their work camps and, consequently, the ensuing layoffs of many workers and the negative impact on their local economy. Furthermore, some legislators complain to the governor and

---

*Contributed by Ron Angelone, former director, Virginia Department of Corrections, and Glen Whorton, assistant director for operations, Nevada Department of Prisons.

prison director about the early-release program (exhibiting their traditional "tough on crime" posture). A sticky political situation has developed, because the "rurals" carry a lot of clout when they band together on an issue. Legislative hearings are imminent on this issue, and the media have begun to clamor for responses to the concerns of rural interest groups and "tough on crime" advocates, who include the staff members at the camps who are at risk of being laid off. The attacks on the program generally relate to one or more of the following categories:

1. "Why doesn't the department close prisons instead of camps, so that rural communities can continue to benefit from the economic influence of salaries and purchases and the public works performed by the inmates?"

2. "Releasing inmates early into the community will place our citizens at risk."

3. "How does the department justify the practice of not operating institutions at their maximum capacity at all times, during good economies as well as bad?"

You, the department's budget analyst, have been instructed by the director to prepare a response to these questions as well as a general position paper on the three-point plan.

## Questions for Discussion

1. What is the rationale for the closing of the camps? Is it basically sound?

2. What would be the effect of closing prisons instead of camps, as desired by the rural people?

3. What is the risk to the community, and is the public's concern legitimate?

4. How can the department defend its practice of not operating prisons at their maximum-capacity levels?

5. What, if any, action(s) should be taken by the director against the staff members in rural areas who appear to be engaging in political "mutiny"?

6. To what extent, if any, should the prison director play the political "game" and begin contacting state legislators to solicit their support of the foregoing proposal?

# The Prison Director
# Versus the Irate Inmate*

The director of the state Department of Prisons has received a grievance from an inmate who indicates that the classification staff at the maximum-security prison has classified him incorrectly. Specifically, the inmate argues that he is serving a sentence for forgery and his offense has been treated (for purposes of

---

*Contributed by Ron Angelone, director, Virginia Department of Corrections, and Glen Whorton, assistant director for operations, Nevada Department of Prisons.

classification) as if it were murder. He also maintains that the staff has begun to retaliate against him because of his grievances regarding his classification placement. The inmate states that if he does not receive satisfaction in regard to the classification, he is going to file suits based on the conditions of confinement at the prison. This is troubling to the director, given the overcrowding that already exists, the physical deficiencies of the maximum-security prison, and the type and extent of programs available there. A review of the inmate's file indicates that he is incarcerated as a habitual offender with three life sentences. The root offenses for the habitual offender findings were indeed forgery. He has been incarcerated only 18 months on the first life sentence. He has four prior felonies for similar offenses in other states. The inmate is 62 years old and in poor health. The file is replete with complaints about other inmates and staff. He has sued the central records staff on one previous occasion claiming that staff misconduct resulted in the mishandling of a request for a speedy trial on a detainer that had been lodged against him. This suit was dismissed when it was discovered that the inmate had lied about having requested the trial. The file also includes numerous disciplinary violations related to refusing to work and possession of unauthorized property. There is no violence in the record or evidence of serious misconduct. The file also discloses that the inmate is embroiled in a dispute with the chief of the prison medical division over his treatment for cancer. The inmate has recently claimed that staff physicians have completely ignored his medical condition and have refused to treat the cancer. The computerized inmate information system indicates that about four months ago the inmate was taken to a local hospital and remained there for approximately one week. A call to the doctor reveals that the inmate's cancer was surgically removed during that visit. A review of classification documents reveals that the staff has correctly scored the inmate's offense on the objective classification instrument. The score for Murder II and Habitual Offender are the same. However, the instrument's computed score on the classification documents indicates that he is a medium-custody inmate. He was assigned to a higher level of custody because of the extremely long sentence that he has to serve. This custody assignment, and the original transfer to the maximum-security prison, was approved by the central classification staff who reviews classification recommendations for the director. You are the director's administrative aide and enjoy the director's trust. She has asked that you prepare a position statement on this matter, representing all relevant viewpoints and possible pitfalls and developing recommendations. You are told, however, that "the bottom line is to do what's right for the inmate."

## Questions for Discussion

1. What are the primary inmate-related issues that the director must deal with: classification or transfer? Was the classification staff technically correct in sending the inmate to a maximum-security institution in the first place?

2. Can the inmate be safely transferred to a lower-level institution? If so, to medium or minimum? (Bear in mind that while being infirm and a relatively old inmate, he is nevertheless serving a lengthy sentence.)

3. If the inmate is transferred, have the director and staff lost any real power in the eyes of other inmates? Why or why not?

4. How does the director deal with these issues without giving an obviously litigious inmate more "ammunition" with which to harass staff or sue the department? Should the director ask the classification team to reconsider the case?

5. What are the staff-related issues the director has to deal with? What are the options in regard to dealing with those issues?

6. Are any broader policy issues presented in this situation? If so, what action do they suggest?

## Summary

This chapter has examined several major issues confronting today's correctional administrators. It is clear that many, if not all, of these issues do not lend themselves to easy or quick resolutions and will continue to pose challenges to today's correctional administrators for many years to come.

## Questions for Review

1. What are the primary substantive and administrative issues facing corrections administrators?

2. What are correctional administrators' roles toward preventing and dealing with sexual coercion?

3. How can prison administrators interdict and treat the drug problem?

4. What are some challenges confronting correctional administrators with respect to special populations: the aging, juvenile, females, the mentally ill, and minority offenders?

5. What are some advantages and disadvantages of privatization?

## Notes

1. Richard P. Seiter, *Correctional Administration: Integrating Theory and Practice* (Upper Saddle River, N.J.: Prentice Hall, 2002), p. 18.

2. Edward E. Rhine, "Probation and Parole Supervision: In Need of a New Narrative," *Corrections Management Quarterly* 1 (1997):71–75.

3. Timothy J. Flanagan, "Correctional Policy and the Long-Term Prisoner, in Timothy Flanagan (ed.), *Long-Term Imprisonment: Policy, Science, and Correctional Practice* (Newbury Park, Calif.: Sage, 1995), p. 249.

4. Edwin W. Zedlewski, "Why Prisons Matter: A Utilitarian Review," *Corrections Management Quarterly* 1 (1997):15–24.

5. Todd R. Clear, "Ten Unintended Consequences of the Growth of Imprisonment," *Corrections Management Quarterly* 1 (1997):25–31.

6. J. Simon and M. M. Freely, "True Crime: The New Penology and Public Discourse on Crime," in T. G. Bloomberg and S. Cohen (eds.), *Punishment and Social Control* (New York: Aldine De Gruyter, 1995).

7. Rhine, "Probation and Parole Supervision," pp. 71–75.

8. Richard P. Seiter, "Offenders and Issues Force Managerial Change," *Corrections Management Quarterly* 1 (1997):iv.

9. U.S. Department of Justice, Bureau of Justice Statistics, "Key Facts at a Glance: Direct Expenditures by Criminal Justice Function," http://www.ojp.usdoj.gov/bjs/glance/tables/exptyptab.htm (accessed June 24, 2002).

10. U.S. Department of Justice, Bureau of Justice Statistics, "Expenditure and Employment Statistics," http://www.ojp.usdoj.gov/bjs/eande.htm (accessed June 24, 2002).

11. Seiter, *Correctional Administration,* p. 22.

12. Ibid., p. 25.

13. Chase Riveland, "The Correctional Leader and Public Policy Skills," *Correctional Management Quarterly* 1 (1997):24.

14. Seiter, *Correctional Administration,* p. 25.

15. Ibid.

16. Robert W. Dumond, "Inmate Sexual Assault: The Plague That Persists," *The Prison Journal* 80 (December 2000):407–414; see also *No Escape: Male Rape in U.S. Prisons* (New York: Human Rights Watch, 2001).

17. Paul W. Tappan, *Crime, Justice, and Correction* (New York: McGraw-Hill, 1960), pp. 678–679.

18. Ibid., p. 678.

19. Ibid.

20. S. Donaldson, "Rape of Incarcerated Americans: A Preliminary Statistical Look," http://www.sspr.org/docs/stats/html (accessed June 22, 2000).

21. Cindy Struckman-Johnson and David Struckman-Johnson, "Sexual Coercion Rates in Seven Midwestern Prison Facilities for Men," *The Prison Journal* 80 (December 2000)379–390.

22. Ibid.

23. Dumond, "Inmate Sexual Assault," p. 408.

24. Leanne Fiftal Alarid, "Sexual Assault and Coercion Among Incarcerated Women Prisoners: Excerpts from Prison Letters," *The Prison Journal* 80 (December 2000):391–406.

25. Jeanne B. Stinchcomb and Vernon B. Fox, *Introduction to Corrections,* 5th ed. (Upper Saddle River, N.J.: Prentice Hall, 1999), pp. 108–109.

26. "United States of America: Florida Reintroduces Chain Gangs," http://www.web.amnesty.org/ai.nsf/index/AMR510021996 (accessed July 1, 2002).

27. See, for example, James F. Anderson, Laronistine Dyson, and Willie Brooks Jr., "Alabama Prison Chain Gangs: Reverting to Archaic Punishment to Reduce Crime and Discipline Offenders," *The Western Journal of Black Studies* 24 (2000), pp. 9–15.

28. Ibid., p. 12.

29. "Inmates No Longer Can Be Chained to 'Hitching Posts'," Associated Press (June 28, 2002).

30. Cheryl Clark and Leslie Kellam, "These Boots Are Made for Women," *Corrections Today* 63 (February 2001):50–54.

31. Faith E. Lutze and David C. Brody, "Mental Abuse as Cruel and Unusual Punishment: Do Boot Camp Prisons Violate the Eighth Amendment?" *Crime and Delinquency* 45 (April 1999):242–255.

32. Ibid., p. 250.

33. Ibid., p. 252.

34. U.S. Department of Justice, Bureau of Justice Statistics, *Corrections Populations in the United States* (Washington, D.C.: Author, 2000), p. 48.

35. Tammerlin Drummond, "Cellblock Seniors: They Have Grown Old and Frail in Prison. Must They Still Be Locked Up?" *Time* (June 21, 1999):60.

36. Seiter, *Correctional Administration,* p. 415.

37. Kathleen Maguire and Ann L. Pastore, eds., *Sourcebook of Criminal Justice Statistics* [Online] Available at http://www.albany.edu/sourcebook/ (accessed July 2, 2002), p. 499.

38. Seiter, *Correctional Administration,* pp. 419–420.

39. Maguire and Pastore, *Sourcebook of Criminal Justice Statistics,* p. 520.

40. Ibid., p. 521.

41. Ibid., p. 420.

42. See Kathleen O'Shea, *Women On the Row: Revelations from Both Sides of the Bars* (Ithaca, N.Y.: Firebrand Books, 2000).

43. Seiter, *Correctional Administration,* p. 420–421.

44. Maguire and Pastore, *Sourcebook of Criminal Justice Statistics,* pp. 543–544.

45. Ibid., pp. 422–425.

46. Ibid.

47. U.S. Department of Justice, Bureau of Justice Statistics Web page, "Prison Statistics," http://www.ojp.usdoj.gov/bjs/prisons.htm (accessed June 24, 2002).

48. See, for example, Coramae Richey Mann, "Racism in the Criminal Justice System: Two Sides of a Controversy," *Criminal Justice Research Bulletin* (Huntsville, Tex.: Sam Houston State University, 1987), 3.

49. See William Wilbanks, *The Myth of a Racist Criminal Justice System* (Belmont, Calif.: Wadsworth, 1987); Joan Petersilia, "Racial Disparities in the Criminal Justice System: Executive Summary of Rand Institute Study, 1983," in Daniel Georges-Abeyle (ed.), *The Criminal Justice System and Blacks* (New York: Clark Boardman Company, 1984), pp. 225–258.

50. U.S. Department of Justice, Bureau of Justice Statistics, "More Than Three-Quarters of Prisoners Had Abused Drugs in the Past," News Release, January 5, 1999 http://www.ojp.usdoj.gov/bjs/pub/press/satsfp97.pr (accessed July 2, 2002).

51. Thomas E. Feucht and Andrew Keyser, *Reducing Drug Use in Prisons: Pennsylvania's Approach* (Washington, D.C.: National Institute of Justice Journal, October 1999), p. 11.

52. Ibid., pp. 11–12.

53. Ibid., pp. 14–15.

54. David Farabee, Michael Prendergast, Jerome Cartier, Harry Wexler, Kevin Knight, and M. Douglas Anglin, "Barriers to Implementing Effective Correctional Drug Treatment Programs," *The Prison Journal* 79 (June 1999):150–162.

55. Ibid., p. 152.

56. Ibid., p. 153.

57. Ibid., pp. 154–155.

58. Camille Camp and George Camp, "Correctional Privatization in Perspective," *The Prison Journal* 65 (1985):14–31.

59. Craig Becker and Mary Dru Stanley, "The Downside of Private Prisons," *The Nation* (June 15, 1985), p. 729.

60. Robert B. Levinson, "Okeechobee: An Evaluation of Privatization in Corrections," *The Prison Journal* 65 (1985):75-94; J. Mullen, "Corrections and the Private Sector," *The Prison Journal* 65 (1985):1-13.

61. Ted Gest, "Prisons for Profit: A Growing Business," *U.S. News and World Report* (July 2, 1984):45-46.

62. Kaduce Lonn Lanza, Karen F. Parker, and Charles W. Thomas, "A Comparative Recidivism Analysis of Releasees from Private and Public Prisons," *Crime and Delinquency* 45 (1999):28-47.

63. Charles Logan, *Private Prisons: Cons and Pros* (New York: Oxford University Press, 1990).

# PART V

# ISSUES SPANNING THE JUSTICE SYSTEM
## Administrative Challenges and Practices

*The six chapters in this part focus on administrative problems or methods spanning the entire justice system. Chapter 13 examines ethical considerations that relate to police, courts, and corrections administration. The rights of criminal justice employees are reviewed in Chapter 14, and Chapter 15 discusses several challenges involving human resources (employee discipline, labor relations, and liability). Chapter 16 discusses financial administration, and Chapter 17 reviews the latest technological hardware and software now in use in criminal justice agencies. Chapter 18, the book's concluding chapter, contemplates what the future holds for criminal justice administrators. With the exception of Chapter 17, case studies are included in each chapter.*

# Chapter 13

# Ethical Considerations

## Key Terms and Concepts

Absolute ethics                    Gratuities
Deontological ethics               Relative ethics
Ethics

## Learning Objectives

As a result of reading this chapter, the student will:

- be able to distinguish between absolute and relative ethics
- be familiar with the utilitarian approach to ethics
- have an understanding of ethics among criminal justice employees
- be familiar with how employees play a role in the ethics of the court system
- know the different tests for the justice system recruit

> *I have no excuse, I was just greedy.*
> —New York Supreme Court Justice-Elect Seymour Thaler,
> convicted of receiving stolen U.S. Treasury bills and perjury, 1972

> *Everything secret degenerates, even the administration of Justice;*
> *nothing is safe that shows it cannot bear discussion and publicity.*
> —Lord Acton

# Introduction

At its root, criminal justice administration is about people and activities; in the end, the primary responsibilities of administrators involve monitoring subordinates' activities to ensure that they act correctly relative to their tasks and responsibilities, and that these duties and responsibilities are conducted in an acceptable and effective manner.

Therefore, this chapter is essentially concerned with what constitutes "correct" behavior in the administration of criminal justice. Individuals and organizations have standards of conduct. In order to understand organizations, it becomes important to comprehend these standards and their etiology.

The chapter opens with a glimpse into the kinds of ethical situations criminal justice employees experience, providing three scenarios that are based on actual cases. Then, we discuss ethics in general, reviewing philosophical foundations and types of ethics.

Next, ethics in policing is examined. Because of their contact with and criticisms by the public, and the unique kinds of vices, crimes, and temptations to which they are directly exposed, the police are given much more attention than are the personnel in the courts or corrections, who are discussed next. Although justice administrators are mentioned throughout, the chapter then looks at some specific challenges that they face, guidelines they must issue, and some tests they can develop for new recruits.

We conclude with six case studies that the reader will find of interest in attempting to understand and resolve ethical quandaries.

# Food for Thought: Some Ethical Dilemmas

To frame the concept of ethics, we begin this chapter with three true scenarios:

> *Police:* Seeing a vehicle weaving across the center line of the highway, Officer A stops the car, approaches the driver's door, and immediately detects a strong odor of alcohol. The motorist is removed from the car and joins Officer A and a backup, Officer B, on the roadside. Officer A decides to use a portable breath test device to confirm his suspicions of DUI, and he gives a sterile plastic mouthpiece to the driver to blow into. The driver attempts to thwart the test by appearing (but failing) to blow into the mouthpiece. Irritated by this attempt, Officer A yanks the mouthpiece away, throws it on the ground, and arrests the driver for DUI. At trial, the driver claimed the mouthpiece was flawed (blocked) so he was unable to blow through it; Officer A testifies under oath that it had not been blocked and as "evidence," he takes a mouthpiece out of his pocket, stating it was the mouthpiece he had used for the test that night. Officer B, sitting in the room, hears this testimony and knows differently, having seen Officer A impatiently throw the mouthpiece on the ground.[1]

EXHIBIT **13.1**
## Who Polices the Police?
*Overcoming the "rat" stigma in internal-affairs assignments*

In the image fueled by countless television police dramas, internal affairs divisions are peopled by self-hating cops whose incompetence on the street has led them to become veritable traitors with few if any friends on the force.

While this perspective is somewhat at odds with reality, assignment to an IA unit still carries enough of a stigma that selecting such personnel is among the most critical, even problematic, decisions made by police executives. In some major-city departments, however, serving as an internal affairs investigator is increasingly viewed as a necessary stepping stone to career advancement and often provides benefits not usually available to those in other areas of policing.

With some 80 percent of the law enforcement agencies in the United States staffed by 25 or fewer sworn officers, there is no generalization about the workings of internal affairs divisions—or perceptions held about them—that would be valid, say policing experts. In small departments, their functions may tend to be limited, while in big departments, such as New York City and Los Angeles, their quality, structure and content can vary widely. Thus, issues such as how to attract top investigators to the unit, how long they remain there, and the message that the assignment conveys to others in the agency are all things with which law enforcement officials must grapple, say observers. . . .

Two views have prevailed. One is that assignment to IA is a part of a ca-reer track, while the other suggests that those assigned to IA will subsequently require protection because of potential enemies. . . .

In 1995, . . . the New York City Police Department, Mayor Rudolph Giuliani and then–Commissioner William J. Bratton unveiled a number of reforms aimed at improving recruitment, training and overall supervision within the Internal Affairs Bureau. The strategies included making assignment to the unit a two-year hitch which would then provide investigators with entry into the Detective Bureau, the Organized Crime Control Bureau or other coveted divisions.

That approach exemplifies what Edwin J. Delattre, dean of the School of Education at Boston University and author of "Character and Cops," cites as a "very old truth about human nature"—namely, that virtue has the best chance of succeeding when it is also advantageous: . . . "Much of the time all of us have mixed motives for our actions, usually more mixed than even the most honest and self-knowledgeable of us fully recognize. Accordingly, the disposition to do 'right when there is no one to make [us] do it but [ourselves]' may be strengthened by awareness that we are not making some permanent sacrifice in behaving rightly."

The majority of departments that have paid attention to the NYPD's strategy have acknowledged that an effective way to draw the best people into IA—both by assignment and volunteering—is by having "good places for them to land and choices of assignment in homicide, organized crime or investigative units after" IAB, said Delattre. . . .

*Source:* Reprinted with permission from *Law Enforcement News*, March 31, 2000, pp. 1, 6. John Jay College of Criminal Justice (CCNY), 555 West 57th St., New York, NY 10019.

*Courts:* For several weeks, a wealthy divorcee receives menacing telephone calls that demand dates and sexual favors. The caller's voice is electronically disguised. The suspect also begins stalking the woman. After working some clues and tailing a suspect, a federal agent finally makes contact with a suspect, determining that he is the chief judge of the state's supreme court. Upon confronting him, the agent is told by the judge to "forget about it, or you'll be checking passports in a remote embassy."[2]

*Corrections:* A corrections officer in a minimum-security facility for young offenders is working the night shift when a youth is admitted. The youth is frightened, as this is his first time in custody, and the officer places him in isolation because the youth told the staff he is feeling suicidal. Over the next several days, the officer develops a friendship with the youth. Looking through the youth's file, the officer learns that the boy does not wish to remain a male; rather, he wants to be a female. One day while doing a routine cell search, the officer observes the youth stuffing women's panties into his pillowcase. With a terrified and pleading look, he explains he prefers them to boxer shorts and begs the officer not to mention this to other staff or youths in the facility. The officer debates what to do; surely the boy would be seriously harangued if others knew of the panties, and it does not seem to be a "big deal"; on the other hand, if the officer does not report the event and the boy's choice of underwear is revealed later on, the officer knows he will lose credibility with other staff and the administration.[3]

Each of these reality-based scenarios poses an ethical dilemma for the criminal justice employee involved. In each case, the officer or agent had to determine the best course of action. In making this determination, the employee had to draw on his or her own ethical foundation and training and even the organization's subculture.

These scenarios should be kept in mind as this chapter examines ethics and many related dilemmas.

# Ethics, Generally

## *Philosophical Foundations*

The term **ethics** is rooted in the ancient Greek idea of character. Ethics involves doing what is right or correct and is generally used to refer to how people should behave in a professional capacity. Many people would argue, however, that no difference should exist between one's professional and personal behavior. Ethical rules of conduct should apply to everything a person does.

A central problem with understanding ethics is the question of "whose ethics" or "which right." This becomes evident when one examines controversial issues such as the death penalty, abortion, use of deadly force, or gun control. How individuals view a particular controversy largely depends on their values, character, or ethics. Both sides on controversies such as these believe they are morally right. These issues demonstrate that in order to understand behavior, the most basic values must be examined and understood.

Another area for examination is that of **deontological ethics,** which does not consider consequences but instead examines one's duty to act. The word *deontology* comes from two Greek roots, *deos* meaning duty, and *logos* meaning study. Thus, deontology means the study of duty. When police officers observe a violation of law, they have a duty to act. Officers frequently use this as an excuse when they issue traffic citations, which, on their face, have little utility and do not produce any great benefit for the rest of society. For example, when an officer writes a traffic citation for a prohibited left turn made at two o'clock in the morning when no traffic is around, the officer is fulfilling a departmental duty to enforce the law. From a utilitarian standpoint (where we judge an action by its consequences), however, little if any good was served. Here, duty prevailed over good consequences.

Immanuel Kant, an eighteenth-century philosopher, expanded the ethics of duty by including the idea of "good will." People's actions must be guided by good intent. In the previous example, the officer who wrote the traffic citation for an improper left turn would be acting unethically if the ticket was a response to a quota or some irrelevant motive. On the other hand, if the citation was issued because the officer truly believed that it would result in some good, it would have been an ethical action.

Some people have expanded this argument even further. Richard Kania[4] argued that police officers should be allowed to freely accept gratuities because such actions would constitute the building blocks of positive social relationships between the police and the public. In this case, duty is used to justify what under normal circumstances would be considered unethical. Conversely, if officers take gratuities for self-gratification rather than to form positive community relationships, then the action would be considered unethical by many.

## *Types of Ethics*

Ethics usually involves standards of fair and honest conduct; what we call conscience, the ability to recognize right from wrong; and actions that are good and proper. There are absolute ethics and relative ethics. **Absolute ethics** has only two sides, something is either good or bad, black or white. Some examples in police ethics would be unethical behaviors such as bribery, extortion, excessive force, and perjury, which nearly everyone would agree are unacceptable behaviors by the police.

**Relative ethics** is more complicated and can have a multitude of sides with varying shades of gray. What is considered ethical behavior by one person may be deemed highly unethical by someone else. Not all ethical issues are clear-cut, however, and communities *do* seem willing at times to tolerate extralegal behavior if there is a greater public good, especially in dealing with problems such as gangs and the homeless. This willingness on the part of the community can be conveyed to the police. Ethical relativism can be said to form an essential part of the community policing movement, discussed more fully later.

A community's acceptance of relative ethics as part of criminal justice may send the wrong message: that there are few boundaries placed on justice system employee behaviors and that, at times, "anything goes" in their fight against crime. As John Kleinig[5] pointed out, giving false testimony to ensure that a public menace is "put away" or the illegal wiretapping of an organized crime figure's telephone might sometimes be viewed as "necessary" and "justified," though illegal. Another example is that many police believe they are compelled to skirt along the edges of the law—or even violate it—in order to arrest drug traffickers. The ethical problem here is that even if the action could be justified as morally proper, it remains illegal. But for many persons, the protection of society overrides other concerns.

This viewpoint—the "principle of double effect"—holds that when one commits an act to achieve a good end, and an inevitable but intended effect is negative, then the act might be justified. A long-standing debate has raged about balancing the rights of individuals against the community's interest in calm and order.

These special areas of ethics can become problematical and controversial when police officers use deadly force or lie and deceive others in their work. Police could justify a whole range of activities that others may deem unethical simply because the consequences resulted in the greatest good for the greatest number—the *utilitarian* approach. If the ends justified the means, perjury would be ethical when committed to prevent a serial killer from being set free to prey on society. In our democratic society, however, the means are just as important, if not more important, than the desired end.

The community—and criminal justice administrators—cannot tolerate completely unethical behavior, but they may seemingly tolerate extralegal behavior if there's a greater public good, especially with gang members and the homeless.

It is no less important today than in the past for criminal justice employees to appreciate and come to grips with ethical considerations. Indeed, ethical issues in policing have been affected by three critical factors[6]: (1) the growing level of temptation stemming from the illicit drug trade; (2) the potentially compromising nature of the organizational culture—a culture that can exalt loyalty over integrity, with a "code of silence" that protects unethical employees; and (3) the challenges posed by decentralization (flattening the organization and pushing decision making downward) through the advent of community oriented policing and problem solving (COPPS, discussed later).

# Ethics in Policing

## *A Primer: The Oral Interview*

During oral interviews for a position in policing, applicants are often placed in a hypothetical situation that tests their ethical beliefs and character. For example, they are asked to assume the role of a police officer who is checking on foot an office supplies retail store that was found to have an unlocked door during early morning hours. Upon leaving the building, the officer observes another officer, Smith, removing a $100 writing pen from a display case and placing it in his uniform pocket. What should the officer do?

This kind of question commonly befuddles the applicant: "Should I rat on my fellow officer? Overlook the matter? Merely tell Smith never to do that again?" Unfortunately, applicants may do a lot of "how am I *supposed* to respond" soul searching and second-guessing with these kinds of questions.

Bear in mind that criminal justice agencies do not wish to hire someone who possesses ethical shortcomings; it is simply too potentially dangerous and expensive, from both a litigation and a morality standpoint, to take the chance of bringing someone into an agency who is corrupt. That is the reason for such questioning and a thorough background investigation of applicants.

Before responding to a scenario like the one concerning Officer Smith, the applicant should consider the following issues: Is this likely to be the first time that Smith has stolen something? Don't the police arrest and jail people for this same kind of behavior?

In short, police administrators should *never* want an applicant to respond that it is all right for an officer to steal. Furthermore, it would be incorrect for an applicant to believe that police do not want an officer to "rat out" another officer. Applicants should never acknowledge that stealing or other such activities are to be overlooked.

## *A "Slippery Slope"? Lying and Deception*

In many cases, no clear line separates acceptable behavior from that which is unacceptable. The two are separated by an expansive "gray" area that comes under relative ethics. Some observers have referred to such illegal behavior as a "slippery slope": People tread on solid or legal ground but at some point slip beyond the acceptable into illegal or unacceptable behavior.

Criminal justice employees lie or deceive for different purposes and under varying circumstances. In some cases, their misrepresentations are accepted as an integral part of a criminal investigation, while in other cases, they are viewed as violations of law. Thomas Barker[7] examined police lying and perjury and developed a taxonomy that centered on accepted lying and deviant lying. *Accepted lying* includes police activities to apprehend or entrap suspects. This type of lying is generally considered to be trickery. *Deviant lying*, on the other hand, refers to occasions when officers commit perjury to convict suspects or are deceptive about some activity that is illegal or unacceptable to the department or public in general.

### Accepted Lying

Deception has long been practiced by the police to ensnare violators and suspects. For many years, it was the principal method used by detectives and police officers to secure confessions and convictions. It is allowed by the law, and to a great extent, it is expected by the public. Gary Marx[8] identified three methods police use to trick a suspect: (1) offering the illegal action as part of a larger, socially acceptable, and legal goal; (2) disguising the illegal action so that the suspect does not know it is illegal; and (3) morally weakening the suspect so that the suspect voluntarily becomes involved.

The courts have long accepted deception as an investigative tool. For example, in *Illinois v. Perkins*,[9] the U.S. Supreme Court ruled that police undercover agents are not required to administer the *Miranda* warning to incarcerated inmates when investigating crimes. Lying, although acceptable by the courts and the public in certain circumstances, does result in an ethical dilemma. It is a dirty means to accomplish a good end; the police use untruths to gain the truth relative to some event.

### Deviant Lying

In their taxonomy of lying, Thomas Barker and David Carter[10] identified two types of deviant lying: lying that serves legitimate purposes and lying that conceals or promotes crimes or illegitimate ends.

Lying that serves legitimate goals occurs when officers lie to secure a conviction, obtain a search warrant, or conceal omissions during an investigation. Barker[11] found that police officers believe that almost one-fourth of their agency would commit perjury in order to secure a conviction in court or to obtain a search warrant. Lying becomes an effective, routine way to side-step legal impediments. When left unchecked by supervisors, managers, and administrators, lying can become organizationally accepted as an effective means to nullify legal entanglements and remove obstacles that stand in the way of convictions. Examples include using the services of nonexistent confidential informants to secure search warrants, concealing that an interrogator went too far, coercing a confession, or perjuring himself or herself to gain a conviction.

Lying to conceal or promote criminality is the most distressing form of deception. Examples range from when the police lie to conceal their using excessive force when arresting a suspect to obscuring the commission of a criminal act.

## *Gratuities*

**Gratuities** are commonly accepted by police officers as a part of their job. Restaurants frequently give officers free or half-price meals and drinks, and some other businesses routinely give officers discounts for services or merchandise. Many police officers and departments accept these gratuities as a part of the job. Other departments prohibit such gifts and discounts but seldom attempt to enforce any relevant policy or regulation. Finally, some departments attempt to ensure that officers do not accept free or discounted services or merchandise and routinely enforce policies or regulations against such behavior.

There are two basic arguments *against* police acceptance of gratuities. First is the slippery slope argument, discussed earlier, which proposes that gratuities are the first step in police corruption. This argument holds that once gratuities are received, police officers' ethics are subverted and they are open to additional breaches of their integrity. Also, officers who accept minor gifts or gratuities are then obligated to provide the donors with some special service or accommodation. Second, some propose that receiving a gratuity is wrong because officers are receiving rewards for services that, as a result of their employment, they are obligated to provide. That is, officers have no legitimate right to accept compensation in the form of a gratuity. If the police ever hope to be accepted as members of a full-fledged profession, then they must address whether the acceptance of gratuities is professional behavior.

Police officers who solicit and receive free gifts were categorized by the Knapp Commission in New York City as "grass-eaters" and "meat-eaters."[12] Grass-eaters are officers who freely accept gratuities and sometimes solicit minor payments and gifts. Meat-eaters, on the other hand, spend a significant portion of the workday aggressively seeking out situations that could be exploited for financial gain. These officers were corrupt and were involved in thefts, drugs, gambling, prostitution, and other criminal activities.

At least in some cases, it seems that taking gratuities may be a first step toward corruption. Gratuities do indeed provide a slippery slope from which officers can easily slide into corruption. The problem is that many officers fail to understand when and where to draw the line. Once a police department decides on a policy, it should ensure that all officers are familiar with that policy. Supervisors and managers must fully understand the department's policy regarding gratuities and emphatically enforce it; once a department draws the line distinguishing what is acceptable, it is responsible for ensuring that the rules are followed.

In a different light, one writer[13] argues that retail store and restaurant owners often feel an indebtedness toward the police, and gratuities provide an avenue of repayment. Thus, gratuities result in social cohesion between the police and businessowners, and the acceptance of gratuities does not necessarily lead to the solicitation of additional gratuities and gifts or corruption.

Figure 13.1 is an example of a policy developed by a western sheriff concerning gratuities.

1. Without the express permission of the Sheriff, members shall not solicit or accept any gift, gratuity, loan, present, or fee where there is any direct or indirect connection between this solicitation or acceptance of such gift and their employment by this office.
2. Members shall not accept, either directly or indirectly, any gift, gratuity, loan, fee or thing of value, the acceptance of which might tend to improperly influence their actions, or that of any other member, in any matter of police business, or which might tend to cast an adverse reflection on the Sheriff's Office.
3. Any unauthorized gift, gratuity, loan, fee, reward or other thing falling into any of these categories coming into the possession of any member shall be forwarded to the member's commander, together with a written report explaining the circumstances connected therewith. The commander will decide the disposition of the gift.

—Washoe County (Nevada) Sheriff's Office

**Figure 13.1**

Washoe County, Nevada, Sheriff's office gratuity policy.

## *Greed and Temptation*

Fundamentally, the expecting and accepting of larger gratuities (setting aside for a moment the debate about whether or not police officers should receive free coffee or meals) and bribes or "shakedowns" are about greed. This greed is perhaps viewed by the individual officer as an entitlement, because of what is perceived as an overall corrupt society, a low-paying job, the kind of work that has to be done, and so on. Mature people, however, simply do not use their position for self-indulgence. Consider the following account, related by Albert A. Seedman,[14] who served from patrol officer to chief of detectives in the New York City Police Department:

> Just before Christmas [in New York City] in 1947, [Captain Ray McGuire and Officer Albert Seedman] helped lug into the office dozens of cartons of toys that had been recovered from a hijacking case. There were dolls, teddy bears, and stuffed animals of all kinds. McGuire, busy overseeing the operation, saw that it was close to three o'clock. He said, "I was going to stop at Macy's to pick up some toys for my girls." One of the detectives mentioned he had to do the same at Macy's. McGuire handed him a twenty-dollar bill. "Pick up a pair of dolls for me, will ya?" If there were two dolls in that office, there were two thousand. Yet I doubt it ever occurred to McGuire that a pair would never be missed. Or that the owner would be delighted to make them a gift.

The habit of not even considering greedy behavior, of not speculating about ways to profit from office, prevents such conduct from "ever occurring" to most officers.[15]

[The author recalls one rainy, cold midwestern night when he was dispatched with two other officers to a robbery scene. An elderly couple had been beaten, robbed, and tied to chairs in their home as a young man ransacked it, took a large amount of cash, and fled. During the offender's flight, he dropped much of the money, some of which was flowing down the curb and into the storm sewer by the time the officers arrived. In pouring rain, the three officers hurriedly collected all the cash that could be retrieved in the yard, flowing down the curb, and—while on their bellies in the deluge—from out of the storm sewer. As with Seedman's story, it never even occurred to the officers to divert any of the couple's funds to their pockets; all that could be located was returned to them. Such accounts, of course, are legion among the police but seldom appear on the front page.]

Edward Tully[16] underscored the vast amount of temptation that confronts today's police officers and what police leaders must do toward combating it:

> Socrates, Mother Teresa, or other revered individuals in our society never had to face the constant stream of ethical problems of a busy cop on the beat. One of the roles of [police leaders] is to create an environment that will help the officer resist the temptations that may lead to misconduct, corruption, or abuse of power. The executive cannot construct a work environment that will completely insulate the officers from the forces which lead to misconduct. The ultimate responsibility for an officer's ethical and moral welfare rests squarely with the officer.

Most citizens have no way of comprehending the amount of temptation that confronts today's police officers. They frequently find themselves alone inside retail businesses after normal business hours, clearing the building after finding an open door or window. A swing or graveyard shift officer could easily plunder considerable booty during these occasions, acquiring everything from clothing to tires for his personal vehicle. At the other end of the spectrum is the potential for huge payoffs from drug traffickers or other big-money offenders who will gladly pay the officer to look away from their crimes. Some officers, of course, find this temptation impossible to overcome.

## *Community Policing*

Community oriented policing and problem solving (COPPS, examined in Chapter 3) is characterized by more frequent and closer contacts with the public, resulting in the minds of many observers in less accountability and, by extension, more opportunities for corruption. Is there a relationship between unethical behavior and COPPS? Should this be a major concern? Probably not. First, only a small fraction of police officers have violated their oath of office throughout history, which includes a long tradition of using discretionary authority. And second, working more closely with the public will also serve to heighten the officers' visibility and trust with the citizenry. COPPS is founded on trust and community interaction. But that is not to say that there should not be scrutiny and accountability.

A case study at chapter's end concerns ethics and community policing.

---

EXHIBIT 13.2
**LAPD Takes Next Step in Developing Monitoring
System for 10,000 Officers**

. . . The Los Angeles Police Department has hired a small information systems consulting firm . . . to develop a monitoring system for its 10,000 officers.

. . . The program will use data-mining techniques to provide a broad statistical overview of an officer's long-term performance, as well as zoom in on specifics to provide detailed breakdowns of an officer's daily activity. Development of such a system is a requirement of a consent decree entered into with the Justice Department. . . .

Officers who use force against suspects far more than average, for ex-

ample, would fall into a red category; those who are less aggressive would be placed in the yellow or green category. . . .

The system is fair and accurate because the firm spent a considerable amount of time studying how law enforcement agencies function. . . .

[The system] will also help departments identify good performers. . . .

*Source:* Reprinted with permission from *Law Enforcement News*, July/August 2001, p. 5. John Jay College of Criminal Justice (CCNY), 555 West 57th St., New York, NY 10019.

---

## *Training, Supervision, Values*

Another key element of ethics in policing is the recruitment and training of police personnel. Like people in other occupations, new officers may learn early on how to steal at a burglary scene or from the body of a dead person, or they may learn how to commit perjury in court, how to cover misdeeds of their peers, how to shake people down, or how to beat people up. Or they may be fortunate enough to work in an agency in which none of these actions is ever suggested to them.

Formal training programs in ethics can help ensure that officers understand their department's code of ethics, elevate the importance of ethics throughout the agency, and underscore top management's support. It is imperative that police administrators see that applicants are thoroughly tested, trained, and exposed to an anticorruption environment by proper role modeling.

No supervision of police officers, no matter how thorough and conscientious, can keep bad cops from doing bad things. There are simply too many police officers and too few supervisors. If there is not enough supervision, then the bad cop will not be afraid. As Marcus Aurelius said, "A man should be upright, not be kept upright." There must be leadership at every level. Line officers are sincere and hard working; their leaders need to ensure that core values are part of the department's operations and become the basis of subordinates' behavior.

The organization's culture is also important in this regard. The police culture often exalts loyalty over integrity. Given the stress usually generated more from within the organization than from outside and the nature of life-and-death decisions they must make daily, even the best officers who simply want to catch criminals may become frustrated and vulnerable to bending the rules for what they view as the greater good of society.

Police agencies must also attempt to shape standards of professional behavior. Many begin to do so by articulating their values, such as "We believe in the sanctity of life," and "We believe that providing superior service to the citizens is our primary responsibility." Other rules try to guide officer behavior, such as not lying or drinking in excess in a public place.

# Ethics in the Courts

## *The Evolution of Standards of Conduct*

The first call during the twentieth century for formalized standards of conduct in the legal profession came in 1906, with Roscoe Pound's speech "The Causes of Popular Dissatisfaction with the Administration of Justice." The American Bar Association (ABA) quickly responded by formulating and approving the Canons of Professional Ethics in 1908 governing lawyers. No separate rules were provided for judges, however.

The first Canons of Judicial Ethics probably grew out of baseball's 1919 scandal in which the World Series was "thrown" to the Chicago White Sox by the Cincinnati Reds. Baseball officials turned to the judiciary for leadership and hired U.S. District Court Judge Kenesaw Mountain Landis as baseball commissioner—a position for which Landis was paid $42,500, compared to his $7,500 earnings per year as a judge. This affair prompted the 1921 ABA convention to pass a resolution of censure against the judge and appoint a committee to propose standards of judicial ethics.[17]

In 1924, the ABA approved the Canons of Judicial Ethics under the leadership of Chief Justice William Howard Taft, and in 1972, the ABA approved a new Model Code of Judicial Conduct; in 1990, the same body adopted a revised Model Code. Nearly all states and the District of Columbia have promulgated standards based on the code. In 1974, the United States Judicial Conference adopted a Code of Conduct for Federal Judges, and Congress has over the years enacted legislation regulating judicial conduct, including the Ethics Reform Act of 1989.

## *The Judge*

Ideally, our judges are flawless. They do not allow emotion or personal biases to creep into their work, treat all cases and individual litigants with an even hand, and employ "justice tempered with mercy." The perfect judge would be like the one described by the eminent Italian legal philosopher Pierro Calamandrei:

The good judge takes equal pains with every case no matter how humble; he knows that important cases and unimportant cases do not exist, for injustice is not one of those poisons which . . . when taken in small doses may produce a salutary effect. Injustice is a dangerous poison even in doses of homeopathic proportions.[18]

Not all judges, of course, can attain this lofty status. Recognizing this fact, nearly 800 years ago King John of England met with his barons on the field of Runnymede and, in the Magna Carta, promised that henceforth he would not "make men justices . . . unless they are such as know the law of the realm and are minded to observe it rightly."[19]

The subject of judicial ethics seemed to arouse little interest until relatively recently. Indeed, from 1890 to 1904, an era of trusts and political corruption, only a few articles were published on the subject of judicial ethics. In contrast, since 1975, more than 900 articles have appeared in magazines and newspapers under the topic of "judges and judicial ethics."

Judges can become engaged in improper conduct or overstep their bounds in many ways: abuse of judicial power (against attorneys or litigants); inappropriate sanctions and dispositions (including showing favoritism or bias); not meeting the standards of impartiality and competence (discourteous behavior, gender bias and harassment, incompetence); conflict of interest (bias; conflicting financial interests or business, social, or family relationships); personal conduct (criminal or sexual misconduct, prejudice, statements of opinion).[20]

Following are examples of some true-to-life ethical dilemmas involving the courts:

1. A judge convinces jailers to release his son on a nonbondable offense.
2. A judge is indicted on charges that he used his office for a racketeering enterprise.
3. Two judges attend the governor's $500 per person inaugural ball.
4. A judge's alleged intemperate treatment of lawyers in the courtroom was spurred by a lawyer's earlier complaints against the judge.
5. A judge is accused of acting with bias in giving a convicted murderer a less severe sentence because the victims were homosexual.
6. A judge whose car bears the bumper sticker "I am a pro-life Democrat" acquits six pro-life demonstrators of trespassing at an abortion clinic on the ground of necessity to protect human life.[21]

These incidents certainly do little to bolster public confidence in the justice system. People expect more from judges, who are "the most highly visible symbol of justice."[22] The quality of the judges determines the quality of justice.

Many judges recoil at the need for a code of judicial conduct or an independent commission to investigate complaints. They dislike being considered suspect and put under regulation. No one likes to be watched, but judges must heed Thomas Jefferson's admonition that everyone in public life should be answerable to someone.[23]

Unfortunately, codes of ethical conduct have not served to eradicate the problems or allay concerns about judges' behavior. Indeed, as three professors of law put it, "The public and the bar appear at times to be more interested in judicial ethics and accountability than the judges are."[24] One judge, who teaches judicial ethics at the National Judicial College in Reno, stated that most judges attending the college admit never having read the Code of Judicial Conduct before seeking judicial office.[25] Some judges also dismiss the need for a judicial conduct code because they believe that it governs aberrant behavior, which, they also believe, is rare among the judiciary. According to the American Judicature Society, however, during one year, 25 judges were suspended from office, and more than 80 judges resigned or retired either before or after formal charges were filed against them; 120 judges also received private censure, admonition, or reprimand.[26]

The Code of Judicial Conduct strives to strike a balance between allowing judges to participate in social and public discourse and prohibiting conduct that would threaten a judge's independence. The essence of judicial independence is that judges' minds, according to John Adams, "should not be distracted with jarring interests; they should not be dependent upon any man, or body of men."[27]

Living by the code is challenging; the key to judicial ethics is to identify the troublesome issues and to sharpen one's sensitivity to them, that is, to create an "ethical alarm system" that responds.[28] Perhaps the most important tenet in the code and the one that is most difficult to apply is that judges should avoid the appearance of impropriety.

By adhering to ethical principles, judges can maintain their independence and follow the ancient charge Moses gave to his judges in Deuteronomy:

> Hear the causes between your brethren, and judge righteously. Ye shall not respect persons in judgment; but ye shall hear the small as well as the great; ye shall not be afraid of the face of man; for the judgment is God's; and for the cause that is too hard for you, bring it unto me, and I will hear it.[29]

## *Lawyers for the Defense*

Defense attorneys, too, must be legally and morally bound to ethical principles as agents of the courts. Elliot Cohen[30] suggested the following moral principles for defense attorneys:

1. Treat others as ends in themselves and not as mere means to winning cases.
2. Treat clients and other professional relations in a similar fashion.
3. Do not deliberately engage in behavior apt to deceive the court as to truth.
4. Be willing, if necessary, to make reasonable personal sacrifices of time, money, and popularity for what you believe to be a morally good cause.
5. Do not give money to, or accept money from, clients for wrongful purposes or in wrongful amounts.
6. Avoid harming others in the course of representing your client.
7. Be loyal to your client and do not betray his confidence.

### *Prosecutors*

Prosecutors can also improve their ethical behavior. Contrary, perhaps, to what is popularly believed, it was decided over a half century ago that the primary duty of a prosecutor is "not that he shall win a case, but that justice shall be done."[31]

Instances of prosecutorial misconduct were reported as early as 1897[32] and are still reported today. One of the leading examples of unethical conduct by a prosecutor was *Miller v. Pate*,[33] in which the prosecutor concealed from the jury in a murder trial the fact that a pair of undershorts with red stains on it were stained not by blood but by paint.

If similar (though not so egregious) kinds of misconduct occur today, one must question why. According to Cohen,[34] the answer is simple: Misconduct works. Oral advocacy is important in the courtroom and can have a powerful effect. Another significant reason for such conduct is the harmless error doctrine, in which an appellate court can affirm a conviction despite the presence of serious misconduct during the trial. Only when appellate courts take a stricter, more consistent approach to this problem will it end.[35]

### *Other Court Employees*

Other court employees have ethical responsibilities as well. Primarily known as "confidential employees," these are justice system functionaries who have a special role in the court system and work closely with a judge or judges. These individuals have a special responsibility to maintain the confidentiality of the court system and thus have a high standard of trust. For example, an appellate court judge's secretary is asked by a good friend who is a lawyer whether or not the judge will be writing the opinion in a certain case. The lawyer may be wishing to attempt to influence the judge through his secretary, renegotiate with an opposing party, or engage in some other improper activity designed to alter the case outcome.[36] Bailiffs, court administrators, court reporters, courtroom clerks, and law clerks would all fit into this category. The judge's secretary, of course, must use his or her own ethical standard in deciding whether to answer the lawyer's question.

It would be improper for a bailiff who is accompanying jurors back from a break in a criminal trial to mention that the judge "sure seems annoyed at the defense attorney" or for a law clerk to tell an attorney friend that the judge she works for prefers reading short bench memos.[37]

## Ethics in Corrections

Corrections personnel confront many of the same ethical dilemmas as police personnel. So, prison and jail administrators, like their counterparts in the police realm, would do well to understand their occupational subculture and its effect on ethical decision making.

The strength of the corrections subculture correlates with the security level of a correctional facility and is strongest in maximum-security institutions. Powerful forces within the correctional system have a stronger influence over the behavior of correctional officers than the administrators of the institution, legislative decrees, or agency policies.[38] Indeed, it has been known for several decades that the exposure to external danger in the workplace creates a remarkable increase in group solidarity.[39]

Some of the job-related stressors for corrections officers are similar to those the police face: the ever-present potential for physical danger, hostility directed at officers by inmates and even by the public, unreasonable role demands, a tedious and unrewarding work environment, and dependence placed on one another to effectively and safely work in their environment.[40] For these reasons, several norms of corrections work have been identified: always go to the aid of an officer in distress; do not "rat"; never make another officer look bad in front of inmates; always support an officer in a dispute with an inmate; always support officer sanctions against inmates; and do not wear a "white hat" (participate in behavior that suggests sympathy or identification with inmates).[41]

Security issues and the way in which individual correctional officers have to rely on each other for their safety makes loyalty to one another a key norm. The proscription against ratting out a colleague is strong. In one documented instance, two officers in the Corcoran, California, state prison blew the whistle on what they considered to be unethical conduct by their colleagues: Officers were alleged to have staged a gladiator-style fight among inmates from different groups in a small exercise yard. The two officers claimed that their colleagues would even place bets on the outcome of the fights and when the fights got out of hand, the officers would fire shots at the inmates. Since the institution had opened in 1988, eight inmates had been shot dead by officers and numerous others had been wounded. The two officers who reported these activities were labeled by colleagues as "rats" and "no-goods" and had their lives threatened; even though they were transferred to other institutions, the labels traveled with them. Four correctional officers were indicted for their alleged involvement in these activities, and were all acquitted in a state prosecution in 2001.[42]

In another case, a female corrections officer at a medium-security institution reported some of her colleagues for sleeping on the night shift. She had first approached them and expressed concern for her safety when they were asleep and told them that if they did not refrain from sleeping, she would have to report them to the superintendent. They continued sleeping, and she reported them. The consequences were severe: Graffiti was written about her on the walls, she received harassing phone calls and letters, her car was vandalized, and some bricks were thrown through the windows of her home.[43]

It would be unfair to suggest that the kind of behavior depicted here reflects the behavior of corrections officers in all places and at all times. The case studies do demonstrate, however, the power and loyalty of the group, and correctional administrators must be cognizant of that power. It is also noteworthy that the corrections subculture, like its police counterpart, provides several positive qualities, particularly in crisis situations, including mutual support and protection, which is essential to the emotional and psychological health of officers involved; there is always the "family" to support you.

# Guiding Decision Making

One of the primary purposes of ethics is to guide decision making.[44] Ethics provides more comprehensive guidelines than law and operational procedures and answers questions that might otherwise go unanswered. When in doubt, justice administrators and employees should be able to consider the ethical consequences of their actions or potential actions to determine how they should proceed. To assist, guidelines must be in place to assist employees when making operational decisions. Criminal justice leaders obviously play a key role in ethics. Not only must they enforce and uphold ethical standards, they must also set an example and see that employees are instructed in the ethical conduct of police business.

Some experts in police ethics lay problems involving employees' ethics, and their lapses in good conduct, squarely at the feet of their leaders; for example, Edward Tully[45] has stated the following:

> Show me a[n] agency with a serious problem of officer misconduct and I will show you a department staffed with too many sergeants not doing their job. [Leaders must] recognize the vital and influential role sergeants play within an organization. They should be selected with care, given as much supervisory training as possible, and included in the decision making process. Sergeants are the custodians of the culture, the leaders and informal disciplinarians of the department, and the individual most officers look to for advice.

Stephen Vicchio[46] added another caveat. Even in communities where all seems to be going well with respect to ethical behavior, trouble may actually be lurking beneath the surface:

> In departments where corruption appears to be low and citizen complaints are minimal, we assume that the officers are people of integrity. Sometimes this is a faulty assumption, particularly if the motivation to do the right thing comes from fear of punishment.

Most efforts to control justice system employee behavior are rooted in statutes and departmental orders and policies. These written directives stipulate inappropriate behavior and, in some cases, behavior or actions that are expected in specific situations. Written directives cannot address every contingency, however, and employees must often use their discretion. These discretionary decisions should be guided by ethics and values. When there is an ethics or policy failure, the resulting behavior is generally considered to be illegal or inappropriate.

# Some Tests for the Justice System Recruit

Following are some tests to help guide the young recruit to decide what is and is not ethical behavior:[47]

- *Test of common sense:* Does the act make sense or would someone look askance at it?
- *Test of publicity:* Would you be willing to see what you did highlighted on the front page of the local newspaper?
- *Test of one's best self:* Will the act fit the concept of one's self at one's best?
- *Test of one's most admired personality:* What would one's parents or minister do in this situation?
- *Test of hurting someone else:* Will it cause pain for someone?
- *Test of foresight:* What is the long-term likely result?

Other questions that the officer might ask are, Is it worth my job and career? Is my decision legal?

Another tool is that of "the Bell, the Book, and the Candle": Do bells or warning buzzers go off as I consider my choice of actions? Does it violate any laws or codes in the statute or ordinance books? Will my decision withstand the light of day, or spotlight of publicity (the candle)?[48]

In sum, all we can do is seek to make the best decisions we can and be a good person and a good justice system employee, one who is consistent and fair. We need to apply the law, the policy, the guidelines, or whatever it is we dispense in our occupation without bias or fear and to the best of our ability, being mindful along the way that others around us may have lost their moral compass and attempt to drag us down with them. To paraphrase Franklin Delano Roosevelt, "Be the best you can, wherever you are, with what you have."

# CASE STUDIES

Following are six case studies,[49] some of which are hypothetical, while others are based on real-life situations. They pose ethically relative (shades-of-gray) dilemmas for command, supervisory, and officer-level personnel.

True ethical dilemmas have no clear or obvious solutions. Oftentimes, *all* choices are no-win in nature. Consider the questions posed at the end of each case study.

Assume that the police have multiple leads that implicate Smith as a pedophile, but they have failed in every attempt to obtain a warrant to search Smith's car and home where evidence might be present. Officer Jones feels frustrated and, early one morning, takes his baton and breaks a rear taillight on Smith's car. The next day he stops Smith for operating his vehicle with a broken taillight; he impounds and inventories the vehicle and finds evidence leading to Smith's conviction on 25 counts of child molestation and possession of pornography. Jones receives accolades for the apprehension.

Queries: Do Officer Jones's "ends" justify the "means"? What if he believes he is justified in "taking bad guys off the streets"? What if he argues that he is correct in this approach because he was molested as a child? What constitutional issues are involved?

Officer Rogers has commenced a problem-solving project in a comparatively affluent neighborhood that is plagued with transients and prostitutes. One of his first activities in scanning the problem is to conduct a rather cursory, door-to-door survey of residents to learn what they know about these problems. At one residence, Miss Larue, recently divorced, seductively dressed in a nightgown, and slightly intoxicated, says she is a cousin of the chief's and asks the officer to come in to talk and have lunch.

Queries: What should Rogers do? Assume further that Rogers's supervisor, Sgt. Tracy Zane, is driving by and witnesses this conversation and sees the officer enter the home. What should Zane do?

There have been problems between rival gang members in one section of the city. Officer Blackwood works with both sides to alleviate the tension and tries hard to develop programs and rapport and to gain gang members' respect. Eventually, the problem calms down. Soon Blackwood begins observing carloads of young men, many of whom are underage, driving around and blatantly drinking. When she confronts them, they tell Blackwood that she should "be cool" about their "harmless" drinking activities because they're cooperating with her and are no longer shooting at each other. They obviously want to take advantage of their new rapport with Blackwood.

Queries: How should Blackwood respond? At what point do/should the police sacrifice their ethical and legal expectations in attempting to develop rapport and calm in the neighborhood?

Officer Burns is known to have extreme difficulty relating to persons of color and others who are socially different from himself. The officer never received any sensitivity or diversity training at the academy or within the department. His supervisor fails to understand the weight of the problem and has little patience with Burns. So, to correct the matter, the supervisor decides to assign Burns to a minority section of town so he will improve his ability to relate to diverse groups. Within a week, Burns responds to a disturbance at a housing project where residents are partying noisily. Burns immediately begins yelling at the residents to quiet down; they fail to respond, so Burns draws his baton and begins poking residents and ordering them to comply with his directions. The crowd immediately turns against Burns, who then has to radio for backup assistance. After the other officers arrive, a fight ensues between them and the residents, and several members of both sides are injured and numerous arrests are made.

Queries: How could the supervisor have dealt better with Burns's lack of sensitivity? What should the supervisor/administration do with Burns? Are there any liability or negligence issues present in this situation?

A municipal court judge borrows money from court employees, publicly endorses and campaigns for a candidate for judicial office, conducts personal business from chambers (displaying and selling antiques), directs other court employees to perform personal errands for him during court hours, suggests to persons appearing before him to contribute to certain charities in lieu of paying fines, and uses court employees to perform translating services at his mother's nursery business.

Queries: Which, if any, of these activities would be unethical? Why? Taken together, would they warrant the judge's being disciplined? Removed from office? (See the outcome at the end of the case studies.)

Dale has worked in the county jail for seven years. He is a dedicated, competent employee, one who is well respected by colleagues and administrators alike. But personal problems have arisen in his life: His wife of 10 years is filing for divorce, and his young daughter has serious behavioral problems. On this particular day, Dale reports for work tired and irritable after dealing with problems at home. One 18-year-old inmate quickly begins to get on his nerves. Small and "yappy," the boy never stops whining, carrying on for several hours with his high-pitched, increasingly maddening talk. Finally, after telling the boy to "shut up or else" several times, Dale loses control and slaps him hard on the face, leaving a welt and a small cut; the blow was loud enough to be heard by other inmates. For the first time, Dale has lost his temper and taken out his frustrations on an inmate. Another officer is sent to cover his post, and Dale goes to the superintendent's office. He recounts the incident, concluding with "I did it, I hit him hard and I deserve to be fired. Or would you let me resign? I'm very sorry it happened this way."

Queries: As the superintendent, what would you do? Fire Dale? Allow him to resign? Take some other course of action? How much weight, if any, should legitimately be given to his personal problems? To what extent, if any, would your decision be guided by the institution's subculture?

You have been employed for two months as a corrections officer at a detention center with about 15 young offenders, most of whom have psychological problems. You are beginning to fit in well and to be invited to other staff members' social functions. During today's lunchtime, you are in the dining room and notice eight of the youths sitting at one table. One of them is an immature 18-year-old whose table manners are disgusting. Today, he decides to pour mounds of ketchup over his meal, swirling it around his plate, and then slurping it into his mouth. He then eats with his mouth open and spits the food across the table when he is talking. You, the other officers, and even other inmates are sickened by his behavior. A fellow officer, Tom, gets up and tugs the boy away from the table by his shirt collar. The officer sets the boy's tray of food on the floor and orders him to get on all fours next to it. "Your manners are disgusting," Tom says, "If you're going to eat like a dog you may as well get down on all fours like a dog; get down there and lick the food off the plate till it's clean." Tom later tells you that he did what he did out of frustration and to use a "shock tactic" to change the boy's behavior.

Queries: What, if anything, should you do in this situation? Did Tom act professionally? Ethically? Should you have intervened on the boy's behalf? What would you do about this incident if you were superintendent of this institution and it was reported to you?

[The earlier case describing the activities of a municipal court judge actually occurred in a Nevada court; the judge was removed from office.]

## Summary

This chapter has examined criminal justice employee behaviors from an ethical standpoint. Ethics form the foundation for behavior. It is important that administrators and subordinates understand ethics and the role ethics plays in their performance of their duties. Agencies must come to grips with the ethical boundaries of police work to ensure that the boundaries are not violated.

Corruption has few easy remedies. As indicated in the chapter's opening quote by Lord Acton, the bad seek to cloak themselves in secrecy. To avoid rotten apples, criminal justice administrators need to maintain high standards for recruitment and training. And to avoid rotten structures, these kinds of agencies need leaders who will not tolerate corruption, institutional procedures for accountability, and systematic investigation of complaints and of suspicious circumstances.[50]

# Questions for Review

1. How would you define ethics? What are examples of relative as well as absolute ethics?
2. Which do you believe are the most difficult ethical dilemmas presented in the case studies? Consider the issues presented in each.
3. Should police accept minor gratuities? Why or why not?
4. How could community policing pose new ethical problems?
5. In what ways can judges, defense attorneys, and prosecutors engage in unethical behaviors?
6. In what substantive ways do the police and corrections subcultures resemble each other?
7. How may corrections officers in prisons be unethical?

# Notes

1. Adapted from John R. Jones and Daniel P. Carlson, *Reputable Conduct: Ethical Issues in Policing and Corrections*, 2d ed. (Upper Saddle River, N.J.: Prentice Hall, 2001), p. 14.
2. This scenario is loosely based on David Gelman, Susan Miller, and Bob Cohn, "The Strange Case of Judge Wachtler," *Newsweek* (November 23, 1992):34-35. Wachtler was later arraigned on charges of attempting to extort money from the woman and threatening her 14-year-old daughter (it was later determined that the judge had been having an affair with the woman, who had recently ended the relationship). After being placed under house arrest with an electronic monitoring bracelet, the judge resigned from the court, which he had served with distinction for two decades.
3. Adapted from Jones and Carlson, *Reputable Conduct*, pp. 162-163.
4. Richard Kania, "Police Acceptance of Gratuities," *Criminal Justice Ethics* 7 (1988): 37-49.
5. John Kleinig, *The Ethics of Policing* (New York: Cambridge University Press, 1996).
6. T. J. O'Malley, "Managing for Ethics: A Mandate for Administrators," *FBI Law Enforcement Bulletin* (April 1997):20-25.
7. David Carter, "Theoretical Dimensions in the Abuse of Authority," in Thomas Barker and David Carter (eds.), *Police Deviance* (Cincinnati: Anderson, 1994), pp. 269-290; also see Thomas Barker and David Carter, "Fluffing Up the Evidence and 'Covering Your Ass': Some Conceptual Notes on Police Lying," *Deviant Behavior*, 11 (1990):61-73.
8. Gary T. Marx, "Who Really Gets Stung? Some Issues Raised by the New Police Undercover Work," *Crime & Delinquency* (1982):165-193.
9. *Illinois v. Perkins*, 110 S.Ct. 2394 (1990).
10. Barker and Carter, *Police Deviance*.
11. Thomas Barker, "An Empirical Study of Police Deviance Other Than Corruption," in Barker and Carter, *Police Deviance*, pp. 123-138.
12. New York City Commission to Investigate Allegations of Police Corruption and the City's Anti-Corruption Procedures, *The Knapp Commission Report on Police Corruption* (New York: George Braziller, 1972), p. 4.
13. Kania, "Police Acceptance of Gratuities," p. 40.

14. Albert A. Seedman and Peter Hellman, *Chief!* (New York: Avon Books, 1974), pp. 43–44.

15. Edwin J. Delattre, *Character and Cops: Ethics in Policing*, 4th ed. (Washington, D.C.: The AEI Press, 2002), p. 41.

16. Edward Tully, "Misconduct, Corruption, Abuse of Power: What Can the Chief Do?" *Beretta USA Leadership Bulletin* Web page, http://www.berettabulletin.com, p. 3 (accessed December 9, 2002).

17. John P. MacKenzie, *The Appearance of Justice* (New York: Scribner's, 1974).

18. Quoted in Frank Greenberg, "The Task of Judging the Judges," *Judicature* 59 (May 1976):464.

19. Ibid., p. 460 (direct quote from the original).

20. For thorough discussions and examples of these areas of potential ethical shortcomings, see Jeffrey M. Shaman, Steven Lubet, and James J. Alfini, *Judicial Conduct and Ethics*, 3d ed. (San Francisco, Calif.: Matthew Bender & Co., 2000).

21. Ibid.

22. Ibid., p. vi.

23. Ibid.

24. Ibid., p. vi.

25. Tim Murphy, "Test Your Ethical Acumen," *Judges' Journal* 8 (1998):34.

26. American Judicature Society, *Judicial Conduct Reporter* 16 (1994):2–3.

27. John Adams, "On Government," quoted in Russell Wheeler, *Judicial Administration: Its Relation to Judicial Independence* (Alexandria, Va.: National Center for State Courts, 1988), p. 112.

28. Shaman, Lubet, and Alfini, *Judicial Conduct and Ethics*, p. viii.

29. Deut. 1:16–17.

30. Elliot D. Cohen, "Pure Legal Advocates and Moral Agents: Two Concepts of a Lawyer in an Adversary System," in Michael C. Braswell, Belinda R. McCarthy, and Bernard J. McCarthy (eds.), *Justice, Crime and Ethics*, 2d ed. (Cincinnati: Anderson, 1996), pp. 131–167.

31. *Berger v. United States*, 295 U.S. 78 (1935).

32. See *Dunlop v. United States*, 165 U.S. 486 (1897), involving a prosecutor's inflammatory statements to the jury.

33. 386 U.S. 1 (1967). In this case, the Supreme Court overturned the defendant's conviction after determining that the prosecutor "deliberately misrepresented the truth."

34. Cohen, "Pure Legal Advocates and Moral Agents," p. 168.

35. Ibid.

36. Cynthia Kelly Conlon and Lisa L. Milord, *The Ethics Fieldbook: Tools for Trainers* (Chicago: American Judicature Society, n.d.), pp. 23–25.

37. Ibid., p. 28.

38. Elizabeth L. Grossi and Bruce L. Berg, "Stress and Job Dissatisfaction Among Correctional Officers: An Unexpected Finding," *International Journal of Offender Therapy and Comparative Criminology* 35 (1991):79.

39. Irving L. Janis, "Group Dynamics Under Conditions of External Danger," in Darwin Cartwright and Alvin Zander (eds.), *Group Dynamics: Research and Theory* (New York: Harper & Row, 1968).

40. Ibid.

41. Ibid., p. 85.

42. CBS News, March 30, 1977; see Jones and Carlson, *Reputable Conduct*, p. 76.

43. Jones and Carlson, *Reputable Conduct*, p. 77.

44. F. K. Fair and W. D. Pilcher, "Morality on the Line: The Role of Ethics in Police Decision-Making," *American Journal of Police*, 10(2) (1991):23–38.

45. Edward Tully, "Misconduct, Corruption, Abuse of Power: What Can the Chief Do?" *Beretta USA Leadership Bulletin*. www.berettabulletin.com (14 January 1998):7.

46. Stephen J. Vicchio, "Ethics and Police Integrity," *FBI Law Enforcement Bulletin* (July 1997):8–12.

47. Kleinig, *The Ethics of Policing*.

48. Ibid.

49. Some of these case studies were adapted from Jones and Carlson, *Reputable Conduct*.

50. Delattre, *Character and Cops*, p. 84.

# Chapter 14

# Rights of Criminal Justice Employees

## Key Terms and Concepts

Americans with Disabilities Act (ADA)

Affirmative action

Bona fide occupational qualifier (BFOQ)

Fair Labor Standards Act (FLSA)

Family and Medical Leave Act (FMLA)

Peace Officers Bill of Rights (POBR)

Reverse discrimination

## Learning Objectives

As a result of reading this chapter, the student will:

- be familiar with laws and rights affecting criminal justice employees
- understand the concept of disparate treatment
- be familiar with effective action plans
- know the elements of a due process claim under U.S. Section 1983
- understand the impact of the Fair Labor Standards Act on criminal justice employees
- understand the impact of sexual harassment in the criminal justice workplace
- know the eligibility requirements for Family and Medical Leave Act benefits
- have an understanding of the Americans with Disabilities Act

*Uneasy lies the head that wears the crown.*

—William Shakespeare

*Good orders make evil men good and bad orders make good men evil.*

—James Harrington

# Introduction

In the past few decades, the rights and obligations of criminal justice employees, like those of workers in the private sector, have changed dramatically. Changes in values, demographics, law, and technology have blurred the line dividing the manager and those who are managed in enforcement, judicial, and correctional agencies. Today's criminal justice employee is far more sophisticated about employee rights.[1] For that reason, and because of attendant liability considerations (discussed in Chapter 15), contemporary criminal justice managers must be more aware of employees' legal rights.

After an overview of the relevant employment laws, we discuss recruitment and hiring issues, age discrimination, affirmative action, discipline and discharge, pay and benefits, and safe workplace issues. Then, we examine constitutional rights of criminal justice employees as determined by the courts regarding free speech, searches and seizures, self-incrimination, religious practices, sexual misconduct, residency requirements, moonlighting, misuse of firearms, alcohol and drugs in the workplace, sexual harassment, and the Americans with Disabilities Act. The chapter concludes with two case studies.

# Overview

Law and litigation affecting criminal justice employees can arise out of federal and state constitutions, statutes, administrative regulations, and judicial interpretations and rulings. Even poorly written employee handbooks or long-standing agency customs or practices may create vested rights. The ripple effect begun by improper or illegal hiring, training, discipline, or discharge can lead not only to poor agency performance and morale, but also to substantial legal and economic liability. It should become apparent in the following overview and the court decisions that follow that utilizing good common sense as well as a sense of fairness will go a long way toward preventing legal problems in the employment relationship.[2]

It should also be noted that the Civil Rights Act of 1991, like its predecessors, may result in further amended versions and changes in public and private sector employment; however, it will take several years for significant decisions to wind their way through the courts for a final determination by the Supreme

Court of the intent and reach of the act. Therefore, this section focuses on presenting the issues rather than on attempting to settle the law in these areas.

- *Fair Labor Standards Act (FLSA; at 29 U.S.C. 203 et seq.):* This act provides minimum salary and overtime provisions covering both public and private sector employees. Part 7(a) contains special provisions for firefighters and police officers. We discuss the FLSA more fully later.

- *Title VII of the Civil Rights Act of 1964 and its Amendments (42 U.S.C. 2000e):* This broadly based act established a federal policy requiring fair employment practices in both the public and private sectors. It prohibited unlawful employment discrimination in the hiring process, discharge, discipline, and working conditions and the unlawful provision of benefits based on race, color, religion, sex, and national origin. Its provisions extend to "hostile work environment" claims based on sexual, racial, or religious harassment.

- *Equal Pay Act [29 U.S.C. 206(d)]:* This legislation provided an alternative remedy to Title VII for sex-based discrimination in wages and benefits when men and women do similar work. It applies the simpler Fair Labor Standards Act procedures to claims. Note that the Equal Pay Act does not mean "comparable worth"—an attempt to determine wages by requiring equal pay for employees whose work is of comparable worth even if the job content is totally different.

- *The Pregnancy Discrimination Act of 1978 [42 U.S.C. Section 2000e(k)]:* This act is an amendment to the scope of sexual discrimination under Title VII. It prohibits unequal treatment of women because of pregnancy or related medical conditions (e.g., nausea). The act requires that employers treat pregnant women like other temporarily disabled employees. The U.S. Supreme Court decided a major case in 1991 that limited employers' ability to exclude women who are pregnant or of childbearing years from certain jobs, under a fetal protection policy.[3]

- *Age Discrimination in Employment Act (29 U.S.C. 623):* This act generally prohibits the unequal treatment of applicants or employees based on their age, if they are age 40 or over, in regard to hiring, firing, receiving benefits, and other conditions of employment.

- *Americans with Disabilities Act of 1990 (ADA) (42 U.S.C. 12112):* The goal of this legislation is to remove barriers that might prevent otherwise qualified individuals with disabilities from enjoying the same employment opportunities available to persons without disabilities. Before the ADA, the Rehabilitation Act of 1973 (see 29 U.S.C. 701) and its amendments prevented similar disability discrimination among public agencies receiving federal funds. The ADA is discussed more fully later.

- *Section 1983 (codified as Title 42, U.S. Code Section 1983):* This major piece of legislation is the instrument by which an employee may sue an employer for civil rights violations based on the deprivation of constitutional rights. It is the most versatile civil rights action and is also the most often used against criminal justice agencies. Section 1983 is discussed more later in Chapter 15.

In addition to the those legislative enactments and state statutes that prohibit various acts of discrimination in employment, there are additional remedies that have tremendous impact on public sector employees. Tort actions (a tort is the infliction of a civil injury) may be brought by public sector employees against their employer for a wide variety of claims, ranging from assault and battery to defamation. Contractual claims may grow out of collective bargaining agreements, which may include procedures for assignments, seniority, due process protections (such as in the Peace Officers' Bill of Rights, discussed later), and grievance procedures. Often the source of the right defines the remedy and the procedure to obtain that remedy. For example, statutes or legal precedents often provide for an aggrieved employee to receive back pay, compensatory damages, injunctive relief, or punitive damages.

# The Employment Relationship

## *Recruitment and Hiring*

Numerous selection methods for hiring police and corrections officers have been tried over the years. Issues in recruitment, selection, and hiring also often involve internal promotions and assignments to special units, such as a special weapons team in a police agency. Requirements concerning age (e.g., the FBI will hire no one older than 37 years of age), height, weight, vision, education, and possession of a valid driver's license have all been utilized over the years in criminal justice. In addition, tests are commonly used to determine intelligence, emotional suitability and stability (using psychological examinations and oral interviews), physical agility, and character (using polygraph examinations and extensive background checks).[4] More recently, drug tests have become frequently used as well (discussed more fully later).

The critical question for such tests is whether or not they validly test the types of skills needed for the job. A companion concern is whether or not the tests are used for discriminatory purposes or have an unequal impact on protected groups (e.g., minorities, the physically challenged). As a result of these considerations, a number of private companies provide valid, reliable examinations for use by the public sector.

## *Disparate Treatment*

It should be emphasized that there is nothing in the law that states that an employer must hire or retain incompetent personnel. In effect, the law does not prohibit discrimination. Thus, it is not unlawful to refuse to hire people who have a record of driving while intoxicated for positions that require driving.

What *is* illegal is to treat people differently because of their age, gender, sex, or other protected status; that is disparate treatment. It is also illegal to deny equal employment opportunities to such persons; that is disparate impact.[5] Federal equal opportunity law prohibits the use of selection procedures for hiring or promotion that have a discriminatory impact on the employment opportunities of women, Hispanics, blacks, or other protected classes. An example of overt discriminatory hiring is reflected in a court decision in 1987 arising out of a situation in a sparsely populated county in Virginia. Four women sued because they were denied positions as courtroom security officer, deputy, and civil process server because of their gender. Sheriffs had refused to hire the women, justifying their decision by contending that being male was a **bona fide occupational qualifier (BFOQ)** for the positions and because the positions were within the "personal staff" of the sheriff, they were exempt from the coverage of Title VII. The Fourth Circuit overturned a lower court decision, finding that the sheriff did not establish that gender was a BFOQ for the positions and that the positions were not part of the sheriff's personal staff (the positions were not high level, policymaking, or advisory in nature). Thus, the refusal to hire the women violated Title VII.[6] There may, however, be a "business justification" for a hiring policy even though it has a disparate impact. For example, in one case an employer required airline attendants to cease flying immediately upon discovering they were pregnant. The court upheld the policy, on the ground that pregnancy could affect one's ability to perform routine duties in an aircraft, thereby jeopardizing the safety of passengers.[7]

A classic example of an apparent neutral employment requirement that actually had a disparate impact on gender, race, and ethnicity was the once-prevalent height requirement used by most public safety agencies. Minimum height requirements of "5 feet, 10 inches or above" were often advertised and effectively operated to exclude most women and many Asians and Hispanics from employment.[8] Such a requirement has gradually been superseded by a "height in proportion to weight" requirement. Nonetheless, other existing physical agility tests serve to discriminate against women and small men with less upper-body strength. One is forced to wonder how many pushups a police officer must do on the job, or be able to do to perform the duties adequately, or how many six-foot walls, ditches, and attics officers must negotiate. (Occasionally, preemployment physical abilities testing becomes ludicrous. For example, the author once allowed a recruiter from a major western city to recruit students in an upper-level criminal justice course. The recruiter said the city's physical test included scaling a six-foot wall; however, he quickly pointed out that testing staff would boost all female applicants over it.)

Litigation is blossoming in this area. In another western city, a woman challenged the police department's physical abilities test as discriminatory and not job related, prompting the agency to hire a Canadian consultant who developed a job-related preemployment agility test (currently used by the Royal Canadian Mounted Police and other agencies across Canada), based on data provided by officers and later computer analyzed for incorporation into the test. In other words, recruits are now tested on the physical demands placed on police officers in that specific community (no pushups or six-foot walls are included).[9]

Discrimination may also exist in promotions and job assignments. As an example of the former, a Nebraska female correctional center worker brought suit alleging that her employer violated her Title VII and equal protection rights by denying her a promotion. The woman was qualified for the higher-level position (assistant center manager for programming), and she also alleged that the center treated women inequitably and unprofessionally, that assertiveness in women was viewed negatively, and that women were assigned clerical duties not assigned to men. The court found that she was indeed denied a promotion because of her sex, in violation of Title VII and the equal protection clause of the Fourteenth Amendment; she was awarded back pay ($7,500), front pay ($122 biweekly until a comparable position became available), general damages, and court costs.[10]

With respect to litigation in the area of job assignments, four female jail matrons who were refused assignments to correctional officer positions in Florida, even though they had been trained and certified as jail officers, were awarded damages. It was ruled that a state regulation prohibiting females in male areas of the jail was discriminatory without proof that gender was a BFOQ.[11] However, a particular assignment may validly exclude one sex. An assignment to work as a decoy female prostitute demonstrates a business necessity for women.[12]

## *How Old Is "Too Old" in Criminal Justice?*

State and public agencies are not immune from age discrimination suits in which arbitrary age restrictions have been found to violate the law. In Florida, a police lieutenant with the state highway patrol with 29 years of service was forced by statute to retire at age 62. The Equal Employment Opportunity Commission (EEOC) brought suit, alleging that Florida's statute violated the Age Discrimination in Employment Act (ADEA). The court held that age should not be a BFOQ, as youthfulness is not a guarantee of public safety. Rather, a physical fitness standard would better serve the purpose of ensuring the ability to perform the tasks of the position.[13]

Indeed, the U.S. Supreme Court rejected mandatory retirement plans for municipal firefighters and police officers.[14] Until 1985, the city of Baltimore had relied on a *federal* police officer and firefighter statute (5 U.S.C. 8335b), an exemption to the ADEA, to establish age limits for appointing and retiring its fire and police officers; the city also contended that age was a BFOQ for doing so. The U.S. Supreme Court said that while Congress had exempted federal employees from application of the ADEA, another agency cannot just adopt the same standards without showing an agency-specific need. Age is not a BFOQ for non-federal firefighters (or, by extension, police officers). The Court also established a "reasonable federal standard" in its 1984 decision in *EEOC v. Wyoming,*[15] in which it overturned a state statute providing for the mandatory retirement of state game wardens at age 55; it held that the ADEA did not require employers to retain unfit employees, only to make individualized determinations about fitness.

## *Criminal Justice and Affirmative Action*

Probably no single employment practice has caused as much controversy as **affirmative action.** The very words bring to mind visions of quotas and of unqualified people being given preferential hiring treatment.[16] Indeed, quotas have been at the center of legal, social, scientific, and political controversy for more than two decades.[17] However, the reality of affirmative action is substantially different from the myth; as a general rule, affirmative action plans give preferred treatment only to affected groups when all other criteria (e.g., education, skills) are equal.[18]

The legal question (and to many persons, a moral one) that arises from affirmative action is this: When does preferential hiring become **reverse discrimination?** The leading case here is *Bakke v. Regents of the University of California,*[19] in 1978, in which Allan Bakke was passed over for medical school admission at the University of California, Davis, partly because the school annually set aside a number of its 100 medical school admissions slots for "disadvantaged" applicants. The Supreme Court held, among other things, that race could be used as a criterion in selection decisions, but it could not be the only criterion.

In a series of cases beginning in 1986,[20] the Supreme Court considered the development and application of affirmative action plans, establishing a two-step inquiry that must be satisfied before an affirmative action plan can be put in place. A plan must have (1) a remedial purpose, to correct past inequities, and there must be (2) a manifest imbalance or significant disparity to justify the plan. The Court, however, emphasized that such plans cannot completely foreclose employment opportunities to nonminority or male candidates.

The validity of such plans is generally determined on a case-by-case basis. For example, the District of Columbia Circuit Court held in 1987 that an affirmative action plan covering the promotion of blacks to management positions in the police department was justified, because only 174 of the 807 positions (22 percent) above the rank of sergeant were filled by blacks, in a city where 60 percent of the labor market was black.[21] Twenty-one past and present nonminority male detectives of the Metropolitan Police Department who were passed over for promotion challenged the department's voluntary affirmative actions plan designed to place "special emphasis" on the hiring and advancement of females and minorities in those employment areas where an "obvious imbalance" in their numbers existed.[22]

The plaintiffs believed that their failure to be promoted was attributable to illegal preferential treatment of blacks and women (reverse discrimination) that violated their rights under Title VII and the due process clause of the Fifth Amendment. The court held that the nonminority and male employees of the department failed to prove that the plan was invalid; a considerable body of evidence showed racial and sexual imbalance at the time the plan was adopted. Also, the plan did not unnecessarily trammel any legitimate interests of the non-minority or male employees since it did not call for displacement or layoff and did not totally exclude them from promotion opportunities.[23]

In summary, then, whenever a criminal justice employer wishes to implement and maintain job requirements, they must be job related. Furthermore, whenever a job requirement discriminates against a protected class, it should have a strong legitimate purpose and be the least restrictive alternative. Finally, attempts to remedy past hiring inequities by such means as affirmative action programs need substantial justification to avoid reverse discrimination.[24]

## *Property Rights in Employment*

The Fourteenth Amendment to the U.S. Constitution provides in part that "No state shall make or enforce any law which shall abridge the privileges or immunities of citizens of the United States; nor shall any State deprive any person of life, liberty, or property without due process of law; nor deny to any person within its jurisdiction the equal protection of the law." Furthermore, the Supreme Court has set forth four elements of a due process claim under Section 1983: (1) A person acting under color of state law (2) deprived an individual (3) of constitutionally protected property (4) without due process of law.[25]

A long line of court cases has established the legal view that public employees have a property interest in their employment. This flies in the face of the old view that employees served "at will" or until their employer, for whatever reason, no longer had need of their services. The Supreme Court has provided some general guidance on how the question of a constitutionally protected property interest is to be resolved:

> To have a property interest in a benefit, a person clearly must have more than an abstract need or desire for it. He must have more than a unilateral expectation of it. He must, instead, have a *legitimate claim of entitlement to it.* It is a purpose of the ancient institution of property to protect those claims *upon which people rely in their daily lives, reliance that must not be arbitrarily undermined* [emphasis added].[26]

The Court has also held that employees are entitled to both a pretermination and a posttermination notice,[27] as well as an opportunity to respond, and that state legislators are free to choose not to confer a property interest in public employment.

The development of a property interest in employment has an important ramification: It means that due process must be exercised by a public entity before terminating or interfering with an employee's property right. What has been established, however, is that a probationary employee has little or no property interest in employment. For example, the Ninth Circuit held that a probationary civil service employee ordinarily has no property interest and could be discharged without a hearing or even "good cause." But in that same decision, the court held that a woman who had passed her six-month probationary period and who had then been promoted to a new position for which there was a probationary period had the legitimate expectation of continued employment.[28]

On the other hand, an Indiana police captain was deemed to have a property interest in his position even though a state statute allowed the city manager to demote without notice. There, a captain of detectives, a Democrat, was demoted by a newly elected Republican mayor. The court determined that the dismissal of even a policymaking public employee for politically motivated reasons is forbidden unless the position inherently encompasses tasks that render political affiliation an appropriate prerequisite for effective performance.[29]

Normally, however, policymaking employees (often called exempt appointments) possess an automatic exception to the contemporary property interest view. These personnel, often elected agency heads, are generally free to hire and fire those employees who are involved in the making of important decisions and policy. Examples of this area include new sheriffs who appoint undersheriffs and wardens who appoint deputy wardens. These subordinate employees have no property interest in their positions and may be asked at any time to leave the agency or revert back to an earlier rank.

This property interest in employment is, of course, generally implied. An example of this implication is found in a Utah case, in which a property interest was found to exist based on an implied contract founded on an employment manual. Due process standards were, therefore, violated when the police department fired an officer without showing good cause or giving him a chance to respond to the charges against him.[30] In a Pennsylvania case, a patrol officer was suspended for 30 days without pay for alleged violations of personnel policies and was not given an opportunity to file a written response to the charges. The court held that the officer's suspension resulted in a deprivation of property.[31]

Also, the property right in one's employment does not have to involve discipline or discharge to afford an employee protections. The claim of a parole officer that he was harassed, humiliated, and interfered with in a deliberate attempt to remove him from his position established a civil rights action for deprivation of property.[32] This decision, against the Illinois Department of Corrections, resulted from allegations that the department engaged in "a deliberate and calculated effort to remove the plaintiff from his position by forcing him to resign, thereby making the protections of the personnel code unavailable to him." As a result, the plaintiff suffered anxiety and stress and eventually went on disability status at substantially reduced pay.[33]

The key questions, then, once a property right is established, are (1) What constitutes adequate grounds for interference with that right? and (2) what is adequate process to sustain that interference?[34]

## Pay and Benefits

The **Fair Labor Standards Act (FLSA)** has had a major impact on criminal justice agencies. One observer referred to the FLSA as the criminal justice administrator's "worst nightmare come true."[35] Initiated in 1938 to establish minimum wages and to require overtime compensation in the private sector, amendments were added in 1974 extending its coverage to state and local governmental employees and including special work period provisions for police and fire employees. In 1976, however, the U.S. Supreme Court ruled that the extension of the act into traditional local and state governmental functions was unconstitutional.[36] In 1985, the Court reversed itself, bringing local police employees under the coverage of the FLSA. In this major (and costly) decision, *Garcia v. San Antonio Transit Authority*,[37] the Court held, 5 to 4, that Congress could impose the requirements of the FLSA on state and local governments.

Criminal justice operations take place 24 hours per day, 7 days per week and often require overtime and participation in off-duty activities such as court appearances and training sessions. The FLSA comes into play when overtime salaries must be paid. It provides that an employer must pay employees time and a half for all hours worked over 40 per week. Overtime must also be paid to personnel for all work in excess of 43 hours in a 7-day cycle or 171 hours in a 28-day period. Public safety employees may accrue a maximum of 240 hours of compensatory or "comp" time, which, if not utilized as leave, must be paid off upon separation from employment at the employee's final rate of pay or at the average pay over the last three years, whichever is greater.[38] Further, employers usually cannot require employees to take compensatory time in lieu of cash.

A recent decision by the U.S. Supreme Court favored administrators in this regard, however. A county in Texas became concerned that after employees reached their cap on comp time accrued, it would be unable to afford to pay them for overtime worked. So the county sought to reduce accrued comp time and implemented a policy under which the employees' supervisor set a maximum number of compensatory hours that could be accumulated. When an employee's accrued amount of comp time approached that maximum, the employee would be asked to take steps to reduce accumulated comp time. If the employee did not do so voluntarily, the supervisor would order the employee to use his comp time at specified times. This policy was attacked in court by 127 deputy sheriffs. The Court held that nothing in the FLSA prohibited employers from instituting such a policy.[39]

An officer who works the night shift must now receive pay for attending training or testifying in court during the day. Further, officers who are ordered to remain at home in anticipation of emergency actions must be compensated. Notably, however, the FLSA's overtime provisions do not apply to persons employed in a bona fide executive, administrative, or professional capacity. In criminal justice, the act has generally been held to apply to detectives and sergeants but not to those of the rank of lieutenant and above.

A companion issue with respect to criminal justice pay and benefits is that of equal pay for equal work. Disparate treatment in pay and benefits can be litigated under Title VII or statutes such as the Equal Pay Act or the equal protection clause. An Ohio case involved matron/dispatchers who performed essentially the same job as jailers but were paid less. This was found to be in violation of the Equal Pay Act and, since discriminatory intent was found, Title VII.[40]

Other criminal justice employee benefits are addressed in Title VII, the ADEA, and the Pregnancy Discrimination Act (PDA). For example, it is illegal to provide less insurance coverage for a female employee who is more likely to use maternity leave or for an older employee who is more liable to use more coverage. Also, an older person or a woman could not be forced to pay higher pension contributions because they might be paying in for a shorter period of time or would be expected to live longer. Regarding pregnancy, the PDA does not require an employer to discriminate in favor of a pregnancy-related condition. It demands only that the employer not treat pregnancy differently from any other temporary medical condition. For example, if an agency has a six-month leave policy for officers who are injured or ill from off-duty circumstances (on-duty circumstances would probably be covered by workers' compensation), that agency would have to provide six months' leave (if needed) for a pregnancy-related condition.[41]

## *Criminal Justice and a Safe Workplace*

It is presently unclear what duties are owed by public employers to their employees in providing a safe workplace. Federal, state, and local governments are exempted from the coverage of the Occupational Safety and Health Act (OSHA), in 29 U.S.C. 652. Nonetheless, criminal justice work is often dangerous, involving the use of force and often occurring in locations outside governmental control. Therefore, workplace safety issues in criminal justice are more likely to revolve around adequacy of training and supervision than physical plants.[42]

The Supreme Court has noted the unique nature and danger of public service employment. In one case, the Court specifically stated that an employee could not bring a Section 1983 civil rights action alleging a workplace so unsafe that it violated the Fourteenth Amendment's due process clause. In this matter, a sewer worker was asphyxiated while clearing a sewer line. His widow alleged that the city knew the sewer was dangerous and that the city had failed to train or supervise the decedent properly.[43]

Other federal courts, especially the federal circuits, however, have ruled inconsistently on the safe workplace issue. One federal circuit held that a constitutional violation could be brought if it was proven that the city actively engaged in conduct that was "deliberately indifferent" to the employee's constitutional rights.[44]

But the Fifth Circuit held differently in a Louisiana case, based on a failure to comply with a court order to have three officers on duty at all times in a prison disciplinary unit.[45] Here, a prison correctional officer in Baton Rouge was the only guard on a dangerous cellblock. While attempting to transfer a handcuffed inmate, the guard got into a scuffle with the inmate and was injured, although not severely. However, he claimed that he received insufficient medical attention and that as a result, he became permanently disabled and that the institution "consciously" and with wanton disregard for his personal safety conspired to have him work alone on the cellblock. He invoked 42 U.S.C. 1983 in his charges, claiming that the institution acted in an indifferent, malicious, and reckless manner toward him, and that he suffered "class-based discrimination." The court held that the guard had no cause of action (no federal or constitutional grounds for litigation).

Liability for an employee's injury, disability, or death is a critical concern for criminal justice agencies. In particular, police and correctional officers often work in circumstances involving violent actions. Although state workers' compensation coverage, disability pensions, life insurance, and survivor pensions are designed to cover such tragedies, such coverage is typically limited and only intended to be remedial. On the other hand, civil tort actions in such cases can have a devastating impact on governmental budgets. Clearly, this is a difficult and costly problem to resolve. It is also an area with moral dilemmas as well. For example, what should be done with a prison intelligence unit that has knowledge of an impending disturbance but fails to alert its officers (who are subsequently injured)? And might a police department with knowledge that its new police vehicles have defective brakes fail to take immediate action for fear that its officers will refuse to drive the vehicles, thus reducing available personnel?[46]

## Constitutional Rights of Criminal Justice Employees

### *Freedom of Speech and Association*

Most, if not all, criminal justice employees, especially police officers, judges, and probation or parole officers, observe and learn much about other citizens; they see people in their most embarrassing and vulnerable moments. Therefore, because of their position in society, criminal justice practitioners pass on information by way of formal or informal conversation that assumes a tremendous air of importance and gravity. In Chapter 2, we quoted a former midwestern police commissioner who described the situation well, commenting that "I'm sorry to say that many police, without realizing they carry such authority, do pass on rumors. The average police officer does not stop to weigh what he or she says." That statement could probably be made about many other types of criminal justice employees as well. Given the delicate nature of their work, they must all guard against being indiscreet with the information they possess.

The 24-hour shift configuration found in criminal justice work serves to exacerbate the grapevine. While on routine patrol, police officers witness many illegal or immoral acts—acts for which citizens would gladly pay the officer for his or her silence. Thus, police officers must closely guard what they verbally pass along to others. Another aspect of the grapevine is the fact that criminal justice personnel, like those in other occupations, can and do complain. Normally, passive grumbling is not unhealthy, but it can take a serious turn when a grapevine is running rampant, incomplete or inaccurate information is being disseminated, or when personnel go public to air their views.

Many criminal justice executives have attempted to harness what their employees say to the public; executives develop and rely on policies and procedures designed to govern employee speech. As will be seen later, on occasion those restrictions will be challenged; a number of court decisions have attempted to define the limits of criminal justice employees' exercise of free speech.

Although the right of freedom of speech is one of the most fundamental of all rights of Americans, the Supreme Court has indicated that "the State has interests as an employer in regulating the speech of its employees that differ significantly from those it possesses in connection with regulation of the speech of the citizenry in general."[47] Thus, the state may impose restrictions on its employees that it would not be able to impose on the citizenry at large. However, these restrictions must be reasonable.[48]

There are two basic situations in which a police regulation may be found to be an unreasonable infringement on the free speech interests of officers.[49] The first occurs when the action is overly broad. A Chicago Police Department rule prohibiting "any activity, conversation, deliberation, or discussion which is derogatory to the Department" is a good example, as such a rule obviously prohibits all criticism of the agency by its officers, even in private conversation.[50] A similar situation arose in New Orleans, where the police department had a regulation that prohibited statements by a police officer that "unjustly criticize or ridicule, or express hatred or contempt toward, or . . . which may be detrimental to, or cast suspicion on the reputation of, or otherwise defame, any person."[51] The regulation was revised and later ruled constitutional.[52]

The second situation in which free speech limitations may be found to be unreasonable is in the way in which the governmental action is applied. Specifically, a police department may be unable to demonstrate that the statements by an officer being disciplined actually adversely affected the operation of the department. A Baltimore regulation prohibiting public criticism of police department action was held to have been unconstitutionally applied to a police officer who was president of the police union and had stated in a television interview that the police commissioner was not leading the department effectively,[53] and that "the bottom is going to fall out of this city."[54]

A related area is that of political activity. As with free speech, governmental agencies may restrict the political behavior of their employees. The rationale is that without such restrictions, employees could be pressured by their superiors to support certain political candidates or engage in political activities, under threat of loss of employment or other adverse action. At the federal level, various types of political activity by federal employees are controlled by the Hatch Act; its constitutionality has been upheld by the U.S. Supreme Court.[55] Many states have similar statutes, often referred to as "little Hatch Acts."

Although it may appear that Supreme Court decisions have laid to rest all controversy in this area, that has not been the case. Two recent cases show lower courts opting to limit the authority of the state to restrict political activities of their employees. In Pawtucket, Rhode Island, two firefighters ran for public office (mayor and city council member), despite a city charter provision prohibiting all political activity by employees (except voting and privately expressing their opinions). The Rhode Island Supreme Court issued an injunction against enforcing the charter provision, on the ground that the provision applied only to *partisan* political activities.[56] In a similar Boston case, however, the court upheld the police department rule on the basis that whether or not the partisan-nonpartisan distinction was crucial was a matter for legislative or administrative determination.[57]

In a Michigan case, a court declared unconstitutional, for being overly broad, two city charter provisions that prohibited contributions to or solicitations for any political purpose by city employees.[58] Clearly, although the Supreme Court seems to be supportive of governmental attempts to limit the political activities of its employees, lower courts seem just as intent to limit the Supreme Court decisions to the facts of those cases.

Could a police officer be disciplined, even discharged, because of his or her political affiliations? The Supreme Court ruled on that question in a case arising out of the Sheriff's Department in Cook County, Illinois.[59] The newly elected sheriff, a Democrat, fired the chief deputy of the process division and a bailiff of the juvenile court because they were Republicans. The Court ruled that it was a violation of the employees' First Amendment rights to discharge them from non-policymaking positions solely on the basis of their political party affiliation.[60]

Nonpolitical associations are also protected by the First Amendment; however, it is common for police departments to prohibit officers from associating with known felons or others of questionable reputation, on the ground that "such associations may expose an officer to irresistible temptations to yield in his obligation to impartially enforce the law, and . . . may give the appearance that the police are not themselves honest and impartial enforcers of the law."[61]

However, rules against association, as with other First Amendment rights, must not be overly broad. A Detroit Police Department regulation prohibiting associating with known criminals or persons charged with crimes, except in connection with regular duties, was declared unconstitutional. The court held that it prohibited some associations that had no bearing on the officers' integrity or public confidence in the officer (e.g., an association with a fellow church member who had been arrested on one occasion years ago, or the befriending of a recently convicted person who wanted to become a productive citizen).[62]

Occasionally, a criminal justice employee will be disciplined for improper association even though it was not demonstrated that the association had a detrimental effect on the employee or the agency. For example, a Maryland court held that a fully qualified police officer who was a practicing nudist could not be fired simply on that basis.[63] On the other hand, a court upheld the discharge of an officer who had had sexual intercourse at a party with a woman he knew to be a nude model at a local "adult theater of known disrepute."[64]

An individual has a fundamental interest in being free to enter into certain intimate or private relationships; nevertheless, freedom of association is not an absolute right. For example, a federal district court held that the dismissal of a married police officer for living with another man's wife was a violation of the officer's privacy and associational rights.[65] Other courts, however, have found that off-duty sexual activity can affect job performance. When a married city police officer allegedly had consensual, private, nonduty, heterosexual relations with single adult women other than his wife in violation of state law criminalizing adultery, the adultery was not a fundamental right. Thus, the officer's extramarital affairs were not protected and the intimate relationship affected the public's perception of the agency.[66]

In another case, a police officer became involved with a city dispatcher who was the wife of a sergeant in the same department. The adulterous officer became eligible for promotion and scored high on the exam. The chief, confirming via an investigation that the officer had in fact been involved in an adulterous relationship with the dispatcher, refused on that basis to promote the officer, as he "would not command respect and trust" from rank-and-file officers and would adversely affect the efficiency and morale of the department. The Texas Supreme Court held that the officer's private, adulterous sexual conduct was not protected by state or federal law; the U.S. Supreme Court denied the appeal.[67]

Finally, the U.S. Court of Appeals for the Sixth Circuit held that a police department could conduct an investigation into the marital sexual relations of a police officer accused of sexual harassment.[68] In this case, there were allegations that the married officer had sexually harassed co-workers and had dated a gang member's mother. The department investigated the accusations, and the officer and his wife brought a Section 1983 action, alleging that the investigation violated their constitutional rights to privacy and freedom of association. The court held that the agency's investigation was reasonable, and, further, that the police department would have been derelict in not investigating the matter.

In summary, police administrators have the constitutional authority to regulate employees' off-duty associational activities, including off-duty sexual conduct that involves a supervisory/subordinate relationship and associations that impact adversely employees' ability to do their jobs or impair the effectiveness and efficiency of the organization.[69]

The First Amendment's reach also includes means of expression other than verbal utterances. The Supreme Court upheld the constitutionality of a regulation of the Suffolk County, New York, Police Department that established several grooming standards (regarding hair, sideburn, and moustache length) for its male officers. In this case, *Kelley v. Johnson*,[70] the Court believed that to make officers easily recognizable to the public and to maintain the esprit de corps within the department, the agency justified the regulations and did not violate any right guaranteed by the First Amendment.

## Searches and Seizures

The Fourth Amendment to the U.S. Constitution protects "the right of the people to be secure in their persons, houses, papers, and effects, against unreasonable searches and seizures." In an important case in 1967, the Supreme Court held that the amendment also protected individuals' reasonable expectations of privacy, not just property interests.[71]

The Fourth Amendment usually applies to police officers when they are at home or off duty in the same manner as it applies to all citizens. Because of the nature of their work, however, police officers can be compelled to cooperate with investigations of their behavior when ordinary citizens would not. Examples would include searches of equipment and lockers provided by the department to the officers. There, the officers have no expectation of privacy that affords or merits protection.[72] Lower courts have established limitations on searches of employees themselves. The rights of prison authorities to search their employees arose in a 1985 Iowa case, in which employees were forced to sign a consent form for searches as a condition of hire; the court disagreed with such a broad policy, ruling that the consent form did not constitute a blanket waiver of all Fourth Amendment rights.[73]

Police officers may also be forced to appear in a lineup, a clear "seizure" of his or her person. Appearance in a lineup normally requires probable cause, but a federal appeals court upheld a police commissioner's ordering of 62 officers to appear in a lineup during an investigation of police brutality, holding that "the governmental interest in the particular intrusion [should be weighed] against the offense to personal dignity and integrity." Again, the court cited the nature of the work, noting that police officers do "not have the full privacy and liberty from police officials that [they] would otherwise enjoy."[74]

## Self-Incrimination

The Supreme Court has also addressed questions concerning the Fifth Amendment as it applies to police officers who are under investigation. In *Garrity v. New Jersey*,[75] a police officer was ordered by the attorney general to answer questions or be discharged. The officer testified that information obtained as a result of his answers was later used to convict him of criminal charges. The Supreme Court held that the information obtained from the officer could not be used against him at his criminal trial, because the Fifth Amendment forbids the use of coerced confessions.

In *Gardner v. Broderick*,[76] a police officer had refused to answer questions asked by a grand jury investigating police misconduct, because he believed his answers might tend to incriminate him. The officer was terminated from his position as result. The Supreme Court ruled that the officer could not be fired for his refusal to waive his constitutional right to remain silent. The Court added, however, that the grand jury could have forced the officer to answer or be terminated for his refusal provided that the officer was informed that his answers would not be used against him later in a criminal case.

As a result of these decisions, it is proper to fire a police officer who refuses to answer questions that are related directly to the performance of his or her duties provided that the officer has been informed that any answers may not be used later in a criminal proceeding. Although there is some diversity of opinion among lower courts on the question of whether or not an officer may be compelled to submit to a polygraph examination, the majority of courts that have considered the question have held that an officer can be required to take the examination.[77]

## Religious Practices

Criminal justice work often requires that personnel are available and on duty 24 hours per day, seven days a week. Although it is not always convenient or pleasant, such shift configurations require that many criminal justice employees work weekends, nights, and holidays. It is generally assumed that one who takes such a position agrees to work such hours and to abide by other such conditions (e.g., carrying a weapon, as in a policing position); it is usually the personnel with the least seniority on the job who must work the most undesirable shifts.

There are occasions when one's religious beliefs are in direct conflict with the requirements of the job. Conflicts can occur between work assignments and attendance at religious services or periods of religious observance. In these situations, the employee may be forced to choose between his or her job and religion. The author is acquainted with a midwestern state trooper whose religion posed another related cause of job-religion conflict: His religion (with which he became affiliated after being hired as a trooper) banned the carrying or use of firearms. The officer chose to give up his weapon, and thus his job. A number of people have chosen to litigate the work-religion conflict rather than accept agency demands.

Title VII of the Civil Rights Act of 1964 prohibits religious discrimination in employment. The act defines religion as including "all aspects of religious . . . practice, as well as belief, unless an employer . . . is unable to reasonably accommodate to an employee's . . . religious . . . practice without undue hardship on the conduct of the employer's business."[78] Thus, Title VII requires reasonable accommodation of religious beliefs, but not to the extent that the employee has complete freedom of religious expression.[79] For example, an Albuquerque firefighter was a Seventh Day Adventist and refused to work Friday or Saturday nights because such shifts interrupted his honoring the Sabbath. He refused to trade shifts or take leave with (as vacation) or without pay, even though existing policy permitted his doing so. Instead, he said that the *department* should make such arrangements for coverage or simply excuse him from his shifts. The department refused to do either, discharging him. The court ruled that the department's accommodations were reasonable and that no further accommodation could be made without causing an undue hardship to the department. His firing was upheld. The court emphasized, however, that future decisions would depend on the facts of the individual case.[80]

A circuit court held that the termination of a Mormon police officer for practicing plural marriage (polygamy) in violation of state law was not a violation of his right to freely exercise his religious beliefs.[81]

## Sexual Misconduct

To be blunt, criminal justice employees have ample opportunity to become engaged in sexual affairs, incidents, trysts, dalliances, or other behavior that is clearly sexual in nature. History (and news accounts) have shown that wearing a uniform, occupying a high or extremely sensitive position, or being sworn to maintain an unblemished and unsullied lifestyle does not mean that all people will do so for all time. Some people are not bashful about their intentions: Several officers have told the author they aspired to police work because they assumed that wearing a uniform made them sexually irresistible. On the civilian side, there are definitely a number of police "groupies," who do in fact chase police officers and others in uniform.

Instances of sexual impropriety in criminal justice work can range from casual flirting while on the job to becoming romantically involved with a foreign agent whose principal aim is to learn delicate matters of national security. And there have been all manner of incidents between those extremes, including the discipline of female police officers who posed nude in magazines. Some major police departments have even been compelled by their mayors to recruit officers for their sexual preference (i.e., homosexuality).

This is a delicate area, one in which discipline can be and has been meted out as police managers attempt to maintain high standards of officer conduct. It has also resulted in litigation, as some officers believe that their right to privacy has been intruded upon.

Officers may be disciplined for impropriety involving adultery and homosexuality. Most court decisions of the 1960s and 1970s agreed that adultery, even when involving an off-duty police officer and occurring in private, could result in disciplinary action,[82] because such behavior brought debilitating criticism on the agency and undermined public confidence in the police. The views of the courts in this area, however, seem to be moderating with the times. A case involving an Internal Revenue Service agent suggested that to uphold disciplinary action for adultery, the government would have to prove that the employing agency was actually discredited.[83] The U.S. Supreme Court more recently appeared to be divided on the issue of extramarital sexual activity in public employment. In 1984, the Sixth Circuit held that a Michigan police officer could not be fired simply because he was living with a woman to whom he was not married (a felony under Michigan law).[84]

The issue of homosexual activity as a ground for termination of public employees arose in an Oklahoma case, in which a state law permitted the discharge of schoolteachers for engaging in "public homosexual activity."[85] A lower court held the law to be unconstitutionally restrictive, and the Supreme Court agreed.[86] Another federal court held that the firing of a bisexual guidance counselor did not deprive the counselor of her First or Fourteenth Amendment rights. The counselor's discussion of her sexual preferences with teachers was not protected by the First Amendment.[87]

## Residency Requirements

In the 1970s and 1980s, interest in residency requirements for governmental employees heightened, especially in communities experiencing economic difficulties.[88] Many governmental agencies now specify that all or certain members in their employ must live within the geographical limits of their employing jurisdiction. In other words, employees must reside within the county or city of employment. Such residency requirements have often been justified by employing agencies, particularly in criminal justice, on the grounds that employees should become familiar with and be visible in the jurisdiction of employment and that they should reside where they are paid by the taxpayers to work. Perhaps the strongest rationale given by employing agencies is that criminal justice employees must live within a certain proximity of their work in order to respond quickly in the event of an emergency.

Prior to 1976, numerous challenges to residency requirements were raised, even after the Michigan Supreme Court ruled that Detroit's residency requirement for police officers was not irrational.[89] Then, in 1976, when the U.S. Supreme Court held that Philadelphia's law requiring firefighters to live in the city did not violate the Constitution, the challenges subsided. The cases now seem to revolve around the question of what constitutes residency. Generally, the police officer must demonstrate that he or she spends a substantial amount of time at the in-city residence.[90] Strong arguments have been made, however, that in areas where housing is unavailable or is exceptionally expensive, a residency requirement is unreasonable.[91]

## Moonlighting

The courts have traditionally supported criminal justice agencies placing limitations on the amount and kind of outside work their employees can perform.[92] For example, police department restrictions on moonlighting range from a complete ban on outside employment to permission to engage in certain forms of work, such as investment counseling, private security, teaching police science courses, and so on. The rationale for agency limitations is that "outside employment seriously interferes with keeping the [police and fire] departments fit and ready for action at all times."[93]

In a Louisiana case, however, firefighters successfully provided evidence that moonlighting had been a common practice for 16 years before the city banned it. No firefighters had ever needed sick leave as a result of injuries acquired while moonlighting, there had never been a problem locating off-duty firefighters to respond to an emergency, and moonlighting had never caused a level of fatigue that was serious enough to impair a firefighter's work. With this evidence, the court invalidated the city ordinance that had sought to prohibit moonlighting.[94]

## Misuse of Firearms

Because of the need to defend themselves or others and be prepared for any exigency, police officers are empowered to use lethal force when justified. Although restricted by the Supreme Court's 1985 decision in *Tennessee v. Garner*[95] (deeming the killing of unarmed, nondangerous suspects as unconstitutional), the possession of, and familiarity with, firearms remains a central aspect of the contemporary officer's role and function. Some officers take this responsibility to the extreme, however, becoming overly reliant on and consumed with their firepower.

Thus, police agencies typically attempt to restrain the use of firearms through written policies and frequent training in "Shoot/Don't Shoot" scenarios. Still, a broad range of potential and actual problems remains with respect to the use and possible misuse of firearms, as the following shows.

In the face of extremely serious potential and real problems and the omnipresent specter of liability suits, police agencies generally have policies regulating the use of handguns and other firearms by their officers, both on and off duty. The courts have held that such regulations need only be reasonable and that the burden rests with the disciplined police officer to show that the regulation was arbitrary and unreasonable.[96] The courts also grant considerable latitude to administrators in determining when their firearms regulations have been violated.[97] Police firearms regulations tend to address three basic issues: (1) requirements for the safeguarding of the weapon, (2) guidelines for carrying the weapon while off duty, and (3) limitations on when the weapon may be fired.[98]

Courts and juries are becoming increasingly harsher in dealing with police officers who misuse their firearms. The current tendency is to "look behind" police shootings in order to determine if the officer acted negligently or the employing agency inadequately trained and supervised the officer/employee. In one case, a federal appeals court approved a $500,000 judgment against the District of Columbia when a police officer who was not in adequate physical shape shot a man in the course of an arrest. The court noted that the District officer had received no fitness training in four years and was physically incapable of subduing the victim. The court noted that had the officer been physically fit and adequately trained in disarmament techniques, a gun would not have been necessary. In his condition, however, the officer posed a "foreseeable risk of harm to others."[99]

Courts have awarded damages against police officers and/or their employers for other acts involving misuse of firearms: An officer shot a person while intoxicated and off duty in a bar;[100] an officer accidentally killed an arrestee with a shotgun while handcuffing him;[101] an unstable officer shot his wife five times and then committed suicide with an off-duty weapon the department required him to carry;[102] and an officer accidentally shot and killed an innocent bystander while pursuing another man at night (the officer had had no instruction on shooting at a moving target, night shooting, or shooting in residential areas).[103]

## *Alcohol and Drugs in the Workplace*

Alcoholism and drug abuse problems have "taken on a life of their own" in contemporary criminal justice; employees must be increasingly wary of the tendency to succumb to these problems, while administrative personnel must be able to recognize and attempt to counsel and treat these current problems.

Indeed, in the aftermath of the early 1990s beating death of Malice Green by a group of Detroit police officers, it was reported that the Detroit Police Department had "high alcoholism rates and pervasive psychological problems connected with the stress of policing a city mired in poverty, drugs, and crime."[104] It was further revealed that while the Detroit Police Department had paid $850,000 to two drug-testing facilities, the department did not have the counseling programs many other cities offer their officers. A psychologist asserted that "There are many, many potential time bombs in that department."[105]

It is obvious, given the extant law of most jurisdictions and the nature of their work, that criminal justice employees must be able to perform their work with a clear head, unaffected by alcohol or drugs.[106] Police departments and prisons will often specify in their manual of policy and procedures that no alcoholic beverages be consumed within a specified period prior to reporting for duty.

Such regulations have been upheld uniformly because of the hazards of the work. A Louisiana court went further, upholding a regulation that prohibited police officers from consuming alcoholic beverages on or off duty to the extent that it caused the officer's behavior to become obnoxious, disruptive, or disorderly.[107] Enforcing such regulations will occasionally result in criminal justice employees being ordered to submit to drug or alcohol tests, discussed next.

### *Drug Testing*

The courts have had several occasions to review criminal justice agency policies requiring employees to submit to urinalysis to determine the presence of drugs or alcohol. It was held as early as 1969 that a firefighter could be ordered to submit to a blood test when the agency had reasonable grounds to believe he was intoxicated, and that it was appropriate for the firefighter to be terminated from employment if he refused to submit to the test.[108]

In March 1989, the U.S. Supreme Court issued two major decisions on drug testing of public employees in the workplace. *Skinner v. Railway Labor Executives Association*[109] and *National Treasury Employees Union v. Von Raab*[110] dealt with drug-testing plans for railroad and U.S. Customs workers, respectively. Under the Fourth Amendment, governmental workers are protected from unreasonable search and seizure, including how drug testing can be conducted. The Fifth Amendment protects federal, state, and local workers from illegal governmental conduct.

In 1983, the Federal Railway Administration promulgated regulations that required railroads to conduct urine and blood tests on their workers following major train accidents. The regulations were challenged, one side arguing that since railroads were privately owned, governmental action, including applying the Fourth Amendment, could not legally be imposed. The Supreme Court disagreed in *Skinner,* ruling that railroads must be viewed as an instrument or agent of the government.

Three of the most controversial drug-testing issues have been whether or not testing should be permitted when there is no indication of a drug problem in the workplace, whether or not the testing methods are reliable, and whether or not a positive test proves on-the-job impairment.[111] The *Von Raab* case addressed all three issues. The U.S. Customs Service implemented a drug-screening program that required urinalysis for employees desiring transfer or promotion to positions that were directly involved in drug interdiction, where carrying a firearm was necessary, or where classified material was handled. Only five of 3,600 employees tested positive. The Treasury Employees Union argued that such an insignificant number of positives created a "suspicionless search" argument; in other words, drug testing was unnecessary and unwarranted. The Supreme Court disagreed, ruling that although only a few employees tested positive, drug use is such a serious problem that the program could continue.

Further, the Court found nothing wrong with the testing protocol. An independent contractor was used. The worker, after discarding outer garments, produced a urine specimen while being observed by a member of the same sex; the sample was signed by the employee, labeled, placed in a plastic bag, sealed and delivered to a lab for testing. The Court found no "grave potential for arbitrary and oppressive interference with the privacy and personal security of the individuals" in this method.

Proving the connection between drug testing and on-the-job impairment has been an ongoing issue. Urinalysis cannot prove when a person testing positive actually used the drug. Therefore, tests may punish and stigmatize a person for extracurricular drug usage that may have no effect on the worker's on-the-job performance.[112] In *Von Raab*, the Court indicated that this dilemma is still no impediment to testing. It stated that the Customs Service had a compelling interest in having a "physically fit" employee with "unimpeachable integrity and judgment."

Together, these two cases may set a new standard for determining the reasonableness of drug testing in the criminal justice workplace. They may legalize many testing programs that formerly would have been risky. *Von Raab* presented three compelling governmental interests that could be weighed against the employee's privacy expectations: the integrity of the work force, public safety, and protection of sensitive information. *Skinner* stated that railroad workers also have diminished expectations of privacy because they are in an industry that is widely regulated to ensure safety.[113]

# Rights of Police Officers

Delineated earlier were several areas (e.g., place of residence, religious practice, freedom of speech, search and seizure) in which criminal justice employees, particularly the police, may encounter treatment by their administrators and the federal courts that is quite different from that received by regular citizens. One does give up certain constitutional rights and privileges by virtue of wearing a justice system uniform. This section looks at how, for the police at least, the pendulum has swung more in the direction of the rank and file.

In the past decade, police officers have insisted on greater procedural safeguards to protect themselves against what they perceive as arbitrary infringement on their rights. These demands have been reflected in statutes enacted in many states, generally known as the **Peace Officers' Bill of Rights (POBR).** This legislation mandates due process rights for peace officers who are the subject of internal investigations that could lead to disciplinary action. These statutes identify the type of information that must be provided to the accused officer, the officer's responsibility to cooperate during the investigation, the officer's right to representation during the process, and the rules and procedures concerning the collection of certain types of evidence. Following are some common provisions of state POBR legislation:

> *Written notice.* The department must provide the officer with written notice of the nature of the investigation, summary of alleged misconduct, and name of investigating officer.
>
> *Right to representation.* The officer may have an attorney or a representative of his or her choosing present during any phase of questioning or hearing.
>
> *Polygraph examination.* The officer may refuse to take a polygraph examination unless the complainant submits to an examination and is determined to be telling the truth. In this case, the officer may be ordered to take a polygraph examination or be subject to disciplinary action.

Officers expect to be treated fairly, honestly, and respectfully during the course of an internal investigation. In turn, the public expects that the agency will develop sound disciplinary policies and conduct thorough inquiries into allegations of misconduct.

It is imperative that administrators become thoroughly familiar with statutes, contract provisions, and existing rules between employer and employee, so that procedural due process requirements can be met, particularly in disciplinary cases in which an employee's property interest might be affected.

Police officers today are also more likely to file a grievance when they believe their rights have been violated. Grievances may cover a broad range of issues, including salaries, overtime, leave, hours of work, allowances, retirement, opportunity for advancement, performance evaluations, workplace conditions, tenure, disciplinary actions, supervisory methods, and administrative practices. The preferred method for settling officers' grievances is through informal discussion: The employee explains his or her grievance to the immediate supervisor. Most complaints can be handled this way. Those complaints that cannot be dealt with informally are usually handled through a more formal grievance process, which may involve several different levels of action.

## Sexual Harassment

Sexual harassment became a major workplace problem in the early 1980s and continued to be so through the 1990s and into the new millennium. To borrow a term from early police authors,[114] many "Neanderthals" in the business of police administration simply do not take the necessary steps to understand the breadth and weight of the matter. If these administrators do not learn the law of sexual harassment *in-house* (through training and education), they may eventually learn the law in the *courthouse*. Indeed, in the 1990s, a number of judgments in excess of a million dollars were made against police agencies for sexual harassment.[115]

Sexual harassment involves unwelcome sexual advances; requests for sexual favors; and other similar verbal, visual, or physical conduct that results in sexual submission being expressed or implied as a condition of employment. It can interfere with an individual's work performance or create an intimidating, hostile, or offensive working environment. The unique aspect of sexual harassment is that, generally speaking, the *victim* defines it in terms of what is offensive. Touching is not required.

Since 1986, workers have had the right to sue for sexual harassment. Until 1998, however, the courts remained silent about the precise meaning of the term; during that year, the U.S. Supreme Court clarified the issue with four historic decisions. The Court made it easier for a person who has been harassed to win a lawsuit but gave employers a greater measure of protection from lawsuits if they have a strong program in place to prevent and discipline harassment.[116] Following is an overview of the impact of each of these four decisions.

The old rule was that to prove harassment, a worker had to show that because she resisted sexual advances she was punished in terms of salary, assignments, or promotions. The new rule is that sexual advances count as harassment even if an employee is otherwise treated well. In this case,[117] a supervisor kept making passes at a subordinate but never punished her; in fact, she was promoted once. The Supreme Court ruled that harassment is defined by the behavior of the manager, not by what subsequently happened to the worker.

Another old rule was that if a manager was not informed that an employee was harassing other workers, the supervisor was not normally responsible for the harasser's actions. The new rule is that the administrator can be held responsible for a harasser's actions unless the company has a strong system of dealing with such problems. This decision[118] involved a Florida lifeguard who, for five years, endured men requesting sexual favors, groping her person, attempting to break into her shower area, and directing vulgar epithets toward her. The Supreme Court held that it is not enough to have a policy against sexual harassment; it must be disseminated and enforced effectively.

Third, the Court made clear that a worker who is being harassed has a duty to report it, beyond merely telling a friend or co-worker. The victim has to inform the person responsible under the sexual harassment policy.[119]

Finally, the Court unanimously held that sexual harassment at work can be illegal and violates federal antidiscrimination law even when the offender and victim are the same sex. In this case,[120] the harassment claim by a male victim stemmed from four months of work on a Gulf of Mexico oil rig, where he was sexually assaulted, battered, touched, and threatened with rape by his direct male supervisor and a second male supervisor. He quit because he feared the harassment would escalate to rape. The ruling allows victims of homosexual harassment to sue in federal court.[121]

# The Family and Medical Leave Act

The **Family and Medical Leave Act (FMLA),** enacted by Public Law 103-3, became effective in August 1993 and is administered and enforced by the U.S. Department of Labor's Wage and Hour Division. FMLA applies to all public agencies, including state, local, and federal employers; local schools; and private sector employers with 50 or more employees in 20 or more workweeks and who are engaged in commerce. FMLA entitles eligible employees to take up to 12 weeks of unpaid, job-protected leave in a 12-month period for specified family and medical reasons.

To be eligible for FMLA benefits, an employee must

- Work for a covered employer
- Have worked for a covered employer for at least 12 months (and have worked at least 1,250 hours during that time)

A covered employer must grant an eligible employee unpaid leave for one or more of the following reasons:

- For the birth and care of a newborn child of the employee
- For placement with the employee of a child for adoption or child care
- To care for an immediate family member with a serious health condition
- To take medical leave when the employee is unable to work because of a serious health condition

A serious health condition means an illness, injury, impairment, or physical or mental condition that involves either any period of incapacitation or treatment, or continuing treatment by a health care provider; this can include any period of inability to work, attend school, or perform regular daily activities.

# The Americans with Disabilities Act (ADA)

Much has been written and many monographs and primers are available concerning the powerful **Americans with Disabilities Act (ADA),** which was signed into law in 1990. Therefore, we only briefly cover the law here; however, those in an administrative capacity are strongly urged to become familiar with the literature in order to avoid conflicts with ADA mandates. The law is applicable to background checks; psychological and medical exams; and agility, drug, and polygraph tests.

While certain agencies in the federal government, such as the Federal Bureau of Investigation, are exempt from the ADA, state and local governments and their agencies are covered by the law. It is critical for administrators to develop written policies and procedures consistent with the ADA and have them in place before a problem arises.[122]

Under the law, criminal justice agencies may not discriminate against qualified individuals with disabilities. A person has a disability under the law if he or she has a mental or physical impairment that substantially limits a major life activity, such as walking, talking, breathing, sitting, standing, or learning.[123] Title I of the ADA makes it illegal to discriminate against persons with disabilities. This mandate applies to the agency's recruitment, hiring, and promotion practices. ADA is not an affirmative action law, so persons with disabilities are not entitled to preference in hiring. However, the law will cause police agencies throughout the United States to adjust and perhaps even completely overhaul their recruitment and selection procedures.

Employers are to provide reasonable accommodation to disabled persons. A reasonable accommodation (80 percent of which have been found to cost less than $100 to effect[124]) can include modifying existing facilities to make them accessible, job restructuring, part-time or modified work schedules, acquiring or modifying equipment, and changing policies. Hiring decisions must be made on whether or not an applicant meets the established prerequisites of the position (e.g., experience or education) and is able to perform the essential functions of the job. Under the law, blanket exclusions of individuals with a particular disability (such as diabetes) are, in most cases, impermissible.

Corrections agencies—jails, prisons, and detention facilities—are also covered by the ADA; programs offered to inmates must be accessible. For example, if a hearing-impaired inmate wished to attend Alcoholics Anonymous meetings, the corrections facility would need to make reasonable accommodation to allow him or her to do so, through such means as providing a sign language interpreter or writing notes as needed.[125]

# CASE STUDIES

The following case studies will help the reader consider some of this chapter's materials concerning sexual harassment and ADA issues.

## A Neanderthal Lives!

You are an administrator in a small, minimum-security facility, where the day shift is composed of four male, veteran officers and one new female officer. The female is a minority, has a college degree from a reputable out-of-state university, and is married to a member of the armed forces. There have been recent reports from your supervisors of obscene and racially offensive remarks and drawings turning up in the female officer's mailbox, but you have not seen any such materials, nor has the female complained to you about such occurrences. Today, however, your day shift sergeant storms into your office with a piece of paper he says was just removed from the conference room bulletin board. It shows a "stick figure" woman and contains several racial slurs and comments to the effect that "women don't belong in this man's business, and you should go back where you came from." The female has seen this material, and the sergeant says she is now in the conference room, crying and very distraught.

### Questions for Discussion

1. What would you do about this situation? Do you ignore it? Call the female officer to your office?
2. What if you bring her in and she indicates that you should just leave the matter alone; do you go ahead and pursue the matter?
3. If you determine which officer is responsible for these materials, what disciplinary action (if any) would you deem warranted? On what grounds?

## At the Heart of the Matter . . .

A police sergeant suffers a heart attack and undergoes a triple heart bypass operation. It is now four years later, and he takes and passes the written and oral examinations for lieutenant but is denied promotion solely because of his heart attack. The agency claims that because lieutenants can be assigned as shift commanders, they must be able to apprehend suspects and to engage in high-speed pursuits. In truth, middle managers in the agency are rarely involved in high levels of physical stress. The officer has exercised regularly and has had a strong performance record prior to and after his heart attack. Medical opinion is that his health is normal for someone his age. The agency has adopted community policing, providing the opportunity for a manager to be assigned to one of several lieutenant positions that do not entail physical exertion. The sergeant sues the agency for violating provisions of the ADA.

### Questions for Discussion

1. Is the sergeant "handicapped" within the meaning of the law?
2. Is the sergeant otherwise qualified for the position of lieutenant?
3. Was the sergeant excluded from the position solely on the basis of a handicap? Explain your answer.
4. Should the sergeant prevail in the suit? If so, on what grounds?[126]

## Summary

After providing an overview of related legislation, this chapter examined several areas of criminal justice employee rights, including the issues of drug testing, privacy, hiring and firing, sexual harassment, disabilities, and peace officers' rights. Criminal justice employers' responsibilities were also discussed.

Being an administrator in the field of criminal justice has never been easy. Unfortunately, the issues facing today's justice administrators have probably never been more difficult or complex.

This chapter clearly demonstrated that these are challenging and, occasionally, litigious times for the justice system; one act of negligence can mean financial disaster for an individual or a supervisor.

## Questions for Review

1. What are criminal justice employees' rights in the workplace according to federal statutes?
2. What is the general employee-employer relationship in criminal justice regarding recruitment and hiring and affirmative action?
3. It has been stated that criminal justice employees have a "property interest" in their jobs as well as a right to a safe workplace. What does this mean?
4. What constitutional rights are implicated for criminal justice employees on the job? (In your response, address whether rights are held regarding freedom of speech, searches and seizures, self-incrimination, and religion.)
5. In what regard is a greater standard of conduct expected of criminal justice employees? (In your response, include discussions of sexual behavior, residency, moonlighting, use of firearms, and alcohol/drug abuse.)

# Notes

1. Robert H. Chaires and Susan A. Lentz, "Criminal Justice Employee Rights: An Overview," *American Journal of Criminal Justice* 13 (April 1995):259.

2. Ibid.

3. See *United Autoworkers v. Johnson Controls,* 111 S.Ct. 1196 (1991).

4. See Kenneth J. Peak, *Policing America: Methods, Issues, Challenges,* 4th ed. (Upper Saddle River, N.J.: Prentice Hall, 2003), Chapter 3.

5. Chaires and Lentz, "Criminal Justice Employee Rights," p. 260.

6. *U.S. v. Gregory,* 818 F.2d 114 (4th Cir. 1987).

7. *Harris v. Pan American,* 649 F.2d 670 (9th Cir. 1988).

8. Chaires and Lentz, "Criminal Justice Employee Rights," p. 267.

9. See Ken Peak, Douglas W. Farenholtz, and George Coxey, "Physical Abilities Testing for Police Officers: A Flexible, Job-Related Approach," *The Police Chief* 59 (January 1992): 52-56.

10. *Shaw v. Nebraska Department of Corrections,* 666 F.Supp. 1330 (N.D. Neb. 1987).

11. *Garrett v. Oskaloosa County,* 734 F.2d 621 (11th Cir. 1984).

12. Chaires and Lentz, "Criminal Justice Employee Rights," p. 268.

13. *EEOC v. State Department of Highway Safety,* 660 F.Supp. 1104 (N.D. Fla. 1986).

14. *Johnson v. Mayor and City Council of Baltimore* (105 S.Ct. 2717 1985).

15. 460 U.S. 226, 103 S.Ct. 1054, 75 L.Ed.2d 18 (1983).

16. Chaires and Lentz, "Criminal Justice Employee Rights," p. 269.

17. Paul J. Spiegelman, "Court-Ordered Hiring Quotas After *Stotts:* A Narrative on the Role of the Moralities of the Web and the Ladder in Employment Discrimination Doctrine," 20 *Harvard Civil Rights Review* 339 (1985):72.

18. Chaires and Lentz, "Criminal Justice Employee Rights," p. 269.

19. *Regents of the University of California v. Bakke,* 98 S.Ct. 2733, 438 U.S. 265, 57 L.Ed.2d (1978).

20. See *Wygant v. Jackson Board of Education,* 106 S.Ct. 1842 (1986).

21. Chaires and Lentz, "Criminal Justice Employee Rights," p. 269.

22. *Ledoux v. District of Columbia,* 820 F.2d 1293 (D.C. Cir. 1987), at 1294.

23. Ibid.

24. Chaires and Lentz, "Criminal Justice Employee Rights," p. 270.

25. See *Parratt v. Taylor,* 451 U.S. 527, 536-37, 101 S.Ct. 1908, 1913-14, 68 L.Ed.2d 420 (1981).

26. *Board of Regents v. Roth,* 408 U.S. at 577, 92 S.Ct. at 2709.

27. *Cleveland Board of Education v. Loudermill,* 470 U.S. 532, 541 (1985).

28. *McGraw v. City of Huntington Beach,* 882 F.2d 384 (9th Cir. 1989).

29. *Lohorn v. Michael,* 913 F.2d 327 (7th Cir. 1990).

30. *Palmer v. City of Monticello* 731 F.Supp. 1503 (D. Utah 1990).

31. *Young v. Municipality of Bethel Park,* 646 F.Supp. 539 (W.D. Penn. 1986).

32. *McAdoo v. Lane,* 564 F.Supp. 1215 (D.C. Ill. 1983).

33. Ibid., at 1217.

34. Chaires and Lentz, "Criminal Justice Employee Rights," p. 273.

35. Lynn Lund, "The 'Ten Commandments' of Risk Management for Jail Administrators," *Detention Reporter* 4 (June 1991):4.

36. *National League of Cities v. Usery,* 426 U.S. 833 (1976).

37. 105 S.Ct. 1005 (1985).

38. Charles R. Swanson, Leonard Territo, and Robert W. Taylor, *Police Administration: Structures, Processes, and Behavior,* 4th ed. (Upper Saddle River, N.J.: Prentice Hall, 1998), p. 278.

39. *Christiansen v. Harris County,* 529 U.S. 576, 120 S. Ct. 1655, 146 L.Ed.2d 621 (2000).

40. *Jurich v. Mahoning County* 31 Fair Emp. Prac. 1275 (BNA) (N.D. Ohio 1983).

41. Chaires and Lentz, "Criminal Justice Employee Rights," p. 280.

42. Ibid.

43. *Collins v. City of Harker Heights,* 112 S.Ct. 1061 (1992).

44. See *Ruge v. City of Bellevue,* 892 F.2d 738 (1989).

45. *Galloway v. State of Louisiana,* 817 F.2d 1154 (5th Cir. 1987).

46. Chaires and Lentz, "Criminal Justice Employee Rights," pp. 280-283.

47. *Pickering v. Board of Education,* 391 U.S. 563 (1968), p. 568.

48. *Keyishian v. Board of Regents,* 385 U.S. 589 (1967).

49. Swanson, Territo, and Taylor, *Police Administration,* p. 394.

50. *Muller v. Conlisk,* 429 F.2d 901 (7th Cir. 1970).

51. *Flynn v. Giarusso,* 321 F.Supp. 1295 (E.D. La. 1971), at p. 1299.

52. *Magri v. Giarusso,* 379 F.Supp. 353 (E.D. La. 1974).

53. Swanson, Territo, and Taylor, *Police Administration,* p. 395.

54. *Brukiewa v. Police Commissioner of Baltimore,* 263 A.2d 210 (Md. 1970).

55. *United Public Workers v. Mitchell,* 330 U.S. 75 (1947); *U.S. Civil Service Commission v. National Association of Letter Carriers,* 413 U.S. 548 (1973).

56. *Magill v. Lynch,* 400 F.Supp. 84 (R.I. 1975).

57. *Boston Police Patrolmen's Association, Inc. v. City of Boston,* 326 N.E.2d 314 (Mass. 1975).

58. *Phillips v. City of Flint,* 225 N.W.2d 780 (Mich. 1975).

59. *Elrod v. Burns,* 427 U.S. 347 (1976); see also, *Ramey v. Harber,* 431 F.Supp 657 (W.D. Va. 1977) and *Branti v. Finkel,* 445 U.S. 507 (1980).

60. *Connick v. Myers,* 461 U.S. 138 (1983); *Jones v. Dodson,* 727 F.2d 1329 (4th Cir. 1984).

61. Swanson, Territo, and Taylor, *Police Administration,* p. 397.

62. *Sponick v. City of Detroit Police Department,* 211 N.W.2d 674 (Mich. 1973), p. 681; but see *Wilson v. Taylor,* 733 F.2d 1539 (11th Cir. 1984).

63. *Bruns v. Pomerleau,* 319 F.Supp. 58 (D. Md. 1970); see also *McMullen v. Carson,* 754 F.2d 936 (11th Cir. 1985), where it was held that a Ku Klux Klansman could not be fired from his position as a records clerk in the sheriff's department simply because he was a Klansman. The court did uphold the dismissal because his active KKK participation threatened to negatively affect the agency's ability to perform its public duties.

64. *Civil Service Commission of Tucson v. Livingston,* 525 P.2d 949 (Ariz. 1974).

65. *Briggs v. North Muskegon Police Department,* 563 F.Supp. 585 (W.D. Mich. 1983), aff'd 746 F.2d 1475 (6th Cir. 1984).

66. *Oliverson v. West Valley City,* 875 F.Supp. 1465 (D. Utah 1995).

67. *Henery v. City of Sherman,* 116 S.Ct. 1098 (1997).

68. See *Hughes v. City of North Olmsted,* 93 F.3d 238 (6th Cir., 1996).

69. Michael J. Bulzomi, "Constitutional Authority to Regulate Off-Duty Relationships: Recent Court Decisions," *FBI Law Enforcement Bulletin* (April 1999):26-32.

70. *425 U.S. 238* (1976).

71. *Katz v. United States,* 389 U.S. 347 (1967).

72. See *People v. Tidwell,* 266 N.E.2d 787 (Ill. 1971).

73. *McDonell v. Hunter,* 611 F.Supp. 1122 (S.D. Iowa, 1985), affd. as mod., 809 F.2d 1302 (8th Cir., 1987).

74. *Biehunik v. Felicetta,* 441 F.2d 228 (1971), p. 230.

75. 385 U.S. 483 (1967).

76. 392 U.S. 273 (1968).

77. See *Gabrilowitz v. Newman,* 582 F.2d 100 (1st Cir. 1978). Cases upholding the department's authority to order a polygraph examination for police officers include *Eshelman v. Blubaum,* 560 P.2d 1283 (Ariz. 1977); *Dolan v. Kelly,* 348 N.Y.S.2d 478 (1973); *Richardson v. City of Pasadena,* 500 S.W.2d 175 (Tex. 1973); *Seattle Police Officer's Guild v. City of Seattle,* 494 P.2d 485 (Wash. 1972); *Roux v. New Orleans Police Department,* 223 So.2d 905 (La. 1969); and *Farmer v. City of Fort Lauderdale,* 427 So.2d 187 (Fla. 1983), *cert. den.,* 104 S.Ct. 74 (1984).

78. 42 U.S.C. 200e(j).

79. *United States v. City of Albuquerque,* 12 EPD 11, 244 (10th Cir. 1976); see also *Trans World Airlines v. Hardison,* 97 S.Ct. 2264 (1977).

80. *United States v. Alburquerque,* 545 F.2d 110 (10th Cir. 1977).

81. *Potter v. Murray City,* 760 F.2d 1065 (10th Cir. 1985).

82. *Faust v. Police Civil Service Commission,* 347 A.2d 765 (Pa. 1975); *Stewart v. Leary,* 293 N.Y.S.2d 573 (1968); *Brewer v. City of Ashland,* 86 S.W.2d 669 (Ky. 1935); *Fabio v. Civil Service Commission of Philadelphia,* 373 A.2d 751 (Pa. 1977).

83. *Major v. Hampton,* 413 F.Supp. 66 (1976).

84. *Briggs v. City of North Muskegon Police Department,* 563 F.Supp. 585 (6th Cir. 1984).

85. *National Gay Task Force v. Bd. of Ed. of Oklahoma City,* 729 F.2d 1270 (10th Cir. 1984).

86. *Board of Education v. National Gay Task Force,* 53 U.S.L.W. 4408, No. 83-2030 (1985).

87. *Rowland v. Mad. River Sch. Dist.,* 730 F.2d 444 (6th Cir. 1984).

88. David J. Schall, "An Investigation into the Relationship Between Municipal Police Residency Requirements, Professionalism, Economic Conditions, and Equal Employment Goals" (unpublished dissertation, The University of Wisconsin–Milwaukee, 1996).

89. *Detroit Police Officers Association v. City of Detroit,* 190 N.W.2d 97 (1971), appeal denied, 405 U.S. 950 (1972).

90. *Miller v. Police Board of City of Chicago,* 349 N.E.2d 544 (Ill. 1976); *Williamson v. Village of Baskin,* 339 So.2d 474 (La. 1976); *Nigro v. Board of Trustees of Alden,* 395 N.Y.S.2d 544 (1977).

91. *State, County, and Municipal Employees Local 339 v. City of Highland Park,* 108 N.W.2d 898 (1961).

92. See, for example, *Cox v. McNamara,* 493 P.2d 54 (Ore. 1972); *Brenckle v. Township of Shaler,* 281 A.2d 920 (Pa. 1972); *Hopwood v. City of Paducah,* 424 S.W.2d 134 (Ky. 1968); *Flood v. Kennedy,* 239 N.Y.S.2d 665 (1963).

93. Richard N. Williams, *Legal Aspects of Discipline by Police Administrators,* Traffic Institute Publication 2705 (Evanston, Ill.: Northwestern University, 1975), p. 4.

94. *City of Crowley Firemen v. City of Crowley,* 264 So.2d 368 (La. 1972).

95. 471 U.S. 1, 105 S.Ct. 1694, 85 L.Ed.2d 1 (1985).

96. See *Lally v. Department of Police,* 306 So.2d 65 (La. 1974).

97. See, for example, *Peters v. Civil Service Commission of Tucson,* 539 P.2d 698 (Ariz. 1977); *Abeyta v. Town of Taos,* 499 F.2d 323 (10th Cir. 1974); *Baumgartner v. Leary,* 311 N.Y.S.2d 468 (1970); *City of Vancouver v. Jarvis,* 455 P.2d 591 (Wash. 1969).

98. Swanson, Territo, and Taylor, *Police Administration,* p. 433.
99. *Parker v. District of Columbia,* 850 F.2d 708 (1988), at 713, 714.
100. *Marusa v. District of Columbia,* 484 F.2d 828 (1973).
101. *Sager v. City of Woodlawn Park,* 543 F.Supp. 282 (D. Colo. 1982).
102. *Bonsignore v. City of New York,* 521 F.Supp. 394 (1981).
103. *Popow v. City of Margate,* 476 F.Supp. 1237 (1979).
104. Eloise Salholz and Frank Washington, "Detroit's Brutal Lessons," *Newsweek* (November 30, 1992):45.
105. Ibid.
106. See *Krolick v. Lowery,* 302 N.Y.S.2d 109 (1969), p. 115; *Hester v. Milledgeville,* 598 F.Supp. 1456, 1457 (M.D.Ga. 1984).
107. *McCracken v. Department of Police,* 337 So.2d 595 (La. 1976).
108. *Krolick v. Lowery.*
109. 489 U.S. 602 (1989).
110. 489 U.S. 656 (1989).
111. Robert J. Alberts and Harvey W. Rubin, "Court's Rulings on Testing Crack Down on Drug Abuse," *Risk Management* 38 (March 1991):36–41.
112. Ibid., p. 38.
113. Ibid., p. 40.
114. A. C. Germann, Frank D. Day, and Robert R. Gallatti, *Introduction to Law Enforcement and Criminal Justice* (Springfield, Ill.: Charles C Thomas, 1976), p. 224.
115. See, for example, Ted Gest and Amy Saltzman, "Harassment: Men on Trial," *U.S. News and World Report* (October 21, 1991):39–40, concerning a $3.1 million award to two former Long Beach, California, female police officers.
116. Marianne Lavelle, "The New Sexual Harassment," *U.S. News and World Report* (July 6, 1998):30–31.
117. *Burlington Industries v. Ellerth,* 118 S.Ct. 2257, 141 L.Ed.2d 633 (1998).
118. *Faragher v. City of Boca Raton,* 118 S.Ct. 2275, 141 L.Ed.2d 662 (1998).
119. *Gebser v. Lago Vista Independent School District,* 118 S.Ct. 1989, 141 L.Ed. 2d 277 (1998).
120. *Oncale v. Sundowner Offshore Services, Inc.,* 523 U.S. 75, 118 S.Ct. 998 (1998).
121. "Court: Harassment Covers Same-Sex Torment," *Associated Press* (March 5, 1998).
122. Paula N. Rubin and Susan W. McCampbell, "The Americans with Disabilities Act and Criminal Justice: Providing Inmate Services," U.S. Department of Justice, National Institute of Justice Research in Action (July 1994):2.
123. Paula N. Rubin, "The Americans With Disabilities Act and Criminal Justice: An Overview," U.S. Department of Justice, National Institute of Justice Research in Action (September 1993):1.
124. U.S. Department of Justice, National Institute of Justice Journal, Research in Action, "Health and Criminal Justice: Strengthening the Relationship" (November 1994):40.
125. Ibid., p. 41.
126. This case study is based on *Kuntz v. City of New Haven,* No. N-90-480 (JGM), March 3, 1993. Kuntz prevailed, was promoted, and won back pay, demonstrating to the court that his possible assignment to field duties would not be dangerous to him, to other police officers, or to the public.

# Chapter 15

# Special Challenges: Discipline, Labor Relations, and Liability

## Key Terms and Concepts

Appeal

Arbitration

Automatic records system

Collective bargaining

Early warning system (EWS)

Esprit de corps

Exonerated

Fact finding

Grievance

Job action

Mediation

Negotiations

Personnel complaint

Title 42 U.S.C. 1983

Tort

Unfounded

## Learning Objectives

As a result of reading this chapter, the student will:

- be familiar with the due process requirements concerning the discharge of public employees
- know the disciplinary actions used by agencies in an investigation of a criminal justice employee
- know the steps taken when a citizen's complaint is filed
- understand the grievance process

- be familiar with collective bargaining and unionization
- know three models used in collective bargaining
- understand the four types of job actions
- know the importance of civil liability and different lawsuits filed against criminal justice practitioners
- be familiar with legislation to protect persons who are victims of others' misuses of authority

> *Discipline must be maintained.*
> —Charles Dickens

> *No man is fit to command another that cannot command himself.*
> —William Penn

# Introduction

Several previous chapters have either implied or stated that the major asset and thus the *major challenge* of any criminal justice agency is its personnel. The ability of such agencies to accomplish their mission ultimately depends on the critically important element of human resources. The expanded labor movement and body of law concerning employees, the increased inclination of citizens to file suit against criminal justice personnel as well as for justice employees to sue their administrators, and the growing willingness of courts and juries to award large cash settlements in such cases—all point to the need for great effort and care to be directed to human resource management. Accordingly, this chapter examines three aspects of human resources/personnel administration that loom large in the administrator's coffer of challenges: discipline, labor relations, and liability.

Because of their power and authority, criminal justice employees, especially the police, are under greater public scrutiny than most other governmental employees. Therefore, this chapter segment examines administrators' responsibilities to *discipline* their employees when warranted. Employee misconduct includes those acts that harm the public, including corruption, harassment, brutality, and civil rights violations. Other violations of agency policy, such as substance abuse and insubordination or even minor violations of dress and punctuality, can also lead to disciplinary action.

In the past 50 years, no force has had a greater impact on the administration of criminal justice agencies than *labor relations.* Labor unions represent a major influence that must be reckoned with by criminal justice administrators. This chapter section discusses how the unionization movement developed, as well as contemporary elements and practices surrounding collective bargaining by labor and management groups.

Finally, the problem of *liability* is closely related to employee discipline, because both can involve misbehavior and harm to others. This chapter section discusses laws and legal concepts (such as negligence and torts) that serve to make criminal justice practitioners legally accountable, both civilly and criminally, for acts of misconduct and negligence.

The chapter concludes with two case studies.

# Disciplinary Policies and Practices

## *Maintaining the Public Trust*

The public's trust and respect are precious commodities and can be quickly lost with improper behavior by criminal justice employees and the improper handling of an allegation of misconduct. Serving communities professionally and with integrity should be the goal of every agency and its employees in order to ensure that trust and respect are maintained. The public expects that criminal justice agencies will make every effort to identify and correct problems and respond to citizens' complaints in an equally judicious, consistent, fair, and equitable manner.

One of the most important responsibilities of criminal justice agencies is implementing sound disciplinary policies and practices and responding to employee misconduct or performance problems at an early stage.

Employee misconduct and violations of departmental policy are the two principal areas in which discipline is involved.[1] Employee misconduct includes those acts that harm the public, including corruption, harassment, brutality, and civil rights violations. Violations of policy may involve a broad range of issues, including substance abuse and insubordination, or minor violations of dress and punctuality.

## *Due Process Requirements*

The well-established, minimum due process requirements for discharging public employees include that employees must

1. Be afforded a public hearing
2. Be present during the presentation of evidence against them and have an opportunity to cross-examine their superiors
3. Have an opportunity to present their own witnesses and other evidence concerning their side of the controversy
4. Be permitted to be represented by counsel
5. Have an impartial referee or hearing officer presiding
6. Have a decision made based on the weight of the evidence introduced during the hearing

Such protections apply to any disciplinary action that can significantly affect a criminal justice employee's reputation and/or future chances for special assignment or promotion. A disciplinary hearing that might result in only a reprimand or short suspension may involve fewer procedural protections than one that could result in more severe sanctions.[2]

When a particular disciplinary action does not include termination or suspension, however, it may still be subject to due process considerations. An example is a Chicago case involving a police officer who was transferred from the Neighborhood Relations Division to less desirable working conditions in the patrol division, with no loss in pay or benefits. The court found that the officer's First Amendment free speech rights were violated as his de facto demotion was in retaliation for his political activities (inviting political opponents of the mayor to a civic function and in retaliation for a speech given there that criticized the police department), and that he was thus entitled to civil damages. The court stated that "Certainly a demotion can be as detrimental to an employee as denial of a promotion."[3]

On the other hand, no due process protection may be required when the property interest (one's job) was fraudulently obtained. Thus, a deputy sheriff was not deprived of due process when he was summarily discharged for lying on his application about a juvenile felony charge, which would have barred him from employment in the first place.[4]

In sum, agency rules and policies should state which due process procedures will be utilized under certain disciplinary situations; the key questions regarding due process are whether or not the employer follows established agency guidelines, and if not, whether the employer has a compelling reason not to.

At times, the administrator will determine that an employee must be disciplined or terminated. What are adequate grounds for discipline or discharge? Grounds can vary widely from agency to agency. Certainly, the agency's formal policies and procedures should specify and control what constitutes proper and improper behavior. Normally, agency practice and custom enter into these decisions. Sometimes administrators will "wink" at the formal policies and procedures, overlooking or only occasionally enforcing certain provisions contained in them. But the failure of the agency to enforce a rule or policy for a long period of time may provide "implied consent" by the employer that such behavior, although officially prohibited, is permissible. (In other words, don't allow an employee to violate the agency's lateness policy for three months and then decide one day to summarily fire him.) Attempts to fire employees for behavior that has been ignored or enforced only infrequently at best may give rise to a defense by the employee.

The hiring of minority employees to meet state hiring goals and then attempting to terminate them as quickly and often as possible violate the employee's Title VII rights. Such a situation occurred in an Indiana case in which it was alleged that black prison correctional officers were hired to fulfill an affirmative action program, only to be fired for disciplinary reasons for which white officers were not discharged.[5]

Generally, violations of an employee's rights in discharge and discipline occur (1) in violation of a protected interest, (2) in retaliation for the exercise of protected conduct, (3) with a discriminatory motive, and (4) with malice.[6]

## A Tradition of Problems in Policing

Throughout its history, policing has experienced problems involving misconduct and corruption. A number of events during the 1990s demonstrated that the problem still exists and requires the attention of police officials. Incidents such as the beating of Rodney King in Los Angeles and Abner Louima in New York by officers, and major corruption scandals in several big-city police departments, have led many people to believe that police misbehavior is at a higher level today than ever before.

Without question, police administrators need to pay close attention to signs of police misconduct and respond quickly and enact policies to guide supervisors on the handling of disciplinary issues. Such policies should ensure that there is certainty, swiftness, fairness, and consistency of punishment when it is warranted,

## Automated Records Systems

There have been many advances in the use of technology in police discipline. In 1991, the Fresno, California, Police Department automated its disciplinary process in an effort to establish a better system for tracking and sanctioning personnel for various offenses.[7] The principal objectives of this **automatic records system** are to assist the chief of police in administering the department in a more equitable fashion and to improve the department's ability to defend its personnel actions. Within minutes, the database provides supervisors with five years of history about standards of discipline for any category of violation. A variety of reports can be produced, showing patterns of incidents for the supervisor.

## Determining the Level and Nature of Action

When an investigation against an employee is sustained, the sanctions and level of discipline must be decided. Management must be careful when recommending and imposing discipline, because of its impact on the overall morale of the agency's employees. If the recommended discipline is viewed by employees as too lenient, it may send the wrong message that the misconduct was insignificant. On the other hand, discipline that is viewed as too harsh may have a demoralizing effect on the officer(s) involved and other agency employees and result in allegations that the leadership is unfair. This alone can have significant impact on the **esprit de corps** or morale of the agency.

In addition to having a disciplinary process that is viewed by employees as fair and consistent, it is also important that discipline is progressive and that more serious sanctions are invoked when repeated violations occur. For example, a third substantiated violation of rude behavior may result in a recommendation for a one-day suspension without pay, but a first offense may be resolved through documented oral counseling or a letter of reprimand. Listed next are disciplinary actions commonly used by agencies in order of their severity.

*Counseling.* This is usually a conversation between the supervisor and employee about a specific aspect of the employee's performance or conduct; it is warranted when an employee has committed a relatively minor infraction or the nature of the offense is such that oral counseling is all that is necessary. For example, an officer who is usually punctual but arrives at briefing 10 minutes late two days in a row may require nothing more than a reminder and warning to correct the problem.

*Documented Oral Counseling.* This is usually the first step in a progressive disciplinary process and is intended to address relatively minor infractions. It occurs when there are no previous reprimands or more severe disciplinary action of the same or similar nature.

*Letters of Reprimand.* These are formal written notices regarding significant misconduct, more serious performance violations, or repeated offenses. It is usually the second step in the formal disciplinary process and is intended to provide the employee and agency with a written record of the violation of behavior; it identifies what specific corrective action must be taken to avoid subsequent, more serious disciplinary steps.

*Suspension.* This is a severe disciplinary action that results in an employee being relieved of duty, often without pay. It is usually administered when an employee commits a serious violation of established rules or after written reprimands have been given and no change in behavior or performance has resulted.

*Demotion.* In this situation, an employee is placed in a position of lower responsibility and pay. It is normally used when an otherwise capable employee is unable to meet the standards required for the higher position, or when the employee has committed a serious act requiring that he or she be removed from a position of management or supervision.

*Transfer.* Many agencies use the disciplinary transfer to deal with problem officers; officers can be transferred to a different location or assignment, and this action is often seen as an effective disciplinary tool.

*Termination.* This is the most severe disciplinary action that can be taken. It usually occurs when previous serious discipline has been imposed and there has been inadequate or no improvement in behavior or performance. It may also occur when an employee commits an offense so serious that continued employment would be inappropriate.

## Positive and Negative Discipline

When policies and procedures are violated, positive or negative disciplinary measures may be imposed. Although different in their philosophy, both seek to accomplish the same purpose: to correct negative behavior and promote the employee's voluntary compliance with departmental policies and procedures.

A positive discipline program (also known as positive counseling) attempts to change employee behavior without invoking punishment. An example of positive discipline or counseling is when an employee ("John") has been nonproductive and nonpunctual, has caused interpersonal problems with co-workers, and/or has other problems on the job. To this point, John has been in control of the situation, on the offensive one might say, while the supervisor ("Jane") and his co-workers have been on the defensive. John is jeopardizing the morale and productivity of the workplace, but the preferred approach is to try to salvage him because of the agency's investment in time, funds, and training.

Finally, Jane calls John into her office. She might begin with a compliment to give him (if indeed she can find one), and then she proceeds to outline all of his workplace shortcomings; this demonstrates to John that Jane "has his number" and is aware of his various problems. Jane explains to him why it is important that he improve (for reasons related to productivity, morale, and so on), and the benefits he might realize from improvement (promotions, pay raises, bonuses). She also outlines what can happen if he does *not* show adequate improvement (demotion, transfer, termination). Now having gained John's attention, she gives him a certain time period (say, 30, 60, or 90 days) in which to improve; she emphasizes, however, that she will be constantly monitoring his progress. She might even ask John to sign a counseling statement form that sets forth all they have discussed, indicating that John has received counseling and understands the situation.

Note that Jane is now on the offensive, thereby putting John on the defensive and in control of his destiny; if he fails to perform, Jane would probably give him a warning, and if the situation continues, he will be terminated. If he sues or files a grievance, Jane has proof that every effort was made to allow John to salvage his position. This is an effective means of giving subordinates an incentive to improve their behavior, while at the same time making the department less vulnerable to successful lawsuits.

Negative discipline is punishment. It is generally used when positive efforts fail or the violation is so serious that punishment is required. Negative discipline varies in its severity and involves documented oral counseling, letter of reprimand, demotion, days off without pay, or even termination.

## Dealing with Complaints

### Complaint Origin
A **personnel complaint** is an allegation of misconduct or illegal behavior against an employee by anyone inside or outside the organization. Internal complaints may come from supervisors who observe officer misconduct, officers who complain about supervisors, supervisors who complain about other supervisors, civilian personnel who complain about officers, and so on. External complaints originate from sources outside the organization and usually involve the public.

Complaints may be received from primary, secondary, and anonymous sources. A victim is a primary source. A secondary source is someone who makes the complaint on behalf of the victim, such as an attorney, school counselor, or parent of a juvenile. An anonymous source complaint derives from an unknown source and may be delivered to the police station via a telephone call or unsigned letter.

Every complaint, regardless of the source, must be accepted and investigated in accordance with established policies and procedures. Anonymous complaints are the most difficult to investigate because there is no opportunity to obtain further information or question the complainant about the allegation. Such complaints can have a negative impact on employee morale, as officers may view such complaints as unjust and frivolous.

### Types and Causes

Complaints may be handled informally or formally, depending on the seriousness of the allegation and preference of the complainant. A formal complaint occurs when a written and signed and/or tape-recorded statement of the allegation is made and the complainant requests to be informed of the investigation's disposition. Figure 15.1 provides an example of a complaint form used to initiate a personnel investigation.

An informal complaint is an allegation of minor misconduct made for informational purposes that can usually be resolved without the need for more formal processes. When a citizen calls the watch commander to complain about the rude behavior of a dispatcher but does not wish to make a formal complaint, the supervisor may simply discuss the incident with the dispatcher and resolve it through informal counseling as long as more serious problems are not discovered and the dispatcher does not have a history of similar complaints.

Few complaints involve acts of physical violence, excessive force, or corruption. Allen Wagner and Scott Decker[8] found that the majority of complaints against officers fall under the general categories of verbal abuse, discourtesy, harassment, improper attitude, and ethnic slurs.[9] Another study[10] found that 42 percent of complaints involved the "verbal conduct" of officers; verbal conduct also accounted for 47 percent of all sustained complaints. The majority of repeated offenses also fell into this category. It is clear that the officers' verbal actions generate a significant number of complaints. Finally, minority citizens and those with less power and fewer resources are more likely than persons with greater power and more resources to file complaints of misconduct and to allege more serious forms of misconduct.[11]

### Receipt and Referral

Administrators should have in place a process for receiving complaints that is clearly delineated by departmental policy and procedures. Generally, a complaint will be made at a police facility and referred to a senior officer in charge to determine its seriousness and need for immediate intervention.

In most cases, the senior officer will determine the nature of the complaint and the employees involved; the matter will be referred to the employee's supervisor to conduct an initial investigation. The supervisor completes the investigation, recommends any discipline, and sends the matter to the Internal Affairs

\*\*\*\*\*\*\*\*\*\*\*\*\*\*\*\*\*\*\*\*\*\*\*\*\*\*\*\*\*\*\*\*\*\*\*\*\*\*\*\*\*\*\*\*\*\*\*\*\*\*\*\*\*\*\*\*\*\*\*\*\*\*\*\*\*\*\*\*\*\*\*\*\*\*\*\*\*\*\*\*\*\*\*\*\*\*\*\*\*\*\*\*\*\*\*\*\*\*\*\*\*

Control Number_____

Date & Time Reported        Location of Interview        Interview

_____        _____        _____Verbal  _____Written  _____Taped

| | |
|---|---|
| Type of Complaint: | \_\_\_\_Force  \_\_\_\_Procedural  \_\_\_\_Conduct<br>\_\_\_\_Other (Specify) |
| Source of Complaint: | \_\_\_\_In Person  \_\_\_\_Mail  \_\_\_\_Telephone<br>\_\_\_\_Other (Specify) |
| Complaint originally<br>Received by: | \_\_\_\_Supervisor  \_\_\_\_On Duty Watch Commander  \_\_\_\_Chief<br>\_\_\_\_IAU  \_\_\_\_Other (Specify) |
| Notifications made:<br>Received by: | _____Division Commander  _____Chief of Police<br>_____On-Call Command Personnel<br>_____Watch Commander  _____Other (Specify) |

Copy of formal personnel complaint given to complainant?  \_\_\_\_Yes \_\_\_\_No

\*\*\*\*\*\*\*\*\*\*\*\*\*\*\*\*\*\*\*\*\*\*\*\*\*\*\*\*\*\*\*\*\*\*\*\*\*\*\*\*\*\*\*\*\*\*\*\*\*\*\*\*\*\*\*\*\*\*\*\*\*\*\*\*\*\*\*\*\*\*\*\*\*\*\*\*\*\*\*\*\*\*\*\*\*\*\*\*\*\*\*\*\*\*\*\*\*\*\*\*\*

Complainant's name:                                    Address:

_____        _____ Zip_____

Residence Phone:                                       Business Phone:

_____        _____ \_\_\_\_

DOB:                Race:                Sex:                Occupation:

_____        _____        _____        _____

\*\*\*\*\*\*\*\*\*\*\*\*\*\*\*\*\*\*\*\*\*\*\*\*\*\*\*\*\*\*\*\*\*\*\*\*\*\*\*\*\*\*\*\*\*\*\*\*\*\*\*\*\*\*\*\*\*\*\*\*\*\*\*\*\*\*\*\*\*\*\*\*\*\*\*\*\*\*\*\*\*\*\*\*\*\*\*\*\*\*\*\*\*\*\*\*\*\*\*\*\*

Location of Occurrence:                                Date & Time of Occurrence:

Member(s) Involved:                                    Member(s) Involved:
(1) _____        (2)_____
(3) _____        (4)_____
Witness(es) Involved:                                  Witness(es) Involved:
(1) _____        (2)_____
(3) _____        (4)_____

\*\*\*\*\*\*\*\*\*\*\*\*\*\*\*\*\*\*\*\*\*\*\*\*\*\*\*\*\*\*\*\*\*\*\*\*\*\*\*\*\*\*\*\*\*\*\*\*\*\*\*\*\*\*\*\*\*\*\*\*\*\*\*\*\*\*\*\*\*\*\*\*\*\*\*\*\*\*\*\*\*\*\*\*\*\*\*\*\*\*\*\*\*\*\*\*\*\*\*\*\*

(1) \_\_\_\_\_  Complainant wishes to make a formal statement and has requested an investigation into the matter with a report back to him/her on the findings and actions.

(2) \_\_\_\_\_  Complainant wishes to advise the Police Department of a problem, understand that some type of action will be taken, but does not request a report back to him/her on the findings and actions.

\*\*\*\*\*\*\*\*\*\*\*\*\*\*\*\*\*\*\*\*\*\*\*\*\*\*\*\*\*\*\*\*\*\*\*\*\*\*\*\*\*\*\*\*\*\*\*\*\*\*\*\*\*\*\*\*\*\*\*\*\*\*\*\*\*\*\*\*\*\*\*\*\*\*\*\*\*\*\*\*\*\*\*\*\*\*\*\*\*\*\*\*\*\*\*\*\*\*\*\*\*

## CITIZEN ADVISEMENTS

(1)  If you have not yet provided the department with a signed written statement or a tape-recorded statement, one may be required in order to pursue the investigation of this matter.

(2)  The complainant(s) and/or witness(es) may be required to take a polygraph examination in order to determine the credibility concerning the allegations made.

(3)  Should the allegations prove to be false, the complainant(s) and/or witness(es) may be liable for criminal and/or civil prosecution.

_____        _____
Signature of Complainant              Date & Time

_____
Signature of Member Receiving Complaint

**Figure 15.1**

Police department formal personnel complaint report form.

Unit (IAU) and the agency head for finalization of the disciplinary process. This method of review ensures that consistent and fair standards of discipline are applied.

### *The Investigative Process*

D. Perez[12] indicated that all but a small percentage of the 17,000 police agencies in the United States have a process for investigation of police misconduct. Generally, the employee's supervisor will conduct a preliminary inquiry of the complaint, commonly known as **fact finding.** Once it is determined that further investigation is necessary, the supervisor may conduct additional questioning of employees and witnesses, obtain written statements from those persons immediately involved in the incident, and gather any evidence that may be necessary for the case, including photographs. Care must be exercised that the accused employee's rights are not violated. The initial investigation would be sent to an appropriate division commander and forwarded to IAU for review.

### *Making a Determination and Disposition*

Once an investigation is completed, the supervisor or IAU officer must make a determination as to the culpability of the accused employee and report same to the administrator. Each allegation should receive a separate adjudication. Following are the categories of dispositions that are commonly used:

- **Unfounded.** The alleged act(s) did not occur.
- **Exonerated.** The act occurred, but it is lawful, proper, justified, and/or in accordance with departmental policies, procedures, rules, and regulations.
- *Not sustained.* There is insufficient evidence to prove or disprove the allegations made.
- *Misconduct not based on the complaint.* Sustainable misconduct was determined but is not a part of the original complaint. For example, a supervisor investigating an allegation of excessive force against an officer may find the force used was within departmental policy, but that the officer made an unlawful arrest.
- *Closed.* An investigation may be halted if the complainant fails to cooperate or it is determined that the action does not fall within the administrative jurisdiction of the police agency.
- *Sustained.* The act did occur and it was a violation of departmental rules and procedures. Sustained allegations include misconduct that falls within the broad outlines of the original allegation(s).

Once a determination of culpability has been made, the complainant should be notified of the department's findings. Details of the investigation or recommended punishment will not be included in the correspondence. As shown in Figure 15.2, the complainant will normally receive only information concerning the outcome of the complaint, including a short explanation of the finding along with an invitation to call the agency if further information is needed.

Police Department
3300 Main Street
Downtown Plaza
Anywhere, USA. 99999
June 20, 2000

Mr. John Doe
2200 Main Avenue
Anywhere, USA.

Re: Internal affairs #000666-98
 Case Closure

Dear Mr. Doe:

Our investigation into your allegations against Officer Smith has been completed. It has been determined that your complaint is SUSTAINED and the appropriate disciplinary action has been taken.

Our department appreciates your bringing this matter to our attention. It is our position that when a problem is identified, it should be corrected as soon as possible. It is our goal to be responsive to the concerns expressed by citizens so as to provide more efficient and effective services.

Your information regarding this incident was helpful and of value in our efforts to attain that goal. Should you have any further questions about this matter, please contact Sergeant Jane Alexander, Internal Affairs, at 555-9999.

Sincerely,


I.M. Boss
Lieutenant
Internal Affairs Unit

**Figure 15.2**

Citizens' notification of discipline letter.

### *Grievances*

Police officers may complain and grieve contractual or other matters about which they are upset or concerned. Following is an overview of the **grievance** process.

Grievance procedures establish a fair and expeditious process for handling employee disputes that are not disciplinary in nature. Grievance procedures involve collective bargaining issues, conditions of employment, or employer-employee relations. More specifically, grievances may cover a broad range of issues, including salaries, overtime, leave, hours of work, allowances, retirement, opportunity for advancement, performance evaluations, workplace conditions, tenure, disciplinary actions, supervisory methods, and administrative practices. Grievance procedures are often established as a part of the collective bargaining process.

The preferred method for settling officers' grievances is through informal discussion, when the employee explains his or her grievance to the immediate supervisor. Most complaints can be handled through this process. Complaints that cannot be dealt with informally are usually handled through a more formal grievance process, as described next. A formal grievance begins with the employee submitting the grievance in writing to the immediate supervisor, as illustrated in Figure 15.3.

Police Department
Formal Grievance Form

Grievance #_____

Employee Name: _____ Work Phone: _____
Department Assigned: _____
Date of Occurrence: _____
Location of Occurrence: _____

Name of:   1.   Department Head:_____

          2.   Division Head:_____

          3.   Immediate Supervisor:_____

Statement of Grievance: _____
_____
_____
_____

Witnesses:_____
_____
_____

What article(s) and or section(s) of the labor agreement of rules and regulations do you believe have been violated? _____
_____
_____
_____

What remedy are you requesting?_____
_____
_____

_____          _____
Employee signature                     Signature of labor representative

**Figure 15.3**

Employee grievance form.

The process for formally handling grievances will vary among agencies and may involve as many as three to six different levels of action. Following is an example of how a grievance may proceed:

> *Level I:* A grievance is submitted in writing to a supervisor. The supervisor will be given five days to respond to the employee's grievance. If the employee is dissatisfied with the response, the grievance moves to the next level.
>
> *Level II:* At this level, the grievance proceeds to the chief executive who will be given a specified time (usually five days) to render a decision.
>
> *Level III:* If the employee is not satisfied with the chief's decision, the grievance may proceed to the city or county manager, as is appropriate. The manager will usually meet with the employee and/or representatives from the bargaining association and attempt to resolve the matter. An additional five to ten days is usually allowed for the manager to render a decision.
>
> *Level IV:* If the grievance is still not resolved, either party may request that the matter be submitted to arbitration. Arbitration involves a neutral, outside person, often selected from a list of arbitrators from the Federal Mediation and Conciliation Service. An arbitrator will conduct a hearing, listen to both parties, and usually render a decision within 20 to 30 days. The decision of the arbitrator can be final and binding. This does not prohibit the employee from appealing the decision to a state court.

Failure to act on grievances quickly may result in serious morale problems within an agency.

### Appealing Disciplinary Measures

**Appeals** processes—frequently outlined in civil service rules and regulations, labor agreements, and departmental policies and procedures—normally follow an officer's chain of command. For example, if an officer disagrees with a supervisor's recommendation for discipline, the first step of an appeal may involve a hearing before the division commander, usually of the rank of captain or deputy chief. The accused employee may be allowed labor representation or an attorney to assist in asking questions of the investigating supervisor, clarifying issues, and presenting new or mitigating evidence. The division commander would have five days to review the recommendation and respond in writing to the employee.

If the employee is still not satisfied, an appeal hearing before the chief executive is granted. This is usually the final step in appeals within the agency. The chief or sheriff communicates a decision in writing to the employee within five to ten days. Depending on labor agreements and civil service rules and regulations, some agencies extend their appeals of discipline beyond the department. For example, employees may bring their issue before the civil service commission or city or county manager for a final review. Employees may also have the right to an independent arbitrator's review of the discipline. The arbitrator's decision is usually binding.

### The Early Warning System

Early identification of and intervention in employee misconduct or performance problems are vital to preventing ongoing and repeated incidents. An **early warning system (EWS)** is designed to identify officers whose behavior is problematic (involving citizen complaints or improper use of force) and provide a form of intervention. The system alerts the department to these individuals and warns the officers, while providing counseling or training to help them change their problematic behavior. Most EWS require three complaints in a given time frame (normally a 12-month period) before intervention is initiated. EWS thus helps agencies respond proactively to patterns of behavior that may lead to more serious problems. EWS may require that the officer's supervisor intervene with early prevention methods such as counseling or training.

In some cases, repeated incidents of violent behavior may require that officers attend anger training or verbal judo sessions to learn how to deescalate confrontational situations. Some preventive measures, such as counseling, remedial training, or temporary change of assignment, may also be used. A referral to an employee assistance program (EAP) to deal with more serious psychological or substance abuse problems is another possible outcome.

## Labor Relations

As indicated in the chapter introduction, *labor relations*—a term that includes the related concepts of *unionization* and *collective bargaining*—pose a major challenge to contemporary criminal justice administrators. This section discusses the unionization movement and the processes of collective bargaining that are currently employed by labor and management.

### Unionization in Policing, Courts, and Corrections

Probably as a result of their difficult working conditions, as well as traditionally low salary and benefits packages, police and corrections employees have elected to band together within their disciplines to fight for improvement. It is probably also accurate to say that a major force in the development and spread of unionization of these two groups was the authoritarian, unilateral, and "do as I say, not as I do" management style that characterized many police and prison administrators of the past.

#### The Movement Begins: Policing

The first campaign to organize the police started shortly after World War I, when the American Federation of Labor (AFL) reversed a long-standing policy and issued charters to police unions in Boston, Washington, D.C., and about 30 other cities. August Vollmer and many other police chiefs promptly condemned this move, insisting that police officers had no more right to unionize than did military personnel. However, many police officers were suffering from the rapid inflation following the outbreak of the war and believed that if their chiefs could not get them long-overdue pay raises, then perhaps unions could. Capitalizing on their sentiments, the fledgling unions signed about 60 percent of all officers in Washington, 75 percent in Boston, and a similar proportion in other cities.[13]

The unions' success was short-lived, however. The Boston police commissioner refused to recognize the union, forbade officers to join it, and filed charges against several union officials. Shortly thereafter, on September 9, 1919, the Boston police initiated their now-famous three-day strike, causing major riots and a furor against the police all across the nation; nine rioters were killed and 23 were seriously injured. During the strike, Massachusetts Governor Calvin Coolidge uttered his long-remembered quote, "There is no right to strike against the public safety by anybody, anywhere, anytime."

During World War II, however, the unionization effort was reignited. Unions issued charters to a few dozen locals all over the country and sent in organizers to help enlist the rank and file. Most police chiefs continued speaking out against unionization, but their subordinates were moved by the thousands to join, sensing the advantage in having unions press for higher wages and benefits.[14] But in a series of rulings, the courts upheld the right of police authorities to ban police unions.

The unions were survived in the early 1950s by many benevolent and fraternal organizations of police. Some were patrolmen's benevolent associations (PBAs), like those formed in New York, Chicago, and Washington, while others were fraternal orders of police (FOPs). During the late 1950s and early 1960s, a new group of rank-and-file association leaders came into power. They were more vocal in articulating their demands. Soon, a majority of the rank and file vocally supported higher salaries and pensions, free legal aid, low-cost insurance, and other services and benefits. Beginning with the granting of public sector **collective bargaining** rights in Wisconsin in 1959, rank-and-file organizations were legally able to insist that their administrators sit down at the bargaining table.[15]

Since its inception, the unionization of the police has flourished. The majority of all U.S. police officers now belong to unions.[16] The International Conference of Police Associations (ICPA) is the largest organization, with more than 100 local and state units representing more than 200,000 officers.[17] George Cole attributed this dramatic rise in union membership to several factors: job dissatisfaction, the belief that the public is hostile to police needs, and an influx of younger officers who hold less traditional views on relations between officers and the department hierarchy.[18]

With some justification, administrators fear that their control over the organization will be reduced as union power increases and that traditional matters within their scope, such as promotion and transfer of personnel, will become enmeshed in union negotiations. And, of course, there is always the specter of police job actions, including work slowdowns, work stoppages (strikes or blue flu), work speedups, or votes of confidence (these are discussed on page 378). The threat of a police work stoppage is real, as a number of strikes by police occurred during the mid-1970s. Several guidelines exist to prevent police strikes:

Police and city administrators need to work toward developing an atmosphere of trust and cooperation; an effective internal communications system must be developed in police agencies and among the police administrator, the city administration, and the union leaders; training must be provided police management, city administration, and union leaders in the area of **negotiation;** and "eleventh-hour" bargaining and negotiation must be eliminated.[19]

### *Corrections Follows the Precedent*

Correctional officers (COs) were probably the last group of public workers to organize. In the early days after authorization of collective bargaining in the 1960s and 1970s, correctional administrators feared that unionization would diminish management authority and undermine staff discipline and prison security. Over the years that collective bargaining has been in place for correctional agencies, however, the early fears have not materialized, and the benefits of shared governance by line staff and management have led to better decisions and higher morale. As with the police, negotiations usually involve pay and benefits for correctional employees, including seniority rights, how staff are selected for overtime, the type of clothing provided to staff by the agency, educational programs, and so forth.

After a contract is negotiated, each prison or community corrections office must implement and administer it. When disputes about the true meaning of a contract arise, management can make a decision, and the union can file a grievance to argue it.[20]

Collective bargaining is now well entrenched in prison and other correctional agency operations, and it will continue to have an impact on policy and practice. There remains some disagreement, however, concerning its implications. Some argue that sharing of power in a correctional setting benefits all parties, and that unions are a powerful voice to the legislature for increases in staffing and budgets. Others maintain that collective bargaining has resulted in a clear distinction between line staff and management, with managers no longer looking out for subordinates because union leadership promotes an adversarial relationship. As James Jacobs and Norma Crotty suggested, "[Collective bargaining] has redefined the prison organization in adversary terms so that wardens are bosses and complaints are grievances."[21]

A major issue with corrections unions involves the right to strike. One can only imagine the chaos that would occur if correctional officers strike. Such unlawful strikes have occurred. The most infamous strike action was in New York State in 1979, when 7,000 correctional workers simultaneously struck the state's 33 prisons. A court found the union in violation of the law, heavily fined the union for the failure of its members to return to work, and jailed union leaders for contempt of court.[22] The strike ended 17 days after it began; the guards gained very few concessions, and salary gains did not offset fines imposed on the strikers.[23]

Finally, another concern regarding collective bargaining is its impact on rehabilitation. Some argue that prison unions, stressing staff safety issues, may overshadow the institution's efforts toward rehabilitation, while also pointing out that rehabilitative programs that improve inmate morale, reduce idleness, and enhance security result in benefits to the staff who work in prison.[24]

Overall, it is not the existence of collective bargaining that seems to have implications for corrections; rather, perhaps much like the unionization with the police, it is the attitude of agency administrators and union leaders and the relationships that develop that pave the direction of the impact. If both parties communicate with and listen to each other, show mutual respect, and are reasonable in their positions, collective bargaining can benefit corrections. If, however, the parties let issues get personal and become overly adversarial, corrections and collective bargaining will experience many negative outcomes.[25]

### *Unionization in the Courts*

The movement to exercise the right to bargain collectively, especially when compared with law enforcement and corrections, has been rare in the courts, occurring on a random, localized basis; however, unified court systems exist in which court personnel are organized statewide, as in Hawaii. Many states adhere generally to model legislation on public employee relation commissions, which provide mediation and fact-finding services and make determinations of unfair labor practices. On occasion, these commissions make decisions that greatly affect the management authority of the judiciary over its personnel.

When a collective bargaining unit exists in a court system, the process has all the basic elements found in other systems: (1) recognition (the employing court recognizes that henceforth employees will be represented by their chosen agent); (2) negotiation (there are established methods for arriving at a collective bargaining agreements, breaking deadlocks, ratifying contracts, etc.); and (3) contract administration (the day-to-day management of a court is accomplished within the framework of the labor contract).[26]

## Collective Bargaining: Types, Relationships, Negotiation, Job Actions

### *Three Models*

Each state is free to decide whether and which public sector employees will have collective bargaining rights and under what terms; therefore, there is considerable variety in collective bargaining arrangements across the nation. In states with comprehensive public sector bargaining laws, the administration of the statute is the responsibility of a state agency such as a Public Employee Relations Board (PERB) or Public Employee Relations Commission (PERC). There are three basic models used in the states: binding arbitration, meet and confer, and bargaining-not-required.[27] Table 15.1 shows the use of these models in the various states.

The *binding arbitration* model is used in 24 states and the District of Columbia. Public employees are given the right to bargain with their employers. If the bargaining reaches an impasse, the matter is submitted to a neutral arbitrator

**TABLE 15.1**    State Collective Bargaining Laws Governing Law Enforcement Officers

| STATE | BINDING ARBITRATION MODEL | MEET-AND-CONFER MODEL | BARGAINING-NOT-REQUIRED MODEL |
|---|---|---|---|
| Alabama | | | X |
| Alaska | X | | |
| Arizona | | | X |
| Arkansas | | | X |
| California | | X | |
| Colorado | | | X |
| Connecticut | X | | |
| Delaware | X | | |
| District of Columbia | X | | |
| Florida | | X | |
| Georgia | | | X |
| Hawaii | X | | |
| Idaho | | | X |
| Illinois | X | | |
| Indiana | | | X |
| Iowa | X | | |
| Kansas | X | | |
| Kentucky | | | X |
| Louisiana | | | X |
| Maine | X | | |
| Maryland | | | X |
| Massachusetts | X | | |
| Michigan | X | | |
| Minnesota | X | | |
| Mississippi | | | X |
| Missouri | | | X |
| Montana | X | | |
| Nebraska | | | X |
| Nevada | X | | |
| New Hampshire | X | | |
| New Jersey | X | | |
| New Mexico | | X | |
| New York | X | | |
| North Carolina | | | X |
| North Dakota | | | X |
| Ohio | X | | |

*(table continues)*

**TABLE 15.1**   State Collective Bargaining Laws Governing Law Enforcement Officers *(continued)*

| STATE | BINDING ARBITRATION MODEL | MEET-AND-CONFER MODEL | BARGAINING-NOT-REQUIRED MODEL |
|---|---|---|---|
| Oklahoma | X | | |
| Oregon | X | | |
| Pennsylvania | X | | |
| Rhode Island | X | | |
| South Carolina | | | X |
| South Dakota | | | X |
| Tennessee | | | X |
| Texas | | | X |
| Utah | | | X |
| Vermont | X | | |
| Virginia | | | X |
| Washington | X | | |
| West Virginia | | | X |
| Wisconsin | X | | |
| Wyoming | | | X |

*Source:* Will Aitchison, *The Rights of Police Officers,* 3rd ed. (Portland, Oregon: Labor Relations Information System, 1996), p. 10.

who decides what the terms and conditions of the new collective bargaining agreement will be.[28]

Only three states use the *meet-and-confer* model, which grants very few rights to public employees. As with the binding arbitration model, criminal justice employees in meet-and-confer states have the right to organize and to select their own bargaining representatives.[29] When an impasse is reached, however, employees are at a distinct disadvantage. Their only legal choices are to accept the employer's best offer, try to influence the offer through political tactics (such as appeals for public support), or take some permissible job action.[30]

The 22 states that follow the *bargaining-not-required* model either do not statutorily require or do not allow collective bargaining by public employees.[31] In the majority of these states, laws permitting public employees to engage in collective bargaining have not been passed.

States with collective bargaining must also address the issue of whether an individual employee must be a member of a union that represents his or her class of employees in a particular organization. In a "closed shop," employees must be dues-paying members or they will be terminated by the employer. "Open" shops, conversely, allow employees a choice of whether or not to join, even though the union has an obligation to represent them.

### *The Bargaining Relationship*

If collective bargaining is legally established, the process of setting up a bargaining relationship is straightforward, although opportunities still exist for disputes. The process for organizing for collective bargaining is as follows: First, a union will begin an organizing drive seeking to get a majority of the class(es) of employees it wants to represent to sign authorization cards. At this point, agency administrators may attempt to convince employees that they are better off without the union. Questions may also arise, such as whether or not certain employees (e.g., police or prison lieutenants) are part of management and therefore ineligible for union representation.

Once a majority ("50 percent plus one" of the eligible employees) have signed cards, the union notifies the criminal justice agency. If management believes that the union has obtained a majority legitimately, it will recognize the union as the bargaining agent of the employees it has sought to represent. Once recognized by the employer, the union will petition the PERB or other body responsible for administering the legislation for certification.

### *Negotiations*

Figure 15.4 depicts a typical configuration of the union and management bargaining teams. Positions shown in the broken-line boxes typically serve in a support role and may or may not actually partake in the bargaining. The management's labor relations manager (lead negotiator) is often an attorney assigned to

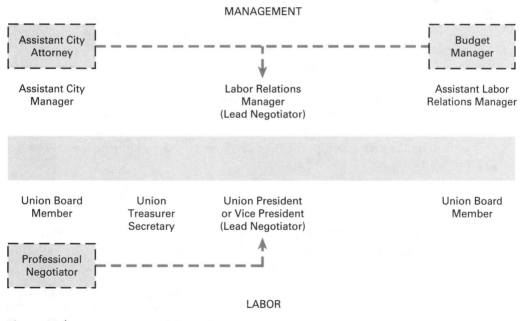

**Figure 15.4**

Union and management collective bargaining teams. *Source:* Jerry Hoover, Chief of Police, Reno, Nevada.

the human resources department, reporting to the city manager or assistant city manager and representing the city in grievances and arbitration matters; management's chief negotiator may also be the director of labor relations or human resources director for the unit of government involved or a professional labor relations specialist. Nor is the union's chief negotiator normally a member of the organization involved; rather, he or she will be a specialist brought in to represent the union's position and providing greater experience, expertise, objectivity, and autonomy. The union's chief negotiator may be accompanied by some people who have conducted surveys on wages and benefits, trends in the consumer price index, and so on.[32]

The agency's chief executive should not appear at the table personally; it is difficult for the chief to represent management one day and then return to work among the employees the next. Rather, management is represented by a key member of the command staff having the executive's confidence.

The issues, and the way in which they are presented, will impact how the negotiations will go. The purpose of bargaining is to produce a bilateral written agreement that will bind both parties during the lifetime of the agreement. Management normally prefers a narrow scope of negotiations because it means less shared power; conversely, the union will opt for the widest possible scope. The number of negotiating sessions may run from one to several dozen, lasting from 30 minutes to 10 or more hours, depending on how close or far apart union and management are when they begin to meet face to face.

In the initial session, the chief negotiator for each party will make an opening statement. Management's representative will often go first, touching on general themes such as the need for patience and the obligation to bargain in good faith. The union's negotiator will generally follow, outlining what the union seeks to achieve under the terms of the new contract. Ground rules for the bargaining may then be reviewed, modified, or developed. The attention then shifts to the terms of the contract that the union is proposing. Both sides need to understand what it is they are attempting to commit each other to. Ultimately, unless a total impasse is reached, agreement will be obtained on the terms of a new contract. The union's membership will vote on the contract as whole. If approved by the membership, the contract then goes before the necessary government officials and bodies for approval.[33]

### In the Event of an Impasse . . .

Even parties bargaining in good faith may not be able to resolve their differences by themselves, and an impasse may result. In such cases, a neutral third party may be introduced to facilitate, suggest, or compel an agreement. Three major forms of impasse resolution are mediation, fact finding, and arbitration.

- **Mediation** occurs when a third party, called the mediator, comes in to help the adversaries with the negotiations.[34] This person may be a professional mediator or someone else in whom both parties have confidence. In most states, mediation may be requested by either labor or management. The mediator's task is to build agreement about the issues involved by reopening communications between the two sides. The mediator cannot compel an agreement, so an advantage of the process is that it preserves collective bargaining by maintaining the decision-making power in the hands of the involved parties.[35]

- **Fact finding** primarily involves the interpretation of facts and the determination of what weight to attach to them. Appointed in the same way as mediators, fact finders also do not have the means to impose a settlement of the dispute. Fact finders may sit alone or as part of a panel normally consisting of three people. The fact-finding hearing is quasi-judicial, although less strict rules of evidence are applied. Both labor and management may be represented by legal counsel, and verbatim transcripts are commonly made. In a majority of cases, the fact finder's recommendations will be made public at some point.[36]

- **Arbitration** is similar to fact finding but differs in that the "end product of arbitration is a final and binding decision that sets the terms of the settlement and with which the parties are legally required to comply."[37] Arbitration may be voluntary or compulsory. It is compulsory when mandated by state law and is binding upon the parties even if one of them is unwilling to comply. It is voluntary when the parties undertake of their own volition to use the procedure. Even when entered into voluntarily, arbitration is compulsory and binding on the parties who have agreed to it.

The establishment of a working agreement between labor and management does not mean that the possibility for conflict no longer exists; the day-to-day administration of the agreement may also be the basis for strife. Questions can arise concerning the interpretation and application of the document and its various clauses, and grievances (discussed earlier) may arise. The sequence of grievance steps will be spelled out in the collective bargaining agreement and would typically include the following five steps: (1) The employee presents the grievance to the immediate supervisor; and, if satisfaction is not achieved, (2) a written grievance is presented to the division commander, then (3) to the chief executive officer, then (4) to the city or county manager, and, finally, (5) to an arbiter, selected according to the rules of the American Arbitration Association.[38]

The burden of proof is on the grieving party, except in disciplinary cases when it is always on the employer. The parties may be represented by counsel at the hearing, and the format will include opening statements by each side, examination and cross-examination of any witnesses, and closing arguments in the reverse order of which opening arguments were made.[39]

### *Job Actions*
A **job action** is an activity by employees to express their dissatisfaction with a particular person, event, or condition or to attempt to influence the outcome of some matter pending before decision makers. Employees seek to create pressure that may shift the course of events to a position more favorable or acceptable to

them.[40] Job actions are of four types: the vote of confidence, work slowdowns, work speedups, and work stoppages.

- *Vote of confidence:* This job action is used sparingly; a vote of no confidence signals employees' collective displeasure with the chief administrator of the agency. Although such votes have no legal standing, they may have high impact as a result of the resulting publicity.
- *Work slowdowns:* Employees continue to work during a slowdown, but they do so at a leisurely pace, causing productivity to fall. As productivity declines, the unit of government is pressured to resume normal work production; for example, a police department may urge officers to issue more citations so revenues are not lost. Citizens may complain to politicians to "get this thing settled."[41]
- *Work speedups:* These involve accelerated activity in the level of services and can foster considerable public resentment. For example, a police department may conduct a "ticket blizzard" to protest a low pay increase, pressure governmental leaders to make more concessions at the bargaining table, or abandon some policy change that affects their working conditions.
- *Work stoppages:* These constitute the most severe job action. The ultimate work stoppage is the strike, or withholding of all employees' services. This tactic is most often used by labor to force management back to the bargaining table when negotiations have reached an impasse. Criminal justice employee strikes are now rare, however. Short of a strike by all employees are briefer work stoppages, known in policing as "blue flu," that last only a few days.

## Civil Liability

No group of workers (with the exception of physicians) is more susceptible to litigation and liability than police and corrections officers. Frequently cast into confrontational situations, and given the complex nature of their work and its requisite training needs, they will from time to time act in a manner that evokes public scrutiny and complaints. The price of failure among public servants can be quite high, in both human and financial terms. Coupled with that is the fact that some police and corrections officers are overzealous and even brutal in their work; they may intentionally or otherwise violate the rights of the citizens they are sworn to protect or the clients they are to detain or supervise. For these inappropriate actions, the public has become quick to file suit for damages for what are perceived to be egregious actions.

Another trend is for such litigants to cast a wide net in their lawsuits, suing not only the principal actors in the incident but supervisors and agency administrators as well; this breadth of suing represents the notion of "vicarious liability" or the doctrine of *respondeat superior,* an old legal maxim meaning "let the master answer." In sum, an employer can be found liable in certain instances for wrongful acts of the employee.[42] Such a case was *McClelland v. Facteau*,[43] in which McClelland was stopped by Officer Facteau for speeding and taken to the city jail; he was not allowed to make any phone calls, was questioned but not advised of his rights, and was beaten and injured by Facteau in the presence of two city police officers who were from different jurisdictions. McClelland sued, claiming that the two police chiefs were directly responsible for his treatment and injuries due to their failure to train and supervise their subordinates properly. Evidence was also produced of prior misbehavior by Facteau. The court ruled that the chiefs could be held liable if they knew of prior misbehavior yet did nothing about it.

Next, we examine torts and negligent behaviors that can lead to civil liability and even incarceration for police and corrections personnel in the justice system; following that is a discussion of two major legislative tools that are used to legally attack such activities: Title 42, U.S. Code Section 1983, and Title 18, U.S. Code, Section 242.

## *Torts and Negligence*

It is important to have a basic understanding of tort liability. A **tort** is the infliction of some injury on one person by another. Three categories of torts generally cover most of the lawsuits filed against criminal justice practitioners: negligence, intentional torts, and constitutional torts.

*Negligence* can arise when a criminal justice employee's conduct creates a danger to others. In other words, the employee did not conduct his or her affairs in a manner so as to avoid subjecting others to a risk of harm and may be held liable for the injuries caused to others.[44]

*Intentional torts* occur when an employee engages in a voluntary act that has a substantial likelihood of resulting in injury to another; examples are assault and battery, false arrest and imprisonment, malicious prosecution, and abuse of process.

*Constitutional torts* involve employees' duty to recognize and uphold the constitutional rights, privileges, and immunities of others; violations of these guarantees may subject the employee to a civil suit, most frequently brought in federal court under 42 U.S. Code Section 1983.[45]

Assault, battery, false imprisonment, false arrest, invasion of privacy, negligence, defamation, and malicious prosecution are examples of torts that are commonly brought against police officers.[46] False arrest is the arrest of a person without probable cause. False imprisonment is the intentional illegal detention of a person, not only in jail but any confinement to a specified area. For example, the police may fail to release an arrested person after a proper bail or bond has been posted, they can delay the arraignment of an arrested person unreasonably, or authorities can fail to release a prisoner after they no longer have authority to hold him or her.[47]

A single act may also be a crime as well as a tort. If Officer Smith, in an unprovoked attack, injures Jones, the state will attempt to punish Smith in a *criminal* action by sending him to jail or prison, fining him, or both. The state would have the burden of proof at criminal trial, having to prove Smith guilty "beyond a reasonable doubt." Furthermore, Jones may sue Smith for money damages in a *civil* action for the personal injury he suffered. In this civil suit, Jones would have the burden of proving Smith's acts were tortious by a "preponderance of the evidence"—a lower standard than that in a criminal court and thus easier to satisfy.

## Section 1983 Legislation

Following the Civil War and in reaction to the activities of the Ku Klux Klan, Congress enacted the Ku Klux Klan Act of 1871, later codified as **Title 42, U.S. Code Section 1983.** It states that

> Every person who, under color of any statute, ordinance, regulation, custom, or usage of any State or Territory, subjects, or causes to be subjected, any citizen of the United States or any other person within the jurisdiction thereof to the deprivation of any rights, privileges, or immunities secured by the Constitution and laws, shall be liable to the party injured in an action at law, suit in equity, or other proper proceeding for redress.

This legislation was intended to provide civil rights protection to all "persons" protected under the act, when a defendant acted "under color of law" (misused power of office), and provided an avenue to the federal courts for relief of alleged civil rights violations.

Section 1983 also allows for a finding of personal liability on the part of police supervisory personnel for inadequate training or if it is proven that they knew, or should have known, of the misconduct of their officers yet failed to take corrective action and prevent future harm.

Such a case was *Brandon v. Allen*,[48] in which two teenagers parked in a "lovers' lane" were approached by an off-duty police officer, Allen, who showed his police identification and demanded that the male exit from the car. Allen struck the male with his fist and stabbed him with a knife and then attempted to break into the car where the female was seated. The young male was able to reenter the car and manage an escape. As the two teenagers sped off, Allen fired a shot at them with his revolver. The shattered windshield glass severely injured the youths to the point that they required plastic surgery. Allen was convicted of criminal charges, and the police chief was also sued under Section 1983. The plaintiffs charged that the chief and others knew of Allen's reputation as an unstable officer; none of the other police officers wished to ride in a patrol car with him. At least two formal charges of misconduct had been filed previously, yet the chief failed to take any remedial action or even to review the disciplinary records of officers when he became chief. The court called this behavior "unjustified inaction," held the police department liable, and allowed the plaintiffs damages. The U.S. Supreme Court upheld this judgment.[49]

Police supervisors have also been found liable for injuries arising out of an official policy or custom of their department. Injuries resulting from a chief's verbal or written support of heavy-handed behavior resulting in the use of excessive force by officers have resulted in such liability.[50]

Whereas Section 1983 is a civil action, Title 18, U.S. Code, Section 242, makes it a *criminal* offense for any person acting under color of law to violate another's civil rights. Section 242 not only applies to police officers, but also to the misconduct of public officials and to the prosecution of judges, bail bond agents, public defenders, and even prosecutors.

## New Areas of Potential Liability

In the 1990s, three areas of potential liability were established, which require knowledge on the part of police administrators: vehicle pursuits, handling computer evidence, and providing information to the public via press releases. A considerable amount of controversy has recently been generated regarding so-called "hot" or vehicle pursuits because of the tremendous potential for injury, property damage, and liability involved. Police administrators are revamping their policies and procedures accordingly. As one sheriff stated, "For so long, administrators thought there was really one lethal weapon they gave their officers, and that was the gun, and yet there was another weapon . . . their car."[51] As one police procedure manual describes it, "The decision by a police officer to pursue a citizen in a motor vehicle is among the most critical that can be made."[52] In sum, pursuit is justified only when the necessity of apprehension outweighs the degree of danger created by the pursuit. That is the reason why there is a nationwide trend by agencies to place more restrictions on pursuits and to have field supervisors (sergeants) call off the chase. It is not uncommon for agency policy to limit the pursuit to two pursuit vehicles: a supervisor and another vehicle authorized by a pursuit monitor.[53]

It is almost impossible today to investigate a fraud, embezzlement, or child pornography case without dealing with some sort of computer evidence. Many police agencies have recruited self-taught experts to fill the role of computer evidence specialists.[54] This increased exposure to computer evidence brings an increase in potential legal liabilities. For example, if a police agency seizes the computer records of an ongoing business, a negative financial impact on the operation of the business may result. Or if it can be shown that the police accidentally destroyed business records through negligence, a criminal investigation might well become the civil suit of the decade.[55] It is crucial that police administrators have personnel trained in the proper procedures for handling computers as well as rules of evidence.[56]

Disseminating public information is another concern. The Louisiana Supreme Court held that police department public information officers (PIOs) can be held liable for unfounded statements they make in news releases. The case involved a defamation suit against the state police, in which the PIO told a reporter that the defendant was running a large-scale illegal gambling operation and bilking customers. The court found that the PIO had no reasonable basis for saying the defendant had cheated customers and thus made injurious statements that he had no reason to believe were true. Although the ruling applies only to PIOs in Louisiana, it could grow to have national implications in the future.[57]

## *Liability of Corrections Personnel*

The liability of corrections workers often centers on their lack of due care for persons in their custody. This responsibility concerns primarily police officers and civilians responsible for inmates in local jails.

When an inmate commits suicide while in custody, police agencies are frequently—and often successfully—sued in state court under negligence and wrongful death claims. The standard used by the courts is whether the agency's act or failure to act created an unusual risk to an inmate. A "special duty" of care exists for police officers to protect inmates suffering from mental disorders and those who are impaired by drugs or alcohol. Foreseeability—the reasonable anticipation that injury or damage may occur—may be found when inmates make statements of intent to commit suicide, have a history of mental illness, are in a vulnerable emotional state, or are at a high level of intoxication or drug dependence.[58]

Suicides are not uncommon among jail inmates; each year, more than 300 jail inmates take their own lives.[59] Inmate suicide rates have also been found to be higher in small jails, and highest in small jails with lower population densities.[60] State courts generally recognize that police officials have a duty of care to persons in their custody.[61] Thus, jail administrators are ultimately responsible for taking reasonable precautions to ensure the health and safety of persons in their custody; they must protect inmates from harm, render medical assistance when necessary, and treat inmates humanely.[62]

Several court decisions have helped establish the duties and guidelines for jail employees concerning the care of their charges. An intoxicated inmate in possession of cigarettes and matches started a fire that resulted in his death; the court stated that "the prisoner may have been voluntarily drunk, but he was not in the cell voluntarily . . . [he] was helpless and the officer knew there was a means of harm on his person." The court concluded the police administration owed a greater duty of care to such an arrestee.[63] Emotionally disturbed arrestees can also create a greater duty for jail personnel. In an Alaskan case, a woman had been arrested for intoxication in a hotel and had trouble talking, standing, and walking; her blood-alcohol content was 0.26 percent. Two and a half hours after her incarceration, officers found her hanging by her sweater from mesh wiring in the cell. The Alaska Supreme Court said the officers knew she was depressed and that in the past few months, one of her sons had been burned to death, another son was stabbed to death, and her mother had died. Thus, the court believed officers should have anticipated her suicide.[64]

In New Mexico, a 17-year-old boy was arrested for armed robbery; he later told his mother he would kill himself before he would go to prison and subsequently tried to cut his wrists with an aluminum can top. The assistant chief ordered the officers to keep watch over him, but he was found dead by hanging the following morning. The state supreme court held that the knowledge officers possess is an important factor in determining liability and negligence in such cases.[65] In a New Jersey case, in which a young man arrested for intoxication was put in a holding cell but officers failed to remove the leather belt that he used to take his life, the court found the officers' conduct could have been a "substantial" factor in his death.[66]

Courts have also found the design of detention facilities as a source of negligence. A Detroit holding cell did not permit officers to observe inmates' movements unless the inmates were standing directly in front of the door, and no electronic monitoring devices were in use. A suicide in this facility led the court to hold that these conditions, and the absence of a detoxification cell, were proximate causes and constituted a building defect.[67] In another incident, an intoxicated college student was placed in a holding cell at the school's public safety building. Forty minutes after being placed in the cell, officers found the man hanging from an overhead heating device by a noose fashioned from his socks and belt. The court found the university liable for operating a defective building and awarded the plaintiff $650,000.[68]

The behavior of jail personnel *after* a suicide or attempted suicide may also indicate a breach of duty. Officers are expected to give all possible aid to an inmate who is injured or has attempted suicide. Thus, when officers found an inmate slumped in a chair with his belt around his neck and left him in that position instead of trying to revive him or call for medical assistance, the court ruled this behavior established a causal link between the officer's inaction and the boy's death.[69]

It is clear that correctional administrators must ensure that their organizations are cognizant of their legal responsibilities and expanded custodial role with their detainees.

# CASE STUDIES

The following two case studies will help the reader apply some of this chapter's materials to real-world issues involving employee rights, law, policy, and decisions concerning whether or not disciplinary action is warranted.

Chapter 5 discussed a relatively new area of law that police administrators must enforce: the 1996 Domestic Violence Offender Gun Ban, which bars police personnel from carrying firearms if they have a misdemeanor conviction for domestic violence. Consider the following situation, and determine how you, the administrator, would handle it from a disciplinary standpoint.

## Lost Love—and a Lost Laborer?

A police officer, Blake, is dispatched to a domestic violence call; on his arrival, a woman runs out of the house screaming, "Help me! He's going to kill me!" Her right eye is swollen. She also tells the officer, "I've had it with his drinking and womanizing and told him to pack up his things and go. That's when he began beating me."

You, a lieutenant, heard the call go out to Blake from Communications, but at shift's end you cannot find any offense report concerning the matter submitted by Blake. You ask Blake about the report, and he tells you that on entering the home, he observed another officer, Carter, who works in your agency, who commented, "Thanks for coming out here, but things are cool now. She slapped me once, and I dealt with it. I admit I got a little out of hand, but it's under control. She's nothing but a cheating, money-grubbing louse." Blake admits that he purposely avoided completing a report, deciding to consider it "like an offsetting penalty in football" and to overlook the matter.

### Questions for Discussion

1. What would you, as the lieutenant and shift commander, do about this situation?
2. Should you call the female victim, or Officer Carter, into your office for an interview?
3. What if you do bring them both in, separately, and they deny that the incident occurred?
4. What if you bring the woman in and, instead, she indicates that she wants to drop the matter, because "it's happened before"; do you go ahead and pursue it?
5. If you determine that Blake is in fact culpable for not reporting the incident, what actions (if any) would you take? On what grounds?

# Campus Conundrum

You are a new administrator in a medium-sized university police department. The campus normally has about 15,000 students, growing to about 25,000 people for home football games. It is a Saturday afternoon and there is such a game, with all police personnel being deployed in the stadium as is customary. Suddenly a sergeant (one who is popular and prone to dumping a load of trouble in your lap and then walking away) storms into your office. He reports that one of your officers—a younger one who has recently undergone a divorce and, as part of his new lifestyle, purchased a motorcycle—has appeared in the football stadium wearing an earring. You also learn that no formal dress code exists for the department.

## Questions for Discussion

1. Should the sergeant ignore the matter?
2. Do you tell the sergeant to have the officer remove the earring?
3. Do you summon the officer to your office (leaving fewer people for crowd control)?
4. What might be a compromise action, until the game is over or until a dress code is enacted?

# Summary

This chapter has examined three aspects of administration that pose serious challenges: discipline, liability, and labor relations. It is clear from this triad of issues that administrators need to understand the current and developing laws that serve to make criminal justice practitioners legally accountable; this need cannot be overstated. It is far better to learn the proper means of discipline, areas of liability, and effective collective bargaining methods through education and training than to learn about these issues as a defendant in a lawsuit.

Criminal justice executives need to be proactive and follow appropriate laws and guidelines as they recruit, hire, train, supervise, and negotiate with their subordinates in order to avoid legal difficulties; for administrators not to do so could place them and their jurisdiction at serious financial, legal, and moral risk.

# Questions for Review

1. List and describe the seven forms of disciplinary actions that may be taken against police officers.
2. Delineate the minimum due process requirements for discharging public employees.

3. Describe the benefits and functions of an early warning system (EWS) for identifying problem officers.

4. Explain the differences between positive and negative discipline.

5. Describe the categories of dispositions that are commonly used with complaints.

6. Provide an example of how a grievance may proceed through its various levels.

7. Explain how unionization began, and its contemporary influence in policing, the courts, and corrections.

8. Describe the three models of collective bargaining and the process that occurs when an impasse is reached.

9. Define tort, Section 1983, and *respondeat superior.*

10. Explain how the following three areas carry the potential for liability: pursuits, computer evidence, and release of public information.

## Notes

1. V. McLaughlin and R. Bing, "Law Enforcement Personnel Selection," *Journal of Police Science and Administration* 15 (1987):271-276.

2. Ibid.

3. *McNamara v. City of Chicago,* 700 F.Supp. 917 (N.D. Ill. 1988), at 919.

4. *White v. Thomas,* 660 F.2d 680 (5th Cir. 1981).

5. *Yarber v. Indiana State Prison,* 713 F.Supp. 271 (N.D. Ind. 1988).

6. Robert H. Chaires and Susan A. Lentz, "Criminal Justice Employee Rights: An Overview," *American Journal of Criminal Justice* 13 (April 1995):273-274.

7. M. Guthrie, "Using Automation to Apply Discipline Fairly," *FBI Law Enforcement Bulletin* 5 (1996):18-21.

8. Allen E. Wagner and Scott H. Decker, "Evaluating Citizen Complaints Against the Police," in R. G. Dunham and G. P. Alpert (eds.), *Critical Issues in Policing: Contemporary Readings* (Prospect Heights, Ill.: Waveland, 1997).

9. Wagner and Decker, "Evaluating Citizen Complaints Against the Police."

10. J. R. Dugan and D. R. Breda, "Complaints About Police Officers: A Comparison Among Types and Agencies," *Journal of Criminal Justice* 19 (1991):165-171.

11. Kim Michelle Lersch, "Police Misconduct and Malpractice: A Critical Analysis of Citizens' Complaints," *Policing* 21 (1998):80-96.

12. D. W. Perez, *Police Review Systems* (Washington, D.C.: Management Information Service, 1992).

13. W. Clinton Terry III, *Policing Society: An Occupational View* (New York: Wiley, 1985), p. 168.

14. Ibid., p. 168.

15. Ibid., pp. 170-171.

16. Samuel Walker, *The Police in America: An Introduction,* 3d ed. (Boston: McGraw-Hill, 1999), p. 368.

17. George F. Cole and Christopher E. Smith, *The American System of Criminal Justice,* 8th ed. (Belmont, Calif.: West/Wadsworth, 1998), p. 240.
18. Ibid., p. 318.
19. Harry W. More Jr., ed., *Critical Issues in Law Enforcement,* 4th ed. (Cincinnati, Ohio: Anderson, 1985), pp. 155–161.
20. Richard P. Seiter, *Correctional Administration: Integrating Theory and Practice* (Upper Saddle River, N.J.: Prentice Hall, 2002), pp. 333–334.
21. James B. Jacobs and Norma Meacham Crotty, *Guard Unions and the Future of Prisons* (Ithaca, N.Y.: Institute of Public Employment, 1978), p. 41.
22. James B. Jacobs, *New Perspectives on Prisons and Imprisonment* (Ithaca, N.Y.: Cornell University Press, 1983), p. 153.
23. Ibid., pp. 154–155.
24. Seiter, *Correctional Administration,* p. 337.
25. Ibid.
26. U.S. Department of Justice, National Institute of Law Enforcement and Criminal Justice, Trial Court Management Series, *Personnel Management* (Washington, D.C.: U.S. Government Printing Office, 1979), pp. 42–47.
27. Will Aitchison, *The Rights of Police Officers,* 3d ed. (Portland, Ore.: Labor Relations Information System, 1996), p. 7.
28. Ibid.
29. Ibid.
30. Ibid., p. 8.
31. Ibid., p. 9.
32. Charles R. Swanson, Leonard Territo, and Robert W. Taylor, *Police Administration: Structures, Processes, and Behavior,* 5th ed. (Upper Saddle River, N.J.: Prentice Hall, 2001), p. 411.
33. Ibid., pp. 415–416.
34. Arnold Zack, *Understanding Fact-Finding and Arbitration in the Public Sector* (Washington, D.C.: U.S. Government Printing Office, 1974), p. 1.
35. Thomas P. Gilroy and Anthony V. Sinicropi, "Impasse Resolution in Public Employment," *Industrial and Labor Relations Review* 25 (July 1971–1972):499.
36. Robert G. Howlett, "Fact Finding: Its Values and Limitations—Comment," Arbitration and the Expanded Role of Neutrals, Proceedings of the Twenty-third Annual Meeting of the National Academy of Arbitrators (Washington, D.C.: Bureau of National Affairs, 1970), p. 156.
37. Zack, *Understanding Fact-Finding,* p. 1.
38. Charles W. Maddox, *Collective Bargaining in Law Enforcement* (Springfield, Ill.: Charles C Thomas, 1975), p. 54.
39. Swanson, Territo, and Taylor, *Police Administration,* p. 422.
40. Ibid., p. 423.
41. Ibid., p. 424.
42. *Monell v. Department of Social Services,* 436 U.S. 658 (1978)
43. 610 F.2d 693 (10th Cir., 1979).
44. H. E. Barrineau III, *Civil Liability in Criminal Justice* (Cincinnati, Ohio: Pilgramage, 1987), p. 58.
45. Ibid., p. 5.
46. Swanson, Territo, and Taylor, *Police Administration,* p. 438.

47. Ibid.

48. 516 F.Supp. 1355 (W.D. Tenn., 1981).

49. *Brandon v. Holt,* 469 U.S. 464, 105 S.Ct. 873 (1985).

50. See, for example, *Black v. Stephens,* 662 F.2d 181 (1991).

51. Oklahoma County Sheriff John Whetsel, quoted in Nicole Marshall, "Hot Pursuit," *Tulsa World* (June 15, 1998):A11.

52. Ronald Palmer, Chief of Police, Tulsa, Oklahoma, Police Department Procedure Manual, June 10, 1998, p. 1.

53. Marshall, "Hot Pursuit," p. A11.

54. Michael R. Anderson, "Reducing Computer Evidence Liability," *Government Technology,* 10 (February 1997):24, 36.

55. Ibid.

56. Ibid.

57. "Be Careful What You Say," *Law Enforcement News* (December 15, 1997):1.

58. Victor E. Kappeler, *Critical Issues in Police Civil Liability,* 2d ed. (Prospect Heights, Ill.: Waveland, 1997), pp. 177–178.

59. U.S. Department of Justice, Bureau of Justice Statistics Web page, *Census of Jails, 1999.* http://www.ojp.usdoj.gov/bjs/ (accessed December 10, 2002).

60. U.S. Department of Justice, Bureau of Justice Statistics Special Report, *Population Density in Local Jails, 1988* (Washington, D.C.: U.S. Government Printing Office, 1991), p. 9.

61. Victor E. Kappeler and Rolando V. delCarmen, "Avoiding Police Liability for Negligent Failure to Prevent Suicide," *The Police Chief* (August 1991):53–59.

62. Ibid., p. 53.

63. *Thomas v. Williams.*

64. *Kanayurak v. North Slope Borough,* 677 P.2d 892 (Alaska 1984).

65. *City of Belen v. Harrell,* 603 P.2d 711 (N.M. 1979).

66. *Hake v. Manchester Township,* 486 A.2d 836 (N.J. 1985).

67. *Davis v. City of Detroit,* 386 N.W.2d 169 (Mich. App. 1986).

68. *Hickey v. Zezulka,* 443 N.W.2d 180 (Mich. App. 1989).

69. *Hake v. Manchester Township.*

# Chapter 16

# Financial Administration

## Key Terms and Concepts

Budget

Budget audit

Budget augmentation

Budget cycle

Budget execution

Budget formulation

Expenditure

Financial accountability

Line-item budgeting

Management accountability

Program accountability

## Learning Objectives

As a result of reading this chapter, the student will:

- be able to define the term *budget*
- understand the concepts of the budget cycle's four steps
- be familiar with the budgeting procedures in the police, courts, and corrections systems
- have examples of different ways in which monies may be acquired
- be able to distinguish between the three different budget formats and the advantages and disadvantages of each
- have examples of how budgets may be augmented

> *How pleasant it is to have money, heigh ho! How pleasant it is to have money.*
>
> —Arthur Hugh Clough

> *Money is like muck, not good except it be spread.*
>
> —Francis Bacon

# Introduction

The importance of financial administration to organizations in this country is unquestioned. Budgets are the key to financial administration; their development involves planning, organizing, directing, and other administrative functions. If unlimited funds were available, planning would not be needed. As Frederick Mosher observed, "Not least among the qualifications of an administrator is [one's] ability as a tactician and gladiator in the budget process."[1]

Just as individuals need to be responsible with their own finances to avoid legal and personal difficulties, so must governmental administrators be responsible stewards of the public's funds.

This chapter presents some of the fundamental elements of the control of fiscal resources through budgeting. It is not intended to prepare the reader to be an expert on fiscal management, but it provides an overview of some of the basic methods and issues surrounding financial administration.

Of the four component parts of financial administration—budgeting, auditing, accounting, and purchasing—budgeting is our primary focus. Included are discussions of budget definitions and uses; the influence of politics and fiscal realities in budgeting, which often lead to constricted financial conditions for the organization; the several elements of the budget process, including formulation, approval, execution, and audit; budget formats; and some strategies for augmenting criminal justice budgets in tight fiscal times.

The chapter concludes with a case study concerning fiscal exigency.

# The Budget

## *A Working Definition*

The word *budget* is derived from the old French *bougette*, meaning a small leather bag or wallet. Initially, it referred to the leather bag in which the chancellor of the exchequer carried documents stating the government's needs and resources to the English Parliament.[2] Later, it came to mean the documents themselves. More recently, **budget** has been defined as a plan stated in financial terms, an estimate of future expenditures, an asking price, a policy statement, the translation of financial resources into human purposes, and a contract between those who appropriate the funds and those who spend them.[3] To some extent, all of these definitions are valid.

In addition, the budget is a management tool, a process, and a political instrument. It is a "comprehensive plan, expressed in financial terms, by which a program is operated for a given period. It includes (1) the services, activities, and projects comprising the program; (2) the resultant expenditure requirements; and (3) the resources available for their support."[4] It is "a plan or schedule adjusting expenses during a certain period to the estimated income for that period."[5] Lester Bittel added:

> A budget is, literally, a financial standard for a particular operation, activity, program, or department. Its data is presented in numerical form, mainly in dollars . . . to be spent for a particular purpose—over a specified period of time. Budgets are derived from planning goals and forecasts.[6]

Although these descriptions are certainly apt, one writer warns that budgets contain an inherently irrational process: "Budgets are based on little more than the past and some guesses."[7]

Financial management of governmental agencies is clearly political. Anything the government does entails the expenditure of public funds.[8] Thus, the single most important political statement that any unit of government makes in a given year is its budget. Essentially, the budget causes administrators to follow the gambler's adage and "put your money where your mouth is."[9] When demands placed on government increase while funds are stable or decline, the competition for funds is keener than usual, forcing justice agencies to make the best case for their budgets. The heads of all departments, if they are doing their jobs well, are also vying for appropriations. Special interest groups, the media, politicians, and the public, with their own views and priorities, often engage in arm twisting during the budgeting process.

# Elements of a Budget

## *The Budget Cycle*

Administrators must think in terms of a **budget cycle,** which in government (and, therefore, all public criminal justice agencies) is typically on a fiscal year basis. Some states have a biennial budget cycle; their legislatures, such as those in Kentucky and Nevada, budget for a two-year period. Normally, however, the fiscal year is a 12-month period that may coincide with a calendar year or, more commonly, will run from July 1 through June 30 of the following year. The federal government's fiscal year is October 1 through September 30. The budget cycle is important because it drives the development of the budget and determines when new monies become available.

The budget cycle consists of four sequential steps, repeated every year at about the same point in time: (1) budget formulation, (2) budget approval, (3) budget execution, and (4) budget audit.

## *Budget Formulation*

Depending on the size and complexity of the organization and the financial condition of the jurisdiction, **budget formulation** can be a relatively simple or exceedingly difficult task; in either case, it is likely to be the most complicated stage of the budgeting process. The administrator must anticipate all types of costs (overtime, gasoline, postage, maintenance contracts) and predict expenses related to major incidents or events that might arise. Certain assumptions based on the previous year's budget can be made, but they are not necessarily accurate. One observer noted that "every expense you budget should be fully supported with the proper and most logical assumptions you can develop. Avoid simply estimating, which is the least supportable form of budgeting."[10] Another criminal justice administrator, discussing budget formulation, added that

> The most important ingredient for any budgeting process is planning. [Administrators] should approach the budget process from the planning standpoint of "How can I best reconcile the [criminal justice] needs of the community with the ability of my jurisdiction to finance them, and then relate those plans in a convincing manner to my governing body for proper financing and execution of programs?" After all, as budget review occurs, the document is taken apart and scrutinized piece by piece or line by line. This fragmentation approach contributes significantly to our inability to defend interrelated programs in an overall budget package.[11]

To illustrate, let us assume that a police department budget is being prepared in a city having a manager form of government. Long before a criminal justice agency (or any other unit of local government) begins to prepare its annual budget, the city manager and/or the staff of the city has made revenue forecasts, considered how much (if any) of the current operating budget will be carried over into the next fiscal year, analyzed how the population of the jurisdiction will grow or shift (affecting demand for public services), and examined other priorities for the coming year. The city manager may also appear before the governing board to obtain information about its fiscal priorities, spending levels, pay raises, new positions, programs, and so on. The city manager may then send all department heads a memorandum outlining the general fiscal guidelines to be followed in preparing their budgets.

On receipt of the city's guidelines for preparing its budget, the heads of functional areas, such as the chief of police, have a planning and research unit (assuming a city large enough to have this level of specialization) prepare an internal budget calendar and an internal fiscal policy memorandum. (Table 16.1 shows an internal budget calendar for a large municipal police department.) This memo may include input from unions and lower supervisory personnel. Each bureau is then given the responsibility for preparing its individual budget request.

In small police departments with little or no functional specialization, the chief may prepare the budget alone or with input from other officers or the city finance officer. In some small agencies, chiefs and sheriffs may not even see their budget or assist in its preparation. Because of tradition, politics, or even

**TABLE 16.1** Budget Preparation Calendar for a Large Police Department

| WHAT SHOULD BE DONE | BY WHOM | ON THESE DATES |
|---|---|---|
| Issue budget instructions and applicable forms | City administrator | November 1 |
| Prepare and issue budget message, with instructions and applicable forms, to unit commanders | Chief of police | November 15 |
| Develop unit budgets with appropriate justification and forward recommended budgets to planning and research unit | Unit commanders | February 1 |
| Review unit budget | Planning and research staff with unit commanders | March 1 |
| Consolidate unit budgets for presentation to chief of police | Planning and research unit | March 15 |
| Review consolidated recommended budget | Chief of police, planning and research staff, and unit commanders | March 30 |
| Obtain department approval of budget | Chief of police | April 15 |
| Forward recommended budget to city administrator | Chief of police | April 20 |
| Review recommended budget by administration | City administrator and chief of police | April 30 |
| Approve revised budget | City administrator | May 5 |
| Forward budget document to city council | City administrator | May 10 |
| Review budget | Budget officer of city council | May 20 |
| Present to council | City administrator and chief of police | June 1 |
| Report back to city administrator | City council | June 5 |
| Review and resubmit to city council | City administrator and chief of police | June 10 |
| Take final action on police budget | City council | June 20 |

Source: National Advisory Commission on Criminal Justice Standards and Goals, *Police*, Washington, D.C.: U.S. Government Printing Office, 1973, p. 137.

laziness, the administrator has abdicated control over the budget. This puts the agency in a precarious position indeed; it will have difficulty engaging in long-term planning and spending money productively for personnel and programs when the executive has to get prior approval from the governing body to buy items such as office supplies.

The planning and research unit then reviews the bureau's budget request for compliance with the budgeting instructions and the chief's and city manager's priorities. Eventually, a consolidated budget is developed for the entire police department and submitted to the chief, who may meet with the planning and research unit and bureau commanders to discuss it. Personalities, politics, priorities, personal agendas, and other issues may need to be addressed; the chief may have to mediate disagreements concerning these matters, sometimes rewarding the loyal and sometimes reducing allotments to the disloyal.[12] Requests for programs, equipment, travel expenses, personnel, or anything else in the draft budget may be deleted, reduced, or enhanced.

The budget is then presented to the city manager. At this point, the chief executive's reputation as a budget framer becomes a factor. If the chief is known to pad the budget heavily, the city manager is far more likely to cut the department's request than if the chief is known to be reasonable in making budget requests, engages in innovative planning, and has a flexible approach to budget negotiations.

The city manager consolidates the police budget request with those from other municipal department heads and then meets with them individually to discuss their requests further. The city manager directs the city finance officer to make any necessary additions or cuts and then to prepare a budget proposal for presentation to the governing body.

The general steps in budget development are shown in Exhibit 16.1.

The courts have a similar budgetary process. In a large court, the process may include five major procedures: (1) developing an internal budgetary policy, (2) reviewing budget submissions, (3) developing a financial strategy, (4) presenting the budget, and (5) monitoring the budget. Figure 16.1 illustrates the relationship of the steps in the process.

## Budget Approval

With the city manager's proposed budget request in hand, the governing board begins its deliberations on the citywide budget. The city manager may appear before the board to answer questions concerning the budget; individual department heads also may be asked to appear. Suggestions for getting monies approved and appropriated include the following:

1. Have a carefully justified budget.
2. Anticipate the environment of the budget hearing by reading news reports and understanding the priorities of the council members. Know what types of questions elected officials are likely to ask.

## Exhibit **16.1**
## Steps in Budget Development

Hal Rubin described how the $550 million budget for the California Highway Patrol (CHP) is typically developed. According to the budget section, "It's an all-year and year-on-year process" that begins at the level of the 99 area commands, where budget requests originate. The requests are dealt with in one of three ways: (1) funded within the department's base budget, (2) disapproved, or (3) carried forward for review by CHP personnel.

At the division level, managers review the area requests, make needed adjustments, and submit a consolidated request to the budget section at headquarters. This section passes input from the field to individual section management staff (e.g., planning and analysis, personnel, training, and communications) for review. Budget section staff meet with individual section management staff. Within two or three months, the budget section identifies proposals for new funding that have department-wide impact and passes them on to the executive level.

The commissioner and aides review the figures along with those from other state departments and agree on a budget to submit to the governor. The governor submits this budget to the legislature, which acts on it and returns it to the governor for signature.

*Source:* Hal Rubin, "Working Out a Budget," *Law and Order* (May 1989):27–28.

3. Determine which "public" will be at the police department's budget hearing and prepare accordingly. Public issues change from time to time; citizens who were outraged over one issue one year may be incensed by another the next.

4. Make good use of graphics in the form of pie charts and histograms but be selective and do not go overboard. Short case studies of successes are normal and add to graphics.

5. Rehearse and critique the presentation many times.

6. Be a political realist.[13]

After everyone scheduled has spoken, the city council gives directions to the city manager to make further cuts in the budget or to reinstate funds or programs cut earlier, and so on. The budget is then approved. It is fair to say that at this stage, budgeting is largely a legislative function that requires some legal action, as a special ordinance or resolution approving the budget is passed each year by the governing board.

The column headings in Table 16.2 indicate (1) the budget amount requested by the chief of police, (2) the amount recommended by the city manager, and (3) the amount finally approved by the city council.

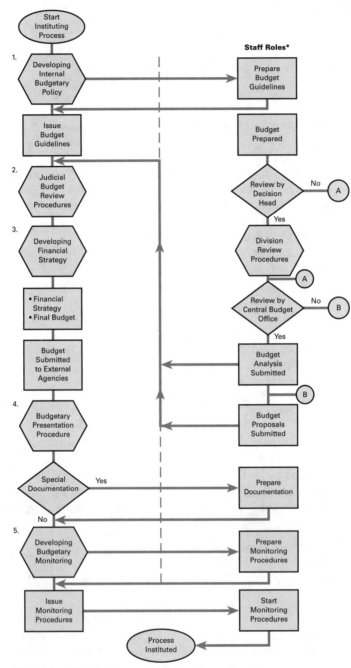

**Figure 16.1**

Steps in a judicial budgetary process.

**TABLE 16.2** Police Operating Budget in a Community of 150,000 Population

| DESCRIPTION | FY 2001–2002 EXPENSES | FY 2002–2003 EXPENSES | FY 2003–2004 DEPT. REQ. | CITY MANAGER | CITY COUNCIL |
|---|---|---|---|---|---|
| **Salaries/Wages** | | | | | |
| Reg. salaries | $14,315,764 | $14,392,639 | $16,221,148 | $16,221,148 | $16,221,148 |
| Overtime | 988,165 | 782,421 | 951,875 | 951,875 | 711,875 |
| Severence pay | 36,194 | 226,465 | 82,000 | –0– | –0– |
| Holiday pay | 395,952 | 591,158 | 698,958 | 698,958 | 698,958 |
| Call back pay | 45,499 | 49,833 | 49,555 | 49,555 | 49,555 |
| Subtotals | 15,781,574 | 16,042,516 | 18,003,536 | 17,921,536 | 17,681,536 |
| **Employee benefits** | | | | | |
| Retirement | 3,345,566 | 3,485,888 | 4,069,521 | 4,069,521 | 4,069,521 |
| Group ins. | 1,256,663 | 1,467,406 | 1,752,718 | 1,752,718 | 1,752,718 |
| Life ins. | 43,797 | 53,164 | 117,590 | 117,396 | 117,396 |
| Disability ins. | 726,885 | 794,686 | 1,346,909 | 1,346,038 | 1,024,398 |
| Uniform allowance | 188,079 | 193,827 | 196,750 | 196,750 | 196,750 |
| Medicare | 77,730 | 80,868 | 100,058 | 99,739 | 99,739 |
| Long-term dis. | 11,583 | 21,974 | 48,517 | 48,517 | 48,517 |
| Subtotals | 5,650,303 | 6,097,813 | 7,583,546 | 7,630,679 | 7,309,039 |
| **Services and supplies** | | | | | |
| Office supp. | 62,357 | 49,292 | 51,485 | 51,485 | 51,485 |
| Operating supp. | 227,563 | 148,569 | 270,661 | 270,661 | 270,661 |
| Repair/Maint. | 248,922 | 195,941 | 233,118 | 233,118 | 233,118 |
| Small tools | 49,508 | 788 | 12,175 | 12,175 | 12,175 |
| Prof. serv. | 337,263 | 290,359 | 334,765 | 334,765 | 334,765 |

*(table continues)*

**TABLE 16.2** *(continued)*

| DESCRIPTION | FY 2001–2002 EXPENSES | FY 2002–2003 EXPENSES | FY 2003–2004 DEPT. REQ. | CITY MANAGER | CITY COUNCIL |
|---|---|---|---|---|---|
| Communication | 287,757 | 223,200 | 392,906 | 392,906 | 392,906 |
| Public utility | 111,935 | 116,773 | 121,008 | 121,008 | 121,008 |
| Rentals | 81,840 | 96,294 | 113,071 | 113,071 | 113,071 |
| Vehicle rental | 834,416 | 1,193,926 | 1,363,278 | 1,363,278 | 1,169,278 |
| Extradition | 20,955 | 22,411 | 20,000 | 20,000 | 20,000 |
| Other travel | 4,649 | 5,123 | 23,500 | 23,500 | 23,500 |
| Advertising | 2,662 | 2,570 | 4,100 | 4,100 | 4,100 |
| Insurance | 328,360 | 595,257 | 942,921 | 942,921 | 942,921 |
| Books/Manuals | 16,285 | 12,813 | 12,404 | 12,404 | 12,404 |
| Employee training | 47,029 | 30,851 | -0- | -0- | -0- |
| Aircraft exp. | -0- | -0- | 15,000 | 15,000 | 15,000 |
| Special inv. | 11,527 | 13,465 | 15,000 | 15,000 | 15,000 |
| Other serv. & supplies | 1,386,201 | 1,039,651 | 1,386,201 | 1,386,201 | 1,386,201 |
| Subtotals | 4,059,229 | 4,037,283 | 5,311,593 | 5,311,593 | 5,117,593 |
| **Capital outlay** | | | | | |
| Machinery and equipment | 572,301 | 102,964 | -0- | -0- | -0- |
| Totals | $26,063,407 | $26,280,576 | $30,898,675 | $30,863,808 | $30,108,168 |

## Budget Execution

The third stage of the process, **budget execution,** has several objectives: (1) to carry out the police department's budgeted objectives for the fiscal year in an orderly manner, (2) to ensure that the department undertakes no financial obligations or commitments other than those funded by the city council, and (3) to provide a periodic accounting of the administrator's stewardship over the department's funds.[14]

Supervision of the budget execution phase is an executive function that requires some type of fiscal control system, usually directed by the city or county manager. Periodic reports on accounts are an important element of budget control; they serve to reduce the likelihood of overspending by identifying areas in which deficits are likely to occur as a result of change in gasoline prices, extensive overtime, natural disasters, and unplanned emergencies (such as riots). A periodic budget status report informs the administrator what percentage of the total budget has been expended to date (Table 16.3).

Prudent administrators normally attempt to manage the budget conservatively for the first eight or nine months of the budget year, holding the line on spending until most fiscal crises have been averted. Because unplanned incidents and natural disasters can wreak havoc with any budget, this conservatism is normally the best course. Then the administrator can plan the most efficient way to allocate funds if emergency funds have not been spent.

## The Audit

The word *audit* means to verify something independently.[15] The basic rationale for an audit has been described by the comptroller general of the United States as follows:

> Governments and agencies entrusted with public resources and the authority for applying them have a responsibility to render a full accounting of their activities. This accountability is inherent in the governmental process and is not always specifically identified by legislative provision. This governmental accountability should identify not only the object for which the public resources have been devoted but also the manner and effect of their application.[16]

After the close of each budget year, the year's **expenditures** are audited to ensure that the agency spent its funds properly. **Budget audits** are designed to investigate three broad areas of accountability: **financial accountability** (focusing on proper fiscal operations and reports of the justice agency), **management accountability** (determining whether funds were utilized efficiently and economically), and **program accountability** (determining whether the city council's goals and objectives were accomplished).[17]

Financial audits determine whether funds were spent legally, the budgeted amount was exceeded, and the financial process proceeded in a legal manner. For example, auditors investigate whether funds transferred between accounts

**TABLE 16.3** A Police Department's Budget Status Report

| LINE ITEM | AMOUNT BUDGETED | EXPENSES TO DATE | AMOUNT ENCUMBERED | BALANCE TO DATE | PERCENTAGE USED |
|---|---|---|---|---|---|
| Salaries | $16,221,148 | $8,427,062.00 | -0- | $7,794,086.00 | 52.0 |
| Professional services | 334,765 | 187,219.61 | $8,014.22 | 139,531.17 | 58.3 |
| Office supplies | 51,485 | 16,942.22 | 3,476.19 | 31,066.59 | 39.7 |
| Repair/Maintenance | 49,317 | 20,962.53 | 1,111.13 | 27,243.34 | 44.8 |
| Communication | 392,906 | 212,099.11 | 1,560.03 | 179,246.86 | 54.4 |
| Utilities | 121,008 | 50,006.15 | 10,952.42 | 60,049.43 | 51.4 |
| Vehicle rental | 1,169,278 | 492,616.22 | 103,066.19 | 573,595.59 | 51.9 |
| Travel | 23,500 | 6,119.22 | 2,044.63 | 15,336.15 | 34.7 |
| Extraditions | 20,000 | 12,042.19 | 262.22 | 7,695.59 | 61.5 |
| Printing/Binding | 36,765 | 15,114.14 | 2,662.67 | 18,988.19 | 48.4 |
| Books/Manuals | 12,404 | 5,444.11 | 614.11 | 6,345.78 | 48.8 |
| Training/Education | 35,695 | 19,661.54 | 119.14 | 15,914.32 | 55.4 |
| Aircraft expense | 15,000 | 8,112.15 | 579.22 | 6,308.63 | 57.9 |
| Special investigation | 15,000 | 6,115.75 | 960.50 | 7,922.75 | 47.2 |
| Machinery | 1,000 | 275.27 | 27.50 | 697.23 | 30.3 |
| Advertising | 4,100 | 1,119.17 | 142.50 | 2,838.33 | 30.8 |

were authorized, grant funds were used properly, computations were made accurately, disbursements were documented, financial transactions followed established procedures, and established competitive bidding procedures were employed.[18]

Justice administrators should welcome auditors' help to identify weaknesses and deficiencies and correct them.

# Budget Formats

The three types of budgets primarily in use today are the line-item (or object-of-expenditure) budget, the performance budget, and the program (or results or outcomes) budget. Two additional types, the planning-programming-budgeting system (PPBS) and the zero-based budget (ZBB), are discussed in the literature but are used to a lesser extent.

## *The Line-Item Budget*

**Line-item** (or object) **budgeting** is the most commonly used budget format. It is the basic system on which all other systems rely because it affords control. It is so named because it breaks down the budget into the major categories commonly used in government (e.g., personnel, equipment, contractual services, commodities, and capital outlay items); every amount of money requested, recommended, appropriated, and expended is associated with a particular item or class of items.[19] In addition, large budget categories will be broken down into smaller line-item budgets (in a police department, examples would include patrol, investigation, communications, or jail function). The line-item format fosters budgetary control because no item escapes scrutiny.[20] Table 16.2 showed a line-item budget for police; see Table 16.4 for a court, Table 16.5 for probation and parole, and Table 16.6 for state prison organizations. Each demonstrates the range of activities and funding needs of each agency. Note in Tables 16.2, 16.5, and 16.6 how a recession affected budgets and requests from year to year in many categories, resulting in severe cuts and even total elimination of items previously funded. Also note some of the ways in which administrators are deviating from the norm in order to save money (e.g., the police budget shows that the department found it to be less expensive to lease its patrol vehicles rather than to buy a huge fleet of its own).

The line-item budget has several strengths and weaknesses. Its strengths include ease of control development, comprehension (especially by elected and other executive branch officials), and administration. Weaknesses are its neglect of long-range planning and its limited ability to evaluate performance. Furthermore, the line-item budget tends to maintain the status quo; ongoing programs are seldom challenged. Line-item budgets are based on history: This year's allocation is based on last year's. Although that allows an inexperienced manager to prepare a budget more easily, it often precludes the reform-minded chief's careful deliberation and planning for the future.

**TABLE 16.4** Operating Budget for a District Court in a County of 300,000 Population

| CATEGORIES | AMOUNTS |
|---|---|
| **Salaries and wages** | |
| Regular salaries | $2,180,792 |
| Part-time temporary | 9,749 |
| Incentive/Longevity | 50,850 |
| Subtotal | $2,241,391 |
| **Employee benefits** | |
| Group insurance | 170,100 |
| Worker comp. | 8,470 |
| Unemployment comp. | 3,220 |
| Retirement | 412,211 |
| Social security | 605 |
| Medicare | 13,503 |
| Subtotal | $608,109 |
| **Services and supplies** | |
| Computers and office equipment | 22,865 |
| Service contracts | 2,000 |
| Minor furniture/Equipment | 1,000 |
| Computer supplies | 10,000 |
| Continuous forms | 4,000 |
| Office supplies | 36,066 |
| Advertising | 50 |
| Copy machine expense | 40,000 |
| Dues and registration | 4,000 |
| Printing | 24,000 |
| Telephone | 16,000 |
| Training | 2,000 |
| Court reporter/Transcript | 235,000 |
| Court reporter per diem | 265,000 |
| Law books/Supplements | 9,000 |
| Jury trials | 75,000 |
| Medical examinations | 80,000 |
| Computerized legal research | 20,000 |
| Travel | 1,500 |
| Subtotal | $847,481 |
| **Child support** | |
| Attorneys and other personnel | $66,480 |
| Court-appointed attorneys | 656,000 |
| Grand juries | 18,600 |
| Family court services | 762,841 |
| Total | $5,200,902 |

**TABLE 16.5** Probation and Parole Budget for a State Serving 3 Million Population

| DESCRIPTION | FY 2001–2002 ACTUAL | FY 2002–2003 AGENCY REQ. | FY 2003–2004 GOV. RECOMM. | LEGIS. APPROVAL |
|---|---|---|---|---|
| Personnel | $13,741,104 | $14,290,523 | $13,620,991 | $13,540,222 |
| Travel | 412,588 | 412,588 | 412,588 | 401,689 |
| Operating expenses | 1,307,020 | 1,395,484 | 1,307,020 | 1,256,787 |
| Equipment | 10,569 | 4,379 | 4,379 | 4,379 |
| Loans to parolees | 4,500 | 4,500 | 4,500 | 4,500 |
| Training | 9,073 | 9,073 | 9,073 | 9,073 |
| Extraditions | 200,000 | 200,000 | 200,000 | 185,000 |
| Client drug tests | 112,962 | 112,962 | 112,962 | 112,962 |
| Home arrest fees | 114,005 | 114,005 | 114,005 | 114,005 |
| Community programs | 50,000 | 50,000 | 50,000 | 47,500 |
| Residential confinement | 496,709 | 500,709 | 496,709 | 487,663 |
| Utilities (paid by building lessors) | | | | |
| Totals | $16,458,530 | $17,094,223 | $16,332,227 | $16,163,780 |

**TABLE 16.6** Operating Budget for a State Medium Security Prison with 1,000 Inmates

| DESCRIPTION | FY 2001–2002 ACTUAL | FY 2002–2003 AGENCY REQ. | FY 2003–2004 GOV. RECOMM. | LEGISLATURE APPROVED |
|---|---|---|---|---|
| **Personnel** | | | | |
| Salaries | $5,051,095 | $5,370,979 | $5,186,421 | $5,105,533 |
| Worker's comp. | 184,362 | 143,462 | 201,198 | 198,016 |
| Retirement | 1,142,010 | 1,174,968 | 1,215,674 | 1,196,028 |
| Recruit tests | 49,447 | 51,528 | 45,692 | 44,972 |
| Insurance | 474,330 | 488,250 | 513,000 | 500,175 |
| Retirement ins. | 30,963 | 31,872 | 35,917 | 35,349 |
| Unemployment comp. | 6,003 | 6,383 | 6,162 | 6,065 |
| Overtime | 165,856 | -0- | -0- | -0- |
| Holiday pay | 150,519 | 158,500 | 154,643 | 151,936 |
| Medicare | 39,965 | 45,140 | 42,225 | 40,948 |
| Shift differential | 95,925 | 101,011 | 98,553 | 96,828 |
| Standby pay | 6,465 | 6,807 | 6,641 | 6,526 |
| Longevity pay | 18,095 | 18,095 | 18,095 | 18,095 |
| Subtotals | $7,415,035 | $7,596,995 | $7,524,221 | $7,400,471 |
| **Services and supplies** | | | | |
| Operating supplies | $180,672 | $277,495 | $180,647 | $214,859 |
| Communications/freight | 4,877 | 5,314 | 5,023 | 5,023 |

| | | | | |
|---|---|---|---|---|
| Printing/copying | 20,900 | 47,222 | 19,016 | 21,527 |
| Equipment repair | 14,385 | 13,542 | 14,817 | 14,817 |
| Vehicle operation | 20,405 | 21,601 | 21,016 | 21,016 |
| Uniforms—custody | 118,122 | 105,976 | 103,237 | 113,856 |
| Inmate clothing | 72,436 | 184,790 | 72,430 | 86,167 |
| Equipment issued | 20,403 | 13,236 | 15,451 | 17,086 |
| Inmate wages | 36,645 | 52,815 | 35,572 | 42,309 |
| Food | 895,897 | 1,299,838 | 895,759 | 1,065,403 |
| Postage | 7,738 | 8,793 | 7,036 | 7,738 |
| Telephone | 24,808 | 23,802 | 22,130 | 24,808 |
| Subscriptions | 382 | 401 | 725 | 401 |
| Hand tools | 110 | 286 | 113 | 113 |
| Subtotals | $1,417,780 | $2,055,111 | $1,392,972 | $1,635,123 |
| **Special equipment** | $116,863 | $34,088 | $12,557 | $13,661 |
| Grounds maint. | 150,098 | 209,003 | 138,560 | 185,843 |
| Inmate law library | 18,564 | 20,115 | 16,419 | 21,836 |
| Special projects | 53,237 | 8,887 | 8,887 | 8,887 |
| Gas and power | 554,478 | 586,604 | 505,823 | 604,335 |
| Water | 60,390 | 69,377 | 52,266 | 67,171 |
| Garbage | 80,035 | 101,240 | 82,436 | 82,436 |
| Canine unit | 13,936 | 2,521 | 4,260 | 2,543 |
| Total | $9,880,416 | $10,683,941 | $9,738,401 | $10,022,306 |

The line-item budget provides ease of control because it clearly indicates the amount budgeted for each item, the amount expended as of a specific date, and the amount still available at that date. (See, for example, Table 16.3.)

Virtually all criminal justice agencies are automated to some extent, whether the financial officer prepares his or her budget using a computerized spreadsheet or a clerk enters information onto a database that will be uploaded to a state's mainframe computer. Some justice agencies use an automated budgeting system (ABS) that can store budget figures, make all necessary calculations for generating a budget request, monitor expenditures from budgets (similar to that shown in Table 16.6), and even generate some reports.

## *The Performance Budget*

The key characteristic of a performance budget is that it relates the volume of work to be done to the amount of money spent.[21] It is input-output oriented, and it increases the responsibility and accountability of the manager for output as opposed to input.[22] This format specifies an organization's activities, using a format similar to that of the line-item budget. It normally measures activities that are easily quantified, such as numbers of traffic citations issued, crimes solved, property recovered, cases heard in the courtroom, and caseloads of probation officers. These activities are then compared to those of the unit that performs the most. This ranking according to activity attempts to allocate funds fairly. Following is an example from a police department: The commander of the traffic accident investigation unit requests an additional three investigators, which the chief approves. Later, the chief might compare the unit's output and costs of the unit to these measures before the three investigators were added to determine how this change affected productivity.[23] An example of the police performance budget is provided in Table 16.7.

The performance budget format could be used in other justice system components as well. The courts could use such performance measures as filing cases, writing opinions, disposing of cases, and accuracy of presentence investigations.

Advantages of the performance budget include a consideration of outputs, the establishment of the costs of various justice agency efforts, improved evaluation of programs and managers, an emphasis on efficiency, increased availability of information for decision making, and the enhancement of budget justification and explanation.[24] The performance budget works best for an assembly line or other organization where work is easily quantifiable, such as paving streets. Its disadvantages include its expense to develop, implement, and operate because of the extensive use of cost accounting techniques and the need for additional staff (Figure 16.2 illustrates the elements used to determine the cost of providing police services); the controversy surrounding attempts to determine appropriate workload and unit cost measures (in criminal justice, although many functions are quantifiable, such reduction of duties to numbers often translates to quotas,

**TABLE 16.7**   Example of a Police Performance Budget

| TOTAL BUDGET | | $ |
|---|---|---|
| **Units/Activities** | | |
| Administration (chief) | Subtotal | $ |
| Strategic planning | | $ |
| Normative planning | | $ |
| Policies and procedures formulation | | $ |
| Etc. | | |
| **Patrol** | Subtotal | $ |
| Calls for service | | $ |
| Citizen contacts | | $ |
| Special details | | $ |
| Etc. | | |
| **Criminal investigation** | Subtotal | $ |
| Suspect apprehension | | $ |
| Recovery of stolen property | | $ |
| Transportation of fugitives | | $ |
| Etc. | | |
| **Traffic services** | Subtotal | $ |
| Accident investigation | | $ |
| Issuance of citations | | $ |
| Public safety speeches | | $ |
| Etc. | | |
| **Juvenile services** | Subtotal | $ |
| Locate runaways/missing juveniles | | $ |
| Arrest of offenders | | $ |
| Referrals and liaison | | $ |
| Etc. | | |
| **Research and development** | Subtotal | $ |
| Perform crime analysis | | $ |
| Prepare annual budget | | $ |
| Prepare annual reports | | $ |
| Etc. | | |

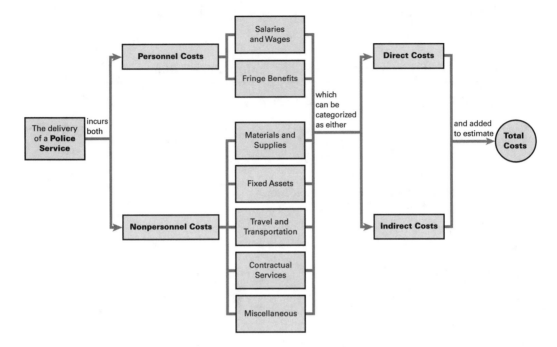

**Figure 16.2**

Elements in the total costs for police services. *Source:* U.S. Department of Justice, National Institute of Justice, *Measuring the Costs of Police Services* (Washington, D.C.: Author, 1982), p. 20.

which are anathema to many people); its emphasis on efficiency rather than effectiveness; and the failure to lend itself to long-range planning.[25]

Determining which functions in criminal justice are more important (and should receive more financial support) is difficult. Therefore, in terms of criminal justice agency budgets, the selection of meaningful work units is difficult and sometimes irrational. How can a justice agency measure its successes? How can it count what does not happen?

## *The Program Budget*

The best-known budget for monitoring the activities of an organization is the *program budget,* developed by the RAND Corporation for the U.S. Department of Defense. This format examines cost units as units of activity rather than as units and subunits within the organization. This budget becomes a planning tool; it demands justification for expenditures for new programs and for deleting old ones that have not met their objectives.

A police agency probably has greater opportunities for creating new community-based programs than do the courts or corrections agencies. Some of these include crime prevention and investigation, drug abuse education, home security, selective enforcement (e.g., drunk driving) programs, and career development for personnel. Each of these endeavors requires instructional materials or special equipment, all of which must be budgeted. For example, traffic accident investigation (TAI) may be a cost area. The program budget emphasizes output measures. Outputs for TAI include the number of accidents worked and enforcement measures taken (such as citations issued, DUI and other arrests made, and public safety speeches given). If the budget for these programs were divided by the units of output, the administrator could determine the relative cost for each unit of output or productivity. The cost of TAI, however, entails more than just the TAI unit; patrol and other support units also engage in this program.

Thus, the program budget is an extremely difficult form to execute and administer because it requires tracking the time of all personnel by activity as well as figuring in the cost of all support services and supplies. For this reason, criminal justice agencies rarely use the program budget.[26] Examples of police and court program budgets are presented in Tables 16.8 and 16.9. Other disadvantages include its cost in terms of time and money to develop, implement, and administer; the difficulty of developing objectives and performance measures; the high cost of data collection; and the resistance of agency managers to developing the skills necessary for directing large-scale, complex programs.[27]

Some advantages of the program budget include its emphasis on the social utility of programs conducted by the agency; its clear relationship between policy objectives and expenditures; its ability to provide justification and explanation of the budget; its establishment of a high degree of accountability; and its format and the wide involvement in formulating objectives, which lead employees at all levels of the organization to understand more thoroughly the importance of their roles and actions.

## PPBS and Zero-Based Budgeting Formats

General Motors used the planning-programming-budgeting system (PPBS) as early as 1924,[28] and the RAND Corporation contributed to its development in a series of studies dating from 1949.[29] By the mid-1950s, several states were using it, and Secretary Robert McNamara introduced PPBS into the Defense Department in the mid-1960s.[30] By 1971, a survey revealed, however, that only 28 percent of the cities and 21 percent of the counties contacted had implemented PPBS or significant elements of it;[31] and in 1971, the federal government announced that it was discontinuing its use.

PPBS treated the three basic budget processes—planning, management, and control—as co-equals. It was predicated on the primacy of planning.[32] This future orientation transformed budgeting from an annual ritual to a "formulation of future goals and policies."[33] The PPBS budget featured a program structure, zero-based budgeting, the use of cost-budget analysis to distinguish between alternatives, and a budgetary horizon, often five years.[34]

**TABLE 16.8**   Example of a Police Program Budget

| *TOTAL BUDGET* | | *$* |
|---|---|---|
| **Program Area** | | |
| Crime prevention | Subtotal | $ |
| Salaries and benefits | | $ |
| Operating expenses | | $ |
| Capital outlay | | $ |
| Miscellaneous | | $ |
| Traffic accident investigation | Subtotal | $ |
| Salaries and benefits | | $ |
| Operating expenses | | $ |
| Capital outlay | | $ |
| Miscellaneous | | $ |
| Traffic accident prevention | Subtotal | $ |
| Salaries and benefits | | $ |
| Operating expenses | | $ |
| Capital outlay | | $ |
| Miscellaneous | | $ |
| Criminal investigation | Subtotal | $ |
| Salaries and benefits | | $ |
| Operating expenses | | $ |
| Capital outlay | | $ |
| Miscellaneous | | $ |
| Juvenile delinquency prevention | Subtotal | $ |
| Salaries and benefits | | $ |
| Operating expenses | | $ |
| Capital outlay | | $ |
| Miscellaneous | | $ |
| Special investigations | Subtotal | $ |
| Salaries and benefits | | $ |
| Operating expenses | | $ |
| Capital outlay | | $ |
| Miscellaneous | | $ |
| Etc. | | |

Associated with PPBS, the zero-based planning and budgeting process requires managers to justify their entire budget request in detail rather than simply to refer to budget amounts established in previous years.[35] That is, each year all budgets begin at zero and must justify any funding. Following Peter Phyrr's use of zero-based budgeting at Texas Instruments, Governor Jimmy Carter adopted it

**TABLE 16.9**   Example of a Court's Program Budget

| TOTAL BUDGET | | $ |
|---|---|---|
| **Program Area** | | |
| Adjudicate criminal cases | Subtotal | $ |
|   Adjudicate felony cases | Total | $ |
|   Adjudicate misdemeanor appeals | Total | $ |
| Adjudicate civil cases | Subtotal | $ |
|   Adjudicate major civil cases | Total | $ |
|   Adjudicate minor civil cases | Total | $ |
|   Adjudicate domestic relations cases | Total | $ |
| Adjudicate juvenile cases | Subtotal | $ |
|   Adjudicate delinquency and dependent and neglect cases | Total | $ |
|   Adjudicate crimes against juveniles | Total | $ |
| Provide alternatives to adjudication | Subtotal | $ |
|   Divert adult offenders | Total | $ |
|   Divert juvenile offenders | Total | $ |
| Provide security | Subtotal | $ |
|   Handle prisoner transport | Total | $ |
|   Provide courtroom security | Total | $ |
|   Etc. | | |

*Source:* U.S. Department of Justice, National Institute of Law Enforcement and Criminal Justice, *Financial Management* (Washington, D.C.: The American University, 1979), p. 41.1.

in Georgia in the early 1970s and then as president implemented it in the federal government for fiscal year 1979. An analysis of this experience at the Department of Agriculture indicates that although its use saved $200,000 in the department's budget, it cost at least 180,000 labor-hours of effort to develop.[36]

It is important to note that few organizations have budgets that are purely one format or another; therefore, it is not unusual to find that because of time, tradition, and personal preferences, a combination of several formats is used.

# Potential Pitfalls in Budgeting

## *The Need for Budgeting Flexibility*

Ancient Greek mythology tells of a highwayman named Procrustes who had an iron bedstead. He measured all who fell into his hands on the bed. If they were too long, their legs were lopped off to fit it. If they were too short, they were stretched to fit the bed. Few criminal justice administrators have not seen their monies and programs laid out on the Procrustesean bed of a state or municipal budget officer and lopped off.

It therefore becomes imperative to build as much flexibility into the planned program and budget as possible. One technique is to make up three budgets: an optimistic one, reflecting the ideal level of service to the jurisdiction and organization; an expected one, giving the most likely level of service that will be funded; and finally, budget plan that will provide a minimum level of service.[37]

To maximize the benefits of using budgets, managers must be able to avoid major pitfalls, which, according to Samuel Certo,[38] include the following:

1. *Placing too much emphasis on relatively insignificant organizational expenses.* In preparing and implementing a budget, managers should allocate more time to deal with significant organizational expenses and less time for relatively insignificant ones. For example, the amount of time spent on developing and implementing a budget for labor costs typically should be more than the amount of time managers spend on developing and implementing a budget for office supplies.

2. *Increasing budgeted expenses year after year without adequate information.* Perhaps the best-known method developed to overcome this potential pitfall is zero-based budgeting.[39]

3. *Ignoring the fact that budgets must be changed periodically.* Administrators must recognize that factors such as the cost of materials, newly developed technology, and demands for services are constantly changing and that budgets should reflect that by being reviewed and modified periodically. The performance budget (discussed earlier) is designed to assist in determining the level of resources to be allocated for each organizational activity.

## *Common Cost and Waste Problems*

To manage costs, administrators must be able to identify areas where waste and costs might be controlled. Louise Tagliaferri[40] identified 14 common cost factors that can be found in most organizations. Note that some costs are simply uncontrollable, but others are within the scope of the manager to reduce or at least maintain within a reasonable range:

| | |
|---|---|
| Absenteeism and turnover | Paperwork |
| Accident loss | Planning and scheduling |
| Direct and indirect labor | Productivity |
| Energy | Product quality |
| Maintenance | Tools and equipment |
| Materials and supplies | Transportation |
| Overtime | Waste |

Tagliaferri also noted that "literally billions of dollars are lost to industry (and criminal justice!) each year through carelessness, inattention, inefficiency, and other cost problems."[41]

## Strategies for Augmenting Criminal Justice Budgets

In difficult fiscal times, criminal justice agencies welcome any means by which they can increase their operating budgets, known as **budget augmentation.** Unfortunately, there are limited opportunities for doing so, especially for courts and corrections agencies; the police have recently fared better in this regard, albeit some measures have been controversial. Prisons and jails do have some income-producing inmate-labor programs (see Chapter 9), and the police can presently draw supplemental funds from several sources.

Federal and general foundation grants are available to police agencies. Police have used them for a variety of purposes, such as vehicle and riot equipment, communications centers, regional crime laboratories, and programs for alcohol accident prevention, rape victims, and the elderly. Potential grantors are located through publications such as the *Federal Directory of Domestic Aid Programs* and by preparing well-conceived grant proposals.

Criminal justice agencies also receive contributions. The Erie County, New York, Sheriff's Office received $5,000 from a local bank to renovate an old van for use in a crime-prevention program. On a larger scale, the New York City Police Foundation has raised money since 1971 for endeavors such as scholarships, a police stress program, and a bomb squad. In one recent year, the foundation raised $1.3 million. Police departments have also raised funds to purchase bulletproof vests and canines and to renovate their facilities.[42]

Huge supplemental revenues for police agencies come from confiscated cash and property involved with narcotics and contraband goods trafficking, racketeering, gambling, and other offenses. States' forfeiture laws allow the police to initiate forfeiture proceedings on seized goods such as airplanes, cash, cars, boats, and guns. These programs can use criminals' assets against them by funding additional law enforcement initiatives.[43]

Extra income also comes from user fees, which some police departments have initiated. These fees for services formerly provided for free, such as unlocking vehicles and responding to false burglar alarms, are controversial. Less controversial have been fees for hooking up burglar alarms to the police alarm board or computer-assisted dispatch system.[44]

Finally, Internal Revenue Service rewards have been paid to police agencies that capture racketeers who have not properly reported their income taxes. The program began in Atlanta, Georgia; the police department approached the IRS about collecting the 10 percent informer's fee on unpaid taxes. Through a special city ordinance, the police department was awarded the informer's fee on behalf of the city. By 1988, the department had filed 31 such claims.[45]

# CASE STUDY

The following case study challenges the reader to consider what he or she would do as an administrator in a city that is experiencing severe financial times—and to confront the question of what kinds of services both inside and outside the agency might be cut or eliminated in order to maintain public safety. This scenario also points out the kinds of "crisis management" that require so much of an administrator's time and preclude the kinds of strategic planning efforts that should be done, as discussed in Chapter 18.

## The Emptying Horn of Plenty

The chief of police in a small (20,000 population) city has experienced nearly a third of the agency's officers leaving in the past year. Budget cuts, attrition, and better salaries in other regional agencies have been the impetus for the departures. Furthermore, the city council is proposing a 15 percent cut in the police budget for the coming year. Citizens are already complaining about delays in police responses and about having to drive to the police department to make complaints or to file reports. The county sheriff has offered in the local newspaper to provide backup for the city when needed, but the chief of police believes the sheriff to be power hungry, and primarily motivated by a desire to absorb the city's police force into his agency. Severe cutbacks have already been made in the DARE and gang prevention programs, and other nonessential services have been terminated. A number of concerts, political rallies, and outdoor events—all of which are normally peaceful—will be held soon during the summer months, requiring considerable amounts of overtime; the chief's view is that "It's better to have us there and not be needed than vice-versa." Federal grants have run out. One of the chief's staff has suggested that the chief propose to the city council a drastic reduction in the city's parks, streets, or fire department budget, those monies being transferred to the police budget. The council, in turn, already wants to explore the possibility of hiring private security services for some events. Exacerbating the situation is the fact that violent crimes are increasing in the jurisdiction.

### Questions for Discussion

1. What measures could the chief implement or propose to the council to slow or eliminate the resignations of sworn personnel?
2. How might the chief obtain more revenues or, alternatively, realize some savings for the department?

3. Should the chief go public with the idea of reducing budgets in the parks or other city departments?
4. How should the chief deal with the local sheriff's offer?

## Summary

This chapter has focused on a singularly important area of financial administration, budgeting, and included its elements, formats, and potential pitfalls. Emphasis was placed on the need for administrators to develop skill in budget formulation and execution.

This chapter also discussed the budget process and different types of budgets. No single budgeting format is best; through tradition and personal preference, a hybrid format normally evolves in an organization. Nor should an administrator, under normal circumstances, surrender control of the organization's budget to another individual or body; the budget is too integral to planning, organizing, and directing programs and operations. In seemingly endless times of fiscal shortages, the justice administrator should attempt to become knowledgeable about opportunities for enhancing the budget through grants, donations, user fees, forfeitures, rewards, and other such means of augmenting the budget. Uncommon times call for uncommon methods.

## Questions for Review

1. What is a budget? How is it used?
2. What is a budget cycle? What is its importance in budgeting?
3. What is involved in formulating a budget? Its approval and its execution?
4. List four types of budget formats used in the past. Which type is used most frequently? What are its major advantages and component parts?
5. How are criminal justice agencies augmenting their budgets? Can additional means be used in this regard? Provide some examples.

## Notes

1. Charles R. Swanson, Leonard Territo, and Robert W. Taylor, *Police Administration: Structures, Processes, and Behavior,* 5th ed. (Upper Saddle River, N.J.: Prentice Hall, 2001), p. 558.

2. See James C. Snyder, "Financial Management and Planning in Local Government," *Atlanta Economic Review* (November/December 1973):43–47.

3. Aaron Wildavsky, *The Politics of the Budgetary Process,* 2d ed. (Boston: Little, Brown, 1974), pp. 1–4.

4. Orin K. Cope, "Operation Analysis—The Basis for Performance Budgeting," in *Performance Budgeting and Unit Cost Accounting for Governmental Units* (Chicago: Municipal Finance Officers Association, 1954), p. 8.

5. Lester R. Bittel, *The McGraw-Hill 36-Hour Management Course* (New York: McGraw-Hill, 1989).

6. Ibid., p. 187.

7. Robert Townsend, *Further Up the Organization: How to Stop Management from Stifling People and Strangling Productivity* (New York: Alfred A. Knofp, 1984), p. 2.

8. Roland N. McKean, *Public Spending* (New York: McGraw-Hill, 1968), p. 1.

9. S. Kenneth Howard, *Changing State Budgeting* (Lexington, Ky.: Council of State Governments, 1973), p. 13.

10. Michael C. Thomsett, *The Little Black Book of Budgets and Forecasts* (New York: AMACOM, a division of the American Management Association, 1988), p. 38.

11. Quoted in V. A. Leonard and Harry W. More, *Police Organization and Management,* 7th ed. (Mineola, N.Y.: Foundation Press, 1987), p. 212.

12. Swanson, Territo, and Taylor, *Police Administration,* p. 567.

13. Adapted, with some changes, from Wildavsky, *The Politics of the Budgetary Process,* pp. 63–123.

14. Lennox L. Moak and Kathryn W. Killian, *A Manual of Techniques for the Preparation, Consideration, Adoption, and Administration of Operating Budgets* (Chicago: Municipal Finance Officers Association, 1973), p. 5, with changes.

15. Lennis M. Knighton, "Four Keys to Audit Effectiveness," *Governmental Finance* 8 (September 1979):3.

16. The Comptroller General of the United States, *Standards for Audit of Governmental Organizations, Programs, Activities, and Functions* (Washington, D.C.: General Accounting Office, 1972), p. 1.

17. Ibid.

18. Peter F. Rousmaniere, ed., *Local Government Auditing* (New York: Council on Municipal Performance, 1979), Tables 1 and 2, pp. 10, 14.

19. Swanson, Territo, and Taylor, *Police Administration,* p. 578.

20. Allen Schick, *Budget Innovation in the States* (Washington, D.C.: Brookings Institution, 1971), pp. 14–15. Schick offers 10 ways in which the line-item budget fosters control.

21. Malchus L. Watlington and Susan G. Dankel, "New Approaches to Budgeting: Are They Worth the Cost?" *Popular Government* 43 (Spring 1978):1.

22. Jesse Burkhead, *Government Budgeting* (New York: Wiley, 1956), p. 11.

23. Larry K. Gaines, Mittie D. Southerland, and John E. Angell, *Police Administration* (New York: McGraw-Hill, 1991), p. 398.

24. Swanson, Territo, and Taylor, *Police Administration,* p. 581.

25. Ibid.

26. Gaines, Southerland, and Angell, *Police Administration,* pp. 396, 398.

27. Ibid., p. 600.

28. David Novick, ed., *Program Budgeting* (New York: Holt, Rinehart and Winston, 1969), p. xxvi.

29. Ibid., p. xxiv.

30. See Council of State Governments, *State Reports on Five-Five-Five* (Chicago: Council of State Governments, 1968).

31. International City Management Association, *Local Government Budgeting, Program Planning and Evaluation* (Urban Data Service Report, 1972):7.

32. Allen Schick, "The Road to PPBS: The Stages of Budget Reform," *Public Administration Review* 26 (December 1966): 244.

33. Ibid.

34. Swanson, Territo, and Taylor, *Police Administration,* p. 583.

35. Peter A. Phyrr, "Zero-Base Budgeting," *Harvard Business Review* (November/December 1970):111–121; see also E. A. Kurbis, "The Case for Zero-Base Budgeting," *CA Magazine* (April 1986):104–105.

36. Joseph S. Wholey, *Zero-Base Budgeting and Program Evaluation* (Lexington, Mass.: Lexington Books, 1978), p. 8.

37. Donald F. Facteau and Joseph E. Gillespie, *Modern Police Administration* (Englewood Cliffs, N.J.: Prentice Hall, 1978), p. 204.

38. Samuel C. Certo, *Principles of Modern Management: Functions and Systems,* 4th ed. (Boston: Allyn & Bacon, 1989):484–485.

39. George S. Minmier, "Zero-Base Budgeting: A New Budgeting Technique for Discretionary Costs," *Mid-South Quarterly Business Review* 14 (October 1976):2–8.

40. Louise E. Tagliaferri, *Creative Cost Improvement for Managers* (New York: Wiley, 1981), p. 7.

41. Ibid., p. 8.

42. Swanson, Territo, and Taylor, *Police Administration,* p. 593.

43. Ibid., p. 595.

44. Ibid.

45. Ibid., p. 596.

# Chapter 17

# Technology Review

## Key Terms and Concepts

Biometrics

Crime mapping

DNA

Drugfire

Gang intelligence systems

Less-than-lethal weapons

Offender management

Pursuit management

Reverse 911

## Learning Objectives

As a result of reading this chapter, the student will:

- be familiar with new and less-than-lethal weapons used by police
- have an understanding of the benefits of crime mapping
- know different techniques and newly developed technologies used by the police to apprehend criminals
- be able to distinguish among the six types of court technologies
- be familiar with the features of Courtroom 21
- be aware of changes in corrections facilities

*God hath made man upright; but they have sought out many inventions.*

*—Ecclesiastes 7:29*

*Everything that can be invented has been invented.*
—Charles H. Duell, Commissioner of Patents, 1899

*There is no reason for any individual to have a computer in their home.*

—Kenneth Olsen, president and founder of
Digital Equipment Corp., 1977

# Introduction

Technology consists primarily of tools to make people more productive. These tools provide administrators with opportunities to reshape the future with increased effectiveness and productivity.[1] Many of today's challenges for administrators involve these technologies. Communications systems that allow criminal justice agencies to share information, a more credible means of identification ensuring that John Doe is really who he says he is, a less-than-lethal weapon that is highly effective, security for the Internet—all these issues existed *before* September 11, 2001.[2]

Leadership is crucial to the development of new technologies. Without a leader championing these innovations, it is unlikely that the impetus needed for the cultural changes that technology requires will exist. Another major challenge for the implementation of new technologies is to ensure that they deliver direct and tangible benefits to everyone and do not leave behind certain groups—the poor, the elderly, the disabled, the non–English speaking—in the rush to use them.

It should be noted that along with all the technologies described in this chapter, a myriad of new issues for the agency administrator are presented. Technology management, staffing considerations, security concerns, and policy implications are all areas that must be examined prior to the technologies' implementation. This technology and the accompanying policy must be consistent with the agency's overall goals and philosophy. The way in which administrators prepare for and address these administrative issues will largely determine the level of success enjoyed by any new technology project.[3] Other related challenges involve acquiring the necessary revenue for funding these technologies, as well as the slowness with which government moves because of the constraints in purchasing.

Because the police component is where the bulk of technological research and development has occurred, and given the nature of the police mission, we begin by examining many new developments in this area. Following that, we review the major types of court technologies that exist or could be expanded for the overall accomplishment of the court mission. Finally, we examine corrections, including what is being done technologically to manage inmates and probationers. The chapter concludes with a brief discussion of the rapidly expanding field of biometrics.

# Policing Technologies

Police officers of the future will function in very different ways from officers of the past. Given the existing and developing technologies described here and what they bode for the future, officers will function with few time and space constraints, because all of them will be equipped with a pager, cellular phone, and laptop computer with software that includes encryption programs and sophisticated databases and search engines. Prior to going on the streets, every rookie will be thoroughly computer literate and able to use crime analysis software.[4] With such tools, it is easy to envision an officer's home, car, or convenience store becoming his or her workplace.

As the saying goes, however, "the fleas come with the dog." There are aspects of the police-technology alliance that can create problems in the foreseeable future. First, many police departments (as well as courts and corrections agencies) lack the in-house computer expertise to install or run the software and equipment. Many police executives believe that they hire people to be police officers only—not to be computer programmers or database experts. Therefore, in many agencies, information technology staff are often civilians and are generally kept away from the operational side of the organization. They understand what computers do, but not necessarily how that capability supports the operational needs of the police officer on the street. Furthermore, the police are also playing "catch-up" to high-tech criminal schemes (such as pornographers and pedophiles who are now on the Web as well as people who steal and trade credit card numbers, rig auctions, create viruses, and devise baby adoption scams).[5] Finally, it should be emphasized that several of the systems described next are expensive and thus cost prohibitive.

## *Recent Developments in Less-Than-Lethal Weapons*

Police departments nationwide continue to look to new techniques that offer a **less-than-lethal weapons** alternative, an "intermediate" weapon between the voice and the gun. Many less-than-lethal alternatives are relatively inexpensive for agencies to adopt and can significantly reduce a department's liability.[6]

The TASER underwent considerable revision in the late 1990s, evolving into a much better tool, and one that is now widely adopted by police agencies. The newer models are handgun shaped, use 26 watts to deliver 50,000 volts (as opposed to the 5- or 6-watt earlier versions) for 5 seconds and can penetrate up to 3 inches of clothing. Their range is up to 21 feet. Even if only one probe sticks to the person, the newer versions will still work most of the time.[7]

Also introduced of late are two types of foam that may hold promise. One is supersticky; intruders are drenched in a substance that, when exposed to the air, turns into taffylike glue. The other creates an avalanche of dense soap bubbles that leaves offenders unable to see or move but still able to breathe. Other chemical compounds, known as "slick'ems" and "stick'ems," make pavements either too sticky or too slippery for vehicles to move.[8]

Strong interest is also present in policing with respect to beanbag rounds (sometimes called kinetic batons) and capture nets. Beanbag rounds (a pellet-loaded bag that unfurls into a spinning pancake) have become extremely popular. They have been adopted by police agencies across the country and have been successfully used to help end a number of standoffs.[9] A Spiderman-style net gun known as the WebShot is designed to wrap and immobilize a suspect. The WebShot gun has been on the market since 1999 and is in trial use with the Los Angeles and San Diego Police Departments. WebShot is ideally used against an unarmed person who is being combative.[10]

The Less Than Lethal program for the National Institute of Justice coordinates research on such weapons, ensuring that they are technically feasible and also practical for police officers. In addition to the WebShot gun, the program recently provided funding for research into the following technologies:

- The Laser Dazzler, a flashlight device designed to disorient or distract suspects with a green laser light
- The Sticky Shocker, a wireless projectile fired from a gas gun that sticks to the subject with glue or a barb that attaches to clothing and delivers an electric shock
- The Ring Airfoil Projectile, a doughnut-shaped, hard-rubber weapon that is under redesign to also disperse a cloud of pepper powder on impact.[11]

Pepper spray, or oleoresin capsicum, is now used by an estimated 90 percent of police agencies, according to the National Institute of Justice.[12] This spray inflames the mucus membranes of the eyes, nose, and mouth, causing a severe burning sensation for 20 minutes or less.[13] The spray is highly effective in subduing suspects without causing undue harm or long-term effects.[14]

Also newly invented (by a member of the Oxnard, California, Police Department's SWAT team) and having promise is "The Option," which offers lethal and less-than-lethal capabilities in a single unit; the weapon has a cylinder of pepper spray that is mounted to the barrel of a pistol or shoulder weapon.[15]

## Crime Mapping

Computerized **crime mapping** has been termed "policing's latest hot topic."[16] For officers on the street, mapping puts street crime into an entirely new perspective; for administrators, it provides a way to involve the community in addressing its own problems by observing trends in neighborhood criminal activity. Crime mapping also offers crime analysts graphic representations of crime-related issues. Furthermore, detectives can use maps to better understand the hunting patterns of serial offenders and to hypothesize where these offenders might live.[17]

Computerized crime mapping combines geographic information from global positioning satellites with crime statistics gathered by the department's computer aided dispatching (CAD) system and demographic data provided by private companies or the U.S. Census Bureau (some agencies acquire information from the Census Bureau's Internet home page). The result is a picture that combines disparate sets of data for a whole new perspective on crime. For example, a map of crimes can be overlaid with maps or layers of causative data: unemployment rates in the areas of high crime, locations of abandoned houses, population density, reports of drug activity, or geographic features (such as alleys, canals, or open fields) that might be contributing factors.[18] Furthermore, the hardware and software are now available to nearly all police agencies, costing just a few thousand dollars.

Following are instances of successful outcomes using crime mapping:

- When an armored car was robbed in Toronto, dispatchers helped officers chase the suspects through a sprawling golf course using the mapping feature of the CAD system.
- The Illinois State Police map fatal accidents throughout the state and show which districts have specific problems. It can correlate those data with citations written, seatbelt usage, and other types of enforcement information.
- The Salinas, California, Police Department maps gang territories and correlates socioeconomic factors with crime-related incidents. Murders are down 61 percent, drive-by shootings by 31 percent, and gang-related assaults, 23 percent.[19]

The NIJ's Crime Mapping Research Center, established in 1997, provides information concerning research, evaluation, and training programs through its website: http://www.ojp.usdoj.gov/cmrc.

## Locating Serial Offenders

Most offenders operate close to home. They tend to concentrate on target-rich environments to "hunt" for their prey. Geographic profiling, a relatively new development in the field of environmental criminology, analyzes the characteristics of such locations as well as the victim encounter, the attack, the murder, and body dumpsites and maps the most probable location of the suspect's home.[20]

Geographic profiling is most effective when used in conjunction with other information. For example, the Washington State Attorney General's office uses a homicide investigation and tracking system (HITS) that includes crime-related databases and links to vice and gang files, sex offender registries, corrections and parole records, and department of motor vehicle databases. HITS can simultaneously scan these databases. When an agency in the state has a major crime in its jurisdiction, the case is loaded into a central system, which scans every database and linking file for connections by comparing eyewitness descriptions of a suspect and vehicle. It then builds a dataset containing profiles of the offender, the victims, and the incidents. The dataset then goes into a geographic information system (GIS), which is described below.[21]

## *Ending High-Speed Pursuits*

Tremendous potential exists for injury, property damage, and liability resulting from high-speed chases by police; indeed, this is such a concern that some agency administrators have developed **pursuit management** policies that completely prohibit such activities by officers.

Tire spikes can be deployed when a fleeing vehicle is approaching and then retracted so that other vehicles and police cars can pass safely. Tire spikes often do not work, however, or result in the suspect losing control of the vehicle (although some spike devices are designed to prevent this by breaking off in the tires and thus deflating them slowly).[22] One device has been developed using a short pulse of electrical current to disrupt electronic devices that are critical to the continued operation of the vehicle ignition system. Once pulsed, the vehicle rolls to a controlled stop similar to the effect of running out of fuel and will not restart until the affected parts are replaced.[23]

## *DNA*

It seems that new success stories involving the use of **DNA** in criminal justice are being reported each day, such as the following:

> A case file in the rape of a 12-year-old Englewood, Colorado, girl was starting to yellow. A sketch of the suspect had not produced anything concrete. Then the Colorado Bureau of Investigation linked a DNA "fingerprint" from the evidence file to a man recently imprisoned for another sexual assault.[24]

Today, some of the nation's most effective crime fighters wear white lab coats instead of blue uniforms and study DNA fingerprinting. Unfortunately, successes such as the Colorado case are severely limited by the scarcity of DNA fingerprints on file.

In the late 1980s, states began passing laws mandating that DNA samples be collected from persons convicted of sexual assault or other violent crimes. These data could then be used to solve existing cases as well as to identify the felons if they committed further crimes after they were released. All 50 states now have such laws and by the end of 1999 had gathered nearly 750,000 DNA samples and made the data accessible to police agencies. The downside is that less than 5 percent of the total number of DNA samples had been analyzed for 13 genetic markers.[25]

The U.S. Department of Justice has stepped in to help the states address their backlog of more than 700,000 DNA samples. The government has funded a private firm to develop and use a process called laser desorption mass spectrometry in conjunction with robotics; this process enables a sample to be analyzed in a matter of seconds. Once this process becomes available, states will be able to handle their backlogs in a matter of months, and DNA will be able to be used much more broadly in identifying, apprehending, and prosecuting criminals.[26]

## *Fingerprints and Mug Shots*

Though perhaps not as exotic as DNA identification, fingerprints are still a reliable means of positively identifying someone. Throughout the country, filing cabinets filled with ink-smeared cards hold the key to countless unsolved crimes, if only the data could be located. Automated fingerprint identification systems (AFIS) allow this legacy of data to be rapidly shared throughout the nation. One such system is the Western Identification Network (www.winid.org), established by nine states as a means to share their 17 million fingerprint records. These states were later joined by local agencies, as well as by the FBI, the Internal Revenue Service, the Secret Service, and the Drug Enforcement Administration. The system can generally provide a match within a few hours and has helped solve more than 5,000 crimes. A digital photo exchange facility, known as WINPHO, is now being added to supplement fingerprint data.[27]

Technology involving mugshots and imaging systems can also be useful for a variety of situations. For example, as a police officer responds to a domestic violence call, the CAD searches the address and finds a restraining order against the ex-husband or boyfriend; moments later a street map and digital mugshot of the suspect appear on the officer's laptop computer screen. The officer is thus aided with an image of the suspect and his criminal history prior to arriving at the scene.[28]

## *Crime Scenes*

Several technologies exist or are being developed relating to crime scene investigations. Three-dimensional computer aided drafting (3-D CAD) software is available for a few hundred dollars. By working in 3-D, CAD users can create scenes that can be viewed from any angle. Suddenly, technical evidence can be visualized by nontechnical observers. Juries can "view" crime scenes and see the location of evidence; they can view just what the witness says he or she saw. Police input the exact dimensions and get a scaled drawing. A 5-day, 40-hour course in 3-D CAD is available for police investigators, traffic accident reconstructionists, and evidence technicians.[29]

Crime scene evidence is often too sketchy to yield an obvious explanation of what happened. New software called Maya™ has been developed for this field, called forensic animation; this software helps experts determine what probably occurred. Maya is so packed with scientific calculations that it can create a virtual house from old police photos and replicate the effects of several types of forces, including gravity: how a fall could or could not have produced massive injuries, how flames spread in a house fire, and the way smoke cuts a pilot's visibility in a plane crash.[30]

The Federal Department of Energy is also testing a prototype laptop computer equipped with digital video and still cameras, laser range finders, and a global positioning system. A detective using it can beam information from a crime scene back to a laboratory to get input from experts. Researchers are also working on a chip that would give police the ability to process more evidence, including DNA samples, at the crime scene, eliminating the risk of contamination enroute to the lab.[31]

## Firearms

Handguns are, and have nearly always been, the weapon of choice for violent criminals, especially those who murder others. Handguns are also used with greatest frequency (in about 7 of every 10 incidents) when police officers are murdered.[32] It is therefore important that administrators adopt every possible technology for training the police in using lethal force against citizens.

### Computer-Assisted Training

A device known as FATS, for firearms training system, is said to be "as close to real life as you can get."[33] Recruits and in-service officers alike use the system. The students are given a high-tech lesson in firearms and can be shown a wide variety of computer-generated scenarios on a movie screen. An instructor at a console can control the scene. Using laser-firing replicas of their actual weapons, they learn not only shooting accuracy but also judgment, when to shoot and when not to shoot. Some sites combine FATS with a driving simulator and have recruits drive to the scene of a bank robbery and then bail out of their car into a FATS scenario.[34]

Recent developments have made firearms simulators even more realistic than the basic FATS system. One version has been developed that has a synchronized "shootback cannon." If an individual on a projection screen pulls a gun and fires toward the trainee, a cannon hanging above the screen pelts him or her with painful 0.68-caliber nylon balls. The newest generation of firearms training systems, which are getting even more realistic and better at breaking down how a trainee reacts under stress, now cost between $25,000 for a small system to $200,000 for a trailer that police departments can move from station to station.[35]

### Using "Fingerprints" of Guns to Solve Cases

Every gun leaves a unique pattern of minute markings on ammunition. If gun makers testfire their weapons before the guns leave their factories and the markings on bullets are catalogued, then the police can use spent ammunition recovered from crime scenes in tracing guns—even when the gun itself is not recovered. This technology could even be taken to the next level: creating an automated database of the fingerprints of new guns. A $45 million multiyear contract was recently awarded to a Montreal, Canada, firm by the U.S. Bureau of Alcohol, Tobacco and Firearms to help fund the development of such technology.[36]

Several problems need to be resolved, however: Criminals can easily use a nail file to scratch a new gun's firing pin; even if the system worked and turned up a serial number, the number could be used to trace the gun to its initial owner, and not necessarily to the criminal; the database would not include the estimated 200 million weapons already in circulation; and gun lobbies would undoubtedly oppose the system as being "suspiciously like a national gun registry."[37]

### *Drugfire: Connecting Guns to Crimes*
**Drugfire** is a federal networked system begun in 1992; it holds images of spent cartridges that can help link weapons to other shootings. It is essentially an imaging system with networked search capabilities. A dedicated microscope is attached to a computer, and an image of the cartridge case primer (the area where the firing pin hits the cartridge) is loaded into the system. The image is stored and accessible to other crime laboratories checking for connections with evidence they hold. Forensic scientists compare fired bullets and used casings to determine whether a firearm in custody was used in other shootings. Since its inception in 1992, more than 1,000 matches have been made by labs around the country using Drugfire, and 68 firearms labs in 19 states and the District of Columbia were linked to Drugfire or are in the planning stages of doing so.[38]

### *"Smart Guns" That Save Lives*
Many police officers have been slain with their own guns. Furthermore, close to 500 children and adolescents are killed in firearms accidents each year, and some 1,400 youngsters commit suicide with guns.[39] Efforts are now underway to create "smart" (or personalized) guns that can be fired only by their rightful owners along with a few other authorized users. Technological options are being explored in several areas; for example, radio signals that enable a weapon to recognize and respond to a transponder worn by the authorized user are being developed. The transponder's range is only a few inches, so the gun would not work for a stranger who steals it. A gun could be designed to recognize up to 50 transponders so a number of officers could fire the weapon if necessary. Although such a system could increase the price of a standard service pistol from $600 to about $900, the development of this system is gaining momentum; states and localities are drafting laws that could require the use of personalized guns.[40]

### *Laser Aiming*
In order to reduce the potential for use of deadly force, many police agencies have begun to authorize and issue laser sights as standard equipment. The high-tech laser system adapts to the officer's firearm by means of replacement grip panels. Packaged within the grips is a sophisticated laser-aiming device that is pressure activated when the officer's gun is drawn. Police agencies have reported that the laser-aiming device clearly adds an additional less-than-lethal force alternative. An officer's verbal commands to a suspect at gunpoint often go unheeded; however, the visual impact of the red laser dot on the suspect's chest has assisted officers in

gaining compliance and even surrender. In addition, lasers have been effective as an alternative sighting method around or over objects.[41]

## Gang Intelligence Systems

The escalating problem of street gangs has prompted many police departments to search for a tool that could help them deal with the problem. Several agencies now use a **gang intelligence system** to collect information in a database, allowing officers to enter and access key pieces of data such as gang names, vehicles, weapons, suspect associates, and incident dates. Even if an officer has a small piece of information to work with, such as a nickname or partial license plate number of a suspect's car, the system's cross-referencing function connects that information to additional information in the database about gang members, their activities, addresses, descriptions, and photos. Officers can even access the database in their patrol cars utilizing laptops. The system also allows photographs to be stored and linked with other information about suspects. A statewide gang intelligence system, California's CAL/GANG, is a relational database that holds and categorizes everything from nicknames to tattoos on suspected or known gang members. This system, which has been credited for solving a number of high-visibility gang crimes, is now being considered by other states, including Florida, which has a significant gang problem.[42]

## Other Technologies

Today, even a small agency can afford a laptop and a modem to send encrypted data to officers in the field.[43] A growing number of U.S. police departments, including small agencies, are using laptop computers with wireless connections to crime and motor vehicle databases. Officers can access court documents, in-house police department records, and a computer aided dispatch system, as well as entering license numbers into their laptop computers. Through various databases, the police can locate drivers with outstanding warrants, expired or suspended licenses, and criminal backgrounds.[44]

Chapter 3 discussed community oriented policing and problem solving (COPPS). Technology can certainly assist in this endeavor. Some cities now employ a sophisticated system that uses an integrated CAD system, mobile data terminals (or MDTS—in-car computers), and message switching and routing tools to collect, store, monitor, and retrieve information needed for COPPS. They can sort data to present information to citizens in an easy-to-understand format at neighborhood meetings.[45]

Some cities are also developing a geographic information system (GIS), which enables officers to plot criminal activity on an electronic map. Layers of information can then be added to the map to create a picture of crime trends.[46]

Some police agencies have begun using a version of a surveying instrument that electronically measures and records distances, angles, elevations, and the names and features of objects. With this system, officers can spend an hour or so getting measurements at major traffic accidents, push a button, and have the system draw lines pertinent to the accident to scale; this process enables officers to get 40 percent more measurements in about 40 percent of the time, thus allowing the traffic flow to resume much more quickly. This system is also being used at major crime scenes. Its only drawback is that it cannot be used in heavy rain or snow.[47]

One tool used routinely during a drunk-driving stop is a small, portable machine that resembles a video-game cartridge used as a breath-screening device. The DUI suspect blows into it, and the officer takes the reading of the amount of alcohol in the suspect's system. Law enforcement officials hope that this device can be adapted so that the test can be used in court. If so, it would save time in transporting DUI suspects, testing them, and finding that their blood level was below the legal limit because of the elapsed time.[48]

Following are brief descriptions of other newly developed technologies for use by the police:

- VINE (Victim Information and Notification Everyday) is an automated notification system that allows registered users to know almost immediately of any change in the status of a particular offender. This information can be sent via telephone, e-mail, or pager to crime victims, usually within 15 minutes of a change in an offender's status. Users can also be notified of release, escape, transfer, sentence expiration date, or death of an inmate.[49]

- Voice recognition: Police reports often require 45 minutes to an hour of writing. A software program uses a police knowledge base combined with report form templates that prompt with questions on the screen and the officer responds verbally. This technology helps police officers input information without having to type it all in.[50]

- An unmanned air vehicle offers a variety of applications to police in narcotics, search and rescue, surveillance, and other types of operations. Furthermore, the vehicle, 6.5 feet in diameter with a 50-horsepower engine enabling it to cruise at 80 knots up to 8,000 feet, has a remote video recorder that can assist SWAT teams and bomb disposal units in viewing dangerous situations without having to place an officer in jeopardy.[51]

- A new video camera has been developed that is so small it can be hidden in a police badge, allowing officers to discreetly videotape every field interrogation, routine traffic stop, and domestic disturbance they encounter. The device, sure to stir a personal liberty debate, could also put a new twist on police brutality litigation.[52]

- Global positioning system (GPS) technology is being utilized by police around the world for finding drowning victims in deep oceans, rivers, and lakes with zero visibility.[53]

- More than 125 police agencies in the United States are using electric bicycles. Appearing to be normal mountain bikes, the flip of a switch provides a

## Exhibit 17.1
## Police Rethink Cruiser Cameras

When they work, they can provide solid evidence of a law enforcement officer's conduct. But when they don't—which seems to be more often the case—any protection offered by a video camera installed in a patrol car is negligible, according to a number of departments that have removed the devices.

Audio and video feeds from cruisers are used increasingly in court to prove or disprove misconduct. . . .

But . . . technical glitches caused by constant use have made the camera-generated evidence worthless in court.

"If there's a breakup or gaps in the tape, it reflects on the professionalism and the credibility of the officer," Mark Davis, an Orange County public defender, told The Los Angeles Times. "If it's not working right, it sort of undermines the whole deal."

The Los Angeles Police Department has removed all of the recording equipment it installed in its fleet a few years ago. . . . The cameras could not be fixed once the company that manufactured them went out of business.

. . . The cameras get a lot of wear and tear . . . and they were often damaged. . . .

Although they have reported significant technical glitches, departments in Newport Beach and Beverly Hills believe the benefits of the camera outweigh the problems. In one case, a Newport Beach officer was cleared when a tape proved that a woman was lying when she claimed to have been sexually assaulted during her arrest on suspicion of drunk driving, said Sgt. Mike McDermott. . . .

While the systems vary, most begin recording automatically when a patrol car's lights and sirens are activated. The camera is mounted on the ceiling of the car next to the rearview mirror, and the recorder is placed in an armored box in the trunk. The sound is turned on manually by pressing a switch in the uniform belt.

But . . . officers would sometimes forget to hit the switch, or the sound was accidentally turned off when it brushed against clothing or objects. At other times, the entire system malfunctioned, producing neither sound nor image. The system's unreliability became frustrating for police, the public and defense attorneys. . . .

During a recent incident, an officer who had his lights and siren on when he collided with another motorist found later that the camera had malfunctioned, failing to capture any of the event on tape. . . .

*Source:* Reprinted with permission from *Law Enforcement News,* November 30, 2000, p. 6. John Jay College of Criminal Justice (CCNY), 555 West 57th St., New York, NY 10019.

turbo power boost of electric power enabling the bike to attain a speed of up to 20 miles per hour, allowing for faster acceleration for climbing hills.[54]

## Reverse 911

**Reverse 911** systems give public safety and police agencies a viable option for alerting the public in times of impending danger, such as escaped or dangerous individuals, missing persons, a string of crimes, or chemical spills. Citizens and businesses can be warned quickly by phone by the system. An operator records a message, brings up a map on a computer screen, designates a target area or chooses a preloaded map area, and the system begins dialing all the numbers in the database within that targeted area and sends the recorded message.[55]

## In Development

Other technologies are being explored by the military that could be used by the police in certain situations:

- A portable, battery-powered sonic rifle fires "bullets" with earsplitting noise; the weapon fires a burst of noise as high as 140 decibels, creating the equivalent of an instant migraine headache.
- A sprayable slime that makes walkways and other surfaces as slippery as ice could be ready for use in 2003.
- The world's foulest odor, termed a "souped up version of human waste" is another possibility.

Each of these projects focuses on exploiting the body's own senses.[56]

# Court Technologies

"Courts *are* their records." This adage captures the essence of the important role played by the courts in serving as the primary repository for the records of the community's arrests, convictions, births, deaths, marriages, divorces, and so on. But in so doing, lawyers, judges, and society generally create a blizzard of paper documents daily, all of which require sorting, filing, and indexing for later retrieval. Many courthouses have file cabinets occupying every inch of wall space, as well as basements filled with boxes of decaying records.

This section reviews the six fundamental types of technology that assist the courts in accomplishing their mission as a repository of information, resolving their paper burden, and improving their overall functioning. We also view a futuristic court that has been created to showcase technological products.

## Six Types

Court technologies can be categorized into six areas: data systems, office automation, court records, testimony, evidence, and legal information.

1. *Data systems* are computer-based tools used to organize information and assist work processes. The court case management system is the most important data system used by the judicial branch. It consists of five essential components: key case information in a highly structured format, computer instructions or programs, computer and telecommunications hardware, people to use and manage the system, and operations procedures to link the work of people with the work of the machines. In addition, courts may use data systems for jury, budget, personnel, and similar functions. Technologies allow remote access to court information and electronic transactions with the court through dial-up lines, kiosks, and the Internet.

2. *Office automation* technology involves tools that improve personnel effectiveness and productivity, including document production, organization of information, communication, financial and statistical analysis, education and planning, and managing work.

3. *Court records* technologies manage the documents filed with the court and include imaging, fax filing, workflow, document management systems, and electronic filing. These technologies improve the efficiency of court staff. Costs are reduced for courts, litigants, and the public as documents can be processed more quickly, and access to information is enhanced dramatically. One of the most common reasons for the failure of electronic systems during the past decade has been the lack of involvement of potential users in the design and development of the system. Electronic filing has the potential to become an exciting advancement for courts that wish to streamline their expanding caseloads.[57] Courts are realizing that computer filing and retrieval of documents can be faster, less expensive, and more accurate and secure than the traditional method; furthermore, computerized documents require far less space to store than paper. Another promising solution to the courts' record-keeping problem is document imaging. Courts enter information into case-processing systems from numerous sources. Some documents submitted directly to the administrator's or clerk's office could be scanned into the imaging system locally. Other documents come from external sources such as attorneys, police and probation agencies, and community services. These documents could be scanned into the system remotely or faxed directly into the system.[58] Imaging has its disadvantages, including its initial cost; difficulty of system implementation (for integration with other systems) and of reading lengthy imaged documents on a computer screen; the impossibility of modifying, manipulating, or copying text in imaged documents; the potential need for additional staff; and the potential for the entire operation to be immobilized by system failures.[59] Figure 17.1 shows a sample page of document imaging.

4. *Testimony* technologies are used to facilitate, capture, store, and reproduce testimony offered in a courtroom. They include audio and video recording, videoconferencing, language translation, and computer-aided transcription. Videoconferencing is becoming one of the most demanded systems in

**Figure 17.1**

A sample document imaging screen. *Source:* National Center for State
Courts, *Court Technology Reports.* Vol. 4. Williamsburg, Va.: Author,
p. 15. Copyright 1992. Used with permission.

today's courts. The primary components of a simple videoconferencing system are television cameras, monitors, microphones, speakers, and a communications network.[60] Courts in at least 30 states use video arraignments for first-appearance felonies and misdemeanors,[61] which represent about three-fourths of new criminal cases each year. Approximately 200 video arraignment sites exist in state court systems today. Video arraignment provides several benefits, including reduced security risks associated with transporting and handling inmates, reduced overcrowding of courthouse holding facilities, improved custody conditions for defendants while they await arraignment, improvements in the overall efficiency of court proceedings, reduced tension levels among guards and prisoners, minimized delays, and reducing or avoiding the commingling of first-time offenders with hardened offenders.[62]

5. *Evidence* technologies assist lawyers in presenting evidence in the courtroom. They allow attorneys to offer clearer and more convincing illustrations of the points they are trying to make to a judge or jury. Tools include sound and visual reinforcement devices, document cameras, computers, and projectors.

6. *Legal information* technologies aid access to case law, statutes, rules, and other legal materials. Large mainframe-based depositories of legal materials

have been supplemented by CD-ROM–based legal collections and legal databases accessed through the Internet.[63]

This list demonstrates that technologies are changing the way the courts work. Clearly, members of the judicial branch—especially chief judges and court administrators—must be knowledgeable about their application, cost, and policy implications, while understanding that some traditional ways of doing things must become obsolete. The electronic filing of information is especially critical for the future of courts, as they attempt to become less laden with, and dependent on, their mountains of paper.

## *Courtroom 21*

The College of William and Mary and the National Center for State Courts unveiled Courtroom 21 in 1994; at that time, it was the most technologically advanced courtroom in the United States, although many of its features are in use today. Nonetheless, this project demonstrates how technology can enrich the legal process by assisting court actors. Courtroom 21 includes the following integrated capabilities[64]:

- *Automatic videorecording of proceedings using ceiling-mounted cameras with voice activation.* There are five ceiling television cameras in the courtroom. When someone in the courtroom speaks, the microphone and camera closest to that person are activated. With cameras properly aimed, the entire courtroom is visible via small video windows, while the person speaking is visible through a large video window.
- *Recorded televised evidence display with analog optical disk storage.* Evidence can be prerecorded on small analog disks for later use at trial. Counsel may present documentary or real evidence to judge and jury via television display. Trial evidence and events may also be preserved on disk for later trial use or for appeals.
- *Remote, two-way television arraignment.* Video arraignment (i.e., teleconferencing) is possible between the bench and some remote site. Audio and video signals are received by the control center and then are sent to the several courtroom computer monitors.
- *Jury box computers.* The jury box contains computers for information display. Each monitor can display documents, real evidence, live or recorded video, transcription, and the usual graphics (charts, diagrams, pictures).
- *LEXIS legal research.* Judges and counsel are provided immediate access to legal resources through the LEXIS online legal database. If an unanticipated legal question arises during trial, judges and counsel can use the computers to consult the database.
- *Video deposition playback facilities.* Because more depositions are being videorecorded by attorneys in preparation for trial, Courtroom 21 has video

deposition playback. To impeach a witness or present expert witness testimony, video depositions can be played on court monitors.

# Corrections Facilities

## *New Demands on Offender Management*

The use of technology behind bars is changing methods of **offender management** as administrators increasingly adopt Web-based systems to manage the flow of information. The old offender-based tracking system was modeled after the way prisons used to work, but new Web-based technology is now used to educate prisoners, treat prisoners who are addicted to drugs or are sex offenders, and provide vocational training. Prison administrators now have to keep accurate records of inmates' purchases for items in the prison store, payments to victims and their families, and other reasons for which money flows in and out of prisoners' bank accounts.[65]

In state-of-the-art prisons, automated systems control access gates and doors, individual cell doors, and the climate in cells and other areas of the prison. Corrections agencies have also used computers to manage inmate records, conduct presentence investigations, supervise offenders in the community, provide instruction to inmates, and train correctional personnel. With computer assistance, jail administrators receive daily reports on court schedules, inmate rosters, time served, statistical reports, maintenance costs, and other data.

The California Department of Corrections (CDC) is one of the largest criminal justice agencies in the world, with 27 state institutions and 38 camps. Managing inmates includes monitoring their movements, medical histories, visitors, restitution fines, and job assignments.[66] The foundation of the CDC's inmate tracking program is an integrated information-sharing system with at least one computer located at each institution. When entering a prison, a new inmate is assigned a unique CDC number; this number helps the staff track the inmate's movements and status at all times. A complex data file that consists of information ranging from medical problems and cell assignment to previous escape history is maintained on each inmate. CDC also accounts for the money an inmate may have arrived with, any money sent to him or her through the mail, and amounts deducted to pay court-ordered restitution fines.[67]

## *Automated Direct Supervision in Jails*

Direct supervision jails are springing up across the country, eschewing typical jail cells with steel bars. Some of these facilities are replacing the bars with barcoded wristbands and state-of-the-art computerized information management systems. As one data communications engineer stated, "Everything from the toilets to the telephones is fully computerized" in these facilities.[68]

The information technology package used in these kinds of facilities includes live-scan fingerprinting, an automated fingerprint identification system, digitized mugshots, and computerized inmate and records management. Each inmate's wristband is keyed into the central computer system, which contains his or her name, physical description, picture, and prisoner number; the system is used to track each inmate's location, visitors, library use, medical treatment, and court appointments. The system is expected to reduce costs, provide a new level of records integrity, and increase the safety of both officers and inmates by allowing the administrators to develop a completely cashless inmate society. Without cash and with limits set on how much an inmate can spend each week, correctional officers hope to curtail contraband problems. This cashless system virtually eliminates the illicit transactions that once were common because the administration can now regulate and monitor the flow of goods and services.[69]

## *"Virtual Visits" to Hospitals and Courtrooms*

Prison and jail inmates make frequent visits to hospitals and courtrooms—all of which pose public safety concerns. In Ohio alone, 40,000 inmate trips to and from medical facilities were eliminated because videoconferencing technology made medical consultations available from within the institution. An onsite prison physician or nurse assists with the physical part of the examination, taking cues from the offsite specialist via video and relaying information, including EKG and blood pressure data.[70]

Increasingly, prisons are using video not only for medical visits, but also for arraignments, parole violation hearings, and distance learning.

## *Kiosk Check-in for Probationers*

A relatively new computer system allows probationers who pose little or no public risk and need little personal supervision to check in from a remote location rather than making a trip to the probation officer's office. The probationers simply push a few buttons at an electronic kiosk to show they have not left town and perhaps breathe into a breathalyzer if abstention from alcohol is a condition of probation. The system is user-friendly, accessible, and works without invading privacy.[71]

The kiosks are strategically located and linked to a network of personal computers in the probation department. During the initial meeting with a probation officer, a probationer's biometric keys (fingerprints, voice, retina scan, signature, hand structure) and a digital photo of the face are captured electronically. They are entered, along with case-specific information, into the database. The system's server can be programmed to expect check ins from several times a day to weekly, monthly, or longer intervals. Specific questions can be written for each client. A probationer may stop at any kiosk, where a biometric sample is taken via scanner and compared to the one collected during enrollment. Once identification is established, the probationer may check in. The kiosk operates every day, serving a maximum of 180 people per day.[72]

## A Body of Evidence: Biometrics

A technology that was growing rapidly even before the September 11 terrorist attacks involves **biometrics:** a system that converts the patterns of the iris, fingertip, hand, or face into a badge of identity. U.S. sales of biometric devices nearly doubled from 2000 to 2001, from $76.8 million to $160.3 million.[73] Employees at some businesses punch in and out by placing their hand on a reader, as do schoolchildren who have their finger-scan verified for enrollment in lunch programs.[74] Although such systems are far from perfect and still contain glitches, they have widespread potential to boost security—and convenience—in this country. These technologies also have their detractors on the ground of privacy, prompting calls for laws that would regulate how biometric data could be collected and used.[75]

## For More Information

Those wishing to learn more about the new developments in technology may find the following World Wide Web address useful: http://www.govtech.net. This resource provides information about new products, solutions to problems, jobs, training resources, and conferences. For Internet access to the National Criminal Justice Reference Service Online, use Telnet to access ncjrsbbs. aspensys.com or Gopher to access ncjrs.aspensys.com. UNOJUST, the United Nations Online Justice Information System, may be reached at http://ncjrs. org/unojust. Many more relevant websites are provided in Appendix I.

## Summary

This chapter has reviewed several exciting technological advances that are in use by or are being developed for police, courts, and corrections organizations. Readers, especially present and future administrators, managers, and supervisors, are encouraged to keep abreast of advances in this area, because the age of computer technology makes almost anything possible.

## Questions for Review

1. What are some of the latest developments in less-than-lethal weapons for the police?
2. Explain how technologies are assisting with crime mapping, locating serial offenders, and high-speed pursuits.
3. What is being done with respect to the forensic arena, including fingerprints, DNA, and crime scenes?

4. What are some of the six major technological capabilities now in use in the nation's courts? What are some of the futuristic technological items or methods found in a twenty-first-century courtroom?

5. Explain what is meant by biometrics, as well as its potential advantages and problems.

## Notes

1. Lawrence P. Webster, "How Technology Can Help Court Leaders Address the Justice Needs of a Multicultural Society in the Twenty-first Century," *The Court Manager* 15(3) (2000):48.

2. Jim McKay, "When the Dust Settles," *Government Technology's Crime and the Tech Effect: Call to Action* (April 2002):5.

3. Gerald W. Schoenle, "Mobile Computing Policy Perspectives: The Buffalo Experience," *The Police Chief* (September 2001):38.

4. Ibid.

5. "Cybergame for the Millennium: Cops 'n Robbers Playin' Hide 'n Seek on the Net," *Police Futurist* 8 (1), (1999):4.

6. "Rethinking Stopping Power," *Law Enforcement News* (November 15, 1999):1, 9.

7. Darren Laur, "More Powerful, but Still Less Lethal," *Law Enforcement Technology* (October 1999):10.

8. John Barry and Tom Morganthau, "Soon, 'Phasers on Stun'," *Newsweek* (February 7, 1994):24-25.

9. Ibid.

10. Luis Cabrera, "Police Explore 'Less-Than-Lethal' Weapons," *Associated Press* (June 19, 2000).

11. Ibid.

12. "Rethinking Stopping Power," *Law Enforcement News* (November 15, 1999):5.

13. "Effectiveness Times Three," *Law Enforcement News* (May 15, 1993):1.

14. Ibid., p. 6.

15. "Rethinking Stopping Power," *Law Enforcement News* (November 15, 1999):5.

16. Lois Pilant, "Computerized Crime Mapping," *The Police Chief* (December 1997):58.

17. Dan Sadler, "Exploring Crime Mapping" (Washington, D.C.: U.S. Department of Justice, National Institute of Justice, Crime Mapping Research Center, 1999), p. 1.

18. Pilant, "Computerized Crime Mapping," p. 58.

19. Ibid., pp. 66-67.

20. Bill McGarigle, "Crime Profilers Gain New Weapons," *Government Technology,* 10 (December 1997):28-29.

21. Ibid.

22. Ibid.

23. Internet, http://www.jaycor.com/arrestor.htm (accessed April 11, 1997).

24. Rutt Bridges, "Catching More Criminals in the DNA Web," *Law Enforcement News* (September 15, 2000):9.

25. Drew Robb, "The Long Net of the Law," *Crime and the Tech Effect* (Folsom, Calif.: Government Technology, April 2001), pp. 44-46.

26. Ibid.

27. Robb, "The Long Net of the Law," p. 46.

28. Corey Grice, "Technologies, Agencies Converge," *Government Technology,* 11 (April 1998):24, 61.

29. Tod Newcombe, "Adding a New Dimension to Crime Reconstruction," *Government Technology,* 9 (August 1996):32.

30. John McCormick, "Scene of the Crime," *Newsweek* (February 28, 2000):60.

31. Joan Raymond, "Forget the Pipe, Sherlock: Gear for Tomorrow's Detectives," *Newsweek* (June 22, 1998):12.

32. Samuel G. Chapman, *Murdered on Duty: The Killing of Police Officers in America,* 2d ed. (Springfield, Ill.: Charles C Thomas, 1998), p. 33.

33. Patrick Joyce, "Firearms Training: As Close to Real as It Gets," *Government Technology,* 8 (July 1995):14–15.

34. Ibid.

35. John McCormick, "On a High-Tech Firing Line," *Newsweek* (December 6, 1999):64.

36. Vanessa O'Connell, "The Next Big Idea: Using 'Fingerprints' of Guns to Solve Cases," *Wall Street Journal* (February 10, 2000):A1.

37. Ibid.

38. Brian Miller, "Spent Cartridges Nail Shooters," *Government Technology,* 9 (October 1996):15.

39. Ted Gest, "Can 'Smart' Guns Save Many Lives?" *U.S. News and World Report* (December 2, 1996):37.

40. Ibid., p. 38.

41. Adam Wollander, "Tactical Technology for the Next Millennium," *Law Enforcement Technology* (April 1998):80.

42. Raymond Dussault, "CAL/GANG Brings Dividends," *Government Technology* (December 1998):124.

43. Tod Newcombe, "Bandwidth Blues," *Government Technology,* 9 (August 1996):1, 52.

44. Kaveh Ghaemian, "Small-Town Cops Wield Big-City Data," *Government Technology,* 9 (September 1996):38.

45. Justine Kavanaugh, "Community Oriented Policing and Technology," *Government Technology,* 9 (March 1996):14.

46. Ibid.

47. Bill McGarigle, "Electronic Mapping Speeds Crime and Traffic Investigations," *Government Technology,* 9 (February 1996):20–21.

48. Justine Kavanaugh, "Drunk Drivers Get a Shot of Technology," *Government Technology,* 9 (March 1996):26.

49. Richard Ehisen, "One Step Ahead," *Government Technology* (April 2002):42.

50. Keith W. Strandberg, "Law Enforcement Computers and Software," *Law Enforcement Technology* (May 1998):40.

51. Richard Morrison, "Eye in the Sky," *Law Enforcement Technology* (June 1998):66.

52. Douglas Page, "Picture This: Oak Ridge National Laboratory (ORNL) Has Developed a Police Shield That Doubles as a Video Camera," *Law Enforcement Technology* (June 1998):70.

53. "The Vanishing," *Government Technology* (July 1998):50.

54. "Utah Offers First Electric Bike School," *Law Enforcement Technology* (December 1998):36.

55. Jim McKay, "Emergency Contact," *Government Technology* (March 2002):38.

56. Seth Hettena, "Military Developing Non-Lethal Weapons," *Associated Press* (March 24, 2002).

57. David J. Egar, "Electronic Filing," paper presented at the Fourth National Court Technology Conference, National Center for State Courts, Nashville, Tennessee, October 1994, p. 3.

58. Carter C. Cowles, National Center for State Courts, "Document Imaging," *Court Technology Reports* 5 (1992):26–27.

59. Carter C. Cowles, "Document Imaging," *Court Technology Bulletin* 7(5) (September/October 1995):5.

60. National Center for State Courts, Court Technology Briefing Paper, "Videoconferencing" (1995):1.

61. Ibid.

62. Ibid., pp. 24–25.

63. Adapted from Webster, "How Technology Can Help Court Leaders Address the Justice Needs of a Multicultural Society in the Twenty-first Century," pp. 48–50.

64. Fredric I. Lederer, "Courtroom 21: A Model Courtroom of the 21st Century," *Court Technology Bulletin,* 6(1) (January/February 1994):1, 5.

65. Shane Peterson, "The Internet Moves Behind Bars," *Government Technology's Crime and the Tech Effect* (April 2001):18.

66. Dona Snow, "Stretching Corrections Resources with Project Management," *Government Technology,* 8 (January 1995):78.

67. Ibid.

68. Raymond Dussault, "Direct Supervision and Records Automation," *Government Technology,* 8 (August 1995):36.

69. Ibid., p. 37.

70. Jim McKay, "Virtual Visits," *Government Technology* (October 2001):46.

71. James Evans, "Kiosk Check In for Probationers," *Government Technology,* 8 (May 1995):42.

72. Ibid., pp. 42, 44.

73. Drew Robb, "Spotlight on Biometrics," *Government Technology's Crime and the Tech Effect: Call to Action* (April 2002):10.

74. Dana Hawkins, "Body of Evidence," *U.S. News and World Report* (February 18, 2002):58.

75. Ibid.

# Chapter 18

# Peeking Over the Rim
## What Lies Ahead?

## Key Terms and Concepts

COPPS

Crime acceleration

Direct supervision jailing

Drivers

Environmental scanning

Restorative justice

Scenario writing

## Learning Objectives

As a result of reading this chapter, the student will:

- know the two major aspects of futures research
- be familiar with the reasons why crime might increase in the future
- understand the difficulties police will face in the future
- be familiar with the changes COPPS might undergo in the future and the questions it will face
- know what skills police officers of the future will possess
- be familiar with the trends that will shape courts in the future
- understand anticipated technologies
- have an idea of how criminal justice personnel will change
- be familiar with community perceptions of prisons

- have an understanding of future issues concerning resources and the overall organization of the criminal justice system

*Where there is no vision the people will perish.*
—Proverbs 29:18

*The future must be shaped or it will impose itself as catastrophe.*
—Henry Kissinger

# Introduction

It has been said that the only thing that is permanent is change. Perhaps more than anything else, the foregoing chapters have demonstrated that even in the relatively tradition-bound domain of criminal justice administration, we certainly live in a dynamic world where society and its problems and challenges are constantly evolving. As a result, our lives will be drastically altered as the world continues to change.

The question at the forefront of our minds is, "What will the future bring?" That troublesome question becomes even more important and ominous when we consider the world's present state of affairs. Our choice is either to ignore the future until it is upon us or to try to anticipate what the future holds and gear our resources to cope with it. Predicting the future is not easy, however. Many variables, such as war, technology, and economic upheaval, can greatly affect otherwise sound predictions and trends. The best we can possibly do in this chapter is render an educated guess.[1]

We begin by considering why it is important to study futures in justice administration, and some of the methods used by futurists for making predictions. Then, the focus shifts to the current and predicted demographic and crime-related changes in our nation, and what all of that portends for the police, including the area of community oriented policing and problem solving (COPPS) and policing methods of the future. Next is a review of some future changes that are envisioned in the courts, and following that is an examination of the corrections field; the latter includes the changing notions of justice, treatment, and custody, as well as changes in corrections personnel and clientele. Also included are future needs of corrections managers and prison construction issues. Then, we review future issues for the entire justice system: personnel, technology, allocation of resources, and the flattening of the organization. The chapter concludes with two case studies.

# Why Study Futures in Justice Administration?

We all think about the future as a normal part of everyday living. We attend classes to better our future life, schedule meetings and appointments, consider our retirement programs, prepare notes for classes and speeches, and even pay our bills as a hedge against problems to come. The trouble is that when the future finally arrives, we often find that it has an embarrassing way of being different from our expectations: We simply did not plan effectively.

The future is therefore a dynamic concept, always changing and making us unsure of what lies ahead. Using driving a car as an analogy, we must constantly look at and be aware of several aspects of the road ahead—our speed and that of other drivers, traffic signals and signs, weather and road conditions—in order to reach our destination. And we *certainly* cannot afford to be in the next century with our eyes firmly fixed on the rearview mirror!

And so it is with criminal justice administration. Historically, the primary role of leaders of criminal justice organizations has been to maintain the status quo. But on close inspection, we realize that reliance on the status quo will not prepare the justice system for the future. Previous chapters of this book, dealing with varied personnel and operational issues, have made clear the need for possessing strategies for future problems. We have learned from terrorist attacks, riots, financial cutbacks, natural and created disasters, strikes, and other exigencies that we must anticipate the future, plan for the unknown, and expect the unforeseen. Still, it is unfortunate that many people, including writers of textbooks devoted to administration and management in general and those examining police, courts, and corrections organizations in specific, completely ignore or give little attention to the future.

The criminal justice community must also plan with an eye toward public approval of its actions. As history has shown with respect to civil unrest—often following what has been perceived as police brutality or shootings or unwarranted court decisions—leaders should consider how destructive and long-lasting civil unrest and perceived social injustice can be. The specter of liability also reminds us of the cost of failure.

In sum, much work remains to be done. For 45,000 years, humankind huddled in the darkness of caves, afraid to take that first step into the light of day. Justice administrators must now be "out in front," paving the way for others to follow, not waiting for someone else to set the pace. Bold leadership is essential today to prepare for future reform. These administrators shoulder the responsibility for seeing that the best and brightest individuals are recruited and trained and become the best they possibly can be in their performance. And they must have a vision for how those individuals—and the ever-evolving high technology that they will be using—may be directed in the most efficient, just manner.

# Predicting the Future

## *Scanning, Scenario Writing, Drivers*

In the past four decades, interest has surged in forecasting the future of criminal justice. William Tafoya[2] called forecasting the "purest form of futuristics," likening it to the headlights of a car being driven in a snowstorm. The lights provide enough illumination to continue, but not enough for the driver to proceed without caution. What lies ahead is unknown. Next, we examine some of the methods that are employed by persons engaged in futures research in their efforts to make the unknown more predictable.

Contemporary futures research has two major aspects: environmental scanning and scenario writing. **Environmental scanning** is an effort to put a social problem under a microscope, with an eye toward the future. We may consult experts, such as demographers, social scientists, technologists and economists for their opinions. A Delphi process may also assist; this gathers experts who look at all possible factors and propose an idea of what will happen in the future. Thus, environmental scanning permits us to identify, track, and assess changes in the environment.[3]

Through scanning, we can examine the factors that seem likely to "drive" the environment. **Drivers** are variables (e.g., economic conditions, demographic shifts, governmental policies, social attitudes, technological advances) that will have a bearing on future conditions. Three categories of drivers will serve to identify possible trends and impacts on the American criminal justice system during this century: (1) social and economic conditions (e.g., size and age of the population, immigration patterns, nature of employment, and lifestyle characteristics); (2) shifts in the amount and type of crimes (including the potential for new types of criminality and for technological advances that might be used for illegal behavior); and (3) possible developments in the criminal justice system itself (e.g., changes in the way the police, courts, and corrections subsystems operate and important innovations).[4]

**Scenario writing** is simply the application of drivers to three primary situations: public tolerance for crime, amount of crime, and the capacity of the criminal justice system to deal with crime. An important consideration is the degree to which each will occur. For example, drivers may be analyzed in a scenario of *low* public tolerance for crime, a *high* amount of crime, and a *high* capacity of the criminal justice system to deal with crime. Conversely, a scenario may include a view of the future in which there is a *high* tolerance for crime, a *low* amount of crime, and a *low* capacity for the system to cope with crime; and so on.

# A Changing Nation

## *Faces of America*

The changing demographics of our nation, and what it bodes for the future, commands the attention of its peacekeepers. Nearly 273 million people are now living in the United States, 51 percent of whom are female. There are about 2.63 persons per household, and about one-fourth (27.6 percent) of all households are headed by one person.[5] While 56 percent of the population is married and lives with a spouse, about 19.4 million adults (9.4 percent) are divorced.[6] These statistics represent threats to societal stability, because the smaller the household, the less the commitment of one person to another, and the less likely deviance will be managed at the household level, thus necessitating governmental intervention. Marriage is our most stable family structure.[7]

Another destabilizing force is the number of people who change where they reside in a given year. The average person moves once every six years, but approximately 17 percent of the population moves each year. Thus, long-term neighborhood stability is the exception rather than the rule. Home ownership—another stability factor—is also a concern, with 72 percent of blacks and Hispanics and 38 percent of whites unable to afford a modestly priced home. Single females fare even worse—57 percent of single white women, 78 percent of black women, and 73 percent of Hispanic women are unable to afford a modestly priced home. Being black or Hispanic and/or being single makes women more susceptible to poverty and criminal victimization.[8]

Furthermore, there is an increasing number of fatherless children, who are more prone to delinquency and other social pathologies. Many problems in crime control are strongly related to father absence: 90 percent of all homeless and runaway youths are from fatherless homes, as are 71 percent of high school dropouts, 70 percent of youths in state institutions, and 75 percent of adolescent patients in substance abuse centers.[9]

We live in a "graying" country as well, where the fastest growing age group is between 55 and 65.[10] The golden years for baby boomers represent this graying of the population. Nearly half (45.2 percent) of women 65 years old and over are widowed; of those, 70.1 percent live alone.[11] The oldest old (persons 85 years old and over) are a small but rapidly growing group and are projected to be the fastest-growing part of the elderly population well into the twenty-first century.[12] The rapid growth of the elderly, particularly the oldest old, represents a triumph of efforts to extend human life, but these age groups also require a large share of special services and public support.[13]

The good news is that the elderly are less likely than younger people to become victims of violence, personal theft, and household crimes and to be injured during a violent crime—but their injuries, with their brittle bones, are more severe. Victimization for the elderly can be permanently disabling. Usually on a fixed income, they cannot always afford the best medical care. They also have a high fear of crime but are less likely than younger people to take protective measures and more likely to report a crime. They are also targeted more often than other people for financial fraud schemes, which can lead to severe depression and other serious health problems. Their isolation leads to a high percentage of their victimization occurring in their homes.[14]

Almost one-third of the current population growth results from legal immigration.[15] An estimated 5 million undocumented immigrants reside in the United States as well, and there is an estimated increase of about 275,000 illegal aliens entering and residing in this country each year. Mexico is the leading country of origin of illegal aliens, with about 2.7 million (or 54 percent) of the illegal immigrant population.[16]

The influence of immigration to America and the growth of minority group populations in general cannot be overstated. America now accepts nearly

1 million newcomers each year (with a net immigration of about 880,000 persons, which could increase or decrease in future years).[17] Immigrants to this nation, however, are not more prone to crime than native-born Americans. Among 18- to 40-year-old men in the United States, immigrants are less likely than native-born Americans to go to prison.[18] However, immigrants pose unique challenges for the police.

## *Crime, Violence, and the Influence of Drugs and Guns*

About 29 million violent and property crime victimizations occur per year in this country.[19] A number of factors contribute to these figures: easy access to firearms, alcohol and substance abuse, drug trafficking, poverty, racial discrimination, and cultural acceptance of violent behavior.

Recent declines in crime have actually made America safer. From 1994 to 1998, the murder rate dropped 30 percent. For other violent crimes, National Crime Victim Survey (NCVS) data showed a 7 percent decline from 1997 to 1998 and a decrease of 26.7 percent from 1993 to 1998, as well as a 12 percent decline in property crimes. Violent crimes are expected to continue to decline.[20] Furthermore, from 1999 to 2000, the violent crime rate fell 15 percent, and the property crime rate fell 10 percent. Violent victimization and property crime rates are the lowest recorded since the NCVS' inception in 1973.[21]

Why this decline in crime? Possible reasons include the tougher sentences imposed on violent criminals by state legislators, and the implementation by local officials of aggressive and intelligent methods of community policing. The effectiveness of good police work and extended incarceration of hardened criminals is beyond dispute. Notwithstanding this recent decline in offenses, serious challenges remain. New criminal types, who are better educated, upscale, older, and increasingly female, will dot the national landscape in the future.

Serious problems with respect to violence remain in the United States. In both the immediate and distant future, police will continue to deal with "the new violence" that has emerged over the past five to ten years. In the past, violence was a means to an end. Revenge, robbery, and jealousy were among the many reasons that people resorted to violence. Today, an entire culture has emerged that sees the use of violence as an end unto itself. The people who make up this culture—gangs, pseudo gangs, well-armed young people, and others—are not going to change their way of thinking or relax their hostility and aggression simply because there is a fluctuation in drug usage or a switch from cocaine to heroin. For these people, the wanton use of violence—aggression for the sake of aggression—is not considered abhorrent behavior. Taken in combination, these factors present challenges for police leaders. Police will have to be trained and educated to understand violent behavior in its more recent form.[22]

Furthermore, the reduction in crime has had minimal, if any, effect on reducing citizen fear of crime. Reducing fear, not simply lowering crime statistics, will be a major challenge facing police leaders in the future. Few police leaders and officers know anything about fear. What is it? How does it work? What is the cycle of fear? How can the police intervene to break the cycle? Why is fear contagious? Do problem solving, partnering, and the implementation of crime control strategies and tactics reduce fear? Officers should be trained in the practical aspects of fear and how to assess causes and levels of individual, neighborhood, and community fear.[23]

Drugs are also a major factor in crime and violence; more than 277,000 offenders are in prison for drug law violations—21 percent of state prisoners and more than 60 percent of federal prisoners. More than 80 percent of state prisoners and 70 percent of federal prisoners have engaged in some form of illicit drug use. One-third of state prison inmates and 22 percent of federal prisoners report they were under the influence of drugs when they committed the crime for which they are in prison.[24]

Most police agencies remain reactive to the drug trade. They perform street corner sweeps, arrest users and low-level dealers, rely on specialists (narcotics units) to assume primary responsibility for enforcement, and participate in regional task forces (generally when funded by the federal government). Police leaders will have to "think out of the box" in the future in response to a changing drug market. A well-planned, strategic approach to the drug trade and problem solving related to drugs will be needed in every agency. More agencies must become involved in teaching employees about drug market analysis and forecasting.

In addition to drugs, two other **crime acceleration** factors—guns and alcohol—might increase the risk of victimization and a general fear of crime. Nearly 200 million guns are in private hands in the United States.[25] Gun violence in the United States is both a criminal justice and a public health problem; firearms are still the weapons most frequently used for murder. They are the weapons of choice in nearly two-thirds of all homicides. Strategies and programs to reduce gun violence include interrupting sources of illegal guns, deterring illegal possession and carrying of guns, and responding to illegal gun use.[26]

Alcohol also remains a major factor in crime and violence, with almost 4 in 10 violent crimes involving alcohol.[27] About one-third of U.S. offenders report that they were using alcohol at the time of their offense.[28]

# What the Future Portends for the Police

What can the nation's police do about demographic changes and still high levels of crime? Can they "hold the line" and reduce the spread of criminality?

Defining solutions to the problems facing future police service is difficult at best. Factors such as locale, political environment, and economics will determine how an agency and its employees will view and react to the future. Additionally, for some police leaders the future is the next fiscal year, while for others it is a three- to five-year span of time toward which they have set into motion a strategic planning process. Still, for others, the future is next Friday and surviving without a crisis until their next day off. Any discussion of the future must include the short term as well as the long term and must give attention to operational issues, administrative issues, the community, and the basic philosophy of policing.[29]

The first priority is for the police to realize that the conventional style of reactive, incident-driven policing employed during the professional era had several drawbacks. That type of police department was hierarchical, impersonal, and rule based, and most important policy decisions were made at the top; line officers made few decisions on their own.

## *Community Oriented Policing and Problem Solving*

Chapter 3 examined the current era of policing, **COPPS;** following are some futuristic issues that remain to be addressed with this program.

First, many fundamental questions remain concerning COPPS. For example, how many police agencies have made a commitment to community policing? How many agencies have demonstrated the link between community policing and the quality of the communities they serve? How many have embraced community policing to gain a share of available federal dollars? Will community policing endure without federal funding?[30]

From 1994 to 2001, the federal Office of Community Oriented Policing Services (COPS), created by the Violent Crime Control and Law Enforcement Act of 1994, spent about $9 billion to help police agencies implement COPPS, adding officers to the beat and providing technical assistance, technology, equipment, and training. By mid-2000, the COPS office had provided funding to 82 percent of America's police departments by awarding more than 30,000 grants to more than 12,000 departments. This included funding more than 105,000 community policing officers and training more than 90,000 officers and citizens.[31] Funding for the COPS office expired in 2000, however, and its future remains uncertain.[32] Any police agency that is currently basing its COPPS efforts on federal funds may find itself in desperate straits in the future.

Another central issue with respect to COPPS concerns community partnerships. Much of society, including the police themselves, has come to realize that the police cannot function independently to address crime and disorder. The challenge to leaders, now and in the future, is to develop meaningful and lasting partnerships rather than the superficial relationships that now exist in many communities. For many police officers, the concept of partnership means simply attending occasional neighborhood association meetings or occasionally visiting neighborhood leaders who live on their beat. Partnerships for the sake of partnership do not endure; they will work only when the mutual benefits to the parties involved are well defined, well understood, and attainable.

Several other issues for the future must be addressed if COPPS is to survive and thrive, including whether police chief executives will change the culture of their agencies, implement the concept, decentralize their department (pushing decision making downward), invest in the necessary technology for locating "hot spots," and develop the necessary mechanisms to support COPPS. These challenges also include recruitment, selection, training, performance appraisals, and reward and promotional systems. It is also necessary that police unions work with administrators to effect the kinds of changes that are needed for COPPS. The answers to these issues could be critical, not only to the future of COPPS, but also to policing and society.

Some futurists see COPPS undergoing a metamorphosis in the near future, including the following changes:

- Ethics will be woven into everything the police do: the hiring process, field training officer programs, decision-making processes. There will be increased emphasis on accountability and integrity within police agencies as policing is elevated to a higher standing, reaching more toward being a true profession, with the majority of officers being required to possess a college degree.
- Formal awards ceremonies will concentrate as much or more on achievements in improving citizens' quality of life than on numbers of felony arrests or other high-risk activities.
- Communications will be greatly improved through internal "Intranets," containing local and agency operational data, phone books, maps, calendars, calls for service, crime data sheets, speeches, newsletters, news releases, and so on.[33]
- Major cities will no longer require policing experience as a requirement to be the chief police executive (who could then be recruited from private industry). The head of the future police agency will essentially be recognized as a CEO with good business sense as a trend toward privatization of certain services becomes more prevalent. Knowledge will continue to increase at lightning speed, forcing the CEO to be involved in trend analysis and forecasting in order to keep ahead of the curve.
- The rigid paramilitary style currently in effect will become obsolete, replaced by work teams consisting of line officers, community members, and business and corporate representatives.
- The current squad structure will give way to more productive, creative teams of officers who, having been empowered with more autonomy, will become efficient problem solvers, thus strengthening ties between the police and the citizenry.
- Neighborhoods will more actively participate in the identification, location, and capture of criminals.

On a more negative note, however, some authors point to what they believe are several *unfavorable* social forces that work against the future of COPPS: local governments being pushed toward a more legalistic, crime-control model of policing; a public that is less willing to pay more taxes to address fundamental social problems; and a public policy that does not allow the police to focus on the root causes of crime, but rather on their symptoms (e.g., criminal conduct) through aggressive strategies rather than through COPPS.[34] Indeed, the landscape of policing is littered with the skeletons of strategies and approaches that died after the departure of a dedicated COPPS chief or sheriff. Although it is hoped that such a fate will not befall COPPS, history has shown it to be a possibility that cannot be ignored.

In sum, several questions for the future of COPPS remain:

- Will police organizations come to believe that they alone cannot control crime and truly enlist the aid of the community in this endeavor?
- Will police chief executives acquire the innovative drive necessary to change the culture of their departments, implement COPPS, flatten the organizational structure of their department, and see that officers' work is properly evaluated?
- Will police executives have the necessary job security to accommodate COPPS? Would at-will employment of chiefs place COPPS at risk?
- Will departments work with their communities, other city agencies, businesses, elected officials, and the media to sustain COPPS?
- Will police unions work with administrators to effect changes needed for COPPS?
- Will police employees who have not yet done so, from top to bottom, sworn and civilian, realize that the traditional "sacred cow," reactive mode of policing has obviously not been successful and cannot work in the future?
- Can those police organizations, from top to bottom, become more customer and value oriented?
- Will police executives and supervisors come to develop the necessary policies and support mechanisms to support COPPS, including recruitment, selection, training, performance appraisals, and reward and promotional systems?
- Will police executives and supervisors begin viewing the patrol officer as a problem-solving specialist? Will they give street officers enough free time and latitude to engage in proactive policing?
- Will police organizations come to view COPPS as a department- and city-wide strategy? Will they invest in technology to support problem-oriented policing?
- Will those agencies attempt to bring diversity into their ranks, reflecting the changing demographics and cultural customs of our society?

## *Participative Management for More Highly Educated Officers*

In the past, the emphasis of police supervision and management was on submission to authority; however, a different set of values and expectations has been established for the future. The autocratic leader of the past will not be effective in the future. As Donald Witham[35] noted, "The watchwords of the new leadership paradigm are coach, inspire, gain commitment, empower, affirm, flexibility, responsibility, self-management, shared power, autonomous teams, and entrepreneurial units."

Police officers of the future will not normally possess military experience and follow its inherent obedience to authority. They will have higher levels of education and will tend to be more independent and less responsive to traditional authoritative approaches to their work. They will have been exposed to more participative, supportive, and humanistic approaches. These officers will want more opportunities to provide input in their work and to address the challenges posed by neighborhood problem solving. In short, they will not want to function like automatons during their tour of duty, blindly following general orders, policies and procedures, and rules and regulations.

These officers will be, according to J. R. Metts,[36] "bright, resourceful, and versatile, cross-trained in law enforcement, firefighting, and paramedical services. Administrators will care less about marksmanship and physical size and more about mental capacity and diplomas."

Changes will not happen overnight, however, because many managers came up through the ranks and will oppose drastic changes to the "old style" of management. As one author observed, "The field of law enforcement management is full of dinosaurs, and they are becoming extinct."[37]

## Future Changes in the Courts

Several critical trends will shape the courts in the next decade, including the following:[38]

- *Increasing demand for culturally appropriate court and justice services:* Over the next 10 years, immigration patterns will result in continued growth in Latino, Middle Eastern, and Asian populations in particular, leading to increasing demand in the trial courts for language and "culture" interpreters, incorporating new forms of dispute resolution, and educating judges and other court actors about cultural diversity.

- *An increasing number of diverse expectations for the courts' role in society:* Complex social and economic problems have several implications, including increased demand for educational materials describing what the courts can and cannot be expected to do, ongoing debate about the role of the judicial branch relative to the other two branches of government, and new types of cases resulting in increasing service demands on courts.

- *Alterations in family composition:* Declining numbers of traditional families will result in courts having to redefine and deal with different kinds of disputes and develop excellent relationships with other public agencies.

- *Polarization of people by class, race, ethnicity, and lifestyle preferences:* Changes in housing and school policies, movement of the white population to suburban areas, the concentration of nonwhite populations in portions of urban areas, and the resulting racial and ethnic tensions will cause a need for different strategies for the courts that serve different geographical area; increased scrutiny of class, racial, ethnic, and lifestyle biases; increased separation of groups into gated communities; and greater demand for cultural sensitivity for court personnel.

• *Increasing demand for acceptance of alternative lifestyles:* Increases in the number of single-member, unrelated-adult, and single-parent families, as well as collections of elderly people and same-sex and nonmarried partnerships, will bring about new areas of law, greater demand for nontraditional family-oriented programs, intolerance and backlash by groups supporting more traditional values, and increased pressures for lifestyle issues to be considered in judicial elections.

• *Increasing manipulation of public opinion about crime and the courts using mass media:* The increasingly competitive nature of the media business will foment general dissatisfaction with the justice system, increased awareness (often distorted) of the court system, more special interest group demands on the courts, difficulty ensuring fair trials in some unusual or sensational cases, and a need to develop better ways to inform the press and the public.

• *Rapidly emerging information and networking technology:* The implications of these trends include a need for increased court participation in designing data-collection and analysis standards, maintaining information network software, making information available to better manage cases, increasing public access to records, changing evidence rules, and changing the method for the compilation, manipulation, and storage of records.

## *Shifts in Philosophy and Practice*

Futurists have been considering needed changes in the courts as their caseloads expand, society demands greater assistance from the courts in addressing its social ills, and technology continues to advance. Looking at current trends, futurist Clement Bezold[39] offered some interesting court-related speculations for the early twenty-first century:

1. Private businesses offering adjudication, arbitration, and mediation will increasingly compete with public courts to resolve disputes more quickly and fairly.

2. The adversary system, which is slow, costly, and fraught with unfairness, will die.

3. The vast majority of judicial decision making (in areas such as small claims, traffic courts, and status offenses) will be by nonlawyer, citizen judges.

4. Courts will be depoliticized. Appointed professional managers will become the norm, and the merit selection of judges will become more commonplace.

5. Courts will increasingly be called on to resolve social problems involving drugs, poverty, and domestic violence, but with little success.

6. Court programs will become increasingly decentralized and closer to client groups.

7. Court organizational structures will become more informal, with less reliance on hierarchical, bureaucratic structures, and with shared leadership.

Certainly not to be overlooked in the courts' future are the impacts of high technology on their internal operations—some of which were discussed in Chapter 17. The following scenario is not uncommon today: The judge, defendants, lawyers, jurors, and members of the press wear headsets that allow them to listen to the extensive audiotaped evidence; the judge turns on "white noise," allowing only himself, defendants, and lawyers to hear conversations, thus allowing all to remain seated during bench conferences; and everyone in the courtroom views documentary evidence on computers, with eight terminals shared by jurors and two shared by the public and press.[40]

The Internet has already transformed the relationship between lawyers and the public, making it easier for the former to locate and interact with the latter. But other substantive changes lie beyond the horizon. A few state supreme courts, for example, are creating websites that offer the prospect of the court becoming a major source of information about its decisions, organization, and other aspects (such as education, communicating with the media, and promoting the court itself).[41]

Some of this technological advancement will increasingly involve the courts in ethical issues, as new life forms are developed at the molecular level and reversible and permanent changes occur in crops, plants, animal life, and human biology.[42] Other developments, such as the six types of court technology described in Chapter 17, will continue to change the way the courts function. Some traditional ways of doing business will become obsolete. Courts must not fall further behind, and they must shape their use of technology to solve the important problems they face.

The two hottest issues in court technology today are electronic filing of documents with the court (where there has been a lack of involvement of users in the design and development of the system) and the integration of criminal justice information systems.[43]

# Corrections and the Future

## *The Changing Nature of "Justice," Treatment, and Custody*

It is important to remember that crime alone does not determine the size of correctional caseloads and institutional populations. Rather, it is the manner in which society responds to criminal behavior. Indeed, the current "justice model" of punishment began in the mid-1970s and emphasizes personal responsibility for crime, "flat" or determinate sentences, swift and sure punishment, and retribution by society. It has done more than anything else to inflate those caseloads and populations.[44]

Furthermore, the movement today is toward **restorative justice,** which is a reaction to the increasingly comprehensive role that government has come to play in apprehending, prosecuting, and punishing criminals—often causing what is perceived by many to be the general exclusion of the victim. Restorative justice seeks to restore at least some of the tangible losses experienced by the victim through negotiated restitution arrangements, as well as the offender's sense of personal accountability for the harm caused by his or her actions. Programs based on restorative justice can be expected to proliferate in the future, especially as victims continue to demand greater representation in the justice process.[45]

Treatment for offenders is also a continuing part of the corrections process—notwithstanding the justice model's influence. The difference with offender treatment of today and that of a more offender-oriented era of the past (known as the "medical model") is that now it is more likely to be offered on a *voluntary* basis, rather than as an inducement for early release. Treatment now takes on a more pragmatic orientation. In contrast to counseling, group therapy, and other forms of treatment, the emphasis today (and likely for the foreseeable future) is placed on developing productive employment skills.[46]

In addition to the changing nature of programs offered by corrections, indications are also on the horizon that the physical features of correctional institutions are beginning to change, especially in local jails, where some of the most antiquated facilities are being razed or modernized, small jails are being consolidated through regionalization, and new architectural and management styles are reflecting the principles of **direct supervision** ("new generation") **jailing.** Both prisons and jails are also becoming more electronically sophisticated; locks and keys are giving way to computers, video cameras, "smart cards," and even satellite surveillance. As corrections administrators are expected to do more with less, methods of tracking inmate movements and purchases through electronic scanning devices are also expanding, as are user fees for services ranging from health care to transportation and even food and lodging.[47]

## Changing Corrections Personnel and Populations

The times are changing with respect to corrections personnel in the areas of recruitment and retention, decision making, and treatment of their charges. Indeed, surveys have identified institutional crowding, staff and funding shortages, and resulting workload increases as the key problems that corrections is anticipated to face in the immediate future.[48]

The ability of corrections administrators to recruit and retain the quality of personnel needed during this new century will largely depend on how well they can accommodate diversity, decentralized decision making, and ongoing career development. The expanding use by government of privatization (discussed in Chapter 12) as an attempt to save money may also affect corrections practices as well as how corrections personnel approach their work: The "threat" of privatization may compel public employees to believe their job security is endangered, thus stimulating them to provide better services at lower cost in the public sector.[49]

The expanding use of computers has also had a substantial impact throughout the corrections field, performing what were previously time-consuming and labor-intensive tasks. Corrections will also be especially challenged to meet the needs of its changing population, including increasing numbers of female offenders (discussed in Chapter 12) as well as those who have AIDS or are physically impaired or elderly. Nor is there expected to be any decline in the number of correctional clients suffering from drug or alcohol addictions or mental disorders.

It is a given that corrections faces some of its toughest hurdles in the twenty-first century. Correctional administrators must anticipate those hurdles. As Jeanne Stinchcomb and Vernon Fox[50] have observed,

> The field of corrections may not be "drowning" . . . but it is rowing upstream amid strong currents. In such a situation, there are three choices: give up, row harder, or reduce the strength of the currents.

The future promises to be both fascinating and frustrating for corrections; perhaps that is "why they call it corrections . . . not perfection."[51]

## *Future Needs of Correctional Managers*

With all of the issues and problems affecting corrections, it is clear that more than ever the effective correctional administrator is one who, in the words of Alvin Cohn,[52] "not only recognizes the inevitability of change, but tries to harness and direct the change process." Cohn suggested that the pedestrian correctional manager reacts to crises, fails to plan, views his or her position as one of a sinecurist (requiring little or no work), and otherwise fails to lead the organization. Conversely, the progressive correctional manager is proactive, views the organization as a system, and plans for and attempts to control its future.[53]

Three significant developments in the fields of business and industry can be transferred to correctional practice. First is *technology*. At the beginning of the twenty-first century, more information is recorded and processed in ways that are faster, more complete, and more accurate than ever before. The second major development is *total quality management,* a philosophy that embraces participative management and moves attention to customers. The third development is *reinventing government,* or finding ways to reduce both the size and complexity of governmental operations. Each of these developments has a critical impact on government but is not always employed by correctional administrators to improve current and projected programs and services.[54]

Cohn believes that the traditional role of correctional managers, much of which revolves around information gathering and case reviewing, may be unnecessary with today's technology; if middle managers and supervisors can be recycled to demonstrate a willingness to change from traditional ways of doing business and incorporate these new developments into their work, restructuring today's correctional agencies will be an easier process.[55]

According to prison expert John DiIulio Jr., prison officials could take three steps to help create better prisons in the short and long terms:

1. Provide continuity in the commissioner's office (and, it should be added, in the warden's office; both have an average tenure that is often less than five years). The high turnover of the past 20 years has fostered a power vacuum at many levels of management.

2. Adopt the practice of unit management as a means of reducing prison violence. In addition to its potential for calming the institution and its residents, unit management leads to fewer staff rotations and allows management to measure performance more effectively. Officers are given more authority and act more like professionals, and morale is boosted.

3. Allow products manufactured by inmates in state prisons to be sold to the federal government. This would eliminate the current endless hours of idleness for inmates. The federal system has a large and ready market for its products.[56]

## *Prison Construction: Coping with Community Perceptions*

Since 1985, the average annual increase in the prison population in the United States has been more than 7 percent. This steady increase has created a correctional crisis for the future.[57] One strategy for addressing this crisis has been (and will likely remain) prison construction. And one issue that has brought criminal justice to the forefront of public policy—and into the living rooms of America—is the effect of prison construction on host communities.

Prison siting involves both the NIMBY (not in my back yard) and LULU (locally unwanted land use) reactions that also appear with proposals to build regionally needed facilities such as homeless shelters, power plants, toxic dumps, halfway houses, all of which are unwanted locally because of their feared impact on the community). Communities' reactions over siting LULU facilities range from having their image tarnished to safety fears and worry over declining property values.[58]

Given the complexities of the issues and emotions involved, it is difficult to predict how communities will react to the proposed opening of LULUs. But when the facility is a *prison,* it is generally assumed that the community will react negatively and with fear. Prison-siting decisions tend to become embroiled in politics, with some leaders seeing the introduction of the prison as a needed economic boost, and others experiencing many fears and concerns.

The impact of prisons on communities can be assessed in two ways: by examining subjective factors (such as attitudes, beliefs, opinions, and perceptions) and/or by evaluating objective indicators (property values, crime rates, employment). Objective factors are mainly used in the promotion of siting a facility, while subjective factors are those offered most in opposition.[59]

For future prison-siting approaches, three sets of issues must be addressed: public confidence, public risk, and shared decision making. Most people are aware of the stigma attached to having a prison in their community, and this awareness can also result in feelings of powerlessness, that the decision to site a prison is a "done deal." In the future, efforts should be made to directly assess and systematically monitor these aspects of siting processes.[60]

But in this same vein, Harry Allen and Clifford Simonsen noted, "We cannot possibly build ourselves out of [a] prison and management crisis."[61] What must be developed first is a logical set of correctional objectives and sentencing policies that have clear goals and wide-ranging options and intermediate sanctions (discussed in Chapter 11).

# The Entire Justice System: Future Issues

## *Personnel Professionalization and Other Issues*

As has been widely reported, the entire future of our nation changed after September 11, 2001. Certainly, many people believe that the justice system must become as professional as possible in order to meet the challenges posed by the threat of terrorism. One trend worth exploring, according to futurist Clyde L. Cronkhite, is the reorganizing of criminal justice agencies into the professional model set by hospitals and universities, where the majority of employees are hired for their expertise and education and can spend an entire career practicing in their field with substantial rewards in pay and recognition. Cronkhite believes that with higher selection, education, and training standards, and employees becoming experts in their fields, less supervision and management would be required. Employees could follow rewarding and challenging career paths that correspond with their interests and talents.[62]

In addition to some personnel matters discussed earlier, other, traditional criminal justice personnel problems are not likely to go away either. Such matters as the need for more women and minorities; unionization and job actions; contract and consolidated policing; civilianization, accreditation, and higher education; and stress recognition and management will not be resolved in the near future. Furthermore, changing societal values, court decisions about the rights of employees, and the Peace Officers' Bill of Rights will make leadership increasingly challenging. Nor will opportunities decline for the police to engage in graft and corruption; therefore, administrators must develop personnel policies that will protect the integrity of the profession.

## *Future High Technology*

We discussed the current state of technology and what is currently in research and development in Chapter 17. The advent of computer crime has certainly changed the world of criminal justice administration, posing new and extraordinary challenges. An estimated 150 million Americans are now plugged into cyberspace, and thousands more enter the online world each day.[63] This high-tech revolution in our homes and offices has opened a whole new world for the criminal element as well. Pornographers and pedophiles are now on the Web, as well as people who trade stolen credit card numbers, rig auctions, create viruses, and devise baby adoption scams, among many other crimes.[64] Computer crimes will increase dramatically, including crimes such as cyberterrorism, identity theft, credit card fraud, consumer fraud, stock market–related fraud, and industrial espionage; these crimes may well become the next national crime-fighting obsessions.[65]

Many criminal justice organizations lack the in-house computer expertise to install or run software and equipment. Many agency executives believe that they hire people only to be police officers, probation officers, court administrators, or whatever—not to be computer programmers or database experts. But the nature of the justice business is changing; people with such skills are not only desirable and valuable, but are also increasingly and rapidly becoming a *necessity* as problem-solving aids.

As noted in Chapter 17, the police are ill prepared to investigate computer-related crimes. They and prosecutors are already playing catch-up to comprehend and investigate a host of evasive criminal schemes.[66]

To meet the future challenges posed by computer crimes, all criminal justice administrators must become better educated, adaptable, and equipped. Training will have to be virtually continuous to address complex threats to society.

## *Allocation of Resources*

If the quality of criminal justice service delivery is to progress, a greater number of leaders will need to know more about resource allocation than they currently do. With the decline in federal funding for additional employees, combined with local, state, and federal belt tightening, greater emphasis will be placed on using available resources as efficiently as possible.

Analysis of workload and resources should be part of every supervisor's and executive's routine functioning. Justifying resources should be based on more than perception and the simple belief that more is better. Once learned, resource allocation is neither overwhelmingly time consuming or difficult. It becomes second nature. With the predicted reduction in federal funds and a tightening of local budgets, a commitment to quality allocation of resources is essential.[67]

On the whole, it is unlikely that local criminal justice budgets will increase substantially in the near future (with the possible exception of terrorism-related activities).[68] Some justice organizations are already attempting to cope with budgetary problems in some new and unique ways, such as employing lobbyists to present their case to state legislatures. Some have also begun generating their own revenue by charging for traditionally free public services, such as automobile accident investigations and response to false alarms by the police.

## *Flattening the Organization*

An area of concern among futurists is organizational structure. Increasing numbers of executives, particularly in the paramilitary, hierarchical police organizations, are beginning to question whether or not the traditional pyramid-shaped bureaucracy will be effective in the future. Indeed, the spread of COPPS has allowed many police executives to flatten their organizations. And, as we discussed in Chapter 2, communication within the pyramid structure often faces many barriers and is frustrated by the levels of bureaucracy; perhaps the organizational structure, the argument goes, could be changed to a more horizontal design to facilitate the flow of information and ideas.

# CASE STUDIES

The following two case studies—concerning strategic planning and the administrator's role within such planning—will assist the reader in considering some of the challenges one faces when looking at the future.

## Gotham City Looks Beyond the Horizon

Gotham City has a number of new department heads, with varying levels of experience. Furthermore, recent crime, budget, and other crises have underscored the need for the city's departments to work more collaboratively and address problems of the future. Accordingly, the city manager is convening a strategic (long-term) planning workshop in one week to bring all department heads together, to orient them concerning the city council's long-term priorities, and to discuss and address problems. Of course, the chief of police will attend and represent the police department.

### Questions for Discussion

1. What kind of information does the chief need?
2. Where will this information be found, and by whom?
3. Using the data that are collected, what are the factors (drivers) that will affect the future of *your* city in its changing environment?
4. What kinds of future challenges would those factors pose for the police in your community?

## A Futures Forum

Assume that your jurisdiction is planning a new, week-long, futures-oriented program, "Leadership Forum for 2010," which will bring professionals together from the business and governmental sectors. Topics to be discussed at the forum include a wide array of area issues, challenges, methods, and concerns. Assume further that you are the county sheriff. After applying and being selected to attend this program, you are advised that you are to make a 60-minute presentation concerning your profession generally, as well as the future challenges facing your organization.

### Questions for Discussion

1. Using some of the materials discussed throughout this book, how would you briefly explain to this group the role of a chief executive officer in a law enforcement organization?

2. What would be some of the important *current* themes and issues that you would take to the forum concerning a law enforcement administrator's job to indicate its complexities and challenges?

3. How would you describe the changing nature of the administrator's role, and the *future* issues and challenges of this position?

## Summary

The cup is half full. The cup is half empty. Should we be optimistic or pessimistic about the nation's future? One thing that is for certain is that our society is changing. This is an exciting and challenging time in the history of criminal justice service. Persons employed in justice-related governmental positions will deal with unforeseen problems caused by new drugs, small but hostile groups of extremists, young people who were raised in an environment of violence, and more. They have the opportunity to deal with these issues supported by advanced technology, highly evolved information resources, better trained employees, and a heightened commitment to interjurisdictional cooperation.

Criminal justice administrators will benefit greatly by anticipating what the future holds, in order that appropriate resources and methods may be brought to bear on the problems ahead. And there is no indication that a significant abatement of today's social problems is looming on the horizon. Criminal justice agencies will be affected in many ways by the social and economic changes to come; they can no longer be resistant to change or unmindful of the future.

## Questions for Review

1. In what ways will there be a demographic shift in America's future?
2. What specific changes in crime are seen for the future?
3. How will community policing and problem solving affect the future of policing?
4. What are some of the major technological changes and problems that futurists anticipate?
5. How will philosophical shifts toward crime and criminals affect custody in the future?
6. What are some problematic personnel issues that loom on the horizon?

## Notes

1. Those wanting to keep abreast of trends and changes should join the World Future Society; its publication, *The Futurist,* is excellent.

2. William L. Tafoya, "The Future of Community Policing," *Crime and Justice International* 13 (July 1997):4–6.

3. Kenneth J. Peak, *Policing America: Methods, Issues, Challenges,* 3rd ed. (Upper Saddle River, N.J.: Prentice Hall, 2000), p. 361.

4. Ibid.

5. U.S. Census Bureau, *Statistics in Brief: Population and Vital Statistics* (Washington, D.C.: Author, 2000).

6. Ibid.

7. Ibid.

8. Ibid., pp. 1–2.

9. Ibid., p. 11.

10. Cicero Wilson, "Economic Shifts That Will Impact Crime Control and Community Mobilization," in U.S. Department of Justice, National Institute of Justice, *What Can the Federal Government Do to Decrease Crime and Revitalize Communities?* (Washington, D.C.: U.S. Department of Justice, 1998), p. 4.

11. U.S. Census Bureau, *Current Population Reports: Marital Status and Living Arrangements* (Washington, D.C.: Author, March 1998), p. 2.

12. Frank B. Hobbs, *The Elderly Population* (Washington, D.C.: U.S. Census Bureau, 1999), p. 2.

13. Konrad M. Kressly, "Golden Years for Baby Boomers: America in the Next Century," *The Harbinger* (January 1998):1.

14. Andrew Karmen, *Crime Victims: An Introduction to Victimology,* 3d ed. (Belmont, Calif.: Wadsworth, 1996), pp. 263–264.

15. U.S. Census Bureau, *Illegal Alien Resident Population* (Washington, D.C.: Author, 2000), p. 1.

16. Ibid., p. 2.

17. Jennifer Cheeseman Day, *National Population Projections* (Washington, D.C.: U.S. Census Bureau, 1999), p. 1.

18. Kristin F. Butcher and Anne Morrison Piehl, "Recent Immigrants: Unexpected Implications for Crime and Incarceration," National Bureau of Economic Research, *NBER Working Papers,* No. 6067 (June 1997):1.

19. U.S. Department of Justice, Bureau of Justice Statistics Press Release, "National Violent Crime Rate Falls More Than 10 Percent—Violent Victimizations Down One-Third Since 1993," August 27, 2000.

20. Ibid., pp. 2–3.

21. U.S. Department of Justice, Bureau of Justice Statistics, *Criminal Victimization 2000: Changes 1999–2000 with Trends 1993–2000* (Washington, D.C.: Author, 2000).

22. Sheldon Greenberg, "Future Issues in Policing: Challenges for Leaders," in Ronald W. Glensor, Mark E. Correia, and Kenneth J. Peak (eds.), *Policing Communities: Understanding Crime and Solving Problems* (Los Angeles: Roxbury, 2000), pp. 315–321.

23. Ibid.

24. U.S. Department of Justice, Bureau of Justice Statistics Press Release, "More Than Three-Quarters of Prisoners Had Abused Drugs in the Past," January 5, 1999.

25. U.S. Department of Justice, National Institute of Justice, *Guns in America: National Survey on Private Ownership and Use of Firearms* (Washington, D.C.: Author, 1997), pp. 1–2.

26. David Sheppard, "Strategies to Reduce Gun Violence," U.S. Department of Justice, Office of Juvenile Justice and Delinquency Prevention Fact Sheet #93 (February 1999):1.

27. U.S. Department of Justice, Bureau of Justice Statistics, *Alcohol and Crime* (Washington, D.C.: Author, 1998), p. 20.

28. Ibid.

29. Greenberg, "Future Issues in Policing," p. 315.

30. Ibid., pp. 318-319.

31. Thomas C. Frazier, "Community Policing Efforts Offer Hope for the Future," *The Police Chief* 67 (August 2000):11.

32. Ibid.

33. Dave Pettinari, "Are We There Yet? The Future of Policing/Sheriffing in Pueblo—Or in Anywhere, America." http://www.policefuturists.org/files/yet.html

34. Roy Roberg, John Crank, and Jack Kuykendall, *Police & Society,* 2d ed. (Los Angeles: Roxbury, 2000), pp. 522-523.

35. Donald C. Witham, "Environmental Scanning Pays Off," *The Police Chief* 58 (March 1991):26-31.

36. J. R. Metts, "Super Cops: The Police Force of Tomorrow," *The Futurist* (October 1985):31-36.

37. D. Story, "What Happens After All the Dinosaurs Are Gone? (The Passing of the Torch)," *Law and Order* 40 (October 1992):47-48.

38. Adapted from John A. Martin and Brenda J. Wagenknecht-Ivey, "Courts 2010: Critical Trends Shaping the Courts in the Next Decade," *The Court Manager* 15(1) (2000):6-16.

39. Adapted from Clement Bezold, "On Futures Thinking and the Courts," *The Court Manager* 6 (Summer 1991):4-11.

40. S. L. Alexander, "A Reality Check on Court/Media Relations," *Judicature* 84 (November-December 2000):146-149.

41. Patrick Schmidt and Paul Martin, "To the Internet and Beyond: State Supreme Courts on the World Wide Web," *Judicature* 84 (May-June 2001):314-318.

42. Franklin Zweig and Diane E. Cowdrey, "Educating Judges for Adjudication of New Life Technologies," *Judicature* 83 (November-December 1999):157.

43. Lawrence P. Webster, "How Technology Can Help Court Leaders Address the Justice Needs of a Multicultural Society in the Twenty-first Century," *The Court Manager* 15 (2000):45-49.

44. For a broader discussion of the justice model, see Jeanne B. Stinchcomb and Vernon B. Fox, *Introduction to Corrections,* 5th ed. (Upper Saddle River, N.J.: Prentice Hall, 1999), pp. 31-34.

45. Ibid., pp. 652-653.

46. Ibid., p. 654.

47. Ibid.

48. U.S. Department of Justice, National Institute of Justice, *NIJ Survey of Wardens and State Commissioners of Corrections* (Washington, D.C.: Author, 1995), p. 2

49. Stinchcomb and Fox, *Introduction to Corrections,* p. 659.

50. Ibid., p. 662.

51. Geno Natalucci-Persichetti, "Maybe That's Why They Call It Corrections," *Corrections Today* 53 (February 1991):26.

52. Alvin W. Cohn, "The Failure of Correctional Management: Recycling the Middle Manager," *Federal Probation* 59(2) (June 1995):10.

53. Ibid.

54. Ibid.

55. Ibid., p. 15.

56. Quoted in ibid.

57. Randy Martin, David Champion, and Todd Gibney, "Community Perceptions About Prison Construction: A Case Study," in Rosemary L. Gido and Ted Alleman (eds.),

*Turnstile Justice: Issues in American Corrections,* 2d ed. (Upper Saddle River, N.J.: Prentice Hall, 2002), pp. 176–207.

58. Ibid.

59. Ibid.

60. Ibid.

61. Harry E. Allen and Clifford E. Simonsen, *Corrections in America: An Introduction,* 9th ed. (Upper Saddle River, N.J.: Prentice Hall, 2001), p. 671.

62. Clyde L. Cronkhite, "American Criminal Justice Trends for the 21st Century," *Crime and Justice International* (July/August 2000):11, 34.

63. Margaret Mannix, "The Web's Dark Side," *U.S. News and World Report* (August 28, 2000):36.

64. Ibid.

65. Pettinari, "Are We There Yet?," p. 3.

66. "Cybergame for the Millennium: Cops 'n Robbers Playin' Hide 'n Seek on the Net," *Police Futurist* 8 (1) (1999):4.

67. Greenberg, "Future Issues in Policing," p. 320.

68. Edward J. Tully, "The Near Future: Implications for Law Enforcement," *FBI Law Enforcement Bulletin,* 55 (July 1986):1.

# Appendix I

# Related Web Sites

*National Institute of Justice*
http://www.ojp.usdoj.gov/nij
A component of the Office of Justice Programs, NIJ is the research agency of the Department of Justice. NIJ supports research, evaluation, and demonstration programs as well as the development of technology. Programs and publications are numerous.

*Bureau of Justice Statistics*
http://www.ojp.usdoj.gov/bjs
This agency is the United States' primary source for criminal justice statistics. BJS collects, analyzes, publishes, and disseminates information on crime, offenders, crime victims, and the operation of justice systems. Numerous publications are available.

*National Law Enforcement and Corrections Technology Center*
http://www.nlectc.org
This site publishes and distributes large collections of free publications concerning computers and software, equipment of all types, weapons and ammunition, and communications.

*The International Association of Chiefs of Police*
http://www.theiacp.org/
Established in 1893, the IACP is the world's oldest and largest organization of police executives (with 16,000 members); it launches programs, conducts research and training, and promulgates standards. Publishes *The Police Chief* monthly.

*Office of Community Oriented Policing Services (COPS)*
http://www.usdoj.gov/cops
Established by Congress with passage of the 1994 Violent Crime Control and Law Enforcement Act, this organization was authorized $8.8 billion over six years for grants to add community policing officers to the streets and to advance community policing. Publishes newsletters, conducts various programs and activities.

*National Judicial College (NJC)*
http://www.judges.org/
A not-for-profit educational corporation located on the campus of the University of Nevada, Reno, the NJC offers many different kinds of short courses for trial court and administrative law judges and court personnel, and cosponsors a Master's of Judicial Studies degree program.

*National Sheriff's Association*
http://www.sheriffs.org
Established in 1940 and serving over 20,000 sheriffs, deputies, jail administrators, corrections officials, court security officers, chiefs of police, and federal law enforcement agents. Provides training, information, and other services. Publishes *Sheriff* magazine monthly and other bulletins.

# Appendix II

# Analects of Confucius and Machiavelli

The writings of two major figures have stood the test of time. The analects (or brief passages) of both Confucius (551-479 B.C.) and Machiavelli (A.D. 1469–1527) are still quite popular today. Many graduate and undergraduate students in a variety of academic disciplines have been compelled to analyze the writings of both, especially Machiavelli's *The Prince*. Both men tend to agree on many points regarding the means of governance, as the following will demonstrate. After reading some analects of each philosopher, we will consider their application to justice administration.

Confucius often emphasized moralism of leaders, saying:

> He who rules by moral force is like the pole-star, which remains in its place while all the lesser stars do homage to it. Govern the people by regulations, keep order among them by chastisements, and they will flee from you, and lose all self-respect. Govern them by moral force, keep order among them..., and they will...come to you of their own accord. If the ruler is upright, all will go well even though he does not give orders. But if he himself is not upright, even though he gives orders, they will not be obeyed.[1]

Confucius also felt that persons who the leader promotes is of no small importance: "Promote those who are worthy, train those who are incompetent; that is the best form of encouragement."[2] He also felt that leaders should learn from and emulate good administrators:

> In the presence of a good man, think all the time how you may learn to equal him. In the presence of a bad man, turn your gaze within! Even when I am walking in a party of no more than three I can always be certain of learning from those I am with. There will be good qualities that I can select for imitation and bad ones that will teach me what requires correction in myself.[3]

Unlike Confucius, Machiavelli is often maligned for being cruel; the "ends justifies the means" philosophy imputed to him even today has cast a pall over his writings. However, although often as biting as the "point of a stiletto"[4] and seemingly ruthless at times ("Men ought either to be caressed or destroyed, since they will seek revenge for minor hurts but will not be able to revenge major ones,"[5] and "If you have to make a choice, to be feared is much safer than to be loved"[6]) he, like Confucius, often spoke of the leader's need to possess character and compassion. For all of his blunt, management-oriented notions of administration, Machiavelli was prudent and pragmatic.

Like Confucius, Machiavelli felt that administrators would do well to follow examples set by other great leaders:

> Men almost always prefer to walk in paths marked out by others and pattern their actions through imitation. A prudent man should always follow the footsteps of the great and imitate those who have been supreme. A prince should read history and reflect on the actions of great men.[7]

Machiavelli's counsel also agreed with that of Confucius in the sense that leaders should surround themselves with persons both knowledgeable and devoted: "The first notion one gets of a prince's intelligence comes from the men around him."[8]

But, again, like Confucius, Machiavelli believed that administrators should be careful of their subordinates' ambition and greed:

> A new prince must always harm those over whom he assumes authority. You cannot stay friends with those who put you in power, because you can never satisfy them as they expected. The man who makes another powerful ruins himself. The reason is that he gets power either by shrewdness or by strength, and both qualities are suspect to the man who has been given the power.[9]

On the need for developing and maintaining good relations with subordinates, he wrote:

> If...a prince...puts his trust in the people, knows how to command, is a man of courage and doesn't lose his head in adversity, and can rouse his people to action by his own example and orders, he will never find himself betrayed, and his foundations will prove to have been well laid. The best fortress of all consists in not being hated by your people. Every prince should prefer to be considered merciful rather than cruel. The prince must have people well disposed toward him; otherwise in times of adversity there's no hope.[10]

In this era of collective bargaining and a rapidly changing workforce, contemporary criminal justice administrators might do well to heed the analects of Confucius and Machiavelli.

Perhaps a leader, in the purest sense, also influences others by example. This characteristic of leadership was recognized in the sixth century B.C. by Lao-Tzu, who wrote:

> The superior leader gets things done
> With very little motion.
> He imparts instruction not through many words

But through a few deeds.
He keeps informed about everything
But interferes hardly at all.
He is a catalyst.
And although things wouldn't get done as well
If he weren't there.
When they succeed he takes no credit.
And because he takes no credit
Credit never leaves him.[11]

# Notes

1. Arthur Waley (trans.), *The Analects of Confucius* (London: George Allen and Unwin, 1938), pp. 88, 173.
2. Ibid., p. 92.
3. Ibid., pp. 105, 127.
4. Robert M. Adams (trans.), *The Prince* (New York: W.W. Norton, 1992), p. xvii.
5. Ibid., p. 7.
6. Ibid., p. 46.
7. Ibid., pp. 15, 41.
8. Ibid., p. 63.
9. Ibid., pp. 5, 11.
10. Ibid., pp. 29, 60.
11. Quoted in Wayne W. Bennett and Karen M. Hess, *Management and Supervision in Law Enforcement,* 3d ed. (Belmont, Calif.: Wadsworth, 2001), p. 63.

# INDEX